DIGITAL TYPE SPCIMENS

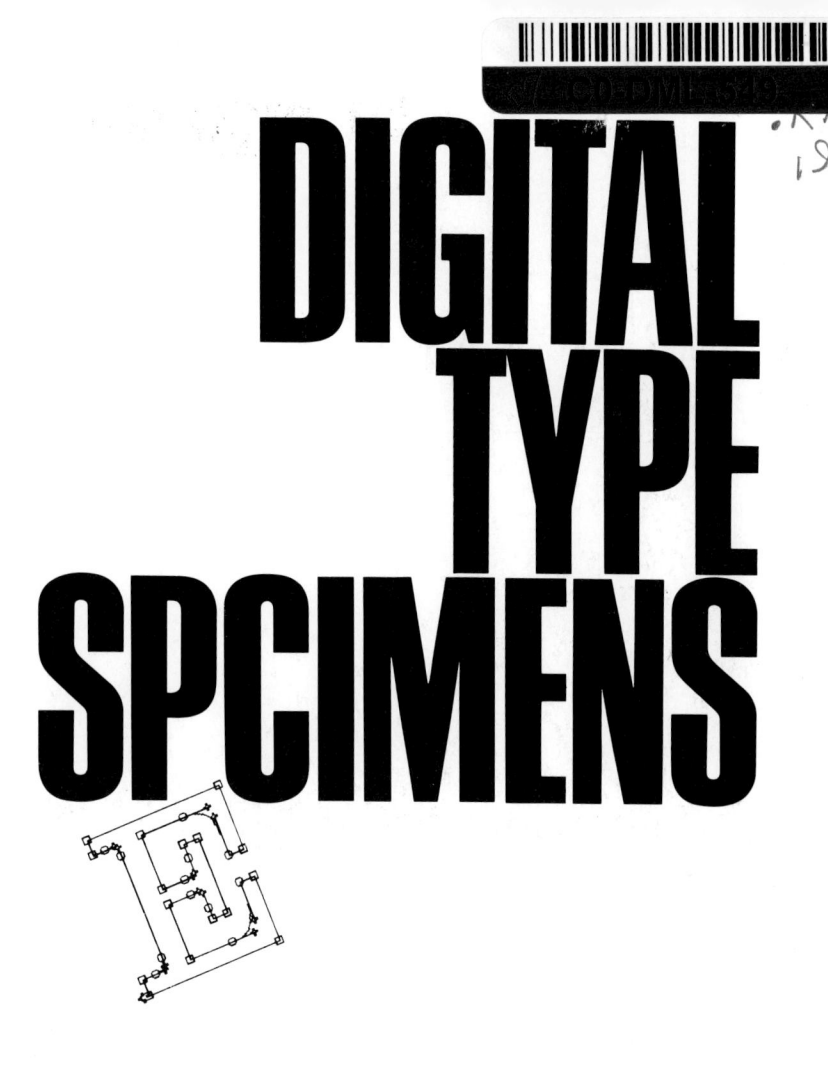

The Designer's Computer Type Book   *by Ben Rosen*

VNR VAN NOSTRAND REINHOLD   NEW YORK

Copyright © 1991 by Van Nostrand Reinhold
Library of Congress Catalog Card Number 90-45216
ISBN 0-442-23501-1

All rights reserved. No part of this work covered by
the copyright hereon may be reproduced or used in any
form by any means—graphic, electronic, or
mechanical, including photocopying, recording, taping,
or information storage and retrieval systems—without
written permission of the publisher.

Printed in the United States of America.

Van Nostrand Reinhold
115 Fifth Avenue
New York, New York 10003

Chapman and Hall
2-6 Boundary Row
London SE1 8HN, England

Thomas Nelson Australia
102 Dodds Street
South Melbourne 3205
Victoria, Australia

Nelson Canada
1120 Birchmount Road
Scarborough, Ontario MIK 5G4, Canada

16 15 14 13 12 11 10 9 8 7 6 5 4 3 2 1

Library of Congress Cataloging-in-Publication Data

Rosen, Ben.
    Digital type specimens: the designer's computer type book / Ben Rosen.
       p. cm.
    Includes index.
    ISBN 0-442-23501-1
    1. Printing—Specimens. 2. Printing, Practical—Layout.
3. Type and type-founding—Data processing. 4. Phototypesetting—
Display type. 5. Desktop publishing. I. Title
Z250.R788 1990
686.2'24—dc20   90-45216
                                          CIP

PREFACE

For some time, there has been an obvious need for a new specimen book of useful, computer-driven digital type specimens selected for design excellence and general availability, shown in a functional, informative format. This book is intended to fill that need. It presents type choices based on the author's experience, presented in ways designed to be most useful for readers choosing, visualizing and specifying type according to their needs.

The goal of this specimen book is to show the best renditions and broadest range of the most useful typefaces generally available, thus offering type users practically and aesthetically satisfying choices. However, the problem of selection has been challenging—there are thousands of typefaces out there: there are modified versions of old metal types from the fifteenth and sixteenth centuries that have been adapted for digitized fonts; special fonts have been drawn for photo projection modes of typesetting, others for digitized type; there are also enhancement techniques that modify digitized type and laser printing is blazing new trails, all of which increase the number of typefaces from which to choose.

Advancing technology further complicates the type industry. New faces are constantly entering the digital type market. Some are extensions of specific design assignments calling for a specialized letterform; others are based on wood type, photolettering, transfer lettering, current calligraphy, or calligraphic models drawn before movable type was invented. All deserve consideration in the compilation of a type specimen book.

No single volume, including this one, contains every available typeface. But this volume presents a rich selection of excellent digital faces that are tastefully designed, visually distinct, skillfully produced and generally available in the U.S. marketplace. Readers using this book in conjunction with my revised edition of *Type and Typography*, a collection of metal type specimens, will also gain access to the finest metal types, some of which have not yet been adapted to digitization.

How many typefaces are necessary? Do designers really use a thousand typefaces in their work? Of course not. A dozen or so judicious type selections become extremely flexible in the hands of a good designer. But *which* dozen or so is the issue. Many designers patiently look through specimen books searching for some connection, some visual message that will signal an appropriate type. A particular face, bypassed many times, may suddenly reveal certain characteristics that are precisely right for a particular job. The thick-thin relationship, the way the serif flows from the stem, roundness, softness, roughness, precision—any of these qualities can lend subtlety or power to a message.

Many of the types available for desktop use are virtual duplicates of those available on the commercial typesetter's market. In this book, to avoid excessive duplication, they are not separated from the faces normally available from commercial typographers. New faces are coming in and going out of existence so rapidly that trying to keep track of them all is an exercise in futility. Already there are programs that offer the intrepid designer the opportunity to design and store individually designed alphabets on relatively low-end electronic equipment. Yet there remains a wealth of fine, useful, and widely accepted typefaces that promise to be with us for a long time to come. These prototypical faces have received the most attention in this publication.

In the opening section of this book, ten beautiful, time-tested typefaces are shown first. They are identified as families and shown in many (though not all) of their variations, including italics, light through bold, condensed through extended and 72 point display to 8 point text sizes in varied leadings. These ten families alone constitute a palette from which excellent typography can be created.

Hundreds of supplementary fonts follow the ten initial type families to support them, enhance them, or stand alone. Fine cursive and calligraphic letterforms are present, followed by classics, eccentrics, ornamentals, romantics, outlines, inlines, and shadow faces. Space allocation and typeface category designations are based on anticipated use and, alas, practical space limitations. No doubt there will be some difference of opinion as to whether certain faces belong where they have been placed—one man's judgment is bound to be open to controversy. Readers are invited to make their own classifications.

Type fonts are represented as complete alphabets with useful punctuation. Source or vendor information is given when available and applicable. A face set on equipment from a vendor shows that vendor's name below it, even if it is not proprietary to that vendor.

The reader will also find basic typecasting information, measurement data and proofreaders' marks which have been included to make this book a useful tool for all who work with type.

In addition to an extensive array of specimens, readers who have worked with metal type will find information to support an easy transition to digital type.

Most people who work with type can do their best without knowing the intricacies of current typesetting technology. Therefore, only limited technical information is offered to acquaint designers and others who use type with the basics of this technology. These limited but substantive fundamentals are included with the intent to provide basic background information about digital type.

Because digital typesetting is a relatively new technology, a brief section on the chronology of typesetting from photo to digital is included. This material will serve to acquaint readers with the nature of various kinds of typegenerating equipment that has had commercial acceptance since 1950. Because changes come along rapidly, making it nearly impossible to keep on the cutting edge of this new discipline, the information is introductory in scope and generic in nature, with major trends and developments presented in broad strokes.

Type needs vary, as do the systems that produce repro copy and the people who use them. The introduction of visually oriented Apple computers has helped many designers with some of the more menial tasks of mechanical preparation. These computers also offer design capabilities previously unavailable to designers without access to the highly sophisticated and very costly computer consoles of the 1960s and early 1970s. Desktop publishing, where high-quality printout is not always critical, is often best served by a minicomputer with a low resolution printer of about three hundred dots per inch. To the ardent designer, on the other hand, low resolution repros may never be acceptable. Clearly, the type requirements for a fine book, a weekly newsletter, a full-color ad in a sophisticated magazine, a design for a cosmetic package or a television commercial for garbage bags could be shown to vary considerably. And while veteran designers neither require nor readily accept advice on type style usage, recent recruits among desktop publishing operators may find the wide choice of fonts offered in this book suggests new and creative approaches.

Over a decade ago, a special issue of *U&LC* was produced, broad in scope and rich in information about the sweeping changes electronic communication was bringing to the field of type and graphics. The group of articles was headed, "WARNING! Perishable Information—read immediately." Today, a decade later, it is still good advice to "read immediately" all the trade publications and current technical information you can find.

To all who have graciously offered a helping hand in response to my many requests during the process of assembling this book, I am hard pressed to fully express my gratitude, but that shall not deter me from trying.

Milton Mandel, president of Centre Typographers, Inc., has extended personal interest, encouragement and heartwarming support in many ways. I am deeply indebted to Mr. Mandel for information and insights about typography gained from rewarding discussions spanning three decades. Nor am I any less indebted to Mr. Mandel for his generous contributions of time and effort, and for authorizing the production of endless stacks of excellent type specimen repros that make up most of this book. Without his largess, I doubt that this volume could have been brought to completion.

Nearly 500 pages of text and display specimens were set in galley form by Harold Chewens of Centre Typographers, Inc., the same Mr. Chewens who, with Mr. Mandel, set the initial linotype and foundry specimens for my first type book, *Type and Typography* in 1960.

I am grateful to Cynthia Hollandsworth, Typographic Advisor to Agfa Compugraphic Division, who found ways in a fiercely busy schedule to obtain and furnish specimens representing many of the finest Agfa Compugraphic typefaces, her own designs among them. I am also pleased to have her monograph on the shift of digital typesetting toward desktop operations, appearing in this book.

My thanks to master type designer Matthew Carter, Vice President of Type Development for Bitstream Inc., who generously arranged for the production of requested type specimens. I am pleased he has shared his observations on the design of type—from punchcutting to digital type—a welcome addition to this work.

Sumner Stone and Fred Brady at Adobe Systems Incorporated, both considerately arranged for the provision of fine Adobe type specimens that add depth to the scope of these type showings.

To Bruce Lehnert of the Linotype Company, my thanks for initiating the participation of his company in this book; to Bruce Brenner and Jim Gutierrez for continuing that interest in practical ways on behalf of the project, I am grateful. The written comments of Messrs. Brenner and Gutierrez on digital type reflects their involvement on the cutting edge of digital type technology.

The International Type Corporation, through the efforts of Allan Haley, has made photo copies of their widely distributed library of typefaces available.

Type specimens from Adobe Systems Incorporated, were set by Keala Hagman; from Bitstream Inc., by Carlton Chin; from Agfa Compugraphic, by Jeff Cote.

My thanks to Rodney Kohn and Barbara Brenner for patient listening and thoughtful responses to my endless questions on matters pertaining to this book and for help in upgrading certain type showings.

For patient, precise and skillfull assistance in the mechanical assembly of this sizable tome, I commend Pamela McPheron.

Finally, there are my editors. Through the efforts of Lilly Kaufman, this project got started; with the help of thankless and unrelenting work by Amanda Miller, it has at last been produced.

To my wife and family, my thanks for putting up with the last few hectic months of preparation.

Here then, is the book. May it serve the reader well in every effort to produce good typography.

CONTENTS

LIST OF TYPE SPECIMENS VI

INTRODUCTION 1

MONOGRAPHS

    From Commercial Type Shops
to Desktop Publishing:
Closing the Gap
Cynthia Hollandsworth 11

    Characters of the Computer
Bruce Brenner and Jim Gutierrez 13

    From Punch to Pixel: Designing
and Making Type
Matthew Carter 14

WORKING WITH DIGITAL TYPE

    Derivations of Type 16
    Digital Type Design 17
    Continuity in Design 17
    Getting Familiar With Type 18
    Measurement Data 19
    The Unit System and the EM 20
    Kerning and Tracking 21
    Copyfitting 21
    The Quick Count 21
    Marking the Copy 22
    Proofreader's Marks 22

THE TYPE SPECIMENS

    The Families of Type 23
    Supplementary Faces 313
    Display Faces
        Scripts and Cursives 480
        Eccentrics, Romantics
and Classics 508
        Outlines and Shadows 520
        Digitized Wood Type 524
    One Line Specimens 526

APPENDIX 534

LIST OF TYPE SPECIMENS

FAMILIES: Display and Text

ITC Avant Garde Gothic Book..... 25
ITC Avant Garde Gothic
  Book Oblique................ 26
ITC Avant Garde Gothic Extra Light 33
ITC Avant Garde Gothic
  Extra Light Oblique........... 34
ITC Avant Garde Gothic Medium .. 38
ITC Avant Garde Gothic
  Medium Oblique.............. 39
ITC Avant Garde Gothic Demi 43
ITC Avant Garde Gothic
  Demi Oblique................ 44
ITC Avant Garde Gothic Bold 48
ITC Avant Garde Gothic
  Bold Oblique................. 49
ITC Avant Garde Gothic
  Alternate Characters.......... 53
Fry's Baskerville 57
ITC New Baskerville Italic 58
ITC New Baskerville Semi Bold.... 65
ITC New Baskerville Semi Bold Italic 66
ITC New Baskerville Bold......... 70
ITC New Baskerville Bold Italic.... 71
ITC New Baskerville Black........ 75
ITC New Baskerville Black Italic ... 76
Bauer Bodoni 81
Bauer Bodoni Italic............... 82
Bauer Bodoni Bold 88
Bauer Bodoni Bold Italic.......... 89
Bauer Bodoni Black 93
Bauer Bodoni Black Italic 94
Bauer Bodoni Bold Condensed..... 98
Bauer Bodoni Black Condensed ... 101
Poster Bodoni Compressed....... 104
Poster Bodoni 107
Poster Bodoni Italic.............. 108
ITC Bookman Light 113
ITC Bookman Light Italic......... 114
ITC Bookman Medium 121
ITC Bookman Medium Italic...... 122
ITC Bookman Demi 126
ITC Bookman Demi Italic......... 127
ITC Bookman Bold 131
ITC Bookman Bold Italic 132
ITC Bookman Swash Characters ... 136
Caslon 540..................... 139
Caslon 540 Italic................. 140
Caslon 224 Medium.............. 147
Caslon 224 Medium Italic......... 148
Caslon 224 Bold 152
Caslon 224 Bold Italic............ 153
Caslon 224 Black 157
Caslon 224 Black Italic............ 158
Caslon Antique.................. 162
Caslon Antique Italic 163
Caslon Open Face................ 167
CG Century Expanded 171
CG Century Expanded Italic....... 172
ITC Century Light................ 179
ITC Century Light Italic........... 180
ITC Century Book................ 184
ITC Century Book Italic 185
Century Bold.................... 189
Century Bold Italic............... 190
New Century Schoolbook Black.... 194
New Century Schoolbook
  Black Italic 195
Century Nova 199
Century Nova Italic 200
ITC Century Bold Condensed 204
ITC Century Bold Condensed Italic 205
Century Bold Condensed 209
Cheltenham..................... 213
Cheltenham Italic................ 214
Cheltenham Bold 221
Cheltenham Bold Italic 222
Cheltenham Bold Condensed 226
Cheltenham Bold Condensed Italic . 227
Cheltenham Bold Extra Condensed . 231
Stempel Garamond.............. 235
Stempel Garamond Italic......... 236
ITC Garamond Light 243
ITC Garamond Light Italic........ 244
ITC Garamond Bold 248
ITC Garamond Bold Italic 249
ITC Garamond Ultra............. 253
ITC Garamond Ultra Italic........ 254
Helvetica 259
Helvetica Italic 260
Helvetica Light.................. 267
Helvetica Light Italic 268
Helvetica Bold................... 274
Helvetica Bold Italic.............. 275
Helvetica Heavy 279
Helvetica Heavy Italic 280
Helvetica Black 284
Helvetica Black Italic 285
Helvetica Ultra Light 290
Helvetica Ultra Light Italic........ 290
Helvetica Thin 290
Helvetica Thin Italic 291
Helvetica Catalog 290
Helvetica Catalog Bold 290
Helvetica Bold No 2.............. 290
Helvetica Black No 2 290
Helvetica Bold Outline............ 290
Helvetica Light Condensed........ 290
Helvetica Light Condensed Italic ... 290
Helvetica Condensed 290
Helvetica Condensed Italic 290
Helvetica Bold Condensed 290
Helvetica Bold Condensed Italic.... 290
Helvetica Black Condensed 290
Helvetica Black Condensed Italic ... 290
Helvetica Bold Condensed Outline . 290
Helvetica Compressed 291
Helvetica Extra Compressed 291
Helvetica Ultra Compressed 291
Helvetica Inserat................ 291
Helvetica Inserat Italic............ 291
Helvetica Light Extended 291
Helvetica Extended............... 291
Helvetica Bold Extended 291
Helvetica Black Extended 291
Helvetica Rounded Bold 291
Helvetica Rounded Bold Italic..... 291
Helvetica Rounded Black 291
Helvetica Rounded Black Italic 291
Helvetica Rounded Bold Outline ... 291
Helvetica Rounded Bold Condensed 291
Helvetica Textbook............... 291
Helvetica Textbook Bold 291
Helvetica Bold Reversed.......... 291
Times......................... 293
Times Italic.................... 294
Times Semi Bold 301
Times Semi Bold Italic........... 302
Times Bold 306
Times Bold Italic 307
Times Extra Bold 311

SUPPLEMENTARY FACES: Display and Text

Aachen Medium 314
Aachen Bold 314
Administer Book................ 314
Administer Book Italic........... 314
Adroit Light 314
Adroit Light Italic............... 314
Abertus Book................... 316
Abertus Book Oblique 316
Abertus Medium................ 316
Abertus Medium Oblique 316
Abertus Bold 316
Abertus Extra Bold.............. 316
Aldus......................... 318
Aldus Italic.................... 318
American Classic................ 318
American Classic Italic........... 318
American Classic Bold 318
American Classic Extra Bold...... 318
ITC American Typewriter Medium . 320
ITC American Typewriter Light.... 320
ITC American Typewriter Bold 320
ITC American Typewriter
  Light Condensed.............. 320
ITC American Typewriter
  Medium Condensed 320
ITC American Typewriter
  Bold Condensed 320
Bitstream Amerigo 322
Bitstream Amerigo Italic 322
Bitstream Amerigo Medium 322
Bitstream Amerigo Medium Italic .. 322
Bitstream Amerigo Bold 322
Bitstream Amerigo Bold Italic..... 322
ITC Bauhaus Medium 324
ITC Bauhaus Light............... 324
ITC Bauhaus Demi............... 324
ITC Bauhaus Bold 324
Belwe Light.................... 324
Belwe Medium 324
Bembo........................ 326
Bembo Italic................... 326
Bembo Medium 326
Bembo Medium Italic 326
Bembo Bold.................... 326
Bembo Bold Italic............... 326

Bembo Bold 326	ITC Elan Black 350	Futura Bold Condensed Italic 372
Bembo Bold Italic 326	ITC Elan Black Italic 350	Futura Extra Black Condensed 372
ITC Berkeley Old Style Book 328	Electra 350	Futura Extra Black Condensed Italic 372
ITC Berkeley Old Style Book Italic . 328	Electra Cursive 350	ITC Galliard 374
ITC Berkeley Old Style Medium . . . 328	Eurostyle 350	ITC Galliard Italic 374
ITC Berkeley Old Style Medium Italic 328	Eurostyle Bold 350	ITC Galliard Bold 374
	Eurostyle Condensed 352	ITC Galliard Bold Italic 374
ITC Berkeley Old Style Bold 328	Eurostyle Bold Condensed 352	ITC Galliard Black 374
ITC Berkeley Old Style Bold Italic . 328	Eurostyle Extended No 2 352	ITC Galliard Black Italic 374
Binny Old Style 330	Eurostyle Bold Extended No 2 352	ITC Galliard Ultra 376
Binny Old Style Italic 330	Fairfield Medium 352	ITC Galliard Ultra Italic 376
Bruce Old Style 330	Fairfield Medium Italic 352	Simoncini Garamond 376
Bruce Old Style Italic 330	ITC Fenice Light 354	Simoncini Garamond Italic 376
Bulmer 330	ITC Fenice Light Italic 354	ITC Garamond Ultra Condensed . . . 376
Bulmer Italic 330	ITC Fenice Regular 354	ITC Garamond Ultra Condensed Italic 376
New Caledonia 332	ITC Fenice Regular Italic 354	
New Caledonia Italic 332	ITC Fenice Bold 354	Adobe Garamond Regular 387
New Caledonia Semi Bold 332	ITC Fenice Bold Italic 354	Adobe Garamond Italic 378
New Caledonia Semi Bold Italic . . . 332	ITC Fenice Ultra 356	Adobe Garamond Semibold 378
New Caledonia Bold 332	ITC Fenice Ultra Italic 356	Adobe Garamond Semibold Italic . . . 378
New Caledonia Bold Italic 332	Floreal Hass Light 356	Adobe Garamond Bold 378
New Caledonia Black 334	Floreal Hass 356	Adobe Garamond Bold Italic 378
New Caledonia Black Italic 334	Floreal Hass Bold 356	Garth Graphic 380
Cartier 334	Floreal Hass Black 356	Garth Graphic Italic 380
Cartier Italic 334	Folio Light 358	Garth Graphic Bold 380
Centaur 334	Folio Light Italic 358	Garth Graphic Bold Italic 380
Centaur Italic (Arrighi) 334	Folio Medium 358	Garth Graphic Extra Bold 380
Bitstream Carmina Medium 336	Folio Bold 358	Garth Graphic Black 380
Bitstream Carmina Medium Italic . . 336	Fournier 358	Goudy Old Style 382
Bitstream Carmina Bold 336	Fournier Italic 358	Goudy Old Style Italic 382
Bitstream Carmina Bold Italic 336	Franklin 360	Goudy Bold 382
Bitstream Carmina Black 336	Franklin Italic 360	Goudy Bold Italic 382
Bitstream Carmina Black Italic 336	Franklin Condensed 360	Goudy Heavyface 382
TSI Caxton Light 338	Franklin Condensed Italic 360	Goudy Heavyface Italic 382
TSI Caxton Light Italic 338	Franklin Wide 360	Monotype Goudy Sans Light 384
TSI Caxton Book 338	Franklin Wide Italic 360	Monotype Goudy Sans Light Italic . 384
TSI Caxton Book Italic 338	Friz Quadrata 362	Monotype Goudy Sans Medium 384
TSI Caxton Bold 338	Friz Quadrata Bold 362	Monotype Goudy Sans Medium Italic 384
TSI Caxton Bold Italic 338	Frontiera 55 362	
Bitstream Charter 340	Frontiera 56 Italic 362	Monotype Goudy Sans Bold 384
Bitstream Charter Italic 340	Frontiera 75 362	Monotype Goudy Sans Extra Bold . . 384
Bitstream Charter Bold 340	Frontiera 76 Italic 362	Granjon 386
Bitstream Charter Bold Italic 340	Frutiger 45 Light 364	Granjon Italic 386
Bitstream Charter Black 340	Frutiger 46 Light Italic 364	Harry Thin 386
Bitstream Charter Black Italic 340	Frutiger 55 364	Harry Plain 386
Cochin 342	Frutiger 56 Italic 364	Harry Heavy 386
Cochin Italic 342	Frutiger 65 Bold 364	Harry Fat 386
Cochin Bold 342	Frutiger 66 Bold Italic 364	Hiroshige Book 388
Cochin Bold Italic 342	Frutiger 75 Black 366	Hiroshige Book Italic 388
Cochin Black 342	Frutiger 76 Black Italic 366	Hiroshige Medium 388
Cochin Black Italic 342	Frutiger 57 Condensed 366	Hiroshige Medium Italic 388
Nicholas Cochin 344	Frutiger 67 Bold Condensed 366	Hiroshige Black 388
Nicholas Cochin Black 344	Frutiger 77 Black Condensed 366	Hiroshige Black Italic 388
Devinne 344	Frutiger 87 Extra Black Condensed . 366	ITC Isbell Book 390
Devinne Italic 344	Futura Light 368	ITC Isbell Book Italic 390
Diotima 344	Futura Light Italic 368	ITC Isbell Medium 390
Diotima Italic 344	Futura Book 368	ITC Isbell Medium Italic 390
Egyptian 505 Light 346	Futura Book Italic 368	ITC Isbell Bold 390
Egyptian 505 346	Futura Medium 368	ITC Isbell Bold Italic 390
Egyptian 505 Medium 346	Futura Medium Italic 368	ITC Isbell Heavy 392
Egyptial 505 Bold 346	Futura Heavy 370	ITC Isbell Heavy Italic 392
Egyptienne F 75 Black 346	Futura Heavy Italic 370	Italia Book (ITC) 392
Egyptienne F 67 Bold Condensed . . 346	Futura Bold 370	Italia Medium (ITC) 392
ITC Elan Book 348	Futura Bold Italic 370	Italia Bold (ITC) 392
ITC Elan Book Italic 348	Futura Extra Black 370	Janson Text 55 394
ITC Elan Medium 348	Futura Extra Black Italic 370	Janson Text 56 Italic 394
ITC Elan Medium Italic 348	Futura Light Condensed 372	Janson Text 75 Bold 394
ITC Elan Bold 348	Futura Medium Condensed 372	Janson Text 76 Bold Italic 394
ITC Elan Bold Italic 348	Futura Bold Condensed 372	Janson Text 95 Black 394

Janson Text 96 Black Italic..........394	Optima Medium...................418	ITC Stone Sans................442
Jenson (Nicholas)..................396	Optima Medium Italic.............418	ITC Stone Sans Italic............442
Kennerly........................396	Optima Demi Bold................418	ITC Stone Sans Semibold.........442
Kennerly Italic...................396	Optima Demi Bold Italic..........418	ITC Stone Sans Semibold Italic....442
Kennerly Bold....................396	Optima Bold.....................420	ITC Stone Sans Bold.............442
Kennerly Bold Italic...............396	Optima Bold Italic................420	ITC Stone Sans Bold Italic........442
ITC Korinna.....................398	Optima Black....................420	ITC Stone Serif.................444
ITC Korinna Kursiv...............398	Optima Black Italic...............420	ITC Stone Serif Italic............444
ITC Korinna Bold.................398	Optima Extra Black...............420	ITC Stone Serif Semibold.........444
ITC Korinna Bold Kursiv..........398	Optima Extra Black Italic.........420	ITC Stone Serif Semibold Italic....444
ITC Korinna Extra Bold..........398	Palatino........................422	ITC Stone Serif Bold.............444
ITC Korinna Extra Bold Kursiv....398	Palatino Italic...................422	ITC Stone Serif Bold Italic.......444
ITC Lubalin Graph Extra Light....400	Palatino Bold....................422	Tekton.........................446
ITC Lubalin Graph	Palatino Bold Italic...............422	Tekton Oblique..................446
Extra Light Oblique...........400	Parsons Regular 422	WTC Thaddeus Regular..........446
ITC Lubalin Graph Book.........400	Parsons Italic....................422	WTC Thaddeus Regular Italic.....446
ITC Lubalin Graph Book Oblique..400	Perpetua........................424	WTC Thaddeus Bold.............446
ITC Lubalin Graph Medium......400	Perpetua Italic...................424	WTC Thaddeus Bold Italic.......446
ITC Lubalin Graph	Perpetua Bold...................424	ITC Tiffany Light................448
Medium Oblique..............400	Perpetua Bold Italic..............424	ITC Tiffany Light Italic..........448
ITC Lubalin Graph Demi.........402	Perpetua Black..................424	ITC Tiffany Medium.............448
ITC Lubalin Graph Demi Oblique .402	Plantin Light....................426	ITC Tiffany Medium Italic.......448
ITC Lubalin Graph Bold..........402	Plantin Light Italic...............426	ITC Tiffany Heavy..............448
ITC Lubalin Graph Bold Oblique ..402	Plantin..........................426	ITC Tiffany Heavy Italic.........448
Lucian.........................402	Plantin Italic....................426	Trajanus........................450
Lucian Bold.....................402	Plantin Bold....................426	Trajanus Italic..................450
Melior..........................404	Plantin Bold Italic...............426	Trajanus Bold...................450
Melior Italic....................404	Primer 54.......................428	Trajanus Bold Italic.............450
Melior Medium..................404	Primer 54 Italic..................428	Trajanus Black...................450
Melior Medium Italic............404	Primer 54 Semi Bold.............428	Trajanus Black Italic.............450
Melior Bold.....................404	Primer 54 Semi Bold Italic.......428	CG Triumvirate Thin.............452
Melior Bold Italic................404	Primer 54 Bold.................428	CG Triumvirate Thin Italic.......452
Minion Regular..................406	Primer 54 Bold Italic.............428	CG Triumvirate Bold.............452
Minion Italic....................406	Raleigh Light....................430	CG Triumvirate Bold Italic.......452
Minion Semibold................406	Raleigh Medium.................430	CG Triumvirate Black............452
Minion Semibold Italic...........406	Raleigh Regular.................430	CG Triumvirate Black Italic......452
Minion Black....................406	Raleigh Bold....................430	Trooper Light...................454
Minion Bold Italic...............406	Raleigh Demi Bold..............430	Trooper Light Italic.............454
ITC Modern No 216 Light........408	Raleigh Extra Bold Condensed.....430	Trooper........................454
ITC Modern No 216 Light Italic...408	Rotis Semi Sans 55..............432	Trooper Italic...................454
ITC Modern No 216 Medium.....408	Rotis Semi Sans 75..............432	Trooper Bold....................454
ITC Modern No 216 Medium Italic 408	Rotis Semi Serif 55..............432	Trooper Black...................454
ITC Modern No 216 Bold........408	Rotis Semi Serif 65..............432	Trump Mediaeval................456
ITC Modern No 216 Bold Italic...408	Rotis Serif 55...................432	Trump Mediaeval Italic..........456
Craw Modern...................410	Rotis Serif 56...................432	Trump Mediaeval Bold...........456
Musketeer Light.................410	TS Scenario Light................434	Trump Mediaeval Bold Italic.....456
Musketeer Demi Bold............410	TS Scenario Light Italic..........434	Trump Mediaeval Black..........456
Musketeer......................410	TS Scenario Demi................434	Univers 45 Light.................458
Musketeer Extra Bold............410	TS Scenario Bold.................434	Univers 46 Light Italic...........458
News Gothic Light...............412	Scotch No 2 434	Univers 55......................458
News Gothic Light Italic.........412	Scotch No 2 Italic...............434	Univers 56 Italic.................458
News Gothic....................412	ITC Serif Gothic Light............436	Univers 65 Bold.................458
News Gothic Bold...............412	ITC Serif Gothic.................436	Univers 66 Bold Italic............458
News Gothic Condensed.........412	ITC Serif Gothic Bold.............436	Univers 75 Black.................460
News Gothic Bold Condensed.....412	ITC Serif Gothic Extra Bold.......436	Univers 76 Black Italic...........460
ITC Novarese Book..............414	ITC Serif Gothic Heavy...........436	Univers 85 Extra Black...........460
ITC Novarese Book Italic.........414	ITC Serif Gothic Black............436	Univers 47 Light Condensed......460
ITC Novarese Medium...........414	ITC Souvenir Light...............438	Univers 48 Light Condensed Italic..460
ITC Novarese Medium Italic......414	ITC Souvenir Light Italic.........438	Univers 57 Condensed...........462
ITC Novarese Bold...............414	ITC Souvenir Medium............438	Univers 58 Condensed Italic......462
ITC Novarese Bold Italic.........414	ITC Souvenir Medium Italic......438	Univers 67 Bold Condensed......462
Antique Olive 416	ITC Souvenir Demi..............438	Univers 68 Bold Condensed Italic .462
Antique Olive Italic..............416	ITC Souvenir Demi Italic.........438	Univers 53 Extended.............462
Antique Olive Medium...........416	ITC Stone Informal..............440	Univers 63 Bold Extended........462
Antique Olive Medium Italic......416	ITC Stone Informal Italic.........440	ITC Usherwood Book............464
Antique Olive Light..............416	ITC Stone Informal Semibold....440	ITC Usherwood Book Italic.......464
Antique Olive Bold..............416	ITC Stone Informal Semibold Italic.440	ITC Usherwood Medium........464
Optima.........................418	ITC Stone Informal Bold.........440	ITC Usherwood Medium Italic....464
Optima Italic...................418	ITC Stone Informal Bold Italic....440	ITC Usherwood Bold............464

ITC Usherwood Bold Italic........ 464	Impuls 491	Lithos Extra Light 513
Utopia Regular 466	Jiffy 491	Lithos Light 513
Utopia Italic 466	Kaufmann 492	Lithos Regular 514
Utopia Semibold................. 466	Kaufmann Bold................. 492	Lithos Bold 514
Utopia Semibold Italic........... 466	Libra 493	Lithos Black 514
Utopia Bold..................... 466	Linoscript 493	London Text 514
Utopia Bold Italic................ 466	Lisbon 494	Luther Fractur 514
Versailles 45 Light 468	Lisbon Italic 494	MacBeth 515
Versailles 46 Light Italic 468	Lisbon Cursive 495	ITC Machine................... 515
Versailles 55 468	Marigold 495	ITC Machine Bold 515
Versailles 56 Italic 468	Medici Script................... 496	McCollough 515
Versailles 95 Black 468	Mistral 496	Mikado Black 515
Versailles 96 Black Italic......... 468	Murray 497	Mique......................... 515
Waldbaum 470	Murray Bold 497	Modern Blackletter............. 515
Waldbaum Italic 470	Nuptial Script.................. 498	New Bostonian 516
Weiss 470	Old Fashion Script 498	Nubian........................ 516
Weiss Italic 470	Ondine........................ 499	Old English.................... 516
Weiss Bold..................... 470	Oxford 499	TS Parsons 516
Weiss Extra Bold................ 470	Park Avenue Script 500	Pierrot 516
ITC Weidemann Book........... 472	Parliament 500	Playbill 516
ITC Weidemann Book Italic...... 472	Piranesi Italic 501	Profil 517
ITC Weidemann Medium 472	Present Script 501	Quartz 45 Light 517
ITC Weidemann Medium Italic.... 472	Quill.......................... 502	Quartz 75 Bold 517
ITC Weidemann Black........... 472	Reporter No 2 502	Rainbow Bass 517
ITC Weidemann Black Italic...... 472	Riviera Script 503	Raphael 517
Windsor Old Style Light......... 474	Sallwey Script 503	Stencil 517
Windsor....................... 474	Shelley Volante Script 504	Stop 518
Windsor Light 474	Signet Roundhand 504	TSI Tango..................... 518
Windsor Elongated 474	Snell Roundhand Black Script..... 505	Tea Chest...................... 518
Worcester Round 474	Stuyvesant 505	Thunderbird Extra Condensed..... 518
Worcester Round Italic 474	Typo Upright 506	Trajan Regular................. 518
ITC Zapf Book Light............ 476	Venture Script................. 506	Trajan Bold 518
ITC Zapf Book Light Italic....... 476	Visigoth 507	Umbra 519
ITC Zapf Book Medium 476		Zarana 519
ITC Zapf Book Medium Italic 476	**DISPLAY: Eccentrics,**	
ITC Zapf Book Demi............ 476	**Romantics and Period Faces**	**DISPLAY: Outlines**
ITC Zapf Book Demi Italic....... 476	Antique 508	Americana Outline............. 520
ITC Zapf International Light 478	American Antique............... 508	ITC Bauhaus Heavy Outline....... 520
ITC Zapf International Light Italic . 478	Calliope Antique................ 508	Bloc 520
ITC Zapf International Medium.... 478	Federal Antique................. 508	Chwast Buffalo
ITC Zapf International	Charlemagne Regular............ 508	Black Condensed Outline....... 520
Medium Italic 478	Charlemagne Bold 508	Cloister Open Face............. 520
ITC Zapf International Demi 478	Chevalier 509	Cooper Black Outline 521
ITC Zapf International Demi Italic . 478	Chisel......................... 509	ITC Franklin Gothic Outline 521
	Chwast Buffalo Black Condensed ... 509	Gill Sans Ultra Bold Outline (KAYO) 521
DISPLAY FACES:	Computer 509	Globe Gothic Outline 521
Scripts and Cursives	Computer Outline 509	Gothic Outline Condensed 521
Ariston 480	Copperplate Light 509	Hobo Outline 522
Ariston Bold 480	Copperplate Heavy.............. 510	ITC Kabel Outline 522
Ariston Extra Bold 481	Davida 510	ITC Korinna Bold Outline 522
Bison 481	Devendra 510	Revue Outline Condensed......... 522
Brush Script.................... 482	Eccentric 510	Revue Shadow................. 522
Calligraphia.................... 482	Engravure 510	Roman Stylus 523
Cascade Script.................. 483	Euclid 510	ITC Souvenir Outline 523
Choc.......................... 483	Euclid Bold 511	Stencil Outline 523
Citadel Script 484	Fantail 511	ITC Serif Gothic Bold Outline..... 523
Commercial Script 484	Fehrle Display 511	Windsor Outline................ 523
Coronet 485	Fette Fraktur Bold 511	Worcester Round Outline 523
Coronet Bold 485	ITC Franklin Gothic Contour 511	
Diskus 486	ITC Franklin Gothic	**DISPLAY: Digitized Wood Type**
Diskus Bold.................... 486	Outline Shadow.............. 512	Cottonwood 524
Dom Casual.................... 487	Ben Franklin Initials............ 512	Ironwood...................... 524
Dom Casual Bold 487	Glenn Shaded 512	Juniper 525
Flemish Script No 2 488	Gold Nugget................... 512	Ponderosa 525
Florentine Script No 2 488	Goudy Handtooled............. 512	
Floridian Script................. 489	Hobo 512	**ONE-LINE SPECIMENS**
French Script................... 489	ITC Kabel Contour 513	Adobe Type Library............ 526
Gando Ronde Script............. 490	Kabel Shaded 513	Bitstream Typeface Library 527
Gavotte Script................. 490	Kismet 513	ITC Typeface Collection.......... 529

Gutenberg examines a press sheet in the engraving above. Below, a page from his celebrated Bible, printed in Mainz, c.1450. Below, right, a current digital type and image-setting work environment.

INTRODUCTION

No technology has contributed more to the enhancement of human aspirations than writing. No system of writing has been more functional, fulfilling and universally accepted than the alphabet. And of all the ways of spreading information visually, nothing came close to displacing printing with metal type as the prime vehicle for the effective use of the alphabet for some five hundred years. Nothing, that is, until now.

Metal type can still be found occasionally among typography buffs and enthusiasts of the art of traditional fine book printing. But by 1950, typesetting had become a mechanically operated photo-optical process, producing repros on light-sensitive receptor surfaces. Later, computers were introduced and developing electronics technology advanced the process further. Computer digitization advanced typesetting yet again, bypassing master negatives and conventional photographic procedures entirely. Laser technology now promises increases in speed and image resolution. Significantly, these new digital technologies have advanced the integration of type with other elements of graphic design, a major step forward in visual communications.

All of these systems of type production can still be found in most major cities, although metal typography is considered more of an art form in some circles. Both photolettering and transfer lettering have come into wide use, performing some of the same functions as typesetting. But it is digital type produced with light and laser projection on highly developed receptor surfaces, that has come to dominate the typesetting industry.

What Is Type?

Type can be described as the product of any technology that enables discrete elements of an alphabet to be combined for effective communication. Its origins can be traced to the middle of the fifteenth century when the earliest type was simply a small metal casting, mostly lead, with a raised letter or punctuation mark on its face. Insignificant in appearance perhaps, but the genius of

This Graduale Romanum, *a fine example of fifteenth century liturgical music books, was printed by Erhard Ratdolt in 1494.*

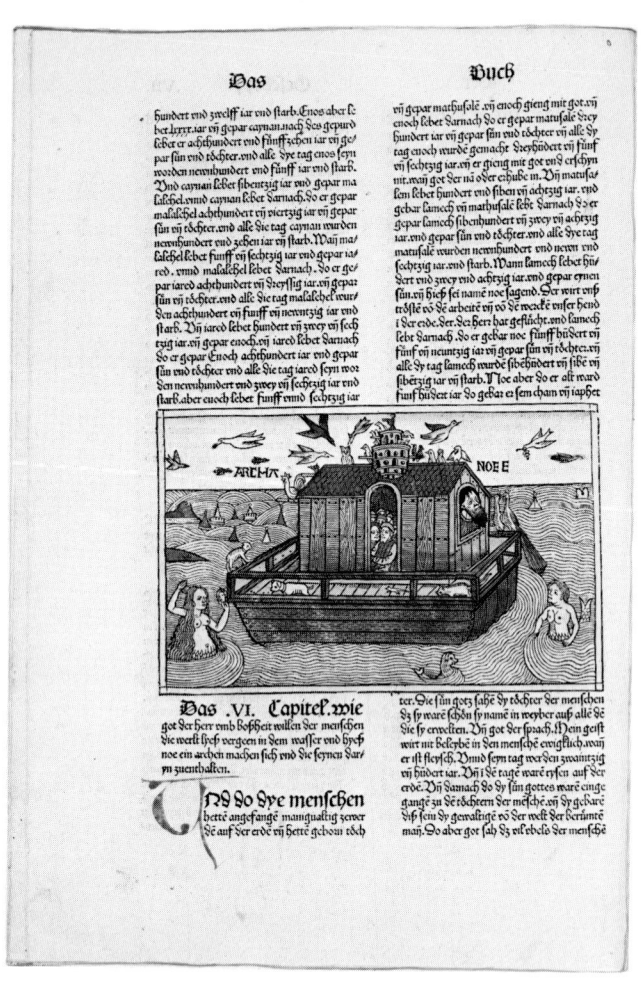

A page from Biblia Germanica *printed in 1483 by Anton Koberger, a major printer and publisher in fifteenth century Nuremberg.*

type was that it rendered the elements of the alphabet uniform, movable and reusable.

Typography, as originally conceived, proved to be a useful craft. Born at the middle of the fifteenth century, movable type produced shock waves that forever altered the way information would be disseminated. Printing with movable type opened a visual channel, through which the creative enthusiasm and humanist values of the Renaissance were expressed. Surviving classical cultural and philosophical concepts, together with both secular and nonsecular attitudes of the East, fed the flood of creativity emerging from the West. With movable type at its disposal, printing was firmly established as an efficient way to provide this wealth of information.

The Legacy of Type

Early in the history of movable type, printing was a scholarly vocation compared to the general level of literacy in fifteenth-century Europe. Printers often possessed profound insights into punch-cutting, molding techniques, printing, writing, historical scholarship of the period, and the varied related disciplines connected with their craft. The new type technology enabled them to reproduce books by the hundreds, with technical and intellectual excellence and hitherto unattainable speed and accuracy. This helped make movable type an attractive invention, and many were drawn to this discipline because of its obvious significance as a prime vehicle of enlightenment.

There were modifications and improvements almost from the beginning, but the basic process remained much the same: cut the punches; make a matrix for each character; pour molten type metal into each mold; duplicate it in sufficient quantities; trim all type to uniform height; sort it out; select and lock the type into a rigid frame; find and use an appropriate ink; cover the type with suitable paper; apply uniform pressure; remove with care. With this process, a printed sheet could be produced over and over. And when that was accomplished: unlock the type, redistribute it, and do it again for the rest of the pages.

Written language was the province of a privileged few before movable type made it available to the common citizen. Movable type was indeed about feeding the growing demand for information. But it also was about power. In the morning of Western civilization, Cadmus,

Beatus
vir ā Seruite dño. Euouae.
qui nō abijt in cōsilio im=
pioꝝ: ⁊ in via peccatoꝝ nō
stetit: et in cathedra pestilē=
tie nō sedit, Sed in lege
dñi volūtas eius: ⁊ in lege ei⁹ meditabit͛ die
ac nocte, Et erit tanqᷓ lignū qđ plantatū est
secus decursus aqᷓrū: qđ fructū suū dabit in
tpe suo, Et foliū ei⁹ nō defluet: ⁊ oīa quecūqᷓ
faciet psperabunt͛, Non sic impij nō sic: sed
tanqᷓ puluis quē proicit ventus a facie terre,
Ideo nō resurgūt impij in iudicio: neqᷓ pctō=
res in cōsilio iustoꝝ, Qm̄ nouit dñs viā iu=
stoꝝ: et iter impioꝝ pibit, Gła pr̄i, Sc d̄d

Quare fremuerūt gētes: ⁊ ꝑpłi meditati
sūt inania, Astiterūt reges tr̄e et prin=
cipes ꝯuenet͛ in vnū: adu͛sus dñm ⁊ adu͛sus
xpm ei⁹, Dirūpam⁹ vincła eoꝝ: ⁊ piciam⁹
a nobis iugū ipoꝝ, Qui habitat in celis irri=
debit eos: et dñs subsannabit eos, Tūc lo=
quet͛ ad eos in ira sua: et in furoꝛe suo cōtur=
babit eos, Ego aūt cōstitutus sū reẍ ab eo

Initials on this Fust and Schoeffer Psalter, vary in color from copy to copy. Produced in Mainz, 1459, they were skillfully printed or stenciled on a pre-printed text. Fust and Schoeffer were partners and successors to Gutenberg.

Nunc ad ægyptiā transeamus ut etiā hinc uideamus rectene an contra gentilium nugas contempsimus & salutarem euāgelii doctrinā secuti sumus: quā maxime nunc neglectis suis sāctissime colit ægyptiis: Vniuersam autem ægyptiorum historiam & theologiam ipsorum seorsū in libro quem sacrum iscripsit Manetus quidam ægyptius græca līgua exquisitissime in mediū edidit. Sed Diodorus etiam siculus uir clarus omnem ut diximus historiam gentium diligenter breuiter ac ordinate congregatam cōscribens ab ægyptiorum theologia totius negotii fecit initiū a quo potius quasi ab illustriore notioreq; græcis q̄ ab ægyptio Maneto: hæc ad uerbum scribenda duximus. De egyptioꝛ theologia.

† A   Ȧsserunt igitur ægyptii in reꝛ omnium originem hoīes primum

A *From* De Praeparatione Evangelica, *the first book printed in Nicolaus Jenson's roman type.*

B *Johann von Speyer, the first printer in Venice, took the name Johannes de Spira. Shown is a detail from Pliny's* Natural History, *printed by de Spira in 1469 with type attributed to Nicolaus Jenson.*

C *Founder of the first printing press in England, William Caxton produced a handsome version of Geoffrey Chaucer's* Canterbury Tales.

D *Excerpt from a work by Francisco Colonna, printed by Aldus Manutius in 1499 with type cut by Griffo.*

ACTENVS DE SITV ET MIRACVLIS terrę aquarumq; & syderum: ac ratione uniuersitatis: atque mensura. Nunc de partibus quanq̄ infinitum id quoq; existimat̄: nec temere sine aliqua reprębēsione tractādū haud ullo in genere uenia iustiore. Si modo mime miꝛ est hominem genitū nō oīa būana nouisse. Quapropter auctorem neminem unū sequar: sed ut queq; ueristimū in quaq; parte arbitrabor: quoniam commune ferme omnibus fuit: ut eos quisq; diligentissime situs disceret: ex quibus ipse prodibat. Ideoq; nec culpabo: nec coarguā

†† B

Here endith the Wyff of Bathes prologe.
And here begynneth her tale.
In olde dayes of kyng Artur
Of Whiche Britons spekith gret honour
Al Was this lond ful filled of fayrye
The elf quene With her ioly companye
Daunced ful ofte in mony a greue mede
This Was the olde opinion as J rede

C

LA SPAVENTEVOLE SILVA, ET CONSTI-
pato Nemore euaso, & gli primi altri lochi per el dolce somno che se hauea per le fesse & prosternate mēbre diffuso relicti, me ritrouai di nouo in uno piu delectabile sito assai piu che el præcedente. Elquale non era de mon ti horridi, & crepidinose rupe intorniato, ne falcato di strumosi iugi. Ma compositamente de grate montagniole di non tropo altecia. Siluose di giouani quercioli, di roburi, fraxini & Carpini, & di frondosi Esculi, & Ilice, & di teneri Coryli, & di Alni, & di Tilie, & di Opio, & de infructuosi Oleastri, dispositi secondo laspecto de

D

a Phoenician prince who understood the uses of power, is said to have introduced written language to ancient Greece. He is identified with the evocative mythological image of casting the alphabet in the role of dragon's teeth, which when sown, sprung to life as armed soldiers. Such was the early understanding of the power of the written word.

Early Type Design

At first, the aim of type designers was to imitate the admired calligraphy of the period. As the craft of producing and printing with movable type entered the 1500s, functional characteristics of type began to affect the way it was designed and produced. Demand for variations in size, weight, style, and visual relationships of letter to letter and space to counterspace all began to bear on the way new types were designed and produced. A vigorous and prolific display of typographic invention appeared.

Many fine U.S. libraries and museums, including the J. Pierpont Morgan Library in New York, the Harvard College Library in Cambridge, MA, the Boston Athenaeum, the John Carter Brown Library in Provi-

†Westvaco, see p. 534.   ††Pierpont Morgan Library, see p. 534.

> LE SEGOND LIVRE. FEVIL. XIX.
>
> LAſpiration a doncques ſon tra=
> uerſant traict ſus la ligne centri=
> que & diametralle, iuſtement au deſ=
> ſus du penyl du corps humain, pour
> nous monſtrer que noſdictes lettres
> Attiques veulent eſtre ſi raiſonable=
> ment faictes, quelles deſirent ſentir
> en elles auec naturelle raiſon, toute
> conuenable proportion, & lart dar=
> chitecture, qui requiert que le corps
> dune maiſon ou dūg Palaix ſoit plus
> eſleue depuis ſon fondement iuſques
> a ſa couuerture, que neſt la dicte cou
> uerture, qui repreſente le chef de tou
> te la maiſon. Si la couuerture dune
> maiſon eſt exceſſiuemēt plusgrande
>
> Ordon=
> nance du
> trauerſāt
> traict au
> corps hu
> main.
>
> Notable
> ſingulier.

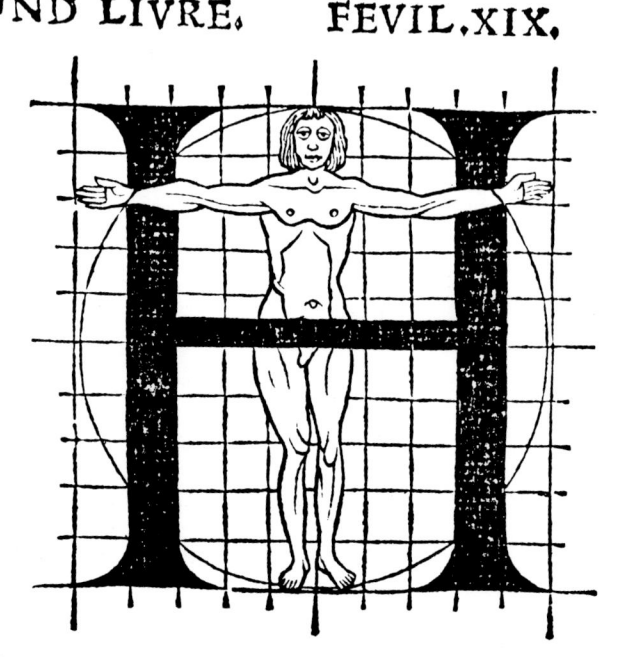

E *Part of a page from Geoffroy Tory's* Champfleury, *a book of language and letters, issued 1529, in France.*

F *Detail of type cut by Philippe Granjean, c.1700, precursor of transitional and modern styles. Granjean's title: King's Royal Punch Cutter.*

G *Lines of verse in Ludovico Arrighi's flowing cursive type, printed in Rome, c.1523.*

H *John Baskerville, self-styled "admirer of the beauty of Letters", produced the face named for him with the help of John Handy, punchcutter.*

dence, The Smithsonian Institution in Washington and the New York Public Library, offer a view of books printed with movable type before 1500. They are known as incunabula, a charming term signifying swaddling clothes, still used to denote the beginning stage of printing with movable type. Firsthand study of early books is a rewarding experience. There is a kind of beauty in these early efforts that eludes verbal description. Early attempts to produce printed books resembling hand written manuscripts are apparent among these ancient examples. Some employ illumination, block prints, or other elements to heighten the illusion of handwritten text.

Type production was nursed, coaxed, cajoled, and otherwise led into more efficient production modes. But for over four hundred years, typesetting was a laborious hand-gathering and -setting system done on a character-by-character basis, line for line, paragraph for paragraph. D. B. Updike (Printing Types), cites sixteenth century reports that work on early type composition and printing on primitive screw type presses was interminable, sometimes beginning at two or three in the morning and continuing until eight or nine in the evening.

LA NAISSANCE DU ROY.

Sous le Regne de Loüis XIII la France ſe voyoit triomphante de toutes parts. Les Hérétiques domptez, la Maiſon d'Auſtriche humiliée, & l'autorite Royale reſtablie, rendoient le Royaume auſſi heureux que floriſſant. Mais il manquoit au Roy un fils qui puſt luy ſuccéder, & vingt-trois ans de mariage ſans enfans luy avoient preſque oſté l'eſpérance d'en avoir jamais. Enfin, Dieu touché des vœux ardents d'un Roy pieux, & d'une vertueuſe Reyne, leur donna un fils, dont la naiſſance ſi peu attenduë, combla de joye tous les François. Ce viſible préſent du Ciel fut un gage certain de la protection Divine, & parut dés ce moment aſſeurer à la France la gloire, où elle eſt parvenue, & la félicité dont elle jouït.

Veggio ne' la mia mente il graue ſcempio
Di quelle genti; e con vittoria grande
Tornarſi lieto il mio Signore in Roma.
Veggio che fiori ogniun d'intorno ſpande;
Veggio le ſpoglie opime andare al tempio

JUVENALIS SATYRA VI. 73

Jamque eadem ſummis pariter, minimiſque libido:
Nec melior pedibus ſilicem quæ conterit atrum;
Quam quæ longorum vehitur cervice Syrorum.
Ut ſpectet ludos, conducit Ogulnia veſtem,
Conducit comites, ſellam, cervical, amicas,
Nutricem, et flavam, cui det mandata, puellam.

A detail, right, from the New York Herald-Tribune of July 3, 1886, the first newspaper to be machine-set with type obtained from the Linotype "Blower". One of the earliest models is shown above.

Mergenthaler's Linotype, Star Base Model 1. Redesigned in 1889, it became the basis for all subsequent Linotype machines.

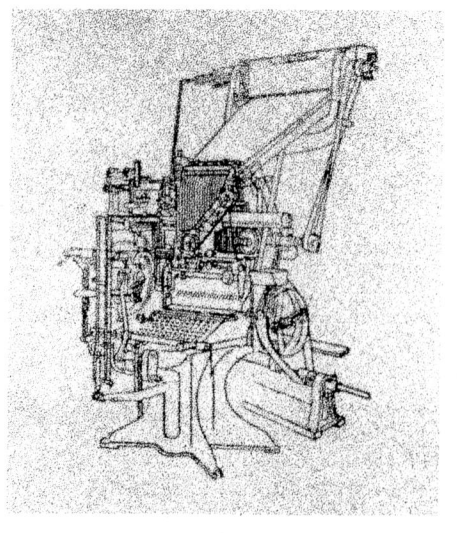

The Mechanization of Typesetting

Work on searching out mechanized ways to set type began in earnest around 1820. For about one hundred years, French, British and American inventors worked at it, with a burst of productivity occurring in the last decades of the nineteenth century. Prototypes of machines to create type mechanically enabled the discipline to survive and eventually prosper.

In the U.S., Ottmar Mergenthaler, a German immigrant, invented commercially acceptable solutions to the troublesome problems of automatic type justification and distribution. He succeeded in setting a few paragraphs of copy for the *New York Tribune* during the summer of 1886. The feat was accomplished on his remarkable invention, the Linotype machine, casting type one line at a time from a row of brass matrices. Machine typesetting was introduced and a pressing need addressed.

The Linotype machine, later fondly known as "the beast", could accept copy, receive type metal, melt it down, and, with the appropriate matrix in place, produce type in the size, style, and measure desired, casting it a whole line at a time. Never mind that the beast was big, heavy, awkward to handle, and at times unbearably hot, or that it made startling sounds, gratuitously groaning and spitting molten type metal unpredictably. There were problems with the cumbersome matrices as well: they were costly, heavy, and demanded large accessible storage spaces. But compared to the tedium of hand-set composition for extensive text-setting, laboriously composed one letter at a time, the Linotype machine was indeed a significant step. Foundries continued to produce the larger display characters as individual types and remained the source for text setting equipment.

The Stage is Set

In the twentieth century, a quiet revolution began and a fundamental change in typesetting technology began to materialize, making traditional type production methods obsolete.

In the periods following the two World Wars, better control of photographic processes and advances in paper, ink, printing technology, and computer development all began to converge; photo-offset lithography grew more efficient and pervasive; typeface design proliferated. World War I had generated an enormous demand for information, but the second World War was followed by an information explosion beyond anything previously experienced. And just in time to connect with this enormous demand, computer driven phototypesetting arrived, full of promise for the electronic information age.

These new technological developments produced consternation in the ranks of the typesetting industry. Production and practice in hot metal type was confronted by wrenching changes brought about by the computer, advanced photo technology, and an increasingly high-tech environment. Invented about 1450, widely practiced until the 1950s, hot metal type all but disappeared from the marketplace by the 1970s.

The New Typesetting Technology

Phototypesetting of the 1950s engaged various mechanical photo-optical systems. Copy was introduced through a keyboard and converted to light impulses by a computer within a printer. These light impulses, directed through master type negatives and optical systems, were projected to create type images on appropriate light-sensitive receptor surfaces.

Digitization of type images followed in less than a decade. At first, master font negatives were used. Fonts were scanned, transferred as lines or dots onto a cathode-ray tube using a digitized light source, and printed as repro copy.

True digital type arrived in the 1970's when it became technically possible to abandon all master film negatives. This was the result of a 1965 invention by Dr. Ing Hell. Under the new system, master art work was scanned, picked up on the video display terminal and transmitted in digital form to magnetic media for storage in a computer. An operator at a video-display terminal then instructed the printer via video signals to produce the desired image.

An argument can be made that all current typesetting processes, while not fully photographic, nevertheless use photo-optics to some degree and thus may be classified as phototype. The laser, for instance, is at least partially dependent on light transmission for its operation, and is included under the phototypesetting umbrella in some publications. For this presentation, however, all type-imaging systems depending on digitization and independent of a master font negative within the printer will be classified as *digital type*.

The Economics of Digital Type

Economics is a strong persuader, and was the major reason for the nearly universal acceptance of the new modes of computerized type. With this technology, commercial typographers no longer required costly, space-consuming typesetting equipment or proving and storage facilities. Rising wages were also a factor—this new system was less labor-intensive. The cost of new typefaces and equipment maintenance was lower. These were irresistible advantages. Furthermore, prime location was no longer so important because electronic information hardly took any more time to travel around the world than around the corner.

Typographers were among the first workers to organize into unions in the U.S. Typography has been a proud trade with a responsible and respected union. As late as the 1960s, typographers were required to learn about typesetting in depth. Overall knowledge of the craft was typically the result of a period of apprenticeship. A developed sensitivity to tasteful typesetting was an attribute sought in typographers and, more often than not, found there.

But aesthetic considerations do not often speed production, and traditional virtues, like dedicated craftsmanship, do not necessarily increase billable output. Inexorably, as society moved along a faster track, typography became more and more about speed of output and compatability with related disciplines.

With computer programs doing much of the work, any good typist became a candidate for a job as typesetter. Under the supervision of skilled and knowledgeable typographers, typists could be trained to be productive typesetters at a fraction of the time and cost demanded by union (or, for that matter, non-union) typographers.

By the 1980s, advanced digital typesetting equipment was capable of exceeding the needs of most commercial typographers—even those with multiple input stations. But the potential for enormous output was there and that was irresistible. There are shops that may never reach the output capability limits of typesetting equipment they own.

Ease of data entry, a sharp and consistent type image, a wide choice of relatively inexpensive type fonts, simple modulation of type image, and an overall economy of operations were all more readily achieved through digital type. General accessibility of the new systems also played a part, allowing nearly anyone who could punch a keyboard to take part in the typesetting process. Companies that formerly went to commercial typographers for their type needs now commonly have their own in-house typesetting facilities. Design firms, ad agencies, public relations firms, and other users of type now set and print much of their own type, or at least keystroke and code it for processing by commercial typographers (frequently referred to as service bureaus), for a relatively small investment. Only those commercial typographers who have long since adapted to digital typesetting methods are finding new sources of business. The subsequent advent of and emphasis on desktop publishing led to further changes in the commercial typesetting business. New services are constantly being devised and offered by commercial type shops in search of new business opportunities.

Enter Phototypesetting

Beginning around 1950, commercially developed phototypesetting equipment began to appear on the market as a practical technology. Nearly 50 years earlier, Mergenthaler among others, made experimental inroads, but their products were neither aesthetically pleasing nor commercially viable. It was Intertype that brought to market the first practical commercial phototypesetter, the *Fotosetter*, in 1949.

Although the Fotosetter was marginally accepted at the time, it was a far cry from later phototypesetting equipment. The engineering challenges of producing functional typesetting equipment overwhelmed the need for aesthetically pleasing output. The type produced on the Fotosetter was anything but heartwarming, and there was heated dialog among designers and typophiles as to whether phototypesetting would ever replace metal type.

Great strides have been made since the earliest phototypesetting models appeared in the marketplace. Advanced phototypesetting and, at its heels, digital type were largely a result of advances in the computer field. Dramatic growth in high speed photographic processes, electronics, and laser technology have all contributed to the near-universal acceptance of current computer-driven, digital typesetting practice.

The descriptions that follow are intended to familiarize the reader with various methods sometimes described as generations of computerized type-setting. Engineering aspects of electronics, digitization, lasers, high-speed photographic techniques, and other high tech processes are beyond the purview of this presentation, which is intended to be an introduction to the basics of current typesetting practice. Moreover, new developments are constantly being introduced—frequent consultation of current material in this rapidly expanding discipline is strongly advised.

Mechanical Photo-Optics

Early phototypesetting equipment like the Mergenthaler Fotosetter and the Monophoto from the Monotype Corporation were designed for use by commercial typographers. They were Rube Goldberg-like, rooted in mechanical technology similar to the metal-type production equipment that preceded them. Because of its many moving parts, the equipment was subject to frequent breakdown, output was slow, and setting options were relatively limited. In addition, the technology was costly, and the ratio of required keystrokes to output was dismal.

The mechanics were ingenious for their time: master alphabets were stored on manually inserted, reusable film negatives. Input copy was entered on a keyboard. Paper tape was introduced, which, when punched, could accept correction, store documents, and drive printers. Inside the printer, a light was projected through the master negative and passed into an optical system. One font master usually created different sizes through lens adjustment. From there it was transferred to a sensitized receptor surface of paper or film. Gears and escape mechanisms moved the receptor surface to a prescribed position, thus securing an orderly exposure of repro copy. The paper or film was then processed as a repro.

The output was a sharply defined photographic image. Punched tape extended the practicality of the system, but speed was not spectacular: no more than a few lines per minute. Rules were rough, and diagonal rules or curved lines were unavailable. The use of film negatives presented storage problems and occasional accumulation of dust which, when projected, produced flaws on printout copy.

Photo-Scan, Digitized

Improvements were added: enhanced electronic functions, lower cost, magnetic data storage, and increasingly sophisticated software were combined to add practicality to phototypesetting. More importantly, computers were incorporated and linked to the printer to produce type images. A monitor was built on a cathode-ray tube, or CRT, and tied to a keyboard to complete the assembly known as a video-display terminal, or VDT.

The fonts, still in the form of master negatives, were scanned and reassembled on a CRT as lines (rasters) or dots (pixels) by means of an electronically driven, digitized light source. From a CRT within the printer, the type image was projected to a film or paper receptor surface and processed. Although digital type was thereby anticipated, such printout is not usually considered true digital type.

Digital CRT Scan

With the ever-growing demand for generating more information faster, photo-optics was bypassed and master film negatives became obsolete. Constantly improving technology allowed original artwork for master fonts to be electronically scanned, stored, and transmitted digitally, directly to magnetic tapes or disks. Each font became a digitized map of the original art from which it was derived and stored in the computer. From there it travelled to a CRT in the printer, which could receive a digital image directly from the VDT. Like familiar television broadcasts, the type image in the printer's CRT was created as a pattern of horizontal lines or dots. The digitized type image was then projected to a paper or film receptor surface. This is the first mode of typesetting commonly referred to as digital type.

These steps were under electronic control, permitting flexibility in type reproportioning and manipulation, and much faster printout rates. Electronics also offered more options for sophisticated creation of graphics as well as type. However, maximum output speeds were seldom sustained, because of unpredictable glitches in the equipment.

Nonetheless, four important advantages remained: 1) far greater font storage capacity; 2) increased output speed; 3) potential for creating continuous-tone photographic images in conjunction with type; 4) greater flexibility in the manipulation of type kerning, extending, condensing, and obliquing. Moreover, all these advantages could be gained in one integrated system. Dramatic price reductions in the late 1980s also played a part in extending the availability of this versatile equipment. Minute point-size gradations, extreme image sharpness, extensive and accessible font storage, and excellent software for sophisticated ruling applications added to the broad acceptance of this typesetting and imaging system.

Digitized Laser Scan

Type-image generation via an electronically controlled laser beam replaced the image-generating CRT and thus became the state-of-the-art digital typesetting system of the 1980s. Using previously developed techniques for the digital storage and transmission of master type fonts, it became possible to abandon all ties to photo-optical typesetting technology.

With digitized laser technology, there is neither a master font negative nor an image generating CRT in the printer. All information is stored and controlled digitally in a computer. A laser beam is electronically directed via computer to burn (print) type images onto the receptor surface in a high-speed scanning action. Travelling line by line across a full page of copy, a laser beam builds the entire type image, one dot at a time along one line at a time, sweeping back and forth at near the speed of light, to produce repro copy directly. No further processing is needed.

Laser output resolution varies, starting from around three hundred dots per inch or DPI, on desktop printers to upwards of five thousand DPI on commercial installations. With all font data stored digitally, size gradations of up to one-tenth of a point are available and extensive reproportioning is possible. The laser scanning operation allows for ease of input and integrated printout of line art and continuous-tone graphics. With a potential repro printout speed of thousands of lines per minute, this appears to be the direction of future development.

Desktop Typesetting

Laser capabilities are also available on relatively simple personal computer systems and on advanced desk-top models. With the demand for expanded type production continuing, and typesetting technology extending its capabilities in speed and output while simultaneously coming down in price, desktop publishing has made the greatest popular inroads yet seen in digital typesetting.

The Apple Mac desktop systems, much more visually oriented and user-friendly than the earlier minicomputer systems released by business machine vendors, have been widely adopted by graphic designers and are also popular as teaching instruments, especially in high school and college graphic design courses. By 1990, cross-licensing of extensive type libraries and broadly compatible software programs have greatly increased the practicality of these computers as viable tools for type and graphic design.

In addition to graphic designers, authors, editors, reporters, executives, secretaries, copywriters, architects, industrial designers—*anyone* who can operate a personal computer—is a candidate to become a typesetter of sorts, and in fairly short order. Having accomplished that, it is only a few short steps for the initiated computer typesetter with an affinity for this medium to learn to integrate line art and continuous-tone graphics.

Software is constantly improving. Now, readily available to all, page-description language programs offer a way to preview, adjust, and control integration of various graphic design elements in the manner employed by many designers. The creative organization of type, format, line art, and continuous tone graphics has become much more responsive to designer control through the use of sophisticated software programs. PostScript, from Adobe Systems Incorporated, is the most widely accepted page-description language on the market; Interpress, a Xerox product; Quark Express, Ventura and Aldus Pagemaker are among competitive programs. New programs continue to be introduced in a seemingly endless procession.

An operator using a desktop work station can now design a publication, set its type, create both line and continuous-tone art, scan and pick up existing art, scaling and positioning all these elements at will. The entire integrated job can then be routed from the computer to a 300 DPI printer to produce a comp or a high resolution laser printer to obtain a camera-ready printout or, if desired, on film negative or even directly onto a printing plate. For this writer, whose graphic design experience goes back over 30 years, this process stops just short of being miraculous.

Using digital equipment, a remarkably fine-tuned body of work is coming from both professional graphic designers and many who are well on their way to becoming professionals. In the design schools, there is lively debate as to whether it is better to teach student designers traditional hands-on approaches to design or the computer-oriented method. Currently most schools offer both approaches and time alone will resolve the issue.

Of course, gaining the skill to set type and manipulate graphic elements is not necessarily the equivalent of becoming a graphic designer, as many desktop operators have discovered. But in our do-it-yourself age, there are software programs to adequately handle simple fliers, newsletters, in-house publications and other forms of visual communication. Frequent production of such publications imparts to the novice the design experience needed to exert increasingly better control over creative processes. Prevailing marketing wisdom holds that this direction will be widely accepted and extended by the end of the century. By that time, a new generation of type-oriented graphic designers, now serving their apprenticeships at desktop work stations, will have developed new aesthetic standards, new ideas about graphics, and advanced ways to enhance visual communications.

**From Commercial Type Shops
to Desktop Publishing: Closing the Gap**
Cynthia Hollandsworth

The change from commercial typography to desktop publishing has many facets: the merger of word processing with typesetting on a low-cost platform, the integration of typography with graphic design, the developments allowing color design on a Macintosh in the PostScript environment. In a word, the difference is *PostScript*, which allows images, color and text to be manipulated simultaneously in fully designed pages.

The implications for all the exciting graphic possibilities of using PostScript on desktop operation are far reaching. For me, the most interesting part is that type and typography have been placed in the hands of the designer. For those who appreciate fine typography this is both a blessing and a curse. The freedom to try many solutions easily and inexpensively will save some designers from making serious design mistakes. However, composing type, as anyone who has done it knows, is a design task in itself. Most designers who have tried to do their own composition have learned to appreciate the careful craftsmanship and experience of professional typographers.

After each technological advance in typography, there has been severe criticism from purists. There have been six major technological advances in type composition in this century: from hand composition to linecasting; to photomatrix; to bitmap; to CRT vector outline; to

---

Cynthia Hollandsworth is the Typographic Advisor to Agfa Corporation, Agfa Compugraphic Division, in Massachusetts. She is a typeface designer, and has released a number of typefaces including AlphaOmega, Hiroshige and ITC Tiepolo. She is also an advisor to the ITC Typeface Review Board.

laser line-and-arc outline; and now to Bezier outline. Criticism notwithstanding, I believe that type has the potential to be set more beautifully today than at any time in history, when used by knowledgeable design professionals. The professional compositor has little trouble moving to the desktop application and creating the same level of quality of typography as always.

Many of the fine compositional features offered on professional systems at the commercial type shop finally have arrived on the desktop. These include significant hyphenation programs, and kerning programs that allow thousands of pair options that can be customized for each individual typeface design. Today PostScript composition is moving to larger Macintoshes and to Sun workstations with enhanced memory and power, which allow the user to accomplish color separated projects in a real-time environment.

Because of PostScript, there is much more design flexibility in headline and display typography than commercial typographers enjoyed. Type that used to be set on a two-inch filmstrip composer can now be composed on the Macintosh, using wonderful programs that allow the designer to move letters to the right or left in tiny increments. A headline can be isolated digitally as a graphic image and modified as if it were a drawing. Using this technique, letters can be joined together into ligatures, modified with swashes and details, such as texture or shadows. These details may be added to quickly produce a headline that would have taken hours or days to design with pen and ink or photographic techniques.

Two things remain to be done to allow users to take full advantage of these developments. First, the world's PostScript library must be vastly expanded. Currently there are only seven hundred PostScript faces that are fully tested and optimized. This is not enough to meet the needs of the advertising typography trade which is accustomed to thousands of design choices. Every new product invites a new typeface design to help set it apart from all the others so the demand for new, high-quality designs never ends.

The second, and by far the larger problem, is that designers who are not typographers by trade must be better educated in the art and craft of typography and type design. In his book *Detail in Typography*, Swiss designer Jost Hochuli identified the hierarchy of typographic knowledge as beginning with letters and letterspacing; words and wordspacing; lines and linespacing; columns; and the appearance of typefaces. There must be an understanding of all of these elements to take advantage of the features and functions available to the desktop typographer. If, for example, there is no awareness of interletter spacing, either in pairs or globally over a text, design errors are inevitable. In the same way, a poor selection of type design for a text can send a subliminal message that conveys something quite different from the intent of the text.

While the principles of typography are relatively simple, the implementation of these concepts must be interpreted over a nearly infinite variety of instances. Imagine how many different letter combinations there are, and multiply this by the number of different typefaces in use, and you will see how complex typography becomes in just the first of Jost Hochuli's principles. The ability to coordinate all the typographic elements into a composition that is harmonious and elegant is a complex combination of craft and taste, requiring training and experience.

How should this massive education project be undertaken? Many manufacturers of type products have created promotional programs to fill some of the needs. Stronger type education in the design schools will help the coming generation of designers. But the burden of mastering the details will fall to the current generation of desktop users to learn on their own.

Beautiful typography can hide a multitude of design sins, while poor typography can ruin the best graphic design. Good typography has the power to communicate selectively, including such feelings as order, calm and peace, causing the reader to be more receptive on a subliminal level. The successful bridge between commercial type shops and desktop publishing is contained in this simple idea: good typography should be common to both disciplines.

Characters of the Computer
Bruce Brenner and Jim Gutierrez

Letterform design is a unique craft that combines fine art with the art of communication; this is the essence of typography. Of course, as with any endeavor, the tools of this trade have changed throughout the centuries as technology progressed. This has never been more evident than in the twentieth century. Hot metal type, phototype and now digital type have been the standard components for designers in their efforts to design and employ type for the past one hundred years. But the past 20 years of digital type technology have amounted to more development and innovation than the sum of advancement during the period from Gutenberg's movable type to Mergenthaler's first Linotype machine, or roughly 450 some years.

The arts of graphic design and typography will be carried into the next century by something seemingly far removed from these traditional elements of communication: the silicon chip, on which computers, laser printers, and imagesetters are based, assist today's designers to enhance their creative processes. Through the power of computers, the artistic cycle of conceptualization, development, and final design is faster, and gets faster still as computers become more powerful. Designers have more time to develop a wider variety of ideas resulting in a rapid exchange of concepts that should ultimately lead to new design movements for the next century. Computers, once thought of as foreign to craftsmanship and aesthetics, are the backbone of today's design houses and are sure to be the fundamental tools for the designers of tomorrow.

Type designed with and for computers has undergone an especially rapid transformation from 1970 through 1990—particularly during the last decade of that period. Even the word *type* has evolved into the generic term *fonts*. Computerized laser imaging has developed to the degree that it can be employed for commercial purposes. In turn, the demand for typefaces in a new medium, *bitmaps* (the elements that ultimately instruct laser devices to position marks on paper, film, or computer screens) has increased.

Early bitmapping efforts were painstaking. To develop a typeface into a bitmapped digital form, hours of hand editing were required to maintain the integrity of the type design. Much as the classically trained type designers drew each character with a pen for specific point sizes, contemporary designers had to "draw" each character for each point size with a computer command. Their work would then be printed by a laser printing device and the quality would be reviewed and accepted or refined. These new processes gave rise to new typographic factors and rules, such as *screen fonts*, *resolution*, and *half-bitting*.

During the same period, "digital drafting" took an evolutionary turn in the form of *outline* or *scalable fonts*. With computerized type, each character's shape was represented by mathematical data, and these in turn could be edited by hand (by actually altering the mathematics of the shape) to achieve the desired type design. These outlines were then scaled by computer algorithms into bitmaps. Again, new rules came into play for the typographer. *Hints* became part of the typographer's jargon, describing the degree of instructions that could be applied to the outlines in order to obtain good typographic quality at low printer resolutions.

These developments in digital typography represent a small renaissance within the type industry. Today's type foundries are constantly developing new typefaces or reviving traditional, time-tested designs. Competing foundries find themselves sharing each other's libraries through cross-licensing agreements. Not only are type designs shared, but type production technologies are exchanged as well. As a result, large type libraries can be developed in months, as opposed to decades. The increasing sophistication of computer type software leads to increased productivity, benefiting the designer, supplier, and customer.

With these developments, clients have changed as well. No longer are companies relying solely on outside graphics firms to design their newsletters, brochures or other literature. Computers give these design customers the ability to develop and create their own original works, fostering an increasing interest in type and type technology among people who were shut out from these activities in the past. With the proliferation of computer use in our society, the demands for graphic communication will increase substantially. More computer users are becoming typographically literate, but it remains the responsibility of trained designers to educate this growing number of type users in the benefits of sound design principles.

The rapid developments in typographic technology provide designers not only with excellent tools for production, but also with a pipeline to computer programmers and engineers, allowing designers to assist in the development of computer tools that they will use. This may lead to computers that are still faster, more powerful, and easier to use. And, as designers gain in production and creativity, the real benefits will reach the person who counts the most: the customer.

At Linotype Company, Bruce Brenner is Manager of Typographic Development and Jim Guiterrez is Manager of Font Licensing Technology.

**From Punch to Pixel:
Designing and Making Type**
Matthew Carter

For much of type's history it has been difficult to see a distinction between type-designing and type-making. How much is art; how much craft? Garamond, Granjon, Fournier, Caslon are usually described as punchcutters, which is to say metalworkers. All had the comprehensive technical mastery that Fournier demanded in the 1760s: "A man cannot be a good punchcutter without being a typographer, that is to say, he must know every detail of the operations involved in typefounding and printing, that he may work with an eye to them."

Designing non-typographic letters was a different matter. Idealized letterforms with rules for their construction were devised by several Renaissance scholars, but beautiful as these often were, they remained theoretical studies with little practical effect on typography, rather like architectural plans too fanciful to build. The meeting of visionary letter design and practical typefounding occurred in an extraordinary project for the reform of French typography begun in the 1690s. The Academy of Sciences, grandiosely charged by Louis XIV with "discovering the secrets of Nature and perfecting the Arts," appointed a committee to study printing, the art that preserves all others. The members of the Bignon Committee have a claim to be the first type designers: they illustrated letterforms in large-scale diagrams, but they could not make type. For this they turned to an experienced punchcutter, Philippe Grandjean. The type that resulted, the *Romain du roi*, had a far-reaching influence, on Fournier and ultimately on Didot and Bodoni.

Of the historical designers who have given their names to styles of type, at least one, John Baskerville, was not himself a punchcutter. He employed a certain John Handy to cut punches under his direction. Handy's name has survived, but in the expansion of typefounding in the nineteenth century the cutters of type became increasingly anonymous. The English typefounder Vincent Figgins II, reminiscing in 1855 about a punchcutter employed by his father, wrote "No one knew his address; but he was supposed to be a tall man, who came in a mysterious way occasionally, whose name no one knew..."

Punchcutters were a secretive lot, as Figgins remarked: "The art had been perpetuated by a kind of Druidical or Masonic induction from the first." Joseph Moxon, in 1683 the first writer on typefounding, found no induction at all: "Letter-cutting is a Handy-Work hitherto kept so conceal'd among the Artificers of it, that I cannot learn any one hath taught it any other; But every one that has used it, Learnt it of his own Genuine Inclination." Joseph Jackson, apprenticed to the great William Caslon, discovered this the hard way. He had bored a hole through the wall in order to spy on his master cutting punches behind locked doors. Having finished a punch on his own initiative, Jackson presented it to Caslon and was rewarded with a good clout and the threat of jail.

By the time of the Private Press movement in England, the separation of type-designing from type-making was complete. The types of the Kelmscott Press designed by William Morris, the Doves Press type of Emery Walker, and several others, were cut by Edward Prince, a free-lance punchcutter in London. The separation of art and craft remained in force after the invention in 1885 of a machine for cutting punches. Frederic Goudy was almost alone among type designers in operating the machine himself; most made drawings and relied on the interpretative skills of specialists to adapt and manufacture their types—grumbling sometimes that bits of their original designs got lost at each successive manufacturing operation, like honey poured from jar to jar.

The fact is that the many specialized operations within a type *factory* eluded the single-handed mastery that a Fournier could exert over a type *foundry*. Some part

---

Matthew Carter is co-founder and Vice-President for Design of Bitstream Inc., a computer type foundry in Cambridge, Massachusetts. He is responsible for the overall design standards of the company and the creation of new type designs, of which the first is Bitstream Charter.

of the work had to be delegated, and with it went some degree of control. The development of photocomposition in the 1960s put a good measure of that control back within the designer's grasp by allowing original drawings to be photographed as the image source of the font. Designs for letters no longer had to be redrawn as engineering blueprints to guide the close-tolerance machining of metal type.

The more direct working methods of photocomposition type design went along with order-of-magnitude economies in font manufacture. With type easier and cheaper to produce, a manufacturers' investment in developing new faces was recouped more quickly. Typographic policies became more adventurous. In the lucrative trade typesetter market, the size and quality of type libraries became important competitive factors.

In the technical generation that followed, powerful digital typesetting systems began to break down the time-honored division of composing rooms into separate text and display departments. Whole-page composition, and typographic refinement programs that kerned headline type, brought the marriage of the big text-type repertories to the display collections, developed originally for film fonts and dry-transfer sheets. Presiding over this union was ITC, purveyors since 1971 of several type designs from the New York photolettering tradition that have the very marketable quality of setting well in both text and display sizes.

"Type-making does not tell its story...it hides its methods." So wrote the scholar-printer Theodore Low De Vinne. The difference between Garamond's *Gros Canon* and Cassandre's Bifur is not one of method—that the former was cut directly in steel while the latter was noodled on the backs of envelopes. The difference is cultural, not technical. Designing type is no more nor less difficult whether "file" means to you a punchcutter's smoothing tool or a bunch of digital data.

Pundits writing at the dawn of photocomposition, and again at the dawn of digital composition, predicted that typographic design would change with typographic technology. That they were wrong, and the changes slight, is probably because the users of the 'new' type were the same people that used the 'old' type. They looked for continuity of result, by cheaper and faster methods. What is novel about the latest typographic technology is its accessibility both to seasoned professionals and to people with no previous experience.

Personal computers, laser printers, page-description languages, and page-layout software, have democratized printing and publishing over the last five years. Fonts of type available in the retail software market are increasingly 'device-independent'. The idea of a font working on a number of different screens and printers is a novel one today, although, like many novelties, it actually represents a return to a former practice. It used to be possible to mix metal types cast at different foundries in the composing stick, and lock them up together in the chase for printing. Since the mechanization of typesetting, fonts have been machine parts that are not interchangeable between manufacturers or equipment models. But the 'open chase' is back in typography and, with it, competition among font makers.

Type design is coming full circle. The early punchcutters had no choice but to be both designers and makers of their types. The distancing of design from manufacture came with the change from craft to industry. That change has now gone into reverse: although type is still an industry, and a growing one, the supply of type is no longer tied exclusively to the supply of typesetting equipment. Once again there are independent 'typefoundries'—casting pixels now instead of lead alloy. The same opportunity that exists for digital typefoundries exists also for individual designers. 'Digital punchcutters' can now design their own letterforms on personal computers and, more importantly, make fonts and proof them immediately on a laser printer or typesetter. Designing, making and selling type are back within the reach of an individual, who can "work with an eye to" all of the operations involved, as Fournier considered so very desirable.

Is the induction into type-designing still as "Druidical" as Figgins said? Will the mysteries, long guarded, be revealed? The soothsayers have not welcomed the uninitiated in the past. This is Fournier: "Those who have embarked upon the task of cutting letters without the preliminary knowledge have invariably failed. We have examples not far to seek who gravely dishonor our profession." Nor would the novice type designer be tempted to experiment by Goudy's "Eccentricity of form from the hand of an artist who is master of himself and of his subject may be pleasing; it becomes only mere affectation when attempted by the ignorant amateur." Happily for Goudy, ignorant amateurs had no practicable way of making their own type in the 1920s. Happily for us, now they do.

Not all typefounders of earlier generations were inhospitable to new ideas and new talent. Some managed to be both mandarin and revolutionary. Charles Peignot, last of a dynasty of founder-designers, presided over French typography during its *belle epoque* between the wars, and in 1954 had the vision to introduce phototypesetting into Europe. Peignot's long career seems to have been dedicated to making typography *interesting*, to himself first and foremost, and to others by example. Looking back in 1975, and urging designers to be more inventive, Peignot asked: "Why should the art of typography be solely severe, esoteric and stiff? I was not bored, working on Bifur with Cassandre.

Adapted from 'Type Design Today' in the AIGA *Journal of Graphic Design*, Volume 6, Number 4, 1989.

Diagram of metal type for the letter H.

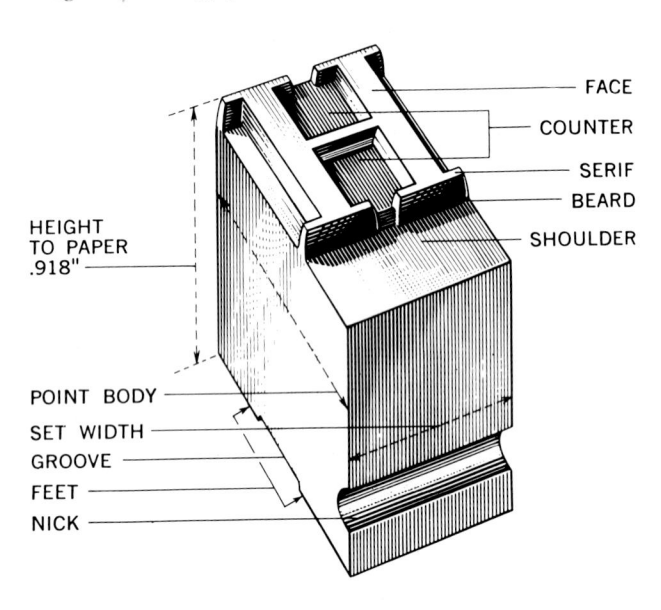

WORKING WITH TYPE

Looking up *type* in most dictionaries will probably yield a definition along these lines: a rectangular piece or block of metal or wood, having on its upper surface a letter or character in relief.

Type as we know it today requires a much broader definition. Type is the imaging of letters of the alphabet, numbers, punctuation and any other graphic devices that together form words, sentences, paragraphs, chapters, and groups of information. It can be used as the basis for designing various publications, signs, displays, film titles, packaging, timekeeping devices, posters, creative graphics, wall decorations and a near-endless list of other applications. Currently, type is produced primarily via program-guided, computer-driven, digitized electronic impulses that direct light and/or laser beams to prepared receptor surfaces where type images are produced at high speed.

Digital type, despite its many similarities to metal type impressions, looks different to the practiced eye. For readers with limited experience in the uses of digital type, some of these differences and similarities will be briefly addressed.

A *typeface* refers to a specific type design, such as Baskerville, Garamond, Helvetica, Palatino, Trooper, Gorilla, and thousands more. Many newer faces are upgraded versions of existing types, others are knockoffs, slightly modified and renamed.

Most faces have been drawn in a variety of styles, such as italic, light, bold, condensed, extended, inline, outline or shaded. The original face plus each of these styles may be considered a *font*.

Derivations of Type

Nearly all Western typefaces are derived from similar sources. The archetypal capital letter is classical Greek (which owes a debt to Phoenician [Semitic] writing models in existence as early as the ninth or tenth century B.C.), from which the stately Roman alphabet of the fourth century A.D. descends. Uncials and early Roman majuscules, followed by half uncials and later Roman minuscules all have been broadly documented. These forms in turn led to the beautifully designed Carolingian minuscules that so strongly influenced the way our alphabet looks today. Inspiring examples can be seen in the *Book of Kells*, the *Lindisfarne Gospels* and other manuscripts rendered in exquisitely written letter forms.

The hand known as *Rotunda*, or Southern Black Letter, appeared in Europe around 1400 and was widely used in secular applications; *Textura*, or Northern Black Letter, of the early 1400s became the nonsecular style of choice. It was a short step to the humanist minuscules, Italic and Fraktur alphabets of the Renaissance. These alphabets were used as models to emulate, exerting a

The letter n *viewed on a monitor during the digitization process.*

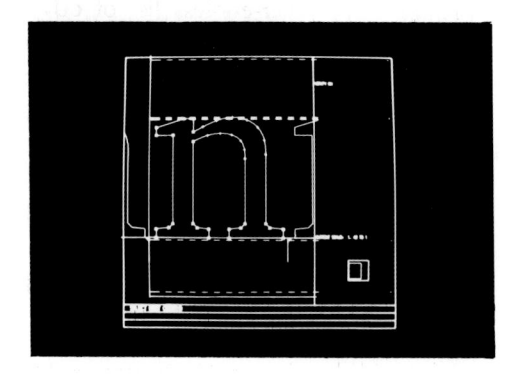

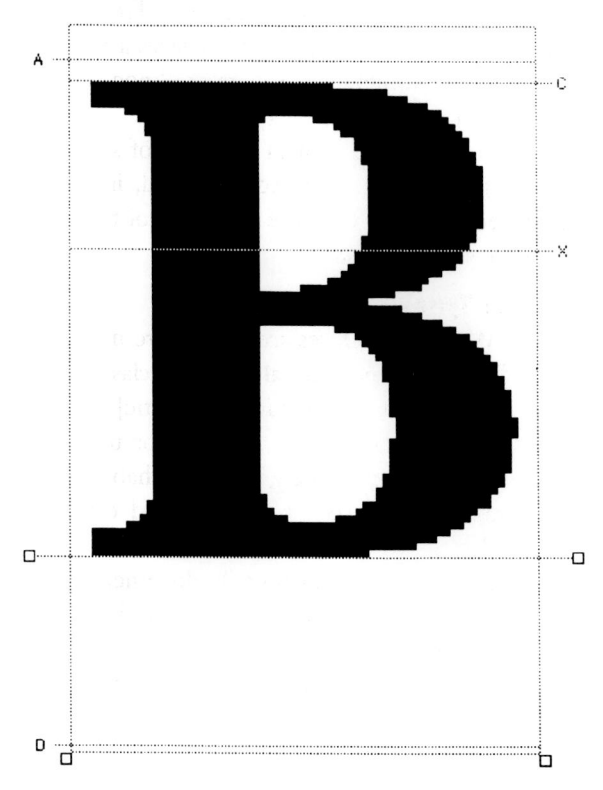

Above, a bitmap printout of a Baskerville Bold cap B *being edited at a 300 DPI resolution level.*

strong influence on the creators of the earliest typefaces put into use.

The Caroline minuscule was greatly admired by Renaissance scribes and scholars just prior to the invention of printing with movable type. Early Italian punchcutters used the minuscule as a model for type design in the production of many secular texts. It was the vertically stroked, angular Textura, originated by twelfth- and thirteenth-century scribes, that German and Dutch punchcutters initially strove to emulate as their type of choice for bibles and religious works. These styles—the graceful humanist minuscules joined with Roman capitals derived from inscriptions on the one hand, together with the Gothic Black Letter on the other—formed the basis of the earliest movable type designs produced in Europe.

Type design has occupied designers for centuries. Many of the successful digital types being introduced today are closely related to and derived from faces that have been most deeply absorbed into Western culture and consciousness. Prototype faces are surprisingly few in number, and while some experts would make other choices, most could agree that Baskerville, Bodoni, Bookman, Caslon, Century, Cheltenham, Garamond, Helvetica, and Times would be reasonable candidates as models for excellence in type design—metal, digital, or otherwise. These faces can be found among the families of type presented in this volume.

Digital Type Design

The design of type has been a substantial and creative accomplishment that nevertheless seems to have been taken for granted by nearly everyone not directly involved in the process. Over the centuries, designers have worked to evolve letterforms that have proven to be practical, highly legible, marketable and traditional, while introducing personalized innovations. Designers of type have consistently sought to respond to the technological and aesthetic dictates of their times while executing their designs with consummate good taste. Among today's type designers the conviction persists that these contradictory criteria can be met with designs that remain fully functional, appealing, beautiful, and unique. The wonder is that they so often succeed. The designers' concepts of appropriate alphabet design form, to a considerable degree, significant facets of the visual identification of their eras.

Continuity In Design

Arbitrary changes in the design of the alphabet could result in hard to read type. Acquired reading skills could become bogged down by a general clogging of existing visual communication channels as a result of type poor in legibility.

Does it follow that digital fonts should be identical

to the familiar hot metal types that preceded them? After all, new technologies usually produce new conditions that eventually result in revised forms. Now that metal type has all but disappeared from the marketplace, how do designers view the challenge of type design for the 1990s?

The best digital type designs are based on the entire experience of type invention, design and development, fine-tuned for legibility, function and aesthetics. Many current types are closely visually related to and based on earlier oldstyle, transitional, and modern models. Some faces are so close in appearance to their antecedents that it often takes a trained eye to recognize the difference. The variations in some current versions of Baskerville, Century, Times and Helvetica, among others, can be subtle indeed. In many cases, type vendors use the same original artwork to create their versions of a given face.

The freedom from design constraints offered first by phototype and more recently by digitization has led to the production of many new typefaces. Some are non-traditional and visually unique in ways that would not have been practical with metal type. The large variety of styles available in faces like Helvetica and Univers and the need for near-perfect fit of formal script faces are all more practical in digital type. The relative ease of re-introducing classic romans like Centaur, Arrighi, Charlemagne, and specialized faces like Visigoth and Tekton extend the designer's palette, encouraging design continuity. In time there will be many more faces as type designers test the limits of practicality.

Getting Familiar with Type

In 1989, *U&LC*, an International Typeface Corporation (ITC) periodical, listed over 115 licensees offering ITC typefaces to commercial typographers and desktop publishers for use with various technologies. Other sources of new typeface design constantly add to the proliferation of new types. The entire Mergenthaler Type Library (also known as the Linotype Library), with many of its faces dating back over one hundred years of metal type production, is being revised to produce new faces for improved performance as digital type. Many more type designs are in progress since there is a trend toward cross-licensing of proprietary faces, a practice that will eventually lead to making virtually every type available from any vendor.

The designer's purpose in gaining extensive type recognition is to become better equipped to make judicious choices for its effective use. The burden of committing a large store of typefaces to memory however, is formidable. Existing faces are frequently refined, or sometimes just changed and renamed, which taxes the memory further. How then to keep track of it all, to recognize and classify this rich store of typographic goods?

Few designers will be able to recognize every face available, but identifying a type by name at a glance is less important than understanding the sources from which it was derived. The finesse with which a typeface has been designed, the visual ambience it creates when used alone or in conjunction with other faces and graphic elements—these are basic tools of typographic design. Perceptive judgements about these aspects of type and ways to apply them, help guide designers toward appropriate and effective communication of subtle shades of imagery. Persuasive presentation of such qualities as dependability, excitement, authority, fun, authenticity, flight or restfulness can enhance the message and thus the effectiveness of most forms of visual communication.

Type, like color, can be categorized according to a few readily recognizable basics. These categories specifically apply to a mere handful of traditional types and script or calligraphic models, but most of the characteristics that help identify and classify all types can be found in these type models. Even exceptions can be better understood by observing their relationship to these basic letterforms. These alphabets have come down to us in three forms:

FORMAL: from which our capital letters derive

CASUAL: represented by lowercase letters in a font

CURSIVE: now seen as italic and script

To these one should add ornamental, eccentric, flourished scripts, romantic, and period styles. They will fit in or close to the following categories which have been widely identified as roman, oldstyle, transitional, modern, sans serif, square serif and script or cursive. This book contains typefaces of each category. Names of a few of these basic faces appear below.

ROMAN: Charlemagne, Perpetua, Palatino

OLDSTYLE: Garamond, Goudy, Jenson

TRANSITIONAL: Caslon, Baskerville, Times

MODERN: Bodoni, Century, Didot

SANS SERIF: Futura, Helvetica, Franklin Gothic

SQUARE SERIF: Beton, Graph, Stymie

SCRIPT: Continental Script, Bank Script

CALLIGRAPHIC: Medici Script, Ondine

To commit these forms to memory, make one selection at a time from each category—Perpetua from the Romans for example. Choosing an alphabet size of no less than 72 point, use tracing paper to compose two or three words that include a variety of both caps and lowercase letters. Your tracing should be as accurate and finely detailed as possible. Pay particular attention to

An engraved and flourished script, in a style popular during the 18th and 19th centuries. Digital types emulate the style but not this level of flourishing.

Measurement Data

English-American Point System

1 pt.	=	1/12 pica	**or**	1/72 inch
6 pts.	=	1/2 pica	**or**	1/12 inch
12 pts.	=	1 pica	**or**	1/6 inch
72 pts.	=	6 picas	**or**	1 inch*

*Seventy-two points measure .996 of an inch.

Didot Point System

12 pts.	=	1 cicero or douze
1 pt.	=	0.3759 mm
8 pts.	=	3.007 mm
12 pts.	=	4.511 mm
1 mm	=	2.66 points
1 m	=	2660 points

Decimal Equivalents

1 inch	=	6 picas
7/8 inch	=	5 picas, 3 points
3/4 inch	=	4 picas, 6 points
5/8 inch	=	3 picas, 9 points
1/2 inch	=	3 picas
3/8 inch	=	2 picas, 3 points
1/4 inch	=	1 pica, 6 points
1/8 inch	=	9 points

straight and diagonal strokes, the various curves, serifs, and differentiations in stroke weight.

When the tracing is as close to perfect as you can make it, transfer the drawing to a paper surface suitable for finished lettering. Then, using a flexible lettering pen or a fine sable brush, ink in the lettering, coming as close to reproduction quality as you can. The time needed for this exercise will vary but should be limited to two hours per word.

To a large extent, contemporary type design is based on these forms. The tracing exercise will help anyone become familiar with the basic groups listed above, in addition to romantic, ornamental, and wood typefaces that have served as models for countless derivative faces. Like the handful of colors that form a basic color wheel, a few type groups can be manipulated to produce an entire spectrum of typographic expression. It is far simpler to deal with a dozen or so visually defined categories of type, instead of thousands of seemingly disconnected types. By examining other types that relate to these basic groups, appealing selections in each category can be more readily identified and recalled. Once you have a grip on the forms that serve as models, you can choose types with much more authority. As for the rest of the typefaces, nearly everything else is variation and adaptation of one or more of these categories.

Measurements

In the United States, type traditionally has been measured in points and picas. But with broader popular usage of desktop applications, it is more common to call for type in inches or millimeters as well as in points and picas, and to use words like *linespacing* instead of *leading*, a term which although still in common use, has become an anachronism. These changes encourage more relaxed nomenclature like column *width* instead of column *measure*, and *vendor* or *supplier*, instead of *foundry*. The shift from these and other typographic buzzwords is an unwelcome change to conservative typophiles. Some of the traditional usage may well remain however. Picas and points, for instance, are convenient units for expressing typographic dimensions and for many, easier to work with than millimeters, inches, and fractions. No doubt new terms will be coined along the way as changing methods lead to new typographic language.

Column width is usually stated in picas and points. A column is defined as a *justified* column of a specified width, or as *flush left* or *flush right*, or *centered* or *random* as shown in the accompanying diagrams.

Another measurement consideration is *x-height*. The x-height of a given font is the height of its lowercase x, and thus represents the visual body size of the font. A type with a large x-height will usually yield greater legibility at any given size. It will also appear larger than a type in the same point size but with a smaller x-height.

The choice of larger or smaller *x-height* is neither *right* nor *wrong* — it is simply a difference to consider in the search for an appropriate face. When legibility and size are constrained by limited space, for instance, or when display copy is used for a poster effect, fonts with a larger x-height often can be used to heighten legibility.

The Unit System and the EM

The *em* designates a square space within a font equivalent to its point size. In a 12-point font, an em would measure 12 points by 12 points. In a 60-point font, an em would measure 60 by 60 points.

The width of each character and the required space between characters and words are measured in *units*. Each character in a font is positioned and measured on an em in relation to a specified number of units. At every point size, each character in a digital font occupies a position representing an em on a grid. The grid is divided into spaces (units) and the number of units can vary considerably depending on the type source. But the number of units remains constant within the font at any type size. Thus, in an 18-unit system, a single unit will always be one-eighteenth of an em. This works to keep the visual relationships of each character closely related whatever the type size. Each letter (and its surrounding spaces) has its own width, expressed in units, with the letter *I* having fewer units than an *M*, and caps more units than lowercase letters. By specifying these units as plus or minus values, designers can exert control over the spacing and texture of type.

Kerning

When type was metal, kerning was a problem. Each letter was cast in position on the type body. To obtain a better fit between certain letters, types were sawn, filed, cut, and otherwise modified. It was a tedious and demanding task, performed one letter at a time. The body would be cut away under part of the face to achieve a better fit. This *kerning* resulted in a partially overhanging face, weakened and subject to many hazards. Phototype eased this chore somewhat by making it possible to cut and paste type images to obtain a more pleasing fit between problematic letter combinations.

With digital type, the problem is diminished further but not eliminated. Each letter in a font is positioned for the best relationship to the rest of the characters in the font. But certain character combinations can cause a problem. In typesetting systems that can be manually manipulated, kerning can be readily accomplished and enhanced to the level of perception and skill of the individual operator. When this work is done at commercial typographers, kerning requirements can result in significant extra costs because of additional time required.

Hxyz Hxyz

Cheltenham and Avant Garde Gothic letters were both set at 72-points and uniformly reduced for the diagram above. Note the marked difference in x-height to cap size.

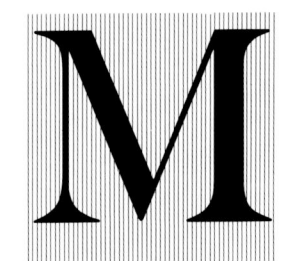

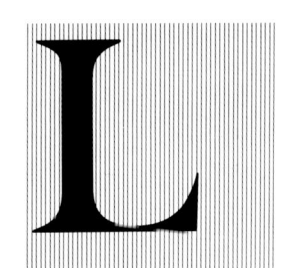

M L

In the schematic diagram, above, the em *is divided vertically into 54 units. Characters vary, occupying more or fewer units. During the type design process, this system helps in the plotting of each character and the spaces within and between letters and words. The unitization of type also helps achieve visual consistency and set width (alphabet length).*

av av LT LT aw aw
no no AT AT fo fo

Commonly kerned pairs of letters above, demonstrate the effects of kerning, a step taken to adjust the space between letters presenting spacing gaps that appear flawed or inconsistent in certain combinations.

Typography is closely allied to the fine arts.
Foundry setting, 1/2 point letterspaced.

Typography is closely allied to the fine arts.
Normal setting, Track 1.

Typography is closely allied to the fine arts.
Medium setting, Track 2.

Typography is closely allied to the fine arts.
Tight setting, Track 3.

Tracking refers to the spacing of any complete text, including letters, spaces between letters and the space between words. The extended, condensed and italicized lines show reproportioning capabilities of digitized typesetting.

Typography is closely allied to the fine arts.
Line extended 10 percent.

Typography is closely allied to the fine arts.
Line condensed 10 percent.

Typography is closely allied to the fine arts.
Line italicized right, 12 degrees.

Copyfitting

When a job requires extensive text setting, an exact character count is not always necessary. Paragraph endings, titling practice, and alterations often defy pinpoint accuracy. A widow (a short word or two at the end of a paragraph, occupying the space needed for a full line of copy) can easily change the best laid plans for an exact line count. But this should not be a problem for the resourceful designer—if a minor change in copy is not an option, there are ways to control the space it will occupy.

Point-size adjustment is one way to achieve a fit. Letterspacing and wordspacing choices, linespacing, column width and vertical and horizontal reproportioning are among the options available when working with digital type. Metal type was not nearly so flexible or so readily changed to accommodate alterations and design adjustments. Which modifications to use and when to use them is the designer's choice. But the finished type product should fully represent the graphic idea visualized by the designer. Experience soon dictates the usage best suited to varied design problems.

Nevertheless, the more accuracy in preparation, the better. When original copy is prepared, it should closely follow the desired finished product. It will be much quicker for a typographer to set a job properly if the typing displays flush or indented paragraphs, accurate capitalization and lowercase letters, correct spelling and punctuation, and other specific details the way you wish them to appear in the finished product. When presenting typewritten copy, it should be double-spaced for clarity and ease of inserting instructions. Even when prepared on a keystroked disk, corresponding typed copy plus detailed specifications and a layout are helpful.

With a fully coded disk, all these details should be covered. Some designers use commercial service typographers to produce repros from disks containing coded copy. Whether a typewriter or a word processor is used to produce original text, conversion into type that will look, fit and function as intended requires a system of clear specification.

Sending copy to a commercial service typographer for high resolution printout requires more in-house preparation and effort than simply keystroking it. Unless the original copy preparation includes coding to control the desired printer output, this must be done by the service typographer, leaving little price advantage in furnishing keystroked but uncoded disks. Some word-processing programs include information on coding requirements, allowing many service typographers to simply insert a customer's disk and run the job.

The Quick Count

For a rough preliminary estimate of how to fit copy to a layout, multiply the number of characters per average line of original copy times the number of lines to be set to determine the total number of characters in the original text.

Next, find a sample of text set in the style and size of your choice, or similar to it. On a piece of tissue, outline the space to be filled and lay it over the selected sample. Count the characters per line and number of lines within the space on the tissue. If the number of characters is a near match to that of your original copy, the enormous flexibility of type probably will allow ways to gain a comfortable and pleasing fit. If it is not, then the type choice, size, linespacing, word or character spacing or original text (or some combination of these) needs adjustment. While far from scientific, this method can produce, with a little experience, a remarkably accurate sense of how near or far your copy may be from a fit. When greater accuracy is required, follow the steps listed below:

1. Count the characters in two or three typical lines of original copy. Letters, punctuation marks, and spaces each count as one.
2. Multiply this count by the number of lines per page, and again by the number of pages of original copy, to get the total character count.
3. After deciding on the typeface and style, refer to the original layout to determine line length and number of characters per line. Consulting type specimens in this book may be helpful.
4. Divide the total number of characters in the original copy by the number of characters per line contained in the chosen type to get the number of lines this type choice will require. If you decide to set a 10- or 11-point type on a 12-point linespace, and the number of lines required is ten, the desired depth would be 10 lines x 12 points per line, for a total of 10 picas in depth, to achieve a proper fit. If fitting problems arise, adjusting the letter-, word-, and linespacing or massaging the layout will help make a perfect fit.

Normally, 10- or 12- or 60-point type takes up a linespace equal to its pointsize unless extra spacing is added. Thus, 10-point type set *solid* (no linespacing added) would set ten points deep for each line, while 10-point type on a 12-point linespace would occupy 12 points per line. Refer to the measurement table to see the relationships of points to pica, points to inch, and picas to inch.

A solid setting of 12 points is designated as *12/12* (spoken as 12 on 12). Any amount of desired linespacing should be specified. Thus, if three points of linespacing on a 12-point face is required, it should be designated as 12/15; if six points were required it would be indicated as 12/18.

Larger faces can be specified accurately by making loose tracing overlays from the specimens shown. Type in this book is shown without extra linespacing, except when this would result in one character overlapping another.

Marking the Copy

Depending on the program used, type preparation on a coded disk allows the designer to set type precisely as desired. Copy that is keystroked but not coded or formatted however, requires accompanying instructions plus a tissue layout to help get the desired setting. When working with a commercial typographer and submitting copy in the form of typewritten sheets, all the applicable information listed below should be included.

SIZE: Order by exact size and linespace—12/16 or 36 point solid for example. "Larger" or "smaller" does not constitute a reasonable specification.

TYPEFACE: Name both the face and its source: Fry's Baskerville, ITC Avant Garde Gothic, Adobe Tekton and so on.

STYLE: Order roman or italic, medium, regular, bold, extra bold condensed or whatever descriptive term is applicable to the specific face you order. Keep in mind what is extra bold for one face may be called black or ultra in another.

LAYOUT: A tracing tissue layout showing positioning and alignment of all elements is often the difference between getting what you want and just missing.

MEASURE: When the width (measure) of a column or line is a factor, the size should be specified on both the original copy and on the layout. Also specify whether columns are to be set justified, flush left or right, centered, or random within limits.

WORDSPACING and LETTERSPACING: Indicate normal, tight, or loose (*foundry*, a metal type term, can be used to designate a loose setting). When using the unit system, specify the number of plus or minus units to use.

CAPITALIZATION: This is done most easily by preparing original copy correctly. If not accurate in the typed copy, mark up for caps, lowercase, initial caps and small caps as desired.

FOUNDRY or VENDOR: For quality control, indicate the name of the foundry or vendor that supplies the type you have selected. Vendor names accompany all showings in this specimen book, because there is more than one version of most of the widely used types available. The differences in rendition of certain typefaces can be considerable, resulting in a poor fit or disappointing appearance.

Proofreaders' Marks

Proofreaders' marks are a simple shorthand method of making copy adjustments and corrections quickly but accurately. Use the traditional ones and they will be understood by nearly everyone who works with type. Invent new ones if they more clearly and accurately express what you want. Some of the most commonly used marks are shown below.

Mark	Symbol	Mark	Symbol
Reset in bold face	*bf*	Insert brackets	[ ]
Reset in Roman	*Rom*	Insert ellipsis	/./././
Push down space	⊥	Let it stand	*stet*
Delete	ℓ	Run in	∽
Insert space	#	Paragraph	¶
Less space	∪	No Paragraph	*no* ¶
Close up entirely	◯	Transpose	*tr.*
Insert period	⊙	Reset in caps	*caps*
Insert colon	:∧	Reset in small caps	*sc*
Insert semi-colon	;∧	Reset in lower case	*lc*
Insert comma	,∧	Reset in italics	*ital*
Insert parentheses	( )	Spell out	*sp.*
Move right	]	Equalize spacing	*eq #*
Move left	[	Align	‖
Indent 1 em	□	Bad letter	X
1 en dash	en	Justify copy	[ ]
1 em dash	em	Flush left copy	[
Insert apostrophe	˅	Flush right copy	]
Insert hyphen	≐	Center copy	][
Insert quotes	˵˶	Break line	⌒

FAMILIES OF TYPE

Family groups offer designers a way to obtain typographic solutions that present a unified appearance even when the copy contains varied information to be presented at different levels of emphasis. Style variations such as weight, roman or italic, condensed, or expanded are conditions that can usually be met while staying within a unified and visually related typeface.

Choosing unrelated types can and often does intrude on clear presentation of content. This is not to say that a variety of disparate types, sizes, column widths, and other variables cannot be used to produce dramatic and effective results — design being what it is, rigid rules must sooner or later be broken. But unless this is done with visual sensitivity, the results can be amateurish and unacceptable.

The following pages show specimens of family typefaces in various styles. They reflect personal opinion and are limited to ten. Shown in a format based on traditional metal type showings, the selections were chosen for utility, design excellence, wide and frequent demand, and general availability. The showings may be viewed as a representative group of time-honored, traditional typefaces, conceived and enhanced by generations of creative type designers. Taken together with the supplemental specimens that follow, they are complete in practical terms, filling the broader needs of most people who work with type. Note that each of the supplementary faces occupies less space than each of the families. Readers should not take this to mean that the supplementary faces are designated as functionally or aesthetically inferior. Indeed, they may well be more useful than the families in certain applications. Space limitations and publishing economics have imposed constraints.

An argument could be made that almost any typeface suitable as a text face could also be adapted for display copy and thus qualify as a family. Current technology can provide size increments as fine as a fraction of a point and contour and reproportioning capabilities previously available only through delicately executed hand lettering or photolettering. Quick to grasp this potential, many designers have used styles formerly designated as display type for offbeat text applications and vice versa. Accordingly, fewer typefaces are shown as only text or display type, with most presented in both forms.

The type families are shown here in full alphabets. Display sizes range from 72 to 18 points, with text showings beginning at 14 points and reducing to ten or eight points. Text showings for the families are set both solid and linespaced in 2- and 4-point increments, as indicated to the left of each text block, helping the reader to visualize final results before specifying.

S	*Times*
E	*Helvetica*
I	*Avant Garde Gothic*
L	*Fry's Baskerville*
I	*Bauer Bodoni*
M	*Century Expanded*
A	*Bookman Swash*
F	*Cheltenham*
O	*Caslon 540*
T	*Stempel Garamond*

b12

ITC Avant Garde Gothic was designed in 1970 by Herb Lubalin and Tom Carnase, as an extension of the logotype for the magazine Avant Garde. The unusual alternate characters follow the display and text showings. The obliques were designed for ITC in Switzerland, by Team 77 of Letterform Research and Design. Oblique alternate characters are not currently available.

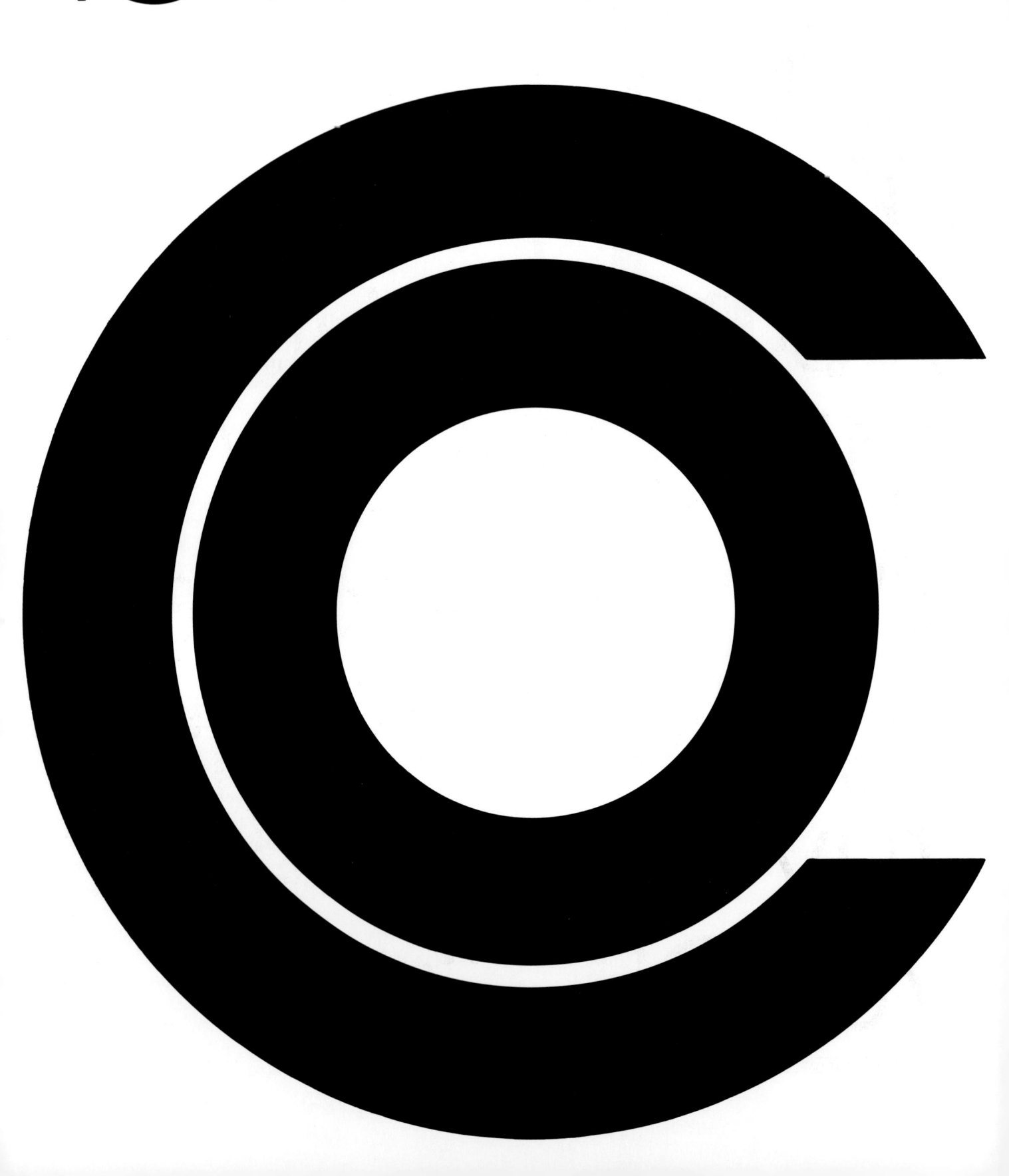

AVANT GARDE GOTHIC FAMILY 25

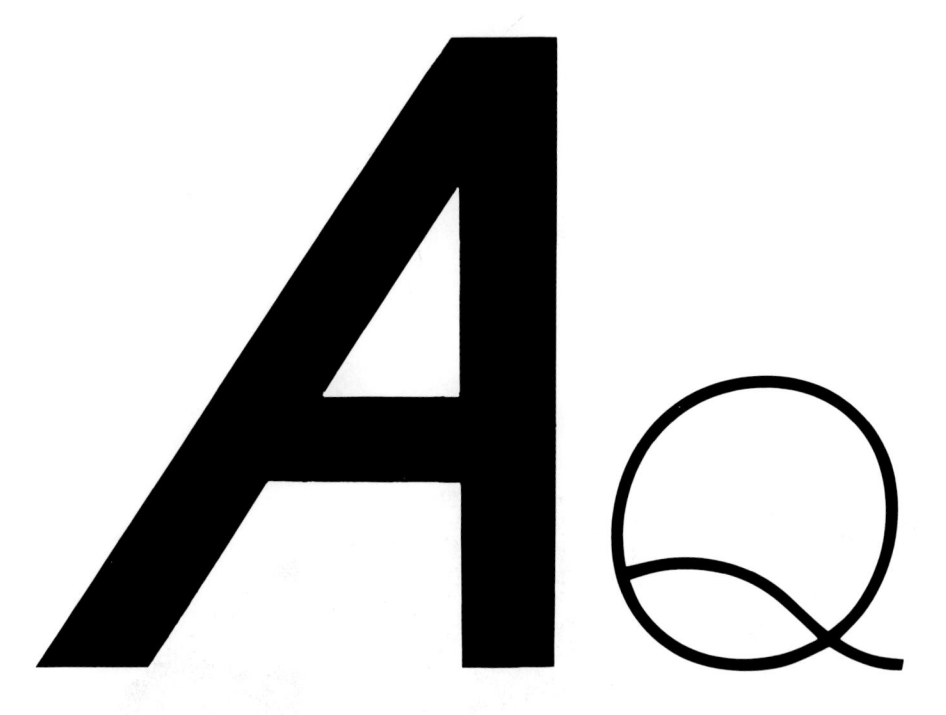

Aa

ABCDEFGHIJKL
MNOPQRSTUV
WXYZ&abcde
fghijklmnopqrs
tuvwxyz123456
7890$.,'""'",;!?

72 POINT ITC AVANT GARDE GOTHIC BOOK   AGFA COMPUGRAPHIC TYPE LIBRARY

ABCDEFGHIJK LMNOPQRSTU VWXYZ&abcd efghijklmnop qrstuvwxyz123 4567890$.,""" ,;!?

72 POINT ITC AVANT GARDE GOTHIC BOOK OBLIQUE   AGFA COMPUGRAPHIC TYPE LIBRARY

ABCDEFGHIJKLMN
OPQRSTUVWXYZ&
abcdefghijklmnop
qrstuvwxyz1234567
890$.,""'";:!?

60 POINT ITC AVANT GARDE GOTHIC** BOOK   MERGENTHALER TYPE LIBRARY

ABCDEFGHIJKLMNO
PQRSTUVWXYZ&ab
cdefghijklmnopqrst
uvwxyz1234567890
$.,""'";:!?

60 POINT ITC AVANT GARDE GOTHIC** BOOK OBLIQUE   MERGENTHALER TYPE LIBRARY

**See page 534

ABCDEFGHIJKLMNOPQRSTUVWXYZ&abcdefghijklmnopqrstuvwxyz1234567890$.,"":;!?

48 POINT ITC AVANT GARDE GOTHIC** BOOK   MERGENTHALER TYPE LIBRARY

ABCDEFGHIJKLMNOPQRSTUVWXYZ&abcdefghijklmnopqrstuvwxyz1234567890$.,"":;!?

48 POINT ITC AVANT GARDE GOTHIC** BOOK OBLIQUE   MERGENTHALER TYPE LIBRARY

ABCDEFGHIJKLMNOPQRSTUVWXYZ&abcdefghijklmnopqrstuvwxyz1234567890$.,"":;!?

36 POINT ITC AVANT GARDE GOTHIC** BOOK   MERGENTHALER TYPE LIBRARY

AVANT GARDE GOTHIC FAMILY 29

ABCDEFGHIJKLMNOPQRSTUVW XYZ&abcdefghijklmnopqrstuvw xyz1234567890$.,""':;!?

36 POINT ITC AVANT GARDE GOTHIC** BOOK OBLIQUE   MERGENTHALER TYPE LIBRARY

ABCDEFGHIJKLMNOPQRSTUVWXYZ&abcdefg hijklmnopqrstuvwxyz1234567890$.,""'':;!?

24 POINT ITC AVANT GARDE GOTHIC** BOOK   MERGENTHALER TYPE LIBRARY

ABCDEFGHIJKLMNOPQRSTUVWXYZ&abcdefgh ijklmnopqrstuvwxyz1234567890$.,""'':;!?

24 POINT ITC AVANT GARDE GOTHIC** BOOK OBLIQUE   MERGENTHALER TYPE LIBRARY

ABCDEFGHIJKLMNOPQRSTUVWXYZ&abcdefghijklmnopqrstuv wxyz1234567890$.,""'':;!?

18 POINT ITC AVANT GARDE GOTHIC** BOOK   MERGENTHALER TYPE LIBRARY

ABCDEFGHIJKLMNOPQRSTUVWXYZ&abcdefghijklmnopqrstuv wxyz1234567890$.,""'':;!?

18 POINT ITC AVANT GARDE GOTHIC** BOOK OBLIQUE   MERGENTHALER TYPE LIBRARY

14/14 OBSERVATIONS ON COMPOSING. Although this essential point has been passed over with little notice by most writers upon this subject, still (so great are the evils resulting from ill-contracted habits, which naturally keep pace with our growth), we cannot avoid pointing out a few instances of the sure consequences attendant on them. There are many persons now employed in the art, who frequently, *with great justice, inveigh in strong terms against the conduct of*

12/12 OBSERVATIONS ON COMPOSING. Although this essential point has been passed over with little notice by most writers upon this subject, still (so great are the evils resulting from ill-contracted habits, which naturally keep pace with our growth), we cannot avoid pointing out a few instances of the sure consequences attendant on them. There are many persons now employed in the art, who frequently, with great justice, inveigh in strong terms against the conduct of those unto whose care they were first entrusted, for suffering them to contract *those ill-becoming postures which are productive of knock knees, round shoulders,*

14/16 OBSERVATIONS ON COMPOSING. Although this essential point has been passed over with little notice by most writers upon this subject, still (so great are the evils resulting from ill-contracted habits, which naturally keep pace with our growth), we cannot avoid pointing out a few instances of the sure consequences attendant *on them. There are many persons now employed in the art, who fre-*

12/14 OBSERVATIONS ON COMPOSING. Although this essential point has been passed over with little notice by most writers upon this subject, still (so great are the evils resulting from ill-contracted habits, which naturally keep pace with our growth), we cannot avoid pointing out a few instances of the sure consequences attendant on them. There are many persons now employed in the art, who frequently, with great justice, *inveigh in strong terms against the conduct of those unto whose care they were*

14/18 OBSERVATIONS ON COMPOSING. Although this essential point has been passed over with little notice by most writers upon this subject, still (so great are the evils resulting from ill-contracted habits, which naturally keep pace with our growth), we cannot *avoid pointing out a few instances of the sure consequences attendant*

12/16 OBSERVATIONS ON COMPOSING. Although this essential point has been passed over with little notice by most writers upon this subject, still (so great are the evils resulting from ill-contracted habits, which naturally keep pace with our growth), we cannot avoid pointing out a few instances of the sure consequences attendant on them. *There are many persons now employed in the art, who frequently, with great justice,*

ITC AVANT GARDE GOTHIC** BOOK   MERGENTHALER TYPE LIBRARY

ABCDEFGHIJKLMNOPQRSTUVWXYZ
ABCDEFGHIJKLMNOPQRSTUVWXYZ
&.,'`-:;!?'""1234567890$
&.,'`-:;!?'""1234567890$
abcdefghijklmnopqrstuvwxyz
abcdefghijklmnopqrstuvwxyz

ABCDEFGHIJKLMNOPQRSTUVWXYZ
ABCDEFGHIJKLMNOPQRSTUVWXYZ
&.,'`-:;!?'""1234567890$
&.,'`-:;!?'""1234567890$
abcdefghijklmnopqrstuvwxyz
abcdefghijklmnopqrstuvwxyz

11/11 OBSERVATIONS ON COMPOSING. Although this essential point has been passed over with little notice by most writers upon this subject, still (so great are the evils resulting from ill-contracted habits, which naturally keep pace with our growth), we cannot avoid pointing out a few instances of the sure consequences attendant on them. There are many persons now employed in the art, who frequently, with great justice, inveigh in strong terms against the conduct of those unto whose care they were first entrusted, for suffering them to contract those ill-becoming postures which are productive of knock knees, round shoulders, and other deformities. *It is deeply to be regretted, that those who undertake so important a charge, are not*

10/10 OBSERVATIONS ON COMPOSING. Although this essential point has been passed over with little notice by most writers upon this subject, still (so great are the evils resulting from ill-contracted habits, which naturally keep pace with our growth), we cannot avoid pointing out a few instances of the sure consequences attendant on them. There are many persons now employed in the art, who frequently, with great justice, inveigh in strong terms against the conduct of those unto whose care they were first entrusted, for suffering them to contract those ill-becoming postures which are productive of knock knees, round shoulders, and other deformities. It is deeply to be regretted, that those who undertake so important a charge, are not better qualified to *fulfil that duty: instead of suffering the tender shoot to grow wild and uncultivated, when the pruning-*

11/13 OBSERVATIONS ON COMPOSING. Although this essential point has been passed over with little notice by most writers upon this subject, still (so great are the evils resulting from ill-contracted habits, which naturally keep pace with our growth), we cannot avoid pointing out a few instances of the sure consequences attendant on them. There are many persons now employed in the art, who frequently, with great justice, inveigh in strong terms against the conduct of those unto whose care they were first entrusted, for suffering them to contract those *ill-becoming postures which are productive of knock knees, round shoulders, and other defor-*

10/12 OBSERVATIONS ON COMPOSING. Although this essential point has been passed over with little notice by most writers upon this subject, still (so great are the evils resulting from ill-contracted habits, which naturally keep pace with our growth), we cannot avoid pointing out a few instances of the sure consequences attendant on them. There are many persons now employed in the art, who frequently, with great justice, inveigh in strong terms against the conduct of those unto whose care they were first entrusted, for suffering them to contract those ill-becoming postures which are productive of knock knees, round shoulders, and other deformities. *It is deeply to be regretted, that those who undertake so important a charge, are not better*

11/15 OBSERVATIONS ON COMPOSING. Although this essential point has been passed over with little notice by most writers upon this subject, still (so great are the evils resulting from ill-contracted habits, which naturally keep pace with our growth), we cannot avoid pointing out a few instances of the sure consequences attendant on them. There are many persons now employed in the art, who frequently, with great *justice, inveigh in strong terms against the conduct of those unto whose care they were first*

10/14 OBSERVATIONS ON COMPOSING. Although this essential point has been passed over with little notice by most writers upon this subject, still (so great are the evils resulting from ill-contracted habits, which naturally keep pace with our growth), we cannot avoid pointing out a few instances of the sure consequences attendant on them. There are many persons now employed in the art, who frequently, with great justice, inveigh in strong terms against the conduct of those unto whose care they were first *entrusted, for suffering them to contract those ill-becoming postures which are productive of knock*

ITC AVANT GARDE GOTHIC** BOOK   MERGENTHALER TYPE LIBRARY

ABCDEFGHIJKLMNOPQRSTUVWXYZ
ABCDEFGHIJKLMNOPQRSTUVWXYZ
&.,"'-:;!?'"''1234567890$
&.,"'-:;!?'"''1234567890$
abcdefghijklmnopqrstuvwxyz
abcdefghijklmnopqrstuvwxyz

ABCDEFGHIJKLMNOPQRSTUVWXYZ
ABCDEFGHIJKLMNOPQRSTUVWXYZ
&.,"'-:;!?'"''1234567890$
&.,"'-:;!?'"''1234567890$
abcdefghijklmnopqrstuvwxyz
abcdefghijklmnopqrstuvwxyz

9/9 OBSERVATIONS ON COMPOSING. Although this essential point has been passed over with little notice by most writers upon this subject, still (so great are the evils resulting from ill-contracted habits, which naturally keep pace with our growth), we cannot avoid pointing out a few instances of the sure consequences attendant on them. There are many persons now employed in the art, who frequently, with great justice, inveigh in strong terms against the conduct of those unto whose care they were first entrusted, for suffering them to contract those ill-becoming postures which are productive of knock knees, round shoulders, and other deformities. It is deeply to be regretted, that those who undertake so important a charge, are not better qualified to fulfil that duty: instead of suffering the tender shoot to grow wild and uncultivated, when the pruning-knife, in a gentle hand, with a little admonition, would have checked its improper growth, and trained it in a right course.

What to a learner may appear fatiguing, time and habit will render easy and familiar; and though to work

8/8 OBSERVATIONS ON COMPOSING. Although this essential point has been passed over with little notice by most writers upon this subject, still (so great are the evils resulting from ill-contracted habits, which naturally keep pace with our growth), we cannot avoid pointing out a few instances of the sure consequences attendant on them. There are many persons now employed in the art, who frequently, with great justice, inveigh in strong terms against the conduct of those unto whose care they were first entrusted, for suffering them to contract those ill-becoming postures which are productive of knock knees, round shoulders, and other deformities. It is deeply to be regretted, that those who undertake so important a charge, are not better qualified to fulfil that duty: instead of suffering the tender shoot to grow wild and uncultivated, when the pruning-knife, in a gentle hand, with a little admonition, would have checked its improper growth, and trained it in a right course.

What to a learner may appear fatiguing, time and habit will render easy and familiar; and though to work with his cases on a level with his breast, may at first tire his arms, yet use will so inure him to it, that it will become afterwards equally unpleasant to work at a low frame. His perseverance in this mode must be strengthened by the reflection, that it will most effectually pre-

9/11 OBSERVATIONS ON COMPOSING. Although this essential point has been passed over with little notice by most writers upon this subject, still (so great are the evils resulting from ill-contracted habits, which naturally keep pace with our growth), we cannot avoid pointing out a few instances of the sure consequences attendant on them. There are many persons now employed in the art, who frequently, with great justice, inveigh in strong terms against the conduct of those unto whose care they were first entrusted, for suffering them to contract those ill-becoming postures which are productive of knock knees, round shoulders, and other deformities. It is deeply to be regretted, that those who undertake so important a charge, are not better qualified to fulfil that duty: instead of suffering the tender shoot to grow wild and uncultivated, when the pruning-knife, in a gentle hand, with a little admonition,

8/10 OBSERVATIONS ON COMPOSING. Although this essential point has been passed over with little notice by most writers upon this subject, still (so great are the evils resulting from ill-contracted habits, which naturally keep pace with our growth), we cannot avoid pointing out a few instances of the sure consequences attendant on them. There are many persons now employed in the art, who frequently, with great justice, inveigh in strong terms against the conduct of those unto whose care they were first entrusted, for suffering them to contract those ill-becoming postures which are productive of knock knees, round shoulders, and other deformities. It is deeply to be regretted, that those who undertake so important a charge, are not better qualified to fulfil that duty: instead of suffering the tender shoot to grow wild and uncultivated, when the pruning-knife, in a gentle hand, with a little admonition, would have checked its improper growth, and trained it in a right course.

What to a learner may appear fatiguing, time and habit will render easy and familiar; and though to work with his cases on a

9/13 OBSERVATIONS ON COMPOSING. Although this essential point has been passed over with little notice by most writers upon this subject, still (so great are the evils resulting from ill-contracted habits, which naturally keep pace with our growth), we cannot avoid pointing out a few instances of the sure consequences attendant on them. There are many persons now employed in the art, who frequently, with great justice, inveigh in strong terms against the conduct of those unto whose care they were first entrusted, for suffering them to contract those ill-becoming postures which are productive of knock knees, round shoulders, and other deformities. It is deeply to be regretted, that those who undertake so important a charge, are not

8/12 OBSERVATIONS ON COMPOSING. Although this essential point has been passed over with little notice by most writers upon this subject, still (so great are the evils resulting from ill-contracted habits, which naturally keep pace with our growth), we cannot avoid pointing out a few instances of the sure consequences attendant on them. There are many persons now employed in the art, who frequently, with great justice, inveigh in strong terms against the conduct of those unto whose care they were first entrusted, for suffering them to contract those ill-becoming postures which are productive of knock knees, round shoulders, and other deformities. It is deeply to be regretted, that those who undertake so important a charge, are not better qualified to fulfil that duty: instead of suffering the tender shoot to grow wild and uncultivated, when the pruning-knife, in a gentle hand, with a

ITC AVANT GARDE GOTHIC** BOOK   MERGENTHALER TYPE LIBRARY

ABCDEFGHIJKLMNOPQRSTUVWXYZ
ABCDEFGHIJKLMNOPQRSTUVWXYZ
&,."-:;!?'"''1234567890$
&,."-:;!?'"''1234567890$
abcdefghijklmnopqrstuvwxyz
abcdefghijklmnopqrstuvwxyz

ABCDEFGHIJKLMNOPQRSTUVWXYZ
ABCDEFGHIJKLMNOPQRSTUVWXYZ
&,."-:;!?'"''1234567890$
&,."-:;!?'"''1234567890$
abcdefghijklmnopqrstuvwxyz
abcdefghijklmnopqrstuvwxyz

AVANT GARDE GOTHIC FAMILY 33

ABCDEFGHIJKL
MNOPQRSTUV
WXYZ&abcde
fghijklmnopqr
stuvwxyz12345
67890$.,'"":;!?

72 POINT ITC AVANT GARDE GOTHIC EXTRA LIGHT   AGFA COMPUGRAPHIC TYPE LIBRARY

ABCDEFGHIJK
LMNOPQRSTU
VWXYZ&abc
defghijklmno
pqrstuvwxyz12
34567890$.,"
";,!?

72 POINT ITC AVANT GARDE GOTHIC EXTRA LIGHT OBLIQUE   AGFA COMPUGRAPHIC TYPE LIBRARY

ABCDEFGHIJKLMNOPQRSTUVWXYZ&abcdefghijklmnopqrstuvwxyz1234567890$.,""-;:!?

48 POINT ITC AVANT GARDE GOTHIC** EXTRA LIGHT   MERGENTHALER TYPE LIBRARY

ABCDEFGHIJKLMNOPQRSTUVWXYZ&abcdefghijklmnopqrstuvwxyz1234567890$.,""-;:!?

48 POINT ITC AVANT GARDE GOTHIC** EXTRA LIGHT OBLIQUE   MERGENTHALER TYPE LIBRARY

ABCDEFGHIJKLMNOPQRSTUVWXYZ&abcdefghijklmnopqrstuvwxyz1234567890$.,""-;:!?

18 POINT ITC AVANT GARDE GOTHIC** EXTRA LIGHT   MERGENTHALER TYPE LIBRARY

ABCDEFGHIJKLMNOPQRSTUVWXYZ&abcdefghijklmnopqrstuvwxyz1234567890$.,""-;:!?

18 POINT ITC AVANT GARDE GOTHIC** EXTRA LIGHT OBLIQUE   MERGENTHALER TYPE LIBRARY

14/14 OBSERVATIONS ON COMPOSING. Although this essential point has been passed over with little notice by most writers upon this subject, still (so great are the evils resulting from ill-contracted habits, which naturally keep pace with our growth), we cannot avoid pointing out a few instances of the sure consequences attendant on them. There are many persons now employed in the art, who frequently, *with great justice, inveigh in strong terms against the conduct of those*

12/12 OBSERVATIONS ON COMPOSING. Although this essential point has been passed over with little notice by most writers upon this subject, still (so great are the evils resulting from ill-contracted habits, which naturally keep pace with our growth), we cannot avoid pointing out a few instances of the sure consequences attendant on them. There are many persons now employed in the art, who frequently, with great justice, inveigh in strong terms against the conduct of those unto whose care they were first entrusted, for suffering them to contract those ill-becoming *postures which are productive of knock knees, round shoulders, and other deform-*

14/16 OBSERVATIONS ON COMPOSING. Although this essential point has been passed over with little notice by most writers upon this subject, still (so great are the evils resulting from ill-contracted habits, which naturally keep pace with our growth), we cannot avoid pointing out a few instances of the sure consequences attendant on *them. There are many persons now employed in the art, who frequently,*

12/14 OBSERVATIONS ON COMPOSING. Although this essential point has been passed over with little notice by most writers upon this subject, still (so great are the evils resulting from ill-contracted habits, which naturally keep pace with our growth), we cannot avoid pointing out a few instances of the sure consequences attendant on them. There are many persons now employed in the art, who frequently, with great justice, inveigh in strong *terms against the conduct of those unto whose care they were first entrusted, for*

14/18 OBSERVATIONS ON COMPOSING. Although this essential point has been passed over with little notice by most writers upon this subject, still (so great are the evils resulting from ill-contracted habits, which naturally keep pace with our growth), we cannot *avoid pointing out a few instances of the sure consequences attendant on*

12/16 OBSERVATIONS ON COMPOSING. Although this essential point has been passed over with little notice by most writers upon this subject, still (so great are the evils resulting from ill-contracted habits, which naturally keep pace with our growth), we cannot avoid pointing out a few instances of the sure consequences attendant on them. There are *many persons now employed in the art, who frequently, with great justice, inveigh in*

ITC AVANT GARDE GOTHIC** EXTRA LIGHT   MERGENTHALER TYPE LIBRARY

ABCDEFGHIJKLMNOPQRSTUVWXYZ
ABCDEFGHIJKLMNOPQRSTUVWXYZ
&,."-;:!?""1234567890$
&,."-;:!?""1234567890$
abcdefghijklmnopqrstuvwxyz
abcdefghijklmnopqrstuvwxyz

ABCDEFGHIJKLMNOPQRSTUVWXYZ
ABCDEFGHIJKLMNOPQRSTUVWXYZ
&,."-;:!?""1234567890$
&,."-;:!?""1234567890$
abcdefghijklmnopqrstuvwxyz
abcdefghijklmnopqrstuvwxyz

AVANT GARDE GOTHIC FAMILY 37

10/10 OBSERVATIONS ON COMPOSING. Although this essential point has been passed over with little notice by most writers upon this subject, still (so great are the evils resulting from ill-contracted habits, which naturally keep pace with our growth), we cannot avoid pointing out a few instances of the sure consequences attendant on them. There are many persons now employed in the art, who frequently, with great justice, inveigh in strong terms against the conduct of those unto whose care they were first entrusted, for suffering them to contract those ill-becoming postures which are productive of knock knees, round shoulders, and other deformities. It is deeply to be regretted, that those who undertake so important a charge, are not better qualified to fulfil that duty: instead of suffering *the tender shoot to grow wild and uncultivated, when the pruning-knife, in a gentle hand, with a little*

8/8 OBSERVATIONS ON COMPOSING. Although this essential point has been passed over with little notice by most writers upon this subject, still (so great are the evils resulting from ill-contracted habits, which naturally keep pace with our growth), we cannot avoid pointing out a few instances of the sure consequences attendant on them. There are many persons now employed in the art, who frequently, with great justice, inveigh in strong terms against the conduct of those unto whose care they were first entrusted, for suffering them to contract those ill-becoming postures which are productive of knock knees, round shoulders, and other deformities. It is deeply to be regretted, that those who undertake so important a charge, are not better qualified to fulfil that duty: instead of suffering the tender shoot to grow wild and uncultivated, when the pruning-knife, in a gentle hand, with a little admonition, would have checked its improper growth, and trained it in a right course.
What to a learner may appear fatiguing, time and habit will render easy and familiar; and though to work with his cases on a level with his breast, may at first tire his arms, yet use will so inure him to it, that it will become afterwards equally unpleasant to work at a low frame. His perseverance in this mode must be strengthened by the *reflection, that it will most effectually prevent his becoming round shouldered, a distinguishing mark by which compositors are in*

10/12 OBSERVATIONS ON COMPOSING. Although this essential point has been passed over with little notice by most writers upon this subject, still (so great are the evils resulting from ill-contracted habits, which naturally keep pace with our growth), we cannot avoid pointing out a few instances of the sure consequences attendant on them. There are many persons now employed in the art, who frequently, with great justice, inveigh in strong terms against the conduct of those unto whose care they were first entrusted, for suffering them to contract those ill-becoming postures which are productive of knock knees, round shoulders, and other deformities. It is deeply to be regretted, that *those who undertake so important a charge, are not better qualified to fulfil that duty: instead of suffering*

8/10 OBSERVATIONS ON COMPOSING. Although this essential point has been passed over with little notice by most writers upon this subject, still (so great are the evils resulting from ill-contracted habits, which naturally keep pace with our growth), we cannot avoid pointing out a few instances of the sure consequences attendant on them. There are many persons now employed in the art, who frequently, with great justice, inveigh in strong terms against the conduct of those unto whose care they were first entrusted, for suffering them to contract those ill-becoming postures which are productive of knock knees, round shoulders, and other deformities. It is deeply to be regretted, that those who undertake so important a charge, are not better qualified to fulfil that duty: instead of suffering the tender shoot to grow wild and uncultivated, when the pruning-knife, in a gentle hand, with a little admonition, would have checked its improper growth, and trained it in a right course.
What to a learner may appear fatiguing, time and habit will *render easy and familiar; and though to work with his cases on a level with his breast, may at first tire his arms, yet use will so inure*

10/14 OBSERVATIONS ON COMPOSING. Although this essential point has been passed over with little notice by most writers upon this subject, still (so great are the evils resulting from ill-contracted habits, which naturally keep pace with our growth), we cannot avoid pointing out a few instances of the sure consequences attendant on them. There are many persons now employed in the art, who frequently, with great justice, inveigh in strong terms against the conduct of those unto whose care they were first entrusted, for suffering *them to contract those ill-becoming postures which are productive of knock knees, round shoulders, and*

8/12 OBSERVATIONS ON COMPOSING. Although this essential point has been passed over with little notice by most writers upon this subject, still (so great are the evils resulting from ill-contracted habits, which naturally keep pace with our growth), we cannot avoid pointing out a few instances of the sure consequences attendant on them. There are many persons now employed in the art, who frequently, with great justice, inveigh in strong terms against the conduct of those unto whose care they were first entrusted, for suffering them to contract those ill-becoming postures which are productive of knock knees, round shoulders, and other deformities. It is deeply to be regretted, that those who undertake so important a charge, are not better qualified to fulfil that duty: instead of suffering the tender *shoot to grow wild and uncultivated, when the pruning-knife, in a gentle hand, with a little admonition, would have checked its*

ITC AVANT GARDE** GOTHIC EXTRA LIGHT   MERGENTHALER TYPE LIBRARY

ABCDEFGHIJKLMNOPQRSTUVWXYZ
ABCDEFGHIJKLMNOPQRSTUVWXYZ
&,"-;!?""1234567890$
&,"-;!?""1234567890$
abcdefghijklmnopqrstuvwxyz
abcdefghijklmnopqrstuvwxyz

ABCDEFGHIJKLMNOPQRSTUVWXYZ
ABCDEFGHIJKLMNOPQRSTUVWXYZ
&,"-;!?""1234567890$
&,"-;!?""1234567890$
abcdefghijklmnopqrstuvwxyz
abcdefghijklmnopqrstuvwxyz

ABCDEFGHIJKL
MNOPQRSTUV
WXYZ&abcde
fghijklmnopqr
stuvwxyz1234
567890$.,""";:!?

72 POINT ITC AVANT GARDE GOTHIC MEDIUM   AGFA COMPUGRAPHIC TYPE LIBRARY

AVANT GARDE GOTHIC FAMILY 39

ABCDEFGHIJK LMNOPQRSTU VWXYZ&abcd efghijklmnop qrstuvwxyz12 34567890$:;!?

72 POINT ITC AVANT GARDE GOTHIC MEDIUM OBLIQUE   AGFA COMPUGRAPHIC TYPE LIBRARY

ABCDEFGHIJKLMNOPQR STUVWXYZ&abcdefghij klmnopqrstuvwxyz1234 567890$.,""":;!?

48 POINT ITC AVANT GARDE GOTHIC** MEDIUM   MERGENTHALER TYPE LIBRARY

ABCDEFGHIJKLMNOPQR STUVWXYZ&abcdefghij klmnopqrstuvwxyz12345 67890$.,""":;!?

48 POINT ITC AVANT GARDE GOTHIC** MEDIUM OBLIQUE   MERGENTHALER TYPE LIBRARY

ABCDEFGHIJKLMNOPQRSTUVWXYZ&abcdefghijklmnopqrstuvwxyz1234567890$.,""":;!?

18 POINT ITC AVANT GARDE GOTHIC** MEDIUM   MERGENTHALER TYPE LIBRARY

ABCDEFGHIJKLMNOPQRSTUVWXYZ&abcdefghijklmnopqrstuvwxyz1234567890$.,""":;!?

18 POINT ITC AVANT GARDE GOTHIC** MEDIUM OBLIQUE   MERGENTHALER TYPE LIBRARY

14/14 OBSERVATIONS ON COMPOSING. Although this essential point has been passed over with little notice by most writers upon this subject, still (so great are the evils resulting from ill-contracted habits, which naturally keep pace with our growth), we cannot avoid pointing out a few instances of the sure consequences attendant on them. There are many persons now employed in the art, *who frequently, with great justice, inveigh in strong terms against the*

12/12 OBSERVATIONS ON COMPOSING. Although this essential point has been passed over with little notice by most writers upon this subject, still (so great are the evils resulting from ill-contracted habits, which naturally keep pace with our growth), we cannot avoid pointing out a few instances of the sure consequences attendant on them. There are many persons now employed in the art, who frequently, with great justice, inveigh in strong terms against the conduct of those unto whose care they were first entrusted, for suffering them to contract *those ill-becoming postures which are productive of knock knees, round*

14/16 OBSERVATIONS ON COMPOSING. Although this essential point has been passed over with little notice by most writers upon this subject, still (so great are the evils resulting from ill-contracted habits, which naturally keep pace with our growth), we cannot avoid pointing out a few instances of the sure consequences *attendant on them. There are many persons now employed in the art,*

12/14 OBSERVATIONS ON COMPOSING. Although this essential point has been passed over with little notice by most writers upon this subject, still (so great are the evils resulting from ill-contracted habits, which naturally keep pace with our growth), we cannot avoid pointing out a few instances of the sure consequences attendant on them. There are many persons now employed in the art, who frequently, with great justice, *inveigh in strong terms against the conduct of those unto whose care they were*

14/18 OBSERVATIONS ON COMPOSING. Although this essential point has been passed over with little notice by most writers upon this subject, still (so great are the evils resulting from ill-contracted habits, which naturally keep pace with our growth), *cannot avoid pointing out a few instances of the sure consequences*

12/16 OBSERVATIONS ON COMPOSING. Although this essential point has been passed over with little notice by most writers upon this subject, still (so great are the evils resulting from ill-contracted habits, which naturally keep pace with our growth), we cannot avoid pointing out a few instances of the sure consequences attendant on them. *There are many persons now employed in the art, who frequently, with great justice,*

ITC AVANT GARDE GOTHIC** MEDIUM   MERGENTHALER TYPE LIBRARY

ABCDEFGHIJKLMNOPQRSTUVWXYZ
ABCDEFGHIJKLMNOPQRSTUVWXYZ
&.,''-:;!?''''1234567890$
&.,''-:;!?''''1234567890$
abcdefghijklmnopqrstuvwxyz
abcdefghijklmnopqrstuvwxyz

ABCDEFGHIJKLMNOPQRSTUVWXYZ
ABCDEFGHIJKLMNOPQRSTUVWXYZ
&.,''-:;!?''''1234567890$
&.,''-:;!?''''1234567890$
abcdefghijklmnopqrstuvwxyz
abcdefghijklmnopqrstuvwxyz

10/10 OBSERVATIONS ON COMPOSING. Although this essential point has been passed over with little notice by most writers upon this subject, still (so great are the evils resulting from ill-contracted habits, which naturally keep pace with our growth), we cannot avoid pointing out a few instances of the sure consequences attendant on them. There are many persons now employed in the art, who frequently, with great justice, inveigh in strong terms against the conduct of those unto whose care they were first entrusted, for suffering them to contract those ill-becoming postures which are productive of knock knees, round shoulders, and other deformities. It is deeply to be regretted, that those who undertake so important a charge, are not better *qualified to fulfill that duty: instead of suffering the tender shoot to grow wild and uncultivated, when*

8/8 OBSERVATIONS ON COMPOSING. Although this essential point has been passed over with little notice by most writers upon this subject, still (so great are the evils resulting from ill-contracted habits, which naturally keep pace with our growth), we cannot avoid pointing out a few instances of the sure consequences attendant on them. There are many persons now employed in the art, who frequently, with great justice, inveigh in strong terms against the conduct of those unto whose care they were first entrusted, for suffering them to contract those ill-becoming postures which are productive of knock knees, round shoulders, and other deformities. It is deeply to be regretted, that those who undertake so important a charge, are not better qualified to fulfill that duty: instead of suffering the tender shoot to grow wild and uncultivated, when the pruning-knife, in a gentle hand, with a little admonition, would have checked its improper growth, and trained it in a right course.
What to a learner may appear fatiguing, time and habit will render easy and familiar; and though to work with his cases on a level with his breast, may at first tire his arms, yet use will so inure him to it, that it will become afterwards equally unpleasant to *work at a low frame. His perseverance in this mode must be strengthened by the reflection, that it will most effectually pre-*

10/12 OBSERVATIONS ON COMPOSING. Although this essential point has been passed over with little notice by most writers upon this subject, still (so great are the evils resulting from ill-contracted habits, which naturally keep pace with our growth), we cannot avoid pointing out a few instances of the sure consequences attendant on them. There are many persons now employed in the art, who frequently, with great justice, inveigh in strong terms against the conduct of those unto whose care they were first entrusted, for suffering them to contract those ill-becoming postures which are productive of knock knees, round shoulders, and other deformities. *It is deeply to be regretted, that those who undertake so important a charge, are not better*

8/10 OBSERVATIONS ON COMPOSING. Although this essential point has been passed over with little notice by most writers upon this subject, still (so great are the evils resulting from ill-contracted habits, which naturally keep pace with our growth), we cannot avoid pointing out a few instances of the sure consequences attendant on them. There are many persons now employed in the art, who frequently, with great justice, inveigh in strong terms against the conduct of those unto whose care they were first entrusted, for suffering them to contract those ill-becoming postures which are productive of knock knees, round shoulders, and other deformities. It is deeply to be regretted, that those who undertake so important a charge, are not better qualified to fulfill that duty: instead of suffering the tender shoot to grow wild and uncultivated, when the pruning-knife, in a gentle hand, with a little admonition, would have checked its improper growth, and trained it in a right course.
What to a learner may appear fatiguing, time and habit will render easy and familiar; and though to work with his cases on

10/14 OBSERVATIONS ON COMPOSING. Although this essential point has been passed over with little notice by most writers upon this subject, still (so great are the evils resulting from ill-contracted habits, which naturally keep pace with our growth), we cannot avoid pointing out a few instances of the sure consequences attendant on them. There are many persons now employed in the art, who frequently, with great justice, inveigh in strong terms against the conduct of those unto whose care they *were first entrusted, for suffering them to contract those ill-becoming postures which are productive*

8/12 OBSERVATIONS ON COMPOSING. Although this essential point has been passed over with little notice by most writers upon this subject, still (so great are the evils resulting from ill-contracted habits, which naturally keep pace with our growth), we cannot avoid pointing out a few instances of the sure consequences attendant on them. There are many persons now employed in the art, who frequently, with great justice, inveigh in strong terms against the conduct of those unto whose care they were first entrusted, for suffering them to contract those ill-becoming postures which are productive of knock knees, round shoulders, and other deformities. It is deeply to be regretted, that those who undertake so important a charge, are not better qualified *to fulfill that duty: instead of suffering the tender shoot to grow wild and uncultivated, when the pruning-knife, in a gentle*

ITC AVANT GARDE GOTHIC** MEDIUM   MERGENTHALER TYPE LIBRARY

ABCDEFGHIJKLMNOPQRSTUVWXYZ
ABCDEFGHIJKLMNOPQRSTUVWXYZ
&.,''-:;!?''''1234567890$
&.,''-:;!?''''1234567890$
abcdefghijklmnopqrstuvwxyz
abcdefghijklmnopqrstuvwxyz

ABCDEFGHIJKLMNOPQRSTUVWXYZ
ABCDEFGHIJKLMNOPQRSTUVWXYZ
&.,''-:;!?''''1234567890$
&.,''-:;!?''''1234567890$
abcdefghijklmnopqrstuvwxyz
abcdefghijklmnopqrstuvwxyz

ABCDEFGHIJK
LMNOPQRSTU
VWXYZ&abc
defghijklmno
pqrstuvwxyz
1234567890O$
.,""":;!?

72 POINT ITC AVANT GARDE GOTHIC DEMI   AGFA COMPUGRAPHIC TYPE LIBRARY

ABCDEFGHIJK
LMNOPQRSTU
VWXYZ&abc
defghijklmno
pqrstuvwxyz
1234567890O$
.,'"";:!?

ABCDEFGHIJKLMNOPQ
RSTUVWXYZ&abcdefg
hijklmnopqrstuvwxyz12
34567890$.,""";!?

48 POINT ITC AVANT GARDE GOTHIC** DEMI   MERGENTHALER TYPE LIBRARY

ABCDEFGHIJKLMNOPQ
RSTUVWXYZ&abcdefg
hijklmnopqrstuvwxyz12
34567890$.,""";!?

48 POINT ITC AVANT GARDE GOTHIC** DEMI OBLIQUE   MERGENTHALER TYPE LIBRARY

ABCDEFGHIJKLMNOPQRSTUVWXYZ&abcdefghijklmnopqrst
uvwxyz1234567890$.,""";!?

18 POINT ITC AVANT GARDE GOTHIC** DEMI   MERGENTHALER TYPE LIBRARY

*ABCDEFGHIJKLMNOPQRSTUVWXYZ&abcdefghijklmnopqrs
tuvwxyz1234567890$.,""";!?*

18 POINT ITC AVANT GARDE GOTHIC** DEMI OBLIQUE   MERGENTHALER TYPE LIBRARY

14/14 OBSERVATIONS ON COMPOSING. Although this essential point has been passed over with little notice by most writers upon this subject, still (so great are the evils resulting from ill-contracted habits, which naturally keep pace with our growth), we cannot avoid pointing out a few instances of the sure consequences attendant on them. There are many persons now employed in the art, *who frequently, with great justice, inveigh in strong terms against the*

12/12 OBSERVATIONS ON COMPOSING. Although this essential point has been passed over with little notice by most writers upon this subject, still (so great are the evils resulting from ill-contracted habits, which naturally keep pace with our growth), we cannot avoid pointing out a few instances of the sure consequences attendant on them. There are many persons now employed in the art, who frequently, with great justice, inveigh in strong terms against the conduct of those unto whose care they were first entrusted, for suffering *them to contract those ill-becoming postures which are productive of knock*

14/16 OBSERVATIONS ON COMPOSING. Although this essential point has been passed over with little notice by most writers upon this subject, still (so great are the evils resulting from ill-contracted habits, which naturally keep pace with our growth), we cannot avoid pointing out a few instances of the sure consequences *attendant on them. There are many persons now employed in*

12/14 OBSERVATIONS ON COMPOSING. Although this essential point has been passed over with little notice by most writers upon this subject, still (so great are the evils resulting from ill-contracted habits, which naturally keep pace with our growth), we cannot avoid pointing out a few instances of the sure consequences attendant on them. There are many persons now employed in the art, who frequently, with *great justice, inveigh in strong terms against the conduct of those unto whose*

14/18 OBSERVATIONS ON COMPOSING. Although this essential point has been passed over with little notice by most writers upon this subject, still (so great are the evils resulting from ill-contracted habits, which naturally keep pace with our growth), *we cannot avoid pointing out a few instances of the sure conse-*

12/16 OBSERVATIONS ON COMPOSING. Although this essential point has been passed over with little notice by most writers upon this subject, still (so great are the evils resulting from ill-contracted habits, which naturally keep pace with our growth), we cannot avoid pointing out a few instances of the sure consequences attendant on them. *There are many persons now employed in the art, who frequently, with*

ITC AVANT GARDE GOTHIC** DEMI MERGENTHALER TYPE LIBRARY

ABCDEFGHIJKLMNOPQRSTUVWXYZ
ABCDEFGHIJKLMNOPQRSTUVWXYZ
&.,''-:;!?''''1234567890$
&.,''-:;!?''''1234567890$
abcdefghijklmnopqrstuvwxyz
abcdefghijklmnopqrstuvwxyz

ABCDEFGHIJKLMNOPQRSTUVWXYZ
ABCDEFGHIJKLMNOPQRSTUVWXYZ
&.,''-:;!?''''1234567890$
&.,''-:;!?''''1234567890$
abcdefghijklmnopqrstuvwxyz
abcdefghijklmnopqrstuvwxyz

AVANT GARDE GOTHIC FAMILY   47

10/10 **OBSERVATIONS ON COMPOSING.** Although this essential point has been passed over with little notice by most writers upon this subject, still (so great are the evils resulting from ill-contracted habits, which naturally keep pace with our growth), we cannot avoid pointing out a few instances of the sure consequences attendant on them. There are many persons now employed in the art, who frequently, with great justice, inveigh in strong terms against the conduct of those unto whose care they were first entrusted, for suffering them to contract those ill-becoming postures which are productive of knock knees, round shoulders, and other deformities. It is deeply to be regretted, that those who undertake so important a *charge, are not better qualified to fulfill that duty: instead of suffering the tender shoot to grow wild*

8/8 **OBSERVATIONS ON COMPOSING.** Although this essential point has been passed over with little notice by most writers upon this subject, still (so great are the evils resulting from ill-contracted habits, which naturally keep pace with our growth), we cannot avoid pointing out a few instances of the sure consequences attendant on them. There are many persons now employed in the art, who frequently, with great justice, inveigh in strong terms against the conduct of those unto whose care they were first entrusted, for suffering them to contract those ill-becoming postures which are productive of knock knees, round shoulders, and other deformities. It is deeply to be regretted, that those who undertake so important a charge, are not better qualified to fulfill that duty: instead of suffering the tender shoot to grow wild and uncultivated, when the pruning-knife, in a gentle hand, with a little admonition, would have checked its improper growth, and trained it in a right course.
  What to a learner may appear fatiguing, time and habit will render easy and familiar; and though to work with his cases on a level with his breast, may at first tire his arms, yet use will so inure him to it, that it will become afterwards equally unpleas-*ant to work at a low frame. His perseverance in this mode must be strengthened by the reflection, that it will most ef-*

10/12 **OBSERVATIONS ON COMPOSING.** Although this essential point has been passed over with little notice by most writers upon this subject, still (so great are the evils resulting from ill-contracted habits, which naturally keep pace with our growth), we cannot avoid pointing out a few instances of the sure consequences attendant on them. There are many persons now employed in the art, who frequently, with great justice, inveigh in strong terms against the conduct of those unto whose care they were first entrusted, for suffering them to contract those ill-becoming postures which are productive of knock knees, round shoulders, *and other deformities. It is deeply to be regretted, that those who undertake so impor-*

8/10 **OBSERVATIONS ON COMPOSING.** Although this essential point has been passed over with little notice by most writers upon this subject, still (so great are the evils resulting from ill-contracted habits, which naturally keep pace with our growth), we cannot avoid pointing out a few instances of the sure consequences attendant on them. There are many persons now employed in the art, who frequently, with great justice, inveigh in strong terms against the conduct of those unto whose care they were first entrusted, for suffering them to contract those ill-becoming postures which are productive of knock knees, round shoulders, and other deformities. It is deeply to be regretted, that those who undertake so important a charge, are not better qualified to fulfill that duty: instead of suffering the tender shoot to grow wild and uncultivated, when the pruning-knife, in a gentle hand, with a little admonition, would have checked its improper growth, and trained it in a right course.
  What to a learner may appear fatiguing, time and habit will render easy and familiar; and though to work with his cases

10/14 **OBSERVATIONS ON COMPOSING.** Although this essential point has been passed over with little notice by most writers upon this subject, still (so great are the evils resulting from ill-contracted habits, which naturally keep pace with our growth), we cannot avoid pointing out a few instances of the sure consequences attendant on them. There are many persons now employed in the art, who frequently, with great justice, inveigh in strong terms against the conduct of those unto *whose care they were first entrusted, for suffering them to contract those ill-becoming postures*

8/12 **OBSERVATIONS ON COMPOSING.** Although this essential point has been passed over with little notice by most writers upon this subject, still (so great are the evils resulting from ill-contracted habits, which naturally keep pace with our growth), we cannot avoid pointing out a few instances of the sure consequences attendant on them. There are many persons now employed in the art, who frequently, with great justice, inveigh in strong terms against the conduct of those unto whose care they were first entrusted, for suffering them to contract those ill-becoming postures which are productive of knock knees, round shoulders, and other deformities. It is deeply to be regretted, that those who undertake so important a charge, are not better qualified *to fulfill that duty: instead of suffering the tender shoot to grow wild and uncultivated, when the pruning-knife, in a gen-*

ITC AVANT GARDE GOTHIC** DEMI   MERGENTHALER TYPE LIBRARY

ABCDEFGHIJKLMNOPQRSTUVWXYZ
ABCDEFGHIJKLMNOPQRSTUVWXYZ
&.,''-:;!?""1234567890$
&.,''-:;!?""1234567890$
abcdefghijklmnopqrstuvwxyz
abcdefghijklmnopqrstuvwxyz

ABCDEFGHIJKLMNOPQRSTUVWXYZ
ABCDEFGHIJKLMNOPQRSTUVWXYZ
&.,''-:;!?""1234567890$
&.,''-:;!?""1234567890$
abcdefghijklmnopqrstuvwxyz
abcdefghijklmnopqrstuvwxyz

ABCDEFGHIJ
KLMNOPQRS
TUVWXYZ&a
bcdefghijklm
nopqrstuvwx
yz123456789
0$.,''""::;!?

72 POINT ITC AVANT GARDE GOTHIC BOLD   AGFA COMPUGRAPHIC TYPE LIBRARY

ABCDEFGHIJ KLMNOPQRS TUVWXYZ&a bcdefghijklm nopqrstuvwx yz123456789 0$.,''"";;!?

72 POINT ITC AVANT GARDE GOTHIC BOLD OBLIQUE   AGFA COMPUGRAPHIC TYPE LIBRARY

AVANT GARDE GOTHIC FAMILY

ABCDEFGHIJKLMNOPQRSTUVWXYZ&abcdefghijklmnopqrstuvwxyz1234567890$.,""":;!?

48 POINT ITC AVANT GARDE GOTHIC** BOLD   MERGENTHALER TYPE LIBRARY

ABCDEFGHIJKLMNOPQRSTUVWXYZ&abcdefghijklmnopqrstuvwxyz1234567890$.,""":;!?

48 POINT ITC AVANT GARDE GOTHIC** BOLD OBLIQUE   MERGENTHALER TYPE LIBRARY

ABCDEFGHIJKLMNOPQRSTUVWXYZ&abcdefghijklmnopqrstuvwxyz1234567890$.,""":;!?

18 POINT ITC AVANT GARDE GOTHIC** BOLD   MERGENTHALER TYPE LIBRARY

ABCDEFGHIJKLMNOPQRSTUVWXYZ&abcdefghijklmnopqrstuvwxyz1234567890$.,""":;!?

18 POINT ITC AVANT GARDE GOTHIC** BOLD OBLIQUE   MERGENTHALER TYPE LIBRARY

AVANT GARDE GOTHIC FAMILY 51

14/14 **OBSERVATIONS ON COMPOSING. Although this essential point has been passed over with little notice by most writers upon this subject, still (so great are the evils resulting from ill-contracted habits, which naturally keep pace with our growth), we cannot avoid pointing out a few instances of the sure consequences attendant on them. There are many persons now em-*ployed in the art, who frequently, with great justice, inveigh in*

12/12 **OBSERVATIONS ON COMPOSING. Although this essential point has been passed over with little notice by most writers upon this subject, still (so great are the evils resulting from ill-contracted habits, which naturally keep pace with our growth), we cannot avoid pointing out a few instances of the sure consequences attendant on them. There are many persons now employed in the art, who frequently, with great justice, inveigh in strong terms against the conduct of those unto whose care they were *first entrusted, for suffering them to contract those ill-becoming postures*

14/16 **OBSERVATIONS ON COMPOSING. Although this essential point has been passed over with little notice by most writers upon this subject, still (so great are the evils resulting from ill-contracted habits, which naturally keep pace with our growth), we cannot avoid pointing out a few instances of the sure con-*sequences attendant on them. There are many persons now em-*

12/14 **OBSERVATIONS ON COMPOSING. Although this essential point has been passed over with little notice by most writers upon this subject, still (so great are the evils resulting from ill-contracted habits, which naturally keep pace with our growth), we cannot avoid pointing out a few instances of the sure consequences attendant on them. There are many persons now employed in the art, *who frequently, with great justice, inveigh in strong terms against the con-*

14/18 **OBSERVATIONS ON COMPOSING. Although this essential point has been passed over with little notice by most writers upon this subject, still (so great are the evils resulting from ill-contracted habits, which naturally keep pace with our growth), *we cannot avoid pointing out a few instances of the sure*

12/16 **OBSERVATIONS ON COMPOSING. Although this essential point has been passed over with little notice by most writers upon this subject, still (so great are the evils resulting from ill-contracted habits, which naturally keep pace with our growth), we cannot avoid pointing out a few instances of the sure consequences attendant on them. *There are many persons now employed in the art,*

ITC AVANT GARDE GOTHIC** BOLD   MERGENTHALER TYPE LIBRARY

ABCDEFGHIJKLMNOPQRSTUVWX
ABCDEFGHIJKLMNOPQRSTUVWX
YZ&.,''-:;!?''""1234567890$
YZ&.,''-:;!?''""1234567890$
abcdefghijklmnopqrstuvwxyz
abcdefghijklmnopqrstuvwxyz

ABCDEFGHIJKLMNOPQRSTUVWXYZ
ABCDEFGHIJKLMNOPQRSTUVWXYZ
&.,''-:;!?''""1234567890$
&.,''-:;!?''""1234567890$
abcdefghijklmnopqrstuvwxyz
abcdefghijklmnopqrstuvwxyz

10/10 OBSERVATIONS ON COMPOSING. Although this essential point has been passed over with little notice by most writers upon this subject, still (so great are the evils resulting from ill-contracted habits, which naturally keep pace with our growth), we cannot avoid pointing out a few instances of the sure consequences attendant on them. There are many persons now employed in the art, who frequently, with great justice, inveigh in strong terms against the conduct of those unto whose care they were first entrusted, for suffering them to contract those ill-becoming postures which are productive of knock knees, round shoulders, and other deformities. It is deeply to be regretted, that those who undertake so important a charge, are not better qualified to fulfill that duty: instead of suffering the tender shoot

8/8 OBSERVATIONS ON COMPOSING. Although this essential point has been passed over with little notice by most writers upon this subject, still (so great are the evils resulting from ill-contracted habits, which naturally keep pace with our growth), we cannot avoid pointing out a few instances of the sure consequences attendant on them. There are many persons now employed in the art, who frequently, with great justice, inveigh in strong terms against the conduct of those unto whose care they were first entrusted, for suffering them to contract those ill-becoming postures which are productive of knock knees, round shoulders, and other deformities. It is deeply to be regretted, that those who undertake so important a charge, are not better qualified to fulfill that duty: instead of suffering the tender shoot to grow wild and uncultivated, when the pruning-knife, in a gentle hand, with a little admonition, would have checked its improper growth, and trained it in a right course.
What to a learner may appear fatiguing, time and habit will render easy and familiar; and though to work with his cases on a level with his breast, may at first tire his arms, yet use will so inure him to it, that it will become afterwards equally unpleasant to work at a low frame. His perseverance in this

10/12 OBSERVATIONS ON COMPOSING. Although this essential point has been passed over with little notice by most writers upon this subject, still (so great are the evils resulting from ill-contracted habits, which naturally keep pace with our growth), we cannot avoid pointing out a few instances of the sure consequences attendant on them. There are many persons now employed in the art, who frequently, with great justice, inveigh in strong terms against the conduct of those unto whose care they were first entrusted, for suffering them to contract those ill-becoming postures which are productive of knock knees, round shoulders, and other deformities. It is deeply to be regretted, that those who undertake so

8/10 OBSERVATIONS ON COMPOSING. Although this essential point has been passed over with little notice by most writers upon this subject, still (so great are the evils resulting from ill-contracted habits, which naturally keep pace with our growth), we cannot avoid pointing out a few instances of the sure consequences attendant on them. There are many persons now employed in the art, who frequently, with great justice, inveigh in strong terms against the conduct of those unto whose care they were first entrusted, for suffering them to contract those ill-becoming postures which are productive of knock knees, round shoulders, and other deformities. It is deeply to be regretted, that those who undertake so important a charge, are not better qualified to fulfill that duty: instead of suffering the tender shoot to grow wild and uncultivated, when the pruning-knife, in a gentle hand, with a little admonition, would have checked its improper growth, and trained it in a right course.
What to a learner may appear fatiguing, time and habit

10/14 OBSERVATIONS ON COMPOSING. Although this essential point has been passed over with little notice by most writers upon this subject, still (so great are the evils resulting from ill-contracted habits, which naturally keep pace with our growth), we cannot avoid pointing out a few instances of the sure consequences attendant on them. There are many persons now employed in the art, who frequently, with great justice, inveigh in strong terms against the conduct of those unto whose care they were first entrusted, for suffering them to contract those ill-becoming pos-

8/12 OBSERVATIONS ON COMPOSING. Although this essential point has been passed over with little notice by most writers upon this subject, still (so great are the evils resulting from ill-contracted habits, which naturally keep pace with our growth), we cannot avoid pointing out a few instances of the sure consequences attendant on them. There are many persons now employed in the art, who frequently, with great justice, inveigh in strong terms against the conduct of those unto whose care they were first entrusted, for suffering them to contract those ill-becoming postures which are productive of knock knees, round shoulders, and other deformities. It is deeply to be regretted, that those who undertake so important a charge, are not better qualified to fulfill that duty: instead of suffering the tender shoot to grow wild and un-

ITC AVANT GARDE GOTHIC** BOLD   MERGENTHALER TYPE LIBRARY

ABCDEFGHIJKLMNOPQRSTUVWXYZ
ABCDEFGHIJKLMNOPQRSTUVWXYZ
&.,"-:;!?""1234567890$
&.,"-:;!?""1234567890$
abcdefghijklmnopqrstuvwxyz
abcdefghijklmnopqrstuvwxyz

ABCDEFGHIJKLMNOPQRSTUVWXYZ
ABCDEFGHIJKLMNOPQRSTUVWXYZ
&.,"-:;!?""1234567890$
&.,"-:;!?""1234567890$
abcdefghijklmnopqrstuvwxyz
abcdefghijklmnopqrstuvwxyz

AVANT GARDE GOTHIC FAMILY 53

AACAO
EAFAFRGA
HTKALALA
LMMNNT
PRRASST
STTHUT
VVVWW

cetvwy

Alternate Characters for Avant Garde Gothic Book

Alternate Characters for Avant Garde Gothic Extra Light

Alternate Characters for Avant Garde Gothic Medium

AVANT GARDE GOTHIC FAMILY 55

AACACO AACACO
EAFAFRGA EAFAFRGA
HTKALAL HTKALAL
LMMNT MMNT
PRRASST PRRASST
STTHUT STTHUT
VVVNW VVVNW
cetvwy cetvwy

Alternate Characters for Avant Garde Gothic Demi   Alternate Characters for Avant Garde Gothic Bold

An excellent version of this classic transitional type, Fry's Baskerville remains unsurpassed. Although it lacks available fonts in italic form, or in a variety of styles, the differing weights offered by the ITC Baskervilles fill the gap very well indeed.

BASKERVILLE FAMILY 57

ABCDEFGHIJ
KLMNOPQRS
TUVWXYZ&a
bcdefghijklmno
pqrstuvwxyz123
4567890$.,"":;!?

72 POINT FRY'S BASKERVILLE   MERGENTHALER TYPE LIBRARY

ABCDEFGHIJKLMNOPQRSTUVWXYZ&abcdefghijklmnopqrstuvwxyz1234567890$.,"":;!?

72 POINT ITC NEW BASKERVILLE** ITALIC   MERGENTHALER TYPE LIBRARY

ABCDEFGHIJKLM
NOPQRSTUVWX
YZ&abcdefghijklmn
opqrstuvwxyz123456
7890$.,""":;!?

60 POINT FRY'S BASKERVILLE   MERGENTHALER TYPE LIBRARY

*ABCDEFGHIJKLM
NOPQRSTUVWXY
Z&abcdefghijklmnopq
rstuvwxyz1234567890$.,""":;!?*

60 POINT ITC NEW BASKERVILLE** ITALIC   MERGENTHALER TYPE LIBRARY

ABCDEFGHIJKLMNOP
QRSTUVWXYZ&abcde
fghijklmnopqrstuvwxyz12
34567890$.,""":;!?

48 POINT FRY'S BASKERVILLE   MERGENTHALER TYPE LIBRARY

*ABCDEFGHIJKLMNOP
QRSTUVWXYZ&abcdef
ghijklmnopqrstuvwxyz123
4567890$.,""":;!?*

48 POINT ITC NEW BASKERVILLE** ITALIC   MERGENTHALER TYPE LIBRARY

ABCDEFGHIJKLMNOPQRST
UVWXYZ&abcdefghijklmnopqr
stuvwxyz1234567890$.,""":;!?

36 POINT FRY'S BASKERVILLE   MERGENTHALER TYPE LIBRARY

ABCDEFGHIJKLMNOPQRSTU VWXYZ&abcdefghijklmnopqrstuv wxyz1234567890$.,""":;!?

36 POINT ITC NEW BASKERVILLE** ITALIC   MERGENTHALER TYPE LIBRARY

ABCDEFGHIJKLMNOPQRSTUVWXYZ&ab cdefghijklmnopqrstuvwxyz1234567890$.,""":;!?

24 POINT FRY'S BASKERVILLE   MERGENTHALER TYPE LIBRARY

ABCDEFGHIJKLMNOPQRSTUVWXYZ&abcd efghijklmnopqrstuvwxyz1234567890$.,""":;!?

24 POINT ITC NEW BASKERVILLE** ITALIC   MERGENTHALER TYPE LIBRARY

ABCDEFGHIJKLMNOPQRSTUVWXYZ&abcdefghijklmnopq rstuvwxyz1234567890$.,""":;!?

18 POINT FRY'S BASKERVILLE   MERGENTHALER TYPE LIBRARY

ABCDEFGHIJKLMNOPQRSTUVWXYZ&abcdefghijklmnopqrstu vwxyz1234567890$.,""":;!?

18 POINT ITC NEW BASKERVILLE** ITALIC   MERGENTHALER TYPE LIBRARY

14/14 Amongst the several mechanic Arts that have engaged my attention, there is no one which I have pursued with so much steadiness and pleasure, as that of Letter-Founding. Having been an early admirer of the beauty of Letters, I became insensibly desirous of contributing to the perfection of them. I formed to myself Ideas of greater accuracy than had yet appeared, and have endeavoured to produce a Sett of Types *according to what I conceived to be their true proportion.*

12/12 Amongst the several mechanic Arts that have engaged my attention, there is no one which I have pursued with so much steadiness and pleasure, as that of Letter-Founding. Having been an early admirer of the beauty of Letters, I became insensibly desirous of contributing to the perfection of them. I formed to myself Ideas of greater accuracy than had yet appeared, and have endeavoured to produce a Sett of Types according to what I conceived to be their true proportion.

Mr. Caslon is an Artist, to whom the Republic of Learning has great obligations; his *ingenuity has left a fairer copy for my emulation, than any other master. In his great variety of*

14/16 Amongst the several mechanic Arts that have engaged my attention, there is no one which I have pursued with so much steadiness and pleasure, as that of Letter-Founding. Having been an early admirer of the beauty of Letters, I became insensibly desirous of contributing to the perfection of them. I formed to myself Ideas of greater ac*curacy than had yet appeared, and have endeavoured to produce a Sett of Types*

12/14 Amongst the several mechanic Arts that have engaged my attention, there is no one which I have pursued with so much steadiness and pleasure, as that of Letter-Founding. Having been an early admirer of the beauty of Letters, I became insensibly desirous of contributing to the perfection of them. I formed to myself Ideas of greater accuracy than had yet appeared, and have endeavoured to produce a Sett of Types according to what I conceived to *be their true proportion.*

Mr. Caslon is an Artist, to whom the Republic

14/18 Amongst the several mechanic Arts that have engaged my attention, there is no one which I have pursued with so much steadiness and pleasure, as that of Letter-Founding. Having been an early admirer of the beauty of Letters, I became insensibly desirous of contrib*uting to the perfection of them. I formed to myself Ideas of greater accuracy than had*

12/16 Amongst the several mechanic Arts that have engaged my attention, there is no one which I have pursued with so much steadiness and pleasure, as that of Letter-Founding. Having been an early admirer of the beauty of Letters, I became insensibly desirous of contributing to the perfection of them. I formed to myself Ideas of greater accuracy than had yet ap*peared, and have endeavoured to produce a Sett of Types according to what I conceived to be their*

FRY'S BASKERVILLE WITH ITC NEW BASKERVILLE** ITALIC   MERGENTHALER TYPE LIBRARY

ABCDEFGHIJKLMNOPQRSTUVW
ABCDEFGHIJKLMNOPQRSTUVW
XYZ&.,"-:;!?""1234567890$
XYZ&.,"-:;!?""1234567890$
abcdefghijklmnopqrstuvwxyz
abcdefghijklmnopqrstuvwxyz

ABCDEFGHIJKLMNOPQRSTUVWXYZ
ABCDEFGHIJKLMNOPQRSTUVWXYZ
&.,"-:;!?""1234567890$
&.,"-:;!?""1234567890$
abcdefghijklmnopqrstuvwxyz
abcdefghijklmnopqrstuvwxyz

BASKERVILLE FAMILY 63

11/11 Amongst the several mechanic Arts that have engaged my attention, there is no one which I have pursued with so much steadiness and pleasure, as that of Letter-Founding. Having been an early admirer of the beauty of Letters, I became insensibly desirous of contributing to the perfection of them. I formed to myself Ideas of greater accuracy than had yet appeared, and have endeavoured to produce a Sett of Types according to what I conceived to be their true proportion.

Mr. Caslon is an Artist, to whom the Republic of Learning has great obligations; his ingenuity has left a fairer copy for my emulation, than any other master. *In his great variety of Characters I intend not to follow him; the Roman and Italic are all I have hitherto attempted; if in these he has left room*

10/10 Amongst the several mechanic Arts that have engaged my attention, there is no one which I have pursued with so much steadiness and pleasure, as that of Letter-Founding. Having been an early admirer of the beauty of Letters, I became insensibly desirous of contributing to the perfection of them. I formed to myself Ideas of greater accuracy than had yet appeared, and have endeavoured to produce a Sett of Types according to what I conceived to be their true proportion.

Mr. Caslon is an Artist, to whom the Republic of Learning has great obligations; his ingenuity has left a fairer copy for my emulation, than any other master. In his great variety of Characters I intend not to follow him; the Roman and Italic are all I have hitherto attempted; *if in these he has left room for improvement, it is probably more owing to that variety which divided his attention, than to any other cause. I honor his merit, and*

11/13 Amongst the several mechanic Arts that have engaged my attention, there is no one which I have pursued with so much steadiness and pleasure, as that of Letter-Founding. Having been an early admirer of the beauty of Letters, I became insensibly desirous of contributing to the perfection of them. I formed to myself Ideas of greater accuracy than had yet appeared, and have endeavoured to produce a Sett of Types according to what I conceived to be their true proportion.

Mr. Caslon is an Artist, to whom the Republic of Learning has great obligations; his ingenuity *has left a fairer copy for my emulation, than any other master. In his great variety of Characters I intend not*

10/12 Amongst the several mechanic Arts that have engaged my attention, there is no one which I have pursued with so much steadiness and pleasure, as that of Letter-Founding. Having been an early admirer of the beauty of Letters, I became insensibly desirous of contributing to the perfection of them. I formed to myself Ideas of greater accuracy than had yet appeared, and have endeavoured to produce a Sett of Types according to what I conceived to be their true proportion.

Mr. Caslon is an Artist, to whom the Republic of Learning has great obligations; his ingenuity has left a fairer copy for my emulation, than any other master. In his great variety of Characters I intend not to follow *him; the Roman and Italic are all I have hitherto attempted; if in these he has left room for improvement, it is*

11/15 Amongst the several mechanic Arts that have engaged my attention, there is no one which I have pursued with so much steadiness and pleasure, as that of Letter-Founding. Having been an early admirer of the beauty of Letters, I became insensibly desirous of contributing to the perfection of them. I formed to myself Ideas of greater accuracy than had yet appeared, and have endeavoured to produce a Sett of Types according to what I con*ceived to be their true proportion.*

Mr. Caslon is an Artist, to whom the Republic of

10/14 Amongst the several mechanic Arts that have engaged my attention, there is no one which I have pursued with so much steadiness and pleasure, as that of Letter-Founding. Having been an early admirer of the beauty of Letters, I became insensibly desirous of contributing to the perfection of them. I formed to myself Ideas of greater accuracy than had yet appeared, and have endeavoured to produce a Sett of Types according to what I conceived to be their true proportion.

Mr. Caslon is an Artist, to whom the Republic of *Learning has great obligations; his ingenuity has left a fairer copy for my emulation, than any other master. In his*

FRY'S BASKERVILLE WITH ITC NEW BASKERVILLE** ITALIC   MERGENTHALER TYPE LIBRARY

ABCDEFGHIJKLMNOPQRSTUVWXYZ
ABCDEFGHIJKLMNOPQRSTUVWXYZ
&.,"-:;!?""1234567890$
&.,'-:;!?""1234567890$
abcdefghijklmnopqrstuvwxyz
abcdefghijklmnopqrstuvwxyz

ABCDEFGHIJKLMNOPQRSTUVWXYZ
ABCDEFGHIJKLMNOPQRSTUVWXYZ
&.,"-:;!?""1234567890$
&.,'-:;!?""1234567890$
abcdefghijklmnopqrstuvwxyz
abcdefghijklmnopqrstuvwxyz

9/9 Amongst the several mechanic Arts that have engaged my attention, there is no one which I have pursued with so much steadiness and pleasure, as that of Letter-Founding. Having been an early admirer of the beauty of Letters, I became insensibly desirous of contributing to the perfection of them. I formed to myself Ideas of greater accuracy than had yet appeared, and have endeavoured to produce a Sett of Types according to what I conceived to be their true proportion.

Mr. Caslon is an Artist, to whom the Republic of Learning has great obligations; his ingenuity has left a fairer copy for my emulation, than any other master. In his great variety of Characters I intend not to follow him; the Roman and Italic are all I have hitherto attempted; if in these he has left room for improvement, it is probably more owing to that variety which divided his attention, than to any other cause. I honor his merit, and only wish to derive some small share of Reputation, from an Art which proves accidentally to have been the object of our mutual pursuit.

After having spent many years, and not a little of my fortune in my endeavours to advance this art; I must own it gives me great

8/8 Amongst the several mechanic Arts that have engaged my attention, there is no one which I have pursued with so much steadiness and pleasure, as that of Letter-Founding. Having been an early admirer of the beauty of Letters, I became insensibly desirous of contributing to the perfection of them. I formed to myself Ideas of greater accuracy than had yet appeared, and have endeavoured to produce a Sett of Types according to what I conceived to be their true proportion.

Mr. Caslon is an Artist, to whom the Republic of Learning has great obligations; his ingenuity has left a fairer copy for my emulation, than any other master. In his great variety of Characters I intend not to follow him; the Roman and Italic are all I have hitherto attempted; if in these he has left room for improvement, it is probably more owing to that variety which divided his attention, than to any other cause. I honor his merit, and only wish to derive some small share of Reputation, from an Art which proves accidentally to have been the object of our mutual pursuit.

After having spent many years, and not a little of my fortune in my endeavours to advance this art; I must own it gives me great Satisfaction, to find that my Edition of Virgil has been so widely accepted by *the students of the printing trades. The many positive comments that I have received in the mail has given me the most enjoyable hours of*

9/11 Amongst the several mechanic Arts that have engaged my attention, there is no one which I have pursued with so much steadiness and pleasure, as that of Letter-Founding. Having been an early admirer of the beauty of Letters, I became insensibly desirous of contributing to the perfection of them. I formed to myself Ideas of greater accuracy than had yet appeared, and have endeavoured to produce a Sett of Types according to what I conceived to be their true proportion.

Mr. Caslon is an Artist, to whom the Republic of Learning has great obligations; his ingenuity has left a fairer copy for my emulation, than any other master. In his great variety of Characters I intend not to follow him; the Roman and Italic are all I have hitherto attempted; if in these he has left room for improvement, it is probably more owing to that variety *which divided his attention, than to any other cause. I honor his merit, and only wish to derive some small share of Reputation,*

8/10 Amongst the several mechanic Arts that have engaged my attention, there is no one which I have pursued with so much steadiness and pleasure, as that of Letter-Founding. Having been an early admirer of the beauty of Letters, I became insensibly desirous of contributing to the perfection of them. I formed to myself Ideas of greater accuracy than had yet appeared, and have endeavoured to produce a Sett of Types according to what I conceived to be their true proportion.

Mr. Caslon is an Artist, to whom the Republic of Learning has great obligations; his ingenuity has left a fairer copy for my emulation, than any other master. In his great variety of Characters I intend not to follow him; the Roman and Italic are all I have hitherto attempted; if in these he has left room for improvement, it is probably more owing to that variety which divided his attention, than to any other cause. I honor his merit, and only wish to derive some small share of Reputation, from an Art which proves accidentally to have *been the object of our mutual pursuit.*

After having spent many years, and not a little of my fortune in my

9/13 Amongst the several mechanic Arts that have engaged my attention, there is no one which I have pursued with so much steadiness and pleasure, as that of Letter-Founding. Having been an early admirer of the beauty of Letters, I became insensibly desirous of contributing to the perfection of them. I formed to myself Ideas of greater accuracy than had yet appeared, and have endeavoured to produce a Sett of Types according to what I conceived to be their true proportion.

Mr. Caslon is an Artist, to whom the Republic of Learning has great obligations; his ingenuity has left a fairer copy for my emulation, than any other master. In his great variety of *Characters I intend not to follow him; the Roman and Italic are all I have hitherto attempted; if in these he has left room for*

8/12 Amongst the several mechanic Arts that have engaged my attention, there is no one which I have pursued with so much steadiness and pleasure, as that of Letter-Founding. Having been an early admirer of the beauty of Letters, I became insensibly desirous of contributing to the perfection of them. I formed to myself Ideas of greater accuracy than had yet appeared, and have endeavoured to produce a Sett of Types according to what I conceived to be their true proportion.

Mr. Caslon is an Artist, to whom the Republic of Learning has great obligations; his ingenuity has left a fairer copy for my emulation, than any other master. In his great variety of Characters I intend not to follow him; the Roman and Italic are all I have hitherto *attempted; if in these he has left room for improvement, it is probably more owing to that variety which divided his attention, than to any other*

FRY'S BASKERVILLE WITH ITC NEW BASKERVILLE** ITALIC   MERGENTHALER TYPE LIBRARY

ABCDEFGHIJKLMNOPQRSTUVWXYZ
ABCDEFGHIJKLMNOPQRSTUVWXYZ
&.,"-:;!?""1234567890$
&.,"-:;!?""1234567890$
abcdefghijklmnopqrstuvwxyz
abcdefghijklmnopqrstuvwxyz

ABCDEFGHIJKLMNOPQRSTUVWXYZ
ABCDEFGHIJKLMNOPQRSTUVWXYZ
&.,"-:;!?""1234567890$
&.,"-:;!?""1234567890$
abcdefghijklmnopqrstuvwxyz
abcdefghijklmnopqrstuvwxyz

ABCDEFGHIJKLMNOPQRSTUVWXYZ&a
bcdefghijklmnopqrstuvwxyz1234567890$"";!?

72 POINT ITC NEW BASKERVILLE** SEMI BOLD   MERGENTHALER TYPE LIBRARY

ABCDEFGHIJK
LMNOPQRSTU
VWXYZ&abcdef
ghijklmnopqrstuv
wxyz123456789
0$.,""",";:!?

72 POINT ITC NEW BASKERVILLE** SEMI BOLD ITALIC   MERGENTHALER TYPE LIBRARY

ABCDEFGHIJKLMNO
PQRSTUVWXYZ&ab
cdefghijklmnopqrstuvw
xyz1234567890$.,""":;!?

48 POINT ITC NEW BASKERVILLE** SEMI BOLD   MERGENTHALER TYPE LIBRARY

*ABCDEFGHIJKLMNOP
QRSTUVWXYZ&abcdef
ghijklmnopqrstuvwxyz123
4567890$.,""":;!?*

48 POINT ITC NEW BASKERVILLE** SEMI BOLD ITALIC   MERGENTHALER TYPE LIBRARY

ABCDEFGHIJKLMNOPQRSTUVWXYZ&abcdefghijklmn
opqrstuvwxyz1234567890$.,""":;!?

18 POINT ITC NEW BASKERVILLE** SEMI BOLD   MERGENTHALER TYPE LIBRARY

*ABCDEFGHIJKLMNOPQRSTUVWXYZ&abcdefghijklmnopqrst
uvwxyz1234567890$.,""":;!?*

18 POINT ITC NEW BASKERVILLE** SEMI BOLD ITALIC   MERGENTHALER TYPE LIBRARY

14/14 Amongst the several mechanic Arts that have engaged my attention, there is no one which I have pursued with so much steadiness and pleasure, as that of Letter-Founding. Having been an early admirer of the beauty of Letters, I became insensibly desirous of contributing to the perfection of them. I formed to myself Ideas of greater accuracy than had yet appeared, and have endeavoured to produce a Sett of Types according to what I conceived to be their true

12/12 Amongst the several mechanic Arts that have engaged my attention, there is no one which I have pursued with so much steadiness and pleasure, as that of Letter-Founding. Having been an early admirer of the beauty of Letters, I became insensibly desirous of contributing to the perfection of them. I formed to myself Ideas of greater accuracy than had yet appeared, and have endeavoured to produce a Sett of Types according to what I conceived to be their true proportion.
  Mr. Caslon is an Artist, to whom the Republic of Learning has great obligations; his ingenuity has left a fairer copy for my emula-

14/16 Amongst the several mechanic Arts that have engaged my attention, there is no one which I have pursued with so much steadiness and pleasure, as that of Letter-Founding. Having been an early admirer of the beauty of Letters, I became insensibly desirous of contributing to the perfection of them. I formed to myself Ideas of greater accuracy than had yet appeared, and have endeavoured to

12/14 Amongst the several mechanic Arts that have engaged my attention, there is no one which I have pursued with so much steadiness and pleasure, as that of Letter-Founding. Having been an early admirer of the beauty of Letters, I became insensibly desirous of contributing to the perfection of them. I formed to myself Ideas of greater accuracy than had yet appeared, and have endeavoured to produce a Sett of Types according to what I conceived to be their true proportion.

14/18 Amongst the several mechanic Arts that have engaged my attention, there is no one which I have pursued with so much steadiness and pleasure, as that of Letter-Founding. Having been an early admirer of the beauty of Letters, I became insensibly desirous of contributing to the perfection of them. I formed to myself Ideas of

12/16 Amongst the several mechanic Arts that have engaged my attention, there is no one which I have pursued with so much steadiness and pleasure, as that of Letter-Founding. Having been an early admirer of the beauty of Letters, I became insensibly desirous of contributing to the perfection of them. I formed to myself Ideas of greater accuracy than had yet appeared, and have endeavoured to produce a Sett of Types

ITC NEW BASKERVILLE** SEMI BOLD   MERGENTHALER TYPE LIBRARY

ABCDEFGHIJKLMNOPQRSTUV
WXYZ&.,"-:;!?""1234567890$
*ABCDEFGHIJKLMNOPQRSTUV
WXYZ&.,"-:;!?""1234567890$*
abcdefghijklmnopqrstuvwxyz
abcdefghijklmnopqrstuvwxyz

ABCDEFGHIJKLMNOPQRSTUVWXYZ
ABCDEFGHIJKLMNOPQRSTUVWXYZ
&.,"-:;!?""1234567890$
&.,"-:;!?""1234567890$
abcdefghijklmnopqrstuvwxyz
abcdefghijklmnopqrstuvwxyz

BASKERVILLE FAMILY 69

10/10 Amongst the several mechanic Arts that have engaged my attention, there is no one which I have pursued with so much steadiness and pleasure, as that of Letter-Founding. Having been an early admirer of the beauty of Letters, I became insensibly desirous of contributing to the perfection of them. I formed to myself Ideas of greater accuracy than had yet appeared, and have endeavoured to produce a Sett of Types according to what I conceived to be their true proportion.

Mr. Caslon is an Artist, to whom the Republic of Learning has great obligations; his ingenuity has left a fairer copy for my emulation, than any other master. In his great variety of Characters I intend not to follow him; the Roman and Italic are all I *have hitherto attempted; if in these he has left room for improvement, it is probably more owing to that variety*

8/8 Amongst the several mechanic Arts that have engaged my attention, there is no one which I have pursued with so much steadiness and pleasure, as that of Letter-Founding. Having been an early admirer of the beauty of Letters, I became insensibly desirous of contributing to the perfection of them. I formed to myself Ideas of greater accuracy than had yet appeared, and have endeavoured to produce a Sett of Types according to what I conceived to be their true proportion.

Mr. Caslon is an Artist, to whom the Republic of Learning has great obligations; his ingenuity has left a fairer copy for my emulation, than any other master. In his great variety of Characters I intend not to follow him; the Roman and Italic are all I have hitherto attempted; if in these he has left room for improvement, it is probably more owing to that variety which divided his attention, than to any other cause. I honor his merit, and only wish to derive some small share of Reputation, from an Art which proves accidentally to have been the object of our mutual pursuit.

After having spent many years, and not a little of my fortune in my endeavours to advance this art; I must own it gives me great *Satisfaction, to find that my Edition of Virgil has been so widely accepted by the students of the printing trades. The many positive*

10/12 Amongst the several mechanic Arts that have engaged my attention, there is no one which I have pursued with so much steadiness and pleasure, as that of Letter-Founding. Having been an early admirer of the beauty of Letters, I became insensibly desirous of contributing to the perfection of them. I formed to myself Ideas of greater accuracy than had yet appeared, and have endeavoured to produce a Sett of Types according to what I conceived to be their true proportion.

Mr. Caslon is an Artist, to whom the Republic of Learning has great obligations; his ingenuity has left a fairer copy for my emulation, than any other *master. In his great variety of Characters I intend not to follow him; the Roman and Italic are all I have hitherto*

8/10 Amongst the several mechanic Arts that have engaged my attention, there is no one which I have pursued with so much steadiness and pleasure, as that of Letter-Founding. Having been an early admirer of the beauty of Letters, I became insensibly desirous of contributing to the perfection of them. I formed to myself Ideas of greater accuracy than had yet appeared, and have endeavoured to produce a Sett of Types according to what I conceived to be their true proportion.

Mr. Caslon is an Artist, to whom the Republic of Learning has great obligations; his ingenuity has left a fairer copy for my emulation, than any other master. In his great variety of Characters I intend not to follow him; the Roman and Italic are all I have hitherto attempted; if in these he has left room for improvement, it is probably more owing to that variety which divided his attention, than to any other cause. I honor his merit, and only wish to derive some small share of Reputation, from an Art *which proves accidentally to have been the object of our mutual pursuit.*

After having spent many years, and not a little of my fortune in my

10/14 Amongst the several mechanic Arts that have engaged my attention, there is no one which I have pursued with so much steadiness and pleasure, as that of Letter-Founding. Having been an early admirer of the beauty of Letters, I became insensibly desirous of contributing to the perfection of them. I formed to myself Ideas of greater accuracy than had yet appeared, and have endeavoured to produce a Sett of Types according to what I conceived to be their true proportion.

Mr. Caslon is an Artist, to whom the Republic of Learning has great obligations; his ingenuity has left a

8/12 Amongst the several mechanic Arts that have engaged my attention, there is no one which I have pursued with so much steadiness and pleasure, as that of Letter-Founding. Having been an early admirer of the beauty of Letters, I became insensibly desirous of contributing to the perfection of them. I formed to myself Ideas of greater accuracy than had yet appeared, and have endeavoured to produce a Sett of Types according to what I conceived to be their true proportion.

Mr. Caslon is an Artist, to whom the Republic of Learning has great obligations; his ingenuity has left a fairer copy for my emulation, than any other master. In his great variety of Characters I intend not to follow him; the Roman and Italic are all I *have hitherto attempted; if in these he has left room for improvement, it is probably more owing to that variety which divided his attention, than*

ITC NEW BASKERVILLE** SEMI BOLD   MERGENTHALER TYPE LIBRARY

ABCDEFGHIJKLMNOPQRSTUVWXYZ
ABCDEFGHIJKLMNOPQRSTUVWXYZ
&.,"-:;!?""1234567890$
&.,"-:;!?""1234567890$
abcdefghijklmnopqrstuvwxyz
abcdefghijklmnopqrstuvwxyz

ABCDEFGHIJKLMNOPQRSTUVWXYZ
ABCDEFGHIJKLMNOPQRSTUVWXYZ
&.,"-:;!?""1234567890$
&.,"-:;!?""1234567890$
abcdefghijklmnopqrstuvwxyz
abcdefghijklmnopqrstuvwxyz

ABCDEFGHIJ
KLMNOPQRS
TUVWXYZ&
abcdefghijklm
nopqrstuvwxyz
1234567890$.,"
:;!?

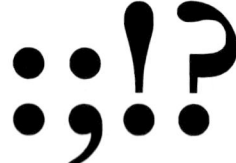

72 POINT ITC NEW BASKERVILLE** BOLD   MERGENTHALER TYPE LIBRARY

ABCDEFGHIJK LMNOPQRSTU VWXYZ&abcde fghijklmnopqrst uvwxyz1234567 890$.,""":;!?

72 POINT ITC NEW BASKERVILLE** BOLD ITALIC   MERGENTHALER TYPE LIBRARY

ABCDEFGHIJKLMNO PQRSTUVWXYZ&ab cdefghijklmnopqrstuv wxyz1234567890$.,""!?

48 POINT ITC NEW BASKERVILLE** BOLD   MERGENTHALER TYPE LIBRARY

BASKERVILLE FAMILY

ABCDEFGHIJKLMNOP
QRSTUVWXYZ&abcde
fghijklmnopqrstuvwxyz12
34567890$.,"":;!?

48 POINT ITC NEW BASKERVILLE** BOLD ITALIC   MERGENTHALER TYPE LIBRARY

ABCDEFGHIJKLMNOPQRSTUVWXYZ&abcdefghijklm
nopqrstuvwxyz1234567890$.,"":;!?

18 POINT ITC NEW BASKERVILLE** BOLD   MERGENTHALER TYPE LIBRARY

ABCDEFGHIJKLMNOPQRSTUVWXYZ&abcdefghijklmnopqr
stuvwxyz1234567890$.,"":;!?

18 POINT ITC NEW BASKERVILLE** BOLD ITALIC   MERGENTHALER TYPE LIBRARY

Detail of incipit page to St. Luke, from the FOUR GOSPELS, drawn in the monastery of St. Martin, in Tours, France during the mid-ninth century.

BASKERVILLE FAMILY 73

14/14 Amongst the several mechanic Arts that have engaged my attention, there is no one which I have pursued with so much steadiness and pleasure, as that of Letter-Founding. Having been an early admirer of the beauty of Letters, I became insensibly desirous of contributing to the perfection of them. I formed to myself Ideas of greater accuracy than had yet appeared, and have endeavoured to produce a Sett of Types according to what I conceived to be

12/12 Amongst the several mechanic Arts that have engaged my attention, there is no one which I have pursued with so much steadiness and pleasure, as that of Letter-Founding. Having been an early admirer of the beauty of Letters, I became insensibly desirous of contributing to the perfection of them. I formed to myself Ideas of greater accuracy than had yet appeared, and have endeavoured to produce a Sett of Types according to what I conceived to be their true proportion.
  Mr. Caslon is an Artist, to whom the Republic of Learning has great obligations; his ingenuity has left a fairer copy for my

14/16 Amongst the several mechanic Arts that have engaged my attention, there is no one which I have pursued with so much steadiness and pleasure, as that of Letter-Founding. Having been an early admirer of the beauty of Letters, I became insensibly desirous of contributing to the perfection of them. I formed to myself Ideas of greater accuracy than had yet appeared, and have en-

12/14 Amongst the several mechanic Arts that have engaged my attention, there is no one which I have pursued with so much steadiness and pleasure, as that of Letter-Founding. Having been an early admirer of the beauty of Letters, I became insensibly desirous of contributing to the perfection of them. I formed to myself Ideas of greater accuracy than had yet appeared, and have endeavoured to produce a Sett of Types according to what I conceived to be their true proportion.

14/18 Amongst the several mechanic Arts that have engaged my attention, there is no one which I have pursued with so much steadiness and pleasure, as that of Letter-Founding. Having been an early admirer of the beauty of Letters, I became insensibly desirous of contributing to the perfection of them. I formed to

12/16 Amongst the several mechanic Arts that have engaged my attention, there is no one which I have pursued with so much steadiness and pleasure, as that of Letter-Founding. Having been an early admirer of the beauty of Letters, I became insensibly desirous of contributing to the perfection of them. I formed to myself Ideas of greater accuracy than had yet appeared, and have endeavoured to produce a Sett of Types

ITC NEW BASKERVILLE** BOLD   MERGENTHALER TYPE LIBRARY

ABCDEFGHIJKLMNOPQRSTUV
ABCDEFGHIJKLMNOPQRSTUV
WXYZ&.,"'-:;!?""1234567890$
WXYZ&.,"'-:;!?""1234567890$
abcdefghijklmnopqrstuvwxyz
abcdefghijklmnopqrstuvwxyz

ABCDEFGHIJKLMNOPQRSTUVWX
ABCDEFGHIJKLMNOPQRSTUVWX
YZ&.,"'-:;!?""1234567890$
YZ&.,"'-:;!?""1234567890$
abcdefghijklmnopqrstuvwxyz
abcdefghijklmnopqrstuvwxyz

10/10 Amongst the several mechanic Arts that have engaged my attention, there is no one which I have pursued with so much steadiness and pleasure, as that of Letter-Founding. Having been an early admirer of the beauty of Letters, I became insensibly desirous of contributing to the perfection of them. I formed to myself Ideas of greater accuracy than had yet appeared, and have endeavoured to produce a Sett of Types according to what I conceived to be their true proportion.

   Mr. Caslon is an Artist, to whom the Republic of Learning has great obligations; his ingenuity has left a fairer copy for my emulation, than any other master. In his great variety of Characters I intend not to follow him; the Roman and Italic are all I *have hitherto attempted; if in these he has left room for improvement, it is probably more owing to that*

8/8 Amongst the several mechanic Arts that have engaged my attention, there is no one which I have pursued with so much steadiness and pleasure, as that of Letter-Founding. Having been an early admirer of the beauty of Letters, I became insensibly desirous of contributing to the perfection of them. I formed to myself Ideas of greater accuracy than had yet appeared, and have endeavoured to produce a Sett of Types according to what I conceived to be their true proportion.

   Mr. Caslon is an Artist, to whom the Republic of Learning has great obligations; his ingenuity has left a fairer copy for my emulation, than any other master. In his great variety of Characters I intend not to follow him; the Roman and Italic are all I have hitherto attempted; if in these he has left room for improvement, it is probably more owing to that variety which divided his attention, than to any other cause. I honor his merit, and only wish to derive some small share of Reputation, from an Art which proves accidentally to have been the object of our mutual pursuit.

   After having spent many years, and not a little of my fortune in my endeavours to advance this art; I must own it gives me *great Satisfaction, to find that my Edition of Virgil has been so widely accepted by the students of printing trades. The many*

10/12 Amongst the several mechanic Arts that have engaged my attention, there is no one which I have pursued with so much steadiness and pleasure, as that of Letter-Founding. Having been an early admirer of the beauty of Letters, I became insensibly desirous of contributing to the perfection of them. I formed to myself Ideas of greater accuracy than had yet appeared, and have endeavoured to produce a Sett of Types according to what I conceived to be their true proportion.

   Mr. Caslon is an Artist, to whom the Republic of Learning has great obligations; his ingenuity has left a fairer copy for my emulation, than any other *master. In his great variety of Characters I intend not to follow him; the Roman and Italic are all I*

8/10 Amongst the several mechanic Arts that have engaged my attention, there is no one which I have pursued with so much steadiness and pleasure, as that of Letter-Founding. Having been an early admirer of the beauty of Letters, I became insensibly desirous of contributing to the perfection of them. I formed to myself Ideas of greater accuracy than had yet appeared, and have endeavoured to produce a Sett of Types according to what I conceived to be their true proportion.

   Mr. Caslon is an Artist, to whom the Republic of Learning has great obligations; his ingenuity has left a fairer copy for my emulation, than any other master. In his great variety of Characters I intend not to follow him; the Roman and Italic are all I have hitherto attempted; if in these he has left room for improvement, it is probably more owing to that variety which divided his attention, than to any other cause. I honor his merit, and only wish to derive some small share of Reputation, from *an Art which proves accidentally to have been the object of our mutual pursuit.*

10/14 Amongst the several mechanic Arts that have engaged my attention, there is no one which I have pursued with so much steadiness and pleasure, as that of Letter-Founding. Having been an early admirer of the beauty of Letters, I became insensibly desirous of contributing to the perfection of them. I formed to myself Ideas of greater accuracy than had yet appeared, and have endeavoured to produce a Sett of Types according to what I conceived to be their true proportion.

   Mr. Caslon is an Artist, to whom the Republic of Learning has great obligations; his ingenuity has left

8/12 Amongst the several mechanic Arts that have engaged my attention, there is no one which I have pursued with so much steadiness and pleasure, as that of Letter-Founding. Having been an early admirer of the beauty of Letters, I became insensibly desirous of contributing to the perfection of them. I formed to myself Ideas of greater accuracy than had yet appeared, and have endeavoured to produce a Sett of Types according to what I conceived to be their true proportion.

   Mr. Caslon is an Artist, to whom the Republic of Learning has great obligations; his ingenuity has left a fairer copy for my emulation, than any other master. In his great variety of Characters I intend not to follow him; the Roman and Italic are all I *have hitherto attempted; if in these he has left room for improvement, it is probably more owing to that variety which divided his*

ITC NEW BASKERVILLE** BOLD   MERGENTHALER TYPE LIBRARY

ABCDEFGHIJKLMNOPQRSTUVWXYZ
ABCDEFGHIJKLMNOPQRSTUVWXYZ
&.,"'-:;!?""1234567890$
&.,"'-:;!?""1234567890$
abcdefghijklmnopqrstuvwxyz
abcdefghijklmnopqrstuvwxyz

ABCDEFGHIJKLMNOPQRSTUVWXYZ
ABCDEFGHIJKLMNOPQRSTUVWXYZ
&.,"'-:;!?""1234567890$
&.,"'-:;!?""1234567890$
abcdefghijklmnopqrstuvwxyz
abcdefghijklmnopqrstuvwxyz

ABCDEFGHIJ
KLMNOPQRS
TUVWXYZ&
abcdefghijklm
nopqrstuvwxy
z1234567890$
.,''"";:!?

72 POINT ITC NEW BASKERVILLE** BLACK   MERGENTHALER TYPE LIBRARY

ABCDEFGHIJKLMNOPQRSTUVWXYZ&abcdefghijklmnopqrstuvwxyz1234567890$.,"";:;!?

72 POINT ITC NEW BASKERVILLE** BLACK ITALIC   MERGENTHALER TYPE LIBRARY

ABCDEFGHIJKLMN
OPQRSTUVWXYZ&
abcdefghijklmnopqrs
tuvwxyz1234567890$
.,""";:!?

48 POINT ITC NEW BASKERVILLE** BLACK   MERGENTHALER TYPE LIBRARY

*ABCDEFGHIJKLMNOP
QRSTUVWXYZ&abcde
fghijklmnopqrstuvwxyz
1234567890$.,""";:!?*

48 POINT ITC NEW BASKERVILLE** BLACK ITALIC   MERGENTHALER TYPE LIBRARY

ABCDEFGHIJKLMNOPQRSTUVWXYZ&abcdefghijkl
mnopqrstuvwxyz1234567890$.,""";:!?

18 POINT ITC NEW BASKERVILLE** BLACK   MERGENTHALER TYPE LIBRARY

*ABCDEFGHIJKLMNOPQRSTUVWXYZ&abcdefghijklmnop
qrstuvwxyz1234567890$.,""";:!?*

18 POINT ITC NEW BASKERVILLE** BLACK ITALIC   MERGENTHALER TYPE LIBRARY

14/14 Amongst the several mechanic Arts that have engaged my attention, there is no one which I have pursued with so much steadiness and pleasure, as that of Letter-Founding. Having been an early admirer of the beauty of Letters, I became insensibly desirous of contributing to the perfection of them. I formed to myself Ideas of greater accuracy than had yet appeared, and have endeavoured to produce a Sett of Types according

14/16 Amongst the several mechanic Arts that have engaged my attention, there is no one which I have pursued with so much steadiness and pleasure, as that of Letter-Founding. Having been an early admirer of the beauty of Letters, I became insensibly desirous of contributing to the perfection of them. I formed to myself Ideas of greater accuracy than had yet ap-

14/18 Amongst the several mechanic Arts that have engaged my attention, there is no one which I have pursued with so much steadiness and pleasure, as that of Letter-Founding. Having been an early admirer of the beauty of Letters, I became insensibly desirous of contributing to the perfection of them.

12/12 Amongst the several mechanic Arts that have engaged my attention, there is no one which I have pursued with so much steadiness and pleasure, as that of Letter-Founding. Having been an early admirer of the beauty of Letters, I became insensibly desirous of contributing to the perfection of them. I formed to myself Ideas of greater accuracy than had yet appeared, and have endeavoured to produce a Sett of Types according to what I conceived to be their true proportion.
Mr. Caslon is an Artist, to whom the Republic of Learning has great obliga-

12/14 Amongst the several mechanic Arts that have engaged my attention, there is no one which I have pursued with so much steadiness and pleasure, as that of Letter-Founding. Having been an early admirer of the beauty of Letters, I became insensibly desirous of contributing to the perfection of them. I formed to myself Ideas of greater accuracy than had yet appeared, and have endeavoured to produce a Sett of Types according to what I conceived to be their true

12/16 Amongst the several mechanic Arts that have engaged my attention, there is no one which I have pursued with so much steadiness and pleasure, as that of Letter-Founding. Having been an early admirer of the beauty of Letters, I became insensibly desirous of contributing to the perfection of them. I formed to myself Ideas of greater accuracy than had yet appeared, and have endeavoured to

---

ITC NEW BASKERVILLE** BLACK   MERGENTHALER TYPE LIBRARY

ABCDEFGHIJKLMNOPQRSTU
ABCDEFGHIJKLMNOPQRSTU
VWXYZ&.,"'-:;!?""''"1234567890$
VWXYZ&.,"'-:;!?""''"1234567890$
abcdefghijklmnopqrstuvwxyz
abcdefghijklmnopqrstuvwxyz

ABCDEFGHIJKLMNOPQRSTUVWX
ABCDEFGHIJKLMNOPQRSTUVWX
YZ&.,"'-:;!?""''"1234567890$
YZ&.,"'-:;!?""''"1234567890$
abcdefghijklmnopqrstuvwxyz
abcdefghijklmnopqrstuvwxyz

BASKERVILLE FAMILY 79

10/10 Amongst the several mechanic Arts that have engaged my attention, there is no one which I have pursued with so much steadiness and pleasure, as that of Letter-Founding. Having been an early admirer of the beauty of Letters, I became insensibly desirous of contributing to the perfection of them. I formed to myself Ideas of greater accuracy than had yet appeared, and have endeavoured to produce a Sett of Types according to what I conceived to be their true proportion.
　Mr. Caslon is an Artist, to whom the Republic of Learning has great obligations; his ingenuity has left a fairer copy for my emulation, than any other master. *In his great variety of Characters I intend not to follow him; the Roman and Italic are all I have hitherto attempted; if in*

8/8 Amongst the several mechanic Arts that have engaged my attention, there is no one which I have pursued with so much steadiness and pleasure, as that of Letter-Founding. Having been an early admirer of the beauty of Letters, I became insensibly desirous of contributing to the perfection of them. I formed to myself Ideas of greater accuracy than had yet appeared, and have endeavoured to produce a Sett of Types according to what I conceived to be their true proportion.
　Mr. Caslon is an Artist, to whom the Republic of Learning has great obligations; his ingenuity has left a fairer copy for my emulation, than any other master. In his great variety of Characters I intend not to follow him; the Roman and Italic are all I have hitherto attempted; if in these he has left room for improvement, it is probably more owing to that variety which divided his attention, than to any other cause. I honor his merit, and only wish to derive some small share of Reputation, from an Art which proves accidentally to have been the object of our mutual pursuit.
　After having spent many years, and not a little of my *fortune in my endeavours to advance this art; I must own it gives me great Satisfaction, to find that my Edition of Virgil*

10/12 Amongst the several mechanic Arts that have engaged my attention, there is no one which I have pursued with so much steadiness and pleasure, as that of Letter-Founding. Having been an early admirer of the beauty of Letters, I became insensibly desirous of contributing to the perfection of them. I formed to myself Ideas of greater accuracy than had yet appeared, and have endeavoured to produce a Sett of Types according to what I conceived to be their true proportion.
　Mr. Caslon is an Artist, to whom the Republic of Learning has great obligations; his ingenuity *has left a fairer copy for my emulation, than any other master. In his great variety of Characters I*

8/10 Amongst the several mechanic Arts that have engaged my attention, there is no one which I have pursued with so much steadiness and pleasure, as that of Letter-Founding. Having been an early admirer of the beauty of Letters, I became insensibly desirous of contributing to the perfection of them. I formed to myself Ideas of greater accuracy than had yet appeared, and have endeavoured to produce a Sett of Types according to what I conceived to be their true proportion.
　Mr. Caslon is an Artist, to whom the Republic of Learning has great obligations; his ingenuity has left a fairer copy for my emulation, than any other master. In his great variety of Characters I intend not to follow him; the Roman and Italic are all I have hitherto attempted; if in these he has left room for improvement, it is probably more owing to that variety which divided his attention, than to any other cause. I *honor his merit, and only wish to derive some small share of Reputation, from an Art which proves accidentally to have*

10/14 Amongst the several mechanic Arts that have engaged my attention, there is no one which I have pursued with so much steadiness and pleasure, as that of Letter-Founding. Having been an early admirer of the beauty of Letters, I became insensibly desirous of contributing to the perfection of them. I formed to myself Ideas of greater accuracy than had yet appeared, and have endeavoured to produce a Sett of Types according to what I conceived to be their true *proportion.*
　Mr. Caslon is an Artist, *to whom the Republic of*

8/12 Amongst the several mechanic Arts that have engaged my attention, there is no one which I have pursued with so much steadiness and pleasure, as that of Letter-Founding. Having been an early admirer of the beauty of Letters, I became insensibly desirous of contributing to the perfection of them. I formed to myself Ideas of greater accuracy than had yet appeared, and have endeavoured to produce a Sett of Types according to what I conceived to be their true proportion.
　Mr. Caslon is an Artist, to whom the Republic of Learning has great obligations; his ingenuity has left a fairer copy for my emulation, than any other master. In his great variety of *Characters I intend not to follow him; the Roman and Italic are all I have hitherto attempted; if in these he has left room*

ITC NEW BASKERVILLE** BLACK　　MERGENTHALER TYPE LIBRARY

ABCDEFGHIJKLMNOPQRSTUVWXYZ
ABCDEFGHIJKLMNOPQRSTUVWXYZ
&.,"‑:;!?""1234567890$
&.,"‑:;!?""1234567890$
abcdefghijklmnopqrstuvwxyz
abcdefghijklmnopqrstuvwxyz

ABCDEFGHIJKLMNOPQRSTUVWXYZ
ABCDEFGHIJKLMNOPQRSTUVWXYZ
&.,"‑:;!?""1234567890$
&.,"‑:;!?""1234567890$
abcdefghijklmnopqrstuvwxyz
abcdefghijklmnopqrstuvwxyz

bro

This enduring version of Bodoni, with its sharply contrasting thick and thin strokes, was produced in 1926 by the Bauer Type Foundry. It is known for its remarkable fidelity to the original versions of Bodoni's types, cut c.1790.

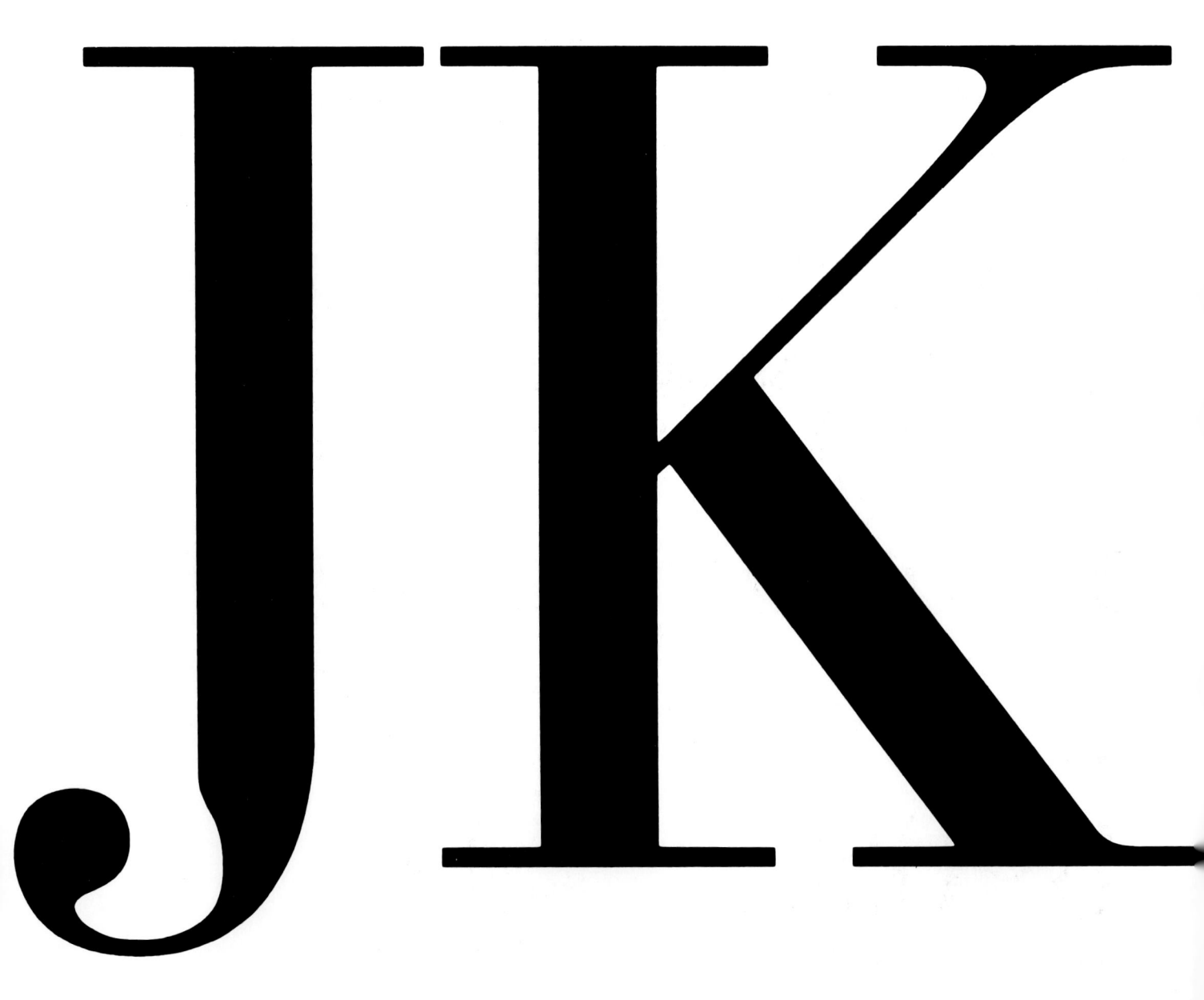

JK

z94

ABCDEFGHIJK
LMNOPQRSTU
VWXYZ&abcde
fghijklmnopqrst
uvwxyz1234567
890$.,"".;:!?

72 POINT BAUER BODONI** MERGENTHALER TYPE LIBRARY

ABCDEFGHIJKL MNOPQRSTUVW XYZ&abcdefghijk lmnopqrstuvwxyz 1234567890$.":!?

72 POINT BAUER BODONI** ITALIC   MERGENTHALER TYPE LIBRARY

ABCDEFGHIJKLMN OPQRSTUVWXYZ& abcdefghijklmnopqrst uvwxyz1234567890$. ",, 66 .,.! ?
,   .;,!

60 POINT BAUER BODONI**   MERGENTHALER TYPE LIBRARY

ABCDEFGHIJKLMN
OPQRSTUVWXYZ&
abcdefghijklmnopqrstu
vwxyz1234567890$;!?

60 POINT BAUER BODONI** ITALIC   MERGENTHALER TYPE LIBRARY

ABCDEFGHIJKLMNOPQ
RSTUVWXYZ&abcdefghij
klmnopqrstuvwxyz1234567
890$.,""":;!?

48 POINT BAUER BODONI**   MERGENTHALER TYPE LIBRARY

ABCDEFGHIJKLMNOPQR
STUVWXYZ&abcdefghijklm
nopqrstuvwxyz1234567890
$.,""":;!?

48 POINT BAUER BODONI** ITALIC   MERGENTHALER TYPE LIBRARY

ABCDEFGHIJKLMNOPQRSTUV
WXYZ&abcdefghijklmnopqrstuvwx
yz1234567890$.,""":;!?

36 POINT BAUER BODONI** MERGENTHALER TYPE LIBRARY

*ABCDEFGHIJKLMNOPQRSTUVW
XYZ&abcdefghijklmnopqrstuvwxyz1
234567890$.,""":;!?*

36 POINT BAUER BODONI** ITALIC MERGENTHALER TYPE LIBRARY

ABCDEFGHIJKLMNOPQRSTUVWXYZ&abcdefgh
ijklmnopqrstuvwxyz1234567890$.,""":;!?

24 POINT BAUER BODONI** MERGENTHALER TYPE LIBRARY

*ABCDEFGHIJKLMNOPQRSTUVWXYZ&abcdefghij
klmnopqrstuvwxyz1234567890$.,""":;!?*

24 POINT BAUER BODONI** ITALIC MERGENTHALER TYPE LIBRARY

ABCDEFGHIJKLMNOPQRSTUVWXYZ&abcdefghijklmnopqrstuvw
xyz1234567890$.,""":;!?

18 POINT BAUER BODONI** MERGENTHALER TYPE LIBRARY

*ABCDEFGHIJKLMNOPQRSTUVWXYZ&abcdefghijklmnopqrstuvwxy
z1234567890$.,""":;!?*

18 POINT BAUER BODONI** ITALIC MERGENTHALER TYPE LIBRARY

14/14 From a translation of a letter to Mr. Francis Rosaspina, in Bologna, by Bodoni dated Sept. 12, 1813:

You received with great courtesy the Rector of this our Imperial Lyceum in Parma; I am happy to think that you will extend the same courtesies to the Censor of said institute. Beside being my friend, and a very worthy ecclesiastic, he is the brother of a great friend of mine, who has a great name in the republic of letters, and among the *sacred orators living. Do please be liberal of your favors to him during the brief stay*

14/16 From a translation of a letter to Mr. Francis Rosaspina, in Bologna, by Bodoni dated Sept. 12, 1813:

You received with great courtesy the Rector of this our Imperial Lyceum in Parma; I am happy to think that you will extend the same courtesies to the Censor of said institute. Beside being my friend, and a very worthy ecclesiastic, he is the brother of a *great friend of mine, who has a great name in the republic of letters, and among the*

14/18 From a translation of a letter to Mr. Francis Rosaspina, in Bologna, by Bodoni dated Sept. 12, 1813:

You received with great courtesy the Rector of this our Imperial Lyceum in Parma; I am happy to think that you will extend the same courtesies to the Censor of said institute. *Beside being my friend, and a very worthy ecclesiastic, he is the brother of a*

12/12 From a translation of a letter to Mr. Francis Rosaspina, in Bologna, by Bodoni dated Sept. 12, 1813:

You received with great courtesy the Rector of this our Imperial Lyceum in Parma; I am happy to think that you will extend the same courtesies to the Censor of said institute. Beside being my friend, and a very worthy ecclesiastic, he is the brother of a great friend of mine, who has a great name in the republic of letters, and among the sacred orators living. Do please be liberal of your favors to him during the brief stay which he is planning to make in this your City, which is counted among the most *cultured in Europe. And now that I have sung the praises of my Recommended, I will mention his*

12/14 From a translation of a letter to Mr. Francis Rosaspina, in Bologna, by Bodoni dated Sept. 12, 1813:

You received with great courtesy the Rector of this our Imperial Lyceum in Parma; I am happy to think that you will extend the same courtesies to the Censor of said institute. Beside being my friend, and a very worthy ecclesiastic, he is the brother of a great friend of mine, who has a great name in the republic of letters, and among the sacred orators *living. Do please be liberal of your favors to him during the brief stay which he is planning to make*

12/16 From a translation of a letter to Mr. Francis Rosaspina, in Bologna, by Bodoni dated Sept. 12, 1813:

You received with great courtesy the Rector of this our Imperial Lyceum in Parma; I am happy to think that you will extend the same courtesies to the Censor of said institute. Beside being my friend, and a very worthy ecclesiastic, he is the brother of a *great friend of mine, who has a great name in the republic of letters, and among the sacred orators*

BAUER BODONI**   MERGENTHALER TYPE LIBRARY

ABCDEFGHIJKLMNOPQRSTUVWXYZ
ABCDEFGHIJKLMNOPQRSTUVWXYZ
&.,''`-:;!?""''1234567890$
&.,''`-:;!?""''1234567890$
abcdefghijklmnopqrstuvwxyz
abcdefghijklmnopqrstuvwxyz

ABCDEFGHIJKLMNOPQRSTUVWXYZ
ABCDEFGHIJKLMNOPQRSTUVWXYZ
&.,''`-:;!?""''1234567890$
&.,''`-:;!?""''1234567890$
abcdefghijklmnopqrstuvwxyz
abcdefghijklmnopqrstuvwxyz

11/11 From a translation of a letter to Mr. Francis Rosaspina, in Bologna, by Bodoni dated Sept. 12, 1813:

You received with great courtesy the Rector of this our Imperial Lyceum in Parma; I am happy to think that you will extend the same courtesies to the Censor of said institute. Beside being my friend, and a very worthy ecclesiastic, he is the brother of a great friend of mine, who has a great name in the republic of letters, and among the sacred orators living. Do please be liberal of your favors to him during the brief stay which he is planning to make in this your City, which is counted among the most cultured in Europe. And now that I have sung the praises of my Recommended, I will mention his name. He is Mr. Abbé Guglielmo Leoni, *very well known in Piedmont, and who holds a distinguished position among the literary men of Bormida*

10/10 From a translation of a letter to Mr. Francis Rosaspina, in Bologna, by Bodoni dated Sept. 12, 1813:

You received with great courtesy the Rector of this our Imperial Lyceum in Parma; I am happy to think that you will extend the same courtesies to the Censor of said institute. Beside being my friend, and a very worthy ecclesiastic, he is the brother of a great friend of mine, who has a great name in the republic of letters, and among the sacred orators living. Do please be liberal of your favors to him during the brief stay which he is planning to make in this your City, which is counted among the most cultured in Europe. And now that I have sung the praises of my Recommended, I will mention his name. He is Mr. Abbé Guglielmo Leoni, very well known in Piedmont, and who holds a distinguished position among the literary men of Bormida and Tanaro. He will give you detailed *news of me, and of my joyful wife, and of our friends; and will add that, as you have already received the most part of my*

11/13 From a translation of a letter to Mr. Francis Rosaspina, in Bologna, by Bodoni dated Sept. 12, 1813:

You received with great courtesy the Rector of this our Imperial Lyceum in Parma; I am happy to think that you will extend the same courtesies to the Censor of said institute. Beside being my friend, and a very worthy ecclesiastic, he is the brother of a great friend of mine, who has a great name in the republic of letters, and among the sacred orators living. Do please be liberal of your favors to him during the brief stay which he is planning to make in this your City, which is counted among the most cultured in Europe. And now that I *have sung the praises of my Recommended, I will mention his name. He is Mr. Abbé Guglielmo Leoni, very*

10/12 From a translation of a letter to Mr. Francis Rosaspina, in Bologna, by Bodoni dated Sept. 12, 1813:

You received with great courtesy the Rector of this our Imperial Lyceum in Parma; I am happy to think that you will extend the same courtesies to the Censor of said institute. Beside being my friend, and a very worthy ecclesiastic, he is the brother of a great friend of mine, who has a great name in the republic of letters, and among the sacred orators living. Do please be liberal of your favors to him during the brief stay which he is planning to make in this your City, which is counted among the most cultured in Europe. And now that I have sung the praises of my Recommended, I will mention his name. He is Mr. Abbé Guglielmo Leoni, very well known in *Piedmont, and who holds a distinguished position among the literary men of Bormida and Tanaro. He will give you*

11/15 From a translation of a letter to Mr. Francis Rosaspina, in Bologna, by Bodoni dated Sept. 12, 1813:

You received with great courtesy the Rector of this our Imperial Lyceum in Parma; I am happy to think that you will extend the same courtesies to the Censor of said institute. Beside being my friend, and a very worthy ecclesiastic, he is the brother of a great friend of mine, who has a great name in the republic of letters, and among the sacred orators living. Do please be liberal of *your favors to him during the brief stay which he is planning to make in this your City, which is counted*

10/14 From a translation of a letter to Mr. Francis Rosaspina, in Bologna, by Bodoni dated Sept. 12, 1813:

You received with great courtesy the Rector of this our Imperial Lyceum in Parma; I am happy to think that you will extend the same courtesies to the Censor of said institute. Beside being my friend, and a very worthy ecclesiastic, he is the brother of a great friend of mine, who has a great name in the republic of letters, and among the sacred orators living. Do please be liberal of your favors to him during the brief stay which he is planning to make in this your City, which is *counted among the most cultured in Europe. And now that I have sung the praises of my Recommended, I will mention his*

BAUER BODONI**   MERGENTHALER TYPE LIBRARY

ABCDEFGHIJKLMNOPQRSTUVWXYZ
ABCDEFGHIJKLMNOPQRSTUVWXYZ
&.,"'-:;!?""''1234567890$
&.,"'-:;!?""''1234567890$
abcdefghijklmnopqrstuvwxyz
abcdefghijklmnopqrstuvwxyz

ABCDEFGHIJKLMNOPQRSTUVWXYZ
ABCDEFGHIJKLMNOPQRSTUVWXYZ
&.,"'-:;!?""''1234567890$
&.,"'-:;!?""''1234567890$
abcdefghijklmnopqrstuvwxyz
abcdefghijklmnopqrstuvwxyz

9/9 From a translation of a letter to Mr. Francis Rosaspina, in Bologna, by Bodoni dated Sept. 12, 1813:

You received with great courtesy the Rector of this our Imperial Lyceum in Parma; I am happy to think that you will extend the same courtesies to the Censor of said institute. Beside being my friend, and a very worthy ecclesiastic, he is the brother of a great friend of mine, who has a great name in the republic of letters, and among the sacred orators living. Do please be liberal of your favors to him during the brief stay which he is planning to make in this your City, which is counted among the most cultured in Europe. And now that I have sung the praises of my Recommended, I will mention his name. He is Mr. Abbé Guglielmo Leoni, very well known in Piedmont, and who holds a distinguished position among the literary men of Bormida and Tanaro. He will give you detailed news of me, and of my joyful wife, and of our friends; and will add that, as you have already received the most part of my Collection, so you will have the remainder. I shall be most happy to hear how you are getting on, and will rejoice to learn that you are enjoying, along with florid health, *a perfect contentment of the soul. Do not be surprised in finding that a friend's hand has written these lines of recommendation, as for some*

8/8 From a translation of a letter to Mr. Francis Rosaspina, in Bologna, by Bodoni dated Sept. 12, 1813:

You received with great courtesy the Rector of this our Imperial Lyceum in Parma; I am happy to think that you will extend the same courtesies to the Censor of said institute. Beside being my friend, and a very worthy ecclesiastic, he is the brother of a great friend of mine, who has a great name in the republic of letters, and among the sacred orators living. Do please be liberal of your favors to him during the brief stay which he is planning to make in this your City, which is counted among the most cultured in Europe. And now that I have sung the praises of my Recommended, I will mention his name. He is Mr. Abbé Guglielmo Leoni, very well known in Piedmont, and who holds a distinguished position among the literary men of Bormida and Tanaro. He will give you detailed news of me, and of my joyful wife, and of our friends; and will add that, as you have already received the most part of my Collection, so you will have the remainder. I shall be most happy to hear how you are getting on, and will rejoice to learn that you are enjoying, along with florid health, a perfect contentment of the soul. Do not be surprised in finding that a friend's hand has written these lines of recommendation, as for some time past I have had recourse to this help, for the reason that I am most busy; nor do I care to encroach upon the time which I need to bring to an end those *typographical enterprises which I conceived, and indeed are now well on their way. Keep your friendship for me.*

9/11 From a translation of a letter to Mr. Francis Rosaspina, in Bologna, by Bodoni dated Sept. 12, 1813:

You received with great courtesy the Rector of this our Imperial Lyceum in Parma; I am happy to think that you will extend the same courtesies to the Censor of said institute. Beside being my friend, and a very worthy ecclesiastic, he is the brother of a great friend of mine, who has a great name in the republic of letters, and among the sacred orators living. Do please be liberal of your favors to him during the brief stay which he is planning to make in this your City, which is counted among the most cultured in Europe. And now that I have sung the praises of my Recommended, I will mention his name. He is Mr. Abbé Guglielmo Leoni, very well known in Piedmont, and who holds a distinguished position among the literary men of Bormida and Tanaro. He will give you detailed news of me, and of my joyful *wife, and of our friends; and will add that, as you have already received the most part of my Collection, so you will have the re-*

8/10 From a translation of a letter to Mr. Francis Rosaspina, in Bologna, by Bodoni dated Sept. 12, 1813:

You received with great courtesy the Rector of this our Imperial Lyceum in Parma; I am happy to think that you will extend the same courtesies to the Censor of said institute. Beside being my friend, and a very worthy ecclesiastic, he is the brother of a great friend of mine, who has a great name in the republic of letters, and among the sacred orators living. Do please be liberal of your favors to him during the brief stay which he is planning to make in this your City, which is counted among the most cultured in Europe. And now that I have sung the praises of my Recommended, I will mention his name. He is Mr. Abbé Guglielmo Leoni, very well known in Piedmont, and who holds a distinguished position among the literary men of Bormida and Tanaro. He will give you detailed news of me, and of my joyful wife, and of our friends; and will add that, as you have already received the most part of my Collection, so you will have the remainder. I shall be most happy to hear how you are getting on, and will rejoice to learn that you are enjoying, along with florid *health, a perfect contentment of the soul. Do not be surprised in finding that a friend's hand has written these lines of recommendation, as for some time past*

9/13 From a translation of a letter to Mr. Francis Rosaspina, in Bologna, by Bodoni dated Sept. 12, 1813:

You received with great courtesy the Rector of this our Imperial Lyceum in Parma; I am happy to think that you will extend the same courtesies to the Censor of said institute. Beside being my friend, and a very worthy ecclesiastic, he is the brother of a great friend of mine, who has a great name in the republic of letters, and among the sacred orators living. Do please be liberal of your favors to him during the brief stay which he is planning to make in this your City, which is counted among the most cultured in Europe. And now that I have sung the praises of my Recommended, I will mention his name. He is *Mr. Abbé Guglielmo Leoni, very well known in Piedmont, and who holds a distinguished position among the literary men of Bormida*

8/12 From a translation of a letter to Mr. Francis Rosaspina, in Bologna, by Bodoni dated Sept. 12, 1813:

You received with great courtesy the Rector of this our Imperial Lyceum in Parma; I am happy to think that you will extend the same courtesies to the Censor of said institute. Beside being my friend, and a very worthy ecclesiastic, he is the brother of a great friend of mine, who has a great name in the republic of letters, and among the sacred orators living. Do please be liberal of your favors to him during the brief stay which he is planning to make in this your City, which is counted among the most cultured in Europe. And now that I have sung the praises of my Recommended, I will mention his name. He is Mr. Abbé Guglielmo Leoni, very well known in Piedmont, and who holds a distinguished position among the literary men of Bormida and Tanaro. He *will give you detailed news of me, and of my joyful wife, and of our friends; and will add that, as you have already received the most part of my*

BAUER BODONI   MERGENTHALER TYPE LIBRARY

ABCDEFGHIJKLMNOPQRSTUVWXYZ
ABCDEFGHIJKLMNOPQRSTUVWXYZ
&.,"'-:;!?""''1234567890$
&.,"'-:;!?""''1234567890$
abcdefghijklmnopqrstuvwxyz
abcdefghijklmnopqrstuvwxyz

ABCDEFGHIJKLMNOPQRSTUVWXYZ
ABCDEFGBRJKLMNOPQRSTUVWXYZ
&.,"'-:;!?""''1234567890$
&.,"'-:;!?""''1234567890$
abcdefghijklmnopqrstuvwxyz
abcdefghijklmnopqrstuvwxyz

ABCDEFGHIJK
LMNOPQRSTU
VWXYZ&abcde
fghijklmnopqrst
uvwxyz1234567
890$.,""":;!?

72 POINT BAUER BODONI** BOLD   MERGENTHALER TYPE LIBRARY

*ABCDEFGHIJK
LMNOPQRSTU
VWXYZ&abcdefg
hijklmnopqrstuvw
xyz1234567890$.
,""".,;:!?*

72 POINT BAUER BODONI** BOLD ITALIC   MERGENTHALER TYPE LIBRARY

ABCDEFGHIJKLMNOPQ
RSTUVWXYZ&abcdefg
hijklmnopqrstuvwxyz12
34567890$.,""":;!?
48 POINT BAUER BODONI** BOLD   MERGENTHALER TYPE LIBRARY

ABCDEFGHIJKLMNOPQ
RSTUVWXYZ&abcdefghij
klmnopqrstuvwxyz123456
7890$.,""":;!?
48 POINT BAUER BODONI** BOLD ITALIC   MERGENTHALER TYPE LIBRARY

ABCDEFGHIJKLMNOPQRSTUVWXYZ&abcdefghijklmnopqrst
uvwxyz1234567890$.,""":;!?
18 POINT BAUER BODONI** BOLD   MERGENTHALER TYPE LIBRARY

ABCDEFGHIJKLMNOPQRSTUVWXYZ&abcdefghijklmnopqrstuv
wxyz1234567890$.,""":;!?
18 POINT BAUER BODONI** BOLD ITALIC   MERGENTHALER TYPE LIBRARY

14/14 From a translation of a letter to Mr. Francis Rosaspina, in Bologna, by Bodoni dated Sept. 12, 1813:

You received with great courtesy the Rector of this our Imperial Lyceum in Parma; I am happy to think that you will extend the same courtesies to the Censor of said institute. Beside being my friend, and a very worthy ecclesiastic, he is the brother of a great friend of mine, who has a great name in the *republic of letters, and among the sacred orators living. Do please be liberal of your*

12/12 From a translation of a letter to Mr. Francis Rosaspina, in Bologna, by Bodoni dated Sept. 12, 1813:

You received with great courtesy the Rector of this our Imperial Lyceum in Parma; I am happy to think that you will extend the same courtesies to the Censor of said institute. Beside being my friend, and a very worthy ecclesiastic, he is the brother of a great friend of mine, who has a great name in the republic of letters, and among the sacred orators living. Do please be liberal of your favors to him during the brief stay which he is planning to *make in this your City; which is counted among the most cultured in Europe. And now that I have*

14/16 From a translation of a letter to Mr. Francis Rosaspina, in Bologna, by Bodoni dated Sept. 12, 1813:

You received with great courtesy the Rector of this our Imperial Lyceum in Parma; I am happy to think that you will extend the same courtesies to the Censor of said institute. Beside being my friend, and a very worthy ecclesiastic, *he is the brother of a great friend of mine, who has a great name in the re-*

12/14 From a translation of a letter to Mr. Francis Rosaspina, in Bologna, by Bodoni dated Sept. 12, 1813:

You received with great courtesy the Rector of this our Imperial Lyceum in Parma; I am happy to think that you will extend the same courtesies to the Censor of said institute. Beside being my friend, and a very worthy ecclesiastic, he is the brother of a great friend of mine, who has a great name in the republic of *letters, and among the sacred orators living. Do please be liberal of your favors to him during the*

14/18 From a translation of a letter to Mr. Francis Rosaspina, in Bologna, by Bodoni dated Sept. 12, 1813:

You received with great courtesy the Rector of this our Imperial Lyceum in Parma; I am happy to think that you will extend the same courtesies to the *Censor of said institute. Beside being my friend, and a very worthy ecclesiastic, he*

12/16 From a translation of a letter to Mr. Francis Rosaspina, in Bologna, by Bodoni dated Sept. 12, 1813:

You received with great courtesy the Rector of this our Imperial Lyceum in Parma; I am happy to think that you will extend the same courtesies to the Censor of said institute. Beside being my friend, and a very worthy ecclesiastic, *he is the brother of a great friend of mine, who has a great name in the republic of letters,*

BAUER BODONI** BOLD   MERGENTHALER TYPE LIBRARY

ABCDEFGHIJKLMNOPQRSTUVWX
ABCDEFGHIJKLMNOPQRSTUVWX
YZ&.,'"-:;!?""1234567890$
YZ&.,'"-:;!?""1234567890$
abcdefghijklmnopqrstuvwxyz
abcdefghijklmnopqrstuvwxyz

ABCDEFGHIJKLMNOPQRSTUVWXYZ
ABCDEFGHIJKLMNOPQRSTUVWXYZ
&.,'"-:;!?""1234567890$
&.,'"-:;!?""1234567890$
abcdefghijklmnopqrstuvwxyz
abcdefghijklmnopqrstuvwxyz

10/10 From a translation of a letter to Mr. Francis Rosaspina, in Bologna, by Bodoni dated Sept. 12, 1813:
You received with great courtesy the Rector of this our Imperial Lyceum in Parma; I am happy to think that you will extend the same courtesies to the Censor of said institute. Beside being my friend, and a very worthy ecclesiastic, he is the brother of a great friend of mine, who has a great name in the republic of letters, and among the sacred orators living. Do please be liberal of your favors to him during the brief stay which he is planning to make in this your City, which is counted among the most cultured in Europe. And now that I have sung the praises of my Recommended, I will mention his name. He is Mr. Abbé Guglielmo Leoni, very well known in Piedmont, and who holds a distinguished position among the literary men of Bormida and Tanaro. *He will give you detailed news of me, and of my*

8/8 From a translation of a letter to Mr. Francis Rosaspina, in Bologna, by Bodoni dated Sept. 12, 1813:
You received with great courtesy the Rector of this our Imperial Lyceum in Parma; I am happy to think that you will extend the same courtesies to the Censor of said institute. Beside being my friend, and a very worthy ecclesiastic, he is the brother of a great friend of mine, who has a great name in the republic of letters, and among the sacred orators living. Do please be liberal of your favors to him during the brief stay which he is planning to make in this your City, which is counted among the most cultured in Europe. And now that I have sung the praises of my Recommended, I will mention his name. He is Mr. Abbé Guglielmo Leoni, very well known in Piedmont, and who holds a distinguished position among the literary men of Bormida and Tanaro. He will give you detailed news of me, and of my joyful wife, and of our friends; and will add that, as you have already received the most part of my Collection, so you will have the remainder. I shall be most happy to hear how you are getting on, and will rejoice to learn that you are enjoying, along with florid health, a perfect contentment of the soul. Do not be surprised in finding that a friend's hand has written these lines of recommendation, as for some time past I have *had recourse to this help, for the reason that I am most busy; nor do I care to encroach upon the time which I need to bring to an end those*

10/12 From a translation of a letter to Mr. Francis Rosaspina, in Bologna, by Bodoni dated Sept. 12, 1813:
You received with great courtesy the Rector of this our Imperial Lyceum in Parma; I am happy to think that you will extend the same courtesies to the Censor of said institute. Beside being my friend, and a very worthy ecclesiastic, he is the brother of a great friend of mine, who has a great name in the republic of letters, and among the sacred orators living. Do please be liberal of your favors to him during the brief stay which he is planning to make in this your City, which is counted among the most cultured in Europe. And now that I have sung the praises of my Recommended, I will mention his name. *He is Mr. Abbé Guglielmo Leoni, very well known in Piedmont, and who holds a distinguished posi-*

8/10 From a translation of a letter to Mr. Francis Rosaspina, in Bologna, by Bodoni dated Sept. 12, 1813:
You received with great courtesy the Rector of this our Imperial Lyceum in Parma; I am happy to think that you will extend the same courtesies to the Censor of said institute. Beside being my friend, and a very worthy ecclesiastic, he is the brother of a great friend of mine, who has a great name in the republic of letters, and among the sacred orators living. Do please be liberal of your favors to him during the brief stay which he is planning to make in this your City, which is counted among the most cultured in Europe. And now that I have sung the praises of my Recommended, I will mention his name. He is Mr. Abbé Guglielmo Leoni, very well known in Piedmont, and who holds a distinguished position among the literary men of Bormida and Tanaro. He will give you detailed news of me, and of my joyful wife, and of our friends; and will add that, as you have already received the most part of my Collection, so you will have the remainder. I shall be *most happy to hear how you are getting on, and will rejoice to learn that you are enjoying, along with florid health, a perfect contentment of the*

10/14 From a translation of a letter to Mr. Francis Rosaspina, in Bologna, by Bodoni dated Sept. 12, 1813:
You received with great courtesy the Rector of this our Imperial Lyceum in Parma; I am happy to think that you will extend the same courtesies to the Censor of said institute. Beside being my friend, and a very worthy ecclesiastic, he is the brother of a great friend of mine, who has a great name in the republic of letters, and among the sacred orators living. Do please be liberal of your favors to him during the brief stay which he is *planning to make in this your City, which is counted among the most cultured in Europe. And now that I have sung the*

8/12 From a translation of a letter to Mr. Francis Rosaspina, in Bologna, by Bodoni dated Sept. 12, 1813:
You received with great courtesy the Rector of this our Imperial Lyceum in Parma; I am happy to think that you will extend the same courtesies to the Censor of said institute. Beside being my friend, and a very worthy ecclesiastic, he is the brother of a great friend of mine, who has a great name in the republic of letters, and among the sacred orators living. Do please be liberal of your favors to him during the brief stay which he is planning to make in this your City, which is counted among the most cultured in Europe. And now that I have sung the praises of my Recommended, I will mention his name. He is Mr. Abbé Guglielmo Leoni, very well known in Piedmont, and who holds *a distinguished position among the literary men of Bormida and Tanaro. He will give you detailed news of me, and of my joyful wife, and of our*

BAUER BODONI** BOLD   MERGENTHALER TYPE LIBRARY

ABCDEFGHIJKLMNOPQRSTUVWXYZ
ABCDEFGHIJKLMNOPQRSTUVWXYZ
&.,"‘-:;!?"" 1234567890$
&.,"‘-:;!?"" 1234567890$
abcdefghijklmnopqrstuvwxyz
abcdefghijklmnopqrstuvwxyz

ABCDEFGHIJKLMNOPQRSTUVWXYZ
ABCDEFGHIJKLMNOPQRSTUVWXYZ
&.,"‘-:;!?"" 1234567890$
&.,"‘-:;!?"" 1234567890$
abcdefghijklmnopqrstuvwxyz
abcdefghijklmnopqrstuvwxyz

ABCDEFGHIJ KLMNOPQRST UVWXYZ&abc defghijklmnop qrstuvwxyz12 34567890$.,"" :;!?

72 POINT BAUER BODONI** BLACK   MERGENTHALER TYPE LIBRARY

ABCDEFGHIJKLMNOPQRSTUVWXYZ&a
bcdefghijklmnopqrstuvwxyz
1234567890$.,'"".;:!?

72 POINT BAUER BODONI** BLACK ITALIC   MERGENTHALER TYPE LIBRARY

ABCDEFGHIJKLMNOPQRSTUVWXYZ&abcdefghijklmnopqrstuvwxyz1234567890$.,""':;!?

48 POINT BAUER BODONI** BLACK   MERGENTHALER TYPE LIBRARY

ABCDEFGHIJKLMNOPQRSTUVWXYZ&abcdefghijklmnopqrstuvwxyz1234567890$.,""':;!?

48 POINT BAUER BODONI** BLACK ITALIC   MERGENTHALER TYPE LIBRARY

ABCDEFGHIJKLMNOPQRSTUVWXYZ&abcdefghijklmnopqrstuvwxyz1234567890$.,""':;!?

18 POINT BAUER BODONI** BLACK   MERGENTHALER TYPE LIBRARY

ABCDEFGHIJKLMNOPQRSTUVWXYZ&abcdefghijklmnopqrstuvwxyz1234567890$.,""':;!?

18 POINT BAUER BODONI** BLACK ITALIC   MERGENTHALER TYPE LIBRARY

14/14 **From a translation of a letter to Mr. Francis Rosaspina, in Bologna, by Bodoni dated Sept. 12, 1813:**
You received with great courtesy the Rector of this our Imperial Lyceum in Parma; I am happy to think that you will extend the same courtesies to the Censor of said institute. Beside being my friend, and a very worthy ecclesiastic, he is the brother of a great friend of mine, who *has a great name in the republic of letters, and among the sacred or-*

14/16 **From a translation of a letter to Mr. Francis Rosaspina, in Bologna, by Bodoni dated Sept. 12, 1813:**
You received with great courtesy the Rector of this our Imperial Lyceum in Parma; I am happy to think that you will extend the same courtesies to the Censor of said institute. Beside being my friend, and a *very worthy ecclesiastic, he is the brother of a great friend of mine,*

14/18 **From a translation of a letter to Mr. Francis Rosaspina, in Bologna, by Bodoni dated Sept. 12, 1813:**
You received with great courtesy the Rector of this our Imperial Lyceum in Parma; I am happy to think that you will extend the same *courtesies to the Censor of said institute. Beside being my friend, and*

12/12 **From a translation of a letter to Mr. Francis Rosaspina, in Bologna, by Bodoni dated Sept. 12, 1813:**
You received with great courtesy the Rector of this our Imperial Lyceum in Parma; I am happy to think that you will extend the same courtesies to the Censor of said institute. Beside being my friend, and a very worthy ecclesiastic, he is the brother of a great friend of mine, who has a great name in the republic of letters, and among the sacred orators living. Do please be liberal of your favors to him during the brief stay *which he is planning to make in this your City, which is counted among the most*

12/14 **From a translation of a letter to Mr. Francis Rosaspina, in Bologna, by Bodoni dated Sept. 12, 1813:**
You received with great courtesy the Rector of this our Imperial Lyceum in Parma; I am happy to think that you will extend the same courtesies to the Censor of said institute. Beside being my friend, and a very worthy ecclesiastic, he is the brother of a great friend of mine, who has a great name *in the republic of letters, and among the sacred orators living. Do please be liberal*

12/16 **From a translation of a letter to Mr. Francis Rosaspina, in Bologna, by Bodoni dated Sept. 12, 1813:**
You received with great courtesy the Rector of this our Imperial Lyceum in Parma; I am happy to think that you will extend the same courtesies to the Censor of said institute. Beside being my friend, and a very *worthy ecclesiastic, he is the brother of a great friend of mine, who has a great*

BAUER BODONI** BLACK   MERGENTHALER TYPE LIBRARY

ABCDEFGHIJKLMNOPQRSTUVW
ABCDEFGHIJKLMNOPQRSTUVW
XYZ&.,"-:;!?"" 1234567890$
XYZ&.,"-:;!?"" 1234567890$
abcdefghijklmnopqrstuvwxyz
abcdefghijklmnopqrstuvwxyz

ABCDEFGHIJKLMNOPQRSTUVWXYZ
ABCDEFGHIJKLMNOPQRSTUVWXYZ
&.,"-:;!?"" 1234567890$
&.,"-:;!?"" 1234567890$
abcdefghijklmnopqrstuvwxyz
abcdefghijklmnopqrstuvwxyz

10/10 From a translation of a letter to Mr. Francis Rosaspina, in Bologna, by Bodoni dated Sept. 12, 1813:

You received with great courtesy the Rector of this our Imperial Lyceum in Parma; I am happy to think that you will extend the same courtesies to the Censor of said institute. Beside being my friend, and a very worthy ecclesiastic, he is the brother of a great friend of mine, who has a great name in the republic of letters, and among the sacred orators living. Do please be liberal of your favors to him during the brief stay which he is planning to make in this your City, which is counted among the most cultured in Europe. And now that I have sung the praises of my Recommended, I will mention his name. He is *Mr. Abbé Guglielmo Leoni, very well known in Piedmont, and who holds a distinguished posi-*

8/8 From a translation of a letter to Mr. Francis Rosaspina, in Bologna, by Bodoni dated Sept. 12, 1813:

You received with great courtesy the Rector of this our Imperial Lyceum in Parma; I am happy to think that you will extend the same courtesies to the Censor of said institute. Beside being my friend, and a very worthy ecclesiastic, he is the brother of a great friend of mine, who has a great name in the republic of letters, and among the sacred orators living. Do please be liberal of your favors to him during the brief stay which he is planning to make in this your City, which is counted among the most cultured in Europe. And now that I have sung the praises of my Recommended, I will mention his name. He is Mr. Abbé Guglielmo Leoni, very well known in Piedmont, and who holds a distinguished position among the literary men of Bormida and Tanaro. He will give you detailed news of me, and of my joyful wife, and of our friends; and will add that, as you have already received the most part of my Collection, so you will have the remainder. I shall be most happy to hear how you are getting on, and will rejoice to learn that you are enjoying, along with florid health, a perfect contentment of the soul. Do not be surprised in finding that a *friend's hand has written these lines of recommendation, as for some time past I have had recourse to this help, for the*

10/12 From a translation of a letter to Mr. Francis Rosaspina, in Bologna, by Bodoni dated Sept. 12, 1813:

You received with great courtesy the Rector of this our Imperial Lyceum in Parma; I am happy to think that you will extend the same courtesies to the Censor of said institute. Beside being my friend, and a very worthy ecclesiastic, he is the brother of a great friend of mine, who has a great name in the republic of letters, and among the sacred orators living. Do please be liberal of your favors to him during the brief stay which he is planning to make in this your City, which is counted among the most cultured in *Europe. And now that I have sung the praises of my Recommended, I will mention his name. He is*

8/10 From a translation of a letter to Mr. Francis Rosaspina, in Bologna, by Bodoni dated Sept. 12, 1813:

You received with great courtesy the Rector of this our Imperial Lyceum in Parma; I am happy to think that you will extend the same courtesies to the Censor of said institute. Beside being my friend, and a very worthy ecclesiastic, he is the brother of a great friend of mine, who has a great name in the republic of letters, and among the sacred orators living. Do please be liberal of your favors to him during the brief stay which he is planning to make in this your City, which is counted among the most cultured in Europe. And now that I have sung the praises of my Recommended, I will mention his name. He is Mr. Abbé Guglielmo Leoni, very well known in Piedmont, and who holds a distinguished position among the literary men of Bormida and Tanaro. He will give you detailed news of me, and of my joyful wife, and of our friends; and will add that, as you have already received the most *part of my Collection, so you will have the remainder. I shall be most happy to hear how you are getting on, and will rejoice*

10/14 From a translation of a letter to Mr. Francis Rosaspina, in Bologna, by Bodoni dated Sept. 12, 1813:

You received with great courtesy the Rector of this our Imperial Lyceum in Parma; I am happy to think that you will extend the same courtesies to the Censor of said institute. Beside being my friend, and a very worthy ecclesiastic, he is the brother of a great friend of mine, who has a great name in the republic of letters, and among the sacred orators living. Do *please be liberal of your favors to him during the brief stay which he is planning to make in this*

8/12 From a translation of a letter to Mr. Francis Rosaspina, in Bologna, by Bodoni dated Sept. 12, 1813:

You received with great courtesy the Rector of this our Imperial Lyceum in Parma; I am happy to think that you will extend the same courtesies to the Censor of said institute. Beside being my friend, and a very worthy ecclesiastic, he is the brother of a great friend of mine, who has a great name in the republic of letters, and among the sacred orators living. Do please be liberal of your favors to him during the brief stay which he is planning to make in this your City, which is counted among the most cultured in Europe. And now that I have sung the praises of my Recommended, I will mention his name. He is Mr. Abbé Guglielmo Leoni, *very well known in Piedmont, and who holds a distinguished position among the literary men of Bormida and Tanaro. He*

BAUER BODONI** BLACK   MERGENTHALER TYPE LIBRARY

ABCDEFGHIJKLMNOPQRSTUVWXYZ
ABCDEFGHIJKLMNOPQRSTUVWXYZ
&.,"-:;!?""1234567890$
&.,"-:;!?""1234567890$
abcdefghijklmnopqrstuvwxyz
abcdefghijklmnopqrstuvwxyz

ABCDEFGHIJKLMNOPQRSTUVWXYZ
ABCDEFGHIJKLMNOPQRSTUVWXYZ
&.,"-:;!?""1234567890$
&.,"-:;!?""1234567890$
abcdefghijklmnopqrstuvwxyz
abcdefghijklmnopqrstuvwxyz

ABCDEFGHIJKLM
NOPQRSTUVWXY
Z&abcdefghijklm
nopqrstuvwxyz12
34567890$.,""'':;!?

72 POINT BAUER BODONI** BOLD CONDENSED   MERGENTHALER TYPE LIBRARY

ABCDEFGHIJKLMNOPQRST
UVWXYZ&abcdefghijklmn
opqrstuvwxyz1234567890$
.,""'':;!?

48 POINT BAUER BODONI** BOLD CONDENSED   MERGENTHALER TYPE LIBRARY

ABCDEFGHIJKLMNOPQRSTUVWXYZ&abcdefghijklmnopqrstuvwxyz12
34567890$.,""'':;!?

18 POINT BAUER BODONI** BOLD CONDENSED   MERGENTHALER TYPE LIBRARY

14/14 **From a translation of a letter to Mr. Francis Rosaspina, in Bologna, by Bodoni dated Sept. 12, 1813:**
You received with great courtesy the Rector of this our Imperial Lyceum in Parma; I am happy to think that you will extend the same courtesies to the Censor of said institute. Beside being my friend, and a very worthy ecclesiastic, he is the brother of a great friend of mine, who has a great name in the republic of letters, and among the sacred orators living. Do please be liberal of your favors to him during the

14/16 **From a translation of a letter to Mr. Francis Rosaspina, in Bologna, by Bodoni dated Sept. 12, 1813:**
You received with great courtesy the Rector of this our Imperial Lyceum in Parma; I am happy to think that you will extend the same courtesies to the Censor of said institute. Beside being my friend, and a very worthy ecclesiastic, he is the brother of a great friend of mine, who has a great name in the republic of letters, and

14/18 **From a translation of a letter to Mr. Francis Rosaspina, in Bologna, by Bodoni dated Sept. 12, 1813:**
You received with great courtesy the Rector of this our Imperial Lyceum in Parma; I am happy to think that you will extend the same courtesies to the Censor of said institute. Beside being my friend, and a very worthy ecclesiastic, he is the

12/12 **From a translation of a letter to Mr. Francis Rosaspina, in Bologna, by Bodoni dated Sept. 12, 1813:**
You received with great courtesy the Rector of this our Imperial Lyceum in Parma; I am happy to think that you will extend the same courtesies to the Censor of said institute. Beside being my friend, and a very worthy ecclesiastic, he is the brother of a great friend of mine, who has a great name in the republic of letters, and among the sacred orators living. Do please be liberal of your favors to him during the brief stay which he is planning to make in this your City, which is counted among the most cultured in Europe. And now that I have sung the praises of my Recom-

12/14 **From a translation of a letter to Mr. Francis Rosaspina, in Bologna, by Bodoni dated Sept. 12, 1813:**
You received with great courtesy the Rector of this our Imperial Lyceum in Parma; I am happy to think that you will extend the same courtesies to the Censor of said institute. Beside being my friend, and a very worthy ecclesiastic, he is the brother of a great friend of mine, who has a great name in the republic of letters, and among the sacred orators living. Do please be liberal of your favors to him during the brief stay which he is

12/16 **From a translation of a letter to Mr. Francis Rosaspina, in Bologna, by Bodoni dated Sept. 12, 1813:**
You received with great courtesy the Rector of this our Imperial Lyceum in Parma; I am happy to think that you will extend the same courtesies to the Censor of said institute. Beside being my friend, and a very worthy ecclesiastic, he is the brother of a great friend of mine, who has a great name in the republic of letters, and among the

---

BAUER BODONI** BOLD CONDENSED   MERGENTHALER TYPE LIBRARY

ABCDEFGHIJKLMNOPQRSTUVWXYZ
&.,"-:;!?""1234567890$
abcdefghijklmnopqrstuvwxyz

ABCDEFGHIJKLMNOPQRSTUVWXYZ
&.,"-:;!?""1234567890$
abcdefghijklmnopqrstuvwxyz

10/10
From a translation of a letter to Mr. Francis Rosaspina, in Bologna, by Bodoni dated Sept. 12, 1813:

You received with great courtesy the Rector of this our Imperial Lyceum in Parma; I am happy to think that you will extend the same courtesies to the Censor of said institute. Beside being my friend, and a very worthy ecclesiastic, he is the brother of a great friend of mine, who has a great name in the republic of letters, and among the sacred orators living. Do please be liberal of your favors to him during the brief stay which he is planning to make in this your City, which is counted among the most cultured in Europe. And now that I have sung the praises of my Recommended, I will mention his name. He is Mr. Abbé Guglielmo Leoni, very well known in Piedmont, and who holds a distinguished position among the literary men of Bormida and Tanaro. He will give you detailed news of me, and of my joyful wife, and of

8/8
From a translation of a letter to Mr. Francis Rosaspina, in Bologna, by Bodoni dated Sept. 12, 1813:

You received with great courtesy the Rector of this our Imperial Lyceum in Parma; I am happy to think that you will extend the same courtesies to the Censor of said institute. Beside being my friend, and a very worthy ecclesiastic, he is the brother of a great friend of mine, who has a great name in the republic of letters, and among the sacred orators living. Do please be liberal of your favors to him during the brief stay which he is planning to make in this your City, which is counted among the most cultured in Europe. And now that I have sung the praises of my Recommended, I will mention his name. He is Mr. Abbé Guglielmo Leoni, very well known in Piedmont, and who holds a distinguished position among the literary men of Bormida and Tanaro. He will give you detailed news of me, and of my joyful wife, and of our friends; and will add that, as you have already received the most part of my Collection, so you will have the remainder. I shall be most happy to hear how you are getting on, and will rejoice to learn that you are enjoying, along with florid health, a perfect contentment of the soul. Do not be surprised in finding that a friend's hand has written these lines of recommendation, as for some time past I have had recourse to this help, for the reason that I am most busy; nor do I care to encroach upon the time which I need to bring to an end those typographical enterprises

10/12
From a translation of a letter to Mr. Francis Rosaspina, in Bologna, by Bodoni dated Sept. 12, 1813:

You received with great courtesy the Rector of this our Imperial Lyceum in Parma; I am happy to think that you will extend the same courtesies to the Censor of said institute. Beside being my friend, and a very worthy ecclesiastic, he is the brother of a great friend of mine, who has a great name in the republic of letters, and among the sacred orators living. Do please be liberal of your favors to him during the brief stay which he is planning to make in this your City, which is counted among the most cultured in Europe. And now that I have sung the praises of my Recommended, I will mention his name. He is Mr. Abbé Guglielmo Leoni, very well known in Piedmont, and who holds a distinguished position

8/10
From a translation of a letter to Mr. Francis Rosaspina, in Bologna, by Bodoni dated Sept. 12, 1813:

You received with great courtesy the Rector of this our Imperial Lyceum in Parma; I am happy to think that you will extend the same courtesies to the Censor of said institute. Beside being my friend, and a very worthy ecclesiastic, he is the brother of a great friend of mine, who has a great name in the republic of letters, and among the sacred orators living. Do please be liberal of your favors to him during the brief stay which he is planning to make in this your City, which is counted among the most cultured in Europe. And now that I have sung the praises of my Recommended, I will mention his name. He is Mr. Abbé Guglielmo Leoni, very well known in Piedmont, and who holds a distinguished position among the literary men of Bormida and Tanaro. He will give you detailed news of me, and of my joyful wife, and of our friends; and will add that, as you have already received the most part of my Collection, so you will have the remainder. I shall be most happy to hear how you are getting on, and will rejoice to learn that you are enjoying, along with florid health, a perfect contentment of the soul. Do

10/14
From a translation of a letter to Mr. Francis Rosaspina, in Bologna, by Bodoni dated Sept. 12, 1813:

You received with great courtesy the Rector of this our Imperial Lyceum in Parma; I am happy to think that you will extend the same courtesies to the Censor of said institute. Beside being my friend, and a very worthy ecclesiastic, he is the brother of a great friend of mine, who has a great name in the republic of letters, and among the sacred orators living. Do please be liberal of your favors to him during the brief stay which he is planning to make in this your City, which is counted among the most cultured in Europe. And now that I have

8/12
From a translation of a letter to Mr. Francis Rosaspina, in Bologna, by Bodoni dated Sept. 12, 1813:

You received with great courtesy the Rector of this our Imperial Lyceum in Parma; I am happy to think that you will extend the same courtesies to the Censor of said institute. Beside being my friend, and a very worthy ecclesiastic, he is the brother of a great friend of mine, who has a great name in the republic of letters, and among the sacred orators living. Do please be liberal of your favors to him during the brief stay which he is planning to make in this your City, which is counted among the most cultured in Europe. And now that I have sung the praises of my Recommended, I will mention his name. He is Mr. Abbé Guglielmo Leoni, very well known in Piedmont, and who holds a distinguished position among the literary men of Bormida and Tanaro. He will give you detailed news of me, and of my joyful wife, and of our

---

BAUER BODONI** BOLD CONDENSED   MERGENTHALER TYPE LIBRARY

ABCDEFGHIJKLMNOPQRSTUVWXYZ
&.,"-:;!?""1234567890$
abcdefghijklmnopqrstuvwxyz

ABCDEFGHIJKLMNOPQRSTUVWXYZ
&.,"-:;!?""1234567890$
abcdefghijklmnopqrstuvwxyz

ABCDEFGHIJKLM
NOPQRSTUVWXY
Z&abcdefghijklm
nopqrstuvwxyz
1234567890$:;!?

72 POINT BAUER BODONI** BLACK CONDENSED   MERGENTHALER TYPE LIBRARY

ABCDEFGHIJKLMNOPQRS
TUVWXYZ&abcdefghijkl
mnopqrstuvwxyz123456
7890$.,""":;!?

48 POINT BAUER BODONI** BLACK CONDENSED   MERGENTHALER TYPE LIBRARY

ABCDEFGHIJKLMNOPQRSTUVWXYZ&abcdefghijklmnopqrstuvwxyz
1234567890$.,""":;!?

18 POINT BAUER BODONI** BLACK CONDENSED   MERGENTHALER TYPE LIBRARY

14/14 From a translation of a letter to Mr. Francis Rosaspina, in Bologna, by Bodoni dated Sept. 12, 1813:

You received with great courtesy the Rector of this our Imperial Lyceum in Parma; I am happy to think that you will extend the same courtesies to the Censor of said institute. Beside being my friend, and a very worthy ecclesiastic, he is the brother of a great friend of mine, who has a great name in the republic of letters, and among the sacred orators living. Do please be liberal of your favors to him

12/12 From a translation of a letter to Mr. Francis Rosaspina, in Bologna, by Bodoni dated Sept. 12, 1813:

You received with great courtesy the Rector of this our Imperial Lyceum in Parma; I am happy to think that you will extend the same courtesies to the Censor of said institute. Beside being my friend, and a very worthy ecclesiastic, he is the brother of a great friend of mine, who has a great name in the republic of letters, and among the sacred orators living. Do please be liberal of your favors to him during the brief stay which he is planning to make in this your City, which is counted among the most cultured in Europe. And now that I have sung the praises of my

14/16 From a translation of a letter to Mr. Francis Rosaspina, in Bologna, by Bodoni dated Sept. 12, 1813:

You received with great courtesy the Rector of this our Imperial Lyceum in Parma; I am happy to think that you will extend the same courtesies to the Censor of said institute. Beside being my friend, and a very worthy ecclesiastic, he is the brother of a great friend of mine, who has a great name in the republic of letters,

12/14 From a translation of a letter to Mr. Francis Rosaspina, in Bologna, by Bodoni dated Sept. 12, 1813:

You received with great courtesy the Rector of this our Imperial Lyceum in Parma; I am happy to think that you will extend the same courtesies to the Censor of said institute. Beside being my friend, and a very worthy ecclesiastic, he is the brother of a great friend of mine, who has a great name in the republic of letters, and among the sacred orators living. Do please be liberal of your favors to him during the brief stay which he

14/18 From a translation of a letter to Mr. Francis Rosaspina, in Bologna, by Bodoni dated Sept. 12, 1813:

You received with great courtesy the Rector of this our Imperial Lyceum in Parma; I am happy to think that you will extend the same courtesies to the Censor of said institute. Beside being my friend, and a very worthy ecclesiastic, he is the

12/16 From a translation of a letter to Mr. Francis Rosaspina, in Bologna, by Bodoni dated Sept. 12, 1813:

You received with great courtesy the Rector of this our Imperial Lyceum in Parma; I am happy to think that you will extend the same courtesies to the Censor of said institute. Beside being my friend, and a very worthy ecclesiastic, he is the brother of a great friend of mine, who has a great name in the republic of letters, and among

BAUER BODONI** BLACK CONDENSED   MERGENTHALER TYPE LIBRARY

ABCDEFGHIJKLMNOPQRSTUVWXYZ
&.,"-:;!?""1234567890$
abcdefghijklmnopqrstuvwxyz

ABCDEFGHIJKLMNOPQRSTUVWXYZ
&.,"-:;!?""1234567890$
abcdefghijklmnopqrstuvwxyz

10/10 From a translation of a letter to Mr. Francis Rosaspina, in Bologna, by Bodoni dated Sept. 12, 1813:

You received with great courtesy the Rector of this our Imperial Lyceum in Parma; I am happy to think that you will extend the same courtesies to the Censor of said institute. Beside being my friend, and a very worthy ecclesiastic, he is the brother of a great friend of mine, who has a great name in the republic of letters, and among the sacred orators living. Do please be liberal of your favors to him during the brief stay which he is planning to make in this your City, which is counted among the most cultured in Europe. And now that I have sung the praises of my Recommended, I will mention his name. He is Mr. Abbé Guglielmo Leoni, very well known in Piedmont, and who holds a distinguished position among the literary men of Bormida and Tanaro. He will give you detailed news of me, and of my joyful wife, and of our

10/12 From a translation of a letter to Mr. Francis Rosaspina, in Bologna, by Bodoni dated Sept. 12, 1813:

You received with great courtesy the Rector of this our Imperial Lyceum in Parma; I am happy to think that you will extend the same courtesies to the Censor of said institute. Beside being my friend, and a very worthy ecclesiastic, he is the brother of a great friend of mine, who has a great name in the republic of letters, and among the sacred orators living. Do please be liberal of your favors to him during the brief stay which he is planning to make in this your City, which is counted among the most cultured in Europe. And now that I have sung the praises of my Recommended, I will mention his name. He is Mr. Abbé Guglielmo Leoni, very well known in Piedmont, and who holds a distinguished position among

10/14 From a translation of a letter to Mr. Francis Rosaspina, in Bologna, by Bodoni dated Sept. 12, 1813:

You received with great courtesy the Rector of this our Imperial Lyceum in Parma; I am happy to think that you will extend the same courtesies to the Censor of said institute. Beside being my friend, and a very worthy ecclesiastic, he is the brother of a great friend of mine, who has a great name in the republic of letters, and among the sacred orators living. Do please be liberal of your favors to him during the brief stay which he is planning to make in this your City, which is counted among the most cultured in Europe. And now that I have

8/8 From a translation of a letter to Mr. Francis Rosaspina, in Bologna, by Bodoni dated Sept. 12, 1813:

You received with great courtesy the Rector of this our Imperial Lyceum in Parma; I am happy to think that you will extend the same courtesies to the Censor of said institute. Beside being my friend, and a very worthy ecclesiastic, he is the brother of a great friend of mine, who has a great name in the republic of letters, and among the sacred orators living. Do please be liberal of your favors to him during the brief stay which he is planning to make in this your City, which is counted among the most cultured in Europe. And now that I have sung the praises of my Recommended, I will mention his name. He is Mr. Abbé Guglielmo Leoni, very well known in Piedmont, and who holds a distinguished position among the literary men of Bormida and Tanaro. He will give you detailed news of me, and of my joyful wife, and of our friends; and will add that, as you have already received the most part of my Collection, so you will have the remainder. I shall be most happy to hear how you are getting on, and will rejoice to learn that you are enjoying, along with florid health, a perfect contentment of the soul. Do not be surprised in finding that a friend's hand has written these lines of recommendation, as for some time past I have had recourse to this help, for the reason that I am most busy; nor do I care to encroach upon the time which I need to bring to an end those typographical enterprises which I conceived, and indeed are

8/10 From a translation of a letter to Mr. Francis Rosaspina, in Bologna, by Bodoni dated Sept. 12, 1813:

You received with great courtesy the Rector of this our Imperial Lyceum in Parma; I am happy to think that you will extend the same courtesies to the Censor of said institute. Beside being my friend, and a very worthy ecclesiastic, he is the brother of a great friend of mine, who has a great name in the republic of letters, and among the sacred orators living. Do please be liberal of your favors to him during the brief stay which he is planning to make in this your City, which is counted among the most cultured in Europe. And now that I have sung the praises of my Recommended, I will mention his name. He is Mr. Abbé Guglielmo Leoni, very well known in Piedmont, and who holds a distinguished position among the literary men of Bormida and Tanaro. He will give you detailed news of me, and of my joyful wife, and of our friends; and will add that, as you have already received the most part of my Collection, so you will have the remainder. I shall be most happy to hear how you are getting on, and will rejoice to learn that you are enjoying, along with florid health, a perfect contentment of the soul. Do not be surprised in finding that a

8/12 From a translation of a letter to Mr. Francis Rosaspina, in Bologna, by Bodoni dated Sept. 12, 1813:

You received with great courtesy the Rector of this our Imperial Lyceum in Parma; I am happy to think that you will extend the same courtesies to the Censor of said institute. Beside being my friend, and a very worthy ecclesiastic, he is the brother of a great friend of mine, who has a great name in the republic of letters, and among the sacred orators living. Do please be liberal of your favors to him during the brief stay which he is planning to make in this your City, which is counted among the most cultured in Europe. And now that I have sung the praises of my Recommended, I will mention his name. He is Mr. Abbé Guglielmo Leoni, very well known in Piedmont, and who holds a distinguished position among the literary men of Bormida and Tanaro. He will give you detailed news of me, and of my joyful wife, and of our friends; and will add that,

---

BAUER BODONI** BLACK CONDENSED   MERGENTHALER TYPE LIBRARY

ABCDEFGHIJKLMNOPQRSTUVWXYZ
&.,"-:;!?""1234567890$
abcdefghijklmnopqrstuvwxyz

ABCDEFGHIJKLMNOPQRSTUVWXYZ
&.,"-:;!?""1234567890$
abcdefghijklmnopqrstuvwxyz

ABCDEFGHIJKLMNOPQ
RSTUVWXYZ&abcdefg
hijklmnopqrstuvwxyz1
234567890$.,""'':;!?

72 POINT POSTER BODONI COMPRESSED   MERGENTHALER TYPE LIBRARY

ABCDEFGHIJKLMNOPQRSTUVWXY
Z&abcdefghijklmnopqrstuvwxyz12
34567890$.,""'':;!?

48 POINT POSTER BODONI COMPRESSED   MERGENTHALER TYPE LIBRARY

ABCDEFGHIJKLMNOPQRSTUVWXYZ&abcdefghijklmnopqrstuvwxyz1234567890$.,""'':;!?

18 POINT POSTER BODONI COMPRESSED   MERGENTHALER TYPE LIBRARY

14/14 **From a translation of a letter to Mr. Francis Rosaspina, in Bologna, by Bodoni dated Sept. 12, 1813:**
You received with great courtesy the Rector of this our Imperial Lyceum in Parma; I am happy to think that you will extend the same courtesies to the Censor of said institute. Beside being my friend, and a very worthy ecclesiastic, he is the brother of a great friend of mine, who has a great name in the republic of letters, and among the sacred orators living. Do please be liberal of your favors to him during the brief stay which he is planning to make in this your City, which is counted among the most cultured in Europe. And now that I have sung the praises of my Recommended, I will mention his name. He

14/16 **From a translation of a letter to Mr. Francis Rosaspina, in Bologna, by Bodoni dated Sept. 12, 1813:**
You received with great courtesy the Rector of this our Imperial Lyceum in Parma; I am happy to think that you will extend the same courtesies to the Censor of said institute. Beside being my friend, and a very worthy ecclesiastic, he is the brother of a great friend of mine, who has a great name in the republic of letters, and among the sacred orators living. Do please be liberal of your favors to him during the brief stay which he is planning to make in this your City, which is counted among

14/18 **From a translation of a letter to Mr. Francis Rosaspina, in Bologna, by Bodoni dated Sept. 12, 1813:**
You received with great courtesy the Rector of this our Imperial Lyceum in Parma; I am happy to think that you will extend the same courtesies to the Censor of said institute. Beside being my friend, and a very worthy ecclesiastic, he is the brother of a great friend of mine, who has a great name in the republic of letters, and among the sacred orators living. Do please be liberal of

12/12 **From a translation of a letter to Mr. Francis Rosaspina, in Bologna, by Bodoni dated Sept. 12, 1813:**
You received with great courtesy the Rector of this our Imperial Lyceum in Parma; I am happy to think that you will extend the same courtesies to the Censor of said institute. Beside being my friend, and a very worthy ecclesiastic, he is the brother of a great friend of mine, who has a great name in the republic of letters, and among the sacred orators living. Do please be liberal of your favors to him during the brief stay which he is planning to make in this your City, which is counted among the most cultured in Europe. And now that I have sung the praises of my Recommended, I will mention his name. He is Mr. Abbé Guglielmo Leoni, very well known in Piedmont, and who holds a distinguished position among the literary men of Bormida and Tanaro. He will give you detailed news of me, and of my joyful wife, and of our friends; and will add that,

12/14 **From a translation of a letter to Mr. Francis Rosaspina, in Bologna, by Bodoni dated Sept. 12, 1813:**
You received with great courtesy the Rector of this our Imperial Lyceum in Parma; I am happy to think that you will extend the same courtesies to the Censor of said institute. Beside being my friend, and a very worthy ecclesiastic, he is the brother of a great friend of mine, who has a great name in the republic of letters, and among the sacred orators living. Do please be liberal of your favors to him during the brief stay which he is planning to make in this your City, which is counted among the most cultured in Europe. And now that I have sung the praises of my Recommended, I will mention his name. He is Mr. Abbé Guglielmo Leoni, very well known in

12/16 **From a translation of a letter to Mr. Francis Rosaspina, in Bologna, by Bodoni dated Sept. 12, 1813:**
You received with great courtesy the Rector of this our Imperial Lyceum in Parma; I am happy to think that you will extend the same courtesies to the Censor of said institute. Beside being my friend, and a very worthy ecclesiastic, he is the brother of a great friend of mine, who has a great name in the republic of letters, and among the sacred orators living. Do please be liberal of your favors to him during the brief stay which he is planning to make in this your City, which is counted among the most cultured in Europe. And now that I

POSTER BODONI COMPRESSED   MERGENTHALER TYPE LIBRARY

ABCDEFGHIJKLMNOPQRSTUVWXYZ
&.,'`-:;!?'"""1234567890$
abcdefghijklmnopqrstuvwxyz

ABCDEFGHIJKLMNOPQRSTUVWXYZ
&.,'`-:;!?'"""1234567890$
abcdefghijklmnopqrstuvwxyz

10/10 From a translation of a letter to Mr. Francis Rosaspina, in Bologna, by Bodoni dated Sept. 12, 1813:

You received with great courtesy the Rector of this our Imperial Lyceum in Parma; I am happy to think that you will extend the same courtesies to the Censor of said institute. Beside being my friend, and a very worthy ecclesiastic, he is the brother of a great friend of mine, who has a great name in the republic of letters, and among the sacred orators living. Do please be liberal of your favors to him during the brief stay which he is planning to make in this your City, which is counted among the most cultured in Europe. And now that I have sung the praises of my Recommended, I will mention his name. He is Mr. Abbé Guglielmo Leoni, very well known in Piedmont, and who holds a distinguished position among the literary men of Bormida and Tanaro. He will give you detailed news of me, and of my joyful wife, and of our friends; and will add that, as you have already received the most part of my Collection, so you will have the remainder. I shall be most happy to hear how you are getting on, and will rejoice to learn that you are enjoying, along with florid health, a perfect contentment of the soul. Do not be surprised in finding that a friend's hand has written these lines of recommendation

8/8 From a translation of a letter to Mr. Francis Rosaspina, in Bologna, by Bodoni dated Sept. 12, 1813:

You received with great courtesy the Rector of this our Imperial Lyceum in Parma; I am happy to think that you will extend the same courtesies to the Censor of said institute. Beside being my friend, and a very worthy ecclesiastic, he is the brother of a great friend of mine, who has a great name in the republic of letters, and among the sacred orators living. Do please be liberal of your favors to him during the brief stay which he is planning to make in this your City, which is counted among the most cultured in Europe. And now that I have sung the praises of my Recommended, I will mention his name. He is Mr. Abbé Guglielmo Leoni, very well known in Piedmont, and who holds a distinguished position among the literary men of Bormida and Tanaro. He will give you detailed news of me, and of my joyful wife, and of our friends; and will add that, as you have already received the most part of my Collection, so you will have the remainder. I shall be most happy to hear how you are getting on, and will rejoice to learn that you are enjoying, along with florid health, a perfect contentment of the soul. Do not be surprised in finding that a friend's hand has written these lines of recommendation, as for some time past I have had recourse to this help, for the reason that I am most busy; nor do I care to encroach upon the time which I need to bring to an end those typographical enterprises which I conceived, and indeed are now well on their way. Keep your friendship for me.

The bearer of this my letter will confirm that I, being very busy with my Typographical Manual, have absolutely no time to write at length, all the more so on account of my uncertain health, which prevents me to bend over my desk for any long time in writing; I only employ myself thus for the strictly indispensable.

You received with great courtesy the Rector of this our Imperial Lyceum in Parma; I am happy to think that you will extend the same courtesies to the Censor of said institute. Beside being my friend,

10/12 From a translation of a letter to Mr. Francis Rosaspina, in Bologna, by Bodoni dated Sept. 12, 1813:

You received with great courtesy the Rector of this our Imperial Lyceum in Parma; I am happy to think that you will extend the same courtesies to the Censor of said institute. Beside being my friend, and a very worthy ecclesiastic, he is the brother of a great friend of mine, who has a great name in the republic of letters, and among the sacred orators living. Do please be liberal of your favors to him during the brief stay which he is planning to make in this your City, which is counted among the most cultured in Europe. And now that I have sung the praises of my Recommended, I will mention his name. He is Mr. Abbé Guglielmo Leoni, very well known in Piedmont, and who holds a distinguished position among the literary men of Bormida and Tanaro. He will give you detailed news of me, and of my joyful wife, and of our friends; and will add that, as you have already received the most part of my Collection, so you will have the remainder. I shall be most happy to hear how you are getting on, and will rejoice to learn that

8/10 From a translation of a letter to Mr. Francis Rosaspina, in Bologna, by Bodoni dated Sept. 12, 1813:

You received with great courtesy the Rector of this our Imperial Lyceum in Parma; I am happy to think that you will extend the same courtesies to the Censor of said institute. Beside being my friend, and a very worthy ecclesiastic, he is the brother of a great friend of mine, who has a great name in the republic of letters, and among the sacred orators living. Do please be liberal of your favors to him during the brief stay which he is planning to make in this your City, which is counted among the most cultured in Europe. And now that I have sung the praises of my Recommended, I will mention his name. He is Mr. Abbé Guglielmo Leoni, very well known in Piedmont, and who holds a distinguished position among the literary men of Bormida and Tanaro. He will give you detailed news of me, and of my joyful wife, and of our friends; and will add that, as you have already received the most part of my Collection, so you will have the remainder. I shall be most happy to hear how you are getting on, and will rejoice to learn that you are enjoying, along with florid health, a perfect contentment of the soul. Do not be surprised in finding that a friend's hand has written these lines of recommendation, as for some time past I have had recourse to this help, for the reason that I am most busy; nor do I care to encroach upon the time which I need to bring to an end those typographical enterprises which I conceived, and indeed are now well on their way. Keep your friendship for me.

The bearer of this my letter will confirm that I, being very busy with my Typographical Manual, have absolutely no time to write at length, all the more so on account of my uncertain health, which

10/14 From a translation of a letter to Mr. Francis Rosaspina, in Bologna, by Bodoni dated Sept. 12, 1813:

You received with great courtesy the Rector of this our Imperial Lyceum in Parma; I am happy to think that you will extend the same courtesies to the Censor of said institute. Beside being my friend, and a very worthy ecclesiastic, he is the brother of a great friend of mine, who has a great name in the republic of letters, and among the sacred orators living. Do please be liberal of your favors to him during the brief stay which he is planning to make in this your City, which is counted among the most cultured in Europe. And now that I have sung the praises of my Recommended, I will mention his name. He is Mr. Abbé Guglielmo Leoni, very well known in Piedmont, and who holds a distinguished position among the literary men of Bormida and Tanaro. He will give you detailed news of

8/12 From a translation of a letter to Mr. Francis Rosaspina, in Bologna, by Bodoni dated Sept. 12, 1813:

You received with great courtesy the Rector of this our Imperial Lyceum in Parma; I am happy to think that you will extend the same courtesies to the Censor of said institute. Beside being my friend, and a very worthy ecclesiastic, he is the brother of a great friend of mine, who has a great name in the republic of letters, and among the sacred orators living. Do please be liberal of your favors to him during the brief stay which he is planning to make in this your City, which is counted among the most cultured in Europe. And now that I have sung the praises of my Recommended, I will mention his name. He is Mr. Abbé Guglielmo Leoni, very well known in Piedmont, and who holds a distinguished position among the literary men of Bormida and Tanaro. He will give you detailed news of me, and of my joyful wife, and of our friends; and will add that, as you have already received the most part of my Collection, so you will have the remainder. I shall be most happy to hear how you are getting on, and will rejoice to learn that you are enjoying, along with florid health, a perfect contentment of the soul. Do not be surprised in finding that a friend's hand has written these lines of recommendation, as for some time past I have had recourse to this help, for the reason that I am most busy; nor do I care to

POSTER BODONI COMPRESSED   MERGENTHALER TYPE LIBRARY

ABCDEFGHIJKLMNOPQRSTUVWXYZ
&.,'`-:;!?''""1234567890$
abcdefghijklmnopqrstuvwxyz

ABCDEFGHIJKLMNOPQRSTUVWXYZ
&.,'`-:;!?''""1234567890$
abcdefghijklmnopqrstuvwxyz

ABCDEFGH
IJKLMNOP
QRSTUVW
XYZ&abcd
efghijklmn
opqrstuvw
xyz1234567
890$.,""66;;!?

72 POINT POSTER BODONI   MERGENTHALER TYPE LIBRARY

ABCDEFGH IJKLMNOP QRSTUVWX YZ&abcdefg hijklmnopq rstuvwxyz1 234567890$,"",,!?;;

72 POINT POSTER BODONI ITALIC   MERGENTHALER TYPE LIBRARY

ABCDEFGHIJKLM
NOPQRSTUVWXY
Z&abcdefghijklm
nopqrstuvwxyz12
34567890$.,""";:!?

48 POINT POSTER BODONI   MERGENTHALER TYPE LIBRARY

ABCDEFGHIJKLM
NOPQRSTUVWXY
Z&abcdefghijklmn
opqrstuvwxyz1234
567890$.,""";:!?

48 POINT POSTER BODONI ITALIC   MERGENTHALER TYPE LIBRARY

ABCDEFGHIJKLMNOPQRSTUVWXYZ&abcdefg-
hijklmnopqrstuvwxyz1234567890$.,""";:!?

18 POINT POSTER BODONI   MERGENTHALER TYPE LIBRARY

*ABCDEFGHIJKLMNOPQRSTUVWXYZ&abcdefgh
ijklmnopqrstuvwxyz1234567890$.,""";:!?*

18 POINT POSTER BODONI ITALIC   MERGENTHALER TYPE LIBRARY

14/14 **From a translation of a letter to a Mr. Francis Rosaspina, in Bologna, by Bodoni dated Sept. 12, 1813:**
You received with great courtesy the Rector of this our Imperial Lyceum in Parma; I am happy to think that you will extend the same courtesies to the Censor of said institute. Beside being *my friend, and a very worthy ecclesiastic, he is the broth-*

12/12 **From a translation of a letter to a Mr. Francis Rosaspina, in Bologna, by Bodoni dated Sept. 12, 1813:**
You received with great courtesy the Rector of this our Imperial Lyceum in Parma; I am happy to think that you will extend the same courtesies to the Censor of said institute. Beside being my friend, and a very worthy ecclesiastic, he is the brother of a great friend of mine, who has a great *name in the republic of letters, and among the sacred orators liv-*

14/16 **From a translation of a letter to a Mr. Francis Rosaspina, in Bologna, by Bodoni dated Sept. 12, 1813:**
You received with great courtesy the Rector of this our Imperial Lyceum in Parma; I am happy to think that you will extend the same *courtesies to the Censor of said institute. Beside being*

12/14 **From a translation of a letter to a Mr. Francis Rosaspina, in Bologna, by Bodoni dated Sept. 12, 1813:**
You received with great courtesy the Rector of this our Imperial Lyceum in Parma; I am happy to think that you will extend the same courtesies to the Censor of said institute. Beside being my *friend, and a very worthy ecclesiastic, he is the brother of a great*

14/18 **From a translation of a letter to a Mr. Francis Rosaspina, in Bologna, by Bodoni dated Sept. 12, 1813:**
You received with great courtesy the Rector of this our Imperial Lyceum in *Parma; I am happy to think that you will extend the same*

12/16 **From a translation of a letter to a Mr. Francis Rosaspina, in Bologna, by Bodoni dated Sept. 12, 1813:**
You received with great courtesy the Rector of this our Imperial Lyceum in Parma; I am happy to think that you will extend the *same courtesies to the Censor of said institute. Beside being my*

POSTER BODONI   MERGENTHALER TYPE LIBRARY

ABCDEFGHIJKLMNOPQRS
ABCDEFGHIJKLMNOPQRS
TUV&.,"-:;!?""1234567890$
TUV&.,"-:;!?""1234567890$
abcdefghijklmnopqrstuvwx
abcdefghijklmnopqrstuvwx

ABCDEFGHIJKLMNOPQRSTUV
ABCDEFGHIJKLMNOPQRSTUV
WXYZ&.,"-:;!?""1234567890$
WXYZ&.,"-:;!?""1234567890$
abcdefghijklmnopqrstuvwxyz
abcdefghijklmnopqrstuvwxyz

10/10 From a translation of a letter to Mr. Francis Rosaspina, in Bologna, by Bodoni dated Sept. 12, 1813:

You received with great courtesy the Rector of this our Imperial Lyceum in Parma; I am happy to think that you will extend the same courtesies to the Censor of said institute. Beside being my friend, and a very worthy ecclesiastic, he is the brother of a great friend of mine, who has a great name in the republic of letters, and among the sacred orators living. Do please be liberal of your favors to him during the brief stay which he is planning to make in this your City, which is *counted among the most cultured in Europe. And now that I have sung the*

8/8 From a translation of a letter to Mr. Francis Rosaspina, in Bologna, by Bodoni dated Sept. 12, 1813:

You received with great courtesy the Rector of this our Imperial Lyceum in Parma; I am happy to think that you will extend the same courtesies to the Censor of said institute. Beside being my friend, and a very worthy ecclesiastic, he is the brother of a great friend of mine, who has a great name in the republic of letters, and among the sacred orators living. Do please be liberal of your favors to him during the brief stay which he is planning to make in this your City, which is counted among the most cultured in Europe. And now that I have sung the praises of my Recommended, I will mention his name. He is Mr. Abbé Guglielmo Leoni, very well known in Piedmont, and who holds a distinguished position among the literary men of Bormida and Tanaro. He will give you detailed news of me, and of my joyful wife, and of our friends; and *will add that, as you have already received the most part of my Collection, so you will have the*

10/12 From a translation of a letter to Mr. Francis Rosaspina, in Bologna, by Bodoni dated Sept. 12, 1813:

You received with great courtesy the Rector of this our Imperial Lyceum in Parma; I am happy to think that you will extend the same courtesies to the Censor of said institute. Beside being my friend, and a very worthy ecclesiastic, he is the brother of a great friend of mine, who has a great name in the republic of letters, and among the sacred orators living. Do please be liberal of your favors to him *during the brief stay which he is planning to make in this your City, which is*

8/10 From a translation of a letter to Mr. Francis Rosaspina, in Bologna, by Bodoni dated Sept. 12, 1813:

You received with great courtesy the Rector of this our Imperial Lyceum in Parma; I am happy to think that you will extend the same courtesies to the Censor of said institute. Beside being my friend, and a very worthy ecclesiastic, he is the brother of a great friend of mine, who has a great name in the republic of letters, and among the sacred orators living. Do please be liberal of your favors to him during the brief stay which he is planning to make in this your City, which is counted among the most cultured in Europe. And now that I have sung the praises of my Recommended, I will mention his name. He is Mr. Abbé Guglielmo Leoni, *very well known in Piedmont, and who holds a distinguished position among the literary men of Bor-*

10/14 From a translation of a letter to Mr. Francis Rosaspina, in Bologna, by Bodoni dated Sept. 12, 1813:

You received with great courtesy the Rector of this our Imperial Lyceum in Parma; I am happy to think that you will extend the same courtesies to the Censor of said institute. Beside being my friend, and a very worthy ecclesiastic, he is the brother of a great friend of mine, who has *a great name in the republic of letters, and among the sacred orators living. Do*

8/12 From a translation of a letter to Mr. Francis Rosaspina, in Bologna, by Bodoni dated Sept. 12, 1813:

You received with great courtesy the Rector of this our Imperial Lyceum in Parma; I am happy to think that you will extend the same courtesies to the Censor of said institute. Beside being my friend, and a very worthy ecclesiastic, he is the brother of a great friend of mine, who has a great name in the republic of letters, and among the sacred orators living. Do please be liberal of your favors to him during the brief stay which he is planning to make in this your City, which is counted *among the most cultured in Europe. And now that I*

POSTER BODONI   MERGENTHALER TYPE LIBRARY

ABCDEFGHIJKLMNOPQRSTUVWXYZ
ABCDEFGHIJKLMNOPQRSTUVWXYZ
&.,"'-:;!?""1234567890$
&.,"'-:;!?""1234567890$
abcdefghijklmnopqrstuvwxyz
abcdefghijklmnopqrstuvwxyz

ABCDEFGHIJKLMNOPQRSTUVWXYZ
ABCDEFGHIJKLMNOPQRSTUVWXYZ
&.,"'-:;!?""1234567890$
&.,"'-:;!?""1234567890$
abcdefghijklmnopqrstuvwxyz
abcdefghijklmnopqrstuvwxyz

LBA
Slapeb

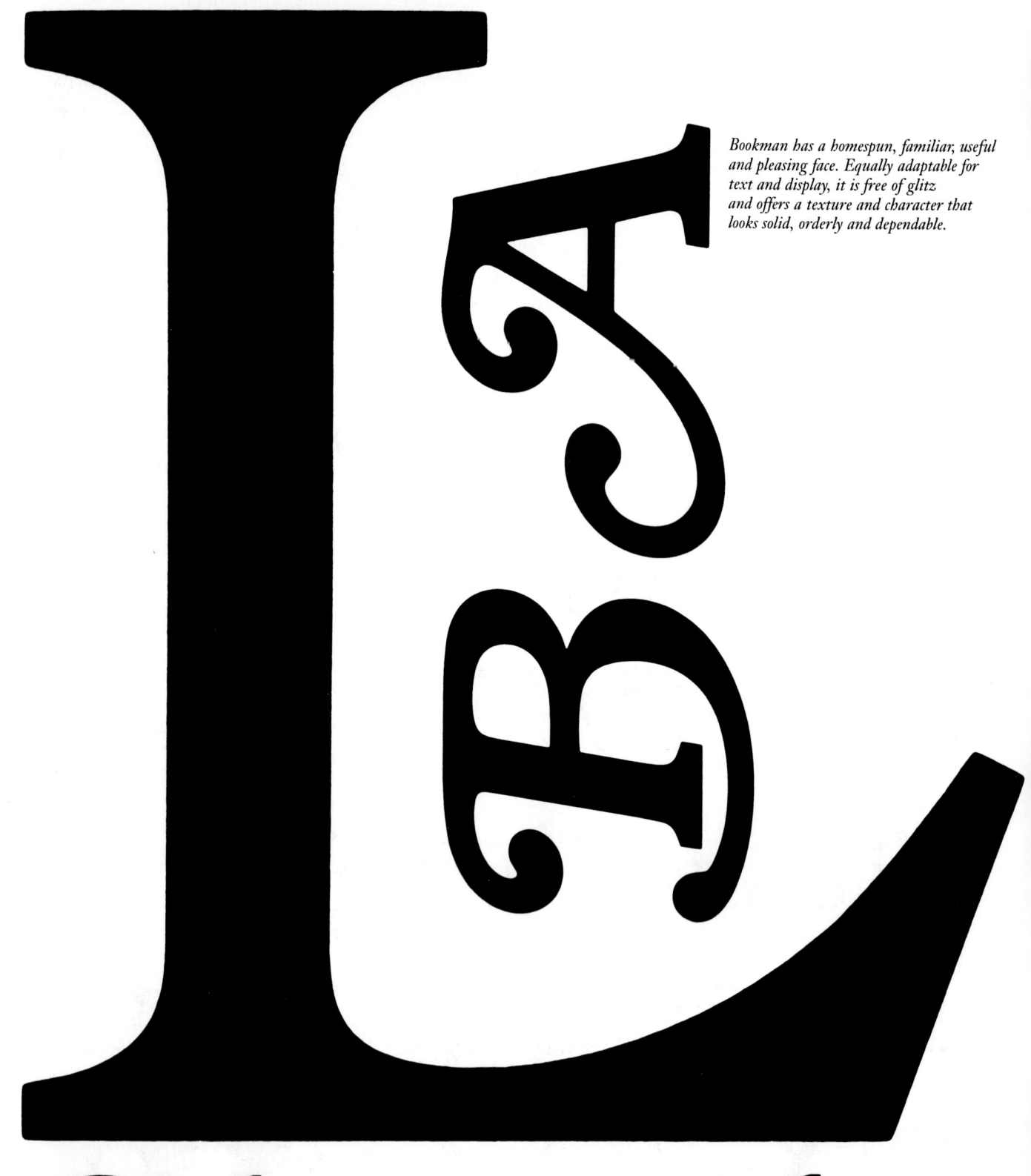

Bookman has a homespun, familiar, useful and pleasing face. Equally adaptable for text and display, it is free of glitz and offers a texture and character that looks solid, orderly and dependable.

&
ABCDEFGHI
JKLMNOPQR
STUVWXYZ
&abcdefghijk
lmnopqrstuv
wxyz123456
7890$.,''"":;!?

72 POINT ITC BOOKMAN LIGHT   AGFA COMPUGRAPHIC TYPE LIBRARY

ABCDEFGHI
JKLMNOPQR
STUVWXYZ
&abcdefghijk
lmnopqrstuv
wxyz123456
7890$.,''"":;!?

ABCDEFGHIJKLM
NOPQRSTUVWXY
Z&abcdefghijklmn
opqrstuvwxyz1234
567890$.,""":;!?

60 POINT ITC BOOKMAN** LIGHT   MERGENTHALER TYPE LIBRARY

ABCDEFGHIJKLM
NOPQRSTUVWXY
Z&abcdefghijklm
nopqrstuvwxyz12
34567890$.,""":;!?

60 POINT ITC BOOKMAN** LIGHT ITALIC   MERGENTHALER TYPE LIBRARY

ABCDEFGHIJKLMNOP
QRSTUVWXYZ&abcde
fghijklmnopqrstuvwxyz
1234567890$.,""":;!?

48 POINT ITC BOOKMAN** LIGHT   MERGENTHALER TYPE LIBRARY

ABCDEFGHIJKLMNOP
QRSTUVWXYZ&abcd
efghijklmnopqrstuvwx
yz1234567890$.,""":;!?

48 POINT ITC BOOKMAN** LIGHT ITALIC   MERGENTHALER TYPE LIBRARY

ABCDEFGHIJKLMNOPQRSTU
VWXYZ&abcdefghijklmnopqrs
tuvwxyz1234567890$.,""":;!?

36 POINT ITC BOOKMAN** LIGHT   MERGENTHALER TYPE LIBRARY

BOOKMAN FAMILY

ABCDEFGHIJKLMNOPQRSTUVWXYZ&abcdefghijklmnopqrstuvwxyz1234567890$.,"":;!?

36 POINT ITC BOOKMAN** LIGHT ITALIC   MERGENTHALER TYPE LIBRARY

ABCDEFGHIJKLMNOPQRSTUVWXYZ&abcdefghijklmnopqrstuvwxyz1234567890$.,"":;!?

24 POINT ITC BOOKMAN** LIGHT   MERGENTHALER TYPE LIBRARY

ABCDEFGHIJKLMNOPQRSTUVWXYZ&abcdefghijklmnopqrstuvwxyz1234567890$.,"":;!?

24 POINT ITC BOOKMAN** LIGHT ITALIC   MERGENTHALER TYPE LIBRARY

ABCDEFGHIJKLMNOPQRSTUVWXYZ&abcdefghijklmnopqrstuvwxyz1234567890$.,"":;!?

18 POINT ITC BOOKMAN** LIGHT   MERGENTHALER TYPE LIBRARY

ABCDEFGHIJKLMNOPQRSTUVWXYZ&abcdefghijklmnopqrstuvwxyz1234567890$.,"":;!?

18 POINT ITC BOOKMAN** LIGHT ITALIC   MERGENTHALER TYPE LIBRARY

BOOKMAN FAMILY

14/14 A Dissertation Upon English Typographical Founders and Founderies., by Edward Rowe Mores, 1778. The late Mr Caslon, the *Coryphæus* of Letterfounders, was not trained to this business. He was originally a *Gun-lock-graver*, and was taken from that instrument to an instrument of very different tendency, *the propagation of the Christian faith.*

In the y. 1720 the London Soc. for promoting Christian Knowl-

12/12 A Dissertation Upon English Typographical Founders and Founderies., by Edward Rowe Mores, 1778. The late Mr Caslon, the *Coryphæus* of Letterfounders, was not trained to this business. He was originally a *Gun-lock-graver*, and was taken from that instrument to an instrument of very different tendency, *the propagation of the Christian faith.*

In the y. 1720 the *London Soc. for promoting Christian Knowledge* in consequence of a representation made by *Mr Salomon Negri a native of Damascus in Syria, well skilled in the oriental lan-*

14/16 A Dissertation Upon English Typographical Founders and Founderies., by Edward Rowe Mores, 1778. The late Mr Caslon, the *Coryphæus* of Letterfounders, was not trained to this business. He was originally a *Gun-lock-graver*, and was taken from that instrument to an instrument of very different tendency, *the propagation of the Christian faith.*

12/14 A Dissertation Upon English Typographical Founders and Founderies., by Edward Rowe Mores, 1778. The late Mr Caslon, the *Coryphæus* of Letterfounders, was not trained to this business. He was originally a *Gun-lock-graver*, and was taken from that instrument to an instrument of very different tendency, *the propagation of the Christian faith.*

In the y. 1720 the London Soc. for promoting Christian Knowledge in conse-

14/18 A Dissertation Upon English Typographical Founders and Founderies., by Edward Rowe Mores, 1778. The late Mr Caslon, the *Coryphæus* of Letterfounders, was not trained to this business. He was originally a *Gun-lock-graver*, *and was taken from that instrument to an instrument of very dif-*

12/16 A Dissertation Upon English Typographical Founders and Founderies., by Edward Rowe Mores, 1778. The late Mr Caslon, the *Coryphæus* of Letterfounders, was not trained to this business. He was originally a *Gun-lock-graver*, and was taken from that instrument to an instrument of very different *tendency, the propagation of the Christian faith.*

ITC BOOKMAN** LIGHT   MERGENTHALER TYPE LIBRARY

ABCDEFGHIJKLMNOPQRSTUV
ABCDEFGHIJKLMNOPQRSTUV
WXYZ&.,"-:;!?""1234567890$
WXYZ&.,"-:;!?""1234567890$
abcdefghijklmnopqrstuvwxyz
abcdefghijklmnopqrstuvwxyz

ABCDEFGHIJKLMNOPQRSTUVWXYZ
ABCDEFGHIJKLMNOPQRSTUVWXYZ
&.,"-:;!?""1234567890$
&.,"-:;!?""1234567890$
abcdefghijklmnopqrstuvwxyz
abcdefghijklmnopqrstuvwxyz

11/11 A Dissertation Upon English Typographical Founders and Founderies., by Edward Rowe Mores, 1778. The late MR CASLON, the *Coryphæus* of Letterfounders, was not trained to this business. He was originally a *Gun-lock-graver*, and was taken from that instrument to an instrument of very different tendency, *the propagation of the Christian faith.*

In the y. 1720 the *London Soc. for promoting Christian Knowledge* in consequence of a representation made by *Mr Salomon Negri* a native of *Damascus* in *Syria*, well skilled in the oriental languages, who had been professor of *Arab.* in places of note for a great *part of his life, deemed it expedient to print for the use of the Eastern churches the N.*

10/10 A Dissertation Upon English Typographical Founders and Founderies., by Edward Rowe Mores, 1778. The late MR CASLON, the *Coryphæus* of Letterfounders, was not trained to this business. He was originally a *Gun-lock-graver*, and was taken from that instrument to an instrument of very different tendency, *the propagation of the Christian faith.*

In the y. 1720 the *London Soc. for promoting Christian Knowledge* in consequence of a representation made by *Mr Salomon Negri* a native of *Damascus* in *Syria*, well skilled in the oriental languages, who had been professor of *Arab.* in places of note for a great part of his life, deemed it expedient to print for the use of the *Eastern churches the N. Test. and Psalt. in the Arab. language for the benefit of the poor Christians*

11/13 A Dissertation Upon English Typographical Founders and Founderies., by Edward Rowe Mores, 1778. The late MR CASLON, the *Coryphæus* of Letterfounders, was not trained to this business. He was originally a *Gun-lock-graver*, and was taken from that instrument to an instrument of very different tendency, *the propagation of the Christian faith.*

In the y. 1720 the *London Soc. for promoting Christian Knowledge* in consequence of a representation made by *Mr Salomon Negri* a native of *Damascus* in *Syria*, well skilled *in the oriental languages, who had been professor of Arab. in places of note for a*

10/12 A Dissertation Upon English Typographical Founders and Founderies., by Edward Rowe Mores, 1778. The late MR CASLON, the *Coryphæus* of Letterfounders, was not trained to this business. He was originally a *Gun-lock-graver*, and was taken from that instrument to an instrument of very different tendency, *the propagation of the Christian faith.*

In the y. 1720 the *London Soc. for promoting Christian Knowledge* in consequence of a representation made by *Mr Salomon Negri* a native of *Damascus* in *Syria*, well skilled in the oriental languages, who had been professor of *Arab.* in *places of note for a great part of his life, deemed it expedient to print for the use of the Eastern*

11/15 A Dissertation Upon English Typographical Founders and Founderies., by Edward Rowe Mores, 1778. The late MR CASLON, the *Coryphæus* of Letterfounders, was not trained to this business. He was originally a *Gun-lock-graver*, and was taken from that instrument to an instrument of very different tendency, *the propagation of the Christian faith.*

In the y. 1720 the *London Soc. for promoting Christian Knowledge* in consequence of a representation made by *Mr Salomon*

10/14 A Dissertation Upon English Typographical Founders and Founderies., by Edward Rowe Mores, 1778. The late MR CASLON, the *Coryphæus* of Letterfounders, was not trained to this business. He was originally a *Gun-lock-graver*, and was taken from that instrument to an instrument of very different tendency, *the propagation of the Christian faith.*

In the y. 1720 the *London Soc. for promoting Christian Knowledge* in consequence of a representation made by *Mr Salomon Negri a native of Damascus in Syria, well skilled in the orien-*

ITC BOOKMAN** LIGHT   MERGENTHALER TYPE LIBRARY

ABCDEFGHIJKLMNOPQRSTUVWXYZ
ABCDEFGHIJKLMNOPQRSTUVWXYZ
&.,"-:;!?""''1234567890$
&.,"-:;!?""''1234567890$
abcdefghijklmnopqrstuvwxyz
abcdefghijklmnopqrstuvwxyz

ABCDEFGHIJKLMNOPQRSTUVWXYZ
ABCDEFGHIJKLMNOPQRSTUVWXYZ
&.,"-:;!?""''1234567890$
&.,"-:;!?""''1234567890$
abcdefghijklmnopqrstuvwxyz
abcdefghijklmnopqrstuvwxyz

9/9 A Dissertation Upon English Typographical Founders and Founderies., by Edward Rowe Mores, 1778. The late Mr Caslon, the *Coryphæus* of Letterfounders, was not trained to this business. He was originally a *Gun-lock-graver*, and was taken from that instrument to an instrument of very different tendency, *the propagation of the Christian faith.*

In the y. 1720 the *London Soc. for promoting Christian Knowledge* in consequence of a representation made by *Mr Salomon Negri* a native of *Damascus* in *Syria*, well skilled in the oriental languages, who had been professor of *Arab.* in places of note for a great part of his life, deemed it expedient to print for the use of the *Eastern* churches *the N. Test.* and *Psalt.* in the *Arab.* language for the benefit of the poor Christians in *Palestine, Syria, Mesopotamia, Arabia* and *Egypt*; the constitution of which countries allows of no printing: and *Mr Caslon* was pitched upon to cut a fount.

He cut the *Eng. Arabic which we see in his specimens. This was after the y. 1721 and before the y.*

8/8 A Dissertation Upon English Typographical Founders and Founderies., by Edward Rowe Mores, 1778. The late Mr Caslon, the *Coryphæus* of Letterfounders, was not trained to this business. He was originally a *Gun-lock-graver*, and was taken from that instrument to an instrument of very different tendency, *the propagation of the Christian faith.*

In the y. 1720 the *London Soc. for promoting Christian Knowledge* in consequence of a representation made by *Mr Salomon Negri* a native of *Damascus* in *Syria*, well skilled in the oriental languages, who had been professor of *Arab.* in places of note for a great part of his life, deemed it expedient to print for the use of the *Eastern* churches *the N. Test.* and *Psalt.* in the *Arab.* language for the benefit of the poor Christians in *Palestine, Syria, Mesopotamia, Arabia* and *Egypt*; the constitution of which countries allows of no printing: and *Mr Caslon* was pitched upon to cut a fount.

He cut the *Eng. Arabic* which we see in his specimens. This was after the y. 1721 and before the y. 1726, in which latter y. the Soc. had procured "two new fonts of Arab. types, viz. One from the Polyglott matrices; and another of a lesser size. He *was originally a Gun-lock-graver, and was taken from that instrument to an instrument of very different tendency, the*

9/11 A Dissertation Upon English Typographical Founders and Founderies., by Edward Rowe Mores, 1778. The late Mr Caslon, the *Coryphæus* of Letterfounders, was not trained to this business. He was originally a *Gun-lock-graver*, and was taken from that instrument to an instrument of very different tendency, *the propagation of the Christian faith.*

In the y. 1720 the *London Soc. for promoting Christian Knowledge* in consequence of a representation made by *Mr Salomon Negri* a native of *Damascus* in *Syria*, well skilled in the oriental languages, who had been professor of *Arab.* in places of note for a great part of his life, deemed it expedient to print for the use of the *Eastern* churches *the N. Test.* and *Psalt.* in the *Arab. language for the benefit of the poor Christians in Palestine, Syria, Mesopotamia, Arabia and Egypt*;

8/10 A Dissertation Upon English Typographical Founders and Founderies., by Edward Rowe Mores, 1778. The late Mr Caslon, the *Coryphæus* of Letterfounders, was not trained to this business. He was originally a *Gun-lock-graver*, and was taken from that instrument to an instrument of very different tendency, *the propagation of the Christian faith.*

In the y. 1720 the *London Soc. for promoting Christian Knowledge* in consequence of a representation made by *Mr Salomon Negri* a native of *Damascus* in *Syria*, well skilled in the oriental languages, who had been professor of *Arab.* in places of note for a great part of his life, deemed it expedient to print for the use of the *Eastern* churches *the N. Test.* and *Psalt.* in the *Arab.* language for the benefit of the poor Christians in *Palestine, Syria, Mesopotamia, Arabia* and *Egypt*; the constitution of which countries allows of no printing: and *Mr Caslon* was pitched upon to cut a fount.

He cut the *Eng. Arabic which we see in his specimens. This was after the y. 1721 and before the y. 1726, in which*

9/13 A Dissertation Upon English Typographical Founders and Founderies., by Edward Rowe Mores, 1778. The late Mr Caslon, the *Coryphæus* of Letterfounders, was not trained to this business. He was originally a *Gun-lock-graver*, and was taken from that instrument to an instrument of very different tendency, *the propagation of the Christian faith.*

In the y. 1720 the *London Soc. for promoting Christian Knowledge* in consequence of a representation made by *Mr Salomon Negri* a native of *Damascus* in *Syria*, well skilled in the oriental languages, who had *been professor of Arab. in places of note for a great part of his life, deemed it expedient to print for the use*

8/12 A Dissertation Upon English Typographical Founders and Founderies., by Edward Rowe Mores, 1778. The late Mr Caslon, the *Coryphæus* of Letterfounders, was not trained to this business. He was originally a *Gun-lock-graver*, and was taken from that instrument to an instrument of very different tendency, *the propagation of the Christian faith.*

In the y. 1720 the *London Soc. for promoting Christian Knowledge* in consequence of a representation made by *Mr Salomon Negri* a native of *Damascus* in *Syria*, well skilled in the oriental languages, who had been professor of *Arab.* in places of note for a great part of his life, deemed it expedient to print for the use of the *Eastern* churches *the N. Test.* and *Psalt. in the Arab. language for the benefit of the poor Christians in Palestine, Syria, Mesopotamia, Arabia and Egypt*;

ITC BOOKMAN** LIGHT   MERGENTHALER TYPE LIBRARY

ABCDEFGHIJKLMNOPQRSTUVWXYZ
ABCDEFGHIJKLMNOPQRSTUVWXYZ
&.,"-:;!?""''1234567890$
&.,"-:;!?""''1234567890$
abcdefghijklmnopqrstuvwxyz
abcdefghijklmnopqrstuvwxyz

ABCDEFGHIJKLMNOPQRSTUVWXYZ
ABCDEFGHIJKLMNOPQRSTUVWXYZ
&.,"-:;!?""''1234567890$
&.,"-:;!?""''1234567890$
abcdefghijklmnopqrstuvwxyz
abcdefghijklmnopqrstuvwxyz

ABCDEFGHI JKLMNOPQ RSTUVWXY Z&abcdefghi jklmnopqrst uvwxyz1234 567890$.,''" :;!?

72 POINT ITC BOOKMAN MEDIUM   AGFA COMPUGRAPHIC TYPE LIBRARY

ABCDEFGHI
JKLMNOPQ
RSTUVWXY
Z&abcdefgh
ijklmnopqrs
tuvwxyz123
4567890$.,
''"".;!?

72 POINT ITC BOOKMAN MEDIUM ITALIC   AGFA COMPUGRAPHIC TYPE LIBRARY

ABCDEFGHIJKLMNO
PQRSTUVWXYZ&abc
defghijklmnopqrstuv
wxyz1234567890$";!?

48 POINT ITC BOOKMAN** MEDIUM   MERGENTHALER TYPE LIBRARY

*ABCDEFGHIJKLMNO
PQRSTUVWXYZ&abc
defghijklmnopqrstuv
wxyz1234567890$";!?*

48 POINT ITC BOOKMAN** MEDIUM ITALIC   MERGENTHALER TYPE LIBRARY

ABCDEFGHIJKLMNOPQRSTUVWXYZ&a
bcdefghijklmnopqrstuvwxyz1234567890
$.,"":;!?

24 POINT ITC BOOKMAN** MEDIUM   MERGENTHALER TYPE LIBRARY

*ABCDEFGHIJKLMNOPQRSTUVWXYZ&a
bcdefghijklmnopqrstuvwxyz1234567890
$.,"":;!?*

24 POINT ITC BOOKMAN** MEDIUM ITALIC   MERGENTHALER TYPE LIBRARY

14/14 A Dissertation Upon English Typographical Founders and Founderies., by Edward Rowe Mores, 1778. The late Mr Caslon, the *Coryphæus* of Letterfounders, was not trained to this business. He was originally a *Gun-lock-graver*, and was taken from that instrument to an instrument of very different tendency, *the propagation of the Christian faith.*

In the y. 1720 the London Soc. for promoting Christian Knowl-

14/16 A Dissertation Upon English Typographical Founders and Founderies., by Edward Rowe Mores, 1778. The late Mr Caslon, the *Coryphæus* of Letterfounders, was not trained to this business. He was originally a *Gun-lock-graver*, and was taken from that instrument to an instrument of very different tendency, *the propagation of the Christian faith.*

14/18 A Dissertation Upon English Typographical Founders and Founderies., by Edward Rowe Mores, 1778. The late Mr Caslon, the *Coryphæus* of Letterfounders, was not trained to this business. He was originally a *Gun-lock-graver, and was taken from that instrument to an instrument of*

12/12 A Dissertation Upon English Typographical Founders and Founderies., by Edward Rowe Mores, 1778. The late Mr Caslon, the *Coryphæus* of Letterfounders, was not trained to this business. He was originally a *Gun-lock-graver*, and was taken from that instrument to an instrument of very different tendency, *the propagation of the Christian faith.*

In the y. 1720 the *London Soc. for promoting Christian Knowledge* in consequence of a representation made by *Mr Salomon Negri a native of Damascus in Syria, well skilled in the*

12/14 A Dissertation Upon English Typographical Founders and Founderies., by Edward Rowe Mores, 1778. The late Mr Caslon, the *Coryphæus* of Letterfounders, was not trained to this business. He was originally a *Gun-lock-graver*, and was taken from that instrument to an instrument of very different tendency, *the propagation of the Christian faith.*

In the y. 1720 the *London Soc. for promoting Christian Knowledge in*

12/16 A Dissertation Upon English Typographical Founders and Founderies., by Edward Rowe Mores, 1778. The late Mr Caslon, the *Coryphæus* of Letterfounders, was not trained to this business. He was originally a *Gun-lock-graver*, and was taken from that instrument to an instrument of very different *tendency, the propagation of the Christian faith.*

ITC BOOKMAN** MEDIUM   MERGENTHALER TYPE LIBRARY

ABCDEFGHIJKLMNOPQRSTUV
ABCDEFGHIJKLMNOPQRSTUV
WXYZ&.,"-:;!?""''1234567890$
WXYZ&.,"-:;!?""''1234567890$
abcdefghijklmnopqrstuvwxyz
abcdefghijklmnopqrstuvwxyz

ABCDEFGHIJKLMNOPQRSTUVWXYZ
ABCDEFGHIJKLMNOPQRSTUVWXYZ
&.,"-:;!?""''1234567890$
&.,"-:;!?""''1234567890$
abcdefghijklmnopqrstuvwxyz
abcdefghijklmnopqrstuvwxyz

10/10 A Dissertation Upon English Typographical Founders and Founderies., by Edward Rowe Mores, 1778. The late MR CASLON, the *Coryphæus* of Letterfounders, was not trained to this business. He was originally a *Gun-lock-graver*, and was taken from that instrument to an instrument of very different tendency, *the propagation of the Christian faith.*

In the y. 1720 the *London Soc. for promoting Christian Knowledge* in consequence of a representation made by *Mr Salomon Negri* a native of *Damascus* in *Syria*, well skilled in the oriental languages, who had been professor of *Arab.* in places of note for a great part of his life, deemed it expedient to print for the use of the *Eastern churches the N. Test. and Psalt. in the Arab. language for the benefit of the poor*

8/8 A Dissertation Upon English Typographical Founders and Founderies., by Edward Rowe Mores, 1778. The late MR CASLON, the *Coryphæus* of Letterfounders, was not trained to this business. He was originally a *Gun-lock-graver*, and was taken from that instrument to an instrument of very different tendency, *the propagation of the Christian faith.*

In the y. 1720 the *London Soc. for promoting Christian Knowledge* in consequence of a representation made by *Mr Salomon Negri* a native of *Damascus* in *Syria*, well skilled in the oriental languages, who had been professor of *Arab.* in places of note for a great part of his life, deemed it expedient to print for the use of the *Eastern* churches *the N. Test.* and *Psalt.* in the *Arab.* language for the benefit of the poor Christians in *Palestine, Syria, Mesopotamia, Arabia* and *Egypt*; the constitution of which countries allows of no printing: and Mr Caslon was pitched upon to cut a fount.

He cut the *Eng. Arabic* which we see in his specimens. This was after the y. 1721 and before the y. 1726, in which latter y. the Soc. had procured "two new fonts of Arab. *types, viz. One from the Polyglott matrices; and another of a lesser size that was cut from the original designs of the*

10/12 A Dissertation Upon English Typographical Founders and Founderies., by Edward Rowe Mores, 1778. The late MR CASLON, the *Coryphæus* of Letterfounders, was not trained to this business. He was originally a *Gun-lock-graver*, and was taken from that instrument to an instrument of very different tendency, *the propagation of the Christian faith.*

In the y. 1720 the *London Soc. for promoting Christian Knowledge* in consequence of a representation made by *Mr Salomon Negri* a native of *Damascus* in *Syria*, well skilled in the oriental languages, who had been professor of *Arab. in places of note for a great part of his life, deemed it expedient to print for the use of the*

8/10 A Dissertation Upon English Typographical Founders and Founderies., by Edward Rowe Mores, 1778. The late MR CASLON, the *Coryphæus* of Letterfounders, was not trained to this business. He was originally a *Gun-lock-graver*, and was taken from that instrument to an instrument of very different tendency, *the propagation of the Christian faith.*

In the y. 1720 the *London Soc. for promoting Christian Knowledge* in consequence of a representation made by *Mr Salomon Negri* a native of *Damascus* in *Syria*, well skilled in the oriental languages, who had been professor of *Arab.* in places of note for a great part of his life, deemed it expedient to print for the use of the *Eastern* churches *the N. Test.* and *Psalt.* in the *Arab.* language for the benefit of the poor Christians in *Palestine, Syria, Mesopotamia, Arabia* and *Egypt*; the constitution of which countries allows of no printing: and Mr Caslon was pitched upon to cut a fount.

He cut the *Eng. Arabic which we see in his specimens.*

10/14 A Dissertation Upon English Typographical Founders and Founderies., by Edward Rowe Mores, 1778. The late MR CASLON, the *Coryphæus* of Letterfounders, was not trained to this business. He was originally a *Gun-lock-graver*, and was taken from that instrument to an instrument of very different tendency, *the propagation of the Christian faith.*

In the y. 1720 the *London Soc. for promoting Christian Knowledge* in consequence of a representation made by *Mr Salomon Negri a native of Damascus in Syria, well skilled in*

8/12 A Dissertation Upon English Typographical Founders and Founderies., by Edward Rowe Mores, 1778. The late MR CASLON, the *Coryphæus* of Letterfounders, was not trained to this business. He was originally a *Gun-lock-graver*, and was taken from that instrument to an instrument of very different tendency, *the propagation of the Christian faith.*

In the y. 1720 the *London Soc. for promoting Christian Knowledge* in consequence of a representation made by *Mr Salomon Negri* a native of *Damascus* in *Syria*, well skilled in the oriental languages, who had been professor of *Arab.* in places of note for a great part of his life, deemed it expedient to print for the use of the *Eastern* churches *the N. Test.* and *Psalt.* in the *Arab.* language *for the benefit of the poor Christians in Palestine, Syria, Mesopotamia,*

ITC BOOKMAN** MEDIUM   MERGENTHALER TYPE LIBRARY

ABCDEFGHIJKLMNOPQRSTUVWXYZ
ABCDEFGHIJKLMNOPQRSTUVWXYZ
&.,"-:;!?''""1234567890$
&.,"-:;!?''""1234567890$
abcdefghijklmnopqrstuvwxyz
abcdefghijklmnopqrstuvwxyz

ABCDEFGHIJKLMNOPQRSTUVWXYZ
ABCDEFGHIJKLMNOPQRSTUVWXYZ
&.,"-:;!?''""1234567890$
&.,"-:;!?''""1234567890$
abcdefghijklmnopqrstuvwxyz
abcdefghijklmnopqrstuvwxyz

ABCDEFGHI
JKLMNOPQ
RSTUVWXY
Z&abcdefghi
jklmnopqrst
uvwxyz123
4567890$.,
'"";!?

ABCDEFGHI
JKLMNOPQ
RSTUVWXY
Z&abcdefgh
ijklmnopqrs
tuvwxyz123
4567890$.,
'"":;!?

ABCDEFGHIJKLMNO
PQRSTUVWXYZ&abc
defghijklmnopqrstuvw
xyz1234567890$":;!?

48 POINT ITC BOOKMAN** DEMI   MERGENTHALER TYPE LIBRARY

*ABCDEFGHIJKLMNO
PQRSTUVWXYZ&abc
defghijklmnopqrstuv
wxyz1234567890$;!?*

48 POINT ITC BOOKMAN** DEMI ITALIC   MERGENTHALER TYPE LIBRARY

ABCDEFGHIJKLMNOPQRSTUVWXYZ&
abcdefghijklmnopqrstuvwxyz123456789
0$.,'"":;!?

24 POINT ITC BOOKMAN** DEMI   MERGENTHALER TYPE LIBRARY

*ABCDEFGHIJKLMNOPQRSTUVWXYZ&
abcdefghijklmnopqrstuvwxyz12345678
90$.,'"":;!?*

24 POINT ITC BOOKMAN** DEMI ITALIC   MERGENTHALER TYPE LIBRARY

14/14 A Dissertation Upon English Typographical Founders and Founderies., by Edward Rowe Mores, 1778. The late MR CASLON, the *Coryphæus* of Letterfounders, was not trained to this business. He was originally a *Gun-lock-graver*, and was taken from that instrument to an instrument of very different tendency, *the propagation of the Christian faith.*

In the y. 1720 the London Soc. for promoting Christian Knowl-

14/16 A Dissertation Upon English Typographical Founders and Founderies., by Edward Rowe Mores, 1778. The late MR CASLON, the *Coryphæus* of Letterfounders, was not trained to this business. He was originally a *Gun-lock-graver*, and was taken from that instrument to an instrument of *very different tendency, the propagation of the Christian*

14/18 A Dissertation Upon English Typographical Founders and Founderies., by Edward Rowe Mores, 1778. The late MR CASLON, the *Coryphæus* of Letterfounders, was not trained to this business. He was originally a *Gun-lock-graver, and was taken from that instrument to an instrument of*

12/12 A Dissertation Upon English Typographical Founders and Founderies., by Edward Rowe Mores, 1778. The late MR CASLON, the *Coryphæus* of Letterfounders, was not trained to this business. He was originally a *Gun-lock-graver*, and was taken from that instrument to an instrument of very different tendency, *the propagation of the Christian faith.*

In the y. 1720 the London Soc. for promoting Christian Knowledge in consequence of a representation made by Mr Salomon Negri a native of Damascus in Syria, well skilled in the

12/14 A Dissertation Upon English Typographical Founders and Founderies., by Edward Rowe Mores, 1778. The late MR CASLON, the *Coryphæus* of Letterfounders, was not trained to this business. He was originally a *Gun-lock-graver*, and was taken from that instrument to an instrument of very different tendency, *the propagation of the Christian faith.*

In the y. 1720 the London Soc. for promoting Christian Knowledge in

12/16 A Dissertation Upon English Typographical Founders and Founderies., by Edward Rowe Mores, 1778. The late MR CASLON, the *Coryphæus* of Letterfounders, was not trained to this business. He was originally a *Gun-lock-graver*, and was taken from that instrument to an instrument of very different tendency, *the propagation of the Christian faith.*

ITC BOOKMAN** DEMI   MERGENTHALER TYPE LIBRARY

ABCDEFGHIJKLMNOPQRSTUV
ABCDEFGHIJKLMNOPQRSTUV
WXYZ&.,"-:;!?""'"1234567890$
WXYZ&.,"-:;!?""'"1234567890$
abcdefghijklmnopqrstuvwxyz
abcdefghijklmnopqrstuvwxyz

ABCDEFGHIJKLMNOPQRSTUVWXYZ
ABCDEFGHIJKLMNOPQRSTUVWXYZ
&.,"-:;!?""'"1234567890$
&.,"-:;!?""'"1234567890$
abcdefghijklmnopqrstuvwxyz
abcdefghijklmnopqrstuvwxyz

10/10 A Dissertation Upon English Typographical Founders and Founderies., by Edward Rowe Mores, 1778. The late MR CASLON, the *Coryphæus* of Letterfounders, was not trained to this business. He was originally a *Gun-lock-graver*, and was taken from that instrument to an instrument of very different tendency, *the propagation of the Christian faith.*

In the y. 1720 the *London Soc. for promoting Christian Knowledge* in consequence of a representation made by *Mr Salomon Negri* a native of *Damascus* in *Syria*, well skilled in the oriental languages, who had been professor of *Arab.* in places of note for a great part of his life, deemed it expedient to print for the use of *the Eastern churches the N. Test. and Psalt. in the Arab. language for the benefit of the poor*

8/8 A Dissertation Upon English Typographical Founders and Founderies., by Edward Rowe Mores, 1778. The late MR CASLON, the *Coryphæus* of Letterfounders, was not trained to this business. He was originally a *Gun-lock-graver*, and was taken from that instrument to an instrument of very different tendency, *the propagation of the Christian faith.*

In the y. 1720 the *London Soc. for promoting Christian Knowledge* in consequence of a representation made by *Mr Salomon Negri* a native of *Damascus* in *Syria*, well skilled in the oriental languages, who had been professor of *Arab.* in places of note for a great part of his life, deemed it expedient to print for the use of the *Eastern* churches *the N. Test.* and *Psalt.* in the *Arab.* language for the benefit of the poor Christians in *Palestine, Syria, Mesopotamia, Arabia* and *Egypt*; the constitution of which countries allows of no printing: and *Mr Caslon* was pitched upon to cut a fount.

He cut the *Eng. Arabic* which we see in his specimens. This was after the y. 1721 and before the y. 1726, in which latter y. the *Soc.* had procured "two new fonts of *Arab. types, viz. One from the Polyglott matrices; and another of a lesser size that was cut from the original designs of*

10/12 A Dissertation Upon English Typographical Founders and Founderies., by Edward Rowe Mores, 1778. The late MR CASLON, the *Coryphæus* of Letterfounders, was not trained to this business. He was originally a *Gun-lock-graver*, and was taken from that instrument to an instrument of very different tendency, *the propagation of the Christian faith.*

In the y. 1720 the *London Soc. for promoting Christian Knowledge* in consequence of a representation made by *Mr Salomon Negri* a native of *Damascus* in *Syria*, well skilled in the oriental languages, who had been professor of *Arab.* in places of note for a great part of his life, deemed it expedient to print for the

8/10 A Dissertation Upon English Typographical Founders and Founderies., by Edward Rowe Mores, 1778. The late MR CASLON, the *Coryphæus* of Letterfounders, was not trained to this business. He was originally a *Gun-lock-graver*, and was taken from that instrument to an instrument of very different tendency, *the propagation of the Christian faith.*

In the y. 1720 the *London Soc. for promoting Christian Knowledge* in consequence of a representation made by *Mr Salomon Negri* a native of *Damascus* in *Syria*, well skilled in the oriental languages, who had been professor of *Arab.* in places of note for a great part of his life, deemed it expedient to print for the use of the *Eastern* churches *the N. Test.* and *Psalt.* in the *Arab.* language for the benefit of the poor Christians in *Palestine, Syria, Mesopotamia, Arabia* and *Egypt*; the constitution of which countries allows of no printing: and *Mr Caslon* was pitched upon to cut a fount.

He cut the *Eng. Arabic which we see in his specimens.*

10/14 A Dissertation Upon English Typographical Founders and Founderies., by Edward Rowe Mores, 1778. The late MR CASLON, the *Coryphæus* of Letterfounders, was not trained to this business. He was originally a *Gun-lock-graver*, and was taken from that instrument to an instrument of very different tendency, *the propagation of the Christian faith.*

In the y. 1720 the *London Soc. for promoting Christian Knowledge* in consequence of a representation made by Mr Salomon Negri a native of Damascus in Syria, well skilled in

8/12 A Dissertation Upon English Typographical Founders and Founderies., by Edward Rowe Mores, 1778. The late MR CASLON, the *Coryphæus* of Letterfounders, was not trained to this business. He was originally a *Gun-lock-graver*, and was taken from that instrument to an instrument of very different tendency, *the propagation of the Christian faith.*

In the y. 1720 the *London Soc. for promoting Christian Knowledge* in consequence of a representation made by *Mr Salomon Negri* a native of *Damascus* in *Syria*, well skilled in the oriental languages, who had been professor of *Arab.* in places of note for a great part of his life, deemed it expedient to print for the use of the *Eastern* churches *the N. Test.* and *Psalt.* in the *Arab.* language for the benefit of the poor Christians in Palestine, Syria, Mesopotamia,

---

ITC BOOKMAN** DEMI   MERGENTHALER TYPE LIBRARY

ABCDEFGHIJKLMNOPQRSTUVWXYZ
ABCDEFGHIJKLMNOPQRSTUVWXYZ
&.,"-:;!?""'"1234567890$
&.,"-:;!?""'"1234567890$
abcdefghijklmnopqrstuvwxyz
abcdefghijklmnopqrstuvwxyz

ABCDEFGHIJKLMNOPQRSTUVWXYZ
ABCDEFGHIJKLMNOPQRSTUVWXYZ
&.,"-:;!?""'"1234567890$
&.,"-:;!?""'"1234567890$
abcdefghijklmnopqrstuvwxyz
abcdefghijklmnopqrstuvwxyz

ABCDEFGH IJKLMNOP QRSTUVWX YZ&abcdefg hijklmnopq rstuvwxyz1 234567890 $.,''""..;!?

72 POINT ITC BOOKMAN BOLD   AGFA COMPUGRAPHIC TYPE LIBRARY

ABCDEFGH
IJKLMNOP
QRSTUVWX
YZ&abcdef
ghijklmnop
qrstuvwxy
z12345678
90$.,''"":;!?

72 POINT ITC BOOKMAN BOLD ITALIC   AGFA COMPUGRAPHIC TYPE LIBRARY

ABCDEFGHIJKLMNOPQRSTUVWXYZ
&abcdefghijklmnopqrstuvwxyz123456
7890$.,"":;!?

24 POINT ITC BOOKMAN** BOLD   MERGENTHALER TYPE LIBRARY

ABCDEFGHIJKLMNOPQRSTUVWXYZ &abcdefghijklmnopqrstuvwxyz1234 567890$.,""'';;!?

24 POINT ITC BOOKMAN** BOLD ITALIC   MERGENTHALER TYPE LIBRARY

ABCDEFGHIJKLMN
OPQRSTUVWXYZ&
abcdefghijklmnopqr
stuvwxyz12345678
90$.,""'';;!?

48 POINT ITC BOOKMAN** BOLD   MERGENTHALER TYPE LIBRARY

*ABCDEFGHIJKLMN
OPQRSTUVWXYZ&
abcdefghijklmnopq
rstuvwxyz1234567
890$.,""'';;!?*

48 POINT ITC BOOKMAN** BOLD ITALIC   MERGENTHALER TYPE LIBRARY

14/14 **A Dissertation Upon English Typographical Founders and Founderies., by Edward Rowe Mores, 1778. The late Mr Caslon, the *Coryphæus* of Letterfounders, was not trained to this business. He was originally a *Gun-lock-graver*, and was taken from that instrument to an instrument of very different tendency, *the propagation of the Christian faith.***
 In the y. 1720 the London

12/12 **A Dissertation Upon English Typographical Founders and Founderies., by Edward Rowe Mores, 1778. The late Mr Caslon, the *Coryphæus* of Letterfounders, was not trained to this business. He was originally a *Gun-lock-graver*, and was taken from that instrument to an instrument of very different tendency, *the propagation of the Christian faith.***
 ***In the y. 1720 the London Soc. for promoting Christian Knowledge* in consequence of a representation *made by Mr Salomon Negri a native of Damascus in Syria*, well skilled**

14/16 **A Dissertation Upon English Typographical Founders and Founderies., by Edward Rowe Mores, 1778. The late Mr Caslon, the *Coryphæus* of Letterfounders, was not trained to this business. He was originally a *Gun-lock-graver*, and was taken from that instrument to *an instrument of very different tendency, the propagation***

12/14 **A Dissertation Upon English Typographical Founders and Founderies., by Edward Rowe Mores, 1778. The late Mr Caslon, the *Coryphæus* of Letterfounders, was not trained to this business. He was originally a *Gun-lock-graver*, and was taken from that instrument to an instrument of very different tendency, *the propagation of the Christian faith.***
 ***In the y. 1720 the London Soc. for promoting Christian Knowledge* in**

14/18 **A Dissertation Upon English Typographical Founders and Founderies., by Edward Rowe Mores, 1778. The late Mr Caslon, the *Coryphæus* of Letterfounders, was not trained to this business. He was originally a *Gun-lock-graver*, and was taken from that instrument to***

12/16 **A Dissertation Upon English Typographical Founders and Founderies., by Edward Rowe Mores, 1778. The late Mr Caslon, the *Coryphæus* of Letterfounders, was not trained to this business. He was originally a *Gun-lock-graver*, and was taken from that instrument to an instrument *of very different tendency, the propagation of the Christian faith.***

ITC BOOKMAN** BOLD   MERGENTHALER TYPE LIBRARY

ABCDEFGHIJKLMNOPQRSTU
ABCDEFGHIJKLMNOPQRSTU
VWX&.,"-:;!?""1234567890$
VWX&.,"-:;!?""1234567890$
abcdefghijklmnopqrstuvwxyz
abcdefghijklmnopqrstuvwxyz

ABCDEFGHIJKLMNOPQRSTUV
ABCDEFGHIJKLMNOPQRSTUV
WXYZ&.,"-:;!?""1234567890$
WXYZ&.,"-:;!?""1234567890$
abcdefghijklmnopqrstuvwxyz
abcdefghijklmnopqrstuvwxyz

10/10 A Dissertation Upon English Typographical Founders and Founderies., by Edward Rowe Mores, 1778. The late Mr Caslon, the *Coryphæus* of Letterfounders, was not trained to this business. He was originally a *Gun-lock-graver*, and was taken from that instrument to an instrument of very different tendency, *the propagation of the Christian faith.*

In the y. 1720 the *London Soc. for promoting Christian Knowledge* in consequence of a representation made by *Mr Salomon Negri* a native of *Damascus* in *Syria*, well skilled in the oriental languages, who had been professor of *Arab.* in places of note for a great part of his life, deemed it expedient to print *for the use of the Eastern churches the N. Test. and Psalt. in the Arab. language for*

8/8 A Dissertation Upon English Typographical Founders and Founderies., by Edward Rowe Mores, 1778. The late Mr Caslon, the *Coryphæus* of Letterfounders, was not trained to this business. He was originally a *Gun-lock-graver*, and was taken from that instrument to an instrument of very different tendency, *the propagation of the Christian faith.*

In the y. 1720 the *London Soc. for promoting Christian Knowledge* in consequence of a representation made by *Mr Salomon Negri* a native of *Damascus* in *Syria*, well skilled in the oriental languages, who had been professor of *Arab.* in places of note for a great part of his life, deemed it expedient to print for the use of the *Eastern* churches *the N. Test.* and *Psalt.* in the *Arab.* language for the benefit of the poor Christians in *Palestine, Syria, Mesopotamia, Arabia* and *Egypt*; the constitution of which countries allows of no printing: and *Mr Caslon* was pitched upon to cut a fount.

He cut the *Eng. Arabic* which we see in his specimens. This was after the y. 1721 and before the y. 1726, in *which latter y. the Soc. had procured "two new fonts of Arab. types, viz. One from the Polyglott matrices;*

10/12 A Dissertation Upon English Typographical Founders and Founderies., by Edward Rowe Mores, 1778. The late Mr Caslon, the *Coryphæus* of Letterfounders, was not trained to this business. He was originally a *Gun-lock-graver*, and was taken from that instrument to an instrument of very different tendency, *the propagation of the Christian faith.*

In the y. 1720 the *London Soc. for promoting Christian Knowledge* in consequence of a representation made by *Mr Salomon Negri* a native of *Damascus* in *Syria*, well skilled in the oriental languages, who had been professor *of Arab. in places of note for a great part of his life, deemed it expedient to*

8/10 A Dissertation Upon English Typographical Founders and Founderies., by Edward Rowe Mores, 1778. The late Mr Caslon, the *Coryphæus* of Letterfounders, was not trained to this business. He was originally a *Gun-lock-graver*, and was taken from that instrument to an instrument of very different tendency, *the propagation of the Christian faith.*

In the y. 1720 the *London Soc. for promoting Christian Knowledge* in consequence of a representation made by *Mr Salomon Negri* a native of *Damascus* in *Syria*, well skilled in the oriental languages, who had been professor of *Arab.* in places of note for a great part of his life, deemed it expedient to print for the use of the *Eastern* churches *the N. Test.* and *Psalt.* in the *Arab.* language for the benefit of the poor Christians in *Palestine, Syria, Mesopotamia, Arabia* and *Egypt*; the constitution of which countries allows of no printing: and Mr Caslon was pitched upon to cut a fount.

10/14 A Dissertation Upon English Typographical Founders and Founderies., by Edward Rowe Mores, 1778. The late Mr Caslon, the *Coryphæus* of Letterfounders, was not trained to this business. He was originally a *Gun-lock-graver*, and was taken from that instrument to an instrument of very different tendency, *the propagation of the Christian faith.*

In the y. 1720 the *London Soc. for promoting Christian Knowledge* in consequence of a representation made by Mr Salomon Negri a native of Damascus in Syria, well

8/12 A Dissertation Upon English Typographical Founders and Founderies., by Edward Rowe Mores, 1778. The late Mr Caslon, the *Coryphæus* of Letterfounders, was not trained to this business. He was originally a *Gun-lock-graver*, and was taken from that instrument to an instrument of very different tendency, *the propagation of the Christian faith.*

In the y. 1720 the *London Soc. for promoting Christian Knowledge* in consequence of a representation made by *Mr Salomon Negri* a native of *Damascus* in *Syria*, well skilled in the oriental languages, who had been professor of *Arab.* in places of note for a great part *of his life, deemed it expedient to print for the use of the Eastern churches the N. Test. and Psalt. in the*

ITC BOOKMAN** BOLD   MERGENTHALER TYPE LIBRARY

ABCDEFGHIJKLMNOPQRSTUVWXYZ
ABCDEFGHIJKLMNOPQRSTUVWXYZ
&.,"-:;!?""1234567890$
&.,"-:;!?""1234567890$
abcdefghijklmnopqrstuvwxyz
abcdefghijklmnopqrstuvwxyz

ABCDEFGHIJKLMNOPQRSTUVWXYZ
ABCDEFGHIJKLMNOPQRSTUVWXYZ
&.,"-:;!?""1234567890$
&.,"-:;!?""1234567890$
abcdefghijklmnopqrstuvwxyz
abcdefghijklmnopqrstuvwxyz

BOOKMAN FAMILY

ABCGKM
NORSThY
&efkmno
rvwy

72 POINT ITC BOOKMAN LIGHT SWASH   AGFA COMPUGRAPHIC TYPE LIBRARY

ABCGKM
NORSThY
Z&ehkmn
opqr

72 POINT ITC BOOKMAN LIGHT ITALIC SWASH   AGFA COMPUGRAPHIC TYPE LIBRARY

BOOKMAN FAMILY

ABCGKMNORSTTh
Y&efKmnorvwy
36 POINT ITC BOOKMAN MEDIUM SWASH   AGFA COMPUGRAPHIC TYPE LIBRARY

ABCGKMNORSTTh
YZ&ehKmnopqr
36 POINT ITC BOOKMAN MEDIUM ITALIC SWASH   AGFA COMPUGRAPHIC TYPE LIBRARY

ABCGKMNORSTTh
Y&efKmnorvwy
36 POINT ITC BOOKMAN DEMI SWASH   AGFA COMPUGRAPHIC TYPE LIBRARY

ABCGKMNORSTTh
YZ&ehKmnopqr
36 POINT ITC BOOKMAN DEMI ITALIC SWASH   AGFA COMPUGRAPHIC TYPE LIBRARY

ABCGKMNORSTTh
Y&efKmnorvwy
36 POINT ITC BOOKMAN BOLD SWASH   AGFA COMPUGRAPHIC TYPE LIBRARY

ABCGKMNORSTTh
YZ&ehKmnopqr
36 POINT ITC BOOKMAN BOLD ITALIC SWASH   AGFA COMPUGRAPHIC TYPE LIBRARY

A 123

&

tuvwxyz

Caslon — eminently legible, traditionally used to convey dignity and purpose — stands as one of the model achievements of type design in the western world. Designed in 1772 by William Caslon, used in the first printed version of the United States constitution, it has had universal acceptance ever since.

CASLON FAMILY 139

fi

ABCDEFGHIJ
KLMNOPQRS
TUVWXYZ&a
bcdefghijklmno
pqrstuvwxyz123
4567890$.,"":;!?

72 POINT CASLON 540   MERGENTHALER TYPE LIBRARY

ABCDEFGHIJ
KLMNOPQRST
UVWXYZ&abcd
efghijklmnopqrstu
vwxyz1234567890$.,"":;!?*

72 POINT CASLON 540 ITALIC   MERGENTHALER TYPE LIBRARY

ABCDEFGHIJKL
MNOPQRSTUVW
XYZ&abcdefghijkl
mnopqrstuvwxyz123
4567890$.,""":;!?

60 POINT CASLON NO. 540   MERGENTHALER TYPE LIBRARY

*ABCDEFGHIJKLM
NOPQRSTUVWXY
Z&abcdefghijklmnopqr
stuvwxyz1234567890
$.,""":;!?*

60 POINT CASLON NO. 540 ITALIC   MERGENTHALER TYPE LIBRARY

ABCDEFGHIJKLMNOPQRSTUVWXYZ&abcdefghijklmnopqrstuvwxyz1234567890$.,""":;!?

48 POINT CASLON NO. 540   MERGENTHALER TYPE LIBRARY

ABCDEFGHIJKLMNOPQRSTUVWXYZ&abcdefghijklmnopqrstuvwxyz1234567890$.,""":;!?

48 POINT CASLON NO. 540 ITALIC   MERGENTHALER TYPE LIBRARY

ABCDEFGHIJKLMNOPQRST
UVWXYZ&abcdefghijklmnopqr
stuvwxyz1234567890$.,""":;!?

36 POINT CASLON NO. 540   MERGENTHALER TYPE LIBRARY

ABCDEFGHIJKLMNOPQRSTU
VWXYZ&abcdefghijklmnopqrstuvw
xyz1234567890$.,"":;!?

36 POINT CASLON NO. 540 ITALIC   MERGENTHALER TYPE LIBRARY

ABCDEFGHIJKLMNOPQRSTUVWXYZ&abcd
efghijklmnopqrstuvwxyz1234567890$.,"":;!?

24 POINT CASLON NO. 540   MERGENTHALER TYPE LIBRARY

ABCDEFGHIJKLMNOPQRSTUVWXYZ&abcdefg
hijklmnopqrstuvwxyz1234567890$.,"":;!?

24 POINT CASLON NO. 540 ITALIC   MERGENTHALER TYPE LIBRARY

ABCDEFGHIJKLMNOPQRSTUVWXYZ&abcdefghijklmnopq
rstuvwxyz1234567890$.,"":;!?

18 POINT CASLON NO. 540   MERGENTHALER TYPE LIBRARY

ABCDEFGHIJKLMNOPQRSTUVWXYZ&abcdefghijklmnopqrstuv
wxyz1234567890$.,"":;!?

18 POINT CASLON NO. 540 ITALIC   MERGENTHALER TYPE LIBRARY

14/14 From a letter to John Baskerville by Benjamin Franklin dated London, 1760:

Let me give you a pleasant Instance of the Prejudice some have entertained against your Work. Soon after I returned, discoursing with a Gentleman concerning the Artists of Birmingham, he said you would [be] a Means of blinding all the Readers in the Nation; for the Strokes of your Letters, being *too thin and narrow, hurt the Eye, and he could never read a Line of them without*

14/16 From a letter to John Baskerville by Benjamin Franklin dated London, 1760:

Let me give you a pleasant Instance of the Prejudice some have entertained against your Work. Soon after I returned, discoursing with a Gentleman concerning the Artists of Birmingham, he said you would [be] a Means of *blinding all the Readers in the Nation; for the Strokes of your Letters, being too thin*

14/18 From a letter to John Baskerville by Benjamin Franklin dated London, 1760:

Let me give you a pleasant Instance of the Prejudice some have entertained against your Work. Soon after I returned, discoursing with a Gentleman *concerning the Artists of Birmingham, he said you would [be] a Means of blinding all*

12/12 From a letter to John Baskerville by Benjamin Franklin dated London, 1760:

Let me give you a pleasant Instance of the Prejudice some have entertained against your Work. Soon after I returned, discoursing with a Gentleman concerning the Artists of Birmingham, he said you would [be] a Means of blinding all the Readers in the Nation; for the Strokes of your Letters, being too thin and narrow, hurt the Eye, and he could never read a Line of them without Pain. "I thought," said I, "you were going to complain of the Gloss of the Paper, some object to." "No, it Is *in the Form and Cut of the Letters themselves; they have not that height and Thickness of the Stroke,*

12/14 From a letter to John Baskerville by Benjamin Franklin dated London, 1760:

Let me give you a pleasant Instance of the Prejudice some have entertained against your Work. Soon after I returned, discoursing with a Gentleman concerning the Artists of Birmingham, he said you would [be] a Means of blinding all the Readers in the Nation; for the Strokes of your Letters, being too thin and narrow, hurt the Eye, and he could never read *a Line of them without Pain. "I thought," said I, "you were going to complain of the Gloss of the*

12/16 From a letter to John Baskerville by Benjamin Franklin dated London, 1760:

Let me give you a pleasant Instance of the Prejudice some have entertained against your Work. Soon after I returned, discoursing with a Gentleman concerning the Artists of Birmingham, he said you would [be] a Means of blinding all the Readers in the Nation; for the *Strokes of your Letters, being too thin and narrow, hurt the Eye, and he could never read a Line of*

CASLON NO. 540   MERGENTHALER TYPE LIBRARY

ABCDEFGHIJKLMNOPQRSTUV
ABCDEFGHIJKLMNOPQRSTUV
WXYZ&.,'‑-:;!?"" 1234567890$
WXYZ&.,'‑-:;!?" "1234567890$
abcdefghijklmnopqrstuvwxyz
abcdefghijklmnopqrstuvwxyz

ABCDEFGHIJKLMNOPQRSTUVWXYZ
ABCDEFGHIJKLMNOPQRSTUVWXYZ
&.,'‑-:;!?"" 1234567890$
&.,'‑-:;!?" "1234567890$
abcdefghijklmnopqrstuvwxyz
abcdefghijklmnopqrstuvwxyz

11/11 From a letter to John Baskerville by Benjamin Franklin dated London, 1760:

Let me give you a pleasant Instance of the Prejudice some have entertained against your Work. Soon after I returned, discoursing with a Gentleman concerning the Artists of Birmingham, he said you would [be] a Means of blinding all the Readers in the Nation; for the Strokes of your Letters, being too thin and narrow, hurt the Eye, and he could never read a Line of them without Pain. "I thought," said I, "you were going to complain of the Gloss of the Paper, some object to." "No, it Is in the Form and Cut of the Letters themselves; they have not that height *and Thickness of the Stroke, which make the common Printing so much the more comfortable to the Eye." You*

10/10 From a letter to John Baskerville by Benjamin Franklin dated London, 1760:

Let me give you a pleasant Instance of the Prejudice some have entertained against your Work. Soon after I returned, discoursing with a Gentleman concerning the Artists of Birmingham, he said you would [be] a Means of blinding all the Readers in the Nation; for the Strokes of your Letters, being too thin and narrow, hurt the Eye, and he could never read a Line of them without Pain. "I thought," said I, "you were going to complain of the Gloss of the Paper, some object to." "No, it Is in the Form and Cut of the Letters themselves; they have not that height and Thickness of the Stroke, which make the common Printing so much the more comfortable to the Eye." You see this Gentleman *was a Connoisseur. In vain I endeavoured to support your character against the Charge; he knew what he felt, and could*

11/13 From a letter to John Baskerville by Benjamin Franklin dated London, 1760:

Let me give you a pleasant Instance of the Prejudice some have entertained against your Work. Soon after I returned, discoursing with a Gentleman concerning the Artists of Birmingham, he said you would [be] a Means of blinding all the Readers in the Nation; for the Strokes of your Letters, being too thin and narrow, hurt the Eye, and he could never read a Line of them without Pain. "I thought," said I, "you were going to complain of the Gloss of the Paper, *some object to." "No, it Is in the Form and Cut of the Letters themselves; they have not that height and Thick-*

10/12 From a letter to John Baskerville by Benjamin Franklin dated London, 1760:

Let me give you a pleasant Instance of the Prejudice some have entertained against your Work. Soon after I returned, discoursing with a Gentleman concerning the Artists of Birmingham, he said you would [be] a Means of blinding all the Readers in the Nation; for the Strokes of your Letters, being too thin and narrow, hurt the Eye, and he could never read a Line of them without Pain. "I thought," said I, "you were going to complain of the Gloss of the Paper, some object to." "No, it Is in the Form and Cut of the Letters themselves; they have not that height and Thickness of the *Stroke, which make the common Printing so much the more comfortable to the Eye." You see this Gentleman was a*

11/15 From a letter to John Baskerville by Benjamin Franklin dated London, 1760:

Let me give you a pleasant Instance of the Prejudice some have entertained against your Work. Soon after I returned, discoursing with a Gentleman concerning the Artists of Birmingham, he said you would [be] a Means of blinding all the Readers in the Nation; for the Strokes of your Letters, being too thin and narrow, *hurt the Eye, and he could never read a Line of them without Pain. "I thought," said I, "you were going*

10/14 From a letter to John Baskerville by Benjamin Franklin dated London, 1760:

Let me give you a pleasant Instance of the Prejudice some have entertained against your Work. Soon after I returned, discoursing with a Gentleman concerning the Artists of Birmingham, he said you would [be] a Means of blinding all the Readers in the Nation; for the Strokes of your Letters, being too thin and narrow, hurt the Eye, and he could never read a Line of them without Pain. "I thought," said I, "you were going to *complain of the Gloss of the Paper, some object to." "No, it Is in the Form and Cut of the Letters themselves; they have not*

CASLON NO. 540   MERGENTHALER TYPE LIBRARY

ABCDEFGHIJKLMNOPQRSTUVWXYZ
ABCDEFGHIJKLMNOPQRSTUVWXYZ
&.,''-:;!?"" 1234567890$
&.,''-:;!?"" 1234567890$
abcdefghijklmnopqrstuvwxyz
abcdefghijklmnopqrstuvwxyz

ABCDEFGHIJKLMNOPQRSTUVWXYZ
ABCDEFGHIJKLMNOPQRSTUVWXYZ
&.,''-:;!?"" 1234567890$
&.,''-:;!?"" 1234567890$
abcdefghijklmnopqrstuvwxyz
abcdefghijklmnopqrstuvwxyz

9/9 From a letter to John Baskerville by Benjamin Franklin dated London, 1760:
Let me give you a pleasant Instance of the Prejudice some have entertained against your Work. Soon after I returned, discoursing with a Gentleman concerning the Artists of Birmingham, he said you would [be] a Means of blinding all the Readers in the Nation; for the Strokes of your Letters, being too thin and narrow, hurt the Eye, and he could never read a Line of them without Pain. "I thought," said I, "you were going to complain of the Gloss of the Paper, some object to." "No, it Is in the Form and Cut of the Letters themselves; they have not that height and Thickness of the Stroke, which make the common Printing so much the more comfortable to the Eye." You see this Gentleman was a *Connoisseur*. In vain I endeavoured to support your character against the Charge; he knew what he felt, and could see the Reason of it, and several other Gentlemen among his Friends had made the same Observation, etc.
Yesterday he called to visit me, when, mischievously bent to try his Judgment, I stept into my Closet, tore off the Top of the capitals, thus

8/8 From a letter to John Baskerville by Benjamin Franklin dated London, 1760:
Let me give you a pleasant Instance of the Prejudice some have entertained against your Work. Soon after I returned, discoursing with a Gentleman concerning the Artists of Birmingham, he said you would [be] a Means of blinding all the Readers in the Nation; for the Strokes of your Letters, being too thin and narrow, hurt the Eye, and he could never read a Line of them without Pain. "I thought," said I, "you were going to complain of the Gloss of the Paper, some object to." "No, it Is in the Form and Cut of the Letters themselves; they have not that height and Thickness of the Stroke, which make the common Printing so much the more comfortable to the Eye." You see this Gentleman was a *Connoisseur*. In vain I endeavoured to support your character against the Charge; he knew what he felt, and could see the Reason of it, and several other Gentlemen among his Friends had made the same Observation, etc.
Yesterday he called to visit me, when, mischievously bent to try his Judgment, I stept into my Closet, tore off the Top of the capitals, thus giving it a disturbing appearance, then presenting to copy to be closely reviewed by the Gentleman to see if the absence of the upper serifs had any affect in his judgement of easily read print. The effect of this change is such that a person looking at the serifs could easily be said to

9/11 From a letter to John Baskerville by Benjamin Franklin dated London, 1760:
Let me give you a pleasant Instance of the Prejudice some have entertained against your Work. Soon after I returned, discoursing with a Gentleman concerning the Artists of Birmingham, he said you would [be] a Means of blinding all the Readers in the Nation; for the Strokes of your Letters, being too thin and narrow, hurt the Eye, and he could never read a Line of them without Pain. "I thought," said I, "you were going to complain of the Gloss of the Paper, some object to." "No, it Is in the Form and Cut of the Letters themselves; they have not that height and Thickness of the Stroke, which make the common Printing so much the more comfortable to the Eye." You see this Gentleman was a *Connoisseur*. In vain I *endeavoured to support your character against the Charge; he knew what he felt, and could see the Reason of it, and several other*

8/10 From a letter to John Baskerville by Benjamin Franklin dated London, 1760:
Let me give you a pleasant Instance of the Prejudice some have entertained against your Work. Soon after I returned, discoursing with a Gentleman concerning the Artists of Birmingham, he said you would [be] a Means of blinding all the Readers in the Nation; for the Strokes of your Letters, being too thin and narrow, hurt the Eye, and he could never read a Line of them without Pain. "I thought," said I, "you were going to complain of the Gloss of the Paper, some object to." "No, it Is in the Form and Cut of the Letters themselves; they have not that height and Thickness of the Stroke, which make the common Printing so much the more comfortable to the Eye." You see this Gentleman was a *Connoisseur*. In vain I endeavoured to support your character against the Charge; he knew what he felt, and could see the Reason of it, and several other Gentlemen among his Friends had made the same Observation, etc.
Yesterday he called to visit me, when, mischievously bent to try his Judgment, I stept into my Closet, tore off the Top of the capitals, thus giving it

9/13 From a letter to John Baskerville by Benjamin Franklin dated London, 1760:
Let me give you a pleasant Instance of the Prejudice some have entertained against your Work. Soon after I returned, discoursing with a Gentleman concerning the Artists of Birmingham, he said you would [be] a Means of blinding all the Readers in the Nation; for the Strokes of your Letters, being too thin and narrow, hurt the Eye, and he could never read a Line of them without Pain. "I thought," said I, "you were going to complain of the Gloss of the Paper, some object to." "No, it Is in the Form and Cut of the Letters themselves; *they have not that height and Thickness of the Stroke, which make the common Printing so much the more comfortable to the Eye." You*

8/12 From a letter to John Baskerville by Benjamin Franklin dated London, 1760:
Let me give you a pleasant Instance of the Prejudice some have entertained against your Work. Soon after I returned, discoursing with a Gentleman concerning the Artists of Birmingham, he said you would [be] a Means of blinding all the Readers in the Nation; for the Strokes of your Letters, being too thin and narrow, hurt the Eye, and he could never read a Line of them without Pain. "I thought," said I, "you were going to complain of the Gloss of the Paper, some object to." "No, it Is in the Form and Cut of the Letters themselves; they have not that height and Thickness of the Stroke, which make the common Printing so much the more comfortable to the Eye." You see *this Gentleman was a Connoisseur. In vain I endeavoured to support your character against the Charge; he knew what he felt, and could see the Reason*

CASLON NO. 540   MERGENTHALER TYPE LIBRARY

ABCDEFGHIJKLMNOPQRSTUVWXYZ
ABCDEFGHIJKLMNOPQRSTUVWXYZ
&.,"-:;!?""1234567890$
&.,"-:;!?""1234567890$
abcdefghijklmnopqrstuvwxyz
abcdefghijklmnopqrstuvwxyz

ABCDEFGHIJKLMNOPQRSTUVWXYZ
ABCDEFGHIJKLMNOPQRSTUVWXYZ
&.,"-:;!?""1234567890$
&.,"-:;!?""1234567890$
abcdefghijklmnopqrstuvwxyz
abcdefghijklmnopqrstuvwxyz

ABCDEFGHIJ
KLMNOPQRS
TUVWXYZ&a
bcdefghijklmn
opqrstuvwxyz
1234567890$.,
"".,;!?

72 POINT CASLON NO. 224** MEDIUM   MERGENTHALER TYPE LIBRARY

ABCDEFGHIJ
KLMNOPQRS
TUVWXYZ&a
bcdefghijklmn
opqrstuvwxyz
1234567890$.,
" ".;!?

72 POINT CASLON NO. 224** MEDIUM ITALIC   MERGENTHALER TYPE LIBRARY

ABCDEFGHIJKLMNOPQRSTUVWXYZ&abcdefghijklmnopqrstuvwxyz1234567890$."";!?

48 POINT CASLON NO. 224** MEDIUM   MERGENTHALER TYPE LIBRARY

ABCDEFGHIJKLMNOPQRSTUVWXYZ&abcdefghijklmnopqrstuvwxyz1234567890$.,"";!?

48 POINT CASLON NO. 224** MEDIUM ITALIC   MERGENTHALER TYPE LIBRARY

ABCDEFGHIJKLMNOPQRSTUVWXYZ&abcdefghijklmnopqrstuvwxyz1234567890$."";!?

24 POINT CASLON NO. 224** MEDIUM   MERGENTHALER TYPE LIBRARY

ABCDEFGHIJKLMNOPQRSTUVWXYZ&abcdefghijklmnopqrstuvwxyz1234567890$.,"":;!?

24 POINT CASLON NO. 224** MEDIUM ITALIC   MERGENTHALER TYPE LIBRARY

14/14

From a letter to John Baskerville by Benjamin Franklin dated London, 1760:

Let me give you a pleasant Instance of the Prejudice some have entertained against your Work. Soon after I returned, discoursing with a Gentleman concerning the Artists of Birmingham, he said you would [be] a Means of blinding all the Readers in the Nation; for the Strokes of your *Letters, being too thin and narrow, hurt the Eye, and he could never*

14/16

From a letter to John Baskerville by Benjamin Franklin dated London, 1760:

Let me give you a pleasant Instance of the Prejudice some have entertained against your Work. Soon after I returned, discoursing with a Gentleman concerning the Artists of Birmingham, he said you would [be] *a Means of blinding all the Readers in the Nation; for the Strokes of your*

14/18

From a letter to John Baskerville by Benjamin Franklin dated London, 1760:

Let me give you a pleasant Instance of the Prejudice some have entertained against your Work. Soon after I returned, discoursing with a *Gentleman concerning the Artists of Birmingham, he said you would*

12/12

From a letter to John Baskerville by Benjamin Franklin dated London, 1760:

Let me give you a pleasant Instance of the Prejudice some have entertained against your Work. Soon after I returned, discoursing with a Gentleman concerning the Artists of Birmingham, he said you would [be] a Means of blinding all the Readers in the Nation; for the Strokes of your Letters, being too thin and narrow, hurt the Eye, and he could never read a Line of them without Pain. "I thought," said I, "you were going to complain of the Gloss of the Paper, *some object to." "No, it Is in the Form and Cut of the Letters themselves; they have*

12/14

From a letter to John Baskerville by Benjamin Franklin dated London, 1760:

Let me give you a pleasant Instance of the Prejudice some have entertained against your Work. Soon after I returned, discoursing with a Gentleman concerning the Artists of Birmingham, he said you would [be] a Means of blinding all the Readers in the Nation; for the Strokes of your Letters, being too thin and narrow, hurt the *Eye, and he could never read a Line of them without Pain. "I thought," said I,*

12/16

From a letter to John Baskerville by Benjamin Franklin dated London, 1760:

Let me give you a pleasant Instance of the Prejudice some have entertained against your Work. Soon after I returned, discoursing with a Gentleman concerning the Artists of Birmingham, he said you would [be] a Means of blinding all the Readers in the Nation; for the Strokes of your *Letters, being too thin and narrow, hurt*

ITC CASLON NO. 224** MEDIUM   MERGENTHALER TYPE LIBRARY

ABCDEFGHIJKLMNOPQRSTUVW
ABCDEFGHIJKLMNOPQRSTUVW
XYZ&.,"-:;!?""1234567890$
XYZ&.,"-:;!?""1234567890$
abcdefghijklmnopqrstuvwxyz
abcdefghijklmnopqrstuvwxyz

ABCDEFGHIJKLMNOPQRSTUVWXYZ
ABCDEFGHIJKLMNOPQRSTUVWXYZ
&.,"-:;!?""1234567890$
&.,"-:;!?""1234567890$
abcdefghijklmnopqrstuvwxyz
abcdefghijklmnopqrstuvwxyz

CASLON FAMILY 151

10/10 From a letter to John Baskerville by Benjamin Franklin dated London, 1760:

Let me give you a pleasant Instance of the Prejudice some have entertained against your Work. Soon after I returned, discoursing with a Gentleman concerning the Artists of Birmingham, he said you would [be] a Means of blinding all the Readers in the Nation; for the Strokes of your Letters, being too thin and narrow, hurt the Eye, and he could never read a Line of them without Pain. "I thought," said I, "you were going to complain of the Gloss of the Paper, some object to." "No, it Is in the Form and Cut of the Letters themselves; they have not that height and Thickness of the Stroke, which make the common Printing so much the more comfortable to *the Eye." You see this Gentleman was a Connoisseur. In vain I endeavoured to support your*

10/12 From a letter to John Baskerville by Benjamin Franklin dated London, 1760:

Let me give you a pleasant Instance of the Prejudice some have entertained against your Work. Soon after I returned, discoursing with a Gentleman concerning the Artists of Birmingham, he said you would [be] a Means of blinding all the Readers in the Nation; for the Strokes of your Letters, being too thin and narrow, hurt the Eye, and he could never read a Line of them without Pain. "I thought," said I, "you were going to complain of the Gloss of the Paper, some object to." "No, it Is in the Form and Cut of the Letters themselves; they have not that *height and Thickness of the Stroke, which make the common Printing so much the more comfort-*

10/14 From a letter to John Baskerville by Benjamin Franklin dated London, 1760:

Let me give you a pleasant Instance of the Prejudice some have entertained against your Work. Soon after I returned, discoursing with a Gentleman concerning the Artists of Birmingham, he said you would [be] a Means of blinding all the Readers in the Nation; for the Strokes of your Letters, being too thin and narrow, hurt the Eye, and he could never read a Line of them without Pain. "I thought," said I, *I, "you were going to complain of the Gloss of the Paper, some object to." "No, it Is in the Form and*

8/8 From a letter to John Baskerville by Benjamin Franklin dated London, 1760:

Let me give you a pleasant Instance of the Prejudice some have entertained against your Work. Soon after I returned, discoursing with a Gentleman concerning the Artists of Birmingham, he said you would [be] a Means of blinding all the Readers in the Nation; for the Strokes of your Letters, being too thin and narrow, hurt the Eye, and he could never read a Line of them without Pain. "I thought," said I, "you were going to complain of the Gloss of the Paper, some object to." "No, it Is in the Form and Cut of the Letters themselves; they have not that height and Thickness of the Stroke, which make the common Printing so much the more comfortable to the Eye." You see this Gentleman was a *Connoisseur. In vain I endeavoured to support your character against the Charge; he knew what he felt, and could see the Reason of it, and several other Gentlemen among his Friends had made the same Observation, etc.*
Yesterday he called to visit me, when, mischievously bent to try his Judgment, I stept into my Closet, tore off the Top of the capitals, thus giving it a disturbing appearance, then presenting the copy to be reviewed by the Gentleman to see if the absence of the upper serifs had any affect in his judgement of easily read

8/10 From a letter to John Baskerville by Benjamin Franklin dated London, 1760:

Let me give you a pleasant Instance of the Prejudice some have entertained against your Work. Soon after I returned, discoursing with a Gentleman concerning the Artists of Birmingham, he said you would [be] a Means of blinding all the Readers in the Nation; for the Strokes of your Letters, being too thin and narrow, hurt the Eye, and he could never read a Line of them without Pain. "I thought," said I, "you were going to complain of the Gloss of the Paper, some object to." "No, it Is in the Form and Cut of the Letters themselves; they have not that height and Thickness of the Stroke, which make the common Printing so much the more comfortable to the Eye." You see this Gentleman was a *Connoisseur. In vain I endeavoured to support your character against the Charge; he knew what he felt, and could see the Reason of it, and several other Gentlemen among his Friends had made the same Observation, etc.*
Yesterday he called to visit me, when, mischievously bent to

8/12 From a letter to John Baskerville by Benjamin Franklin dated London, 1760:

Let me give you a pleasant Instance of the Prejudice some have entertained against your Work. Soon after I returned, discoursing with a Gentleman concerning the Artists of Birmingham, he said you would [be] a Means of blinding all the Readers in the Nation; for the Strokes of your Letters, being too thin and narrow, hurt the Eye, and he could never read a Line of them without Pain. "I thought," said I, "you were going to complain of the Gloss of the Paper, some object to." "No, it Is in the Form and Cut of the Letters themselves; they have not that height and Thickness of the Stroke, which make the common Printing so much the more *comfortable to the Eye." You see this Gentleman was a Connoisseur. In vain I endeavoured to support your character*

ITC CASLON NO. 224** MEDIUM   MERGENTHALER TYPE LIBRARY

ABCDEFGHIJKLMNOPQRSTUVWXYZ
ABCDEFGHIJKLMNOPQRSTUVWXYZ
&.,"-:;!?""1234567890$
&.,"-:;!?""1234567890$
abcdefghijklmnopqrstuvwxyz
abcdefghijklmnopqrstuvwxyz

ABCDEFGHIJKLMNOPQRSTUVWXYZ
ABCDEFGHIJKLMNOPQRSTUVWXYZ
&.,"-:;!?""1234567890$
&.,"-:;!?""1234567890$
abcdefghijklmnopqrstuvwxyz
abcdefghijklmnopqrstuvwxyz

ABCDEFGHIJ
KLMNOPQRS
TUVWXYZ&a
bcdefghijklmn
opqrstuvwxyz
1234567890$
.,"":;!?

72 POINT CASLON NO. 224** BOLD   MERGENTHALER TYPE LIBRARY

ABCDEFGHIJ
KLMNOPQRS
TUVWXYZ&a
bcdefghijklmn
opqrstuvwxyz
1234567890$
.,"":;!?

72 POINT CASLON NO. 224** BOLD ITALIC   MERGENTHALER TYPE LIBRARY

ABCDEFGHIJKLMNOPQRSTUVWXYZ&abcdefghijklmnopqrstuvwxyz1234567890$";!?

48 POINT CASLON NO. 224** BOLD   MERGENTHALER TYPE LIBRARY

ABCDEFGHIJKLMNOPQRSTUVWXYZ&abcdefghijklmnopqrstuvwxyz1234567890$.,"";!?

48 POINT CASLON NO. 224** BOLD ITALIC   MERGENTHALER TYPE LIBRARY

ABCDEFGHIJKLMNOPQRSTUVWXYZ&abcdefghijklmnopqrstuvwxyz1234567890$"";!?

24 POINT CASLON NO. 224** BOLD   MERGENTHALER TYPE LIBRARY

ABCDEFGHIJKLMNOPQRSTUVWXYZ&abcdefghijklmnopqrstuvwxyz1234567890$.,"";!?

24 POINT CASLON NO. 224** BOLD ITALIC   MERGENTHALER TYPE LIBRARY

14/14 From a letter to John Baskerville by Benjamin Franklin dated London, 1760:

Let me give you a pleasant Instance of the Prejudice some have entertained against your Work. Soon after I returned, discoursing with a Gentleman concerning the Artists of Birmingham, he said you would [be] a Means of blinding all the Readers in the Nation; for the Strokes of your *Letters, being too thin and narrow, hurt the Eye, and he could never*

12/12 From a letter to John Baskerville by Benjamin Franklin dated London, 1760:

Let me give you a pleasant Instance of the Prejudice some have entertained against your Work. Soon after I returned, discoursing with a Gentleman concerning the Artists of Birmingham, he said you would [be] a Means of blinding all the Readers in the Nation; for the Strokes of your Letters, being too thin and narrow, hurt the Eye, and he could never read a Line of them without Pain. "I thought," said I, "you were going to complain of the Gloss of the Paper, *some object to." "No, it Is in the Form and Cut of the Letters themselves; they*

14/16 From a letter to John Baskerville by Benjamin Franklin dated London, 1760:

Let me give you a pleasant Instance of the Prejudice some have entertained against your Work. Soon after I returned, discoursing with a Gentleman concerning the Artists of Birmingham, he said you would [be] *a Means of blinding all the Readers in the Nation; for the Strokes of*

12/14 From a letter to John Baskerville by Benjamin Franklin dated London, 1760:

Let me give you a pleasant Instance of the Prejudice some have entertained against your Work. Soon after I returned, discoursing with a Gentleman concerning the Artists of Birmingham, he said you would [be] a Means of blinding all the Readers in the Nation; for the Strokes of your Letters, being too thin and narrow, hurt the Eye, *and he could never read a Line of them without Pain. "I thought," said I, "you*

14/18 From a letter to John Baskerville by Benjamin Franklin dated London, 1760:

Let me give you a pleasant Instance of the Prejudice some have entertained against your Work. Soon after I returned, discoursing with a *Gentleman concerning the Artists of Birmingham, he said you would*

12/16 From a letter to John Baskerville by Benjamin Franklin dated London, 1760:

Let me give you a pleasant Instance of the Prejudice some have entertained against your Work. Soon after I returned, discoursing with a Gentleman concerning the Artists of Birmingham, he said you would [be] a Means of blinding all the Readers in the *Nation; for the Strokes of your Letters, being too thin and narrow, hurt the Eye,*

ITC CASLON NO. 224** BOLD   MERGENTHALER TYPE LIBRARY

ABCDEFGHIJKLMNOPQRSTUVW
ABCDEFGHIJKLMNOPQRSTUVW
XYZ&.,"-:;!?""1234567890$
XYZ&.,"-:;!?""1234567890$
abcdefghijklmnopqrstuvwxyz
abcdefghijklmnopqrstuvwxyz

ABCDEFGHIJKLMNOPQRSTUVWXYZ
ABCDEFGHIJKLMNOPQRSTUVWXYZ
&.,"-:;!?""1234567890$
&.,"-:;!?""1234567890$
abcdefghijklmnopqrstuvwxyz
abcdefghijklmnopqrstuvwxyz

10/10 From a letter to John Baskerville by Benjamin Franklin dated London, 1760:

Let me give you a pleasant Instance of the Prejudice some have entertained against your Work. Soon after I returned, discoursing with a Gentleman concerning the Artists of Birmingham, he said you would [be] a Means of blinding all the Readers in the Nation; for the Strokes of your Letters, being too thin and narrow, hurt the Eye, and he could never read a Line of them without Pain. "I thought," said I, "you were going to complain of the Gloss of the Paper, some object to." "No, it Is in the Form and Cut of the Letters themselves; they have not that height and Thickness of the Stroke, which make the common Printing so much the more comfortable to the Eye." *You see this Gentleman was a Connoisseur. In vain I endeavoured to support*

10/12 From a letter to John Baskerville by Benjamin Franklin dated London, 1760:

Let me give you a pleasant Instance of the Prejudice some have entertained against your Work. Soon after I returned, discoursing with a Gentleman concerning the Artists of Birmingham, he said you would [be] a Means of blinding all the Readers in the Nation; for the Strokes of your Letters, being too thin and narrow, hurt the Eye, and he could never read a Line of them without Pain. "I thought," said I, "you were going to complain of the Gloss of the Paper, some object to." "No, it Is in the Form and Cut of the Letters themselves; they have *not that height and Thickness of the Stroke, which make the common Printing so much the more*

10/14 From a letter to John Baskerville by Benjamin Franklin dated London, 1760:

Let me give you a pleasant Instance of the Prejudice some have entertained against your Work. Soon after I returned, discoursing with a Gentleman concerning the Artists of Birmingham, he said you would [be] a Means of blinding all the Readers in the Nation; for the Strokes of your Letters, being too thin and narrow, hurt the Eye, and he could never read a Line of them without Pain. "I *thought," said I, "you were going to complain of the Gloss of the Paper, some object to." "No, it Is*

8/8 From a letter to John Baskerville by Benjamin Franklin dated London, 1760:

Let me give you a pleasant Instance of the Prejudice some have entertained against your Work. Soon after I returned, discoursing with a Gentleman concerning the Artists of Birmingham, he said you would [be] a Means of blinding all the Readers in the Nation; for the Strokes of your Letters, being too thin and narrow, hurt the Eye, and he could never read a Line of them without Pain. "I thought," said I, "you were going to complain of the Gloss of the Paper, some object to." "No, it is in the Form and Cut of the Letters themselves; they have not that height and Thickness of the Stroke, which make the common Printing so much the more comfortable to the Eye." You see this Gentleman was a *Connoisseur.* In vain I endeavoured to support your character against the Charge; he knew what he felt, and could see the Reason of it, and several other Gentlemen among his Friends had made the same Observation, etc.

Yesterday he called to visit me, when, mischievously bent to try his Judgment, I stept into my Closet, tore off the Top of the capitals, thus giving it a disturbing appearance, then presenting *to copy to be reviewed by the Gentleman to see if the absence of the upper serifs had any affect in his judgement of easily read*

8/10 From a letter to John Baskerville by Benjamin Franklin dated London, 1760:

Let me give you a pleasant Instance of the Prejudice some have entertained against your Work. Soon after I returned, discoursing with a Gentleman concerning the Artists of Birmingham, he said you would [be] a Means of blinding all the Readers in the Nation; for the Strokes of your Letters, being too thin and narrow, hurt the Eye, and he could never read a Line of them without Pain. "I thought," said I, "you were going to complain of the Gloss of the Paper, some object to." "No, it Is in the Form and Cut of the Letters themselves; they have not that height and Thickness of the Stroke, which make the common Printing so much the more comfortable to the Eye." You see this Gentleman was a *Connoisseur.* In vain I endeavoured to support your character against the Charge; he knew what he felt, and could see the Reason of it, and several other Gentlemen among his Friends *made the same Observation, etc.*

Yesterday he called to visit me, when, mischievously bent to

8/12 From a letter to John Baskerville by Benjamin Franklin dated London, 1760:

Let me give you a pleasant Instance of the Prejudice some have entertained against your Work. Soon after I returned, discoursing with a Gentleman concerning the Artists of Birmingham, he said you would [be] a Means of blinding all the Readers in the Nation; for the Strokes of your Letters, being too thin and narrow, hurt the Eye, and he could never read a Line of them without Pain. "I thought," said I, "you were going to complain of the Gloss of the Paper, some object to." "No, it Is in the Form and Cut of the Letters themselves; they have not that height and Thickness of the Stroke, which make the common Printing so much the more *comfortable to the Eye." You see this Gentleman was a Connoisseur. In vain I endeavoured to support your character*

ITC CASLON NO. 224** BOLD   MERGENTHALER TYPE LIBRARY

ABCDEFGHIJKLMNOPQRSTUVWXYZ
ABCDEFGHIJKLMNOPQRSTUVWXYZ
&.,"-:;!?""1234567890$
&.,"-:;!?""*1234567890$*
abcdefghijklmnopqrstuvwxyz
abcdefghijklmnopqrstuvwxyz

ABCDEFGHIJKLMNOPQRSTUVWXYZ
ABCDEFGHIJKLMNOPQRSTUVWXYZ
&.,"-:;!?""1234567890$
&.,"-:;!?""*1234567890$*
abcdefghijklmnopqrstuvwxyz
abcdefghijklmnopqrstuvwxyz

ABCDEFGHIJ KLMNOPQRS TUVWXYZ&a bcdefghijklmn opqrstuvwxyz 1234567890$.,"";;!?

72 POINT CASLON NO. 224** BLACK   MERGENTHALER TYPE LIBRARY

ABCDEFGHIJKLMNOPQRSTUVWXYZ&a bcdefghijklmnopqrstuvwxyz 1234567890$.,""";:!?

72 POINT CASLON NO. 224** BLACK ITALIC   MERGENTHALER TYPE LIBRARY

ABCDEFGHIJKLMNOPQRSTUVWXYZ&a bcdefghijklmnopqrstuvwxyz1234567890$. ,"";:!?

24 POINT CASLON NO. 224** BLACK   MERGENTHALER TYPE LIBRARY

ABCDEFGHIJKLMN
OPQRSTUVWXYZ&
abcdefghijklmnopqrs
tuvwxyz1234567890
$.,'""：；!?

48 POINT CASLON NO. 224** BLACK   MERGENTHALER TYPE LIBRARY

ABCDEFGHIJKLMN
OPQRSTUVWXYZ&
abcdefghijklmnopqrs
tuvwxyz1234567890
$.,'""：；!?

48 POINT CASLON NO. 224** BLACK ITALIC   MERGENTHALER TYPE LIBRARY

ABCDEFGHIJKLMNOPQRSTUVWXYZ&a
bcdefghijklmnopqrstuvwxyz1234567890$
.,'"":;!?

24 POINT CASLON NO. 224** BLACK ITALIC   MERGENTHALER TYPE LIBRARY

14/14 From a letter to John Baskerville by Mr. Benjamin Franklin dated London, 1760:

Let me give you a pleasant Instance of the Prejudice some have entertained against your Work. Soon after I returned, discoursing with a Gentleman concerning the Artists of Birmingham, he said you would [be] a Means of blinding all the Readers in the Nation; for the *Strokes of your Letters, being too thin and narrow, hurt the Eye,*

14/16 From a letter to John Baskerville by Mr. Benjamin Franklin dated London, 1760:

Let me give you a pleasant Instance of the Prejudice some have entertained against your Work. Soon after I returned, discoursing with a Gentleman concerning the Artists of Birmingham, he said you *would [be] a Means of blinding all the Readers in the Nation; for the*

14/18 From a letter to John Baskerville by Mr. Benjamin Franklin dated London, 1760:

Let me give you a pleasant Instance of the Prejudice some have entertained against your Work. Soon after I returned, discoursing *with a Gentleman concerning the Artists of Birmingham, he said*

12/12 From a letter to John Baskerville by Benjamin Franklin dated London, 1760:

Let me give you a pleasant Instance of the Prejudice some have entertained against your Work. Soon after I returned, discoursing with a Gentleman concerning the Artists of Birmingham, he said you would [be] a Means of blinding all the Readers in the Nation; for the Strokes of your Letters, being too thin and narrow, hurt the Eye, and he could never read a Line of them without Pain. "I thought," said I, "you were going to *complain of the Gloss of the Paper, some object to." "No, it Is in the Form and Cut*

12/14 From a letter to John Baskerville by Benjamin Franklin dated London, 1760:

Let me give you a pleasant Instance of the Prejudice some have entertained against your Work. Soon after I returned, discoursing with a Gentleman concerning the Artists of Birmingham, he said you would [be] a Means of blinding all the Readers in the Nation; for the Strokes of your Letters, being too thin *and narrow, hurt the Eye, and he could never read a Line of them without Pain.*

12/16 From a letter to John Baskerville by Benjamin Franklin dated London, 1760:

Let me give you a pleasant Instance of the Prejudice some have entertained against your Work. Soon after I returned, discoursing with a Gentleman concerning the Artists of Birmingham, he said you would [be] a Means of blinding all the Readers in the Nation; for the *Strokes of your Letters, being too thin*

ITC CASLON NO. 224** BLACK   MERGENTHALER TYPE LIBRARY

ABCDEFGHIJKLMNOPQRSTUV
ABCDEFGHIJKLMNOPQRSTUV
WXYZ&.,"-:;!?""1234567890$
WXYZ&.,"-:;!?""1234567890$
abcdefghijklmnopqrstuvwxyz
abcdefghijklmnopqrstuvwxyz

ABCDEFGHIJKLMNOPQRSTUVWXYZ
ABCDEFGHIJKLMNOPQRSTUVWXYZ
&.,"-:;!?""1234567890$
&.,"-:;!?""1234567890$
abcdefghijklmnopqrstuvwxyz
abcdefghijklmnopqrstuvwxyz

CASLON FAMILY

10/10 From a letter to John Baskerville by Benjamin Franklin dated London, 1760:

Let me give you a pleasant Instance of the Prejudice some have entertained against your Work. Soon after I returned, discoursing with a Gentleman concerning the Artists of Birmingham, he said you would [be] a Means of blinding all the Readers in the Nation; for the Strokes of your Letters, being too thin and narrow, hurt the Eye, and he could never read a Line of them without Pain. "I thought," said I, "you were going to complain of the Gloss of the Paper, some object to." "No, it Is in the Form and Cut of the Letters themselves; they have not that height and Thickness of the Stroke, which make the common *Printing so much the more comfortable to the Eye." You see this Gentleman was a Connois-*

8/8 From a letter to John Baskerville by Benjamin Franklin dated London, 1760:

Let me give you a pleasant Instance of the Prejudice some have entertained against your Work. Soon after I returned, discoursing with a Gentleman concerning the Artists of Birmingham, he said you would [be] a Means of blinding all the Readers in the Nation; for the Strokes of your Letters, being too thin and narrow, hurt the Eye, and he could never read a Line of them without Pain. "I thought," said I, "you were going to complain of the Gloss of the Paper, some object to." "No, it Is in the Form and Cut of the Letters themselves; they have not that height and Thickness of the Stroke, which make the common Printing so much the more comfortable to the Eye." You see this Gentleman was a *Connoisseur.* In vain I endeavoured to support your character against the Charge; he knew what he felt, and could see the Reason of it, and several other Gentlemen among his Friends had made the same Observation, etc.

Yesterday he called to visit me, when, mischievously bent to try his Judgment, I stept into my Closet, tore off the Top of the *capitals, thus giving it a disturbing appearance, then presenting to copy to be reviewed by the Gentleman to see if the*

10/12 From a letter to John Baskerville by Benjamin Franklin dated London, 1760:

Let me give you a pleasant Instance of the Prejudice some have entertained against your Work. Soon after I returned, discoursing with a Gentleman concerning the Artists of Birmingham, he said you would [be] a Means of blinding all the Readers in the Nation; for the Strokes of your Letters, being too thin and narrow, hurt the Eye, and he could never read a Line of them without Pain. "I thought," said I, "you were going to complain of the Gloss of the Paper, some object to." "No, it Is in the Form and Cut of the Letters *themselves; they have not that height and Thickness of the Stroke, which make the common*

8/10 From a letter to John Baskerville by Benjamin Franklin dated London, 1760:

Let me give you a pleasant Instance of the Prejudice some have entertained against your Work. Soon after I returned, discoursing with a Gentleman concerning the Artists of Birmingham, he said you would [be] a Means of blinding all the Readers in the Nation; for the Strokes of your Letters, being too thin and narrow, hurt the Eye, and he could never read a Line of them without Pain. "I thought," said I, "you were going to complain of the Gloss of the Paper, some object to." "No, it Is in the Form and Cut of the Letters themselves; they have not that height and Thickness of the Stroke, which make the common Printing so much the more comfortable to the Eye." You see this Gentleman was a *Connoisseur.* In vain I endeavoured to support your character against the Charge; he knew what he felt, and could see the Reason of it, and several *other Gentlemen among his Friends had made the same Observation, etc.*

10/14 From a letter to John Baskerville by Benjamin Franklin dated London, 1760:

Let me give you a pleasant Instance of the Prejudice some have entertained against your Work. Soon after I returned, discoursing with a Gentleman concerning the Artists of Birmingham, he said you would [be] a Means of blinding all the Readers in the Nation; for the Strokes of your Letters, being too thin and narrow, hurt the Eye, and he could never read a Line of them without Pain. *"I thought," said I, "you were going to complain of the Gloss of the Paper, some object*

8/12 From a letter to John Baskerville by Benjamin Franklin dated London, 1760:

Let me give you a pleasant Instance of the Prejudice some have entertained against your Work. Soon after I returned, discoursing with a Gentleman concerning the Artists of Birmingham, he said you would [be] a Means of blinding all the Readers in the Nation; for the Strokes of your Letters, being too thin and narrow, hurt the Eye, and he could never read a Line of them without Pain. "I thought," said I, "you were going to complain of the Gloss of the Paper, some object to." "No, it Is in the Form and Cut of the Letters themselves; they have not that height and Thickness of the Stroke, which make *the common Printing so much the more comfortable to the Eye." You see this Gentleman was a Connoisseur. In vain I*

ITC CASLON NO. 224** BLACK   MERGENTHALER TYPE LIBRARY

ABCDEFGHIJKLMNOPQRSTUVWXYZ
ABCDEFGHIJKLMNOPQRSTUVWXYZ
&.,"-:;!?'""1234567890$
&.,"-:;!?'""1234567890$
abcdefghijklmnopqrstuvwxyz
abcdefghijklmnopqrstuvwxyz

ABCDEFGHIJKLMNOPQRSTUVWXYZ
ABCDEFGHIJKLMNOPQRSTUVWXYZ
&.,"-:;!?'""1234567890$
&.,"-:;!?'""1234567890$
abcdefghijklmnopqrstuvwxyz
abcdefghijklmnopqrstuvwxyz

ABCDEFGHIJK
LMNOPQRST
UVWXYZ&abcde
fghijklmnopqrstuv
wxyz1234567890$.,
"".;!?

72 POINT CASLON ANTIQUE   MERGENTHALER TYPE LIBRARY

ABCDEFGHIJK LMNOPQRST UVWXYZ&abcd efghijklmnopqrstuv wxyz1234567890$.,"":;!?

72 POINT CASLON ANTIQUE ITALIC   MERGENTHALER TYPE LIBRARY

ABCDEFGHIJKLMNOP
QRSTUVWXYZ&abcdefg
hijklmnopqrstuvwxyz1234567
890$.,"":;!?

48 POINT CASLON ANTIQUE   MERGENTHALER TYPE LIBRARY

ABCDEFGHIJKLMNOP
QRSTUVWXYZ&abcdef
ghijklmnopqrstuvwxyz123456
7890$.,"":;!?

48 POINT CASLON ANTIQUE ITALIC   MERGENTHALER TYPE LIBRARY

ABCDEFGHIJKLMNOPQRSTUVWXYZ&abcd
efghijklmnopqrstuvwxyz1234567890$.,"":;!?

24 POINT CASLON ANTIQUE   MERGENTHALER TYPE LIBRARY

ABCDEFGHIJKLMNOPQRSTUVWXYZ&abcd
efghijklmnopqrstuvwxyz1234567890$.,"":;!?

24 POINT CASLON ANTIQUE ITALIC   MERGENTHALER TYPE LIBRARY

CASLON FAMILY 165

14/14 From a letter to John Baskerville by Benjamin Franklin dated London, 1760:

Let me give you a pleasant Instance of the Prejudice some have entertained against your Work. Soon after I returned, discoursing with a Gentleman concerning the Artists of Birmingham, he said you would [be] a Means of blinding all the Readers in the Nation; for the Strokes of your Letters, being too thin and narrow, hurt the Eye, and he could never read a Line of them without Pain. *"I thought," said I, "you were going to complain of the Gloss of the Paper, some*

14/16 From a letter to John Baskerville by Benjamin Franklin dated London, 1760:

Let me give you a pleasant Instance of the Prejudice some have entertained against your Work. Soon after I returned, discoursing with a Gentleman concerning the Artists of Birmingham, he said you would [be] a Means of blinding all the Readers in the Nation; for the Strokes of your Letters, *being too thin and narrow, hurt the Eye, and he could never read a Line of them without*

14/18 From a letter to John Baskerville by Benjamin Franklin dated London, 1760:

Let me give you a pleasant Instance of the Prejudice some have entertained against your Work. Soon after I returned, discoursing with a Gentleman concerning the Artists of Birmingham, he said you would *[be] a Means of blinding all the Readers in the Nation; for the Strokes of your Letters,*

12/12 From a letter to John Baskerville by Benjamin Franklin dated London, 1760:

Let me give you a pleasant Instance of the Prejudice some have entertained against your Work. Soon after I returned, discoursing with a Gentleman concerning the Artists of Birmingham, he said you would [be] a Means of blinding all the Readers in the Nation; for the Strokes of your Letters, being too thin and narrow, hurt the Eye, and he could never read a Line of them without Pain. "I thought," said I, "you were going to complain of the Gloss of the Paper, some object to." "No, it Is in the Form and Cut of the Letters *themselves; they have not that height and Thickness of the Stroke, which make the common Printing so*

12/14 From a letter to John Baskerville by Benjamin Franklin dated London, 1760:

Let me give you a pleasant Instance of the Prejudice some have entertained against your Work. Soon after I returned, discoursing with a Gentleman concerning the Artists of Birmingham, he said you would [be] a Means of blinding all the Readers in the Nation; for the Strokes of your Letters, being too thin and narrow, hurt the Eye, and he could never read a Line of them without Pain. *"I thought," said I, "you were going to complain of the Gloss of the Paper, some object to."*

12/16 From a letter to John Baskerville by Benjamin Franklin dated London, 1760:

Let me give you a pleasant Instance of the Prejudice some have entertained against your Work. Soon after I returned, discoursing with a Gentleman concerning the Artists of Birmingham, he said you would [be] a Means of blinding all the Readers in the Nation; for the Strokes of your *Letters, being too thin and narrow, hurt the Eye, and he could never read a Line of them without Pain. "I*

CASLON ANTIQUE   MERGENTHALER TYPE LIBRARY

ABCDEFGHIJKLMNOPQRSTUVW
ABCDEFGHIJKLMNOPQRSTUVW
XYZ&.,"-:;!?""1234567890$
XYZ&.,"-:;!?""1234567890$
abcdefghijklmnopqrstuvwxyz
abcdefghijklmnopqrstuvwxyz

ABCDEFGHIJKLMNOPQRSTUVWXYZ
ABCDEFGHIJKLMNOPQRSTUVWXYZ
&.,"-:;!?""1234567890$
&.,"-:;!?""1234567890$
abcdefghijklmnopqrstuvwxyz
abcdefghijklmnopqrstuvwxyz

10/10 From a letter to John Baskerville by Benjamin Franklin dated London, 1760:

Let me give you a pleasant Instance of the Prejudice some have entertained against your Work. Soon after I returned, discoursing with a Gentleman concerning the Artists of Birmingham, he said you would [be] a Means of blinding all the Readers in the Nation; for the Strokes of your Letters, being too thin and narrow, hurt the Eye, and he could never read a Line of them without Pain. "I thought," said I, "you were going to complain of the Gloss of the Paper, some object to." "No, it Is in the Form and Cut of the Letters themselves; they have not that height and Thickness of the Stroke, which make the common Printing so much the more comfortable to the Eye." You see this Gentleman was a *Connoisseur*. *In vain I endeavoured to support your character against the Charge; he knew what he felt, and could see the Reason of it, and several other Gentlemen among his Friends*

10/12 From a letter to John Baskerville by Benjamin Franklin dated London, 1760:

Let me give you a pleasant Instance of the Prejudice some have entertained against your Work. Soon after I returned, discoursing with a Gentleman concerning the Artists of Birmingham, he said you would [be] a Means of blinding all the Readers in the Nation; for the Strokes of your Letters, being too thin and narrow, hurt the Eye, and he could never read a Line of them without Pain. "I thought," said I, "you were going to complain of the Gloss of the Paper, some object to." "No, it Is in the Form and Cut of the Letters themselves; they have not that height and Thickness of the Stroke, which make the common Printing so much the more *comfortable to the Eye." You see this Gentleman was a Connoisseur. In vain I endeavoured to support your character*

10/14 From a letter to John Baskerville by Benjamin Franklin dated London, 1760:

Let me give you a pleasant Instance of the Prejudice some have entertained against your Work. Soon after I returned, discoursing with a Gentleman concerning the Artists of Birmingham, he said you would [be] a Means of blinding all the Readers in the Nation; for the Strokes of your Letters, being too thin and narrow, hurt the Eye, and he could never read a Line of them without Pain. "I thought," said I, "you were going to complain of the Gloss of the Paper, some *object to." "No, it Is in the Form and Cut of the Letters themselves; they have not that height and Thickness of the*

8/8 From a letter to John Baskerville by Benjamin Franklin dated London, 1760:

Let me give you a pleasant Instance of the Prejudice some have entertained against your Work. Soon after I returned, discoursing with a Gentleman concerning the Artists of Birmingham, he said you would [be] a Means of blinding all the Readers in the Nation; for the Strokes of your Letters, being too thin and narrow, hurt the Eye, and he could never read a Line of them without Pain. "I thought," said I, "you were going to complain of the Gloss of the Paper, some object to." "No, it Is in the Form and Cut of the Letters themselves; they have not that height and Thickness of the Stroke, which make the common Printing so much the more comfortable to the Eye." You see this Gentleman was a *Connoisseur*. In vain I endeavoured to support your character against the Charge; he knew what he felt, and could see the Reason of it, and several other Gentlemen among his Friends had made the same Observation, etc.

Yesterday he called to visit me, when, mischievously bent to try his Judgment, I stept into my Closet, tore off the Top of the capitals, thus giving it a disturbing appearance, then presenting to copy to be reviewed by the Gentleman to see if the absence of the upper serifs had any affect in his judgement of easily read print. The effect of this change is such that a person looking at the serifs could find the line disturbing to the viewer. The effect of *this change is so considerable, that a learned man who reads for his enjoyment could no longer comprehend the printed word without stopping to*

8/10 From a letter to John Baskerville by Benjamin Franklin dated London, 1760:

Let me give you a pleasant Instance of the Prejudice some have entertained against your Work. Soon after I returned, discoursing with a Gentleman concerning the Artists of Birmingham, he said you would [be] a Means of blinding all the Readers in the Nation; for the Strokes of your Letters, being too thin and narrow, hurt the Eye, and he could never read a Line of them without Pain. "I thought," said I, "you were going to complain of the Gloss of the Paper, some object to." "No, it Is in the Form and Cut of the Letters themselves; they have not that height and Thickness of the Stroke, which make the common Printing so much the more comfortable to the Eye." You see this Gentleman was a *Connoisseur*. In vain I endeavoured to support your character against the Charge; he knew what he felt, and could see the Reason of it, and several other Gentlemen among his Friends had made the same Observation, etc.

Yesterday he called to visit me, when, mischievously bent to try his Judgment, I stept into my Closet, tore off the Top of the capitals, thus *giving it a disturbing appearance, then presenting to copy to be reviewed by the Gentleman to see if the absence of the upper serifs had any affect in his*

8/12 From a letter to John Baskerville by Benjamin Franklin dated London, 1760:

Let me give you a pleasant Instance of the Prejudice some have entertained against your Work. Soon after I returned, discoursing with a Gentleman concerning the Artists of Birmingham, he said you would [be] a Means of blinding all the Readers in the Nation; for the Strokes of your Letters, being too thin and narrow, hurt the Eye, and he could never read a Line of them without Pain. "I thought," said I, "you were going to complain of the Gloss of the Paper, some object to." "No, it Is in the Form and Cut of the Letters themselves; they have not that height and Thickness of the Stroke, which make the common Printing so much the more comfortable to the Eye." You see this Gentleman was a *Connoisseur*. In vain I endeavoured to support your character against the Charge; he knew what he felt, and could *see the Reason of it, and several other Gentlemen among his Friends had made the same Observation, etc.*

CASLON ANTIQUE   MERGENTHALER TYPE LIBRARY

ABCDEFGHIJKLMNOPQRSTUVWXYZ
ABCDEFGHIJKLMNOPQRSTUVWXYZ
&.,"-:;!?""1234567890$
&.,"-:;!?""1234567890$
abcdefghijklmnopqrstuvwxyz
abcdefghijklmnopqrstuvwxyz

ABCDEFGHIJKLMNOPQRSTUVWXYZ
ABCDEFGHIJKLMNOPQRSTUVWXYZ
&.,"-:;!?""1234567890$
&.,"-:;!?""1234567890$
abcdefghijklmnopqrstuvwxyz
abcdefghijklmnopqrstuvwxyz

ABCDEFGHIJ
KLMNOPQRS
TUVWXYZ&
abcdefghijklmnopq
rstuvwxyz123456
7890$.,""";:!?

72 POINT CASLON OPEN FACE   MERGENTHALER TYPE LIBRARY

ABCDEFGHIJKLMN
OPQRSTUVWXYZ&
abcdefghijklmnopqrstuvwxyz
1234567890$.,""";:!?

48 POINT CASLON OPEN FACE   MERGENTHALER TYPE LIBRARY

14/14 From a letter to John Baskerville by Benjamin Franklin dated London, 1760:

Let me give you a pleasant Instance of the Prejudice some have entertained against your Work. Soon after I returned, discoursing with a Gentleman concerning the Artists of Birmingham, he said you would [be] a Means of blinding all the Readers in the Nation; for the Strokes of your Letters, being too thin and narrow, hurt the Eye, and he could never read a Line of them without Pain. "I thought," said I, "you were going to complain of the

12/12 From a letter to John Baskerville by Benjamin Franklin dated London, 1760:

Let me give you a pleasant Instance of the Prejudice some have entertained against your Work. Soon after I returned, discoursing with a Gentleman concerning the Artists of Birmingham, he said you would [be] a Means of blinding all the Readers in the Nation; for the Strokes of your Letters, being too thin and narrow, hurt the Eye, and he could never read a Line of them without Pain. "I thought," said I, "you were going to complain of the Gloss of the Paper, some object to." "No, it Is in the Form and Cut of the Letters themselves; they have not that height and Thickness of the Stroke, which make the

14/16 From a letter to John Baskerville by Benjamin Franklin dated London, 1760:

Let me give you a pleasant Instance of the Prejudice some have entertained against your Work. Soon after I returned, discoursing with a Gentleman concerning the Artists of Birmingham, he said you would [be] a Means of blinding all the Readers in the Nation; for the Strokes of your Letters, being too thin and narrow, hurt the Eye, and he could never read a

12/14 From a letter to John Baskerville by Benjamin Franklin dated London, 1760:

Let me give you a pleasant Instance of the Prejudice some have entertained against your Work. Soon after I returned, discoursing with a Gentleman concerning the Artists of Birmingham, he said you would [be] a Means of blinding all the Readers in the Nation; for the Strokes of your Letters, being too thin and narrow, hurt the Eye, and he could never read a Line of them without Pain. "I thought," said I, "you were going to complain of the Gloss of the Paper,

14/18 From a letter to John Baskerville by Benjamin Franklin dated London, 1760:

Let me give you a pleasant Instance of the Prejudice some have entertained against your Work. Soon after I returned, discoursing with a Gentleman concerning the Artists of Birmingham, he said you would [be] a Means of blinding all the Readers in the Nation; for the Strokes of

12/16 From a letter to John Baskerville by Benjamin Franklin dated London, 1760:

Let me give you a pleasant Instance of the Prejudice some have entertained against your Work. Soon after I returned, discoursing with a Gentleman concerning the Artists of Birmingham, he said you would [be] a Means of blinding all the Readers in the Nation; for the Strokes of your Letters, being too thin and narrow, hurt the Eye, and he could never read a Line

CASLON OPEN FACE   MERGENTHALER TYPE LIBRARY

ABCDEFGHIJKLMNOPQRSTUVWXYZ
&.,"-:;!?""1234567890$
abcdefghijklmnopqrstuvwxyz

ABCDEFGHIJKLMNOPQRSTUVWXYZ
&.,"-:;!?""1234567890$
abcdefghijklmnopqrstuvwxyz

CASLON FAMILY

10/10 From a letter to John Baskerville by Benjamin Franklin dated London, 1760:

Let me give you a pleasant Instance of the Prejudice some have entertained against your Work. Soon after I returned, discoursing with a Gentleman concerning the Artists of Birmingham, he said you would [be] a Means of blinding all the Readers in the Nation; for the Strokes of your Letters, being too thin and narrow, hurt the Eye, and he could never read a Line of them without Pain. "I thought," said I, "you were going to complain of the Gloss of the Paper, some object to." "No, it Is in the Form and Cut of the Letters themselves; they have not that height and Thickness of the Stroke, which make the common Printing so much the more comfortable to the Eye." You see this Gentleman was a Connoisseur. In vain I endeavoured to support your character against the Charge; he knew what he felt, and could see the Reason of it, and several other

8/8 From a letter to John Baskerville by Benjamin Franklin dated London, 1760:

Let me give you a pleasant Instance of the Prejudice some have entertained against your Work. Soon after I returned, discoursing with a Gentleman concerning the Artists of Birmingham, he said you would [be] a Means of blinding all the Readers in the Nation; for the Strokes of your Letters, being too thin and narrow, hurt the Eye, and he could never read a Line of them without Pain. "I thought," said I, "you were going to complain of the Gloss of the Paper, some object to." "No, it Is in the Form and Cut of the Letters themselves; they have not that height and Thickness of the Stroke, which make the common Printing so much the more comfortable to the Eye." You see this Gentleman was a Connoisseur. In vain I endeavoured to support your character against the Charge; he knew what he felt, and could see the Reason of it, and several other Gentlemen among his Friends had made the same Observation, etc.

Yesterday he called to visit me, when, mischievously bent to try his Judgment, I stept into my Closet, tore off the Top of the capitals, thus giving it a disturbing appearance, then presenting to copy to be reviewed by the Gentleman to see if the absence of the upper serifs had any affect in his judgement of easily read print. The effect of this change is such that a person looking at the serifs could find the line disturbing to the viewer. The effect of this change is so considerable, that a learned man who reads

10/12 From a letter to John Baskerville by Benjamin Franklin dated London, 1760:

Let me give you a pleasant Instance of the Prejudice some have entertained against your Work. Soon after I returned, discoursing with a Gentleman concerning the Artists of Birmingham, he said you would [be] a Means of blinding all the Readers in the Nation; for the Strokes of your Letters, being too thin and narrow, hurt the Eye, and he could never read a Line of them without Pain. "I thought," said I, "you were going to complain of the Gloss of the Paper, some object to." "No, it Is in the Form and Cut of the Letters themselves; they have not that height and Thickness of the Stroke, which make the common Printing so much the more comfortable to the Eye." You see this Gentleman was a Connoisseur. In vain I endeavoured to

8/10 From a letter to John Baskerville by Benjamin Franklin dated London, 1760:

Let me give you a pleasant Instance of the Prejudice some have entertained against your Work. Soon after I returned, discoursing with a Gentleman concerning the Artists of Birmingham, he said you would [be] a Means of blinding all the Readers in the Nation; for the Strokes of your Letters, being too thin and narrow, hurt the Eye, and he could never read a Line of them without Pain. "I thought," said I, "you were going to complain of the Gloss of the Paper, some object to." "No, it Is in the Form and Cut of the Letters themselves; they have not that height and Thickness of the Stroke, which make the common Printing so much the more comfortable to the Eye." You see this Gentleman was a Connoisseur. In vain I endeavoured to support your character against the Charge; he knew what he felt, and could see the Reason of it, and several other Gentlemen among his Friends had made the same Observation, etc.

Yesterday he called to visit me, when, mischievously bent to try his Judgment, I stept into my Closet, tore off the Top of the capitals, thus giving it a disturbing appearance, then presenting to copy to be reviewed by

10/14 From a letter to John Baskerville by Benjamin Franklin dated London, 1760:

Let me give you a pleasant Instance of the Prejudice some have entertained against your Work. Soon after I returned, discoursing with a Gentleman concerning the Artists of Birmingham, he said you would [be] a Means of blinding all the Readers in the Nation; for the Strokes of your Letters, being too thin and narrow, hurt the Eye, and he could never read a Line of them without Pain. "I thought," said I, "you were going to complain of the Gloss of the Paper, some object to." "No, it Is in the Form and Cut of the Letters themselves; they have not that height and

8/12 From a letter to John Baskerville by Benjamin Franklin dated London, 1760:

Let me give you a pleasant Instance of the Prejudice some have entertained against your Work. Soon after I returned, discoursing with a Gentleman concerning the Artists of Birmingham, he said you would [be] a Means of blinding all the Readers in the Nation; for the Strokes of your Letters, being too thin and narrow, hurt the Eye, and he could never read a Line of them without Pain. "I thought," said I, "you were going to complain of the Gloss of the Paper, some object to." "No, it Is in the Form and Cut of the Letters themselves; they have not that height and Thickness of the Stroke, which make the common Printing so much the more comfortable to the Eye." You see this Gentleman was a Connoisseur. In vain I endeavoured to support your character against the Charge; he knew what he felt, and could see the Reason of it, and several other Gentlemen

CASLON OPEN FACE   MERGENTHALER TYPE LIBRARY

ABCDEFGHIJKLMNOPQRSTUVWXYZ
&.,"-:;!?""1234567890$
abcdefghijklmnopqrstuvwxyz

ABCDEFGHIJKLMNOPQRSTUVWXYZ
&.,"-:;!?""1234567890$
abcdefghijklmnopqrstuvwxyz

M
476

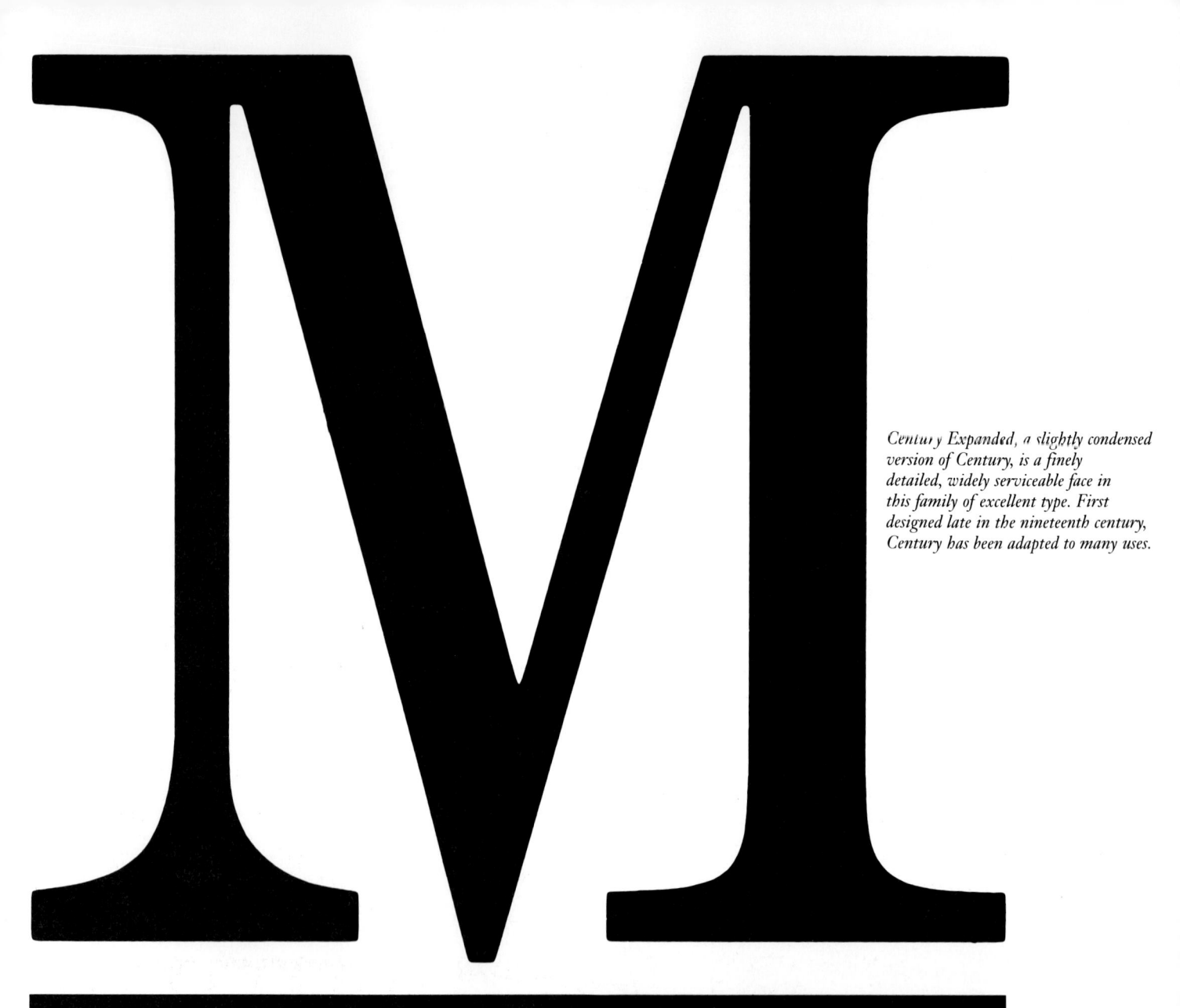

Century Expanded, a slightly condensed version of Century, is a finely detailed, widely serviceable face in this family of excellent type. First designed late in the nineteenth century, Century has been adapted to many uses.

CENTURY FAMILY 171

gesfar

ABCDEFGHI
JKLMNOPQR
STUVWXYZ&
abcdefghijklmn
opqrstuvwxyz
1234567890$.,"
"..!?
.,;:

72 POINT CG CENTURY EXPANDED   AGFA COMPUGRAPHIC TYPE LIBRARY

ABCDEFGHI
JKLMNOPQR
STUVWXYZ&
abcdefghijklmn
opqrstuvwxyz
1234567890$.,"
"".,!?

ABCDEFGHIJKL
MNOPQRSTUVW
XYZ&abcdefghijkl
mnopqrstuvwxyz12
34567890$.,"":;!?

60 POINT CENTURY EXPANDED   MERGENTHALER TYPE LIBRARY

ABCDEFGHIJKL
MNOPQRSTUVW
XYZ&abcdefghijkl
mnopqrstuvwxyz12
34567890$.,"":;!?

60 POINT CENTURY EXPANDED ITALIC   MERGENTHALER TYPE LIBRARY

ABCDEFGHIJKLMNO
PQRSTUVWXYZ&abc
defghijklmnopqrstuvwx
yz1234567890$.,""":;!?

48 POINT CENTURY EXPANDED   MERGENTHALER TYPE LIBRARY

ABCDEFGHIJKLMNO
PQRSTUVWXYZ&abc
defghijklmnopqrstuvwx
yz1234567890$.,""":;!?

48 POINT CENTURY EXPANDED ITALIC   MERGENTHALER TYPE LIBRARY

ABCDEFGHIJKLMNOPQRS
TUVWXYZ&abcdefghijklmno
pqrstuvwxyz1234567890$.,""";:!?

36 POINT CENTURY EXPANDED   MERGENTHALER TYPE LIBRARY

ABCDEFGHIJKLMNOPQRS
TUVWXYZ&abcdefghijklmno
pqrstuvwxyz1234567890$.,""";:!?

36 POINT CENTURY EXPANDED ITALIC   MERGENTHALER TYPE LIBRARY

ABCDEFGHIJKLMNOPQRSTUVWXYZ&a
bcdefghijklmnopqrstuvwxyz1234567890$.,""";:
!?

24 POINT CENTURY EXPANDED   MERGENTHALER TYPE LIBRARY

ABCDEFGHIJKLMNOPQRSTUVWXYZ&a
bcdefghijklmnopqrstuvwxyz1234567890$.,""";:
!?

24 POINT CENTURY EXPANDED ITALIC   MERGENTHALER TYPE LIBRARY

ABCDEFGHIJKLMNOPQRSTUVWXYZ&abcdefghijklmno
pqrstuvwxyz1234567890$.,""";:!?

18 POINT CENTURY EXPANDED   MERGENTHALER TYPE LIBRARY

ABCDEFGHIJKLMNOPQRSTUVWXYZ&abcdefghijklmno
pqrstuvwxyz1234567890$.,""";:!?

18 POINT CENTURY EXPANDED ITALIC   MERGENTHALER TYPE LIBRARY

CENTURY FAMILY

14/14 From a letter by Benjamin Franklin to B. Vaughan Esq. dated April 21, 1785:

If the Irish can manufacture cottons, stuffs and silks, and linens, and cutlery, and toys, and books etc. etc. etc., so as to sell them cheaper in England than the *manufacturers* of England sell them, is not this good for the people of England who are not *manufacturers? and will not even the manufacturers themselves share the benefit? Since if cottons are cheaper,*

14/16 From a letter by Benjamin Franklin to B. Vaughan Esq. dated April 21, 1785:

If the Irish can manufacture cottons, stuffs and silks, and linens, and cutlery, and toys, and books etc. etc. etc., so as to sell them cheaper in England than the *manufacturers* of England sell them, is not this good for *the people of England who are not manufacturers? and will not even the*

14/18 From a letter by Benjamin Franklin to B. Vaughan Esq. dated April 21, 1785:

If the Irish can manufacture cottons, stuffs and silks, and linens, and cutlery, and toys, and books etc. etc. etc., so as to sell them cheaper in *England than the manufacturers of England sell them, is not this good*

12/12 From a letter by Benjamin Franklin to B. Vaughan Esq. dated April 21, 1785:

If the Irish can manufacture cottons, stuffs and silks, and linens, and cutlery, and toys, and books etc. etc. etc., so as to sell them cheaper in England than the *manufacturers* of England sell them, is not this good for the people of England who are not *manufacturers?* and will not even the manufacturers themselves share the benefit? Since if cottons are cheaper, all the other manufacturers who wear cottons will save in that article, and so of the rest. If books *can be had much cheaper from Ireland, (which I believe for I bought Blackstone*

12/14 From a letter by Benjamin Franklin to B. Vaughan Esq. dated April 21, 1785:

If the Irish can manufacture cottons, stuffs and silks, and linens, and cutlery, and toys, and books etc. etc. etc., so as to sell them cheaper in England than the *manufacturers* of England sell them, is not this good for the people of England who are not *manufacturers?* and will not even the manufacturers themselves share the benefit? *Since if cottons are cheaper, all the other manufacturers who wear cottons will save*

12/16 From a letter by Benjamin Franklin to B. Vaughan Esq. dated April 21, 1785:

If the Irish can manufacture cottons, stuffs and silks, and linens, and cutlery, and toys, and books etc. etc. etc., so as to sell them cheaper in England than the *manufacturers* of England sell them, is not this good for the people of England who are not *manufacturers? and will not even the manufacturers themselves share the benefit?*

CENTURY EXPANDED   MERGENTHALER TYPE LIBRARY

ABCDEFGHIJKLMNOPQRSTUV
ABCDEFGHIJKLMNOPQRSTUV
WXYZ&.,"-:;!?""1234567890$
WXYZ&.,"-:;!?""1234567890$
abcdefghijklmnopqrstuvwxyz
abcdefghijklmnopqrstuvwxyz

ABCDEFGHIJKLMNOPQRSTUVW
ABCDEFGHIJKLMNOPQRSTUVW
XYZ&.,"-:;!?""1234567890$
XYZ&.,"-:;!?""1234567890$
abcdefghijklmnopqrstuvwxyz
abcdefghijklmnopqrstuvwxyz

CENTURY FAMILY 177

11/11 From a letter by Benjamin Franklin to B. Vaughan Esq. dated April 21, 1785:

If the Irish can manufacture cottons, stuffs and silks, and linens, and cutlery, and toys, and books etc. etc. etc., so as to sell them cheaper in England than the *manufacturers* of England sell them, is not this good for the people of England who are not *manufacturers*? and will not even the manufacturers themselves share the benefit? Since if cottons are cheaper, all the other manufacturers who wear cottons will save in that article, and so of the rest. If books can be had much cheaper from Ireland, (which I believe for I bought Blackstone there for 24/- when *it was sold in England at four guineas) is not this an advantage not to English booksellers*

10/10 From a letter by Benjamin Franklin to B. Vaughan Esq. dated April 21, 1785:

If the Irish can manufacture cottons, stuffs and silks, and linens, and cutlery, and toys, and books etc. etc. etc., so as to sell them cheaper in England than the *manufacturers* of England sell them, is not this good for the people of England who are not *manufacturers*? and will not even the manufacturers themselves share the benefit? Since if cottons are cheaper, all the other manufacturers who wear cottons will save in that article, and so of the rest. If books can be had much cheaper from Ireland, (which I believe for I bought Blackstone there for 24/- when it was sold in England at four guineas) is not this an advantage not to English booksellers indeed, but to *English readers and to learning. And of all the complaints perhaps these booksellers are least*

11/13 From a letter by Benjamin Franklin to B. Vaughan Esq. dated April 21, 1785:

If the Irish can manufacture cottons, stuffs and silks, and linens, and cutlery, and toys, and books etc. etc. etc., so as to sell them cheaper in England than the *manufacturers* of England sell them, is not this good for the people of England who are not *manufacturers*? and will not even the manufacturers themselves share the benefit? Since if cottons are cheaper, all the other manufacturers who wear cottons will save in that article, and so of the rest. If books can be *had much cheaper from Ireland, (which I believe for I bought Blackstone there for 24/- when*

10/12 From a letter by Benjamin Franklin to B. Vaughan Esq. dated April 21, 1785:

If the Irish can manufacture cottons, stuffs and silks, and linens, and cutlery, and toys, and books etc. etc. etc., so as to sell them cheaper in England than the *manufacturers* of England sell them, is not this good for the people of England who are not *manufacturers*? and will not even the manufacturers themselves share the benefit? Since if cottons are cheaper, all the other manufacturers who wear cottons will save in that article, and so of the rest. If books can be had much cheaper from Ireland, (which I believe for I bought Blackstone there for 24/- when *it was sold in England at four guineas) is not this an advantage not to English booksellers indeed, but to*

11/15 From a letter by Benjamin Franklin to B. Vaughan Esq. dated April 21, 1785:

If the Irish can manufacture cottons, stuffs and silks, and linens, and cutlery, and toys, and books etc. etc. etc., so as to sell them cheaper in England than the *manufacturers* of England sell them, is not this good for the people of England who are not *manufacturers*? and will not even the manufacturers themselves share *the benefit? Since if cottons are cheaper, all the other manufacturers who wear cottons will save*

10/14 From a letter by Benjamin Franklin to B. Vaughan Esq. dated April 21, 1785:

If the Irish can manufacture cottons, stuffs and silks, and linens, and cutlery, and toys, and books etc. etc. etc., so as to sell them cheaper in England than the *manufacturers* of England sell them, is not this good for the people of England who are not *manufacturers*? and will not even the manufacturers themselves share the benefit? Since if cottons are cheaper, all the other manufacturers who wear cot*tons will save in that article, and so of the rest. If books can be had much cheaper from Ireland,*

CENTURY EXPANDED   MERGENTHALER TYPE LIBRARY

ABCDEFGHIJKLMNOPQRSTUVWXYZ
ABCDEFGHIJKLMNOPQRSTUVWXYZ
&.,"-:;!?""1234567890$
&.,"-:;!?""1234567890$
abcdefghijklmnopqrstuvwxyz
abcdefghijklmnopqrstuvwxyz

ABCDEFGHIJKLMNOPQRSTUVWXYZ
ABCDEFGHIJKLMNOPQRSTUVWXYZ
&.,"-:;!?""1234567890$
&.,"-:;!?""1234567890$
abcdefghijklmnopqrstuvwxyz
abcdefghijklmnopqrstuvwxyz

9/9 From a letter by Benjamin Franklin to B. Vaughan Esq. dated April 21, 1785:

If the Irish can manufacture cottons, stuffs and silks, and linens, and cutlery, and toys, and books etc. etc. etc., so as to sell them cheaper in England than the *manufacturers* of England sell them, is not this good for the people of England who are not *manufacturers*? and will not even the manufacturers themselves share the benefit? Since if cottons are cheaper, all the other manufacturers who wear cottons will save in that article, and so of the rest. If books can be had much cheaper from Ireland, (which I believe for I bought Blackstone there for 24/- when it was sold in England at four guineas) is not this an advantage not to English booksellers indeed, but to English readers and to learning. And of all the complaints perhaps these booksellers are least worthy of consideration. The catalogue you last sent me amazes me by the high prices (said to be the lowest) affixed to each article. And one can scarce see a *new book, without observing the excessive artifices may use of to puff up a paper of verses into a pamphlet, a*

8/8 From a letter by Benjamin Franklin to B. Vaughan Esq. dated April 21, 1785:

If the Irish can manufacture cottons, stuffs and silks, and linens, and cutlery, and toys, and books etc. etc. etc., so as to sell them cheaper in England than the *manufacturers* of England sell them, is not this good for the people of England who are not *manufacturers*? and will not even the manufacturers themselves share the benefit? Since if cottons are cheaper, all the other manufacturers who wear cottons will save in that article, and so of the rest. If books can be had much cheaper from Ireland, (which I believe for I bought Blackstone there for 24/- when it was sold in England at four guineas) is not this an advantage not to English booksellers indeed, but to English readers and to learning. And of all the complaints perhaps these booksellers are least worthy of consideration. The catalogue you last sent me amazes me by the high prices (said to be the lowest) affixed to each article. And one can scarce see a new book, without observing the excessive artifices may use of to puff up a paper of verses into a pamphlet, a pamphlet into an octavo, and an octavo into a quarto, with scab boardings, white lines, sparse titles of chapters, and exorbitant *margins, to such a degree, that the selling of paper seems now the object and printing on it only the pretence. I enclose the copy of a*

9/11 From a letter by Benjamin Franklin to B. Vaughan Esq. dated April 21, 1785:

If the Irish can manufacture cottons, stuffs and silks, and linens, and cutlery, and toys, and books etc. etc. etc., so as to sell them cheaper in England than the *manufacturers* of England sell them, is not this good for the people of England who are not *manufacturers*? and will not even the manufacturers themselves share the benefit? Since if cottons are cheaper, all the other manufacturers who wear cottons will save in that article, and so of the rest. If books can be had much cheaper from Ireland, (which I believe for I bought Blackstone there for 24/- when it was sold in England at four guineas) is not this an advantage not to English booksellers indeed, but to English readers and to *learning. And of all the complaints perhaps these booksellers are least worthy of consideration. The catalogue*

8/10 From a letter by Benjamin Franklin to B. Vaughan Esq. dated April 21, 1785:

If the Irish can manufacture cottons, stuffs and silks, and linens, and cutlery, and toys, and books etc. etc. etc., so as to sell them cheaper in England than the *manufacturers* of England sell them, is not this good for the people of England who are not *manufacturers*? and will not even the manufacturers themselves share the benefit? Since if cottons are cheaper, all the other manufacturers who wear cottons will save in that article, and so of the rest. If books can be had much cheaper from Ireland, (which I believe for I bought Blackstone there for 24/- when it was sold in England at four guineas) is not this an advantage not to English booksellers indeed, but to English readers and to learning. And of all the complaints perhaps these booksellers are least worthy of consideration. The catalogue you last sent me amazes me by the high prices (said to be the lowest) affixed to each article. And one *can scarce see a new book, without observing the excessive artifices may use of to puff up a paper of verses into a pamphlet, a*

9/13 From a letter by Benjamin Franklin to B. Vaughan Esq. dated April 21, 1785:

If the Irish can manufacture cottons, stuffs and silks, and linens, and cutlery, and toys, and books etc. etc. etc., so as to sell them cheaper in England than the *manufacturers* of England sell them, is not this good for the people of England who are not *manufacturers*? and will not even the manufacturers themselves share the benefit? Since if cottons are cheaper, all the other manufacturers who wear cottons will save in that article, and so of the rest. If books can be had much cheaper from Ireland, (which I believe for *I bought Blackstone there for 24/- when it was sold in England at four guineas) is not this an advantage not to*

8/12 From a letter by Benjamin Franklin to B. Vaughan Esq. dated April 21, 1785:

If the Irish can manufacture cottons, stuffs and silks, and linens, and cutlery, and toys, and books etc. etc. etc., so as to sell them cheaper in England than the *manufacturers* of England sell them, is not this good for the people of England who are not *manufacturers*? and will not even the manufacturers themselves share the benefit? Since if cottons are cheaper, all the other manufacturers who wear cottons will save in that article, and so of the rest. If books can be had much cheaper from Ireland, (which I believe for I bought Blackstone there for 24/- when it was sold in England at four guineas) is not this an advantage not to English *booksellers indeed, but to English readers and to learning. And of all the complaints perhaps these booksellers are least worthy of*

CENTURY EXPANDED   MERGENTHALER TYPE LIBRARY

ABCDEFGHIJKLMNOPQRSTUVWXYZ
ABCDEFGHIJKLMNOPQRSTUVWXYZ
&.,"-:;!?""1234567890$
&.,"-:;!?""1234567890$
abcdefghijklmnopqrstuvwxyz
abcdefghijklmnopqrstuvwxyz

ABCDEFGHIJKLMNOPQRSTUVWXYZ
ABCDEFGHIJKLMNOPQRSTUVWXYZ
&.,"-:;!?""1234567890$
&.,"-:;!?""1234567890$
abcdefghijklmnopqrstuvwxyz
abcdefghijklmnopqrstuvwxyz

ABCDEFGHIJK
LMNOPQRSTU
VWXYZ&abcde
fghijklmnopqrs
tuvwxyz12345
67890$.,''"":;!?

72 POINT ITC CENTURY LIGHT   AGFA COMPUGRAPHIC TYPE LIBRARY

CENTURY FAMILY

ABCDEFGHIJ
KLMNOPQRST
UVWXYZ&abc
defghijklmnop
qrstuvwxyz123
4567890$.,''""
.,!?

72 POINT ITC CENTURY LIGHT ITALIC AGFA COMPUGRAPHIC TYPE LIBRARY

ABCDEFGHIJKLMNOP
QRSTUVWXYZ&abcdef
ghijklmnopqrstuvwxyz1
234567890$.,""':;!?

48 POINT ITC CENTURY** LIGHT MERGENTHALER TYPE LIBRARY

ABCDEFGHIJKLMNOP
QRSTUVWXYZ&abcdef
ghijklmnopqrstuvwxyz
1234567890$.,""'':;!?

48 POINT ITC CENTURY** LIGHT ITALIC MERGENTHALER TYPE LIBRARY

ABCDEFGHIJKLMNOPQRSTUVWXYZ&abcdefg
hijklmnopqrstuvwxyz1234567890$.,""'':;!?

24 POINT ITC CENTURY** LIGHT MERGENTHALER TYPE LIBRARY

ABCDEFGHIJKLMNOPQRSTUVWXYZ&abcde
fghijklmnopqrstuvwxyz1234567890$.,""'':;!?

24 POINT ITC CENTURY** LIGHT ITALIC MERGENTHALER TYPE LIBRARY

14/14 From a letter by Benjamin Franklin to B. Vaughan Esq. dated April 21, 1785:
If the Irish can manufacture cottons, stuffs and silks, and linens, and cutlery, and toys, and books etc. etc. etc., so as to sell them cheaper in England than the *manufacturers* of England sell them, is not this good for the people of England who are not *manufacturers*? and will not even the manufacturers themselves share the benefit? Since if *cottons are cheaper, all the other manufacturers who wear cottons*

12/12 From a letter by Benjamin Franklin to B. Vaughan Esq. dated April 21, 1785:
If the Irish can manufacture cottons, stuffs and silks, and linens, and cutlery, and toys, and books etc. etc. etc., so as to sell them cheaper in England than the *manufacturers* of England sell them, is not this good for the people of England who are not *manufacturers*? and will not even the manufacturers themselves share the benefit? Since if cottons are cheaper, all the other manufacturers who wear cottons will save in that article, and so of the rest. If books can be had much cheaper from Ireland, *(which I believe for I bought Blackstone there for 24/- when it was sold in England*

14/16 From a letter by Benjamin Franklin to B. Vaughan Esq. dated April 21, 1785:
If the Irish can manufacture cottons, stuffs and silks, and linens, and cutlery, and toys, and books etc. etc. etc., so as to sell them cheaper in England than the *manufacturers* of England sell them, is not this good for the people of England who are not *manufacturers*? *and will not even the manufacturers themselves share the benefit? Since*

12/14 From a letter by Benjamin Franklin to B. Vaughan Esq. dated April 21, 1785:
If the Irish can manufacture cottons, stuffs and silks, and linens, and cutlery, and toys, and books etc. etc. etc., so as to sell them cheaper in England than the *manufacturers* of England sell them, is not this good for the people of England who are not *manufacturers*? and will not even the manufacturers themselves share the benefit? Since if cottons are cheaper, *all the other manufacturers who wear cottons will save in that article, and so of the*

14/18 From a letter by Benjamin Franklin to B. Vaughan Esq. dated April 21, 1785:
If the Irish can manufacture cottons, stuffs and silks, and linens, and cutlery, and toys, and books etc. etc. etc., so as to sell them cheaper in England than the *manufacturers* of England sell *them, is not this good for the people of England who are not manufactur-*

12/16 From a letter by Benjamin Franklin to B. Vaughan Esq. dated April 21, 1785:
If the Irish can manufacture cottons, stuffs and silks, and linens, and cutlery, and toys, and books etc. etc. etc., so as to sell them cheaper in England than the *manufacturers* of England sell them, is not this good for the people of England who are not *manufacturers*? and *will not even the manufacturers themselves share the benefit? Since if cottons*

ITC CENTURY** LIGHT   MERGENTHALER TYPE LIBRARY

ABCDEFGHIJKLMNOPQRSTUVW
ABCDEFGHIJKLMNOPQRSTUVW
XYZ&.,"-:;!?"" 1234567890$
XYZ&.,'-:;!?"" 1234567890$
abcdefghijklmnopqrstuvwxyz
abcdefghijklmnopqrstuvwxyz

ABCDEFGHIJKLMNOPQRSTUVWXYZ
ABCDEFGHIJKLMNOPQRSTUVWXYZ
&.,"-:;!?"" 1234567890$
&.,'-:;!?"" 1234567890$
abcdefghijklmnopqrstuvwxyz
abcdefghijklmnopqrstuvwxyz

CENTURY FAMILY 183

10/10 From a letter by Benjamin Franklin to B. Vaughan Esq. dated April 21, 1785:

If the Irish can manufacture cottons, stuffs and silks, and linens, and cutlery, and toys, and books etc. etc. etc., so as to sell them cheaper in England than the *manufacturers* of England sell them, is not this good for the people of England who are not *manufacturers*? and will not even the manufacturers themselves share the benefit? Since if cottons are cheaper, all the other manufacturers who wear cottons will save in that article, and so of the rest. If books can be had much cheaper from Ireland, (which I believe for I bought Blackstone there for 24/- when it was sold in England at four guineas) is not this an advantage not to English booksellers indeed, but to English readers *and to learning. And of all the complaints perhaps these booksellers are least worthy of consideration.*

8/8 From a letter by Benjamin Franklin to B. Vaughan Esq. dated April 21, 1785:

If the Irish can manufacture cottons, stuffs and silks, and linens, and cutlery, and toys, and books etc. etc. etc., so as to sell them cheaper in England than the *manufacturers* of England sell them, is not this good for the people of England who are not *manufacturers*? and will not even the manufacturers themselves share the benefit? Since if cottons are cheaper, all the other manufacturers who wear cottons will save in that article, and so of the rest. If books can be had much cheaper from Ireland, (which I believe for I bought Blackstone there for 24/- when it was sold in England at four guineas) is not this an advantage not to English booksellers indeed, but to English readers and to learning. And of all the complaints perhaps these booksellers are least worthy of consideration. The catalogue you last sent me amazes me by the high prices (said to be the lowest) affixed to each article. And one can scarce see a new book, without observing the excessive artifices may use of to puff up a paper of verses into a pamphlet, a pamphlet into an octavo, and an octavo into a quarto, with scab boardings, white lines, sparse titles of chapters, and exorbitant margins, to such a degree, that the selling *of paper seems now the object and printing on it only the pretence. I enclose the copy of a page in a late comedy. Between*

10/12 From a letter by Benjamin Franklin to B. Vaughan Esq. dated April 21, 1785:

If the Irish can manufacture cottons, stuffs and silks, and linens, and cutlery, and toys, and books etc. etc. etc., so as to sell them cheaper in England than the *manufacturers* of England sell them, is not this good for the people of England who are not *manufacturers*? and will not even the manufacturers themselves share the benefit? Since if cottons are cheaper, all the other manufacturers who wear cottons will save in that article, and so of the rest. If books can be had much cheaper from Ireland, (which I believe for I bought Blackstone there for 24/- when it was sold in *England at four guineas) is not this an advantage not to English booksellers indeed, but to English*

8/10 From a letter by Benjamin Franklin to B. Vaughan Esq. dated April 21, 1785:

If the Irish can manufacture cottons, stuffs and silks, and linens, and cutlery, and toys, and books etc. etc. etc., so as to sell them cheaper in England than the *manufacturers* of England sell them, is not this good for the people of England who are not *manufacturers*? and will not even the manufacturers themselves share the benefit? Since if cottons are cheaper, all the other manufacturers who wear cottons will save in that article, and so of the rest. If books can be had much cheaper from Ireland, (which I believe for I bought Blackstone there for 24/- when it was sold in England at four guineas) is not this an advantage not to English booksellers indeed, but to English readers and to learning. And of all the complaints perhaps these booksellers are least worthy of consideration. The catalogue you last sent me amazes me by the high prices (said to be the lowest) affixed to each article. And one can scarce see a new *book, without observing the excessive artifices may use of to puff up a paper of verses into a pamphlet, a pamphlet into an octavo,*

10/14 From a letter by Benjamin Franklin to B. Vaughan Esq. dated April 21, 1785:

If the Irish can manufacture cottons, stuffs and silks, and linens, and cutlery, and toys, and books etc. etc. etc., so as to sell them cheaper in England than the *manufacturers* of England sell them, is not this good for the people of England who are not *manufacturers*? and will not even the manufacturers themselves share the benefit? Since if cottons are cheaper, all the other manufacturers who wear cottons will save in *that article, and so of the rest. If books can be had much cheaper from Ireland, (which I believe for I*

8/12 From a letter by Benjamin Franklin to B. Vaughan Esq. dated April 21, 1785:

If the Irish can manufacture cottons, stuffs and silks, and linens, and cutlery, and toys, and books etc. etc. etc., so as to sell them cheaper in England than the *manufacturers* of England sell them, is not this good for the people of England who are not *manufacturers*? and will not even the manufacturers themselves share the benefit? Since if cottons are cheaper, all the other manufacturers who wear cottons will save in that article, and so of the rest. If books can be had much cheaper from Ireland, (which I believe for I bought Blackstone there for 24/- when it was sold in England at four guineas) is not this an advantage not to English booksellers indeed, *but to English readers and to learning. And of all the complaints perhaps these booksellers are least worthy of consideration. The*

ITC CENTURY** LIGHT   MERGENTHALER TYPE LIBRARY

ABCDEFGHIJKLMNOPQRSTUVWXYZ
ABCDEFGHIJKLMNOPQRSTUVWXYZ
&.,"-:;!?""1234567890$
&,"-:;!?""1234567890$
abcdefghijklmnopqrstuvwxyz
abcdefghijklmnopqrstuvwxyz

ABCDEFGHIJKLMNOPQRSTUVWXYZ
ABCDEFGHIJKLMNOPQRSTUVWXYZ
&.,"-:;!?""1234567890$
&,"-:;!?""1234567890$
abcdefghijklmnopqrstuvwxyz
abcdefghijklmnopqrstuvwxyz

ABCDEFGHIJ
KLMNOPQRST
UVWXYZ&abc
defghijklmnop
qrstuvwxyz12
34567890$.,''
'':;!?

72 POINT ITC CENTURY BOOK   AGFA COMPUGRAPHIC TYPE LIBRARY

ABCDEFGHIJ
KLMNOPQRS
TUVWXYZ&a
bcdefghijklmn
opqrstuvwxyz
1234567890$.,
'',"".,:!?

CENTURY FAMILY

ABCDEFGHIJKLMNOP
QRSTUVWXYZ&abcdef
ghijklmnopqrstuvwxyz1
234567890$.,""'';!?

48 POINT ITC CENTURY** BOOK   MERGENTHALER TYPE LIBRARY

ABCDEFGHIJKLMNOP
QRSTUVWXYZ&abcdef
ghijklmnopqrstuvwxyz1
234567890$.,""'';!?

48 POINT ITC CENTURY** BOOK ITALIC   MERGENTHALER TYPE LIBRARY

ABCDEFGHIJKLMNOPQRSTUVWXYZ&abcde
fghijklmnopqrstuvwxyz1234567890$.,""'';!?

24 POINT ITC CENTURY** BOOK   MERGENTHALER TYPE LIBRARY

*ABCDEFGHIJKLMNOPQRSTUVWXYZ&abcd
efghijklmnopqrstuvwxyz1234567890$.,""'';!?*

24 POINT ITC CENTURY** BOOK ITALIC   MERGENTHALER TYPE LIBRARY

CENTURY FAMILY 187

14/14 From a letter by Benjamin Franklin to B. Vaughan Esq. dated April 21, 1785:

If the Irish can manufacture cottons, stuffs and silks, and linens, and cutlery, and toys, and books etc. etc. etc., so as to sell them cheaper in England than the *manufacturers* of England sell them, is not this good for the people of England who are not *manufacturers*? and will not even the manufacturers themselves share the benefit? *Since if cottons are cheaper, all the other manufacturers who wear*

14/16 From a letter by Benjamin Franklin to B. Vaughan Esq. dated April 21, 1785:

If the Irish can manufacture cottons, stuffs and silks, and linens, and cutlery, and toys, and books etc. etc. etc., so as to sell them cheaper in England than the *manufacturers* of England sell them, is not this good for the people of England who are not *manufacturers? and will not even the manufacturers themselves share the bene-*

14/18 From a letter by Benjamin Franklin to B. Vaughan Esq. dated April 21, 1785:

If the Irish can manufacture cottons, stuffs and silks, and linens, and cutlery, and toys, and books etc. etc. etc., so as to sell them cheaper in England than the *manufacturers* of England sell them, *is not this good for the people of England who are not manu-*

12/12 From a letter by Benjamin Franklin to B. Vaughan Esq. dated April 21, 1785:

If the Irish can manufacture cottons, stuffs and silks, and linens, and cutlery, and toys, and books etc. etc. etc., so as to sell them cheaper in England than the *manufacturers* of England sell them, is not this good for the people of England who are not *manufacturers*? and will not even the manufacturers themselves share the benefit? Since if cottons are cheaper, all the other manufacturers who wear cottons will save in that article, and so of the rest. If books can be had *much cheaper from Ireland, (which I believe for I bought Blackstone there for 24/-*

12/14 From a letter by Benjamin Franklin to B. Vaughan Esq. dated April 21, 1785:

If the Irish can manufacture cottons, stuffs and silks, and linens, and cutlery, and toys, and books etc. etc. etc., so as to sell them cheaper in England than the *manufacturers* of England sell them, is not this good for the people of England who are not *manufacturers*? and will not even the manufacturers themselves share the benefit? Since if *cottons are cheaper, all the other manufacturers who wear cottons will save in that*

12/16 From a letter by Benjamin Franklin to B. Vaughan Esq. dated April 21, 1785:

If the Irish can manufacture cottons, stuffs and silks, and linens, and cutlery, and toys, and books etc. etc. etc., so as to sell them cheaper in England than the *manufacturers* of England sell them, is not this good for the people of England who are not *manufacturers*? and will not even the manufacturers themselves share the benefit? Since if

ITC CENTURY** BOOK   MERGENTHALER TYPE LIBRARY

ABCDEFGHIJKLMNOPQRSTUVW
ABCDEFGHIJKLMNOPQRSTUVW
XYZ&.,"-:;!?""1234567890$
XYZ&.,"-:;!?""1234567890$
abcdefghijklmnopqrstuvwxyz
abcdefghijklmnopqrstuvwxyz

ABCDEFGHIJKLMNOPQRSTUVWXYZ
ABCDEFGHIJKLMNOPQRSTUVWXYZ
&.,"-:;!?""1234567890$
&.,"-:;!?""1234567890$
abcdefghijklmnopqrstuvwxyz
abcdefghijklmnopqrstuvwxyz

10/10 From a letter by Benjamin Franklin to B. Vaughan Esq. dated April 21, 1785:

If the Irish can manufacture cottons, stuffs and silks, and linens, and cutlery, and toys, and books etc. etc. etc., so as to sell them cheaper in England than the *manufacturers* of England sell them, is not this good for the people of England who are not *manufacturers*? and will not even the manufacturers themselves share the benefit? Since if cottons are cheaper, all the other manufacturers who wear cottons will save in that article, and so of the rest. If books can be had much cheaper from Ireland, (which I believe for I bought Blackstone there for 24/- when it was sold in England at four guineas) is not this an advantage not to English booksellers indeed, but to English readers *and to learning. And of all the complaints perhaps these booksellers are least worthy of consideration.*

10/12 From a letter by Benjamin Franklin to B. Vaughan Esq. dated April 21, 1785:

If the Irish can manufacture cottons, stuffs and silks, and linens, and cutlery, and toys, and books etc. etc. etc., so as to sell them cheaper in England than the *manufacturers* of England sell them, is not this good for the people of England who are not *manufacturers*? and will not even the manufacturers themselves share the benefit? Since if cottons are cheaper, all the other manufacturers who wear cottons will save in that article, and so of the rest. If books can be had much cheaper from Ireland, (which I believe for I bought Blackstone there for 24/- when it was sold in *England at four guineas) is not this an advantage not to English booksellers indeed, but to English*

10/14 From a letter by Benjamin Franklin to B. Vaughan Esq. dated April 21, 1785:

If the Irish can manufacture cottons, stuffs and silks, and linens, and cutlery, and toys, and books etc. etc. etc., so as to sell them cheaper in England than the *manufacturers* of England sell them, is not this good for the people of England who are not *manufacturers*? and will not even the manufacturers themselves share the benefit? Since if cottons are cheaper, all the other manufacturers who wear cottons will *save in that article, and so of the rest. If books can be had much cheaper from Ireland, (which I believe for*

ITC CENTURY** BOOK   MERGENTHALER TYPE LIBRARY

ABCDEFGHIJKLMNOPQRSTUVWXYZ
ABCDEFGHIJKLMNOPQRSTUVWXYZ
&.,"'-:;!?"" 1234567890$
&.,"'-:;!?"" 1234567890$
abcdefghijklmnopqrstuvwxyz
abcdefghijklmnopqrstuvwxyz

8/8 From a letter by Benjamin Franklin to B. Vaughan Esq. dated April 21, 1785:

If the Irish can manufacture cottons, stuffs and silks, and linens, and cutlery, and toys, and books etc. etc. etc., so as to sell them cheaper in England than the *manufacturers* of England sell them, is not this good for the people of England who are not *manufacturers*? and will not even the manufacturers share the benefit? Since if cottons are cheaper, all the other manufacturers who wear cottons will save in that article, and so of the rest. If books can be had much cheaper from Ireland, (which I believe for I bought Blackstone there for 24/- when it was sold in England at four guineas) is not this an advantage not to English booksellers indeed, but to English readers and to learning. And of all the complaints perhaps these booksellers are least worthy of consideration. The catalogue you last sent me amazes me by the high prices (said to be the lowest) affixed to each article. And one can scarce see a new book, without observing the excessive artifices may use of to puff up a paper of verses into a pamphlet, a pamphlet into an octavo, and an octavo into a quarto, with scab boardings, white lines, sparse titles of chapters, and exorbitant margins, to *such a degree, that the selling of paper seems now the object and printing on it only the pretence. I enclose the copy of a page in a*

8/10 From a letter by Benjamin Franklin to B. Vaughan Esq. dated April 21, 1785:

If the Irish can manufacture cottons, stuffs and silks, and linens, and cutlery, and toys, and books etc. etc. etc., so as to sell them cheaper in England than the *manufacturers* of England sell them, is not this good for the people of England who are not *manufacturers*? and will not even the manufacturers themselves share the benefit? Since if cottons are cheaper, all the other manufacturers who wear cottons will save in that article, and so of the rest. If books can be had much cheaper from Ireland, (which I believe for I bought Blackstone there for 24/- when it was sold in England at four guineas) is not this an advantage not to English booksellers indeed, but to English readers and to learning. And of all the complaints perhaps these booksellers are least worthy of consideration. The catalogue you last sent me amazes me by the high prices (said to be the lowest) affixed to each article. And one can *scarce see a new book, without observing the excessive artifices may use of to puff up a paper of verses into a pamphlet, a*

8/12 From a letter by Benjamin Franklin to B. Vaughan Esq. dated April 21, 1785:

If the Irish can manufacture cottons, stuffs and silks, and cutlery, and toys, and books etc. etc. etc., so as to sell them cheaper in England than the *manufacturers* of England sell them, is not this good for the people of England who are not *manufacturers*? and will not even the manufacturers themselves share the benefit? Since if cottons are cheaper, all the other manufacturers who wear cottons will save in that article, and so of the rest. If books can be had much cheaper from Ireland, (which I believe for I bought Blackstone there for 24/- when it was sold in England at four guineas) is not this an advantage not to English booksellers *indeed, but to English readers and to learning. And of all the complaints perhaps these booksellers are least worthy of consid-*

ABCDEFGHIJKLMNOPQRSTUVWXYZ
ABCDEFGHIJKLMNOPQRSTUVWXYZ
&.,"'-:;!?"" 1234567890$
&.,"'-:;!?"" 1234567890$
abcdefghijklmnopqrstuvwxyz
abcdefghijklmnopqrstuvwxyz

ABCDEFGHIJ KLMNOPQRS TUVWXYZ&a bcdefghijklmn opqrstuvwxyz1 234567890$.,"":; !?

72 POINT CENTURY BOLD   MERGENTHALER TYPE LIBRARY

ABCDEFGHIJ KLMNOPQRS TUVWXYZ&a bcdefghijklmno pqrstuvwxyz123 4567890$.,"":;!?

72 POINT CENTURY BOLD ITALIC   MERGENTHALER TYPE LIBRARY

CENTURY FAMILY

ABCDEFGHIJKLMN
OPQRSTUVWXYZ&a
bcdefghijklmnopqrstuv
wxyz1234567890$.,"":;!?

48 POINT CENTURY BOLD   MERGENTHALER TYPE LIBRARY

*ABCDEFGHIJKLMNO
PQRSTUVWXYZ&abc
defghijklmnopqrstuvwx
yz1234567890$.,"":;!?*

48 POINT CENTURY BOLD ITALIC   MERGENTHALER TYPE LIBRARY

ABCDEFGHIJKLMNOPQRSTUVWXYZ&
abcdefghijklmnopqrstuvwxyz1234567890$.,
"":;!?

24 POINT CENTURY BOLD   MERGENTHALER TYPE LIBRARY

*ABCDEFGHIJKLMNOPQRSTUVWXYZ&a
bcdefghijklmnopqrstuvwxyz1234567890$.,"":
;!?*

24 POINT CENTURY BOLD ITALIC   MERGENTHALER TYPE LIBRARY

14/14 From a letter by Benjamin Franklin to B. Vaughan Esq. dated April 21, 1785:

If the Irish can manufacture cottons, stuffs and silks, and linens, and cutlery, and toys, and books etc. etc. etc., so as to sell them cheaper in England than the *manufacturers* of England sell them, is not this good for the people of England who are not *manufacturers?* *and will not even the manufacturers themselves share the benefit? Since*

12/12 From a letter by Benjamin Franklin to B. Vaughan Esq. dated April 21, 1785:

If the Irish can manufacture cottons, stuffs and silks, and linens, and cutlery, and toys, and books etc. etc. etc., so as to sell them cheaper in England than the *manufacturers* of England sell them, is not this good for the people of England who are not *manufacturers?* and will not even the manufacturers themselves share the benefit? Since if cottons are cheaper, all the other manufacturers who wear cottons will save in that article, and so of the rest. *If books can be had much cheaper from Ireland, (which I believe for I bought*

14/16 From a letter by Benjamin Franklin to B. Vaughan Esq. dated April 21, 1785:

If the Irish can manufacture cottons, stuffs and silks, and linens, and cutlery, and toys, and books etc. etc. etc., so as to sell them cheaper in England than the *manufacturers* of England sell them, is *not this good for the people of England who are not manufacturers?*

12/14 From a letter by Benjamin Franklin to B. Vaughan Esq. dated April 21, 1785:

If the Irish can manufacture cottons, stuffs and silks, and linens, and cutlery, and toys, and books etc. etc. etc., so as to sell them cheaper in England than the *manufacturers* of England sell them, is not this good for the people of England who are not *manufacturers?* and will not even the manufacturers themselves share *the benefit? Since if cottons are cheaper, all the other manufacturers who wear cot-*

14/18 From a letter by Benjamin Franklin to B. Vaughan Esq. dated April 21, 1785:

If the Irish can manufacture cottons, stuffs and silks, and linens, and cutlery, and toys, and books etc. etc. etc., so as to sell them *cheaper in England than the manufacturers of England sell them, is*

12/16 From a letter by Benjamin Franklin to B. Vaughan Esq. dated April 21, 1785:

If the Irish can manufacture cottons, stuffs and silks, and linens, and cutlery, and toys, and books etc. etc. etc., so as to sell them cheaper in England than the *manufacturers* of England sell them, is not this good for the people of England *who are not manufacturers? and will not even the manufacturers themselves share*

CENTURY BOLD MERGENTHALER TYPE LIBRARY

ABCDEFGHIJKLMNOPQRSTUV
ABCDEFGHIJKLMNOPQRSTUV
WXYZ&.,'"-:;!?"" 1234567890$
WXYZ&.,'"-:;!?"" 1234567890$
abcdefghijklmnopqrstuvwxyz
abcdefghijklmnopqrstuvwxyz

ABCDEFGHIJKLMNOPQRSTUVW
ABCDEFGHIJKLMNOPQRSTUVW
XYZ&.,'"-:;!?"" 1234567890$
XYZ&.,'"-:;!?"" 1234567890$
abcdefghijklmnopqrstuvwxyz
abcdefghijklmnopqrstuvwxyz

CENTURY FAMILY 193

10/10 From a letter by Benjamin Franklin to B. Vaughan Esq. dated April 21, 1785:

If the Irish can manufacture cottons, stuffs and silks, and linens, and cutlery, and toys, and books etc. etc. etc., so as to sell them cheaper in England than the *manufacturers* of England sell them, is not this good for the people of England who are not *manufacturers*? and will not even the manufacturers themselves share the benefit? Since if cottons are cheaper, all the other manufacturers who wear cottons will save in that article, and so of the rest. If books can be had much cheaper from Ireland, (which I believe for I bought Blackstone there for 24/- when it was sold in England at four guineas) is not this an advantage not to English *booksellers indeed, but to English readers and to learning. And of all the complaints perhaps these*

8/8 From a letter by Benjamin Franklin to B. Vaughan Esq. dated April 21, 1785:

If the Irish can manufacture cottons, stuffs and silks, and linens, and cutlery, and toys, and books etc. etc. etc., so as to sell them cheaper in England than the *manufacturers* of England sell them, is not this good for the people of England who are not *manufacturers*? and will not even the manufacturers themselves share the benefit? Since if cottons are cheaper, all the other manufacturers who wear cottons will save in that article, and so of the rest. If books can be had much cheaper from Ireland, (which I believe for I bought Blackstone there for 24/- when it was sold in England at four guineas) is not this an advantage not to English booksellers indeed, but to English readers and to learning. And of all the complaints perhaps these booksellers are least worthy of consideration. The catalogue you last sent me amazes me by the high prices (said to be the lowest) affixed to each article. And one can scarce see a new book, without observing the excessive artifices may use of to puff up a paper of verses into a pamphlet, a pamphlet into an octavo, and an octavo into a quarto, with scab boardings, *white lines, sparse titles of chapters, and exorbitant margins, to such a degree, that the selling of paper seems now the object*

10/12 From a letter by Benjamin Franklin to B. Vaughan Esq. dated April 21, 1785:

If the Irish can manufacture cottons, stuffs and silks, and linens, and cutlery, and toys, and books etc. etc. etc., so as to sell them cheaper in England than the *manufacturers* of England sell them, is not this good for the people of England who are not *manufacturers*? and will not even the manufacturers themselves share the benefit? Since if cottons are cheaper, all the other manufacturers who wear cottons will save in that article, and so of the rest. If books can be had much cheaper from Ireland, (which I believe for I bought Blackstone *there for 24/- when it was sold in England at four guineas) is not this an advantage not to English*

8/10 From a letter by Benjamin Franklin to B. Vaughan Esq. dated April 21, 1785:

If the Irish can manufacture cottons, stuffs and silks, and linens, and cutlery, and toys, and books etc. etc. etc., so as to sell them cheaper in England than the *manufacturers* of England sell them, is not this good for the people of England who are not *manufacturers*? and will not even the manufacturers themselves share the benefit? Since if cottons are cheaper, all the other manufacturers who wear cottons will save in that article, and so of the rest. If books can be had much cheaper from Ireland, (which I believe for I bought Blackstone there for 24/- when it was sold in England at four guineas) is not this an advantage not to English booksellers indeed, but to English readers and to learning. And of all the complaints perhaps these booksellers are least worthy of consideration. The catalogue you last sent me amazes me by the high prices (said to be *the lowest) affixed to each article. And one can scarce see a new book, without observing the excessive artifices may use of to*

10/14 From a letter by Benjamin Franklin to B. Vaughan Esq. dated April 21, 1785:

If the Irish can manufacture cottons, stuffs and silks, and linens, and cutlery, and toys, and books etc. etc. etc., so as to sell them cheaper in England than the *manufacturers* of England sell them, is not this good for the people of England who are not *manufacturers*? and will not even the manufacturers themselves share the benefit? Since if cottons are cheaper, all the other manufacturers *who wear cottons will save in that article, and so of the rest. If books can be had much cheaper from*

8/12 From a letter by Benjamin Franklin to B. Vaughan Esq. dated April 21, 1785:

If the Irish can manufacture cottons, stuffs and silks, and linens, and cutlery, and toys, and books etc. etc. etc., so as to sell them cheaper in England than the *manufacturers* of England sell them, is not this good for the people of England who are not *manufacturers*? and will not even the manufacturers themselves share the benefit? Since if cottons are cheaper, all the other manufacturers who wear cottons will save in that article, and so of the rest. If books can be had much cheaper from Ireland, (which I believe for I bought Blackstone there for 24/- when it was sold in England at four guineas) is not this *an advantage not to English booksellers indeed, but to English readers and to learning. And of all the complaints perhaps*

CENTURY BOLD   MERGENTHALER TYPE LIBRARY

ABCDEFGHIJKLMNOPQRSTUVWXYZ
ABCDEFGHIJKLMNOPQRSTUVWXYZ
&.,"-:;!?""1234567890$
&.,"-:;!?""1234567890$
abcdefghijklmnopqrstuvwxyz
abcdefghijklmnopqrstuvwxyz

ABCDEFGHIJKLMNOPQRSTUVWXYZ
ABCDEFGHIJKLMNOPQRSTUVWXYZ
&.,"-:;!?""1234567890$
&.,"-:;!?""1234567890$
abcdefghijklmnopqrstuvwxyz
abcdefghijklmnopqrstuvwxyz

ABCDEFGH
IJKLMNOP
QRSTUVWX
YZ&abcdefg
hijklmnopq
rstuvwxyz1
234567890$.
,""";:!?

72 POINT NEW CENTURY SCHOOLBOOK BLACK   MERGENTHALER TYPE LIBRARY

ABCDEFGHIJKLMNOPQRSTUVWXY
Z&abcdefghijklmnopqrstuvwxyz123
4567890$.,""";:!?

24 POINT NEW CENTURY SCHOOLBOOK BLACK   MERGENTHALER TYPE LIBRARY

CENTURY FAMILY 195

ABCDEFGHI
JKLMNOPQ
RSTUVWXY
Z&abcdefgh
ijklmnopqr
stuvwxyz123
4567890$.,""
:;!?

72 POINT NEW CENTURY SCHOOLBOOK BLACK ITALIC   MERGENTHALER TYPE LIBRARY

ABCDEFGHIJKLMNOPQRSTUVWXY
Z&abcdefghijklmnopqrstuvwxyz1234
567890$.,"":;!?*

24 POINT NEW CENTURY SCHOOLBOOK BLACK ITALIC   MERGENTHALER TYPE LIBRARY

ABCDEFGHIJKL
MNOPQRSTUVWX
YZ&abcdefghijkl
mnopqrstuvwxyz1
234567890$.,""";:!?

48 POINT NEW CENTURY SCHOOLBOOK BLACK   MERGENTHALER TYPE LIBRARY

ABCDEFGHIJKLM
NOPQRSTUVWXY
Z&abcdefghijklm
nopqrstuvwxyz123
4567890$.,""";:!?

48 POINT NEW CENTURY SCHOOLBOOK BLACK ITALIC   MERGENTHALER TYPE LIBRARY

14/14 **From a letter by Benjamin Franklin to B. Vaughan Esq. dated April 21, 1785:**

If the Irish can manufacture cottons, stuffs and silks, and linens, and cutlery, and toys, and books etc. etc. etc., so as to sell them cheaper in England than the *manufacturers* of England sell them, is not this good for the people of *England who are not manufacturers? and will not even*

12/12 **From a letter by Benjamin Franklin to B. Vaughan Esq. dated April 21, 1785:**

If the Irish can manufacture cottons, stuffs and silks, and linens, and cutlery, and toys, and books etc. etc. etc., so as to sell them cheaper in England than the *manufacturers* of England sell them, is not this good for the people of England who are not *manufacturers?* and will not even the manufacturers themselves share the benefit? *Since if cottons are cheaper, all the other manufacturers who wear cot-*

14/16 **From a letter by Benjamin Franklin to B. Vaughan Esq. dated April 21, 1785:**

If the Irish can manufacture cottons, stuffs and silks, and linens, and cutlery, and toys, and books etc. etc. etc., so as to sell them cheaper in England than the *manufacturers* of England sell them, is not this good for the people of Eng-

12/14 **From a letter by Benjamin Franklin to B. Vaughan Esq. dated April 21, 1785:**

If the Irish can manufacture cottons, stuffs and silks, and linens, and cutlery, and toys, and books etc. etc. etc., so as to sell them cheaper in England than the *manufacturers* of England sell them, is not this good for the people of England who are not *manufacturers?* and will not even the manufactur-

14/18 **From a letter by Benjamin Franklin to B. Vaughan Esq. dated April 21, 1785:**

If the Irish can manufacture cottons, stuffs and silks, and linens, and cutlery, and toys, and books etc. etc. etc., so as *to sell them cheaper in England than the manufacturers*

12/16 **From a letter by Benjamin Franklin to B. Vaughan Esq. dated April 21, 1785:**

If the Irish can manufacture cottons, stuffs and silks, and linens, and cutlery, and toys, and books etc. etc. etc., so as to sell them cheaper in England than the *manufacturers of England sell them, is not this good for the people of Eng-*

NEW CENTURY SCHOOLBOOK BLACK   MERGENTHALER TYPE LIBRARY

ABCDEFGHIJKLMNOPQRST
ABCDEFGHIJKLMNOPQRST
UVWX&.,"-:;!?""1234567890$
UVWX&.,"-:;!?""1234567890$
abcdefghijklmnopqrstuvwxy
abcdefghijklmnopqrstuvwxy

ABCDEFGHIJKLMNOPQRSTUV
ABCDEFGHIJKLMNOPQRSTUV
WXYZ&.,"-:;!?""1234567890$
WXYZ&.,"-:;!?""1234567890$
abcdefghijklmnopqrstuvwxyz
abcdefghijklmnopqrstuvwxyz

10/10 From a letter by Benjamin Franklin to B. Vaughan Esq. dated April 21, 1785:

If the Irish can manufacture cottons, stuffs and silks, and linens, and cutlery, and toys, and books etc. etc. etc., so as to sell them cheaper in England than the *manufacturers* of England sell them, is not this good for the people of England who are not *manufacturers*? and will not even the manufacturers themselves share the benefit? Since if cottons are cheaper, all the other manufacturers who wear cottons will save in that article, and so of the rest. *If books can be had much cheaper from Ireland, (which I believe for I bought Blackstone there for 24/- when it was sold in England at four guineas) is not this an*

10/12 From a letter by Benjamin Franklin to B. Vaughan Esq. dated April 21, 1785:

If the Irish can manufacture cottons, stuffs and silks, and linens, and cutlery, and toys, and books etc. etc. etc., so as to sell them cheaper in England than the *manufacturers* of England sell them, is not this good for the people of England who are not *manufacturers*? and will not even the manufacturers themselves share the benefit? Since if cottons are cheaper, all the other manufacturers who wear cottons will save in that article, and so of the rest. *If books can be had much cheaper from Ireland, (which I believe for I bought*

10/14 From a letter by Benjamin Franklin to B. Vaughan Esq. dated April 21, 1785:

If the Irish can manufacture cottons, stuffs and silks, and linens, and cutlery, and toys, and books etc. etc. etc., so as to sell them cheaper in England than the *manufacturers* of England sell them, is not this good for the people of England who are not *manufacturers*? and will not even the manufacturers themselves share *the benefit? Since if cottons are cheaper, all the other manufacturers who wear cot-*

8/8 From a letter by Benjamin Franklin to B. Vaughan Esq. dated April 21, 1785:

If the Irish can manufacture cottons, stuffs and silks, and linens, and cutlery, and toys, and books etc. etc. etc., so as to sell them cheaper in England than the *manufacturers* of England sell them, is not this good for the people of England who are not *manufacturers*? and will not even the manufacturers themselves share the benefit? Since if cottons are cheaper, all the other manufacturers who wear cottons will save in that article, and so of the rest. If books can be had much cheaper from Ireland, (which I believe for I bought Blackstone there for 24/- when it was sold in England at four guineas) is not this an advantage not to English booksellers indeed, but to English readers and to learning. And of all the complaints perhaps these booksellers are least worthy of consideration. The catalogue you last sent me amazes me by the high prices (said to be the lowest) affixed to each article. And one can scarce *see a new book, without observing the excessive artifices may use of to puff up a paper of verses into a*

8/10 From a letter by Benjamin Franklin to B. Vaughan Esq. dated April 21, 1785:

If the Irish can manufacture cottons, stuffs and silks, and linens, and cutlery, and toys, and books etc. etc. etc., so as to sell them cheaper in England than the *manufacturers* of England sell them, is not this good for the people of England who are not *manufacturers*? and will not even the manufacturers themselves share the benefit? Since if cottons are cheaper, all the other manufacturers who wear cottons will save in that article, and so of the rest. If books can be had much cheaper from Ireland, (which I believe for I bought Blackstone there for 24/- when it was sold in England at four guineas) is not this an advantage not to English booksellers indeed, but to English readers and to learning. And of all the *complaints perhaps these booksellers are least worthy of consideration. The catalogue you last sent*

8/12 From a letter by Benjamin Franklin to B. Vaughan Esq. dated April 21, 1785:

If the Irish can manufacture cottons, stuffs and silks, and linens, and cutlery, and toys, and books etc. etc. etc., so as to sell them cheaper in England than the *manufacturers* of England sell them, is not this good for the people of England who are not *manufacturers*? and will not even the manufacturers themselves share the benefit? Since if cottons are cheaper, all the other manufacturers who wear cottons will save in that article, and so of the rest. If books can be had much cheaper from Ireland, *(which I believe for I bought Blackstone there for 24/- when it was sold in England at four guineas) is not*

NEW CENTURY SCHOOLBOOK BLACK   MERGENTHALER TYPE LIBRARY

ABCDEFGHIJKLMNOPQRSTUVWXYZ
ABCDEFGHIJKLMNOPQRSTUVWXYZ
&.,"-:;!?""1234567890$
&.,"-:;!?""1234567890$
abcdefghijklmnopqrstuvwxyz
abcdefghijklmnopqrstuvwxyz

ABCDEFGHIJKLMNOPQRSTUVWXYZ
ABCDEFGHIJKLMNOPQRSTUVWXYZ
&.,"-:;!?""1234567890$
&.,"-:;!?""1234567890$
abcdefghijklmnopqrstuvwxyz
abcdefghijklmnopqrstuvwxyz

ABCDEFGHIJKLM
NOPQRSTUVWXY
Z&abcdefghijklmno
pqrstuvwxyz123456
7890$.,"":;!?

72 POINT CENTURY NOVA   MERGENTHALER TYPE LIBRARY

ABCDEFGHIJKL MNOPQRSTUVW XYZ&abcdefghijklm nopqrstuvwxyz1234 567890$.,""'.,;!?

72 POINT CENTURY NOVA ITALIC   MERGENTHALER TYPE LIBRARY

ABCDEFGHIJKLMNOPQRS
TUVWXYZ&abcdefghijklmno
pqrstuvwxyz1234567890$.,""":;
!?

48 POINT CENTURY NOVA   MERGENTHALER TYPE LIBRARY

*ABCDEFGHIJKLMNOPQRS
TUVWXYZ&abcdefghijklmno
pqrstuvwxyz1234567890$.,""":;
!?*

48 POINT CENTURY NOVA ITALIC   MERGENTHALER TYPE LIBRARY

ABCDEFGHIJKLMNOPQRSTUVWXYZ&abcdefghijklm
nopqrstuvwxyz1234567890$.,"":;!?

24 POINT CENTURY NOVA   MERGENTHALER TYPE LIBRARY

*ABCDEFGHIJKLMNOPQRSTUVWXYZ&abcdefghijkl
mnopqrstuvwxyz1234567890$.,"":;!?*

24 POINT CENTURY NOVA ITALIC   MERGENTHALER TYPE LIBRARY

14/14 From a letter by Benjamin Franklin to B. Vaughan Esq. dated April 21, 1785:
If the Irish can manufacture cottons, stuffs and silks, and linens, and cutlery, and toys, and books etc. etc. etc., so as to sell them cheaper in England than the *manufacturers* of England sell them, is not this good for the people of England who are not *manufacturers*? and will not even the manufacturers themselves share the benefit? Since if cottons are cheaper, all the other manufacturers who wear cottons will save in that article, and so of the rest. If books can be had much cheaper

12/12 From a letter by Benjamin Franklin to B. Vaughan Esq. dated April 21, 1785:
If the Irish can manufacture cottons, stuffs and silks, and linens, and cutlery, and toys, and books etc. etc. etc., so as to sell them cheaper in England than the *manufacturers* of England sell them, is not this good for the people of England who are not *manufacturers*? and will not even the manufacturers themselves share the benefit? Since if cottons are cheaper, all the other manufacturers who wear cottons will save in that article, and so of the rest. If books can be had much cheaper from Ireland, (which I believe for I bought Blackstone there for 24/- when it was sold in *England at four guineas) is not this an advantage not to English booksellers indeed, but to English*

14/16 From a letter by Benjamin Franklin to B. Vaughan Esq. dated April 21, 1785:
If the Irish can manufacture cottons, stuffs and silks, and linens, and cutlery, and toys, and books etc. etc. etc., so as to sell them cheaper in England than the *manufacturers* of England sell them, is not this good for the people of England who are not *manufacturers*? and will not even the manufacturers *themselves share the benefit? Since if cottons are cheaper, all the other manufacturers who*

12/14 From a letter by Benjamin Franklin to B. Vaughan Esq. dated April 21, 1785:
If the Irish can manufacture cottons, stuffs and silks, and linens, and cutlery, and toys, and books etc. etc. etc., so as to sell them cheaper in England than the *manufacturers* of England sell them, is not this good for the people of England who are not *manufacturers*? and will not even the manufacturers themselves share the benefit? Since if cottons are cheaper, all the other manufacturers who wear cottons will *save in that article, and so of the rest. If books can be had much cheaper from Ireland, (which I believe for I*

14/18 From a letter by Benjamin Franklin to B. Vaughan Esq. dated April 21, 1785:
If the Irish can manufacture cottons, stuffs and silks, and linens, and cutlery, and toys, and books etc. etc. etc., so as to sell them cheaper in England than the *manufacturers* of England sell them, is not this good for the *people of England who are not manufacturers? and will not even the manufacturers*

12/16 From a letter by Benjamin Franklin to B. Vaughan Esq. dated April 21, 1785:
If the Irish can manufacture cottons, stuffs and silks, and linens, and cutlery, and toys, and books etc. etc. etc., so as to sell them cheaper in England than the *manufacturers* of England sell them, is not this good for the people of England who are not *manufacturers*? and will not even the manufacturers them*selves share the benefit? Since if cottons are cheaper, all the other manufacturers who wear cottons will*

CENTURY NOVA   MERGENTHALER TYPE LIBRARY

ABCDEFGHIJKLMNOPQRSTUVWXYZ
ABCDEFGHIJKLMNOPQRSTUVWXYZ
&.,"-:;!?""1234567890$
&.,"-:;!?""1234567890$
abcdefghijklmnopqrstuvwxyz
abcdefghijklmnopqrstuvwxyz

ABCDEFGHIJKLMNOPQRSTUVWXYZ
ABCDEFGHIJKLMNOPQRSTUVWXYZ
&.,"-:;!?""1234567890$
&.,"-:;!?""1234567890$
abcdefghijklmnopqrstuvwxyz
abcdefghijklmnopqrstuvwxyz

CENTURY FAMILY 203

10/10 From a letter by Benjamin Franklin to B. Vaughan Esq. dated April 21, 1785:

If the Irish can manufacture cottons, stuffs and silks, and linens, and cutlery, and toys, and books etc. etc. etc., so as to sell them cheaper in England than the *manufacturers* of England sell them, is not this good for the people of England who are not *manufacturers*? and will not even the manufacturers themselves share the benefit? Since if cottons are cheaper, all the other manufacturers who wear cottons will save in that article, and so of the rest. If books can be had much cheaper from Ireland, (which I believe for I bought Blackstone there for 24/- when it was sold in England at four guineas) is not this an advantage not to English booksellers indeed, but to English readers and to learning. And of all the complaints perhaps these booksellers are least worthy of consideration. The catalogue you *last sent me amazes me by the high prices (said to be the lowest) affixed to each article. And one can scarce see a new book,*

8/8 From a letter by Benjamin Franklin to B. Vaughan Esq. dated April 21, 1785:

If the Irish can manufacture cottons, stuffs and silks, and linens, and cutlery, and toys, and books etc. etc. etc., so as to sell them cheaper in England than the *manufacturers* of England sell them, is not this good for the people of England who are not *manufacturers*? and will not even the manufacturers themselves share the benefit? Since if cottons are cheaper, all the other manufacturers who wear cottons will save in that article, and so of the rest. If books can be had much cheaper from Ireland, (which I believe for I bought Blackstone there for 24/- when it was sold in England at four guineas) is not this an advantage not to English booksellers indeed, but to English readers and to learning. And of all the complaints perhaps these booksellers are least worthy of consideration. The catalogue you last sent me amazes me by the high prices (said to be the lowest) affixed to each article. And one can scarce see a new book, without observing the excessive artifices may use of to puff up a paper of verses into a pamphlet, a pamphlet into an octavo, and an octavo into a quarto, with scab boardings, white lines, sparse titles of chapters, and exorbitant margins, to such a degree, *that the selling of paper seems now the object and printing on it only the pretence. I enclose the copy of a page in a late comedy. Between every two lines there is a white space equal to another line. You have a law, I think, against butchers blowing of veal to make it look fatter; why not one against booksellers blowing of books to make them look bigger. All this to yourself; you can easily guess the reason.*

10/12 From a letter by Benjamin Franklin to B. Vaughan Esq. dated April 21, 1785:

If the Irish can manufacture cottons, stuffs and silks, and linens, and cutlery, and toys, and books etc. etc. etc., so as to sell them cheaper in England than the *manufacturers* of England sell them, is not this good for the people of England who are not *manufacturers*? and will not even the manufacturers themselves share the benefit? Since if cottons are cheaper, all the other manufacturers who wear cottons will save in that article, and so of the rest. If books can be had much cheaper from Ireland, (which I believe for I bought Blackstone there for 24/- when it was sold in England at four guineas) is not this an advantage not to English booksellers indeed, but to English *readers and to learning. And of all the complaints perhaps these booksellers are least worthy of consideration. The cata-*

8/10 From a letter by Benjamin Franklin to B. Vaughan Esq. dated April 21, 1785:

If the Irish can manufacture cottons, stuffs and silks, and linens, and cutlery, and toys, and books etc. etc. etc., so as to sell them cheaper in England than the *manufacturers* of England sell them, is not this good for the people of England who are not *manufacturers*? and will not even the manufacturers themselves share the benefit? Since if cottons are cheaper, all the other manufacturers who wear cottons will save in that article, and so of the rest. If books can be had much cheaper from Ireland, (which I believe for I bought Blackstone there for 24/- when it was sold in England at four guineas) is not this an advantage not to English booksellers indeed, but to English readers and to learning. And of all the complaints perhaps these booksellers are least worthy of consideration. The catalogue you last sent me amazes me by the high prices (said to be the lowest) affixed to each article. And one can scarce see a new book, without observing the excessive artifices may use of to puff up a paper of verses into a pamphlet, a pamphlet into an octavo, and an octavo into a quarto, with scab boardings, white lines, sparse titles of chapters, and exorbitant margins, to such a degree, *that the selling of paper seems now the object and printing on it only the pretence. I enclose the copy of a page in a late comedy. Between every two lines*

10/14 From a letter by Benjamin Franklin to B. Vaughan Esq. dated April 21, 1785:

If the Irish can manufacture cottons, stuffs and silks, and linens, and cutlery, and toys, and books etc. etc. etc., so as to sell them cheaper in England than the *manufacturers* of England sell them, is not this good for the people of England who are not *manufacturers*? and will not even the manufacturers themselves share the benefit? Since if cottons are cheaper, all the other manufacturers who wear cottons will save in that article, and so of the rest. If books can be had much cheaper from *Ireland, (which I believe for I bought Blackstone there for 24/- when it was sold in England at four guineas) is not this an*

8/12 From a letter by Benjamin Franklin to B. Vaughan Esq. dated April 21, 1785:

If the Irish can manufacture cottons, stuffs and silks, and linens, and cutlery, and toys, and books etc. etc. etc., so as to sell them cheaper in England than the *manufacturers* of England sell them, is not this good for the people of England who are not *manufacturers*? and will not even the manufacturers themselves share the benefit? Since if cottons are cheaper, all the other manufacturers who wear cottons will save in that article, and so of the rest. If books can be had much cheaper from Ireland, (which I believe for I bought Blackstone there for 24/- when it was sold in England at four guineas) is not this an advantage not to English booksellers indeed, but to English readers and to learning. And of all the complaints perhaps these booksellers are least worthy of consideration. The catalogue you last sent me amazes me by the high prices (said to be the lowest) *affixed to each article. And one can scarce see a new book, without observing the excessive artifices may use of to puff up a paper of verses into a pamphlet, a*

CENTURY NOVA   MERGENTHALER TYPE LIBRARY

ABCDEFGHIJKLMNOPQRSTUVWXYZ
ABCDEFGHIJKLMNOPQRSTUVWXYZ
&.,"-:;!?""1234567890$
&.,"-:;!?""1234567890$
abcdefghijklmnopqrstuvwxyz
abcdefghijklmnopqrstuvwxyz

ABCDEFGHIJKLMNOPQRSTUVWXYZ
ABCDEFGHIJKLMNOPQRSTUVWXYZ
&.,"-:;!?""1234567890$
&.,"-:;!?""1234567890$
abcdefghijklmnopqrstuvwxyz
abcdefghijklmnopqrstuvwxyz

ABCDEFGHIJKL
MNOPQRSTUVW
XYZ&abcdefghijk
lmnopqrstuvwxyz
1234567890$.,""":
;!?

72 POINT ITC CENTURY** BOLD CONDENSED   MERGENTHALER TYPE LIBRARY

ABCDEFGHIJKLMNOPQRSTUVWXYZ&abcdefghijklmnopqrstuvwxyz1234567890$.,"":;!?

72 POINT ITC CENTURY** BOLD CONDENSED ITALIC   MERGENTHALER TYPE LIBRARY

ABCDEFGHIJKLMNOPQ
RSTUVWXYZ&abcdefghi
jklmnopqrstuvwxyz1234
567890$.,""":;!?

48 POINT ITC CENTURY** BOLD CONDENSED   MERGENTHALER TYPE LIBRARY

*ABCDEFGHIJKLMNOPQ
RSTUVWXYZ&abcdefghi
jklmnopqrstuvwxyz1234
567890$.,""":;!?*

48 POINT ITC CENTURY** BOLD CONDENSED ITALIC   MERGENTHALER TYPE LIBRARY

ABCDEFGHIJKLMNOPQRSTUVWXYZ&abcdefghij
klmnopqrstuvwxyz1234567890$.,"":;!?

24 POINT ITC CENTURY** BOLD CONDENSED   MERGENTHALER TYPE LIBRARY

*ABCDEFGHIJKLMNOPQRSTUVWXYZ&abcdefghij
klmnopqrstuvwxyz1234567890$.,"":;!?*

24 POINT ITC CENTURY** BOLD CONDENSED ITALIC   MERGENTHALER TYPE LIBRARY

CENTURY FAMILY 207

14/14 From a letter by Benjamin Franklin to B. Vaughan Esq. dated April 21, 1785:

If the Irish can manufacture cottons, stuffs and silks, and linens, and cutlery, and toys, and books etc. etc. etc., so as to sell them cheaper in England than the *manufacturers* of England sell them, is not this good for the people of England who are not *manufacturers*? and will not even the manufacturers themselves share the benefit? Since if cottons are cheaper, *all the other manufacturers who wear cottons will save in that article, and so*

14/16 From a letter by Benjamin Franklin to B. Vaughan Esq. dated April 21, 1785:

If the Irish can manufacture cottons, stuffs and silks, and linens, and cutlery, and toys, and books etc. etc. etc., so as to sell them cheaper in England than the *manufacturers* of England sell them, is not this good for the people of England who are not *manufacturers*? and will not *even the manufacturers themselves share the benefit? Since if cottons are*

14/18 From a letter by Benjamin Franklin to B. Vaughan Esq. dated April 21, 1785:

If the Irish can manufacture cottons, stuffs and silks, and linens, and cutlery, and toys, and books etc. etc. etc., so as to sell them cheaper in England than the *manufacturers* of England sell them, is *not this good for the people of England who are not manufacturers? and will*

12/12 From a letter by Benjamin Franklin to B. Vaughan Esq. dated April 21, 1785:

If the Irish can manufacture cottons, stuffs and silks, and linens, and cutlery, and toys, and books etc. etc. etc., so as to sell them cheaper in England than the *manufacturers* of England sell them, is not this good for the people of England who are not *manufacturers*? and will not even the manufacturers themselves share the benefit? Since if cottons are cheaper, all the other manufacturers who wear cottons will save in that article, and so of the rest. If books can be had much cheaper from Ireland, (which I believe *for I bought Blackstone there for 24/- when it was sold in England at four guineas) is not*

12/14 From a letter by Benjamin Franklin to B. Vaughan Esq. dated April 21, 1785:

If the Irish can manufacture cottons, stuffs and silks, and linens, and cutlery, and toys, and books etc. etc. etc., so as to sell them cheaper in England than the *manufacturers* of England sell them, is not this good for the people of England who are not *manufacturers*? and will not even the manufacturers themselves share the benefit? Since if cottons are cheaper, all the *other manufacturers who wear cottons will save in that article, and so of the rest. If books*

12/16 From a letter by Benjamin Franklin to B. Vaughan Esq. dated April 21, 1785:

If the Irish can manufacture cottons, stuffs and silks, and linens, and cutlery, and toys, and books etc. etc. etc., so as to sell them cheaper in England than the *manufacturers* of England sell them, is not this good for the people of England who are not *manufacturers*? and will *not even the manufacturers themselves share the benefit? Since if cottons are cheaper, all the*

ITC CENTURY** BOLD CONDENSED   MERGENTHALER TYPE LIBRARY

ABCDEFGHIJKLMNOPQRSTUVWXYZ
ABCDEFGHIJKLMNOPQRSTUVWXYZ
&.,"-:;!?""1234567890$
&.,"-:;!?""1234567890$
abcdefghijklmnopqrstuvwxyz
abcdefghijklmnopqrstuvwxyz

ABCDEFGHIJKLMNOPQRSTUVWXYZ
ABCDEFGHIJKLMNOPQRSTUVWXYZ
&.,"-:;!?""1234567890$
&.,"-:;!?""1234567890$
abcdefghijklmnopqrstuvwxyz
abcdefghijklmnopqrstuvwxyz

CENTURY FAMILY

10/10 From a letter by Benjamin Franklin to B. Vaughan Esq. dated April 21, 1785:

If the Irish can manufacture cottons, stuffs and silks, and linens, and cutlery, and toys, and books etc. etc. etc., so as to sell them cheaper in England than the *manufacturers* of England sell them, is not this good for the people of England who are not *manufacturers*? and will not even the manufacturers themselves share the benefit? Since if cottons are cheaper, all the other manufacturers who wear cottons will save in that article, and so of the rest. If books can be had much cheaper from Ireland, (which I believe for I bought Blackstone there for 24/- when it was sold in England at four guineas) is not this an advantage not to English booksellers indeed, but to English readers and to learning. And of all the complaints perhaps these *booksellers are least worthy of consideration. The catalogue you last sent me amazes me by the high prices*

8/8 From a letter by Benjamin Franklin to B. Vaughan Esq. dated April 21, 1785:

If the Irish can manufacture cottons, stuffs and silks, and linens, and cutlery, and toys, and books etc. etc. etc., so as to sell them cheaper in England than the *manufacturers* of England sell them, is not this good for the people of England who are not *manufacturers*? and will not even the manufacturers themselves share the benefit? Since if cottons are cheaper, all the other manufacturers who wear cottons will save in that article, and so of the rest. If books can be had much cheaper from Ireland, (which I believe for I bought Blackstone there for 24/- when it was sold in England at four guineas) is not this an advantage not to English booksellers indeed, but to English readers and to learning. And of all the complaints perhaps these booksellers are least worthy of consideration. The catalogue you last sent me amazes me by the high prices (said to be the lowest) affixed to each article. And one can scarce see a new book, without observing the excessive artifices may use of to puff up a paper of verses into a pamphlet, a pamphlet into an octavo, and an octavo into a quarto, with scab boardings, white lines, sparse titles of chapters, and exorbitant margins, to such a degree, that the selling of paper seems now the object and printing on it only the pretence. I enclose *the copy of a page in a late comedy. Between every two lines there is a white space equal to another line. You have a law, I think, against*

10/12 From a letter by Benjamin Franklin to B. Vaughan Esq. dated April 21, 1785:

If the Irish can manufacture cottons, stuffs and silks, and linens, and cutlery, and toys, and books etc. etc. etc., so as to sell them cheaper in England than the *manufacturers* of England sell them, is not this good for the people of England who are not *manufacturers*? and will not even the manufacturers themselves share the benefit? Since if cottons are cheaper, all the other manufacturers who wear cottons will save in that article, and so of the rest. If books can be had much cheaper from Ireland, (which I believe for I bought Blackstone there for 24/- when it was sold in England at four guineas) is not this an advantage *not to English booksellers indeed, but to English readers and to learning. And of all the complaints perhaps these*

8/10 From a letter by Benjamin Franklin to B. Vaughan Esq. dated April 21, 1785:

If the Irish can manufacture cottons, stuffs and silks, and linens, and cutlery, and toys, and books etc. etc. etc., so as to sell them cheaper in England than the *manufacturers* of England sell them, is not this good for the people of England who are not *manufacturers*? and will not even the manufacturers themselves share the benefit? Since if cottons are cheaper, all the other manufacturers who wear cottons will save in that article, and so of the rest. If books can be had much cheaper from Ireland, (which I believe for I bought Blackstone there for 24/- when it was sold in England at four guineas) is not this an advantage not to English booksellers indeed, but to English readers and to learning. And of all the complaints perhaps these booksellers are least worthy of consideration. The catalogue you last sent me amazes me by the high prices (said to be the lowest) affixed to each article. And one can scarce see a new book, without observing the excessive artifices may use of to *puff up a paper of verses into a pamphlet, a pamphlet into an octavo, and an octavo into a quarto, with scab boardings, white lines, sparse*

10/14 From a letter by Benjamin Franklin to B. Vaughan Esq. dated April 21, 1785:

If the Irish can manufacture cottons, stuffs and silks, and linens, and cutlery, and toys, and books etc. etc. etc., so as to sell them cheaper in England than the *manufacturers* of England sell them, is not this good for the people of England who are not *manufacturers*? and will not even the manufacturers themselves share the benefit? Since if cottons are cheaper, all the other manufacturers who wear cottons will save in that article, and so of the rest. If *books can be had much cheaper from Ireland, (which I believe for I bought Blackstone there for 24/- when it was*

8/12 From a letter by Benjamin Franklin to B. Vaughan Esq. dated April 21, 1785:

If the Irish can manufacture cottons, stuffs and silks, and linens, and cutlery, and toys, and books etc. etc. etc., so as to sell them cheaper in England than the *manufacturers* of England sell them, is not this good for the people of England who are not *manufacturers*? and will not even the manufacturers themselves share the benefit? Since if cottons are cheaper, all the other manufacturers who wear cottons will save in that article, and so of the rest. If books can be had much cheaper from Ireland, (which I believe for I bought Blackstone there for 24/- when it was sold in England at four guineas) is not this an advantage not to English booksellers indeed, but to English readers and to learning. And *of all the complaints perhaps these booksellers are least worthy of consideration. The catalogue you last sent me amazes me by the high*

ITC CENTURY® BOLD CONDENSED   MERGENTHALER TYPE LIBRARY

ABCDEFGHIJKLMNOPQRSTUVWXYZ
ABCDEFGHIJKLMNOPQRSTUVWXYZ
&.,"-:;!?""1234567890$
&.,"-:;!?""1234567890$
abcdefghijklmnopqrstuvwxyz
abcdefghijklmnopqrstuvwxyz

ABCDEFGHIJKLMNOPQRSTUVWXYZ
ABCDEFGHIJKLMNOPQRSTUVWXYZ
&.,"-:;!?""1234567890$
&.,"-:;!?""1234567890$
abcdefghijklmnopqrstuvwxyz
abcdefghijklmnopqrstuvwxyz

CENTURY FAMILY

ABCDEFGHIJKLMNOPQRSTUVWXYZ&abcdefghijklmnopqrstuvwxyz1234567890$.,""'';:!?

72 POINT CENTURY BOLD CONDENSED   MERGENTHALER TYPE LIBRARY

ABCDEFGHIJKLMNOPQRSTUVWXYZ&abcdefghijklmnopqrstuvwxyz1234567890$.,""'';:!?

48 POINT CENTURY BOLD CONDENSED   MERGENTHALER TYPE LIBRARY

ABCDEFGHIJKLMNOPQRSTUVWXYZ&abcdefghijklmnopqrstuvwxyz1234567890$.,""'';:!?

24 POINT CENTURY BOLD CONDENSED   MERGENTHALER TYPE LIBRARY

NOTE: *Mergenthaler Century Bold Condensed is considerably more condensed than ITC Century Bold Condensed.*

14/14 From a letter by Benjamin Franklin to B. Vaughan Esq. dated April 21, 1785:

If the Irish can manufacture cottons, stuffs and silks, and linens, and cutlery, and toys, and books etc. etc. etc., so as to sell them cheaper in England than the manufacturers of England sell them, is not this good for the people of England who are not manufacturers? and will not even the manufacturers themselves share the benefit? Since if cottons are cheaper, all the other manufacturers who wear cottons will save in that article, and so of the rest. If books can be had much cheaper from Ireland, (which I be-

14/16 From a letter by Benjamin Franklin to B. Vaughan Esq. dated April 21, 1785:

If the Irish can manufacture cottons, stuffs and silks, and linens, and cutlery, and toys, and books etc. etc. etc., so as to sell them cheaper in England than the manufacturers of England sell them, is not this good for the people of England who are not manufacturers? and will not even the manufacturers themselves share the benefit? Since if cottons are cheaper, all the other manufacturers who wear cottons will save in

14/18 From a letter by Benjamin Franklin to B. Vaughan Esq. dated April 21, 1785:

If the Irish can manufacture cottons, stuffs and silks, and linens, and cutlery, and toys, and books etc. etc. etc., so as to sell them cheaper in England than the manufacturers of England sell them, is not this good for the people of England who are not manufacturers? and will not even the manufacturers themselves share the bene-

12/12 From a letter by Benjamin Franklin to B. Vaughan Esq. dated April 21, 1785:

If the Irish can manufacture cottons, stuffs and silks, and linens, and cutlery, and toys, and books etc. etc. etc., so as to sell them cheaper in England than the manufacturers of England sell them, is not this good for the people of England who are not manufacturers? and will not even the manufacturers themselves share the benefit? Since if cottons are cheaper, all the other manufacturers who wear cottons will save in that article, and so of the rest. If books can be had much cheaper from Ireland, (which I believe for I bought Blackstone there for 24/- when it was sold in England at four guineas) is not this an advantage not to English booksellers indeed, but to English readers and to learning.

12/14 From a letter by Benjamin Franklin to B. Vaughan Esq. dated April 21, 1785:

If the Irish can manufacture cottons, stuffs and silks, and linens, and cutlery, and toys, and books etc. etc. etc., so as to sell them cheaper in England than the manufacturers of England sell them, is not this good for the people of England who are not manufacturers? and will not even the manufacturers themselves share the benefit? Since if cottons are cheaper, all the other manufacturers who wear cottons will save in that article, and so of the rest. If books can be had much cheaper from Ireland, (which I believe for I bought Blackstone

12/16 From a letter by Benjamin Franklin to B. Vaughan Esq. dated April 21, 1785:

If the Irish can manufacture cottons, stuffs and silks, and linens, and cutlery, and toys, and books etc. etc. etc., so as to sell them cheaper in England than the manufacturers of England sell them, is not this good for the people of England who are not manufacturers? and will not even the manufacturers themselves share the benefit? Since if cottons are cheaper, all the other manufacturers who wear cottons will save in that article,

---

CENTURY BOLD CONDENSED   MERGENTHALER TYPE LIBRARY

ABCDEFGHIJKLMNOPQRSTUVWXYZ
&.,"-:;!?""1234567890$
abcdefghijklmnopqrstuvwxyz

ABCDEFGHIJKLMNOPQRSTUVWXYZ
&.,"-:;!?""1234567890$
abcdefghijklmnopqrstuvwxyz

CENTURY FAMILY 211

10/10 From a letter by Benjamin Franklin to B. Vaughan Esq. dated April 21, 1785:

If the Irish can manufacture cottons, stuffs and silks, and linens, and cutlery, and toys, and books etc. etc. etc., so as to sell them cheaper in England than the manufacturers of England sell them, is not this good for the people of England who are not manufacturers? and will not even the manufacturers themselves share the benefit? Since if cottons are cheaper, all the other manufacturers who wear cottons will save in that article, and so of the rest. If books can be had much cheaper from Ireland, (which I believe for I bought Blackstone there for 24/- when it was sold in England at four guineas) is not this an advantage not to English booksellers indeed, but to English readers and to learning. And of all the complaints perhaps these booksellers are least worthy of consideration. The catalogue you last sent me amazes me by the high prices (said to be the lowest) affixed to each article. And one can scarce see a new book, without observing the excessive artifices may use of to puff

10/12 From a letter by Benjamin Franklin to B. Vaughan Esq. dated April 21, 1785:

If the Irish can manufacture cottons, stuffs and silks, and linens, and cutlery, and toys, and books etc. etc. etc., so as to sell them cheaper in England than the manufacturers of England sell them, is not this good for the people of England who are not manufacturers? and will not even the manufacturers themselves share the benefit? Since if cottons are cheaper, all the other manufacturers who wear cottons will save in that article, and so of the rest. If books can be had much cheaper from Ireland, (which I believe for I bought Blackstone there for 24/- when it was sold in England at four guineas) is not this an advantage not to English booksellers indeed, but to English readers and to learning. And of all the complaints perhaps these booksellers are least worthy of consideration. The catalogue you last sent me amazes me by the high prices (said to be

10/14 From a letter by Benjamin Franklin to B. Vaughan Esq. dated April 21, 1785:

If the Irish can manufacture cottons, stuffs and silks, and linens, and cutlery, and toys, and books etc. etc. etc., so as to sell them cheaper in England than the manufacturers of England sell them, is not this good for the people of England who are not manufacturers? and will not even the manufacturers themselves share the benefit? Since if cottons are cheaper, all the other manufacturers who wear cottons will save in that article, and so of the rest. If books can be had much cheaper from Ireland, (which I believe for I bought Blackstone there for 24/- when it was sold in England at four guineas) is not this an advantage not to English booksellers indeed,

CENTURY BOLD CONDENSED MERGENTHALER TYPE LIBRARY

ABCDEFGHIJKLMNOPQRSTUVWXYZ
&.,''-:;!?""''1234567890$
abcdefghijklmnopqrstuvwxyz

8/8 From a letter by Benjamin Franklin to B. Vaughan Esq. dated April 21, 1785:
If the Irish can manufacture cottons, stuffs and silks, and linens, and cutlery, and toys, and books etc. etc. etc., so as to sell them cheaper in England than the manufacturers of England sell them, is not this good for the people of England who are not manufacturers? and will not even the manufacturers themselves share the benefit? Since if cottons are cheaper, all the other manufacturers who wear cottons will save in that article, and so of the rest. If books can be had much cheaper from Ireland, (which I believe for I bought Blackstone there for 24/- when it was sold in England at four guineas) is not this an advantage not to English booksellers indeed, but to English readers and to learning. And of all the complaints perhaps these booksellers are least worthy of consideration. The catalogue you last sent me amazes me by the high prices (said to be the lowest) affixed to each article. And one can scarce see a new book, without observing the excessive artifices may use of to puff up a paper of verses into a pamphlet, a pamphlet into an octavo, and an octavo into a quarto, with scab boardings, white lines, sparse titles of chapters, and exorbitant margins, to such a degree, that the selling of paper seems now the object and printing on it only the pretence. I enclose the copy of a page in a late comedy. Between every two lines there is a white space equal to another line. You have a law, I think, against butchers blowing of veal to make it look fatter; why not one against booksellers blowing of books to make them look bigger. All this to yourself; you can easily guess the reason.
My grandson is a little indisposed, but sends you two pamphlets, Figaro and Le

8/10 From a letter by Benjamin Franklin to B. Vaughan Esq. dated April 21, 1785:
If the Irish can manufacture cottons, stuffs and silks, and linens, and cutlery, and toys, and books etc. etc. etc., so as to sell them cheaper in England than the manufacturers of England sell them, is not this good for the people of England who are not manufacturers? and will not even the manufacturers themselves share the benefit? Since if cottons are cheaper, all the other manufacturers who wear cottons will save in that article, and so of the rest. If books can be had much cheaper from Ireland, (which I believe for I bought Blackstone there for 24/- when it was sold in England at four guineas) is not this an advantage not to English booksellers indeed, but to English readers and to learning. And of all the complaints perhaps these booksellers are least worthy of consideration. The catalogue you last sent me amazes me by the high prices (said to be the lowest) affixed to each article. And one can scarce see a new book, without observing the excessive artifices may use of to puff up a paper of verses into a pamphlet, a pamphlet into an octavo, and an octavo into a quarto, with scab boardings, white lines, sparse titles of chapters, and exorbitant margins, to such a degree, that the selling of paper seems now the object and printing on it only the pretence. I enclose the copy of a page in a late comedy. Between every two lines there is a white space equal to another line. You have a law,

8/12 From a letter by Benjamin Franklin to B. Vaughan Esq. dated April 21, 1785:
If the Irish can manufacture cottons, stuffs and silks, and linens, and cutlery, and toys, and books etc. etc. etc., so as to sell them cheaper in England than the manufacturers of England sell them, is not this good for the people of England who are not manufacturers? and will not even the manufacturers themselves share the benefit? Since if cottons are cheaper, all the other manufacturers who wear cottons will save in that article, and so of the rest. If books can be had much cheaper from Ireland, (which I believe for I bought Blackstone there for 24/- when it was sold in England at four guineas) is not this an advantage not to English booksellers indeed, but to English readers and to learning. And of all the complaints perhaps these booksellers are least worthy of consideration. The catalogue you last sent me amazes me by the high prices (said to be the lowest) affixed to each article. And one can scarce see a new book, without observing the excessive artifices may use of to puff up a paper of verses into a pamphlet, a pamphlet into an octavo, and an octavo into a

ABCDEFGHIJKLMNOPQRSTUVWXYZ
&.,''-:;!?""''1234567890$
abcdefghijklmnopqrstuvwxyz

ITC Cheltenham is a revival based on the popular 1900s version, which never fully lost currency. It combines warmth, and individuality with high legibility. Cheltenham is characteristic of types in wide use in the 1920s.

ijk E

CHELTENHAM FAMILY 213

zf

ABCDEFGHIJ
KLMNOPQRS
TUVWXYZ&
abcdefghijklmnopq
rstuvwxyz1234567
890$.,"":;!?

72 POINT CHELTENHAM   MERGENTHALER TYPE LIBRARY

ABCDEFGHIJKLMNOPQRSTUVWXYZ&abcdefghijklmnopqrstuvwxyz1234567890$.,"":;!?

72 POINT CHELTENHAM ITALIC   MERGENTHALER TYPE LIBRARY

ABCDEFGHIJKL
MNOPQRSTUV
WXYZ&abcdefghijkl
mnopqrstuvwxyz12345
67890$.,"":;!?

60 POINT CHELTENHAM   MERGENTHALER TYPE LIBRARY

ABCDEFGHIJKL
MNOPQRSTUVW
XYZ&abcdefghijklmn
opqrstuvwxyz12345678
90$.,"":;!?

60 POINT CHELTENHAM ITALIC   MERGENTHALER TYPE LIBRARY

ABCDEFGHIJKLMNO
PQRSTUVWXYZ&abc
defghijklmnopqrstuvwxyz123
4567890$.,""":;!?

48 POINT CHELTENHAM   MERGENTHALER TYPE LIBRARY

*ABCDEFGHIJKLMNOP
QRSTUVWXYZ&abcdef
ghijklmnopqrstuvwxyz123456
7890$.,""":;!?*

48 POINT CHELTENHAM ITALIC   MERGENTHALER TYPE LIBRARY

ABCDEFGHIJKLMNOPQRST
UVWXYZ&abcdefghijklmnopqrst
uvwxyz1234567890$.,""":;!?

36 POINT CHELTENHAM   MERGENTHALER TYPE LIBRARY

*ABCDEFGHIJKLMNOPQRST
UVWXYZ&abcdefghijklmnopqrstuv
wxyz1234567890$.,""":;!?*

36 POINT CHELTENHAM ITALIC   MERGENTHALER TYPE LIBRARY

ABCDEFGHIJKLMNOPQRSTUVWXYZ&a
bcdefghijklmnopqrstuvwxyz1234567890$.,""":;!?

24 POINT CHELTENHAM   MERGENTHALER TYPE LIBRARY

*ABCDEFGHIJKLMNOPQRSTUVWXYZ&abc
defghijklmnopqrstuvwxyz1234567890$.,""":;!?*

24 POINT CHELTENHAM ITALIC   MERGENTHALER TYPE LIBRARY

ABCDEFGHIJKLMNOPQRSTUVWXYZ&abcdefghijklmnopqr
stuvwxyz1234567890$.,""":;!?

18 POINT CHELTENHAM   MERGENTHALER TYPE LIBRARY

*ABCDEFGHIJKLMNOPQRSTUVWXYZ&abcdefghijklmnopqrstu
vwxyz1234567890$.,""":;!?*

18 POINT CHELTENHAM ITALIC   MERGENTHALER TYPE LIBRARY

CHELTENHAM FAMILY

14/14 Type is defined as a right-angled, prism-shaped piece of metal, having for its face a letter or character, usually in high relief, adapted for use in letter-press printing; and type in the aggregate is described as an assemblage of the characters used for printing. In a single type the chief points to be described are the face, counter, stem, hair-line, serif, beard or neck, shoulder, body or shank, pin-mark, nick, feet, and groove.

The accompanying diagram of a piece of *type (fig. 2) shows its face, body, nick, groove, feet, and pin-mark; and the plan of the*

12/12 Type is defined as a right-angled, prism-shaped piece of metal, having for its face a letter or character, usually in high relief, adapted for use in letter-press printing; and type in the aggregate is described as an assemblage of the characters used for printing. In a single type the chief points to be described are the face, counter, stem, hair-line, serif, beard or neck, shoulder, body or shank, pin-mark, nick, feet, and groove.

The accompanying diagram of a piece of type (fig. 2) shows its face, body, nick, groove, feet, and pin-mark; and the plan of the face (fig. 3) shows the stem, hair-line, serif, counter, beard, and shoulder.

The body (or shank) of a piece of type is the metal between the shoulder and the feet (described later),

14/16 Type is defined as a right-angled, prism-shaped piece of metal, having for its face a letter or character, usually in high relief, adapted for use in letter-press printing; and type in the aggregate is described as an assemblage of the characters used for printing. In a single type the chief points to be described are the face, counter, stem, hair-line, serif, beard or neck, shoulder, body or *shank, pin-mark, nick, feet, and groove.*

The accompanying diagram of a piece of

12/14 Type is defined as a right-angled, prism-shaped piece of metal, having for its face a letter or character, usually in high relief, adapted for use in letter-press printing; and type in the aggregate is described as an assemblage of the characters used for printing. In a single type the chief points to be described are the face, counter, stem, hair-line, serif, beard or neck, shoulder, body or shank, pin-mark, nick, feet, and groove.

The accompanying diagram of a piece of type *(fig. 2) shows its face, body, nick, groove, feet, and pin-mark; and the plan of the face (fig. 3) shows the*

14/18 Type is defined as a right-angled, prism-shaped piece of metal, having for its face a letter or character, usually in high relief, adapted for use in letter-press printing; and type in the aggregate is described as an assemblage of the characters used for printing. In a single type the chief points to be *described are the face, counter, stem, hairline, serif, beard or neck, shoulder, body or*

12/16 Type is defined as a right-angled, prism-shaped piece of metal, having for its face a letter or character, usually in high relief, adapted for use in letter-press printing; and type in the aggregate is described as an assemblage of the characters used for printing. In a single type the chief points to be described are the face, counter, stem, hair-line, serif, beard or neck, shoulder, body or shank, pin-mark, nick, feet, *and groove.*

The accompanying diagram of a piece of type (fig.

CHELTENHAM   MERGENTHALER TYPE LIBRARY

ABCDEFGHIJKLMNOPQRSTUV
ABCDEFGHIJKLMNOPQRSTUV
WXYZ&.,"-:;!?""1234567890$
WXYZ&.,"-:;!?""1234567890$
abcdefghijklmnopqrstuvwxyz
abcdefghijklmnopqrstuvwxyz

ABCDEFGHIJKLMNOPQRSTUVW
ABCDEFGHIJKLMNOPQRSTUVW
XYZ&.,"-:;!?""1234567890$
XYZ&.,"-:;!?""1234567890$
abcdefghijklmnopqrstuvwxyz
abcdefghijklmnopqrstuvwxyz

CHELTENHAM FAMILY 219

11/11 Type is defined as a right-angled, prism-shaped piece of metal, having for its face a letter or character, usually in high relief, adapted for use in letter-press printing; and type in the aggregate is described as an assemblage of the characters used for printing. In a single type the chief points to be described are the face, counter, stem, hair-line, serif, beard or neck, shoulder, body or shank, pin-mark, nick, feet, and groove.

The accompanying diagram of a piece of type (fig. 2) shows its face, body, nick, groove, feet, and pin-mark; and the plan of the face (fig. 3) shows the stem, hair-line, serif, counter, beard, and shoulder.

The body (or shank) of a piece of type is the metal between the shoulder and the feet (described later), and *the term "body" is also used to denote the size or thickness of types, leads, etc. The pin-mark is an indentation on the*

10/10 Type is defined as a right-angled, prism-shaped piece of metal, having for its face a letter or character, usually in high relief, adapted for use in letter-press printing; and type in the aggregate is described as an assemblage of the characters used for printing. In a single type the chief points to be described are the face, counter, stem, hair-line, serif, beard or neck, shoulder, body or shank, pin-mark, nick, feet, and groove.

The accompanying diagram of a piece of type (fig. 2) shows its face, body, nick, groove, feet, and pin-mark; and the plan of the face (fig. 3) shows the stem, hair-line, serif, counter, beard, and shoulder.

The body (or shank) of a piece of type is the metal between the shoulder and the feet (described later), and the term "body" is also used to denote the size or thickness of types, leads, etc. The pin-mark is an indentation on the upper part of the body, *made by the pin in casting. The nick is the groove across the lower part of the body of the type, and is a guide to the position in*

11/13 Type is defined as a right-angled, prism-shaped piece of metal, having for its face a letter or character, usually in high relief, adapted for use in letter-press printing; and type in the aggregate is described as an assemblage of the characters used for printing. In a single type the chief points to be described are the face, counter, stem, hair-line, serif, beard or neck, shoulder, body or shank, pin-mark, nick, feet, and groove.

The accompanying diagram of a piece of type (fig. 2) shows its face, body, nick, groove, feet, and pin-mark; and the plan of the face (fig. 3) shows the stem, hair-line, serif, counter, beard, and shoulder.

The body (or shank) of a piece of type is the metal between the shoulder and the feet (described later), and the

10/12 Type is defined as a right-angled, prism-shaped piece of metal, having for its face a letter or character, usually in high relief, adapted for use in letter-press printing; and type in the aggregate is described as an assemblage of the characters used for printing. In a single type the chief points to be described are the face, counter, stem, hair-line, serif, beard or neck, shoulder, body or shank, pin-mark, nick, feet, and groove.

The accompanying diagram of a piece of type (fig. 2) shows its face, body, nick, groove, feet, and pin-mark; and the plan of the face (fig. 3) shows the stem, hair-line, serif, counter, beard, and shoulder.

The body (or shank) of a piece of type is the metal between the shoulder and the feet (described later), and the term "body" *is also used to denote the size or thickness of types, leads, etc. The pin-mark is an indentation on the upper part of the body,*

11/15 Type is defined as a right-angled, prism-shaped piece of metal, having for its face a letter or character, usually in high relief, adapted for use in letter-press printing; and type in the aggregate is described as an assemblage of the characters used for printing. In a single type the chief points to be described are the face, counter, stem, hair-line, serif, beard or neck, shoulder, body or shank, pin-mark, nick, feet, and groove.

The accompanying diagram of a piece of type (fig. 2) *shows its face, body, nick, groove, feet, and pin-mark; and the plan of the face (fig. 3) shows the stem, hair-line, serif,*

10/14 Type is defined as a right-angled, prism-shaped piece of metal, having for its face a letter or character, usually in high relief, adapted for use in letter-press printing; and type in the aggregate is described as an assemblage of the characters used for printing. In a single type the chief points to be described are the face, counter, stem, hair-line, serif, beard or neck, shoulder, body or shank, pin-mark, nick, feet, and groove.

The accompanying diagram of a piece of type (fig. 2) shows its face, body, nick, groove, feet, and pin-mark; and the plan of the face (fig. 3) shows the stem, hair-line, serif, counter, beard, *and shoulder.*

The body (or shank) of a piece of type is the metal between the

CHELTENHAM   MERGENTHALER TYPE LIBRARY

ABCDEFGHIJKLMNOPQRSTUVWXYZ
ABCDEFGHIJKLMNOPQRSTUVWXYZ
&.,"-:;!?""1234567890$
&.,"-:;!?""1234567890$
abcdefghijklmnopqrstuvwxyz
abcdefghijklmnopqrstuvwxyz

ABCDEFGHIJKLMNOPQRSTUVWXYZ
ABCDEFGHIJKLMNOPQRSTUVWXYZ
&.,"-:;!?""1234567890$
&.,"-:;!?""1234567890$
abcdefghijklmnopqrstuvwxyz
abcdefghijklmnopqrstuvwxyz

9/9 Type is defined as a right-angled, prism-shaped piece of metal, having for its face a letter or character, usually in high relief, adapted for use in letter-press printing; and type in the aggregate is described as an assemblage of the characters used for printing. In a single type the chief points to be described are the face, counter, stem, hair-line, serif, beard or neck, shoulder, body or shank, pin-mark, nick, feet, and groove.

The accompanying diagram of a piece of type (fig. 2) shows its face, body, nick, groove, feet, and pin-mark; and the plan of the face (fig. 3) shows the stem, hair-line, serif, counter, beard, and shoulder.

The body (or shank) of a piece of type is the metal between the shoulder and the feet (described later), and the term "body" is also used to denote the size or thickness of types, leads, etc. The pin-mark is an indentation on the upper part of the body, made by the pin in casting. The nick is the groove across the lower part of the body of the type, and is a guide to the position in which it is to be set up. The feet are the projections on each side of the groove on which the type stands, the groove being the hollow left between the feet where formerly was the jet.

The face of a type is the letter on its upper end which carries the ink to

8/8 Type is defined as a right-angled, prism-shaped piece of metal, having for its face a letter or character, usually in high relief, adapted for use in letter-press printing; and type in the aggregate is described as an assemblage of the characters used for printing. In a single type the chief points to be described are the face, counter, stem, hair-line, serif, beard or neck, shoulder, body or shank, pin-mark, nick, feet, and groove.

The accompanying diagram of a piece of type (fig. 2) shows its face, body, nick, groove, feet, and pin-mark; and the plan of the face (fig. 3) shows the stem, hair-line, serif, counter, beard, and shoulder.

The body (or shank) of a piece of type is the metal between the shoulder and the feet (described later), and the term "body" is also used to denote the size or thickness of types, leads, etc. The pin-mark is an indentation on the upper part of the body, made by the pin in casting. The nick is the groove across the lower part of the body of the type, and is a guide to the position in which it is to be set up. The feet are the projections on each side of the groove on which the type stands, the groove being the hollow left between the feet where formerly was the jet.

The face of a type is the letter on its upper end which carries the ink to be impressed upon the paper; the counter is the cavity left by the surrounding lines of the face. The pin-mark is an indentation on the upper part of the body. The *groove across the lower part of the body of the type is a guide to the position in which it is to be set up. The feet are the projections on each side of the groove on*

9/11 Type is defined as a right-angled, prism-shaped piece of metal, having for its face a letter or character, usually in high relief, adapted for use in letter-press printing; and type in the aggregate is described as an assemblage of the characters used for printing. In a single type the chief points to be described are the face, counter, stem, hair-line, serif, beard or neck, shoulder, body or shank, pin-mark, nick, feet, and groove.

The accompanying diagram of a piece of type (fig. 2) shows its face, body, nick, groove, feet, and pin-mark; and the plan of the face (fig. 3) shows the stem, hair-line, serif, counter, beard, and shoulder.

The body (or shank) of a piece of type is the metal between the shoulder and the feet (described later), and the term "body" is also used to denote the size or thickness of types, leads, etc. The pin-mark is an indentation on the upper part of the body, made by the pin in casting. *The nick is the groove across the lower part of the body of the type, and is a guide to the position in which it is to be set up. The feet are*

8/10 Type is defined as a right-angled, prism-shaped piece of metal, having for its face a letter or character, usually in high relief, adapted for use in letter-press printing; and type in the aggregate is described as an assemblage of the characters used for printing. In a single type the chief points to be described are the face, counter, stem, hair-line, serif, beard or neck, shoulder, body or shank, pin-mark, nick, feet, and groove.

The accompanying diagram of a piece of type (fig. 2) shows its face, body, nick, groove, feet, and pin-mark; and the plan of the face (fig. 3) shows the stem, hair-line, serif, counter, beard, and shoulder.

The body (or shank) of a piece of type is the metal between the shoulder and the feet (described later), and the term "body" is also used to denote the size or thickness of types, leads, etc. The pin-mark is an indentation on the upper part of the body, made by the pin in casting. The nick is the groove across the lower part of the body of the type, and is a guide to the position in which it is to be set up. The feet are the projections on each side of the groove on which the type stands, the groove being the hollow left between the feet where formerly was the jet.

The face of a type is the letter on its upper end which carries the ink to be

9/13 Type is defined as a right-angled, prism-shaped piece of metal, having for its face a letter or character, usually in high relief, adapted for use in letter-press printing; and type in the aggregate is described as an assemblage of the characters used for printing. In a single type the chief points to be described are the face, counter, stem, hair-line, serif, beard or neck, shoulder, body or shank, pin-mark, nick, feet, and groove.

The accompanying diagram of a piece of type (fig. 2) shows its face, body, nick, groove, feet, and pin-mark; and the plan of the face (fig. 3) shows the stem, hair-line, serif, counter, beard, and shoulder.

The body (or shank) of a piece of type is the metal between the *shoulder and the feet (described later), and the term "body" is also used to denote the size or thickness of types, leads, etc. The pin-mark is an*

8/12 Type is defined as a right-angled, prism-shaped piece of metal, having for its face a letter or character, usually in high relief, adapted for use in letter-press printing; and type in the aggregate is described as an assemblage of the characters used for printing. In a single type the chief points to be described are the face, counter, stem, hair-line, serif, beard or neck, shoulder, body or shank, pin-mark, nick, feet, and groove.

The accompanying diagram of a piece of type (fig. 2) shows its face, body, nick, groove, feet, and pin-mark; and the plan of the face (fig. 3) shows the stem, hair-line, serif, counter, beard, and shoulder.

The body (or shank) of a piece of type is the metal between the shoulder and the feet (described later), and the term "body" is also used to denote the size or thickness of types, leads, etc. The pin-mark is an indentation on the upper part of the body, made by the pin in casting. The nick is the groove across the lower part of the body of the type, and is a guide to the position in which it is to be set up.

CHELTENHAM   MERGENTHALER TYPE LIBRARY

ABCDEFGHIJKLMNOPQRSTUVWXYZ
ABCDEFGHIJKLMNOPQRSTUVWXYZ
&.,"-:;!?""1234567890$
&.,"-:;!?""1234567890$
abcdefghijklmnopqrstuvwxyz
abcdefghijklmnopqrstuvwxyz

ABCDEFGHIJKLMNOPQRSTUVWXYZ
ABCDEFGHIJKLMNOPQRSTUVWXYZ
&.,"-:;!?""1234567890$
&.,"-:;!?""1234567890$
abcdefghijklmnopqrstuvwxyz
abcdefghijklmnopqrstuvwxyz

ABCDEFGHIJ KLMNOPQRS TUVWXYZ&a bcdefghijklmno pqrstuvwxyz12 34567890$.,""":;!?

72 POINT CHELTENHAM BOLD MERGENTHALER TYPE LIBRARY

¹⁴⁄₁₄ **Type is defined as a right-angled, prism-shaped piece of metal, having for its face a letter or character, usually in high relief, adapted for use in letter-press printing; and type in the aggregate is described as an assemblage of the characters used for printing. In a single type the chief points to be described are the face, counter, stem, hair-line, serif, beard or neck, shoulder, body or shank, pin-*mark, nick, feet, and groove.***

The accompanying diagram of a

¹⁴⁄₁₆ **Type is defined as a right-angled, prism-shaped piece of metal, having for its face a letter or character, usually in high relief, adapted for use in letter-press printing; and type in the aggregate is described as an assemblage of the characters used for printing. In a single type the chief points to be described are the face, *counter, stem, hair-line, serif, beard or neck, shoulder, body or shank, pin-***

¹⁴⁄₁₈ **Type is defined as a right-angled, prism-shaped piece of metal, having for its face a letter or character, usually in high relief, adapted for use in letter-press printing; and type in the aggregate is described as an assemblage of the characters used for *printing. In a single type the chief points to be described are the face,***

¹²⁄₁₂ **Type is defined as a right-angled, prism-shaped piece of metal, having for its face a letter or character, usually in high relief, adapted for use in letter-press printing; and type in the aggregate is described as an assemblage of the characters used for printing. In a single type the chief points to be described are the face, counter, stem, hair-line, serif, beard or neck, shoulder, body or shank, pin-mark, nick, feet, and groove.**

The accompanying diagram of a piece of type (fig. 2) shows its face, body, nick, groove, feet, and pin-mark; and the plan of *the face (fig. 3) shows the stem, hair-line, serif, counter, beard, and shoulder.*

¹²⁄₁₄ **Type is defined as a right-angled, prism-shaped piece of metal, having for its face a letter or character, usually in high relief, adapted for use in letter-press printing; and type in the aggregate is described as an assemblage of the characters used for printing. In a single type the chief points to be described are the face, counter, stem, hair-line, serif, beard or neck, shoulder, body or shank, pin-mark, nick, feet, and groove.**

The accompanying diagram of a piece of type (fig. 2) shows its face, body, nick,

¹²⁄₁₆ **Type is defined as a right-angled, prism-shaped piece of metal, having for its face a letter or character, usually in high relief, adapted for use in letter-press printing; and type in the aggregate is described as an assemblage of the characters used for printing. In a single type the chief points to be described are the face, counter, stem, hair-line, serif, beard or neck, shoulder, body or shank, pin-mark, nick, feet, and groove.**

CHELTENHAM BOLD   MERGENTHALER TYPE LIBRARY

ABCDEFGHIJKLMNOPQRSTUV
ABCDEFGHIJKLMNOPQRSTUV
WXYZ&.,"-:;!?""'"1234567890$
WXYZ&.,"-:;!?""'"1234567890$
abcdefghijklmnopqrstuvwxyz
abcdefghijklmnopqrstuvwxyz

ABCDEFGHIJKLMNOPQRSTUVW
ABCDEFGHIJKLMNOPQRSTUVW
XYZ&.,"-:;!?""'"1234567890$
XYZ&.,"-:;!?""'"1234567890$
abcdefghijklmnopqrstuvwxyz
abcdefghijklmnopqrstuvwxyz

CHELTENHAM FAMILY 225

10/10 Type is defined as a right-angled, prism-shaped piece of metal, having for its face a letter or character, usually in high relief, adapted for use in letter-press printing; and type in the aggregate is described as an assemblage of the characters used for printing. In a single type the chief points to be described are the face, counter, stem, hair-line, serif, beard or neck, shoulder, body or shank, pin-mark, nick, feet, and groove.

The accompanying diagram of a piece of type (fig. 2) shows its face, body, nick, groove, feet, and pin-mark; and the plan of the face (fig. 3) shows the stem, hair-line, serif, counter, beard, and shoulder.

The body (or shank) of a piece of type is the metal between the shoulder and the feet (described later), *and the term "body" is also used to denote the size or thickness of types, leads, etc. The pin-mark is an*

10/12 Type is defined as a right-angled, prism-shaped piece of metal, having for its face a letter or character, usually in high relief, adapted for use in letter-press printing; and type in the aggregate is described as an assemblage of the characters used for printing. In a single type the chief points to be described are the face, counter, stem, hair-line, serif, beard or neck, shoulder, body or shank, pin-mark, nick, feet, and groove.

The accompanying diagram of a piece of type (fig. 2) shows its face, body, nick, groove, feet, and pin-mark; and the plan of the face (fig. 3) shows the stem, hair-line, serif, counter, beard, and shoulder.

The body (or shank) of a piece of type is the metal between the shoulder and the feet (described later),

10/14 Type is defined as a right-angled, prism-shaped piece of metal, having for its face a letter or character, usually in high relief, adapted for use in letter-press printing; and type in the aggregate is described as an assemblage of the characters used for printing. In a single type the chief points to be described are the face, counter, stem, hair-line, serif, beard or neck, shoulder, body or shank, pin-mark, nick, feet, and groove.

The accompanying diagram of a piece of type (fig. 2) *shows its face, body, nick, groove, feet, and pin-mark; and the plan of the face (fig. 3) shows the*

CHELTENHAM BOLD   MERGENTHALER TYPE LIBRARY

ABCDEFGHIJKLMNOPQRSTUVWXYZ
ABCDEFGHIJKLMNOPQRSTUVWXYZ
&.,"‑‑:;!?"""1234567890$
&.,"‑‑:;!?"""1234567890$
abcdefghijklmnopqrstuvwxyz
abcdefghijklmnopqrstuvwxyz

8/8 Type is defined as a right-angled, prism-shaped piece of metal, having for its face a letter or character, usually in high relief, adapted for use in letter-press printing; and type in the aggregate is described as an assemblage of the characters used for printing. In a single type the chief points to be described are the face, counter, stem, hair-line, serif, beard or neck, shoulder, body or shank, pin-mark, nick, feet, and groove.

The accompanying diagram of a piece of type (fig. 2) shows its face, body, nick, groove, feet, and pin-mark; and the plan of the face (fig. 3) shows the stem, hair-line, serif, counter, beard, and shoulder.

The body (or shank) of a piece of type is the metal between the shoulder and the feet (described later), and the term "body" is also used to denote the size or thickness of types, leads, etc. The pin-mark is an indentation on the upper part of the body, made by the pin in casting. The nick is the groove across the lower part of the body of the type, and is a guide to the position in which it is to be set up. The feet are the projections on each side of the groove on which the type stands, the groove being the hollow left between the feet where formerly was the jet.

The face of a type is the letter on its upper end which carries the ink to be impressed upon the paper; the counter is the cavity left by

8/10 Type is defined as a right-angled, prism-shaped piece of metal, having for its face a letter or character, usually in high relief, adapted for use in letter-press printing; and type in the aggregate is described as an assemblage of the characters used for printing. In a single type the chief points to be described are the face, counter, stem, hair-line, serif, beard or neck, shoulder, body or shank, pin-mark, nick, feet, and groove.

The accompanying diagram of a piece of type (fig. 2) shows its face, body, nick, groove, feet, and pin-mark; and the plan of the face (fig. 3) shows the stem, hair-line, serif, counter, beard, and shoulder.

The body (or shank) of a piece of type is the metal between the shoulder and the feet (described later), and the term "body" is also used to denote the size or thickness of types, leads, etc. The pin-mark is an indentation on the upper part of the body, made by the pin in casting. The nick is the groove across the lower part of the *body of the type, and is a guide to the position in which it is to be set up. The feet are the projections on each side of the groove on*

8/12 Type is defined as a right-angled, prism-shaped piece of metal, having for its face a letter or character, usually in high relief, adapted for use in letter-press printing; and type in the aggregate is described as an assemblage of the characters used for printing. In a single type the chief points to be described are the face, counter, stem, hair-line, serif, beard or neck, shoulder, body or shank, pin-mark, nick, feet, and groove.

The accompanying diagram of a piece of type (fig. 2) shows its face, body, nick, groove, feet, and pin-mark; and the plan of the face (fig. 3) shows the stem, hair-line, serif, counter, beard, and shoulder.

The body (or shank) of a piece of type is the metal between the *shoulder and the feet (described later), and the term "body" is also used to denote the size or thickness of types, leads, etc. The pin-*

ABCDEFGHIJKLMNOPQRSTUVWXYZ
ABCDEFGHIJKLMNOPQRSTUVWXYZ
&.,"‑‑:;!?"""1234567890$
&.,"‑‑:;!?"""1234567890$
abcdefghijklmnopqrstuvwxyz
abcdefghijklmnopqrstuvwxyz

ABCDEFGHIJKL
MNOPQRSTUVW
XYZ&abcdefghijk
lmnopqrstuvwxy
z1234567890$.,"":
;!?

72 POINT CHELTENHAM BOLD CONDENSED   MERGENTHALER TYPE LIBRARY

ABCDEFGHIJKLM NOPQRSTUVWXY Z&abcdefghijklm nopqrstuvwxyz12 34567890$.,""";!?

72 POINT CHELTENHAM BOLD CONDENSED ITALIC   MERGENTHALER TYPE LIBRARY

ABCDEFGHIJKLMNOPQRS
TUVWXYZ&abcdefghijkl
mnopqrstuvwxyz1234567
890$.,""'":;!?

48 POINT CHELTENHAM BOLD CONDENSED   MERGENTHALER TYPE LIBRARY

*ABCDEFGHIJKLMNOPQRST
UVWXYZ&abcdefghijklmn
opqrstuvwxyz1234567890
$.,""'":;!?*

48 POINT CHELTENHAM BOLD CONDENSED ITALIC   MERGENTHALER TYPE LIBRARY

ABCDEFGHIJKLMNOPQRSTUVWXYZ&abcdefghij
klmnopqrstuvwxyz1234567890$.,""'":;!?

24 POINT CHELTENHAM BOLD CONDENSED   MERGENTHALER TYPE LIBRARY

*ABCDEFGHIJKLMNOPQRSTUVWXYZ&abcdefghijkl
mnopqrstuvwxyz1234567890$.,""'";!?*

24 POINT CHELTENHAM BOLD CONDENSED ITALIC   MERGENTHALER TYPE LIBRARY

CHELTENHAM FAMILY 229

14/14 **Type is defined as a right-angled, prism-shaped piece of metal, having for its face a letter or character, usually in high relief, adapted for use in letter-press printing; and type in the aggregate is described as an assemblage of the characters used for printing. In a single type the chief points to be described are the face, counter, stem, hair-line, serif, beard or neck, shoulder, body or shank, pin-mark, nick, feet, and groove.**

The accompanying diagram of a piece

14/16 **Type is defined as a right-angled, prism-shaped piece of metal, having for its face a letter or character, usually in high relief, adapted for use in letter-press printing; and type in the aggregate is described as an assemblage of the characters used for printing. In a single type the chief points to be described are the face, *counter, stem, hair-line, serif, beard or neck, shoulder, body or shank, pin-***

14/18 **Type is defined as a right-angled, prism-shaped piece of metal, having for its face a letter or character, usually in high relief, adapted for use in letter-press printing; and type in the aggregate is described as an assemblage of the characters used for printing. *In a single type the chief points to be described are the face, counter,***

12/12 Type is defined as a right-angled, prism-shaped piece of metal, having for its face a letter or character, usually in high relief, adapted for use in letter-press printing; and type in the aggregate is described as an assemblage of the characters used for printing. In a single type the chief points to be described are the face, counter, stem, hair-line, serif, beard or neck, shoulder, body or shank, pin-mark, nick, feet, and groove.

The accompanying diagram of a piece of type (fig. 2) shows its face, body, nick, groove, feet, and pin-mark; and the plan of the face (fig. 3) shows the stem, hair-line, serif, counter, beard, and shoulder.

12/14 Type is defined as a right-angled, prism-shaped piece of metal, having for its face a letter or character, usually in high relief, adapted for use in letter-press printing; and type in the aggregate is described as an assemblage of the characters used for printing. In a single type the chief points to be described are the face, counter, stem, hair-line, serif, beard or neck, shoulder, body or shank, pin-mark, nick, feet, and groove.

The accompanying diagram of a piece of type (fig. 2) shows its face, body, nick, groove,

12/16 Type is defined as a right-angled, prism-shaped piece of metal, having for its face a letter or character, usually in high relief, adapted for use in letter-press printing; and type in the aggregate is described as an assemblage of the characters used for printing. In a single type the chief points to be described are the face, counter, stem, hair-line, *serif, beard or neck, shoulder, body or shank, pin-mark, nick, feet, and groove.*

CHELTENHAM BOLD CONDENSED   MERGENTHALER TYPE LIBRARY

ABCDEFGHIJKLMNOPQRSTUVWXYZ
ABCDEFGHIJKLMNOPQRSTUVWXYZ
&.,"-:;!?""1234567890$
&.,"-:;!?""1234567890$
abcdefghijklmnopqrstuvwxyz
abcdefghijklmnopqrstuvwxyz

ABCDEFGHIJKLMNOPQRSTUVWXYZ
ABCDEFGHIJKLMNOPQRSTUVWXYZ
&.,"-:;!?""1234567890$
&.,"-:;!?""1234567890$
abcdefghijklmnopqrstuvwxyz
abcdefghijklmnopqrstuvwxyz

10/10 Type is defined as a right-angled, prism-shaped piece of metal, having for its face a letter or character, usually in high relief, adapted for use in letter-press printing; and type in the aggregate is described as an assemblage of the characters used for printing. In a single type the chief points to be described are the face, counter, stem, hair-line, serif, beard or neck, shoulder, body or shank, pin-mark, nick, feet, and groove.

The accompanying diagram of a piece of type (fig. 2) shows its face, body, nick, groove, feet, and pin-mark; and the plan of the face (fig. 3) shows the stem, hair-line, serif, counter, beard, and shoulder.

The body (or shank) of a piece of type is the metal between the shoulder and the feet (described later), and the term "body" is also used to denote the size or thickness of types, leads, etc. The pin-mark is an indent-

8/8 Type is defined as a right-angled, prism-shaped piece of metal, having for its face a letter or character, usually in high relief, adapted for use in letter-press printing; and type in the aggregate is described as an assemblage of the characters used for printing. In a single type the chief points to be described are the face, counter, stem, hair-line, serif, beard or neck, shoulder, body or shank, pin-mark, nick, feet, and groove.

The accompanying diagram of a piece of type (fig. 2) shows its face, body, nick, groove, feet, and pin-mark; and the plan of the face (fig. 3) shows the stem, hair-line, serif, counter, beard, and shoulder.

The body (or shank) of a piece of type is the metal between the shoulder and the feet (described later), and the term "body" is also used to denote the size or thickness of types, leads, etc. The pin-mark is an indentation on the upper part of the body, made by the pin in casting. The nick is the groove across the lower part of the body of the type, and is a guide to the position in which it is to be set up. The feet are the projections on each side of the groove on which the type stands, the groove being the hollow left between the feet where formerly was the jet.

The face of a type is the letter on its upper end which carries the ink to be impressed upon the paper; the counter is the cavity left by the

10/12 Type is defined as a right-angled, prism-shaped piece of metal, having for its face a letter or character, usually in high relief, adapted for use in letter-press printing; and type in the aggregate is described as an assemblage of the characters used for printing. In a single type the chief points to be described are the face, counter, stem, hair-line, serif, beard or neck, shoulder, body or shank, pin-mark, nick, feet, and groove.

The accompanying diagram of a piece of type (fig. 2) shows its face, body, nick, groove, feet, and pin-mark; and the plan of the face (fig. 3) shows the stem, hair-line, serif, counter, beard, and shoulder.

The body (or shank) of a piece of type is the metal between the shoulder and the feet (described later), and

8/10 Type is defined as a right-angled, prism-shaped piece of metal, having for its face a letter or character, usually in high relief, adapted for use in letter-press printing; and type in the aggregate is described as an assemblage of the characters used for printing. In a single type the chief points to be described are the face, counter, stem, hair-line, serif, beard or neck, shoulder, body or shank, pin-mark, nick, feet, and groove.

The accompanying diagram of a piece of type (fig. 2) shows its face, body, nick, groove, feet, and pin-mark; and the plan of the face (fig. 3) shows the stem, hair-line, serif, counter, beard, and shoulder.

The body (or shank) of a piece of type is the metal between the shoulder and the feet (described later), and the term "body" is also used to denote the size or thickness of types, leads, etc. The pin-mark is an indentation on the upper part of the body, made by the pin in casting. The nick is the groove across the lower part of the body of *the type, and is a guide to the position in which it is to be set up. The feet are the projections on each side of the groove on which the type*

10/14 Type is defined as a right-angled, prism-shaped piece of metal, having for its face a letter or character, usually in high relief, adapted for use in letter-press printing; and type in the aggregate is described as an assemblage of the characters used for printing. In a single type the chief points to be described are the face, counter, stem, hair-line, serif, beard or neck, shoulder, body or shank, pin-mark, nick, feet, and groove.

The accompanying diagram of a piece of type (fig. 2) *shows its face, body, nick, groove, feet, and pin-mark; and the plan of the face (fig. 3) shows the stem, hair-*

8/12 Type is defined as a right-angled, prism-shaped piece of metal, having for its face a letter or character, usually in high relief, adapted for use in letter-press printing; and type in the aggregate is described as an assemblage of the characters used for printing. In a single type the chief points to be described are the face, counter, stem, hair-line, serif, beard or neck, shoulder, body or shank, pin-mark, nick, feet, and groove.

The accompanying diagram of a piece of type (fig. 2) shows its face, body, nick, groove, feet, and pin-mark; and the plan of the face (fig. 3) shows the stem, hair-line, serif, counter, beard, and shoulder.

The body (or shank) of a piece of type is the metal between the *shoulder and the feet (described later), and the term "body" is also used to denote the size or thickness of types, leads, etc. The pin-mark is*

CHELTENHAM BOLD CONDENSED   MERGENTHALER TYPE LIBRARY

ABCDEFGHIJKLMNOPQRSTUVWXYZ
ABCDEFGHIJKLMNOPQRSTUVWXYZ
&.,"-:;!?""1234567890$
&.,"-:;!?""1234567890$
abcdefghijklmnopqrstuvwxyz
abcdefghijklmnopqrstuvwxyz

ABCDEFGHIJKLMNOPQRSTUVWXYZ
ABCDEFGHIJKLMNOPQRSTUVWXYZ
&.,"-:;!?""1234567890$
&.,"-:;!?""1234567890$
abcdefghijklmnopqrstuvwxyz
abcdefghijklmnopqrstuvwxyz

ABCDEFGHIJKLMNOP
QRSTUVWXYZ&abcd
efghijklmnopqrstuvw
xyz1234567890$.,""":
;!?

72 POINT CHELTENHAM BOLD EXTRA CONDENSED   MERGENTHALER TYPE LIBRARY

ABCDEFGHIJKLMNOPQRSTUVW
XYZ&abcdefghijklmnopqrstuvw
xyz1234567890$.,""":;!?

48 POINT CHELTENHAM BOLD EXTRA CONDENSED   MERGENTHALER TYPE LIBRARY

ABCDEFGHIJKLMNOPQRSTUVWXYZ&abcdefghijklmnopqrstuvwx
yz1234567890$.,""":;!?

24 POINT CHELTENHAM BOLD EXTRA CONDENSED   MERGENTHALER TYPE LIBRARY

14/14 Type is defined as a right-angled, prism-shaped piece of metal, having for its face a letter or character, usually in high relief, adapted for use in letter-press printing; and type in the aggregate is described as an assemblage of the characters used for printing. In a single type the chief points to be described are the face, counter, stem, hair-line, serif, beard or neck, shoulder, body or shank, pin-mark, nick, feet, and groove.

The accompanying diagram of a piece of type (fig. 2) shows its face, body, nick, groove, feet, and pin-mark; and the plan of the face (fig. 3) shows the stem, hair-line, serif, counter, beard, and shoulder.

12/12 Type is defined as a right-angled, prism-shaped piece of metal, having for its face a letter or character, usually in high relief, adapted for use in letter-press printing; and type in the aggregate is described as an assemblage of the characters used for printing. In a single type the chief points to be described are the face, counter, stem, hair-line, serif, beard or neck, shoulder, body or shank, pin-mark, nick, feet, and groove.

The accompanying diagram of a piece of type (fig. 2) shows its face, body, nick, groove, feet, and pin-mark; and the plan of the face (fig. 3) shows the stem, hair-line, serif, counter, beard, and shoulder.

The body (or shank) of a piece of type is the metal between the shoulder and the feet (described later), and the term "body" is also used to denote the size or thickness of types,

14/16 Type is defined as a right-angled, prism-shaped piece of metal, having for its face a letter or character, usually in high relief, adapted for use in letter-press printing; and type in the aggregate is described as an assemblage of the characters used for printing. In a single type the chief points to be described are the face, counter, stem, hair-line, serif, beard or neck, shoulder, body or shank, pin-mark, nick, feet, and groove.

The accompanying diagram of a piece of type (fig. 2) shows its face, body, nick, groove, feet, and pin-

12/14 Type is defined as a right-angled, prism-shaped piece of metal, having for its face a letter or character, usually in high relief, adapted for use in letter-press printing; and type in the aggregate is described as an assemblage of the characters used for printing. In a single type the chief points to be described are the face, counter, stem, hair-line, serif, beard or neck, shoulder, body or shank, pin-mark, nick, feet, and groove.

The accompanying diagram of a piece of type (fig. 2) shows its face, body, nick, groove, feet, and pin-mark; and the plan of the face (fig. 3) shows the stem, hair-line, serif, counter, beard, and shoulder.

14/18 Type is defined as a right-angled, prism-shaped piece of metal, having for its face a letter or character, usually in high relief, adapted for use in letter-press printing; and type in the aggregate is described as an assemblage of the characters used for printing. In a single type the chief points to be described are the face, counter, stem, hair-line, serif, beard or neck, shoulder, body or shank, pin-mark, nick, feet, and groove.

12/16 Type is defined as a right-angled, prism-shaped piece of metal, having for its face a letter or character, usually in high relief, adapted for use in letter-press printing; and type in the aggregate is described as an assemblage of the characters used for printing. In a single type the chief points to be described are the face, counter, stem, hair-line, serif, beard or neck, shoulder, body or shank, pin-mark, nick, feet, and groove.

The accompanying diagram of a piece of type (fig. 2) shows its face, body, nick, groove, feet, and pin-mark; and the plan of

CHELTENHAM BOLD EXTRA CONSENSED   MERGENTHALER TYPE LIBRARY

ABCDEFGHIJKLMNOPQRSTUVWXYZ
&.,'"-:;!?""'1234567890$
abcdefghijklmnopqrstuvwxyz

ABCDEFGHIJKLMNOPQRSTUVWXYZ
&.,'"-:;!?""'1234567890$
abcdefghijklmnopqrstuvwxyz

CHELTENHAM FAMILY 233

10/10 Type is defined as a right-angled, prism-shaped piece of metal, having for its face a letter or character, usually in high relief, adapted for use in letter-press printing; and type in the aggregate is described as an assemblage of the characters used for printing. In a single type the chief points to be described are the face, counter, stem, hair-line, serif, beard or neck, shoulder, body or shank, pin-mark, nick, feet, and groove.

The accompanying diagram of a piece of type (fig. 2) shows its face, body, nick, groove, feet, and pin-mark; and the plan of the face (fig. 3) shows the stem, hair-line, serif, counter, beard, and shoulder.

The body (or shank) of a piece of type is the metal between the shoulder and the feet (described later), and the term "body" is also used to denote the size or thickness of types, leads, etc. The pin-mark is an indentation on the upper part of the body, made by the pin in casting. The nick is the groove across the lower part of the body of the type, and is a guide to the position in which it is to be set up. The feet are the projections on each side of the groove on which the type stands, the groove being the hollow left between the feet where formerly was the jet.

8/8 Type is defined as a right-angled, prism-shaped piece of metal, having for its face a letter or character, usually in high relief, adapted for use in letter-press printing; and type in the aggregate is described as an assemblage of the characters used for printing. In a single type the chief points to be described are the face, counter, stem, hair-line, serif, beard or neck, shoulder, body or shank, pin-mark, nick, feet, and groove.

The accompanying diagram of a piece of type (fig. 2) shows its face, body, nick, groove, feet, and pin-mark; and the plan of the face (fig. 3) shows the stem, hair-line, serif, counter, beard, and shoulder.

The body (or shank) of a piece of type is the metal between the shoulder and the feet (described later), and the term "body" is also used to denote the size or thickness of types, leads, etc. The pin-mark is an indentation on the upper part of the body, made by the pin in casting. The nick is the groove across the lower part of the body of the type, and is a guide to the position in which it is to be set up. The feet are the projections on each side of the groove on which the type stands, the groove being the hollow left between the feet where formerly was the jet.

The face of a type is the letter on its upper end which carries the ink to be impressed upon the paper; the counter is the cavity left by the surrounding lines of the face.

Type is defined as a right-angled, prism-shaped piece of metal, having for its face a letter or character, usually in high relief, adapted for use in letter-press printing; and type in the aggregate is described as an assemblage of the characters used for printing. In a single type the chief points to be described are the face, counter, stem, hair-line, serif, beard or neck, shoulder, body or shank, pin-mark, nick, feet, and groove.

10/12 Type is defined as a right-angled, prism-shaped piece of metal, having for its face a letter or character, usually in high relief, adapted for use in letter-press printing; and type in the aggregate is described as an assemblage of the characters used for printing. In a single type the chief points to be described are the face, counter, stem, hair-line, serif, beard or neck, shoulder, body or shank, pin-mark, nick, feet, and groove.

The accompanying diagram of a piece of type (fig. 2) shows its face, body, nick, groove, feet, and pin-mark; and the plan of the face (fig. 3) shows the stem, hair-line, serif, counter, beard, and shoulder.

The body (or shank) of a piece of type is the metal between the shoulder and the feet (described later), and the term "body" is also used to denote the size or thickness of types, leads, etc. The pin-mark is an indentation on the upper part of the body, made by the pin in casting. The nick is the groove across the lower part of the body of the type, and is a guide to the position in which it is to be set up. The feet are the projections on each side

8/10 Type is defined as a right-angled, prism-shaped piece of metal, having for its face a letter or character, usually in high relief, adapted for use in letter-press printing; and type in the aggregate is described as an assemblage of the characters used for printing. In a single type the chief points to be described are the face, counter, stem, hair-line, serif, beard or neck, shoulder, body or shank, pin-mark, nick, feet, and groove.

The accompanying diagram of a piece of type (fig. 2) shows its face, body, nick, groove, feet, and pin-mark; and the plan of the face (fig. 3) shows the stem, hair-line, serif, counter, beard, and shoulder.

The body (or shank) of a piece of type is the metal between the shoulder and the feet (described later), and the term "body" is also used to denote the size or thickness of types, leads, etc. The pin-mark is an indentation on the upper part of the body, made by the pin in casting. The nick is the groove across the lower part of the body of the type, and is a guide to the position in which it is to be set up. The feet are the projections on each side of the groove on which the type stands, the groove being the hollow left between the feet where formerly was the jet.

The face of a type is the letter on its upper end which carries the ink to be impressed upon the paper; the counter is the cavity left by the surrounding lines of the face.

Type is defined as a right-angled, prism-shaped piece of metal, having for its face a letter

10/14 Type is defined as a right-angled, prism-shaped piece of metal, having for its face a letter or character, usually in high relief, adapted for use in letter-press printing; and type in the aggregate is described as an assemblage of the characters used for printing. In a single type the chief points to be described are the face, counter, stem, hair-line, serif, beard or neck, shoulder, body or shank, pin-mark, nick, feet, and groove.

The accompanying diagram of a piece of type (fig. 2) shows its face, body, nick, groove, feet, and pin-mark; and the plan of the face (fig. 3) shows the stem, hair-line, serif, counter, beard, and shoulder.

The body (or shank) of a piece of type is the metal between the shoulder and the feet (described later), and the term "body" is also used to denote the size or thickness of types, leads, etc. The pin-mark is an indentation

8/12 Type is defined as a right-angled, prism-shaped piece of metal, having for its face a letter or character, usually in high relief, adapted for use in letter-press printing; and type in the aggregate is described as an assemblage of the characters used for printing. In a single type the chief points to be described are the face, counter, stem, hair-line, serif, beard or neck, shoulder, body or shank, pin-mark, nick, feet, and groove.

The accompanying diagram of a piece of type (fig. 2) shows its face, body, nick, groove, feet, and pin-mark; and the plan of the face (fig. 3) shows the stem, hair-line, serif, counter, beard, and shoulder.

The body (or shank) of a piece of type is the metal between the shoulder and the feet (described later), and the term "body" is also used to denote the size or thickness of types, leads, etc. The pin-mark is an indentation on the upper part of the body, made by the pin in casting. The nick is the groove across the lower part of the body of the type, and is a guide to the position in which it is to be set up. The feet are the projections on each side of the groove on which the type stands, the groove being the hollow left between the feet where formerly

---

CHELTENHAM BOLD EXTRA CONDENSED   MERGENTHALER TYPE LIBRARY

ABCDEFGHIJKLMNOPQRSTUVWXYZ
&.,"'-:;!?"'"1234567890$
abcdefghijklmnopqrstuvwxyz

ABCDEFGHIJKLMNOPQRSTUVWXYZ
&.,"'-:;!?"'"1234567890$
abcdefghijklmnopqrstuvwxyz

Stempel Garamond was selected as the outstanding version of Garamond. This popular type has been widely produced, with varying degrees of fidelity, by nearly every foundry and vendor since 1900. Another fine example is the Adobe Garamond, a recent release.

ABCDEFGHIJ
KLMNOPQRS
TUVWXYZ&a
bcdefghijklmno
pqrstuvwxyz123
4567890$.,"":;!?

72 POINT STEMPEL GARAMOND*   MERGENTHALER TYPE LIBRARY

*See page 534

ABCDEFGHIJ
KLMNOPQRS
TUVWXYZ&a
bcdefghijklmnop
qrstuvwxyz1234
567890$.,"":;!?

72 POINT STEMPEL GARAMOND* ITALIC   MERGENTHALER TYPE LIBRARY

ABCDEFGHIJKL
MNOPQRSTUV
WXYZ&abcdefghij
klmnopqrstuvwxyz
1234567890$.,""":;!?

60 POINT STEMPEL GARAMOND* MERGENTHALER TYPE LIBRARY

ABCDEFGHIJKL
MNOPQRSTUVW
XYZ&abcdefghijkl
mnopqrstuvwxyz12
34567890$.,""":;!?

60 POINT STEMPEL GARAMOND* ITALIC MERGENTHALER TYPE LIBRARY

ABCDEFGHIJKLMNO
PQRSTUVWXYZ&abcd
efghijklmnopqrstuvwxyz
1234567890$.,""":;!?

48 POINT STEMPEL GARAMOND*   MERGENTHALER TYPE LIBRARY

*ABCDEFGHIJKLMNO
PQRSTUVWXYZ&abcd
efghijklmnopqrstuvwxyz1
234567890$.,""":;!?*

48 POINT STEMPEL GARAMOND* ITALIC   MERGENTHALER TYPE LIBRARY

ABCDEFGHIJKLMNOPQRS
TUVWXYZ&abcdefghijklmno
pqrstuvwxyz1234567890$.,""":;!?

36 POINT STEMPEL GARAMOND*   MERGENTHALER TYPE LIBRARY

*ABCDEFGHIJKLMNOPQRST
UVWXYZ&abcdefghijklmnopqr
stuvwxyz1234567890$.,""":;!?*

36 POINT STEMPEL GARAMOND* ITALIC   MERGENTHALER TYPE LIBRARY

ABCDEFGHIJKLMNOPQRSTUVWXYZ&a
bcdefghijklmnopqrstuvwxyz1234567890$.,""":;
!?

24 POINT STEMPEL GARAMOND*   MERGENTHALER TYPE LIBRARY

*ABCDEFGHIJKLMNOPQRSTUVWXYZ&ab
cdefghijklmnopqrstuvwxyz1234567890$.,""":;!?*

24 POINT STEMPEL GARAMOND* ITALIC   MERGENTHALER TYPE LIBRARY

ABCDEFGHIJKLMNOPQRSTUVWXYZ&abcdefghijklmno
pqrstuvwxyz1234567890$.,""":;!?

18 POINT STEMPEL GARAMOND*   MERGENTHALER TYPE LIBRARY

*ABCDEFGHIJKLMNOPQRSTUVWXYZ&abcdefghijklmnopq
rstuvwxyz1234567890$.,""":;!?*

18 POINT STEMPEL GARAMOND* ITALIC   MERGENTHALER TYPE LIBRARY

14/14 From a letter by Benjamin Franklin to Noah Webster dated Dec. 26, 1789:

In examining the English Books, that were printed between the Restoration and the Accession of George the 2d, we may observe, that all *Substantives* were begun with a capital, in which we imitated our Mother Tongue, the German. This was more particularly useful to those, who were not well acquainted with the English; *there being such a prodigious Number of our Words, that are both Verbs and*

12/12 From a letter by Benjamin Franklin to Noah Webster dated Dec. 26, 1789:

In examining the English Books, that were printed between the Restoration and the Accession of George the 2d, we may observe, that all *Substantives* were begun with a capital, in which we imitated our Mother Tongue, the German. This was more particularly useful to those, who were not well acquainted with the English; there being such a prodigious Number of our Words, that are both *Verbs* and *Substantives,* and spelt in the same manner, tho' often accented differently *in Pronunciation.*
This Method has, by the Fancy of Printers,

14/16 From a letter by Benjamin Franklin to Noah Webster dated Dec. 26, 1789:

In examining the English Books, that were printed between the Restoration and the Accession of George the 2d, we may observe, that all *Substantives* were begun with a capital, in which we imitated our Mother Tongue, the German. This was more *particularly useful to those, who were not well acquainted with the English;*

12/14 From a letter by Benjamin Franklin to Noah Webster dated Dec. 26, 1789:

In examining the English Books, that were printed between the Restoration and the Accession of George the 2d, we may observe, that all *Substantives* were begun with a capital, in which we imitated our Mother Tongue, the German. This was more particularly useful to those, who were not well acquainted with the English; there being such a *prodigious Number of our Words, that are both Verbs and Substantives, and spelt in the*

14/18 From a letter by Benjamin Franklin to Noah Webster dated Dec. 26, 1789:

In examining the English Books, that were printed between the Restoration and the Accession of George the 2d, we may observe, that all *Substantives* were begun with a capital, in *which we imitated our Mother Tongue, the German. This was more particu-*

12/16 From a letter by Benjamin Franklin to Noah Webster dated Dec. 26, 1789:

In examining the English Books, that were printed between the Restoration and the Accession of George the 2d, we may observe, that all *Substantives* were begun with a capital, in which we imitated our Mother Tongue, the German. This was more particularly useful to those, who were not well acquainted with the English; there being such a

STEMPEL GARAMOND* — MERGENTHALER TYPE LIBRARY

ABCDEFGHIJKLMNOPQRSTUV
ABCDEFGHIJKLMNOPQRSTUV
WXYZ&.,"-:;!?""1234567890$
WXYZ&.,"-:;!?""1234567890$
abcdefghijklmnopqrstuvwxyz
abcdefghijklmnopqrstuvwxyz

ABCDEFGHIJKLMNOPQRSTUVW
ABCDEFGHIJKLMNOPQRSTUVW
XYZ&.,"-:;!?""1234567890$
XYZ&.,"-:;!?""1234567890$
abcdefghijklmnopqrstuvwxyz
abcdefghijklmnopqrstuvwxyz

11/11 From a letter by Benjamin Franklin to Noah Webster dated Dec. 26, 1789:

In examining the English Books, that were printed between the Restoration and the Accession of George the 2d, we may observe, that all *Substantives* were begun with a capital, in which we imitated our Mother Tongue, the German. This was more particularly useful to those, who were not well acquainted with the English; there being such a prodigious Number of our Words, that are both *Verbs* and *Substantives,* and spelt in the same manner, tho' often accented differently in Pronunciation.

This Method has, by the Fancy of Printers, of *late Years been laid aside, from an Idea, that suppressing the Capitals shows the Character to*

10/10 From a letter by Benjamin Franklin to Noah Webster dated Dec. 26, 1789:

In examining the English Books, that were printed between the Restoration and the Accession of George the 2d, we may observe, that all *Substantives* were begun with a capital, in which we imitated our Mother Tongue, the German. This was more particularly useful to those, who were not well acquainted with the English; there being such a prodigious Number of our Words, that are both *Verbs* and *Substantives,* and spelt in the same manner, tho' often accented differently in Pronunciation.

This Method has, by the Fancy of Printers, of late Years been laid aside, from an Idea, that suppressing the Capitals shows the Character to greater Advantage; *those Letters prominent above the line disturbing its even regular Appearance. The Effect of this Change*

11/13 From a letter by Benjamin Franklin to Noah Webster dated Dec. 26, 1789:

In examining the English Books, that were printed between the Restoration and the Accession of George the 2d, we may observe, that all *Substantives* were begun with a capital, in which we imitated our Mother Tongue, the German. This was more particularly useful to those, who were not well acquainted with the English; there being such a prodigious Number of our Words, that are both *Verbs* and *Substantives,* and spelt in the same manner, tho' often accented differently *in Pronunciation.*

This Method has, by the Fancy of Printers, of

10/12 From a letter by Benjamin Franklin to Noah Webster dated Dec. 26, 1789:

In examining the English Books, that were printed between the Restoration and the Accession of George the 2d, we may observe, that all *Substantives* were begun with a capital, in which we imitated our Mother Tongue, the German. This was more particularly useful to those, who were not well acquainted with the English; there being such a prodigious Number of our Words, that are both *Verbs* and *Substantives,* and spelt in the same manner, tho' often accented differently in Pronunciation.

This Method has, by the Fancy of Printers, of late *Years been laid aside, from an Idea, that suppressing the Capitals shows the Character to greater Advan-*

11/15 From a letter by Benjamin Franklin to Noah Webster dated Dec. 26, 1789:

In examining the English Books, that were printed between the Restoration and the Accession of George the 2d, we may observe, that all *Substantives* were begun with a capital, in which we imitated our Mother Tongue, the German. This was more particularly useful to those, who were not well acquainted with the English; there *being such a prodigious Number of our Words, that are both Verbs and Substantives, and spelt in*

10/14 From a letter by Benjamin Franklin to Noah Webster dated Dec. 26, 1789:

In examining the English Books, that were printed between the Restoration and the Accession of George the 2d, we may observe, that all *Substantives* were begun with a capital, in which we imitated our Mother Tongue, the German. This was more particularly useful to those, who were not well acquainted with the English; there being such a prodigious Number of our Words, that are both *Verbs* and *Substantives,* and spelt *in the same manner, tho' often accented differently in Pronunciation.*

STEMPEL GARAMOND*   MERGENTHALER TYPE LIBRARY

ABCDEFGHIJKLMNOPQRSTUVWXYZ
ABCDEFGHIJKLMNOPQRSTUVWXYZ
&.,"'-:;!?""1234567890$
&.,"'-:;!?""1234567890$
abcdefghijklmnopqrstuvwxyz
abcdefghijklmnopqrstuvwxyz

ABCDEFGHIJKLMNOPQRSTUVWXYZ
ABCDEFGHIJKLMNOPQRSTUVWXYZ
&.,"'-:;!?""1234567890$
&.,"'-:;!?""1234567890$
abcdefghijklmnopqrstuvwxyz
abcdefghijklmnopqrstuvwxyz

9/9 From a letter by Benjamin Franklin to Noah Webster dated Dec. 26, 1789:
   In examining the English Books, that were printed between the Restoration and the Accession of George the 2d, we may observe, that all *Substantives* were begun with a capital, in which we imitated our Mother Tongue, the German. This was more particularly useful to those, who were not well acquainted with the English; there being such a prodigious Number of our Words, that are both *Verbs* and *Substantives*, and spelt in the same manner, tho' often accented differently in Pronunciation.
   This Method has, by the Fancy of Printers, of late Years been laid aside, from an Idea, that suppressing the Capitals shows the Character to greater Advantage; those Letters prominent above the line disturbing its even regular Appearance. The Effect of this Change is so considerable, that a learned Man of France, who used to read our Books, tho' not perfectly acquainted with our Language, in Conversation *with me on the Subject of our Authors, attributed the greater Obscurity he found in our modern Books, compared with*

8/8 From a letter by Benjamin Franklin to Noah Webster dated Dec. 26, 1789:
   In examining the English Books, that were printed between the Restoration and the Accession of George the 2d, we may observe, that all *Substantives* were begun with a capital, in which we imitated our Mother Tongue, the German. This was more particularly useful to those, who were not well acquainted with the English; there being such a prodigious Number of our Words, that are both *Verbs* and *Substantives*, and spelt in the same manner, tho' often accented differently in Pronunciation.
   This Method has, by the Fancy of Printers, of late Years been laid aside, from an Idea, that suppressing the Capitals shows the Character to greater Advantage; those Letters prominent above the line disturbing its even regular Appearance. The Effect of this Change is so considerable, that a learned Man of France, who used to read our Books, tho' not perfectly acquainted with our Language, in Conversation with me on the Subject of our Authors, attributed the greater Obscurity he found in our modern Books, compared with those of the Period above mentioned, to a Change of Style for the worse in our Writers, of which Mistake I convinced him, by marking for him *each Substantive with a Capital in a Paragraph, which he then easily understood, tho' before he could not comprehend it. This shows the*

9/11 From a letter by Benjamin Franklin to Noah Webster dated Dec. 26, 1789:
   In examining the English Books, that were printed between the Restoration and the Accession of George the 2d, we may observe, that all *Substantives* were begun with a capital, in which we imitated our Mother Tongue, the German. This was more particularly useful to those, who were not well acquainted with the English; there being such a prodigious Number of our Words, that are both *Verbs* and *Substantives*, and spelt in the same manner, tho' often accented differently in Pronunciation.
   This Method has, by the Fancy of Printers, of late Years been laid aside, from an Idea, that suppressing the Capitals shows the Character to greater Advantage; those Letters *prominent above the line disturbing its even regular Appearance. The Effect of this Change is so considerable, that a*

8/10 From a letter by Benjamin Franklin to Noah Webster dated Dec. 26, 1789:
   In examining the English Books, that were printed between the Restoration and the Accession of George the 2d, we may observe, that all *Substantives* were begun with a capital, in which we imitated our Mother Tongue, the German. This was more particularly useful to those, who were not well acquainted with the English; there being such a prodigious Number of our Words, that are both *Verbs* and *Substantives*, and spelt in the same manner, tho' often accented differently in Pronunciation.
   This Method has, by the Fancy of Printers, of late Years been laid aside, from an Idea, that suppressing the Capitals shows the Character to greater Advantage; those Letters prominent above the line disturbing its even regular Appearance. The Effect of this Change is so considerable, that a learned Man of France, who used to read our Books, tho' not perfectly acquainted with our Language, in Conversation *with me on the Subject of our Authors, attributed the greater Obscurity he found in our modern Books, compared with those of the*

9/13 From a letter by Benjamin Franklin to Noah Webster dated Dec. 26, 1789:
   In examining the English Books, that were printed between the Restoration and the Accession of George the 2d, we may observe, that all *Substantives* were begun with a capital, in which we imitated our Mother Tongue, the German. This was more particularly useful to those, who were not well acquainted with the English; there being such a prodigious Number of our Words, that are both *Verbs* and *Substantives*, and spelt in the same manner, tho' often accented differently in Pronunciation.
   This Method has, by the Fancy of Printers, of late Years been laid aside, from an Idea, that suppressing the Capitals

8/12 From a letter by Benjamin Franklin to Noah Webster dated Dec. 26, 1789:
   In examining the English Books, that were printed between the Restoration and the Accession of George the 2d, we may observe, that all *Substantives* were begun with a capital, in which we imitated our Mother Tongue, the German. This was more particularly useful to those, who were not well acquainted with the English; there being such a prodigious Number of our Words, that are both *Verbs* and *Substantives*, and spelt in the same manner, tho' often accented differently in Pronunciation.
   This Method has, by the Fancy of Printers, of late Years been laid aside, from an Idea, that suppressing the Capitals shows the Character to greater Advantage; those Letters prominent above the line *disturbing its even regular Appearance. The Effect of this Change is*

STEMPEL GARAMOND* · MERGENTHALER TYPE LIBRARY

ABCDEFGHIJKLMNOPQRSTUVWXYZ
ABCDEFGHIJKLMNOPQRSTUVWXYZ
&.,"‘-:;!?''""1234567890$
&.,"‘-:;!?''""1234567890$
abcdefghijklmnopqrstuvwxyz
abcdefghijklmnopqrstuvwxyz

ABCDEFGHIJKLMNOPQRSTUVWXYZ
ABCDEFGHIJKLMNOPQRSTUVWXYZ
&.,"‘-:;!?''""1234567890$
&.,"‘-:;!?''""1234567890$
abcdefghijklmnopqrstuvwxyz
abcdefghijklmnopqrstuvwxyz

ABCDEFGHIJKL
MNOPQRSTUV
WXYZ&abcdefg
hijklmnopqrstu
vwxyz12345678
90$.,""‚;!?

72 POINT ITC GARAMOND** LIGHT   MERGENTHALER TYPE LIBRARY

Note that Stempel Garamond display caps are larger, and their x-height smaller than ITC Garamond. Another excellent version of Garamond has been released by Adobe, see p. 378.

ABCDEFGHIJKL
MNOPQRSTUV
WXYZ&abcdefg
hijklmnopqrstuv
wxyz12345678
90$.,""":;!?

72 POINT ITC GARAMOND** LIGHT ITALIC   MERGENTHALER TYPE LIBRARY

ABCDEFGHIJKLMNOPQRSTUVWXYZ&abcdefghijklmnopqrstuvwxyz1234567890$.,""":;!?

48 POINT ITC GARAMOND** LIGHT   MERGENTHALER TYPE LIBRARY

ABCDEFGHIJKLMNOPQRSTUVWXYZ&abcdefghijklmnopqrstuvwxyz1234567890$.,""":;!?

48 POINT ITC GARAMOND** LIGHT ITALIC   MERGENTHALER TYPE LIBRARY

ABCDEFGHIJKLMNOPQRSTUVWXYZ&abcdefghijklmnopqrstuvwxyz1234567890$.,""":;!?

24 POINT ITC GARAMOND** LIGHT   MERGENTHALER TYPE LIBRARY

ABCDEFGHIJKLMNOPQRSTUVWXYZ&abcdefghijklmnopqrstuvwxyz1234567890$.,""":;!?

24 POINT ITC GARAMOND** LIGHT ITALIC   MERGENTHALER TYPE LIBRARY

14/14 From a letter by Benjamin Franklin to Noah Webster dated Dec. 26, 1789:

In examining the English Books, that were printed between the Restoration and the Accession of George the 2d, we may observe, that all *Substantives* were begun with a capital, in which we imitated our Mother Tongue, the German. This was more particularly useful to those, who were not well acquainted with the English; there being such a *prodigious Number of our Words, that are both Verbs and Substantives, and*

14/16 From a letter by Benjamin Franklin to Noah Webster dated Dec. 26, 1789:

In examining the English Books, that were printed between the Restoration and the Accession of George the 2d, we may observe, that all *Substantives* were begun with a capital, in which we imitated our Mother Tongue, the German. This was more particularly useful to *those, who were not well acquainted with the English; there being such a pro-*

14/18 From a letter by Benjamin Franklin to Noah Webster dated Dec. 26, 1789:

In examining the English Books, that were printed between the Restoration and the Accession of George the 2d, we may observe, that all *Substantives* were begun with a capital, in which we imitated our Mother Tongue, the German. *This was more particularly useful to*

12/12 From a letter by Benjamin Franklin to Noah Webster dated Dec. 26, 1789:

In examining the English Books, that were printed between the Restoration and the Accession of George the 2d, we may observe, that all *Substantives* were begun with a capital, in which we imitated our Mother Tongue, the German. This was more particularly useful to those, who were not well acquainted with the English; there being such a prodigious Number of our Words, that are both *Verbs* and *Substantives,* and spelt in the same manner, tho' often accented differently in the *Pronunciation.*
This Method has, by the Fancy of Printers, of

12/14 From a letter by Benjamin Franklin to Noah Webster dated Dec. 26, 1789:

In examining the English Books, that were printed between the Restoration and the Accession of George the 2d, we may observe, that all *Substantives* were begun with a capital, in which we imitated our Mother Tongue, the German. This was more particularly useful to those, who were not well acquainted with the English; there being such a prodigious *Number of our Words, that are both Verbs and Substantives, and spelt in the same manner,*

12/16 From a letter by Benjamin Franklin to Noah Webster dated Dec. 26, 1789:

In examining the English Books, that were printed between the Restoration and the Accession of George the 2d, we may observe, that all *Substantives* were begun with a capital, in which we imitated our Mother Tongue, the German. This was more particularly useful to *those, who were not well acquainted with the English; there being such a prodigious*

ITC GARAMOND** LIGHT   MERGENTHALER TYPE LIBRARY

ABCDEFGHIJKLMNOPQRSTUVWXYZ
ABCDEFGHIJKLMNOPQRSTUVWXYZ
&.,"-:;!?"" 1234567890$
&.,"-:;!?"" 1234567890$
abcdefghijklmnopqrstuvwxyz
abcdefghijklmnopqrstuvwxyz

ABCDEFGHIJKLMNOPQRSTUVWXYZ
ABCDEFGHIJKLMNOPQRSTUVWXYZ
&.,"-:;!?"" 1234567890$
&.,"-:;!?"" 1234567890$
abcdefghijklmnopqrstuvwxyz
abcdefghijklmnopqrstuvwxyz

GARAMOND FAMILY 247

10/10 From a letter by Benjamin Franklin to Noah Webster dated Dec. 26, 1789:

In examining the English Books, that were printed between the Restoration and the Accession of George the 2d, we may observe, that all *Substantives* were begun with a capital, in which we imitated our Mother Tongue, the German. This was more particularly useful to those, who were not well acquainted with the English; there being such a prodigious Number of our Words, that are both *Verbs* and *Substantives,* and spelt in the same manner, tho' often accented differently in Pronunciation.

This Method has, by the Fancy of Printers, of late Years been laid aside, from an Idea, that suppressing the Capitals shows the Character to greater Advantage; *those Letters prominent above the line disturbing its even regular Appearance. The Effect of this Change is so*

8/8 From a letter by Benjamin Franklin to Noah Webster dated Dec. 26, 1789:

In examining the English Books, that were printed between the Restoration and the Accession of George the 2d, we may observe, that all *Substantives* were begun with a capital, in which we imitated our Mother Tongue, the German. This was more particularly useful to those, who were not well acquainted with the English; there being such a prodigious Number of our Words, that are both *Verbs* and *Substantives,* and spelt in the same manner, tho' often accented differently in Pronunciation.

This Method has, by the Fancy of Printers, of late Years been laid aside, from an Idea, that suppressing the Capitals shows the Character to greater Advantage; those Letters prominent above the line disturbing its even regular Appearance. The Effect of this Change is so considerable, that a learned Man of France, who used to read our Books, tho' not perfectly acquainted with our Language, in Conversation with me on the Subject of our Authors, attributed the greater Obscurity he found in our modern Books, compared with those of the Period above mentioned, to a Change of Style for the worse in our Writers, of which Mistake I convinced him, by marking for him each *Substantive with a Capital in a Paragraph, which he then easily understood, tho' before he could not comprehend it. This shows the*

10/12 From a letter by Benjamin Franklin to Noah Webster dated Dec. 26, 1789:

In examining the English Books, that were printed between the Restoration and the Accession of George the 2d, we may observe, that all *Substantives* were begun with a capital, in which we imitated our Mother Tongue, the German. This was more particularly useful to those, who were not well acquainted with the English; there being such a prodigious Number of our Words, that are both *Verbs* and *Substantives,* and spelt in the same manner, tho' often accented differently in Pronunciation.

This Method has, by the Fancy of Printers, of late Years *been laid aside, from an Idea, that suppressing the Capitals shows the Character to greater Advantage;*

8/10 From a letter by Benjamin Franklin to Noah Webster dated Dec. 26, 1789:

In examining the English Books, that were printed between the Restoration and the Accession of George the 2d, we may observe, that all *Substantives* were begun with a capital, in which we imitated our Mother Tongue, the German. This was more particularly useful to those, who were not well acquainted with the English; there being such a prodigious Number of our Words, that are both *Verbs* and *Substantives,* and spelt in the same manner, tho' often accented differently in Pronunciation.

This Method has, by the Fancy of Printers, of late Years been laid aside, from an Idea, that suppressing the Capitals shows the Character to greater Advantage; those Letters prominent above the line disturbing its even regular Appearance. The Effect of this Change is so considerable, that a learned Man of France, who used to read our Books, tho' not perfectly acquainted with our Language, in Conversa-*tion with me on the Subject of our Authors, attributed the greater Obscurity he found in our modern Books, compared with those of the*

10/14 From a letter by Benjamin Franklin to Noah Webster dated Dec. 26, 1789:

In examining the English Books, that were printed between the Restoration and the Accession of George the 2d, we may observe, that all *Substantives* were begun with a capital, in which we imitated our Mother Tongue, the German. This was more particularly useful to those, who were not well acquainted with the English; there being such a prodigious Number of our Words, that are both *Verbs* and *Substantives,* and spelt in *the same manner, tho' often accented differently in Pronunciation.*

8/12 From a letter by Benjamin Franklin to Noah Webster dated Dec. 26, 1789:

In examining the English Books, that were printed between the Restoration and the Accession of George the 2d, we may observe, that all *Substantives* were begun with a capital, in which we imitated our Mother Tongue, the German. This was more particularly useful to those, who were not well acquainted with the English; there being such a prodigious Number of our Words, that are both *Verbs* and *Substantives,* and spelt in the same manner, tho' often accented differently in Pronunciation.

This Method has, by the Fancy of Printers, of late Years been laid aside, from an Idea, that suppressing the Capitals shows the Character *to greater Advantage; those Letters prominent above the line disturbing its even regular Appearance. The Effect of this Change is so*

ITC GARAMOND** LIGHT   MERGENTHALER TYPE LIBRARY

ABCDEFGHIJKLMNOPQRSTUVWXYZ
ABCDEFGHIJKLMNOPQRSTUVWXYZ
&.,''-:;!?''''1234567890$
&.,''-:;!?''''1234567890$
abcdefghijklmnopqrstuvwxyz
abcdefghijklmnopqrstuvwxyz

ABCDEFGHIJKLMNOPQRSTUVWXYZ
ABCDEFGHIJKLMNOPQRSTUVWXYZ
&.,''-:;!?''''1234567890$
&.,''-:;!?''''1234567890$
abcdefghijklmnopqrstuvwxyz
abcdefghijklmnopqrstuvwxyz

ABCDEFGHIJK LMNOPQRSTU VWXYZ&abcd efghijklmnop qrstuvwxyz12 34567890$.,""": ;!?

72 POINT ITC GARAMOND** BOLD   MERGENTHALER TYPE LIBRARY

ABCDEFGHIJK LMNOPQRST UVWXYZ&ab cdefghijklmn opqrstuvwxyz 1234567890$., ""'',;!?

72 POINT ITC GARAMOND** BOLD ITALIC   MERGENTHALER TYPE LIBRARY

ABCDEFGHIJKLMNOPQRSTUVWXYZ&abcdefghijklmnopqrstuvwxyz1234567890$.,""*:;!?

48 POINT ITC GARAMOND** BOLD   MERGENTHALER TYPE LIBRARY

ABCDEFGHIJKLMNOPQRSTUVWXYZ&abcdefghijklmnopqrstuvwxyz1234567890$.,"":;!?*

48 POINT ITC GARAMOND** BOLD ITALIC   MERGENTHALER TYPE LIBRARY

ABCDEFGHIJKLMNOPQRSTUVWXYZ&abcdefghijklmnopqrstuvwxyz1234567890$"":;!?

24 POINT ITC GARAMOND** BOLD   MERGENTHALER TYPE LIBRARY

ABCDEFGHIJKLMNOPQRSTUVWXYZ&abcdefghijklmnopqrstuvwxyz1234567890$.,"":;!?

24 POINT ITC GARAMOND** BOLD ITALIC   MERGENTHALER TYPE LIBRARY

GARAMOND FAMILY 251

14/14 From a letter by Benjamin Franklin to Noah Webster dated Dec. 26, 1789:

In examining the English Books, that were printed between the Restoration and the Accession of George the 2d, we may observe, that all *Substantives* were begun with a capital, in which we imitated our Mother Tongue, the German. This was more particularly useful *to those, who were not well acquainted with the English; there*

14/16 From a letter by Benjamin Franklin to Noah Webster dated Dec. 26, 1789:

In examining the English Books, that were printed between the Restoration and the Accession of George the 2d, we may observe, that all *Substantives* were begun with a capital, in which we imitated *our Mother Tongue, the German. This was more particularly useful*

14/18 From a letter by Benjamin Franklin to Noah Webster dated Dec. 26, 1789:

In examining the English Books, that were printed between the Restoration and the Accession of George the 2d, we may observe, *that all Substantives were begun with a capital, in which we imi-*

12/12 From a letter by Benjamin Franklin to Noah Webster dated Dec. 26, 1789:

In examining the English Books, that were printed between the Restoration and the Accession of George the 2d, we may observe, that all *Substantives* were begun with a capital, in which we imitated our Mother Tongue, the German. This was more particularly useful to those, who were not well acquainted with the English; there being such a prodigious Number of our Words, that are both *Verbs* and *Substantives,* and spelt *in the same manner, tho' often accented differently in Pronunciation.*

12/14 From a letter by Benjamin Franklin to Noah Webster dated Dec. 26, 1789:

In examining the English Books, that were printed between the Restoration and the Accession of George the 2d, we may observe, that all *Substantives* were begun with a capital, in which we imitated our Mother Tongue, the German. This was more particularly useful to those, who were not well acquainted *with the English; there being such a prodigious Number of our Words, that are*

12/16 From a letter by Benjamin Franklin to Noah Webster dated Dec. 26, 1789:

In examining the English Books, that were printed between the Restoration and the Accession of George the 2d, we may observe, that all *Substantives* were begun with a capital, in which we imitated our Mother Tongue, the German. *This was more particularly useful to those, who were not well acquainted*

ITC GARAMOND** BOLD   MERGENTHALER TYPE LIBRARY

ABCDEFGHIJKLMNOPQRSTUVW
ABCDEFGHIJKLMNOPQRSTUVW
XYZ&.,"-:;!?""1234567890$
XYZ&.,"-:;!?""1234567890$
abcdefghijklmnopqrstuvwxyz
abcdefghijklmnopqrstuvwxyz

ABCDEFGHIJKLMNOPQRSTUVWXYZ
ABCDEFGHIJKLMNOPQRSTUVWXYZ
&.,"-:;!?""1234567890$
&.,"-:;!?""1234567890$
abcdefghijklmnopqrstuvwxyz
abcdefghijklmnopqrstuvwxyz

10/10 From a letter by Benjamin Franklin to Noah Webster dated Dec. 26, 1789:

In examining the English Books, that were printed between the Restoration and the Accession of George the 2d, we may observe, that all *Substantives* were begun with a capital, in which we imitated our Mother Tongue, the German. This was more particularly useful to those, who were not well acquainted with the English; there being such a prodigious Number of our Words, that are both *Verbs* and *Substantives,* and spelt in the same manner, tho' often accented differently in Pronunciation.

This Method has, by the Fancy of Printers, of late Years been laid aside, from an Idea, that suppressing the Capitals shows the Character to greater Advantage; those Letters prominent

8/8 From a letter by Benjamin Franklin to Noah Webster dated Dec. 26, 1789:

In examining the English Books, that were printed between the Restoration and the Accession of George the 2d, we may observe, that all *Substantives* were begun with a capital, in which we imitated our Mother Tongue, the German. This was more particularly useful to those, who were not well acquainted with the English; there being such a prodigious Number of our Words, that are both *Verbs* and *Substantives,* and spelt in the same manner, tho' often accented differently in Pronunciation.

This Method has, by the Fancy of Printers, of late Years been laid aside, from an Idea, that suppressing the Capitals shows the Character to greater Advantage; those Letters prominent above the line disturbing its even regular Appearance. The Effect of this Change is so considerable, that a learned Man of France, who used to read our Books, tho' not perfectly acquainted with our Language, in Conversation with me on the Subject of our Authors, attributed the greater Obscurity he found in our modern Books, compared with those of the *Period above mentioned, to a Change of Style for the worse in our Writers, of which Mistake I convinced him, by mark-*

10/12 From a letter by Benjamin Franklin to Noah Webster dated Dec. 26, 1789:

In examining the English Books, that were printed between the Restoration and the Accession of George the 2d, we may observe, that all *Substantives* were begun with a capital, in which we imitated our Mother Tongue, the German. This was more particularly useful to those, who were not well acquainted with the English; there being such a prodigious Number of our Words, that are both *Verbs* and *Substantives,* and spelt in the same manner, tho' often accented differently in Pronunciation.

This Method has, by the Fancy of Printers, of late Years been laid aside, from an Idea, that

8/10 From a letter by Benjamin Franklin to Noah Webster dated Dec. 26, 1789:

In examining the English Books, that were printed between the Restoration and the Accession of George the 2d, we may observe, that all *Substantives* were begun with a capital, in which we imitated our Mother Tongue, the German. This was more particularly useful to those, who were not well acquainted with the English; there being such a prodigious Number of our Words, that are both *Verbs* and *Substantives,* and spelt in the same manner, tho' often accented differently in Pronunciation.

This Method has, by the Fancy of Printers, of late Years been laid aside, from an Idea, that suppressing the Capitals shows the Character to greater Advantage; those Letters prominent above the line disturbing its even regular Appearance. The Effect of this Change is so considerable, that a learned Man of *France, who used to read our Books, tho' not perfectly acquainted with our Language, in Conversation with me on*

10/14 From a letter by Benjamin Franklin to Noah Webster dated Dec. 26, 1789:

In examining the English Books, that were printed between the Restoration and the Accession of George the 2d, we may observe, that all *Substantives* were begun with a capital, in which we imitated our Mother Tongue, the German. This was more particularly useful to those, who were not well acquainted with the English; there being such a prodigious Number of our Words, *that are both Verbs and Substantives, and spelt in the same manner, tho' often accented differ-*

8/12 From a letter by Benjamin Franklin to Noah Webster dated Dec. 26, 1789:

In examining the English Books, that were printed between the Restoration and the Accession of George the 2d, we may observe, that all *Substantives* were begun with a capital, in which we imitated our Mother Tongue, the German. This was more particularly useful to those, who were not well acquainted with the English; there being such a prodigious Number of our Words, that are both *Verbs* and *Substantives,* and spelt in the same manner, tho' often accented differently in Pronunciation.

This Method has, by the Fancy of Printers, of late Years been *laid aside, from an Idea, that suppressing the Capitals shows the Character to greater Advantage; those Letters*

ITC GARAMOND** BOLD MERGENTHALER TYPE LIBRARY

ABCDEFGHIJKLMNOPQRSTUVWXYZ
ABCDEFGHIJKLMNOPQRSTUVWXYZ
&.,"-:;!?""1234567890$
&.,"-:;!?""1234567890$
abcdefghijklmnopqrstuvwxyz
abcdefghijklmnopqrstuvwxyz

ABCDEFGHIJKLMNOPQRSTUVWXYZ
ABCDEFGHIJKLMNOPQRSTUVWXYZ
&.,"-:;!?""1234567890$
&.,"-:;!?""1234567890$
abcdefghijklmnopqrstuvwxyz
abcdefghijklmnopqrstuvwxyz

ABCDEFGHIJ KLMNOPQR STUVWXYZ &abcdefghij klmnopqrst uvwxyz1234 567890$.,"":; !?

72 POINT ITC GARAMOND** ULTRA   MERGENTHALER TYPE LIBRARY

ABCDEFGHIJ KLMNOPQRS TUVWXYZ&a bcdefghijklm nopqrstuvwx yz12345678 90$.,""";:!?

72 POINT ITC GARAMOND** ULTRA ITALIC   MERGENTHALER TYPE LIBRARY

ABCDEFGHIJKLMNOPQRSTUVWXYZ&a
bcdefghijklmnopqrstuvwxyz12345678
90$.,"";:!?

24 POINT ITC GARAMOND** ULTRA   MERGENTHALER TYPE LIBRARY

ABCDEFGHIJKLMN
OPQRSTUVWXYZ&
abcdefghijklmnopq
rstuvwxyz1234567
890$.,""":;!?

48 POINT ITC GARAMOND** ULTRA   MERGENTHALER TYPE LIBRARY

ABCDEFGHIJKLMN
OPQRSTUVWXYZ&
abcdefghijklmnopq
rstuvwxyz1234567
890$.," ":;!?

48 POINT ITC GARAMOND** ULTRA ITALIC   MERGENTHALER TYPE LIBRARY

ABCDEFGHIJKLMNOPQRSTUVWXYZ&a
bcdefghijklmnopqrstuvwxyz12345678
90$.," ":;!?

24 POINT ITC GARAMOND** ULTRA ITALIC   MERGENTHALER TYPE LIBRARY

14/14 From a letter by Mr. Benjamin Franklin to Noah Webster dated Dec. 26, 1789:

In examining the English Books, that were printed between the Restoration and the Accession of George the 2d, we may observe, that all *Substantives* were begun with a capital, in which we imitated our Mother Tongue, the German. *This was more particularly useful to those, who were not*

12/12 From a letter by Benjamin Franklin to Noah Webster dated Dec. 26, 1789:

In examining the English Books, that were printed between the Restoration and the Accession of George the 2d, we may observe, that all *Substantives* were begun with a capital, in which we imitated our Mother Tongue, the German. This was more particularly useful to those, who were not well acquainted with the English; there being such a prodigious Number of our Words, that are both *Verbs and Substantives, and spelt in the same manner, tho' often accented*

14/16 From a letter by Mr. Benjamin Franklin to Noah Webster dated Dec. 26, 1789:

In examining the English Books, that were printed between the Restoration and the Accession of George the 2d, we may observe, that all *Substantives* were begun with a capital, *in which we imitated our Mother Tongue, the German.*

12/14 From a letter by Benjamin Franklin to Noah Webster dated Dec. 26, 1789:

In examining the English Books, that were printed between the Restoration and the Accession of George the 2d, we may observe, that all *Substantives* were begun with a capital, in which we imitated our Mother Tongue, the German. This was more particularly useful to those, who were *not well acquainted with the English; there being such a prodigious*

14/18 From a letter by Mr. Benjamin Franklin to Noah Webster dated Dec. 26, 1789:

In examining the English Books, that were printed between the Restoration and the Accession of George the 2d, *may observe, that all Substantives were begun with a capital,*

12/16 From a letter by Benjamin Franklin to Noah Webster dated Dec. 26, 1789:

In examining the English Books, that were printed between the Restoration and the Accession of George the 2d, we may observe, that all *Substantives* were begun with a capital, in which we imitated our Mother Tongue, the German. *This was more particularly useful to those, who*

ITC GARAMOND** ULTRA   MERGENTHALER TYPE LIBRARY

ABCDEFGHIJKLMNOPQRSTUV
ABCDEFGHIJKLMNOPQRSTUV
WXYZ&.,"-:;!?""1234567890$
WXYZ&.,"-:;!?""1234567890$
abcdefghijklmnopqrstuvwxyz
abcdefghijklmnopqrstuvwxyz

ABCDEFGHIJKLMNOPQRSTUVW
ABCDEFGHIJKLMNOPQRSTUVW
XYZ&.,"-:;!?""1234567890$
XYZ&.,"-:;!?""1234567890$
abcdefghijklmnopqrstuvwxyz
abcdefghijklmnopqrstuvwxyz

10/10 From a letter by Benjamin Franklin to Noah Webster dated Dec. 26, 1789:

In examining the English Books, that were printed between the Restoration and the Accession of George the 2d, we may observe, that all *Substantives* were begun with a capital, in which we imitated our Mother Tongue, the German. This was more particularly useful to those, who were not well acquainted with the English; there being such a prodigious Number of our Words, that are both *Verbs* and *Substantives*, and spelt in the same manner, tho' often accented differently in Pronunciation.

This Method has, by the Fancy of Printers, of late Years been laid aside, from an Idea, that suppressing the Capitals shows the

8/8 From a letter by Benjamin Franklin to Noah Webster dated Dec. 26, 1789:

In examining the English Books, that were printed between the Restoration and the Accession of George the 2d, we may observe, that all *Substantives* were begun with a capital, in which we imitated our Mother Tongue, the German. This was more particularly useful to those, who were not well acquainted with the English; there being such a prodigious Number of our Words, that are both *Verbs* and *Substantives*, and spelt in the same manner, tho' often accented differently in Pronunciation.

This Method has, by the Fancy of Printers, of late Years been laid aside, from an Idea, that suppressing the Capitals shows the Character to greater Advantage; those Letters prominent above the line disturbing its even regular Appearance. The Effect of this Change is so considerable, that a learned Man of France, who used to read our Books, tho' not perfectly acquainted with our Language, in Conversation with me on the Subject of our Authors, attributed the greater Obscurity he found in our modern *Books, compared with those of the Period above mentioned, to a Change of Style for the worse in our Writers,*

10/12 From a letter by Benjamin Franklin to Noah Webster dated Dec. 26, 1789:

In examining the English Books, that were printed between the Restoration and the Accession of George the 2d, we may observe, that all *Substantives* were begun with a capital, in which we imitated our Mother Tongue, the German. This was more particularly useful to those, who were not well acquainted with the English; there being such a prodigious Number of our Words, that are both *Verbs* and *Substantives,* and spelt in the same manner, tho' often accented differently in *Pronunciation.*

This Method has, by the Fancy of Printers,

8/10 From a letter by Benjamin Franklin to Noah Webster dated Dec. 26, 1789:

In examining the English Books, that were printed between the Restoration and the Accession of George the 2d, we may observe, that all *Substantives* were begun with a capital, in which we imitated our Mother Tongue, the German. This was more particularly useful to those, who were not well acquainted with the English; there being such a prodigious Number of our Words, that are both *Verbs* and *Substantives,* and spelt in the same manner, tho' often accented differently in Pronunciation.

This Method has, by the Fancy of Printers, of late Years been laid aside, from an Idea, that suppressing the Capitals shows the Character to greater Advantage; those Letters prominent above the line disturbing its even regular Appearance. The Effect of this Change is so consider*able, that a learned Man of France, who used to read our Books, tho' not perfectly acquainted with our Lan-*

10/14 From a letter by Benjamin Franklin to Noah Webster dated Dec. 26, 1789:

In examining the English Books, that were printed between the Restoration and the Accession of George the 2d, we may observe, that all *Substantives* were begun with a capital, in which we imitated our Mother Tongue, the German. This was more particularly useful to those, who were not well acquainted with the English; there being such a pro*digious Number of our Words, that are both Verbs and Substantives, and spelt in the*

8/12 From a letter by Benjamin Franklin to Noah Webster dated Dec. 26, 1789:

In examining the English Books, that were printed between the Restoration and the Accession of George the 2d, we may observe, that all *Substantives* were begun with a capital, in which we imitated our Mother Tongue, the German. This was more particularly useful to those, who were not well acquainted with the English; there being such a prodigious Number of our Words, that are both *Verbs* and *Substantives,* and spelt in the same manner, tho' often accented differently in Pronunciation.

This Method has, by the Fancy of Printers, of late Years *been laid aside, from an Idea, that suppressing the Capitals shows the Character to greater Advantage; those*

ITC GARAMOND** ULTRA   MERGENTHALER TYPE LIBRARY

ABCDEFGHIJKLMNOPQRSTUVWXYZ
ABCDEFGHIJKLMNOPQRSTUVWXYZ
&.,"-:;!?""1234567890$
&.,"-:;!?""1234567890$
abcdefghijklmnopqrstuvwxyz
abcdefghijklmnopqrstuvwxyz

ABCDEFGHIJKLMNOPQRSTUVWXYZ
ABCDEFGHIJKLMNOPQRSTUVWXYZ
&.,"-:;!?""1234567890$
&.,"-:;!?""1234567890$
abcdefghijklmnopqrstuvwxyz
abcdefghijklmnopqrstuvwxyz

RSGrand5

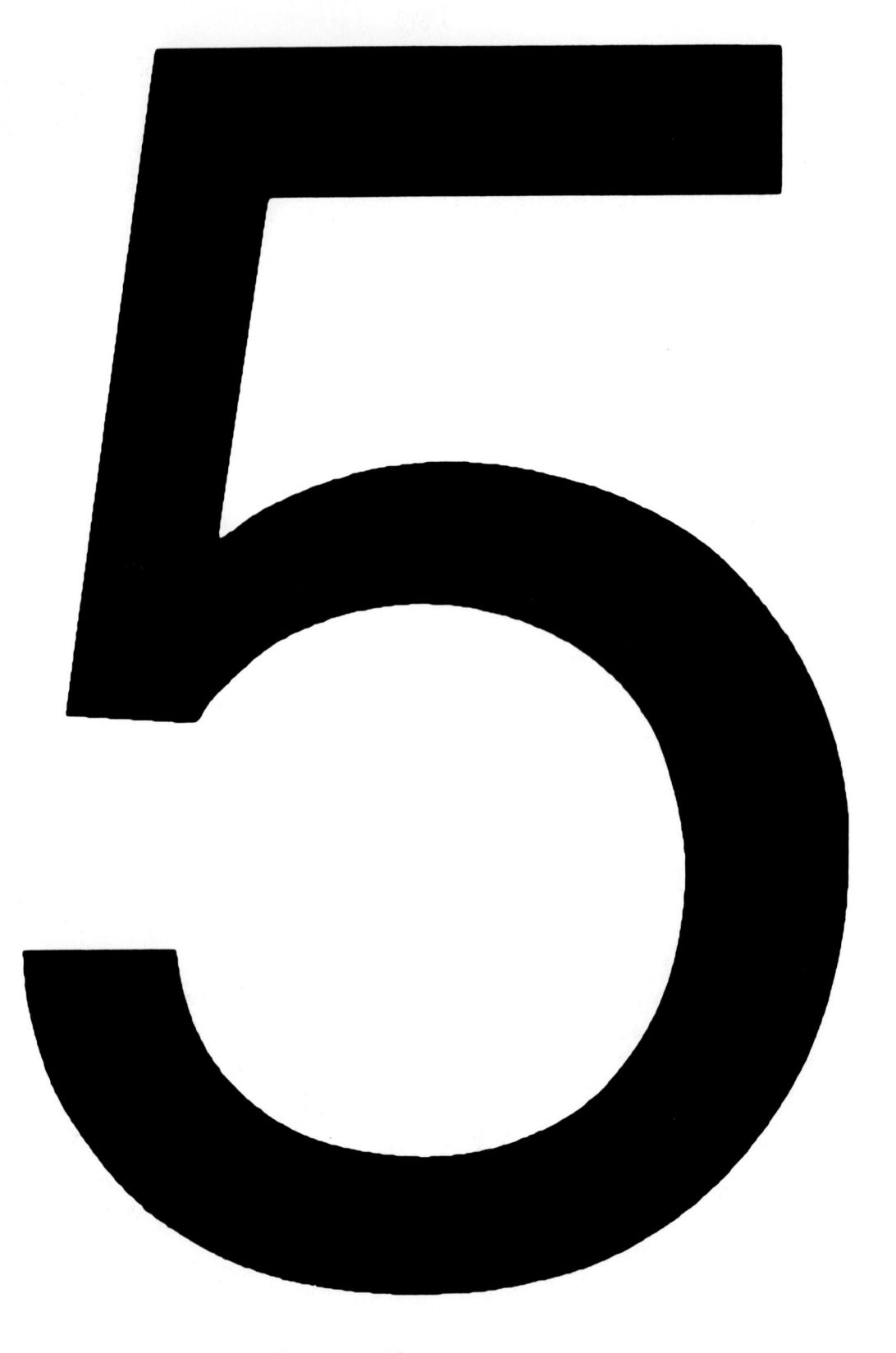

At this writing, Helvetica is, and for some time has been, the most widely used type in the world. Designed in 1957 by Max Miedinger, it quickly became a favorite among designers. The subtlety of its thick-to-thin relationships, the beautifully defined character in both capital and lower case letters, and the exceptional legibility in its form make it a type for all seasons.

HELVETICA FAMILY 259

tuqrs

ABCDEFGHIJK
LMNOPQRSTU
VWXYZ&abcde
fghijklmnopqrst
uvwxyz1234567
890$.,"":;!?

72 POINT HELVETICA* MERGENTHALER TYPE LIBRARY

ABCDEFGHIJK LMNOPQRSTU VWXYZ&abcde fghijklmnopqrst uvwxyz1234567 890$.,"";:!?

72 POINT HELVETICA* ITALIC   MERGENTHALER TYPE LIBRARY

ABCDEFGHIJKLM
NOPQRSTUVWXY
Z&abcdefghijklmnop
qrstuvwxyz1234567
890$.,""":;!?

60 POINT HELVETICA*   MERGENTHALER TYPE LIBRARY

ABCDEFGHIJKLM
NOPQRSTUVWXY
Z&abcdefghijklmno
pqrstuvwxyz12345
67890$.,""":;!?

60 POINT HELVETICA* ITALIC   MERGENTHALER TYPE LIBRARY

HELVETICA FAMILY

ABCDEFGHIJKLMNOPQRSTUVWXYZ&abcdefghijklmnopqrstuvwxyz1234567890$.,""":;!?

48 POINT HELVETICA*   MERGENTHALER TYPE LIBRARY

ABCDEFGHIJKLMNOPQRSTUVWXYZ&abcdefghijklmnopqrstuvwxyz1234567890$.,""":;!?

48 POINT HELVETICA* ITALIC   MERGENTHALER TYPE LIBRARY

ABCDEFGHIJKLMNOPQRSTUVWXYZ&abcdefghijklmnopqrstuvwxyz1234567890$.,""":;!?

36 POINT HELVETICA*   MERGENTHALER TYPE LIBRARY

ABCDEFGHIJKLMNOPQRSTU
VWXYZ&abcdefghijklmnopqrstu
vwxyz1234567890$.,""":;!?

36 POINT HELVETICA* ITALIC   MERGENTHALER TYPE LIBRARY

ABCDEFGHIJKLMNOPQRSTUVWXYZ&abcd
efghijklmnopqrstuvwxyz1234567890$.,""":;!?

24 POINT HELVETICA*   MERGENTHALER TYPE LIBRARY

ABCDEFGHIJKLMNOPQRSTUVWXYZ&abcd
efghijklmnopqrstuvwxyz1234567890$.,""":;!?

24 POINT HELVETICA* ITALIC   MERGENTHALER TYPE LIBRARY

ABCDEFGHIJKLMNOPQRSTUVWXYZ&abcdefghijklmnopqrs
tuvwxyz1234567890$.,""":;!?

18 POINT HELVETICA*   MERGENTHALER TYPE LIBRARY

ABCDEFGHIJKLMNOPQRSTUVWXYZ&abcdefghijklmnopqrs
tuvwxyz1234567890$.,""":;!?

18 POINT HELVETICA* ITALIC   MERGENTHALER TYPE LIBRARY

14/14 Typography is closely allied to the fine arts, and types have always reflected the taste or feeling of their time. The charm of the early Italian types has perhaps never been equalled; and the like is true of the Renaissance manuscripts on which they were based — and of many other departments of art in that same wonderful time. Note, too, the relation of the French manuscripts and types of a slightly later *date to the manuscripts and types of the Italian Renaissance.*

14/16 Typography is closely allied to the fine arts, and types have always reflected the taste or feeling of their time. The charm of the early Italian types has perhaps never been equalled; and the like is true of the Renaissance manuscripts on which they were based — and of many other departments of art in that same wonderful time. Note, *too, the relation of the French manuscripts and types of a slightly later*

14/18 Typography is closely allied to the fine arts, and types have always reflected the taste or feeling of their time. The charm of the early Italian types has perhaps never been equalled; and the like is true of the Renaissance manuscripts on which they were based — *and of many other departments of art in that same wonderful time. Note,*

12/12 Typography is closely allied to the fine arts, and types have always reflected the taste or feeling of their time. The charm of the early Italian types has perhaps never been equalled; and the like is true of the Renaissance manuscripts on which they were based — and of many other departments of art in that same wonderful time. Note, too, the relation of the French manuscripts and types of a slightly later date to the manuscripts and the types of the Italian Renaissance.
In spite of the increasing interest in the history of printing, and the attention paid in *many quarters to the work of famous typographers, a knowledge of standards among*

12/14 Typography is closely allied to the fine arts, and types have always reflected the taste or feeling of their time. The charm of the early Italian types has perhaps never been equalled; and the like is true of the Renaissance manuscripts on which they were based — and of many other departments of art in that same wonderful time. Note, too, the relation of the French manuscripts and types of a slightly later date to the manuscripts and the *types of the Italian Renaissance.*
In spite of the increasing interest in the

12/16 Typography is closely allied to the fine arts, and types have always reflected the taste or feeling of their time. The charm of the early Italian types has perhaps never been equalled; and the like is true of the Renaissance manuscripts on which they were based — and of many other departments of art in that same wonderful time. Note, too, the relation *of the French manuscripts and types of a slightly later date to the manuscripts and*

HELVETICA®   MERGENTHALER TYPE LIBRARY

ABCDEFGHIJKLMNOPQRSTUVW
ABCDEFGHIJKLMNOPQRSTUVW
XYZ&.,''-:;!?''''1234567890$
XYZ&.,''-:;!?''''1234567890$
abcdefghijklmnopqrstuvwxyz
abcdefghijklmnopqrstuvwxyz

ABCDEFGHIJKLMNOPQRSTUVWXYZ
ABCDEFGHIJKLMNOPQRSTUVWXYZ
&.,''-:;!?''''1234567890$
&.,''-:;!?''''1234567890$
abcdefghijklmnopqrstuvwxyz
abcdefghijklmnopqrstuvwxyz

11/11 Typography is closely allied to the fine arts, and types have always reflected the taste or feeling of their time. The charm of the early Italian types has perhaps never been equalled; and the like is true of the Renaissance manuscripts on which they were based — and of many other departments of art in that same wonderful time. Note, too, the relation of the French manuscripts and types of a slightly later date to the manuscripts and the types of the Italian Renaissance.

In spite of the increasing interest in the history of printing, and the attention paid in many quarters to the work of famous typographers, a knowledge of standards among the rank and file *of printers is still greatly lacking. To the average printer of today, type is type, printing is printing*

10/10 Typography is closely allied to the fine arts, and types have always reflected the taste or feeling of their time. The charm of the early Italian types has perhaps never been equalled; and the like is true of the Renaissance manuscripts on which they were based — and of many other departments of art in that same wonderful time. Note, too, the relation of the French manuscripts and types of a slightly later date to the manuscripts and the types of the Italian Renaissance.

In spite of the increasing interest in the history of printing, and the attention paid in many quarters to the work of famous typographers, a knowledge of standards among the rank and file of printers is still greatly lacking. To the average printer of today, type is *type, printing is printing — it is all about alike; and he concerns himself only with alleged labour-saving*

11/13 Typography is closely allied to the fine arts, and types have always reflected the taste or feeling of their time. The charm of the early Italian types has perhaps never been equalled; and the like is true of the Renaissance manuscripts on which they were based — and of many other departments of art in that same wonderful time. Note, too, the relation of the French manuscripts and types of a slightly later date to the manuscripts and the types of the Italian Renaissance.

In spite of the increasing interest in the history of printing, and the attention paid in many quarters *to the work of famous typographers, a knowledge of standards among the rank and*

10/12 Typography is closely allied to the fine arts, and types have always reflected the taste or feeling of their time. The charm of the early Italian types has perhaps never been equalled; and the like is true of the Renaissance manuscripts on which they were based — and of many other departments of art in that same wonderful time. Note, too, the relation of the French manuscripts and types of a slightly later date to the manuscripts and the types of the Italian Renaissance.

In spite of the increasing interest in the history of printing, and the attention paid in many quarters to the work of famous typographers, a knowledge of *standards among the rank and file of printers is still greatly lacking. To the average printer of today, type*

11/15 Typography is closely allied to the fine arts, and types have always reflected the taste or feeling of their time. The charm of the early Italian types has perhaps never been equalled; and the like is true of the Renaissance manuscripts on which they were based — and of many other departments of art in that same wonderful time. Note, too, the relation of the French manuscripts and types of a slightly later date to the manuscripts *and the types of the Italian Renaissance.*

In spite of the increasing interest in the history

10/14 Typography is closely allied to the fine arts, and types have always reflected the taste or feeling of their time. The charm of the early Italian types has perhaps never been equalled; and the like is true of the Renaissance manuscripts on which they were based — and of many other departments of art in that same wonderful time. Note, too, the relation of the French manuscripts and types of a slightly later date to the manuscripts and the types of the Italian Renaissance.

In spite of the increasing interest in the history of printing, and the attention paid in many quarters to

HELVETICA*   MERGENTHALER TYPE LIBRARY

ABCDEFGHIJKLMNOPQRSTUVWXYZ
ABCDEFGHIJKLMNOPQRSTUVWXYZ
&.,''-:;!?''''1234567890$
&.,''-:;!?''''1234567890$
abcdefghijklmnopqrstuvwxyz
abcdefghijklmnopqrstuvwxyz

ABCDEFGHIJKLMNOPQRSTUVWXYZ
ABCDEFGHIJKLMNOPQRSTUVWXYZ
&.,''-:;!?''''1234567890$
&.,''-:;!?''''1234567890$
abcdefghijklmnopqrstuvwxyz
abcdefghijklmnopqrstuvwxyz

9/9 Typography is closely allied to the fine arts, and types have always reflected the taste or feeling of their time. The charm of the early Italian types has perhaps never been equalled; and the like is true of the Renaissance manuscripts on which they were based — and of many other departments of art in that same wonderful time. Note, too, the relation of the French manuscripts and types of a slightly later date to the manuscripts and the types of the Italian Renaissance.

In spite of the increasing interest in the history of printing, and the attention paid in many quarters to the work of famous typographers, a knowledge of standards among the rank and file of printers is still greatly lacking. To the average printer of today, type is type, printing is printing — it is all about alike; and he concerns himself only with alleged labour-saving contrivances, or new type-faces that ensure convenience at the expense of proper design. In a more advanced class is to be found the printer who, knowing something of the historical side of printing and realizing *intellectually that there is a standard of excellence, yet has never considered the question as applying in any practical*

8/8 Typography is closely allied to the fine arts, and types have always reflected the taste or feeling of their time. The charm of the early Italian types has perhaps never been equalled; and the like is true of the Renaissance manuscripts on which they were based — and of many other departments of art in that same wonderful time. Note, too, the relation of the French manuscripts and types of a slightly later date to the manuscripts and the types of the Italian Renaissance.

In spite of the increasing interest in the history of printing, and the attention paid in many quarters to the work of famous typographers, a knowledge of standards among the rank and file of printers is still greatly lacking. To the average printer of today, type is type, printing is printing — it is all about alike; and he concerns himself only with alleged labour-saving contrivances, or new type-faces that ensure convenience at the expense of proper design. In a more advanced class is to be found the printer who, knowing something of the historical side of printing and realizing intellectually that there is a standard of excellence, yet has never considered the question as applying in any practical way to himself or his work.

Typography is closely allied to the fine arts, and types have always reflected the taste or feeling of their time. The charm of the

9/11 Typography is closely allied to the fine arts, and types have always reflected the taste or feeling of their time. The charm of the early Italian types has perhaps never been equalled; and the like is true of the Renaissance manuscripts on which they were based — and of many other departments of art in that same wonderful time. Note, too, the relation of the French manuscripts and types of a slightly later date to the manuscripts and the types of the Italian Renaissance.

In spite of the increasing interest in the history of printing, and the attention paid in many quarters to the work of famous typographers, a knowledge of standards among the rank and file of printers is still greatly lacking. To the average printer of today, type is type, printing is printing — it is all about alike; and he concerns himself only with alleged *labour-saving contrivances, or new type-faces that ensure convenience at the expense of proper design. In a more*

8/10 Typography is closely allied to the fine arts, and types have always reflected the taste or feeling of their time. The charm of the early Italian types has perhaps never been equalled; and the like is true of the Renaissance manuscripts on which they were based — and of many other departments of art in that same wonderful time. Note, too, the relation of the French manuscripts and types of a slightly later date to the manuscripts and the types of the Italian Renaissance.

In spite of the increasing interest in the history of printing, and the attention paid in many quarters to the work of famous typographers, a knowledge of standards among the rank and file of printers is still greatly lacking. To the average printer of today, type is type, printing is printing — it is all about alike; and he concerns himself only with alleged labour-saving contrivances, or new type-faces that ensure convenience at the expense of proper design. In a more advanced class is to be found the printer who, knowing *something of the historical side of printing and realizing intellectually that there is a standard of excellence, yet has never consid-*

9/13 Typography is closely allied to the fine arts, and types have always reflected the taste or feeling of their time. The charm of the early Italian types has perhaps never been equalled; and the like is true of the Renaissance manuscripts on which they were based — and of many other departments of art in that same wonderful time. Note, too, the relation of the French manuscripts and types of a slightly later date to the manuscripts and the types of the Italian Renaissance.

In spite of the increasing interest in the history of printing, and the attention paid in many quarters to the work of famous typographers, a knowledge of standards among *the rank and file of printers is still greatly lacking. To the average printer of today, type is type, printing is printing —*

8/12 Typography is closely allied to the fine arts, and types have always reflected the taste or feeling of their time. The charm of the early Italian types has perhaps never been equalled; and the like is true of the Renaissance manuscripts on which they were based — and of many other departments of art in that same wonderful time. Note, too, the relation of the French manuscripts and types of a slightly later date to the manuscripts and the types of the Italian Renaissance.

In spite of the increasing interest in the history of printing, and the attention paid in many quarters to the work of famous typographers, a knowledge of standards among the rank and file of printers is still greatly lacking. To the average printer of today, type *is type, printing is printing — it is all about alike; and he concerns himself only with alleged labour-saving contrivances, or new*

HELVETICA*   MERGENTHALER TYPE LIBRARY

ABCDEFGHIJKLMNOPQRSTUVWXYZ
ABCDEFGHIJKLMNOPQRSTUVWXYZ
&..,''-:;!?''''1234567890$
&..,''-:;!?''''1234567890$
abcdefghijklmnopqrstuvwxyz
abcdefghijklmnopqrstuvwxyz

ABCDEFGHIJKLMNOPQRSTUVWXYZ
ABCDEFGHIJKLMNOPQRSTUVWXYZ
&..,''-:;!?''''1234567890$
&..,''-:;!?''''1234567890$
abcdefghijklmnopqrstuvwxyz
abcdefghijklmnopqrstuvwxyz

ABCDEFGHIJK
LMNOPQRSTU
VWXYZ&abcdef
ghijklmnopqrstu
vwxyz12345678
90$.,"":;!?

72 POINT HELVETICA* LIGHT   MERGENTHALER TYPE LIBRARY

ABCDEFGHIJK
LMNOPQRSTU
VWXYZ&abcdef
ghijklmnopqrstu
vwxyz12345678
90$.,"":;!?

72 POINT HELVETICA* LIGHT ITALIC   MERGENTHALER TYPE LIBRARY

HELVETICA FAMILY 269

ABCDEFGHIJKLM
NOPQRSTUVWXYZ
&abcdefghijklmnop
qrstuvwxyz1234567
890$.,""":;!?

60 POINT HELVETICA* LIGHT   MERGENTHALER TYPE LIBRARY

*ABCDEFGHIJKLM
NOPQRSTUVWXYZ
&abcdefghijklmnop
qrstuvwxyz1234567
890$.,""":;!?*

60 POINT HELVETICA* LIGHT ITALIC   MERGENTHALER TYPE LIBRARY

ABCDEFGHIJKLMNOP
QRSTUVWXYZ&abcdefg
hijklmnopqrstuvwxyz123
4567890$.,""":;!?

48 POINT HELVETICA® LIGHT   MERGENTHALER TYPE LIBRARY

*ABCDEFGHIJKLMNOP
QRSTUVWXYZ&abcdefg
hijklmnopqrstuvwxyz123
4567890$.,""":;!?*

48 POINT HELVETICA® LIGHT ITALIC   MERGENTHALER TYPE LIBRARY

ABCDEFGHIJKLMNOPQRSTU
VWXYZ&abcdefghijklmnopqrstu
vwxyz1234567890$.,""":;!?

36 POINT HELVETICA® LIGHT   MERGENTHALER TYPE LIBRARY

ABCDEFGHIJKLMNOPQRSTU VWXYZ&abcdefghijklmnopqrstu vwxyz1234567890$.,""":;!?

36 POINT HELVETICA* LIGHT ITALIC   MERGENTHALER TYPE LIBRARY

ABCDEFGHIJKLMNOPQRSTUVWXYZ&abcdef ghijklmnopqrstuvwxyz1234567890$.,""":;!?

24 POINT HELVETICA* LIGHT   MERGENTHALER TYPE LIBRARY

ABCDEFGHIJKLMNOPQRSTUVWXYZ&abcdef ghijklmnopqrstuvwxyz1234567890$.,""":;!?

24 POINT HELVETICA* LIGHT ITALIC   MERGENTHALER TYPE LIBRARY

ABCDEFGHIJKLMNOPQRSTUVWXYZ&abcdefghijklmnopqrst uvwxyz1234567890$.,""":;!?

18 POINT HELVETICA* LIGHT   MERGENTHALER TYPE LIBRARY

ABCDEFGHIJKLMNOPQRSTUVWXYZ&abcdefghijklmnopqrst uvwxyz1234567890$.,""":;!?

18 POINT HELVETICA* LIGHT ITALIC   MERGENTHALER TYPE LIBRARY

272 HELVETICA FAMILY

14/14 Typography is closely allied to the fine arts, and types have always reflected the taste or feeling of their time. The charm of the early Italian types has perhaps never been equalled; and the like is true of the Renaissance manuscripts on which they were based — and of many other departments of art in that same wonderful time. Note, too, the relation of the French manuscripts and types of a *slightly later date to the manuscripts and types of the Italian Renaissance.*

14/16 Typography is closely allied to the fine arts, and types have always reflected the taste or feeling of their time. The charm of the early Italian types has perhaps never been equalled; and the like is true of the Renaissance manuscripts on which they were based — and of many other departments of art in that same wonderful *time. Note, too, the relation of the French manuscripts and types of a*

14/18 Typography is closely allied to the fine arts, and types have always reflected the taste or feeling of their time. The charm of the early Italian types has perhaps never been equalled; and the like is true of the Renaissance manuscripts on which they were based — and of many other departments of art in that same wonderful

12/12 Typography is closely allied to the fine arts, and types have always reflected the taste or feeling of their time. The charm of the early Italian types has perhaps never been equalled; and the like is true of the Renaissance manuscripts on which they were based — and of many other departments of art in that same wonderful time. Note, too, the relation of the French manuscripts and types of a slightly later date to the manuscripts and types of the Italian Renaissance.
  In spite of the increasing interest in the history of printing, and the attention paid in *many quarters to the work of famous typographers, a knowledge of standards among*

12/14 Typography is closely allied to the fine arts, and types have always reflected the taste or feeling of their time. The charm of the early Italian types has perhaps never been equalled; and the like is true of the Renaissance manuscripts on which they were based — and of many other departments of art in that same wonderful time. Note, too, the relation of the French manuscripts and types of a slightly later date to the manuscripts and the *types of the Italian Renaissance.*
  In spite of the increasing interest in the

12/16 Typography is closely allied to the fine arts, and types have always reflected the taste or feeling of their time. The charm of the early Italian types has perhaps never been equalled; and the like is true of the Renaissance manuscripts on which they were based — and of many other departments of art in that same wonderful time. Note, too, the relation *of the French manuscripts and types of a slightly later date to the manuscripts and*

HELVETICA* LIGHT   MERGENTHALER TYPE LIBRARY

ABCDEFGHIJKLMNOPQRSTUVWX
ABCDEFGHIJKLMNOPQRSTUVWX
YZ&.,''-:;!?''''1234567890$
YZ&.,''-:;!?''''1234567890$
abcdefghijklmnopqrstuvwxyz
abcdefghijklmnopqrstuvwxyz

ABCDEFGHIJKLMNOPQRSTUVWXYZ
ABCDEFGHIJKLMNOPQRSTUVWXYZ
&.,''-:;!?''''1234567890$
&.,''-:;!?''''1234567890$
abcdefghijklmnopqrstuvwxyz
abcdefghijklmnopqrstuvwxyz

10/10 Typography is closely allied to the fine arts, and types have always reflected the taste or feeling of their time. The charm of the early Italian types has perhaps never been equalled; and the like is true of the Renaissance manuscripts on which they were based — and of many other departments of art in that same wonderful time. Note, too, the relation of the French manuscripts and types of a slightly later date to the manuscripts and the types of the Italian Renaissance.

In spite of the increasing interest in the history of printing, and the attention paid in many quarters to the work of famous typographers, a knowledge of standards among the rank and file of printers is still greatly lacking. To the average printer of today, type *is type, printing is printing — it is all about alike; and he concerns himself only with alleged labour-saving*

10/12 Typography is closely allied to the fine arts, and types have always reflected the taste or feeling of their time. The charm of the early Italian types has perhaps never been equalled; and the like is true of the Renaissance manuscripts on which they were based — and of many other departments of art in that same wonderful time. Note, too, the relation of the French manuscripts and types of a slightly later date to the manuscripts and the types of the Italian Renaissance.

In spite of the increasing interest in the history of printing, and the attention paid in many quarters to the work of famous typographers, a knowledge of *standards among the rank and file of printers is still greatly lacking. To the average printer of today, type*

10/14 Typography is closely allied to the fine arts, and types have always reflected the taste or feeling of their time. The charm of the early Italian types has perhaps never been equalled; and the like is true of the Renaissance manuscripts on which they were based — and of many other departments of art in that same wonderful time. Note, too, the relation of the French manuscripts and types of a slightly later date to the manuscripts and the types of the Italian Renaissance.

In spite of the increasing interest in the history of printing, and the attention paid in many quarters to

8/8 Typography is closely allied to the fine arts, and types have always reflected the taste or feeling of their time. The charm of the early Italian types has perhaps never been equalled; and the like is true of the Renaissance manuscripts on which they were based — and of many other departments of art in that same wonderful time. Note, too, the relation of the French manuscripts and types of a slightly later date to the manuscripts and the types of the Italian Renaissance.

In spite of the increasing interest in the history of printing, and the attention paid in many quarters to the work of famous typographers, a knowledge of standards among the rank and file of printers is still greatly lacking. To the average printer of today, type is type, printing is printing — it is all about alike; and he concerns himself only with alleged labour-saving contrivances, or new typefaces that ensure convenience at the expense of proper design. In a more advanced class is to be found the printer who, knowing something of the historical side of printing and realizing intellectually that there is a standard of excellence, yet has never considered the question as applying in any practical way to himself or his work.

Typography is closely allied to the fine arts, and types have always reflected the taste or feeling of their time. The charm of the

8/10 Typography is closely allied to the fine arts, and types have always reflected the taste or feeling of their time. The charm of the early Italian types has perhaps never been equalled; and the like is true of the Renaissance manuscripts on which they were based — and of many other departments of art in that same wonderful time. Note, too, the relation of the French manuscripts and types of a slightly later date to the manuscripts and the types of the Italian Renaissance.

In spite of the increasing interest in the history of printing, and the attention paid in many quarters to the work of famous typographers, a knowledge of standards among the rank and file of printers is still greatly lacking. To the average printer of today, type is type, printing is printing — it is all about alike; and he concerns himself only with alleged labour-saving contrivances, or new typefaces that ensure convenience at the expense of proper design. In a more advanced class is to be found the printer who, knowing *something of the historical side of printing and realizing intellectually that there is a standard of excellence, yet has never consid-*

8/12 Typography is closely allied to the fine arts, and types have always reflected the taste or feeling of their time. The charm of the early Italian types has perhaps never been equalled; and the like is true of the Renaissance manuscripts on which they were based — and of many other departments of art in that same wonderful time. Note, too, the relation of the French manuscripts and types of a slightly later date to the manuscripts and the types of the Italian Renaissance.

In spite of the increasing interest in the history of printing, and the attention paid in many quarters to the work of famous typographers, a knowledge of standards among the rank and file of printers is still greatly lacking. To the average printer of today, type *is type, printing is printing — it is all about alike; and he concerns himself only with alleged labour-saving contrivances, or new type-*

HELVETICA* LIGHT   MERGENTHALER TYPE LIBRARY

ABCDEFGHIJKLMNOPQRSTUVWXYZ
ABCDEFGHIJKLMNOPQRSTUVWXYZ
&.,"-:;!?""1234567890$
&.,"-:;!?""1234567890$
abcdefghijklmnopqrstuvwxyz
abcdefghijklmnopqrstuvwxyz

ABCDEFGHIJKLMNOPQRSTUVWXYZ
ABCDEFGHIJKLMNOPQRSTUVWXYZ
&.,"-:;!?""1234567890$
&.,"-:;!?""1234567890$
abcdefghijklmnopqrstuvwxyz
abcdefghijklmnopqrstuvwxyz

ABCDEFGHIJ
KLMNOPQRST
UVWXYZ&abc
defghijklmnop
qrstuvwxyz123
4567890$.,"":;!?

72 POINT HELVETICA* BOLD   MERGENTHALER TYPE LIBRARY

ABCDEFGHIJKLMNOPQRSTUVWXYZ&abcdefghijklmnopqrstuvwxyz1234567890$.,"":;!?

72 POINT HELVETICA* BOLD ITALIC   MERGENTHALER TYPE LIBRARY

ABCDEFGHIJKLMNOPQRSTUVWXYZ&abcdefghijklmnopqrstuvwxyz1234567890$.,""":;!?

48 POINT HELVETICA* BOLD   MERGENTHALER TYPE LIBRARY

ABCDEFGHIJKLMNOPQRSTUVWXYZ&abcdefghijklmnopqrstuvwxyz1234567890$.,""":;!?

48 POINT HELVETICA* BOLD ITALIC   MERGENTHALER TYPE LIBRARY

ABCDEFGHIJKLMNOPQRSTUVWXYZ&abcdefghijklmnopqrstuvwxyz1234567890$.,";!?

24 POINT HELVETICA* BOLD   MERGENTHALER TYPE LIBRARY

ABCDEFGHIJKLMNOPQRSTUVWXYZ&abcdefghijklmnopqrstuvwxyz1234567890$.,""":;!?

24 POINT HELVETICA* BOLD ITALIC   MERGENTHALER TYPE LIBRARY

14/14 **Typography is closely allied to the fine arts, and types have always reflected the taste or feeling of their time. The charm of the early Italian types has perhaps never been equalled; and the like is true of the Renaissance manuscripts on which they were based — and of many other departments of art in that same wonderful time. Note, too, the relation of the French man-*uscripts and types of a slightly later date to the manuscripts and types***

12/12 **Typography is closely allied to the fine arts, and types have always reflected the taste or feeling of their time. The charm of the early Italian types has perhaps never been equalled; and the like is true of the Renaissance manuscripts on which they were based — and of many other departments of art in that same wonderful time. Note, too, the relation of the French manuscripts and types of a slightly later date to the manuscripts and the types of the Italian Renaissance.**
   In spite of the increasing interest in the *history of printing, and the attention paid in many quarters to the work of famous*

14/16 **Typography is closely allied to the fine arts, and types have always reflected the taste or feeling of their time. The charm of the early Italian types has perhaps never been equalled; and the like is true of the Renaissance manuscripts on which they were based — and of many other departments of art in *that same wonderful time. Note, too, the relation of the French man-***

12/14 **Typography is closely allied to the fine arts, and types have always reflected the taste or feeling of their time. The charm of the early Italian types has perhaps never been equalled; and the like is true of the Renaissance manuscripts on which they were based — and of many other departments of art in that same wonderful time. Note, too, the relation of the French manuscripts and types of a *slightly later date to the manuscripts and the types of the Italian Renaissance.***

14/18 **Typography is closely allied to the fine arts, and types have always reflected the taste or feeling of their time. The charm of the early Italian types has perhaps never been equalled; and the like is true of the Renaissance manuscripts *on which they were based — and of many other departments of art in***

12/16 **Typography is closely allied to the fine arts, and types have always reflected the taste or feeling of their time. The charm of the early Italian types has perhaps never been equalled; and the like is true of the Renaissance manuscripts on which they were based — and of many other departments of art in that same *wonderful time. Note, too, the relation of the French manuscripts and types of a***

HELVETICA* BOLD   MERGENTHALER TYPE LIBRARY

ABCDEFGHIJKLMNOPQRSTUVW
ABCDEFGHIJKLMNOPQRSTUVW
XYZ&.,"-:;!?""1234567890$
XYZ&.,"-:;!?""1234567890$
abcdefghijklmnopqrstuvwxyz
abcdefghijklmnopqrstuvwxyz

ABCDEFGHIJKLMNOPQRSTUVWXYZ
ABCDEFGHIJKLMNOPQRSTUVWXYZ
&.,"-:;!?""1234567890$
&.,"-:;!?""1234567890$
abcdefghijklmnopqrstuvwxyz
abcdefghijklmnopqrstuvwxyz

10/10 Typography is closely allied to the fine arts, and types have always reflected the taste or feeling of their time. The charm of the early Italian types has perhaps never been equalled; and the like is true of the Renaissance manuscripts on which they were based — and of many other departments of art in that same wonderful time. Note, too, the relation of the French manuscripts and types of a slightly later date to the manuscripts and the types of the Italian Renaissance.

In spite of the increasing interest in the history of printing, and the attention paid in many quarters to the work of famous typographers, a knowledge of standards among the rank and file of printers is still greatly lacking. To the average *printer of today, type is type, printing is printing — it is all about alike; and he concerns himself only*

8/8 Typography is closely allied to the fine arts, and types have always reflected the taste or feeling of their time. The charm of the early Italian types has perhaps never been equalled; and the like is true of the Renaissance manuscripts on which they were based — and of many other departments of art in that same wonderful time. Note, too, the relation of the French manuscripts and types of a slightly later date to the manuscripts and the types of the Italian Renaissance.

In spite of the increasing interest in the history of printing, and the attention paid in many quarters to the work of famous typographers, a knowledge of standards among the rank and file of printers is still greatly lacking. To the average printer of today, type is type, printing is printing — it is all about alike; and he concerns himself only with alleged labour-saving contrivances, or new type-faces that ensure convenience at the expense of proper design. In a more advanced class is to be found the printer who, knowing something of the historical side of printing and realizing intellectually that there is a standard of excellence, yet has never considered the question as applying in any practical way to himself or his work.

Typography is closely allied to the fine arts, and types have always reflected the taste or feeling of their time. The charm of

10/12 Typography is closely allied to the fine arts, and types have always reflected the taste or feeling of their time. The charm of the early Italian types has perhaps never been equalled; and the like is true of the Renaissance manuscripts on which they were based — and of many other departments of art in that same wonderful time. Note, too, the relation of the French manuscripts and types of a slightly later date to the manuscripts and the types of the Italian Renaissance.

In spite of the increasing interest in the history of printing, and the attention paid in many quarters to the work of famous typographers, a *knowledge of standards among the rank and file of printers is still greatly lacking. To the average*

8/10 Typography is closely allied to the fine arts, and types have always reflected the taste or feeling of their time. The charm of the early Italian types has perhaps never been equalled; and the like is true of the Renaissance manuscripts on which they were based — and of many other departments of art in that same wonderful time. Note, too, the relation of the French manuscripts and types of a slightly later date to the manuscripts and the types of the Italian Renaissance.

In spite of the increasing interest in the history of printing, and the attention paid in many quarters to the work of famous typographers, a knowledge of standards among the rank and file of printers is still greatly lacking. To the average printer of today, type is type, printing is printing — it is all about alike; and he concerns himself only with alleged labour-saving contrivances, or new type-faces that ensure convenience at the expense of proper design. In a more advanced class is to be *found the printer who, knowing something of the historical side of printing and realizing intellectually that there is a*

10/14 Typography is closely allied to the fine arts, and types have always reflected the taste or feeling of their time. The charm of the early Italian types has perhaps never been equalled; and the like is true of the Renaissance manuscripts on which they were based — and of many other departments of art in that same wonderful time. Note, too, the relation of the French manuscripts and types of a slightly later date to the manuscripts and the types of the Italian Renaissance.

In spite of the increasing interest in the history of printing, and the attention paid in many quar-

8/12 Typography is closely allied to the fine arts, and types have always reflected the taste or feeling of their time. The charm of the early Italian types has perhaps never been equalled; and the like is true of the Renaissance manuscripts on which they were based — and of many other departments of art in that same wonderful time. Note, too, the relation of the French manuscripts and types of a slightly later date to the manuscripts and the types of the Italian Renaissance.

In spite of the increasing interest in the history of printing, and the attention paid in many quarters to the work of famous typographers, a knowledge of standards among the rank and file of printers is still greatly lacking. To the average printer of *today, type is type, printing is printing — it is all about alike; and he concerns himself only with alleged labour-saving con-*

HELVETICA* BOLD   MERGENTHALER TYPE LIBRARY

ABCDEFGHIJKLMNOPQRSTUVWXYZ
ABCDEFGHIJKLMNOPQRSTUVWXYZ
&.,''-:;!?''""1234567890$
&.,''-:;!?''""1234567890$
abcdefghijklmnopqrstuvwxyz
abcdefghijklmnopqrstuvwxyz

ABCDEFGHIJKLMNOPQRSTUVWXYZ
ABCDEFGHIJKLMNOPQRSTUVWXYZ
&.,''-:;!?''""1234567890$
&.,''-:;!?''""1234567890$
abcdefghijklmnopqrstuvwxyz
abcdefghijklmnopqrstuvwxyz

ABCDEFGHIJ KLMNOPQRS TUVWXYZ&ab cdefghijklmn opqrstuvwxy z1234567890$.,'"":;!?

72 POINT HELVETICA* HEAVY   MERGENTHALER TYPE LIBRARY

ABCDEFGHIJKLMNOPQRSTUVWXYZ&abcdefghijklmnopqrstuvwxyz1234567890$.,"":;!?

72 POINT HELVETICA* HEAVY ITALIC   MERGENTHALER TYPE LIBRARY

ABCDEFGHIJKLMNO
PQRSTUVWXYZ&abc
defghijklmnopqrstuv
wxyz1234567890$";!?

48 POINT HELVETICA* HEAVY   MERGENTHALER TYPE LIBRARY

*ABCDEFGHIJKLMNO
PQRSTUVWXYZ&abc
defghijklmnopqrstuv
wxyz1234567890$";!?*

48 POINT HELVETICA* HEAVY ITALIC   MERGENTHALER TYPE LIBRARY

ABCDEFGHIJKLMNOPQRSTUVWXYZ&ab
cdefghijklmnopqrstuvwxyz1234567890$
.,""":;!?

24 POINT HELVETICA* HEAVY   MERGENTHALER TYPE LIBRARY

*ABCDEFGHIJKLMNOPQRSTUVWXYZ&a
bcdefghijklmnopqrstuvwxyz1234567890
$.,""":;!?*

24 POINT HELVETICA* HEAVY ITALIC   MERGENTHALER TYPE LIBRARY

14/14 Typography is closely allied to the fine arts, and types have always reflected the taste or feeling of their time. The charm of the early Italian types has perhaps never been equalled; and the like is true of the Renaissance manuscripts on which they were based — and of many other departments of art in that same wonderful time. Note, too, *the relation of the French manuscripts and types of a slightly*

14/16 Typography is closely allied to the fine arts, and types have always reflected the taste or feeling of their time. The charm of the early Italian types has perhaps never been equalled; and the like is true of the Renaissance manuscripts on which they were based — and of many *other departments of art in that same wonderful time. Note, too,*

14/18 Typography is closely allied to the fine arts, and types have always reflected the taste or feeling of their time. The charm of the early Italian types has perhaps never been equalled; and the like is true of the Renaissance *sance manuscripts on which they were based — and of many*

12/12 Typography is closely allied to the fine arts, and types have always reflected the taste or feeling of their time. The charm of the early Italian types has perhaps never been equalled; and the like is true of the Renaissance manuscripts on which they were based — and of many other departments of art in that same wonderful time. Note, too, the relation of the French manuscripts and types of a slightly later date to the manuscripts and the types of the Italian Renaissance.
In spite of the increasing interest in the history of printing, and the atten-

12/14 Typography is closely allied to the fine arts, and types have always reflected the taste or feeling of their time. The charm of the early Italian types has perhaps never been equalled; and the like is true of the Renaissance manuscripts on which they were based — and of many other departments of art in that same wonderful time. Note, too, the relation of the French manuscripts *and types of a slightly later date to the manuscripts and the types of the Ital-*

12/16 Typography is closely allied to the fine arts, and types have always reflected the taste or feeling of their time. The charm of the early Italian types has perhaps never been equalled; and the like is true of the Renaissance manuscripts on which they were based — and of many other departments of art *in that same wonderful time. Note, too, the relation of the French manuscripts*

HELVETICA* HEAVY   MERGENTHALER TYPE LIBRARY

ABCDEFGHIJKLMNOPQRSTUV
ABCDEFGHIJKLMNOPQRSTUV
WXYZ&.,'‐-:;!?""1234567890$
WXYZ&.,'‐-:;!?""1234567890$
abcdefghijklmnopqrstuvwxyz
abcdefghijklmnopqrstuvwxyz

ABCDEFGHIJKLMNOPQRSTUVWXYZ
ABCDEFGHIJKLMNOPQRSTUVWXYZ
&.,'‐-:;!?""1234567890$
&.,'‐-:;!?""1234567890$
abcdefghijklmnopqrstuvwxyz
abcdefghijklmnopqrstuvwxyz

HELVETICA FAMILY 283

10/10 **Typography is closely allied to the fine arts, and types have always reflected the taste or feeling of their time. The charm of the early Italian types has perhaps never been equalled; and the like is true of the Renaissance manuscripts on which they were based — and of many other departments of art in that same wonderful time. Note, too, the relation of the French manuscripts and types of a slightly later date to the manuscripts and the types of the Italian Renaissance.**

In spite of the increasing interest in the history of printing, and the attention paid in many quarters to the work of famous typographers, a knowledge of standards among the rank and *file of printers is still greatly lacking. To the average printer of today, type is type, printing*

8/8 **Typography is closely allied to the fine arts, and types have always reflected the taste or feeling of their time. The charm of the early Italian types has perhaps never been equalled; and the like is true of the Renaissance manuscripts on which they were based — and of many other departments of art in that same wonderful time. Note, too, the relation of the French manuscripts and types of a slightly later date to the manuscripts and the types of the Italian Renaissance.**

In spite of the increasing interest in the history of printing, and the attention paid in many quarters to the work of famous typographers, a knowledge of standards among the rank and file of printers is still greatly lacking. To the average printer of today, type is type, printing is printing — it is all about alike; and he concerns himself only with alleged labour-saving contrivances, or new type-faces that ensure convenience at the expense of proper design. In a more advanced class is to be found the printer who, knowing something of the historical side of printing and realizing intellectually that there is a standard of excel-*lence, yet has never considered the question as applying in any practical way to himself or his work.*

10/12 **Typography is closely allied to the fine arts, and types have always reflected the taste or feeling of their time. The charm of the early Italian types has perhaps never been equalled; and the like is true of the Renaissance manuscripts on which they were based — and of many other departments of art in that same wonderful time. Note, too, the relation of the French manuscripts and types of a slightly later date to the manuscripts and the types of the Italian Renaissance.**

In spite of the increasing interest in the history of printing, and the attention paid in many *quarters to the work of famous typographers, a knowledge of standards among the rank and*

8/10 **Typography is closely allied to the fine arts, and types have always reflected the taste or feeling of their time. The charm of the early Italian types has perhaps never been equalled; and the like is true of the Renaissance manuscripts on which they were based — and of many other departments of art in that same wonderful time. Note, too, the relation of the French manuscripts and types of a slightly later date to the manuscripts and the types of the Italian Renaissance.**

In spite of the increasing interest in the history of printing, and the attention paid in many quarters to the work of famous typographers, a knowledge of standards among the rank and file of printers is still greatly lacking. To the average printer of today, type is type, printing is printing — it is all about alike; and he concerns himself only with alleged labour-saving contrivances, or new type-faces *that ensure convenience at the expense of proper design. In a more advanced class is to be found the printer who,*

10/14 **Typography is closely allied to the fine arts, and types have always reflected the taste or feeling of their time. The charm of the early Italian types has perhaps never been equalled; and the like is true of the Renaissance manuscripts on which they were based — and of many other departments of art in that same wonderful time. Note, too, the relation of the French manuscripts and types of a slightly later date to the manuscripts and the types of *the Italian Renaissance.***

In spite of the increasing interest in the his-

8/12 **Typography is closely allied to the fine arts, and types have always reflected the taste or feeling of their time. The charm of the early Italian types has perhaps never been equalled; and the like is true of the Renaissance manuscripts on which they were based — and of many other departments of art in that same wonderful time. Note, too, the relation of the French manuscripts and types of a slightly later date to the manuscripts and the types of the Italian Renaissance.**

In spite of the increasing interest in the history of printing, and the attention paid in many quarters to the work of famous typographers, a knowledge of standards among *the rank and file of printers is still greatly lacking. To the average printer of today, type is type, printing is printing*

HELVETICA® HEAVY   MERGENTHALER TYPE LIBRARY

ABCDEFGHIJKLMNOPQRSTUVWXYZ
ABCDEFGHIJKLMNOPQRSTUVWXYZ
&.,'‑:;!?'"1234567890$
&.,'‑:;!?'"1234567890$
abcdefghijklmnopqrstuvwxyz
abcdefghijklmnopqrstuvwxyz

ABCDEFGHIJKLMNOPQRSTUVWXYZ
ABCDEFGHIJKLMNOPQRSTUVWXYZ
&.,'‑:;!?'"1234567890$
&.,'‑:;!?'"1234567890$
abcdefghijklmnopqrstuvwxyz
abcdefghijklmnopqrstuvwxyz

ABCDEFGHI
JKLMNOPQR
STUVWXYZ
&abcdefghij
klmnopqrstu
vwxyz12345
67890$,""„;!?

72 POINT HELVETICA* BLACK   MERGENTHALER TYPE LIBRARY

ABCDEFGHI JKLMNOPQR STUVWXYZ &abcdefghij klmnopqrstu vwxyz12345 67890$,"",;!?

72 POINT HELVETICA* BLACK ITALIC   MERGENTHALER TYPE LIBRARY

HELVETICA FAMILY

ABCDEFGHIJKLMN
OPQRSTUVWXYZ&
abcdefghijklmnopqr
stuvwxyz12345678
90$.,""";!?

48 POINT HELVETICA* BLACK   MERGENTHALER TYPE LIBRARY

ABCDEFGHIJKLMN
OPQRSTUVWXYZ&
abcdefghijklmnopqr
stuvwxyz123456789
0$.,""";!?

48 POINT HELVETICA* BLACK ITALIC   MERGENTHALER TYPE LIBRARY

HELVETICA FAMILY 287

ABCDEFGHIJKLMNOPQRSTUVWXYZ &abcdefghijklmnopqrstuvwxyz12345 67890$.,""":;!?

24 POINT HELVETICA® BLACK MERGENTHALER TYPE LIBRARY

ABCDEFGHIJKLMNOPQRSTUVWXYZ &abcdefghijklmnopqrstuvwxyz123456 7890$.,""":;!?

24 POINT HELVETICA® BLACK ITALIC MERGENTHALER TYPE LIBRARY

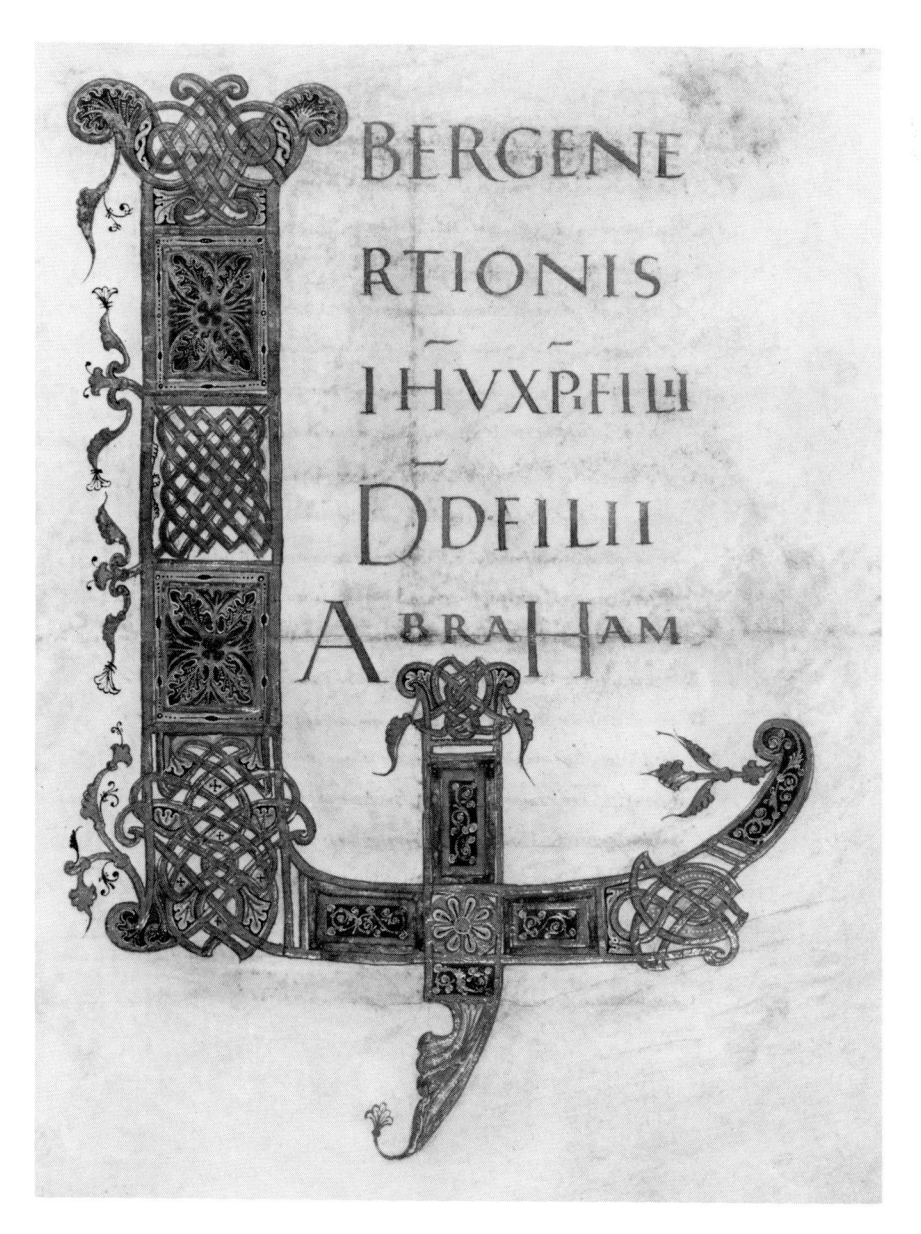

The initial page of the Gospel of St. Matthew from the FOUR GOSPELS, was lettered more than a thousand years ago by scribes in Tours, France. It remains a high point of Western calligraphy, standing in interesting relation to Helvetica, one of today's most widely used family of types.

14/14 **Typography is closely allied to the fine arts, and types have always reflected the taste or feeling of their time. The charm of the early Italian types has perhaps never been equalled; and the like is true of the Renaissance manuscripts on which they were based — and of many other departments of art in that same wonderful time. Note, too, the relation of the French manuscripts**

12/12 **Typography is closely allied to the fine arts, and types have always reflected the taste or feeling of their time. The charm of the early Italian types has perhaps never been equalled; and the like is true of the Renaissance manuscripts on which they were based — and of many other departments of art in that same wonderful time. Note, too, the relation of the French manuscripts and types of a slightly later date to the manuscripts and the types of *the Italian Renaissance.***
In spite of the increasing interest

14/16 **Typography is closely allied to the fine arts, and types have always reflected the taste or feeling of their time. The charm of the early Italian types has perhaps never been equalled; and the like is true of the Renaissance manuscripts on which they were based —** *and of many other departments of art in that same wonderful*

12/14 **Typography is closely allied to the fine arts, and types have always reflected the taste or feeling of their time. The charm of the early Italian types has perhaps never been equalled; and the like is true of the Renaissance manuscripts on which they were based — and of many other departments of art in that same wonderful time. Note, too, the** *relation of the French manuscripts and types of a slightly later date to*

14/18 **Typography is closely allied to the fine arts, and types have always reflected the taste or feeling of their time. The charm of the early Italian types has perhaps never been equalled; and the like is true of *the Renaissance manuscripts* on which they were based —**

12/16 **Typography is closely allied to the fine arts, and types have always reflected the taste or feeling of their time. The charm of the early Italian types has perhaps never been equalled; and the like is true of the Renaissance manuscripts on which they were based — and of many** *other departments of art in that same wonderful time.* **Note, too, the**

HELVETICA® BLACK   MERGENTHALER TYPE LIBRARY

ABCDEFGHIJKLMNOPQRSTU
ABCDEFGHIJKLMNOPQRSTU
VWXY&.,"-:;!?""1234567890$
VWXY&.,"-:;!?""1234567890$
abcdefghijklmnopqrstuvwxyz
abcdefghijklmnopqrstuvwxyz

ABCDEFGHIJKLMNOPQRSTUVWX
ABCDEFGHIJKLMNOPQRSTUVWX
YZ&.,"-:;!?""1234567890$
YZ&.,"-:;!?""1234567890$
abcdefghijklmnopqrstuvwxyz
abcdefghijklmnopqrstuvwxyz

10/10 Typography is closely allied to the fine arts, and types have always reflected the taste or feeling of their time. The charm of the early Italian types has perhaps never been equalled; and the like is true of the Renaissance manuscripts on which they were based — and of many other departments of art in that same wonderful time. Note, too, the relation of the French manuscripts and types of a slightly later date to the manuscripts and the types of the Italian Renaissance.

In spite of the increasing interest in the history of printing, and the attention paid in many quarters to the work of famous typographers, *a knowledge of standards among the rank and file of printers is still greatly*

8/8 Typography is closely allied to the fine arts, and types have always reflected the taste or feeling of their time. The charm of the early Italian types has perhaps never been equalled; and the like is true of the Renaissance manuscripts on which they were based — and of many other departments of art in that same wonderful time. Note, too, the relation of the French manuscripts and types of a slightly later date to the manuscripts and the types of the Italian Renaissance.

In spite of the increasing interest in the history of printing, and the attention paid in many quarters to the work of famous typographers, a knowledge of standards among the rank and file of printers is still greatly lacking. To the average printer of today, type is type, printing is printing — it is all about alike; and he concerns himself only with alleged labour-saving contrivances, or new type-faces that ensure convenience at the expense of proper design. In a more advanced class is to be found the printer who, knowing something of the historical side of printing and realizing *intellectually that there is a standard of excellence, yet has never considered the question as applying in*

10/12 Typography is closely allied to the fine arts, and types have always reflected the taste or feeling of their time. The charm of the early Italian types has perhaps never been equalled; and the like is true of the Renaissance manuscripts on which they were based — and of many other departments of art in that same wonderful time. Note, too, the relation of the French manuscripts and types of a slightly later date to the manuscripts and the types of the Italian Renaissance.

In spite of the increasing interest in the *history of printing, and the attention paid in many quarters to the work of famous typog-*

8/10 Typography is closely allied to the fine arts, and types have always reflected the taste or feeling of their time. The charm of the early Italian types has perhaps never been equalled; and the like is true of the Renaissance manuscripts on which they were based — and of many other departments of art in that same wonderful time. Note, too, the relation of the French manuscripts and types of a slightly later date to the manuscripts and the types of the Italian Renaissance.

In spite of the increasing interest in the history of printing, and the attention paid in many quarters to the work of famous typographers, a knowledge of standards among the rank and file of printers is still greatly lacking. To the average printer of today, type is type, printing is printing — it is all about alike; and he concerns himself only with alleged labour-saving contrivances, or new type-faces that ensure convenience at the expense of proper design. *In a more advanced*

10/14 Typography is closely allied to the fine arts, and types have always reflected the taste or feeling of their time. The charm of the early Italian types has perhaps never been equalled; and the like is true of the Renaissance manuscripts on which they were based — and of many other departments of art in that same wonderful time. Note, too, the relation of the French manuscripts and types of a slightly later date to *the manuscripts and the types of the Italian Renaissance.*

8/12 Typography is closely allied to the fine arts, and types have always reflected the taste or feeling of their time. The charm of the early Italian types has perhaps never been equalled; and the like is true of the Renaissance manuscripts on which they were based — and of many other departments of art in that same wonderful time. Note, too, the relation of the French manuscripts and types of a slightly later date to the manuscripts and the types of the Italian Renaissance.

In spite of the increasing interest in the history of printing, and the attention paid in many quarters to the work of famous typographers, a knowledge of *standards among the rank and file of printers is still greatly lacking. To the average printer of today, type is*

HELVETICA* BLACK   MERGENTHALER TYPE LIBRARY

ABCDEFGHIJKLMNOPQRSTUVWXYZ
ABCDEFGHIJKLMNOPQRSTUVWXYZ
&.,'‘-:;!?'"""1234567890$
&.,'‘-:;!?'"""1234567890$
abcdefghijklmnopqrstuvwxyz
abcdefghijklmnopqrstuvwxyz

ABCDEFGHIJKLMNOPQRSTUVWXYZ
ABCDEFGHIJKLMNOPQRSTUVWXYZ
&.,'‘-:;!?'"""1234567890$
&.,'‘-:;!?'"""1234567890$
abcdefghijklmnopqrstuvwxyz
abcdefghijklmnopqrstuvwxyz

HELVETICA FAMILY, 36 VARIATIONS

Helvetica* ultra light
abcdefghijklmnopqrstuvwxyz ABCDEFGHIJKLMNOPQRSTUVWXYZ 1234567890 .,:;''&!?

Helvetica* ultra light italic
abcdefghijklmnopqrstuvwxyz ABCDEFGHIJKLMNOPQRSTUVWXYZ 1234567890 .,:;''&!?

Helvetica* thin
abcdefghijklmnopqrstuvwxyz ABCDEFGHIJKLMNOPQRSTUVWXYZ 1234567890 .,:;''&!?

Helvetica* thin italic
abcdefghijklmnopqrstuvwxyz ABCDEFGHIJKLMNOPQRSTUVWXYZ 1234567890 .,:;''&!?

Helvetica* Catalogue roman
abcdefghijklmnopqrstuvwxyz ABCDEFGHIJKLMNOPQRSTUVWXYZ 1234567890 .,:;''&!?

Helvetica* Catalogue bold
abcdefghijklmnopqrstuvwxyz ABCDEFGHIJKLMNOPQRSTUVWXYZ 1234567890 .,:;''&!?

Helvetica* bold No. 2
abcdefghijklmnopqrstuvwxyz ABCDEFGHIJKLMNOPQRSTUVWXYZ 1234567890 .,:;''&!?

Helvetica* black No. 2
abcdefghijklmnopqrstuvwxyz ABCDEFGHIJKLMNOPQRSTUVWXYZ 1234567890 :;''&!?

Helvetica* bold outline
abcdefghijklmnopqrstuvwxyz ABCDEFGHIJKLMNOPQRSTUVWXYZ 1234567890 .,:;''&!?

Helvetica* light condensed
abcdefghijklmnopqrstuvwxyz ABCDEFGHIJKLMNOPQRSTUVWXYZ 1234567890 .,:;''&!?

Helvetica* light condensed italic
abcdefghijklmnopqrstuvwxyz ABCDEFGHIJKLMNOPQRSTUVWXYZ 1234567890 .,:;''&!?

Helvetica* condensed
abcdefghijklmnopqrstuvwxyz ABCDEFGHIJKLMNOPQRSTUVWXYZ 1234567890 .,:;''&!?

Helvetica* condensed italic
abcdefghijklmnopqrstuvwxyz ABCDEFGHIJKLMNOPQRSTUVWXYZ 1234567890 .,:;''&!?

Helvetica* bold condensed
abcdefghijklmnopqrstuvwxyz ABCDEFGHIJKLMNOPQRSTUVWXYZ 1234567890 .,:;''&!?

Helvetica* bold condensed italic
abcdefghijklmnopqrstuvwxyz ABCDEFGHIJKLMNOPQRSTUVWXYZ 1234567890 .,:;''&!?

Helvetica* black condensed
abcdefghijklmnopqrstuvwxyz ABCDEFGHIJKLMNOPQRSTUVWXYZ 1234567890 .,:;''&!?

Helvetica* black condensed italic
abcdefghijklmnopqrstuvwxyz ABCDEFGHIJKLMNOPQRSTUVWXYZ 1234567890 .,:;''&!?

Helvetica* bold condensed outline
abcdefghijklmnopqrstuvwxyz ABCDEFGHIJKLMNOPQRSTUVWXYZ 1234567890 .,:;''&!?

MERGENTHALER TYPE LIBRARY

Helvetica* compressed
abcdefghijklmnopqrstuvwxyz
ABCDEFGHIJKLMNOPQRSTUVWXYZ
1234567890 .,:;''&!?

Helvetica* extra compressed
abcdefghijklmnopqrstuvwxyz
ABCDEFGHIJKLMNOPQRSTUVWXYZ
1234567890 .,:;''&!?

Helvetica* ultra compressed
abcdefghijklmnopqrstuvwxyz
ABCDEFGHIJKLMNOPQRSTUVWXYZ
1234567890 .,:;''&!?

Helvetica* Inserat
abcdefghijklmnopqrstuvwxyz
ABCDEFGHIJKLMNOPQRSTUVWXYZ
1234567890 .,:;''&!?

Helvetica* Inserat italic
abcdefghijklmnopqrstuvwxyz
ABCDEFGHIJKLMNOPQRSTUVWXYZ
1234567890 .,:;''&!?

Helvetica* light extended
abcdefghijklmnopqrstuvwxyz ABCDEFGHIJKLMNOPQRSTUVWXYZ 1234567890 .,:;''&!?

Helvetica* extended
abcdefghijklmnopqrstuvwxyz ABCDEFGHIJKLMNOPQRSTUVWXYZ 1234567890 :;''&!?

Helvetica* bold extended
abcdefghijklmnopqrstuvwxyz ABCDEFGHIJKLMNOPQRSTUVWXYZ 1234567890 .,:;''&!?

Helvetica* black extended
abcdefghijklmnopqrstuvwxyz ABCDEFGHIJKLMNOPQRSTUVWXYZ 1234567890 .,:;

Helvetica* Rounded bold
abcdefghijklmnopqrstuvwxyz ABCDEFGHIJKLMNOPQRSTUVWXYZ 1234567890 .,:;''&!?

Helvetica* Rounded bold italic
abcdefghijklmnopqrstuvwxyz ABCDEFGHIJKLMNOPQRSTUVWXYZ 1234567890 .,:;''&!?

Helvetica* Rounded black
abcdefghijklmnopqrstuvwxyz ABCDEFGHIJKLMNOPQRSTUVWXYZ 1234567890 .,:;''&!?

Helvetica* Rounded black italic
abcdefghijklmnopqrstuvwxyz ABCDEFGHIJKLMNOPQRSTUVWXYZ 1234567890 .,:;''&!?

Helvetica* Rounded bold outline
abcdefghijklmnopqrstuvwxyz ABCDEFGHIJKLMNOPQRSTUVWXYZ 1234567890 .,:;''&!?

Helvetica* Rounded bold condensed
abcdefghijklmnopqrstuvwxyz ABCDEFGHIJKLMNOPQRSTUVWXYZ 1234567890 .,:;''&!?

Helvetica* Textbook roman
abcdefghijklmnopqrstuvwxyz ABCDEFGHIJKLMNOPQRSTUVWXYZ 1234567890 .,:;''&!?

Helvetica* Textbook bold
abcdefghijklmnopqrstuvwxyz ABCDEFGHIJKLMNOPQRSTUVWXYZ 1234567890 .,:;''&!?

Helvetica* bold reversed
abcdefghijklmnopqrstuvwxyz ABCDEFGHIJKLMNOPQRSTUVWXYZ 1234567890 .,:;''&!?

MERGENTHALER TYPE LIBRARY

Times Roman is the second most widely used typeface. In 1932, "The Times" of London commissioned the design of a new typeface. Under the able direction of Stanley Morison, a face originally called New Times Roman was produced and soon became one of the most widely accepted types of the twentieth century, used in many languages and in all parts of the world.

p56

ABCDEFGHIJK
LMNOPQRSTU
VWXYZ&abcde
fghijklmnopqrstu
vwxyz123456789
0$.,"":;!?

72 POINT TIMES* MERGENTHALER TYPE LIBRARY

ABCDEFGHIJKLMNOP
QRSTUVWXYZ&abcdef
ghijklmnopqrstuvwxyz123
4567890$.,""":;!?

48 POINT TIMES*   MERGENTHALER TYPE LIBRARY

ABCDEFGHIJKLMNOPQ
RSTUVWXYZ&abcdefghij
klmnopqrstuvwxyz1234567
890$.,""":;!?

48 POINT TIMES* ITALIC   MERGENTHALER TYPE LIBRARY

ABCDEFGHIJKLMNOPQRSTU
VWXYZ&abcdefghijklmnopqrstu
vwxyz1234567890$.,""":;!?

36 POINT TIMES*   MERGENTHALER TYPE LIBRARY

ABCDEFGHIJKLMNOPQRSTUV WXYZ&abcdefghijklmnopqrstuvw xyz1234567890$.," ":;!?

36 POINT TIMES* ITALIC   MERGENTHALER TYPE LIBRARY

ABCDEFGHIJKLMNOPQRSTUVWXYZ&abcde fghijklmnopqrstuvwxyz1234567890$.," ":;!?

24 POINT TIMES*   MERGENTHALER TYPE LIBRARY

ABCDEFGHIJKLMNOPQRSTUVWXYZ&abcdefg hijklmnopqrstuvwxyz1234567890$.," ":;!?

24 POINT TIMES* ITALIC   MERGENTHALER TYPE LIBRARY

ABCDEFGHIJKLMNOPQRSTUVWXYZ&abcdefghijklmnopqrst uvwxyz1234567890$.," ":;!?

18 POINT TIMES*   MERGENTHALER TYPE LIBRARY

ABCDEFGHIJKLMNOPQRSTUVWXYZ&abcdefghijklmnopqrstuvw xyz1234567890$.," ":;!?

18 POINT TIMES* ITALIC   MERGENTHALER TYPE LIBRARY

14/14 To cast off manuscript with accuracy and precision, is a task of a disagreeable nature, which requires great attention and mature deliberation. The trouble and difficulty is much increased, when the copy is not only irregularly written (which is too frequently the case), but also abounds with interlineations, erasures, and variations in the sizes of paper. To surmount these defects the closest application and attention is required; yet, at times, so *numerous are the alterations and additions, that they not unfrequently baffle*

12/12 To cast off manuscript with accuracy and precision, is a task of a disagreeable nature, which requires great attention and mature deliberation. The trouble and difficulty is much increased, when the copy is not only irregularly written (which is too frequently the case), but also abounds with interlineations, erasures, and variations in the sizes of paper. To surmount these defects the closest application and attention is required; yet, at times, so numerous are the alterations and additions, that they not unfrequently baffle the skill and judgment of the most experienced calculators of copy. Such an imper*fect and slovenly mode of sending works to the press (which is generally attended with unpleas-*

14/16 To cast off manuscript with accuracy and precision, is a task of a disagreeable nature, which requires great attention and mature deliberation. The trouble and difficulty is much increased, when the copy is not only irregularly written (which is too frequently the case), but also abounds with interlineations, erasures, and variations in the sizes of paper. To surmount *these defects the closest application and attention is required; yet, at times, so*

12/14 To cast off manuscript with accuracy and precision, is a task of a disagreeable nature, which requires great attention and mature deliberation. The trouble and difficulty is much increased, when the copy is not only irregularly written (which is too frequently the case), but also abounds with interlineations, erasures, and variations in the sizes of paper. To surmount these defects the closest application and attention is required; yet, at times, so numerous are the *alterations and additions, that they not unfrequently baffle the skill and judgment of the most*

14/18 To cast off manuscript with accuracy and precision, is a task of a disagreeable nature, which requires great attention and mature deliberation. The trouble and difficulty is much increased, when the copy is not only irregularly written (which is too frequently the case), but also abounds *with interlineations, erasures, and variations in the sizes of paper. To surmount*

12/16 To cast off manuscript with accuracy and precision, is a task of a disagreeable nature, which requires great attention and mature deliberation. The trouble and difficulty is much increased, when the copy is not only irregularly written (which is too frequently the case), but also abounds with interlineations, erasures, and variations in the sizes of paper. To surmount these *defects the closest application and attention is required; yet, at times, so numerous are the*

TIMES*   MERGENTHALER TYPE LIBRARY

ABCDEFGHIJKLMNOPQRSTUVWX
ABCDEFGHIJKLMNOPQRSTUVWX
YZ&.,''-:;!?''""1234567890$
YZ&.,''-:;!?''""1234567890$
abcdefghijklmnopqrstuvwxyz
abcdefghijklmnopqrstuvwxyz

ABCDEFGHIJKLMNOPQRSTUVWXYZ
ABCDEFGHIJKLMNOPQRSTUVWXYZ
&.,''-:;!?''""1234567890$
&.,''-:;!?''""1234567890$
abcdefghijklmnopqrstuvwxyz
abcdefghijklmnopqrstuvwxyz

TIMES FAMILY 299

11/11 To cast off manuscript with accuracy and precision, is a task of a disagreeable nature, which requires great attention and mature deliberation. The trouble and difficulty is much increased, when the copy is not only irregularly written (which is too frequently the case), but also abounds with interlineations, erasures, and variations in the sizes of paper. To surmount these defects the closest application and attention is required; yet, at times, so numerous are the alterations and additions, that they not unfrequently baffle the skill and judgment of the most experienced calculators of copy. Such an imperfect and slovenly mode of sending works to the press (which is generally attended with unpleasant consequences to all parties) cannot be too strongly deprecated by all admirers of the art.

10/10 To cast off manuscript with accuracy and precision, is a task of a disagreeable nature, which requires great attention and mature deliberation. The trouble and difficulty is much increased, when the copy is not only irregularly written (which is too frequently the case), but also abounds with interlineations, erasures, and variations in the sizes of paper. To surmount these defects the closest application and attention is required; yet, at times, so numerous are the alterations and additions, that they not unfrequently baffle the skill and judgment of the most experienced calculators of copy. Such an imperfect and slovenly mode of sending works to the press (which is generally attended with unpleasant consequences to all parties) cannot be too strongly deprecated by all admirers of the art.
The first thing necessary is to take a comprehensive view of the copy, and to notice whether it is written even, if

11/13 To cast off manuscript with accuracy and precision, is a task of a disagreeable nature, which requires great attention and mature deliberation. The trouble and difficulty is much increased, when the copy is not only irregularly written (which is too frequently the case), but also abounds with interlineations, erasures, and variations in the sizes of paper. To surmount these defects the closest application and attention is required; yet, at times, so numerous are the alterations and additions, that they not unfrequently baffle the skill and judgment of the most experienced calculators of copy. Such an imperfect and slovenly *mode of sending works to the press (which is generally attended with unpleasant consequences to all*

10/12 To cast off manuscript with accuracy and precision, is a task of a disagreeable nature, which requires great attention and mature deliberation. The trouble and difficulty is much increased, when the copy is not only irregularly written (which is too frequently the case), but also abounds with interlineations, erasures, and variations in the sizes of paper. To surmount these defects the closest application and attention is required; yet, at times, so numerous are the alterations and additions, that they not unfrequently baffle the skill and judgment of the most experienced calculators of copy. Such an imperfect and slovenly mode of sending works to the press (which is generally attended with unpleasant consequences to all *parties) cannot be too strongly deprecated by all admirers of the art.*

11/15 To cast off manuscript with accuracy and precision, is a task of a disagreeable nature, which requires great attention and mature deliberation. The trouble and difficulty is much increased, when the copy is not only irregularly written (which is too frequently the case), but also abounds with interlineations, erasures, and variations in the sizes of paper. To surmount these defects the closest application and attention is required; yet, at times, so numerous are the *alterations and additions, that they not unfrequently baffle the skill and judgment of the most experienced*

10/14 To cast off manuscript with accuracy and precision, is a task of a disagreeable nature, which requires great attention and mature deliberation. The trouble and difficulty is much increased, when the copy is not only irregularly written (which is too frequently the case), but also abounds with interlineations, erasures, and variations in the sizes of paper. To surmount these defects the closest application and attention is required; yet, at times, so numerous are the alterations and additions, that they not unfrequently baffle the skill and judgment of the most *experienced calculators of copy. Such an imperfect and slovenly mode of sending works to the press (which is*

TIMES*   MERGENTHALER TYPE LIBRARY

ABCDEFGHIJKLMNOPQRSTUVWXYZ
ABCDEFGHIJKLMNOPQRSTUVWXYZ
&.,'`-:;!?''""1234567890$
&.,'`-:;!?''""1234567890$
abcdefghijklmnopqrstuvwxyz
abcdefghijklmnopqrstuvwxyz

ABCDEFGHIJKLMNOPQRSTUVWXYZ
ABCDEFGHIJKLMNOPQRSTUVWXYZ
&.,'`-:;!?''""1234567890$
&.,'`-:;!?''""1234567890$
abcdefghijklmnopqrstuvwxyz
abcdefghijklmnopqrstuvwxyz

9/9 To cast off manuscript with accuracy and precision, is a task of a disagreeable nature, which requires great attention and mature deliberation. The trouble and difficulty is much increased, when the copy is not only irregularly written (which is too frequently the case), but also abounds with interlineations, erasures, and variations in the sizes of paper. To surmount these defects the closest application and attention is required; yet, at times, so numerous are the alterations and additions, that they not unfrequently baffle the skill and judgment of the most experienced calculators of copy. Such an imperfect and slovenly mode of sending works to the press (which is generally attended with unpleasant consequences to all parties) cannot be too strongly deprecated by all admirers of the art.

The first thing necessary is to take a comprehensive view of the copy, and to notice whether it is written even, if it has many interlineations, etc. also the number of break lines, and whether divided into chapters and sub-heads, in order that allowance may be made for them in the calculation, so that the plan of the work *may not afterwards be infringed on. These observations should be entered as a memorandum, on a separate piece of paper, to*

8/8 To cast off manuscript with accuracy and precision, is a task of a disagreeable nature, which requires great attention and mature deliberation. The trouble and difficulty is much increased, when the copy is not only irregularly written (which is too frequently the case), but also abounds with interlineations, erasures, and variations in the sizes of paper. To surmount these defects the closest application and attention is required; yet, at times, so numerous are the alterations and additions, that they not unfrequently baffle the skill and judgment of the most experienced calculators of copy. Such an imperfect and slovenly mode of sending works to the press (which is generally attended with unpleasant consequences to all parties) cannot be too strongly deprecated by all admirers of the art.

The first thing necessary is to take a comprehensive view of the copy, and to notice whether it is written even, if it has many interlineations, etc. also the number of break lines, and whether divided into chapters and sub-heads, in order that allowance may be made for them in the calculation, so that the plan of the work may not afterwards be infringed on. These observations should be entered as a memorandum, on a separate piece of paper, to assist the memory, and save the trouble of re-examining the manuscript.

This preparation being made, we then take that part of the copy for our calculation which comes nearest to the general tendency of the writing,

9/11 To cast off manuscript with accuracy and precision, is a task of a disagreeable nature, which requires great attention and mature deliberation. The trouble and difficulty is much increased, when the copy is not only irregularly written (which is too frequently the case), but also abounds with interlineations, erasures, and variations in the sizes of paper. To surmount these defects the closest application and attention is required; yet, at times, so numerous are the alterations and additions, that they not unfrequently baffle the skill and judgment of the most experienced calculators of copy. Such an imperfect and slovenly mode of sending works to the press (which is generally attended with unpleasant consequences to all parties) cannot be too strongly deprecated by all admirers of the art.

The first thing necessary is to take a comprehensive view of *the copy, and to notice whether it is written even, if it has many interlineations, etc. also the number of break lines, and whether*

8/10 To cast off manuscript with accuracy and precision, is a task of a disagreeable nature, which requires great attention and mature deliberation. The trouble and difficulty is much increased, when the copy is not only irregularly written (which is too frequently the case), but also abounds with interlineations, erasures, and variations in the sizes of paper. To surmount these defects the closest application and attention is required; yet, at times, so numerous are the alterations and additions, that they not unfrequently baffle the skill and judgment of the most experienced calculators of copy. Such an imperfect and slovenly mode of sending works to the press (which is generally attended with unpleasant consequences to all parties) cannot be too strongly deprecated by all admirers of the art.

The first thing necessary is to take a comprehensive view of the copy, and to notice whether it is written even, if it has many interlineations, etc. also the number of break lines, and whether divided into chapters and sub-heads, in order that allowance may be made for them in the *calculation, so that the plan of the work may not afterwards be infringed on. These observations should be entered as a memorandum, on a*

9/13 To cast off manuscript with accuracy and precision, is a task of a disagreeable nature, which requires great attention and mature deliberation. The trouble and difficulty is much increased, when the copy is not only irregularly written (which is too frequently the case), but also abounds with interlineations, erasures, and variations in the sizes of paper. To surmount these defects the closest application and attention is required; yet, at times, so numerous are the alterations and additions, that they not unfrequently baffle the skill and judgment of the most experienced calculators of copy. Such an imperfect and slovenly mode of sending works to the press (which is generally attended with *unpleasant consequences to all parties) cannot be too strongly deprecated by all admirers of the art.*

8/12 To cast off manuscript with accuracy and precision, is a task of a disagreeable nature, which requires great attention and mature deliberation. The trouble and difficulty is much increased, when the copy is not only irregularly written (which is too frequently the case), but also abounds with interlineations, erasures, and variations in the sizes of paper. To surmount these defects the closest application and attention is required; yet, at times, so numerous are the alterations and additions, that they not unfrequently baffle the skill and judgment of the most experienced calculators of copy. Such an imperfect and slovenly mode of sending works to the press (which is generally attended with unpleasant consequences to all parties) cannot be too strongly deprecated by all admirers of the art.

The first thing necessary is to take a comprehensive view of the copy, and to notice whether it is written even, if it has many interlineations,

TIMES*   MERGENTHALER TYPE LIBRARY

ABCDEFGHIJKLMNOPQRSTUVWXYZ
ABCDEFGHIJKLMNOPQRSTUVWXYZ
&.,'`-:;!?'"" 1234567890$
&.,'`-:;!?'"" 1234567890$
abcdefghijklmnopqrstuvwxyz
abcdefghijklmnopqrstuvwxyz

ABCDEFGHIJKLMNOPQRSTUVWXYZ
ABCDEFGHIJKLMNOPQRSTUVWXYZ
&.,'`-:;!?'"" 1234567890$
&.,'`-:;!?'"" 1234567890$
abcdefghijklmnopqrstuvwxyz
abcdefghijklmnopqrstuvwxyz

ABCDEFGHIJ KLMNOPQRST UVWXYZ&abc defghijklmnopqr stuvwxyz123456 7890$.,"":;!?

72 POINT TIMES* SEMI BOLD   MERGENTHALER TYPE LIBRARY

*ABCDEFGHIJ
KLMNOPQRST
UVWXYZ&abc
defghijklmnopqr
stuvwxyz1234567
890$.,"":;!?*

72 POINT TIMES® SEMI BOLD ITALIC   MERGENTHALER TYPE LIBRARY

ABCDEFGHIJKLMNOPQRSTUVWXYZ&abcdefghijklmnopqrstuvwxyz1234567890$.,""":;!?

48 POINT TIMES* SEMI BOLD   MERGENTHALER TYPE LIBRARY

ABCDEFGHIJKLMNOPQRSTUVWXYZ&abcdefghijklmnopqrstuvwxyz1234567890$.,""":;!?

48 POINT TIMES* SEMI BOLD ITALIC   MERGENTHALER TYPE LIBRARY

ABCDEFGHIJKLMNOPQRSTUVWXYZ&abcdefghijklmnopqrstuvwxyz1234567890$.,""":;!?

24 POINT TIMES* SEMI BOLD   MERGENTHALER TYPE LIBRARY

ABCDEFGHIJKLMNOPQRSTUVWXYZ&abcdefghijklmnopqrstuvwxyz1234567890$.,""":;!?

24 POINT TIMES* SEMI BOLD ITALIC   MERGENTHALER TYPE LIBRARY

304 TIMES FAMILY

14/14   To cast off manuscript with accuracy and precision, is a task of a disagreeable nature, which requires great attention and mature deliberation. The trouble and difficulty is much increased, when the copy is not only irregularly written (which is too frequently the case), but also abounds with interlineations, erasures, and variations in the sizes of paper. To surmount these defects the closest ap*plication and attention is required; yet, at times, so numerous are the alterations*

12/12   To cast off manuscript with accuracy and precision, is a task of a disagreeable nature, which requires great attention and mature deliberation. The trouble and difficulty is much increased, when the copy is not only irregularly written (which is too frequently the case), but also abounds with interlineations, erasures, and variations in the sizes of paper. To surmount these defects the closest application and attention is required; yet, at times, so numerous are the alterations and additions, that they not unfrequently baffle the skill and judgment of the most experienced calculators of copy. Such an imperfect and slovenly mode of sending works to the

14/16   To cast off manuscript with accuracy and precision, is a task of a disagreeable nature, which requires great attention and mature deliberation. The trouble and difficulty is much increased, when the copy is not only irregularly written (which is too frequently the case), but also abounds with interlineations, erasures, and *variations in the sizes of paper. To surmount these defects the closest applica-*

12/14   To cast off manuscript with accuracy and precision, is a task of a disagreeable nature, which requires great attention and mature deliberation. The trouble and difficulty is much increased, when the copy is not only irregularly written (which is too frequently the case), but also abounds with interlineations, erasures, and variations in the sizes of paper. To surmount these defects the closest application and attention is required; yet, at *times, so numerous are the alterations and additions, that they not unfrequently baffle*

14/18   To cast off manuscript with accuracy and precision, is a task of a disagreeable nature, which requires great attention and mature deliberation. The trouble and difficulty is much increased, when the copy is not only irregularly written (which is too fre*quently the case), but also abounds with interlineations, erasures, and varia-*

12/16   To cast off manuscript with accuracy and precision, is a task of a disagreeable nature, which requires great attention and mature deliberation. The trouble and difficulty is much increased, when the copy is not only irregularly written (which is too frequently the case), but also abounds with interlineations, erasures, and variations in the sizes of *paper. To surmount these defects the closest application and attention is required; yet, at*

TIMES® SEMI BOLD   MERGENTHALER TYPE LIBRARY

ABCDEFGHIJKLMNOPQRSTUVW
ABCDEFGHIJKLMNOPQRSTUVW
XYZ&.,''-:;!?''""1234567890$
XYZ&.,''-:;!?''""1234567890$
abcdefghijklmnopqrstuvwxyz
abcdefghijklmnopqrstuvwxyz

ABCDEFGHIJKLMNOPQRSTUVWXYZ
ABCDEFGHIJKLMNOPQRSTUVWXYZ
&.,''-:;!?''""1234567890$
&.,''-:;!?''""1234567890$
abcdefghijklmnopqrstuvwxyz
abcdefghijklmnopqrstuvwxyz

TIMES FAMILY 305

10/10   To cast off manuscript with accuracy and precision, is a task of a disagreeable nature, which requires great attention and mature deliberation. The trouble and difficulty is much increased, when the copy is not only irregularly written (which is too frequently the case), but also abounds with interlineations, erasures, and variations in the sizes of paper. To surmount these defects the closest application and attention is required; yet, at times, so numerous are the alterations and additions, that they not unfrequently baffle the skill and judgment of the most experienced calculators of copy. Such an imperfect and slovenly mode of sending works to the press (which is generally attended with unpleasant consequences to all parties) cannot be too strongly deprecated by all admirers of the art.
The first thing necessary is to take a comprehensive view of the copy, and to notice whether it is written even,

8/8   To cast off manuscript with accuracy and precision, is a task of a disagreeable nature, which requires great attention and mature deliberation. The trouble and difficulty is much increased, when the copy is not only irregularly written (which is too frequently the case), but also abounds with interlineations, erasures, and variations in the sizes of paper. To surmount these defects the closest application and attention is required; yet, at times, so numerous are the alterations and additions, that they not unfrequently baffle the skill and judgment of the most experienced calculators of copy. Such an imperfect and slovenly mode of sending works to the press (which is generally attended with unpleasant consequences to all parties) cannot be too strongly deprecated by all admirers of the art.
   The first thing necessary is to take a comprehensive view of the copy, and to notice whether it is written even, if it has many interlineations, etc. also the number of break lines, and whether divided into chapters and sub-heads, in order that allowance may be made for them in the calculation, so that the plan of the work may not afterwards be infringed on. These observations should be entered as a memorandum, on a separate piece of paper, to assist the memory, and save the trouble of re-examining the manuscript.
This preparation being made, we then take that part of the copy for our calculation which comes nearest to the general tendency of the

10/12   To cast off manuscript with accuracy and precision, is a task of a disagreeable nature, which requires great attention and mature deliberation. The trouble and difficulty is much increased, when the copy is not only irregularly written (which is too frequently the case), but also abounds with interlineations, erasures, and variations in the sizes of paper. To surmount these defects the closest application and attention is required; yet, at times, so numerous are the alterations and additions, that they not unfrequently baffle the skill and judgment of the most experienced calculators of copy. Such an imperfect and slovenly mode of sending works to the press (which is generally attended with *unpleasant consequences to all parties) cannot be too strongly deprecated by all admirers of the art.*

8/10   To cast off manuscript with accuracy and precision, is a task of a disagreeable nature, which requires great attention and mature deliberation. The trouble and difficulty is much increased, when the copy is not only irregularly written (which is too frequently the case), but also abounds with interlineations, erasures, and variations in the sizes of paper. To surmount these defects the closest application and attention is required; yet, at times, so numerous are the alterations and additions, that they not unfrequently baffle the skill and judgment of the most experienced calculators of copy. Such an imperfect and slovenly mode of sending works to the press (which is generally attended with unpleasant consequences to all parties) cannot be too strongly deprecated by all admirers of the art.
   The first thing necessary is to take a comprehensive view of the copy, and to notice whether it is written even, if it has many interlineations, etc. also the number of break lines, and whether divided into chapters and sub-heads, in order that allowance may be made *for them in the calculation, so that the plan of the work may not afterwards be infringed on. These observations should be entered as a*

10/14   To cast off manuscript with accuracy and precision, is a task of a disagreeable nature, which requires great attention and mature deliberation. The trouble and difficulty is much increased, when the copy is not only irregularly written (which is too frequently the case), but also abounds with interlineations, erasures, and variations in the sizes of paper. To surmount these defects the closest application and attention is required; yet, at times, so numerous are the alterations and additions, that they not unfrequently baffle the *skill and judgment of the most experienced calculators of copy. Such an imperfect and slovenly mode of sending*

8/12   To cast off manuscript with accuracy and precision, is a task of a disagreeable nature, which requires great attention and mature deliberation. The trouble and difficulty is much increased, when the copy is not only irregularly written (which is too frequently the case), but also abounds with interlineations, erasures, and variations in the sizes of paper. To surmount these defects the closest application and attention is required; yet, at times, so numerous are the alterations and additions, that they not unfrequently baffle the skill and judgment of the most experienced calculators of copy. Such an imperfect and slovenly mode of sending works to the press (which is generally attended with unpleasant consequences to all parties) cannot be too strongly deprecated by all admirers of the art.
The first thing necessary is to take a comprehensive view of the copy, and to notice whether it is written even, if it has many interlinea-

TIMES® SEMI BOLD   MERGENTHALER TYPE LIBRARY

ABCDEFGHIJKLMNOPQRSTUVWXYZ
ABCDEFGHIJKLMNOPQRSTUVWXYZ
&.,'‘-:;!?’"" 1234567890$
&.,'‘-:;!?’"" 1234567890$
abcdefghijklmnopqrstuvwxyz
abcdefghijklmnopqrstuvwxyz

ABCDEFGHIJKLMNOPQRSTUVWXYZ
ABCDEFGHIJKLMNOPQRSTUVWXYZ
&.,'‘-:;!?’"" 1234567890$
&.,'‘-:;!?’"" 1234567890$
abcdefghijklmnopqrstuvwxyz
abcdefghijklmnopqrstuvwxyz

ABCDEFGHIJKLMNOPQRSTUVWXYZ&abcdefghijklmnopqrstuvwxyz1234567890$.,""'';!?

72 POINT TIMES* BOLD   MERGENTHALER TYPE LIBRARY

ABCDEFGHIJK
LMNOPQRSTU
VWXYZ&abcdef
ghijklmnopqrstuv
wxyz1234567890
$.,"":;!?

72 POINT TIMES® BOLD ITALIC   MERGENTHALER TYPE LIBRARY

ABCDEFGHIJKLMNOPQRSTUVWXYZ&abcdefghijklmnopqrstuvwxyz1234567890$.,""":;!?

48 POINT TIMES* BOLD   MERGENTHALER TYPE LIBRARY

ABCDEFGHIJKLMNOPQRSTUVWXYZ&abcdefghijklmnopqrstuvwxyz1234567890$.,""":;!?

48 POINT TIMES* BOLD ITALIC   MERGENTHALER TYPE LIBRARY

ABCDEFGHIJKLMNOPQRSTUVWXYZ&abcdefghijklmnopqrstuvwxyz1234567890$.,""":;!?

24 POINT TIMES* BOLD   MERGENTHALER TYPE LIBRARY

ABCDEFGHIJKLMNOPQRSTUVWXYZ&abcdefghijklmnopqrstuvwxyz1234567890$.,""":;!?

24 POINT TIMES* BOLD ITALIC   MERGENTHALER TYPE LIBRARY

TIMES FAMILY 309

14/14 **To cast off manuscript with accuracy and precision, is a task of a disagreeable nature, which requires great attention and mature deliberation. The trouble and difficulty is much increased, when the copy is not only irregularly written (which is too frequently the case), but also abounds with interlineations, erasures, and variations in the sizes of paper. To surmount these defects the closest application and attention is required; yet, at times, so numerous are the alterations**

12/12 **To cast off manuscript with accuracy and precision, is a task of a disagreeable nature, which requires great attention and mature deliberation. The trouble and difficulty is much increased, when the copy is not only irregularly written (which is too frequently the case), but also abounds with interlineations, erasures, and variations in the sizes of paper. To surmount these defects the closest application and attention is required; yet, at times, so numerous are the alterations and additions, that they not unfrequently baffle the skill and judgment of the most experienced calculators of copy. Such an imperfect and slovenly mode of sending works to the press**

14/16 **To cast off manuscript with accuracy and precision, is a task of a disagreeable nature, which requires great attention and mature deliberation. The trouble and difficulty is much increased, when the copy is not only irregularly written (which is too frequently the case), but also abounds with interlineations, erasures, and variations in the sizes of paper. To surmount these defects the closest application**

12/14 **To cast off manuscript with accuracy and precision, is a task of a disagreeable nature, which requires great attention and mature deliberation. The trouble and difficulty is much increased, when the copy is not only irregularly written (which is too frequently the case), but also abounds with interlineations, erasures, and variations in the sizes of paper. To surmount these defects the closest application and attention is required; yet, at times, so numerous are the alterations and additions, that they not unfrequently baffle the**

14/18 **To cast off manuscript with accuracy and precision, is a task of a disagreeable nature, which requires great attention and mature deliberation. The trouble and difficulty is much increased, when the copy is not only irregularly written (which is too frequently the case), but also abounds with interlineations, erasures, and variations**

12/16 **To cast off manuscript with accuracy and precision, is a task of a disagreeable nature, which requires great attention and mature deliberation. The trouble and difficulty is much increased, when the copy is not only irregularly written (which is too frequently the case), but also abounds with interlineations, erasures, and variations in the sizes of paper. To surmount these defects the closest application and attention is required; yet, at**

TIMES® BOLD   MERGENTHALER TYPE LIBRARY

ABCDEFGHIJKLMNOPQRSTUVW
ABCDEFGHIJKLMNOPQRSTUVW
XYZ&.,'"-:;!?""1234567890$
XYZ&.,'"-:;!?""1234567890$
abcdefghijklmnopqrstuvwxyz
abcdefghijklmnopqrstuvwxyz

ABCDEFGHIJKLMNOPQRSTUVWXYZ
ABCDEFGHIJKLMNOPQRSTUVWXYZ
&.,'"-:;!?""1234567890$
&.,'"-:;!?""1234567890$
abcdefghijklmnopqrstuvwxyz
abcdefghijklmnopqrstuvwxyz

10/10 To cast off manuscript with accuracy and precision, is a task of a disagreeable nature, which requires great attention and mature deliberation. The trouble and difficulty is much increased, when the copy is not only irregularly written (which is too frequently the case), but also abounds with interlineations, erasures, and variations in the sizes of paper. To surmount these defects the closest application and attention is required; yet, at times, so numerous are the alterations and additions, that they not unfrequently baffle the skill and judgment of the most experienced calculators of copy. Such an imperfect and slovenly mode of sending works to the press (which is generally attended with unpleasant consequences to all parties) cannot be too strongly deprecated by all admirers of the art.

The first thing necessary is to take a comprehensive view of the copy, and to notice whether it is written even,

8/8 To cast off manuscript with accuracy and precision, is a task of a disagreeable nature, which requires great attention and mature deliberation. The trouble and difficulty is much increased, when the copy is not only irregularly written (which is too frequently the case), but also abounds with interlineations, erasures, and variations in the sizes of paper. To surmount these defects the closest application and attention is required; yet, at times, so numerous are the alterations and additions, that they not unfrequently baffle the skill and judgment of the most experienced calculators of copy. Such an imperfect and slovenly mode of sending works to the press (which is generally attended with unpleasant consequences to all parties) cannot be too strongly deprecated by all admirers of the art.

The first thing necessary is to take a comprehensive view of the copy, and to notice whether it is written even, if it has many interlineations, etc. also the number of break lines, and whether divided into chapters and sub-heads, in order that allowance may be made for them in the calculation, so that the plan of the work may not afterwards be infringed on. These observations should be entered as a memorandum, on a separate piece of paper, to assist the memory, and save the trouble of re-examining the manuscript.

This preparation being made, we then take that part of the copy for our calculation which comes nearest to the general tendency of the

10/12 To cast off manuscript with accuracy and precision, is a task of a disagreeable nature, which requires great attention and mature deliberation. The trouble and difficulty is much increased, when the copy is not only irregularly written (which is too frequently the case), but also abounds with interlineations, erasures, and variations in the sizes of paper. To surmount these defects the closest application and attention is required; yet, at times, so numerous are the alterations and additions, that they not unfrequently baffle the skill and judgment of the most experienced calculators of copy. Such an imperfect and slovenly mode of sending works to the press (which is generally attended *with unpleasant consequences to all parties) cannot be too strongly deprecated by all admirers of the art.*

8/10 To cast off manuscript with accuracy and precision, is a task of a disagreeable nature, which requires great attention and mature deliberation. The trouble and difficulty is much increased, when the copy is not only irregularly written (which is too frequently the case), but also abounds with interlineations, erasures, and variations in the sizes of paper. To surmount these defects the closest application and attention is required; yet, at times, so numerous are the alterations and additions, that they not unfrequently baffle the skill and judgment of the most experienced calculators of copy. Such an imperfect and slovenly mode of sending works to the press (which is generally attended with unpleasant consequences to all parties) cannot be too strongly deprecated by all admirers of the art.

The first thing necessary is to take a comprehensive view of the copy, and to notice whether it is written even, if it has many interlineations, etc. also the number of break lines, and whether divided into chapters and sub-heads, in order that allowance may be made *for them in the calculation, so that the plan of the work may not afterwards be infringed on. These observations should be entered as a*

10/14 To cast off manuscript with accuracy and precision, is a task of a disagreeable nature, which requires great attention and mature deliberation. The trouble and difficulty is much increased, when the copy is not only irregularly written (which is too frequently the case), but also abounds with interlineations, erasures, and variations in the sizes of paper. To surmount these defects the closest application and attention is required; yet, at times, so numerous are the alterations and additions, that they not unfrequently baffle the *skill and judgment of the most experienced calculators of copy. Such an imperfect and slovenly mode of sending*

8/12 To cast off manuscript with accuracy and precision, is a task of a disagreeable nature, which requires great attention and mature deliberation. The trouble and difficulty is much increased, when the copy is not only irregularly written (which is too frequently the case), but also abounds with interlineations, erasures, and variations in the sizes of paper. To surmount these defects the closest application and attention is required; yet, at times, so numerous are the alterations and additions, that they not unfrequently baffle the skill and judgment of the most experienced calculators of copy. Such an imperfect and slovenly mode of sending works to the press (which is generally attended with unpleasant consequences to all parties) cannot be too strongly deprecated by all admirers of the art.

The first thing necessary is to take a comprehensive view of the copy, and to notice whether it is written even, if it has many interlinea-

TIMES® BOLD   MERGENTHALER TYPE LIBRARY

ABCDEFGHIJKLMNOPQRSTUVWXYZ
ABCDEFGHIJKLMNOPQRSTUVWXYZ
&.,'"-:;!?"" "1234567890$
&.,'"-:;!?"" "1234567890$
abcdefghijklmnopqrstuvwxyz
abcdefghijklmnopqrstuvwxyz

ABCDEFGHIJKLMNOPQRSTUVWXYZ
ABCDEFGHIJKLMNOPQRSTUVWXYZ
&.,'"-:;!?"" "1234567890$
&.,'"-:;!?"" "1234567890$
abcdefghijklmnopqrstuvwxyz
abcdefghijklmnopqrstuvwxyz

ABCDEFGHIJ
KLMNOPQRS
TUVWXYZ&a
bcdefghijklmn
opqrstuvwxyz1
234567890$.:;!?

72 POINT TIMES* EXTRA BOLD   MERGENTHALER TYPE LIBRARY

ABCDEFGHIJKLMN
OPQRSTUVWXYZ&
abcdefghijklmnopqrst
uvwxyz1234567890$:;!?

48 POINT TIMES* EXTRA BOLD   MERGENTHALER TYPE LIBRARY

12/12 **To cast off manuscript with accuracy and precision, is a task of a disagreeable nature, which requires great attention and mature deliberation. The trouble and difficulty is much increased, when the copy is not only irregularly written (which is too frequently the case), but also abounds with interlineations, erasures, and variations in the sizes of paper. To surmount these defects the closest application and attention is required; yet, at times, so numerous are the alterations and additions, that they not unfrequently baffle the skill and judgment of the most experienced calculators of copy. Such an imperfect and slovenly mode of**

12/14 **To cast off manuscript with accuracy and precision, is a task of a disagreeable nature, which requires great attention and mature deliberation. The trouble and difficulty is much increased, when the copy is not only irregularly written (which is too frequently the case), but also abounds with interlineations, erasures, and variations in the sizes of paper. To surmount these defects the closest application and attention is required; yet, at times, so numerous are the alterations and additions, that they not un-**

12/16 **To cast off manuscript with accuracy and precision, is a task of a disagreeable nature, which requires great attention and mature deliberation. The trouble and difficulty is much increased, when the copy is not only irregularly written (which is too frequently the case), but also abounds with interlineations, erasures, and variations in the sizes of paper. To surmount these defects the closest application and attention is re-**

10/10 **To cast off manuscript with accuracy and precision, is a task of a disagreeable nature, which requires great attention and mature deliberation. The trouble and difficulty is much increased, when the copy is not only irregularly written (which is too frequently the case), but also abounds with interlineations, erasures, and variations in the sizes of paper. To surmount these defects the closest application and attention is required; yet, at times, so numerous are the alterations and additions, that they not unfrequently baffle the skill and judgment of the most experienced calculators of copy. Such an imperfect and slovenly mode of sending works to the press (which is generally attended with unpleasant consequences to all parties) cannot be too strongly deprecated by all admirers of the art.**
The first thing necessary is to take a comprehen-

10/12 **To cast off manuscript with accuracy and precision, is a task of a disagreeable nature, which requires great attention and mature deliberation. The trouble and difficulty is much increased, when the copy is not only irregularly written (which is too frequently the case), but also abounds with interlineations, erasures, and variations in the sizes of paper. To surmount these defects the closest application and attention is required; yet, at times, so numerous are the alterations and additions, that they not unfrequently baffle the skill and judgment of the most experienced calculators of copy. Such an imperfect and slovenly mode of sending works to the press (which is generally attended with unpleasant consequences to all parties) cannot be too strongly depre-**

10/14 **To cast off manuscript with accuracy and precision, is a task of a disagreeable nature, which requires great attention and mature deliberation. The trouble and difficulty is much increased, when the copy is not only irregularly written (which is too frequently the case), but also abounds with interlineations, erasures, and variations in the sizes of paper. To surmount these defects the closest application and attention is required; yet, at times, so numerous are the alterations and additions, that they not unfrequently baffle the skill and judgment of the most experienced calculators of copy. Such an imperfect**

TIMES® EXTRA BOLD   MERGENTHALER TYPE LIBRARY

ABCDEFGHIJKLMNOPQRSTUVWXYZ
&.,"-:;!?""1234567890$
abcdefghijklmnopqrstuvwxyz

ABCDEFGHIJKLMNOPQRSTUVWXYZ
&.,"-:;!?""1234567890$
abcdefghijklmnopqrstuvwxyz

Supplementary Faces

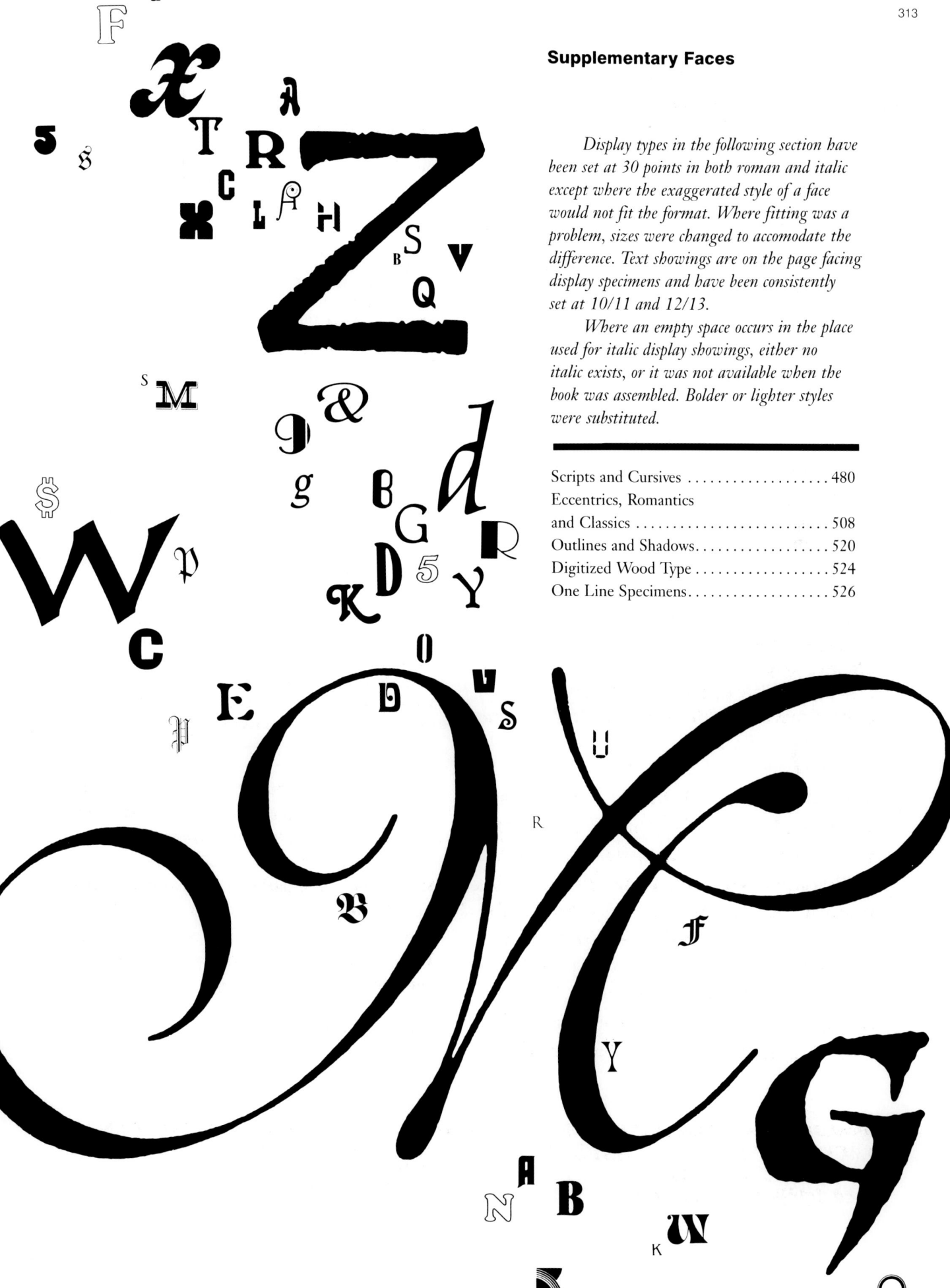

Display types in the following section have been set at 30 points in both roman and italic except where the exaggerated style of a face would not fit the format. Where fitting was a problem, sizes were changed to accomodate the difference. Text showings are on the page facing display specimens and have been consistently set at 10/11 and 12/13.

Where an empty space occurs in the place used for italic display showings, either no italic exists, or it was not available when the book was assembled. Bolder or lighter styles were substituted.

Scripts and Cursives 480
Eccentrics, Romantics
and Classics 508
Outlines and Shadows 520
Digitized Wood Type 524
One Line Specimens 526

SUPPLEMENTARY FACES

ABCDEFGHIJKLMNOPQRSTUVWXYZ&
abcdefghijklmnopqrstuvwxyz
1234567890$.,'''":;!?

AACHEN MEDIUM   AGFA COMPUGRAPHIC TYPE LIBRARY

ABCDEFGHIJKLMNOPQRSTUVWXYZ&
abcdefghijklmnopqrstuvwxyz
1234567890$.,'''":;!?

AACHEN BOLD   AGFA COMPUGRAPHIC TYPE LIBRARY

ABCDEFGHIJKLMNOPQRSTUVWX
YZ&abcdefghijklmnopqrstuvwxyz
1234567890$.,'''":;!?

ADMINISTER BOOK   AGFA COMPUGRAPHIC TYPE LIBRARY

*ABCDEFGHIJKLMNOPQRSTUVWXYZ
&abcdefghijklmnopqrstuvwxyz
1234567890$.,'''":;!?*

ADMINISTER BOOK ITALIC   AGFA COMPUGRAPHIC TYPE LIBRARY

ABCDEFGHIJKLMNOPQRSTUVWXYZ
&abcdefghijklmnopqrstuvwxyz
1234567890$.,'''":;!?

ADROIT LIGHT   AGFA COMPUGRAPHIC TYPE LIBRARY

*ABCDEFGHIJKLMNOPQRSTUVWXYZ
&abcdefghijklmnopqrstuvwxyz
1234567890$.,'''":;!?*

ADROIT LIGHT ITALIC   AGFA COMPUGRAPHIC TYPE LIBRARY

SUPPLEMENTARY FACES 315

12/13 **Now, since architects, painters & others at times are wont to set an inscription on lofty walls, it will make for the merit of the work that they form the letters correctly. Accordingly I am minded here to treat briefly of this. And first I will give rules for a Latin Alphabet, and then for one of our common Text: since it is of these two sorts of letters we customarily make use in such work; and first, for the Roman letters: Draw for each a square of uniform size, in which the letter is to be contained. But when you draw in it the heavier limb of the letter, make this of the width of a tenth part of the square, and the lighter a third as wide as the heavier:**

10/11 **Now, since architects, painters & others at times are wont to set an inscription on lofty walls, it will make for the merit of the work that they form the letters correctly. Accordingly I am minded here to treat briefly of this. And first I will give rules for a Latin Alphabet, and then for one of our common Text: since it is of these two sorts of letters we customarily make use in such work; and first, for the Roman letters: Draw for each a square of uniform size, in which the letter is to be contained. But when you draw in it the heavier limb of the letter, make this of the width of a tenth part of the square, and the lighter a third as wide as the heavier: to follow this rule for all letters of the Alphabet. First, make an A after this fashion: Indicate the angles of the square by the letters a. b. c. d. (and so do for all the rest of the letters): then divide the square by two lines bisecting one ano**

AACHEN MEDIUM WITH BOLD   AGFA COMPUGRAPHIC TYPE LIBRARY

12/13 It is still a matter of conjecture whether Johann Gutenberg was the first to conceive the principle of casting moveable [i.e., separate] metal types which he could arrange in words and sentences so that he could impress their faces on paper. There is, however, hardly a doubt, judging at least from the evidence available, that he was the first to make practical use of the idea, and that it is do to his in genious application of it that the profound art of typography was born. Whether he cast his letters in molds of sand or in metal matrices, is a question *not really material at this time; it is the far-reaching results of his inspiration that most*

10/11 It is still a matter of conjecture whether Johann Gutenberg was the first to conceive the principle of casting moveable [i.e., separate] metal types which he could arrange in words and sentences so that he could impress their faces on paper. There is, however, hardly a doubt, judging at least from the evidence available, that he was the first to make practical use of the idea, and that it is do to his ingenious application of it that the profound art of typography was born. Whether he cast his letters in molds of sand or in metal matrices, is a question not really material at this time; it is the far-reaching results of his inspiration that most concern us in this discussion. It seems quite probable that Gutenberg at first had little more in mind than a desire to find some expedient *by which to supplement with explanatory text the illustrations cut on wood blocks--some method that w*

ADMINISTER BOOK WITH BOOK ITALIC   AGFA COMPUGRAPHIC TYPE LIBRARY

12/13 It is still a matter of conjecture whether Johann Gutenberg was the first to conceive the principle of casting moveable [i.e., separate] metal types which he could arrange in words and sentences so that he could impress their faces on paper. There is, however, hardly a doubt, judging at least from the evidence available, that he was the first to make practical use of the idea, and that it is do to his in genious application of it that the profound art of typography was born. Whether he cast his letters in molds of sand or in metal matrices, is a question not really *material at this time; it is the far-reaching results of his inspiration that most concern*

10/11 It is still a matter of conjecture whether Johann Gutenberg was the first to conceive the principle of casting moveable [i.e., separate] metal types which he could arrange in words and sentences so that he could impress their faces on paper. There is, however, hardly a doubt, judging at least from the evidence available, that he was the first to make practical use of the idea, and that it is do to his ingenious application of it that the profound art of typography was born. Whether he cast his letters in molds of sand or in metal matrices, is a question not really material at this time; it is the far-reaching results of his inspiration that most concern us in this discussion. It seems quite probable that Gutenberg at first had little more in mind than a desire to find some expedient by which *to supplement with explanatory text the illustrations cut on wood blocks --some method that would avoid the labor of engra*

ADROIT LIGHT WITH LIGHT ITALIC   AGFA COMPUGRAPHIC TYPE LIBRARY

SUPPLEMENTARY FACES

ABCDEFGHIJKLMNOPQRSTUVWXYZ&
abcdefghijklmnopqrstuvwxyz
1234567890$.,""'':;!?

ALBERTUS BOOK   AGFA COMPUGRAPHIC TYPE LIBRARY

ABCDEFGHIJKLMNOPQRSTUVWXYZ&
abcdefghijklmnopqrstuvwxyz
1234567890$.,""'':;!?

ALBERTUS BOOK OBLIQUE   AGFA COMPUGRAPHIC TYPE LIBRARY

**ABCDEFGHIJKLMNOPQRSTUVWXYZ
&abcdefghijklmnopqrstuvwxyz
1234567890$.,""'':;!?**

ALBERTUS MEDIUM   AGFA COMPUGRAPHIC TYPE LIBRARY

ABCDEFGHIJKLMNOPQRSTUVWXYZ&
abcdefghijklmnopqrstuvwxyz
1234567890$.,""'':;!?

ALBERTUS MEDIUM OBLIQUE   AGFA COMPUGRAPHIC TYPE LIBRARY

**ABCDEFGHIJKLMNOPQRSTUVWXY
Z&abcdefghijklmnopqrstuvwxyz
1234567890$.,""'':;!?**

ALBERTUS BOLD   AGFA COMPUGRAPHIC TYPE LIBRARY

**ABCDEFGHIJKLMNOPQRSTUVWX
YZ&abcdefghijklmnopqrstuvwxyz
1234567890$.,""'':;!?**

ALBERTUS EXTRA BOLD   AGFA COMPUGRAPHIC TYPE LIBRARY

SUPPLEMENTARY FACES 317

12/13 Lying in my bed, on the morning of the Feast of Kings, when I had had my sleep and rest, & my stomach had readily digested its light and pleasant repast, in the year that was reckoned as MDXXIII, I fell to musing and set the wheel of my memory awhirl thinking on a thousand little conceits, some serious and some joyous, among which there came to my mind a certain Antique letter which I had lately made for my lord the Treasurer for War, Maistre Jehan Groslier, Counsellor and Secretary to our Lord the King, lover of well-made letters and of all learned persons, by whom also he is much *loved & esteemed on both this & the other side of the mountains. And whilst thinking of this Attic*

10/11 Lying in my bed, on the morning of the Feast of Kings, when I had had my sleep and rest, & my stomach had readily digested its light and pleasant repast, in the year that was reckoned as MDXXIII, I fell to musing and set the wheel of my memory awhirl thinking on a thousand little conceits, some serious and some joyous, among which there came to my mind a certain Antique letter which I had lately made for my lord the Treasurer for War, Maistre Jehan Groslier, Counsellor and Secretary to our Lord the King, lover of well-made letters and of all learned persons, by whom also he is much loved & esteemed on both this & the other side of the mountains. And whilst thinking of this Attic Letter, there came of a sudden into my memory a pithy passage in the first book & eighth chapter of the DeOfficiis of Cicero, where *it is written: Non nobis solum nati sumus; ortusque nostri partem patria vendicat, partem amici. Which is to say, in*

ALBERTUS BOOK WITH BOOK OBLIQUE   AGFA COMPUGRAPHIC TYPE LIBRARY

12/13 **Lying in my bed, on the morning of the Feast of Kings, when I had had my sleep and rest, & my stomach had readily digested its light and pleasant repast, in the year that was reckoned as MDXXIII, I fell to musing and set the wheel of my memory awhirl thinking on a thousand little conceits, some serious and some joyous, among which there came to my mind a certain Antique letter which I had lately made for my lord the Treasurer for War, Maistre Jehan Groslier, Counsellor and Secretary to our Lord the King, lover of well-made letters and of all learned persons, by whom also he is much *loved & esteemed on both this & the other side of the mountains. And whilst thinking of this***

10/11 **Lying in my bed, on the morning of the Feast of Kings, when I had had my sleep and rest, & my stomach had readily digested its light and pleasant repast, in the year that was reckoned as MDXXIII, I fell to musing and set the wheel of my memory awhirl thinking on a thousand little conceits, some serious and some joyous, among which there came to my mind a certain Antique letter which I had lately made for my lord the Treasurer for War, Maistre Jehan Groslier, Counsellor and Secretary to our Lord the King, lover of well-made letters and of all learned persons, by whom also he is much loved & esteemed on both this & the other side of the mountains. And whilst thinking of this Attic Letter, there came of a sudden into my memory a pithy passage in the first book & eighth chapter of the DeOfficiis of *Cicero, where it is written: Non nobis solum nati sumus; ortusque nostri partem patria vendicat, partem amici.***

ALBERTUS MEDIUM WITH MEDIUM OBLIQUE   AGFA COMPUGRAPHIC TYPE LIBRARY

12/13 **Lying in my bed, on the morning of the Feast of Kings, when I had had my sleep and rest, & my stomach had readily digested its light and pleasant repast, in the year that was reckoned as MDXXIII, I fell to musing and set the wheel of my memory awhirl thinking on a thousand little conceits, some serious and some joyous, among which there came to my mind a certain Antique letter which I had lately made for my lord the Treasurer for War, Maistre Jehan Groslier, Counsellor and Secretary to our Lord the King, lover of well-made letters and of all learned persons, by whom also he is much loved & esteemed on both this & the other side of the**

10/11 **Lying in my bed, on the morning of the Feast of Kings, when I had had my sleep and rest, & my stomach had readily digested its light and pleasant repast, in the year that was reckoned as MDXXIII, I fell to musing and set the wheel of my memory awhirl thinking on a thousand little conceits, some serious and some joyous, among which there came to my mind a certain Antique letter which I had lately made for my lord the Treasurer for War, Maistre Jehan Groslier, Counsellor and Secretary to our Lord the King, lover of well-made letters and of all learned persons, by whom also he is much loved & esteemed on both this & the other side of the mountains. And whilst thinking of this Attic Letter, there came of a sudden into my memory a pithy passage in the first book & eighth chapter of the DeOfficiis of Cicero, where it is written: Non nobis solum nati sumus; ortusque**

ALBERTUS BOLD WITH EXTRA BOLD   AGFA COMPUGRAPHIC TYPE LIBRARY

ABCDEFGHIJKLMNOPQRSTUVWXYZ&abcdefghijklmnopqrstuvwxyz1234567890$.,''"":;!?
ALDUS* MERGENTHALER TYPE LIBRARY

ABCDEFGHIJKLMNOPQRSTUVWXYZ&abcdefghijklmnopqrstuvwxyz1234567890$.,''"":;!?
ALDUS* ITALIC MERGENTHALER TYPE LIBRARY

ABCDEFGHIJKLMNOPQRSTUVWXYZ&abcdefghijklmnopqrstuvwxyz1234567890$.,''"":;!?
AMERICAN CLASSIC AGFA COMPUGRAPHIC TYPE LIBRARY

ABCDEFGHIJKLMNOPQRSTUVWXYZ&abcdefghijklmnopqrstuvwxyz1234567890$.,''"":;!?
AMERICAN CLASSIC ITALIC AGFA COMPUGRAPHIC TYPE LIBRARY

ABCDEFGHIJKLMNOPQRSTUVWXYZ&abcdefghijklmnopqrstuvwxyz1234567890$.,''"":;!?
AMERICAN CLASSIC BOLD AGFA COMPUGRAPHIC TYPE LIBRARY

ABCDEFGHIJKLMNOPQRSTUVWXYZ&abcdefghijklmnopqrstuvwxyz1234567890$.,''"":;!?
AMERICAN CLASSIC EXTRA BOLD AGFA COMPUGRAPHIC TYPE LIBRARY

SUPPLEMENTARY FACES 319

12/13 In type-founding, types are cast in moulds containing at one end a copper matrix of the character. The aperture through which the melted metal is injected is at the end of the mould opposite the matrix, and a piece as long as the type, called the jet, extends through the aperture from the bottom of the type. Thus imperfections in the metal and variations of temperature spend themselves in the jet, leaving the body of the type comparatively perfect. The types thus cast go through various processes, such as breaking off the jet and ploughing in its place a shallow groove across the foot, *thus leaving each type two "feet" to stand upon, "rubbing," etc.; and at last, set up in*

10/11 In type-founding, types are cast in moulds containing at one end a copper matrix of the character. The aperture through which the melted metal is injected is at the end of the mould opposite the matrix, and a piece as long as the type, called the jet, extends through the aperture from the bottom of the type. Thus imperfections in the metal and variations of temperature spend themselves in the jet, leaving the body of the type comparatively perfect. The types thus cast go through various processes, such as breaking off the jet and ploughing in its place a shallow groove across the foot, thus leaving each type two "feet" to stand upon, "rubbing," etc.; and at last, set up in long rows, they pass under the eye of an expert, who, as he examines them carefully with a glass, rejects all in which he detects any imperfections. In *these processes an average of 10 per cent, is eliminated; so that of 100 lbs. cast only 90 lbs. are actually fit for*

ALDUS* WITH ITALIC   MERGENTHALER TYPE LIBRARY

12/13 Now, since architects, painters & others at times are wont to set an inscription on lofty walls, it will make for the merit of the work that they form the letters correctly. Accordingly I am minded here to treat briefly of this. And first I will give rules for a Latin Alphabet, and then for one of our common Text: since it is of these two sorts of letters we customarily make use in such work; and first, for the Roman letters: Draw for each a square of uniform size, in which the letter is *to be contained. But when you draw in it the heavier limb of the letter, ma*

10/11 Now, since architects, painters & others at times are wont to set an inscription on lofty walls, it will make for the merit of the work that they form the letters correctly. Accordingly I am minded here to treat briefly of this. And first I will give rules for a Latin Alphabet, and then for one of our common Text: since it is of these two sorts of letters we customarily make use in such work; and first, for the Roman letters: Draw for each a square of uniform size, in which the letter is to be contained. But when you draw in it the heavier limb of the letter, make this of the width of a tenth part of the square, and the lighter a third as wide as the heavier: to follow this rule for *all letters of the Alphabet. First, make an A after this fashion: Indicate the angles of the*

AMERICAN CLASSIC WITH ITALIC   AGFA COMPUGRAPHIC TYPE LIBRARY

12/13 Now, since architects, painters & others at times are wont to set an inscription on lofty walls, it will make for the merit of the work that they form the letters correctly. Accordingly I am minded here to treat briefly of this. And first I will give rules for a Latin Alphabet, and then for one of our common Text: since it is of these two sorts of letters we customarily make use in such work; and first, for the Roman letters: Draw for each a square of uniform **size, in which the letter is to be contained. But when you draw in it th**

10/11 Now, since architects, painters & others at times are wont to set an inscription on lofty walls, it will make for the merit of the work that they form the letters correctly. Accordingly I am minded here to treat briefly of this. And first I will give rules for a Latin Alphabet, and then for one of our common Text: since it is of these two sorts of letters we customarily make use in such work; and first, for the Roman letters: Draw for each a square of uniform size, in which the letter is to be contained. But when you draw in it the heavier limb of the letter, make this of the width of a tenth part of the square, and the lighter a third as wide as **the heavier: to follow this rule for all letters of the Alphabet. First, make an A after**

AMERICAN CLASSIC BOLD WITH EXTRA BOLD   AGFA COMPUGRAPHIC TYPE LIBRARY

ABCDEFGHIJKLMNOPQRSTUVW
XYZ&abcdefghijklmnopqrstuvwx
yz1234567890$.,""":;!?

ITC AMERICAN TYPEWRITER** MEDIUM   MERGENTHALER TYPE LIBRARY

ABCDEFGHIJKLMNOPQRSTUVWX
YZ&abcdefghijklmnopqrstuvwxyz1
234567890$.,""":;!?

ITC AMERICAN TYPEWRITER** LIGHT   MERGENTHALER TYPE LIBRARY

**ABCDEFGHIJKLMNOPQRSTU
VWXYZ&abcdefghijklmnopqr
stuvwxyz1234567890$.,""":;!?**

ITC AMERICAN TYPEWRITER** BOLD   MERGENTHALER TYPE LIBRARY

ABCDEFGHIJKLMNOPQRSTUVWXYZ&abcdef
ghijklmnopqrstuvwxyz1234567890$.,""":;!?

ITC AMERICAN TYPEWRITER** LIGHT CONDENSED   MERGENTHALER TYPE LIBRARY

ABCDEFGHIJKLMNOPQRSTUVWXYZ&abcde
fghijklmnopqrstuvwxyz1234567890$.,""":;!?

ITC AMERICAN TYPEWRITER** MEDIUM CONDENSED   MERGENTHALER TYPE LIBRARY

**ABCDEFGHIJKLMNOPQRSTUVWXYZ&ab
cdefghijklmnopqrstuvwxyz1234567890$.,
""":;!?**

ITC AMERICAN TYPEWRITER** BOLD CONDENSED   MERGENTHALER TYPE LIBRARY

SUPPLEMENTARY FACES 321

12/13 Typography is closely allied to the fine arts, and types have always reflected the taste or feeling of their time. The charm of the early Italian types has perhaps never been equalled; and the like is true of the Renaissance manuscripts on which they were based — and of many other departments of art in that same wonderful time. Note, too, the relation of the French manuscripts and types of a slightly later date to the manuscripts and the types of the Italian Renaissance.

In spite of the increasing interest in the history of printing, and the attention paid in many quarters to the work of fa-

10/11 Typography is closely allied to the fine arts, and types have always reflected the taste or feeling of their time. The charm of the early Italian types has perhaps never been equalled; and the like is true of the Renaissance manuscripts on which they were based — and of many other departments of art in that same wonderful time. Note, too, the relation of the French manuscripts and types of a slightly later date to the manuscripts and the types of the Italian Renaissance.

In spite of the increasing interest in the history of printing, and the attention paid in many quarters to the work of famous typographers, a knowledge of standards among the rank and file of printers is still greatly lacking. To the average printer of today, type is type, printing is printing — it is all about alike; and he concerns himself only

ITC AMERICAN TYPEWRITER** MEDIUM WITH LIGHT   MERGENTHALER TYPE LIBRARY

12/13 **Typography is closely allied to the fine arts, and types have always reflected the taste or feeling of their time. The charm of the early Italian types has perhaps never been equalled; and the like is true of the Renaissance manuscripts on which they were based — and of many other departments of art in that same wonderful time. Note, too, the relation of the French manuscripts and types of a slightly later date to the manuscripts and the types of the** Italian Renaissance.

In spite of the increasing interest in the history of

10/11 **Typography is closely allied to the fine arts, and types have always reflected the taste or feeling of their time. The charm of the early Italian types has perhaps never been equalled; and the like is true of the Renaissance manuscripts on which they were based — and of many other departments of art in that same wonderful time. Note, too, the relation of the French manuscripts and types of a slightly later date to the manuscripts and the types of the Italian Renaissance.**

In spite of the increasing interest in the history of printing, and the attention paid in many quarters to the work of famous ographers, a knowledge of standards among the rank and file of printers is still greatly lacking. To the average printer of today,

ITC AMERICAN TYPEWRITER** BOLD WITH LIGHT CONDENSED   MERGENTHALER TYPE LIBRARY

12/13 Typography is closely allied to the fine arts, and types have always reflected the taste or feeling of their time. The charm of the early Italian types has perhaps never been equalled; and the like is true of the Renaissance manuscripts on which they were based — and of many other departments of art in that same wonderful time. Note, too, the relation of the French manuscripts and types of a slightly later date to the manuscripts and the types of the Italian Renaissance.

In spite of the increasing interest in the history of printing, and the attention paid in many quarters to the work of famous typographers, a knowledge of **standards among the rank and file of printers is still greatly lacking. To the average printer of**

10/11 Typography is closely allied to the fine arts, and types have always reflected the taste or feeling of their time. The charm of the early Italian types has perhaps never been equalled; and the like is true of the Renaissance manuscripts on which they were based — and of many other departments of art in that same wonderful time. Note, too, the relation of the French manuscripts and types of a slightly later date to the manuscripts and the types of the Italian Renaissance.

In spite of the increasing interest in the history of printing, and the attention paid in many quarters to the work of famous typographers, a knowledge of standards among the rank and file of printers is still greatly lacking. To the average printer of today, type is type, printing is printing — it is all about alike; and he concerns himself only with alleged labour-saving contrivances, or new type-faces that ensure convenience at the **expense of proper design. In a more advanced class is to be found the printer who, knowing something of the historical**

ITC AMERICAN TYPEWRITER** MEDIUM CONDENSED WITH BOLD CONDENSED   MERGENTHALER TYPE LIBRARY

ABCDEFGHIJKLMNOPQRSTUVWXYZ&abcdefghijklmnopqrstuvwxyz124567890$.,""":;!?ñfiflå

BITSTREAM AMERIGO®   BITSTREAM TYPEFACE LIBRARY

ABCDEFGHIJKLMNOPQRSTUVWXYZ&abcdefghijklmnopqrstuvwxyz1234567890$.,""":;!?ñfiflå

BITSTREAM AMERIGO ITALIC   BITSTREAM TYPEFACE LIBRARY

ABCDEFGHIJKLMNOPQRSTUVWXYZ&abcdefghijklmnopqrstuvwxyz1234567890$.,""":;!?ñfiflå

BITSTREAM AMERIGO MEDIUM   BITSTREAM TYPEFACE LIBRARY

ABCDEFGHIJKLMNOPQRSTUVWXYZ&abcdefghijklmnopqrstuvwxyz1234567890$.,""":;!?ñfiflå

BITSTREAM AMERIGO MEDIUM ITALIC   BITSTREAM TYPEFACE LIBRARY

ABCDEFGHIJKLMNOPQRSTUVWXYZ&abcdefghijklmnopqrstuvwxyz1234567890$.,""":;!?ñfiflå

BITSTREAM AMERIGO BOLD   BITSTREAM TYPEFACE LIBRARY

ABCDEFGHIJKLMNOPQRSTUVWXYZ&abcdefghijklmnopqrstuvwxyz1234567890$.,""":;!?ñfiflå

BITSTREAM AMERIGO BOLD ITALIC   BITSTREAM TYPEFACE LIBRARY

12/13 It is still a matter of conjecture whether Johann Gutenberg was the first to conceive the principle of casting movable [i.e., separate] metal types which he could arrange in words and sentences so that he could impress their faces on paper. There is, however, hardly a doubt, judging at least from the evidence available, that he was the first to make practical use of the idea, and that it is due to his ingenious application of it that the profound art of typography was born. Whether he cast his letters in molds of sand or in metal matrices, is a question not really material at this time; it is the far-reaching *results of his inspiration that most concern us in this discussion. It seems quite probable that Gutenberg*

10/11 It is still a matter of conjecture whether Johann Gutenberg was the first to conceive the principle of casting movable [i.e., separate] metal types which he could arrange in words and sentences so that he could impress their faces on paper. There is, however, hardly a doubt, judging at least from the evidence available, that he was the first to make practical use of the idea, and that it is due to his ingenious application of it that the profound art of typography was born. Whether he cast his letters in molds of sand or in metal matrices, is a question not really material at this time; it is the far-reaching results of his inspiration that most concern us in this discussion. It seems quite probable that Gutenberg at first had little more in mind than a desire to find some expedient by which to supplement with explanatory text the illustrations *cut on wood blocks–some method that would avoid the labor of engraving the text itself, some device that would*

BITSTREAM AMERIGO® WITH ITALIC   BITSTREAM TYPEFACE LIBRARY

12/13 **It is still a matter of conjecture whether Johann Gutenberg was the first to conceive the principle of casting movable [i.e., separate] metal types which he could arrange in words and sentences so that he could impress their faces on paper. There is, however, hardly a doubt, judging at least from the evidence available, that he was the first to make practical use of the idea, and that it is due to his ingenious application of it that the profound art of typography was born. Whether he cast his letters in molds of sand or in metal matrices, is a question not really material at this time; it is the far-reaching *results of his inspiration that most concern us in this discussion. It seems quite probable that Gutenberg***

10/11 **It is still a matter of conjecture whether Johann Gutenberg was the first to conceive the principle of casting movable [i.e., separate] metal types which he could arrange in words and sentences so that he could impress their faces on paper. There is, however, hardly a doubt, judging at least from the evidence available, that he was the first to make practical use of the idea, and that it is due to his ingenious application of it that the profound art of typography was born. Whether he cast his letters in molds of sand or in metal matrices, is a question not really material at this time; it is the far-reaching results of his inspiration that most concern us in this discussion. It seems quite probable that Gutenberg at first had little more in mind than a desire to find some expedient by which to supplement with explanatory text the illustrations *cut on wood blocks–some method that would avoid the labor of engraving the text itself, some device that would***

BITSTREAM AMERIGO MEDIUM WITH MEDIUM ITALIC   BITSTREAM TYPEFACE LIBRARY

12/13 **It is still a matter of conjecture whether Johann Gutenberg was the first to conceive the principle of casting movable [i.e., separate] metal types which he could arrange in words and sentences so that he could impress their faces on paper. There is, however, hardly a doubt, judging at least from the evidence available, that he was the first to make practical use of the idea, and that it is due to his ingenious application of it that the profound art of typography was born. Whether he cast his letters in molds of sand or in metal matrices, is a question not really material at this time; it is the far-reaching *reaching results of his inspiration that most concern us in the discussion. It seems quite probable***

10/11 **It is still a matter of conjecture whether Johann Gutenberg was the first to conceive the principle of casting movable [i.e., separate] metal types which he could arrange in words and sentences so that he could impress their faces on paper. There is, however, hardly a doubt, judging at least from the evidence available, that he was the first to make practical use of the idea, and that it is due to his ingenious application of it that the profound art of typography was born. Whether he cast his letters in molds of sand or in metal matrices, is a question not really material at this time; it is the far-reaching results of his inspiration that most concern us in this discussion. It seems quite probable that Gutenberg at first had little more in mind than a desire to find some expedient by which to supplement with explanatory text the illustrations *cut on wood blocks–some method that would avoid the labor of engraving the text itself, some device that would***

BITSTREAM AMERIGO BOLD WITH BOLD ITALIC   BITSTREAM TYPEFACE LIBRARY

ABCDEFGHIJKLMNOPQRSTUVWXYZ&ab
cdefghijklmnopqrstuvwxyz1234567890
$.,''"";:!?

ITC BAUHAUS** MEDIUM   MERGENTHALER TYPE LIBRARY

ABCDEFGHIJKLMNOPQRSTUVWXYZ&a
bcdefghijklmnopqrstuvwxyz123456789
0$.,''"";:!?

ITC BAUHAUS** LIGHT   MERGENTHALER TYPE LIBRARY

ABCDEFGHIJKLMNOPQRSTUVWXYZ&a
bcdefghijklmnopqrstuvwxyz12345678
90$.,''"";:!?

ITC BAUHAUS** DEMI   MERGENTHALER TYPE LIBRARY

ABCDEFGHIJKLMNOPQRSTUVWXYZ&
abcdefghijklmnopqrstuvwxyz123456
7890$.,''"";:!?

ITC BAUHAUS** BOLD   MERGENTHALER TYPE LIBRARY

ABCDEFGHIJKLMNOPQRSTUVWXYZ
&abcdefghijklmnopqrstuvwxyz123456
7890$.,''"";:!?

BELWE LIGHT   MERGENTHALER TYPE LIBRARY

ABCDEFGHIJKLMNOPQRSTUVWX
YZ&abcdefghijklmnopqrstuvwxyz1
234567890$.,''"";:!?

BELWE MEDIUM   MERGENTHALER TYPE LIBRARY

12/13 In type-founding, types are cast in moulds containing at one end a copper matrix of the character. The aperture through which the melted metal is injected is at the end of the mould opposite the matrix, and a piece as long as the type, called the jet, extends through the aperture from the bottom of the type. Thus imperfections in the metal and variations of temperature spend themselves in the jet, leaving the body of the type comparatively perfect. The types thus cast go through various processes, such as breaking off the jet and ploughing in its place a shallow groove across the foot, thus leaving each type two "feet" to stand upon, "rubbing," etc.; and

10/11 In type-founding, types are cast in moulds containing at one end a copper matrix of the character. The aperture through which the melted metal is injected is at the end of the mould opposite the matrix, and a piece as long as the type, called the jet, extends through the aperture from the bottom of the type. Thus imperfections in the metal and variations of temperature spend themselves in the jet, leaving the body of the type comparatively perfect. The types thus cast go through various processes, such as breaking off the jet and ploughing in its place a shallow groove across the foot, thus leaving each type two "feet" to stand upon, "rubbing," etc.; and at last, set up in long rows, they pass under the eye of an expert, who, as he examines them carefully with a glass, rejects all in which he detects any imperfections. In these processes an average of 10 per cent. is eliminated; so that of 100 lbs. cast only 90 lbs. are actually fit

ITC BAUHAUS** MEDIUM WITH LIGHT   MERGENTHALER TYPE LIBRARY

12/13 **In type-founding, types are cast in moulds containing at one end a copper matrix of the character. The aperture through which the melted metal is injected is at the end of the mould opposite the matrix, and a piece as long as the type, called the jet, extends through the aperture from the bottom of the type. Thus imperfections in the metal and variations of temperature spend themselves in the jet, leaving the body of the type comparatively perfect. The types thus cast go through various processes, such as breaking off the jet and ploughing in its place a shallow groove across the foot, thus leaving each type two "feet" to stand upon, "rubbing," etc.; and at last, set**

10/11 **In type-founding, types are cast in moulds containing at one end a copper matrix of the character. The aperture through which the melted metal is injected is at the end of the mould opposite the matrix, and a piece as long as the type, called the jet, extends through the aperture from the bottom of the type. Thus imperfections in the metal and variations of temperature spend themselves in the jet, leaving the body of the type comparatively perfect. The types thus cast go through various processes, such as breaking off the jet and ploughing in its place a shallow groove across the foot, thus leaving each type two "feet" to stand upon, "rubbing," etc.; and at last, set up in long rows, they pass under the eye of an expert, who, as he examines them carefully with a glass, rejects all in which he detects any imperfections. In these processes an average of 10 per cent. is eliminated; so that of 100 lbs. cast only 90 lbs. are**

ITC BAUHAUS** DEMI WITH BOLD   MERGENTHALER TYPE LIBRARY

12/13 Now, since architects, painters & others at times are wont to set an inscription on lofty walls, it will make for the merit of the work that they form the letters correctly. Accordingly I am minded here to treat briefly of this. And first I will give rules for a Latin Alphabet, and then for one of our common Text: since it is of these two sorts of letters we customarily make use in such work; and first, for the Roman letters: Draw for each a square of uniform size, in which the letter is to be contained. But when you draw in it the heavier limb of the letter, make this of the width of a **tenth part of the square, and the lighter a third as wide as the heavier: to follow this**

10/11 Now, since architects, painters & others at times are wont to set an inscription on lofty walls, it will make for the merit of the work that they form the letters correctly. Accordingly I am minded here to treat briefly of this. And first I will give rules for a Latin Alphabet, and then for one of our common Text: since it is of these two sorts of letters we customarily make use in such work; and first, for the Roman letters: Draw for each a square of uniform size, in which the letter is to be contained. But when you draw in it the heavier limb of the letter, make this of the width of a tenth part of the square, and the lighter a third as wide as the heavier: to follow this rule for all letters of the Alphabet.

First, make an A after this fashion: Indicate the **angles of the square by the letters a. b. c. d. (and so do for all the rest of the letters): then divide the**

BELWE LIGHT WITH MEDIUM   MERGENTHALER TYPE LIBRARY

ABCDEFGHIJKLMNOPQRSTUVWXYZ&abcdefghijklmnopqrstuvwxyz1234567890$.,'""::;!?

BEMBO**   MERGENTHALER TYPE LIBRARY

ABCDEFGHIJKLMNOPQRSTUVWXYZ&abcdefghijklmnopqrstuvwxyz1234567890$.,'""::;!?

BEMBO** ITALIC   MERGENTHALER TYPE LIBRARY

ABCDEFGHIJKLMNOPQRSTUVWXYZ&abcdefghijklmnopqrstuvwxyz1234567890$.,'""::;!?

BEMBO** MEDIUM   MERGENTHALER TYPE LIBRARY

ABCDEFGHIJKLMNOPQRSTUVWXYZ&abcdefghijklmnopqrstuvwxyz1234567890$.,'""::;!?

BEMBO** MEDIUM ITALIC   MERGENTHALER TYPE LIBRARY

ABCDEFGHIJKLMNOPQRSTUVWXYZ&abcdefghijklmnopqrstuvwxyz1234567890$.,'""::;!?

BEMBO** BOLD   MERGENTHALER TYPE LIBRARY

ABCDEFGHIJKLMNOPQRSTUVWXYZ&abcdefghijklmnopqrstuvwxyz1234567890$.,'""::;!?

BEMBO** BOLD ITALIC   MERGENTHALER TYPE LIBRARY

SUPPLEMENTARY FACES 327

12/13 The invention of printing, one of the most momentous events in the history of civilization, has been the subject of most controversy. The rival claims of Gutenberg and Coster have been argued with considerable acrimony by a number of authorities. While the weight of opinion has credited the invention to Gutenberg, the case of the German has not been absolutely conclusive. In the first place, there exists no piece of printing in which the name of Gutenberg appears as the printer. In the second place, there was known no trustworthy printed or written *evidence dated during the contemporary period. And, in the third place, the cause of Gutenberg suf-*

10/11 The invention of printing, one of the most momentous events in the history of civilization, has been the subject of most controversy. The rival claims of Gutenberg and Coster have been argued with considerable acrimony by a number of authorities. While the weight of opinion has credited the invention to Gutenberg, the case of the German has not been absolutely conclusive. In the first place, there exists no piece of printing in which the name of Gutenberg appears as the printer. In the second place, there was known no trustworthy printed or written evidence dated during the contemporary period. And, in the third place, the cause of Gutenberg suffered severe prejudice through the discovery by Hessels that a large proportion of the documents, on which his case had been based, were *rank forgeries, inspired by the over-enthusiastic nationalism of Bodmann, the archivist at Mentz.*

BEMBO** WITH ITALIC   MERGENTHALER TYPE LIBRARY

12/13 The invention of printing, one of the most momentous events in the history of civilization, has been the subject of most controversy. The rival claims of Gutenberg and Coster have been argued with considerable acrimony by a number of authorities. While the weight of opinion has credited the invention to Gutenberg, the case of the German has not been absolutely conclusive. In the first place, there exists no piece of printing in which the name of Gutenberg appears as the printer. In the second place, there was known no trustworthy printed or written *evidence dated during the contemporary period. And, in the third place, the cause of Gutenberg suf-*

10/11 The invention of printing, one of the most momentous events in the history of civilization, has been the subject of most controversy. The rival claims of Gutenberg and Coster have been argued with considerable acrimony by a number of authorities. While the weight of opinion has credited the invention to Gutenberg, the case of the German has not been absolutely conclusive. In the first place, there exists no piece of printing in which the name of Gutenberg appears as the printer. In the second place, there was known no trustworthy printed or written evidence dated during the contemporary period. And, in the third place, the cause of Gutenberg suffered severe prejudice through the discovery by Hessels that a large proportion of the documents, on which his case had been based, were *rank forgeries, inspired by the over-enthusiastic nationalism of Bodmann, the archivist at Mentz.*

BEMBO** MEDIUM WITH MEDIUM ITALIC   MERGENTHALER TYPE LIBRARY

12/13 **The invention of printing, one of the most momentous events in the history of civilization, has been the subject of most controversy. The rival claims of Gutenberg and Coster have been argued with considerable acrimony by a number of authorities. While the weight of opinion has credited the invention to Gutenberg, the case of the German has not been absolutely conclusive. In the first place, there exists no piece of printing in which the name of Gutenberg appears as the printer. In the second place, there was *known no trustworthy printed or written evidence dated during the contemporary period.***

10/11 **The invention of printing, one of the most momentous events in the history of civilization, has been the subject of most controversy. The rival claims of Gutenberg and Coster have been argued with considerable acrimony by a number of authorities. While the weight of opinion has credited the invention to Gutenberg, the case of the German has not been absolutely conclusive. In the first place, there exists no piece of printing in which the name of Gutenberg appears as the printer. In the second place, there was known no trustworthy printed or written evidence dated during the contemporary period. And, in the third place, the cause of Gutenberg suffered severe prejudice through the discovery by Hessels *that a large proportion of the documents, on which his case had been based, were rank forgeries, inspired by***

BEMBO** BOLD WITH BOLD ITALIC   MERGENTHALER TYPE LIBRARY

SUPPLEMENTARY FACES

ABCDEFGHIJKLMNOPQRSTUVWXYZ&abcdefghijklmnopqrstuvwxyz1234567890$.,""'':;!?

ITC BERKELEY OLD STYLE** BOOK   MERGENTHALER TYPE LIBRARY

ABCDEFGHIJKLMNOPQRSTUVWXYZ&abcdefghijklmnopqrstuvwxyz1234567890$.,""'':;!?

ITC BERKELEY OLD STYLE** BOOK ITALIC   MERGENTHALER TYPE LIBRARY

ABCDEFGHIJKLMNOPQRSTUVWXYZ&abcdefghijklmnopqrstuvwxyz1234567890$.,""'':;!?

ITC BERKELEY OLD STYLE** MEDIUM   MERGENTHALER TYPE LIBRARY

ABCDEFGHIJKLMNOPQRSTUVWXYZ&abcdefghijklmnopqrstuvwxyz1234567890$.,""'':;!?

ITC BERKELEY OLD STYLE** MEDIUM ITALIC   MERGENTHALER TYPE LIBRARY

ABCDEFGHIJKLMNOPQRSTUVWXYZ&abcdefghijklmnopqrstuvwxyz1234567890$.,""'':;!?

ITC BERKELEY OLD STYLE** BOLD   MERGENTHALER TYPE LIBRARY

ABCDEFGHIJKLMNOPQRSTUVWXYZ&abcdefghijklmnopqrstuvwxyz1234567890$.,""'':;!?

ITC BERKELEY OLD STYLE** BOLD ITALIC   MERGENTHALER TYPE LIBRARY

SUPPLEMENTARY FACES 329

12/13 It is still a matter of conjecture whether Johann Gutenberg was the first to conceive the principle of casting movable [i.e., separate] metal types which he could arrange in words and sentences so that he could impress their faces on paper. There is, however, hardly a doubt, judging at least from the evidence available, that he was the first to make practical use of the idea, and that it is due to his ingenious application of it that the profound art of typography was born.

Whether he cast his letters in molds of sand or in metal matrices, is a question not really material at this time; it is the far-reaching results of his *inspiration that most concern us in this discussion. It seems quite probable that Gutenberg at first had*

10/11 It is still a matter of conjecture whether Johann Gutenberg was the first to conceive the principle of casting movable [i.e., separate] metal types which he could arrange in words and sentences so that he could impress their faces on paper. There is, however, hardly a doubt, judging at least from the evidence available, that he was the first to make practical use of the idea, and that it is due to his ingenious application of it that the profound art of typography was born.

Whether he cast his letters in molds of sand or in metal matrices, is a question not really material at this time; it is the far-reaching results of his inspiration that most concern us in this discussion. It seems quite probable that Gutenberg at first had little more in mind than a desire to find some expedient by which to supplement with explan*atory text the illustrations cut on wood blocks — some method that would avoid the labor of engraving the text itself, some*

ITC BERKELEY OLD STYLE** BOOK WITH BOOK ITALIC   MERGENTHALER TYPE LIBRARY

12/13 It is still a matter of conjecture whether Johann Gutenberg was the first to conceive the principle of casting movable [i.e., separate] metal types which he could arrange in words and sentences so that he could impress their faces on paper. There is, however, hardly a doubt, judging at least from the evidence available, that he was the first to make practical use of the idea, and that it is due to his ingenious application of it that the profound art of typography was born.

Whether he cast his letters in molds of sand or in metal matrices, is a question not really *material at this time; it is the far-reaching results of his inspiration that most concern us in this dis-*

10/11 It is still a matter of conjecture whether Johann Gutenberg was the first to conceive the principle of casting movable [i.e., separate] metal types which he could arrange in words and sentences so that he could impress their faces on paper. There is, however, hardly a doubt, judging at least from the evidence available, that he was the first to make practical use of the idea, and that it is due to his ingenious application of it that the profound art of typography was born.

Whether he cast his letters in molds of sand or in metal matrices, is a question not really material at this time; it is the far-reaching results of his inspiration that most concern us in this discussion. It seems quite probable that Gutenberg at first had little more in mind than a desire to find some expedient by which to supplement *with explanatory text the illustrations cut on wood blocks — some method that would avoid the labor of engraving*

ITC BERKELEY OLD STYLE** MEDIUM WITH MEDIUM ITALIC   MERGENTHALER TYPE LIBRARY

12/13 **It is still a matter of conjecture whether Johann Gutenberg was the first to conceive the principle of casting movable [i.e., separate] metal types which he could arrange in words and sentences so that he could impress their faces on paper. There is, however, hardly a doubt, judging at least from the evidence available, that he was the first to make practical use of the idea, and that it is due to his ingenious application of it that the profound art of typography was born.**

Whether he cast his letters in molds of sand or in metal matrices, is a question not *really material at this time; it is the far-reaching results of his inspiration that most concern*

10/11 **It is still a matter of conjecture whether Johann Gutenberg was the first to conceive the principle of casting movable [i.e., separate] metal types which he could arrange in words and sentences so that he could impress their faces on paper. There is, however, hardly a doubt, judging at least from the evidence available, that he was the first to make practical use of the idea, and that it is due to his ingenious application of it that the profound art of typography was born.**

Whether he cast his letters in molds of sand or in metal matrices, is a question not really material at this time; it is the far-reaching results of his inspiration that most concern us in this discussion. It seems quite probable that Gutenberg at first had little more in mind than a desire to find some expedient by which to *supplement with explanatory text the illustrations cut on wood blocks — some method that would avoid the labor*

ITC BERKELEY OLD STYLE** BOLD WITH BOLD ITALIC   MERGENTHALER TYPE LIBRARY

ABCDEFGHIJKLMNOPQRSTU VWXYZ&abcdefghijklmnopqrstu vwxyz1234567890$.,"":;!?

BINNY OLD STYLE   MERGENTHALER TYPE LIBRARY

ABCDEFGHIJKLMNOPQRSTU VWXYZ&abcdefghijklmnopqrstuv wxyz1234567890$.,"":;!?

BINNY OLD STYLE ITALIC   MERGENTHALER TYPE LIBRARY

ABCDEFGHIJKLMNOPQRSTUV WXYZ&abcdefghijklmnopqrstuvwx yz1234567890$.,"":;!?

BRUCE OLD STYLE   MERGENTHALER TYPE LIBRARY

ABCDEFGHIJKLMNOPQRSTUV WXYZ&abcdefghijklmnopqrstuvwxyz 1234567890$.,"":;!?

BRUCE OLD STYLE ITALIC   MERGENTHALER TYPE LIBRARY

ABCDEFGHIJKLMNOPQRSTUVWXY Z&abcdefghijklmnopqrstuvwxyz1234567 890$.,"":;!?

BULMER   MERGENTHALER TYPE LIBRARY

ABCDEFGHIJKLMNOPQRSTUVWXYZ &abcdefghijklmnopqrstuvwxyz1234567890 $.,"":;!?

BULMER ITALIC   MERGENTHALER TYPE LIBRARY

SUPPLEMENTARY FACES 331

12/13 Now, since architects, painters & others at times are wont to set an inscription on lofty walls, it will make for the merit of the work that they form the letters correctly. Accordingly I am minded here to treat briefly of this. And first I will give rules for a Latin Alphabet, and then for one of our common Text: since it is of these two sorts of letters we customarily make use in such work; and first, for the Roman letters: Draw for each a square of uniform size, in which the letter is to be contained. But when you draw in it the *heavier limb of the letter, make this of the width of a tenth part of the square, and the*

10/11 Now, since architects, painters & others at times are wont to set an inscription on lofty walls, it will make for the merit of the work that they form the letters correctly. Accordingly I am minded here to treat briefly of this. And first I will give rules for a Latin Alphabet, and then for one of our common Text: since it is of these two sorts of letters we customarily make use in such work; and first, for the Roman letters: Draw for each a square of uniform size, in which the letter is to be contained. But when you draw in it the heavier limb of the letter, make this of the width of a tenth part of the square, and the lighter a third as wide as the heavier: to follow this rule for all letters of the Alphabet.
First, make an A after this fashion: Indicate the angles of the square by the letters a. b. c. d. (and so

BINNY OLD STYLE WITH ITALIC   MERGENTHALER TYPE LIBRARY

12/13 The invention of printing, one of the most momentous events in the history of civilization, has been the subject of most controversy. The rival claims of Gutenberg and Coster have been argued with considerable acrimony by a number of authorities. While the weight of opinion has credited the invention to Gutenberg, the case of the German has not been absolutely conclusive. In the first place, there exists no piece of printing in which the name of Gutenberg appears as the printer. In the second place, there was known no trustwor-*thy printed or written evidence dated during the contemporary period. And, in the third*

10/11 The invention of printing, one of the most momentous events in the history of civilization, has been the subject of most controversy. The rival claims of Gutenberg and Coster have been argued with considerable acrimony by a number of authorities. While the weight of opinion has credited the invention to Gutenberg, the case of the German has not been absolutely conclusive. In the first place, there exists no piece of printing in which the name of Gutenberg appears as the printer. In the second place, there was known no trustworthy printed or written evidence dated during the contemporary period. And, in the third place, the cause of Gutenberg suffered severe prejudice through the discovery by Hessels that a large proportion of the docu-*ments, on which his case had been based, were rank forgeries, inspired by the over-enthusiastic nationalism*

BRUCE OLD STYLE WITH ITALIC   MERGENTHALER TYPE LIBRARY

12/13 The invention of printing, one of the most momentous events in the history of civilization, has been the subject of most controversy. The rival claims of Gutenberg and Coster have been argued with considerable acrimony by a number of authorities. While the weight of opinion has credited the invention to Gutenberg, the case of the German has not been absolutely conclusive. In the first place, there exists no piece of printing in which the name of Gutenberg appears as the printer. In the second place, there was known no trustworthy printed or written evidence dated during the contemporary period. And, in the third *place, the cause of Gutenberg suffered severe prejudice through the discovery by Hessels that a large*

10/11 The invention of printing, one of the most momentous events in the history of civilization, has been the subject of most controversy. The rival claims of Gutenberg and Coster have been argued with considerable acrimony by a number of authorities. While the weight of opinion has credited the invention to Gutenberg, the case of the German has not been absolutely conclusive. In the first place, there exists no piece of printing in which the name of Gutenberg appears as the printer. In the second place, there was known no trustworthy printed or written evidence dated during the contemporary period. And, in the third place, the cause of Gutenberg suffered severe prejudice through the discovery by Hessels that a large proportion of the documents, on which his case had been based, were rank forgeries, inspired by the over-enthusiastic nationalism of Bodmann, the archivist at Mentz.
The circumstantial evidence, however, has all pointed to

BULMER WITH ITALIC   MERGENTHALER TYPE LIBRARY

SUPPLEMENTARY FACES

ABCDEFGHIJKLMNOPQRSTUVWXYZ&abcdefghijklmnopqrstuvwxyz1234567890$.,""":;!?

NEW CALEDONIA*   MERGENTHALER TYPE LIBRARY

ABCDEFGHIJKLMNOPQRSTUVWXYZ&abcdefghijklmnopqrstuvwxyz1234567890$.,""":;!?

NEW CALEDONIA* ITALIC   MERGENTHALER TYPE LIBRARY

ABCDEFGHIJKLMNOPQRSTUVWXYZ&abcdefghijklmnopqrstuvwxyz1234567890$.,""":;!?

NEW CALEDONIA* SEMI BOLD   MERGENTHALER TYPE LIBRARY

ABCDEFGHIJKLMNOPQRSTUVWXYZ&abcdefghijklmnopqrstuvwxyz1234567890$.,""":;!?

NEW CALEDONIA* SEMI BOLD ITALIC   MERGENTHALER TYPE LIBRARY

ABCDEFGHIJKLMNOPQRSTUVWXYZ&abcdefghijklmnopqrstuvwxyz1234567890$.,""":;!?

NEW CALEDONIA* BOLD   MERGENTHALER TYPE LIBRARY

ABCDEFGHIJKLMNOPQRSTUVWXYZ&abcdefghijklmnopqrstuvwxyz1234567890$.,""":;!?

NEW CALEDONIA* BOLD ITALIC   MERGENTHALER TYPE LIBRARY

SUPPLEMENTARY FACES 333

12/13 In type-founding, types are cast in moulds containing at one end a copper matrix of the character. The aperture through which the melted metal is injected is at the end of the mould opposite the matrix, and a piece as long as the type, called the jet, extends through the aperture from the bottom of the type. Thus imperfections in the metal and variations of temperature spend themselves in the jet, leaving the body of the type comparatively perfect. The types thus cast go through various processes, such as breaking off the jet and ploughing in its place a shallow groove across the foot, thus *leaving each type two "feet" to stand upon, "rubbing," etc.; and at last, set up in long rows,*

10/11 In type-founding, types are cast in moulds containing at one end a copper matrix of the character. The aperture through which the melted metal is injected is at the end of the mould opposite the matrix, and a piece as long as the type, called the jet, extends through the aperture from the bottom of the type. Thus imperfections in the metal and variations of temperature spend themselves in the jet, leaving the body of the type comparatively perfect. The types thus cast go through various processes, such as breaking off the jet and ploughing in its place a shallow groove across the foot, thus leaving each type two "feet" to stand upon, "rubbing," etc.; and at last, set up in long rows, they pass under the eye of an expert, who, as he examines them carefully with a glass, rejects all in which he detects any imperfections. In these processes *an average of 10 per cent, is eliminated; so that of 100 lbs. cast only 90 lbs. are actually fit for delivery.*

NEW CALEDONIA* WITH ITALIC   MERGENTHALER TYPE LIBRARY

12/13 In type-founding, types are cast in moulds containing at one end a copper matrix of the character. The aperture through which the melted metal is injected is at the end of the mould opposite the matrix, and a piece as long as the type, called the jet, extends through the aperture from the bottom of the type. Thus imperfections in the metal and variations of temperature spend themselves in the jet, leaving the body of the type comparatively perfect. The types thus cast go through various processes, such as breaking off the jet and ploughing in its place a shallow *groove across the foot, thus leaving each type two "feet" to stand upon, "rubbing," etc.; and*

10/11 In type-founding, types are cast in moulds containing at one end a copper matrix of the character. The aperture through which the melted metal is injected is at the end of the mould opposite the matrix, and a piece as long as the type, called the jet, extends through the aperture from the bottom of the type. Thus imperfections in the metal and variations of temperature spend themselves in the jet, leaving the body of the type comparatively perfect. The types thus cast go through various processes, such as breaking off the jet and ploughing in its place a shallow groove across the foot, thus leaving each type two "feet" to stand upon, "rubbing," etc.; and at last, set up in long rows, they pass under the eye of an expert, who, as he examines them carefully with a glass, rejects all in which he detects *any imperfections. In these processes an average of 10 per cent, is eliminated; so that of 100 lbs. cast only 90*

NEW CALEDONIA* SEMI BOLD WITH SEMI BOLD ITALIC   MERGENTHALER TYPE LIBRARY

12/13 **In type-founding, types are cast in moulds containing at one end a copper matrix of the character. The aperture through which the melted metal is injected is at the end of the mould opposite the matrix, and a piece as long as the type, called the jet, extends through the aperture from the bottom of the type. Thus imperfections in the metal and variations of temperature spend themselves in the jet, leaving the body of the type comparatively perfect. The types thus cast go through various processes, such as breaking off the jet and ploughing in its *place a shallow groove across the foot, thus leaving each type two "feet" to stand upon,***

10/11 In type-founding, types are cast in moulds containing at one end a copper matrix of the character. The aperture through which the melted metal is injected is at the end of the mould opposite the matrix, and a piece as long as the type, called the jet, extends through the aperture from the bottom of the type. Thus imperfections in the metal and variations of temperature spend themselves in the jet, leaving the body of the type comparatively perfect. The types thus cast go through various processes, such as breaking off the jet and ploughing in its place a shallow groove across the foot, thus leaving each type two "feet" to stand upon, "rubbing," etc.; and at last, set up in long rows, they pass under the eye of an expert, who, as he examines them carefully with a glass, rejects all in which he detects any imperfections. In these processes an

NEW CALEDONIA* BOLD WITH BOLD ITALIC   MERGENTHALER TYPE LIBRARY

SUPPLEMENTARY FACES

ABCDEFGHIJKLMNOPQRSTUVW
XYZ&abcdefghijklmnopqrstuvwxyz
1234567890$.,"":;!?

NEW CALEDONIA* BLACK   MERGENTHALER TYPE LIBRARY

ABCDEFGHIJKLMNOPQRSTUVWX YZ&abcdefghijklmnopqrstuvwxyz1234567890$.,"":;!?

NEW CALEDONIA* BLACK ITALIC   MERGENTHALER TYPE LIBRARY

ABCDEFGHIJKLMNOPQRSTUVWXYZ&abc
defghijklmnopqrstuvwxyz1234567890$.,"":;!?

CARTIER   MERGENTHALER TYPE LIBRARY

ABCDEFGHIJKLMNOPQRSTUVWXYZ&abc
defghijklmnopqrstuvwxyz1234567890$.,"":;!?

CARTIER ITALIC   MERGENTHALER TYPE LIBRARY

ABCDEFGHIJKLMNOPQRSTUVWXYZ
&abcdefghijklmnopqrstuvwxyz1234567890$.,
"":;!?

CENTAUR**   MERGENTHALER TYPE LIBRARY

ABCDEFGHIJKLMNOPQRSTUVWXYZ&abcd efghijklmnopqrstuvwxyz1234567890$.,"":;!?

(This face was designed to function as italic for Centaur.)

ARRIGHI**   MERGENTHALER TYPE LIBRARY

SUPPLEMENTARY FACES 335

12/13 **Lying in my bed, on the morning of the Feast of Kings, when I had had my sleep and rest, & my stomach had readily digested its light and pleasant repast, in the year that was reckoned as MDXXIII, I fell to musing and set the wheel of my memory awhirl thinking on a thousand little conceits, some serious & some joyous, among which there came to my mind a certain Antique letter which I had lately made for my lord the Treasurer for War, Maistre Jehan Groslier, Counsellor and Secretary to our Lord the King, *lover of well-made letters and of all learned persons, by whom also he***

10/11 **Lying in my bed, on the morning of the Feast of Kings, when I had had my sleep and rest, & my stomach had readily digested its light and pleasant repast, in the year that was reckoned as MDXXIII, I fell to musing and set the wheel of my memory awhirl thinking on a thousand little conceits, some serious & some joyous, among which there came to my mind a certain Antique letter which I had lately made for my lord the Treasurer for War, Maistre Jehan Groslier, Counsellor and Secretary to our Lord the King, lover of well-made letters and of all learned persons, by whom also he is much loved & esteemed on both this & the other side of the mountains. And whilst thinking of this Attic *Letter, there came of a sudden into my memory a pithy passage in the first book & eighth chapter***

NEW CALEDONIA* BLACK WITH BLACK ITALIC   MERGENTHALER TYPE LIBRARY

12/13 Lying in my bed, on the morning of the Feast of Kings, when I had had my sleep and rest, & my stomach had readily digested its light and pleasant repast, in the year that was reckoned as MDXXIII, I fell to musing and set the wheel of my memory awhirl thinking on a thousand little conceits, some serious & some joyous, among which there came to my mind a certain Antique letter which I had lately made for my lord the Treasurer for War, Maistre Jehan Groslier, Counsellor and Secretary to our Lord the King, lover of well-made letters and of all learned persons, by whom also he is much loved & esteemed on both this & the other side of the *mountains. And whilst thinking of this Attic Letter, there came of a sudden into my memory a pithy passage in the first book &*

10/11 Lying in my bed, on the morning of the Feast of Kings, when I had had my sleep and rest, & my stomach had readily digested its light and pleasant repast, in the year that was reckoned as MDXXIII, I fell to musing and set the wheel of my memory awhirl thinking on a thousand little conceits, some serious & some joyous, among which there came to my mind a certain Antique letter which I had lately made for my lord the Treasurer for War, Maistre Jehan Groslier, Counsellor and Secretary to our Lord the King, lover of well-made letters and of all learned persons, by whom also he is much loved & esteemed on both this & the other side of the mountains. And whilst thinking of this Attic Letter, there came of a sudden into my memory a pithy passage in the first book & eighth chapter of the DeOfficiis of Cicero, where it is written: Non nobis solum nati sumus; ortusque nostri partem *patria vendicat, partem amici. Which is to say, in substance, that we are not born into this world for ourselves alone, but to serve & give pleasure to*

CARTIER WITH ITALIC   MERGENTHALER TYPE LIBRARY

12/13 Lying in my bed, on the morning of the Feast of Kings, when I had had my sleep and rest, & my stomach had readily digested its light and pleasant repast, in the year that was reckoned as MDXXIII, I fell to musing and set the wheel of my memory awhirl thinking on a thousand little conceits, some serious & some joyous, among which there came to my mind a certain Antique letter which I had lately made for my lord the Treasurer for War, Maistre Jehan Groslier, Counsellor and Secretary to our Lord the King, lover of well-made letters and of all learned persons, by whom also he is much loved & esteemed on both this & the other side of the mountains. And whilst thinking of this Attic Letter, there *came of a sudden into my memory a pithy passage in the first book & eighth chapter of the DeOfficiis of Cicero, where it is written:*

10/11 Lying in my bed, on the morning of the Feast of Kings, when I had had my sleep and rest, & my stomach had readily digested its light and pleasant repast, in the year that was reckoned as MDXXIII, I fell to musing and set the wheel of my memory awhirl thinking on a thousand little conceits, some serious & some joyous, among which there came to my mind a certain Antique letter which I had lately made for my lord the Treasurer for War, Maistre Jehan Groslier, Counsellor and Secretary to our Lord the King, lover of well-made letters and of all learned persons, by whom also he is much loved & esteemed on both this & the other side of the mountains. And whilst thinking of this Attic Letter, there came of a sudden into my memory a pithy passage in the first book & eighth chapter of the DeOfficiis of Cicero, where it is written: Non nobis solum nati sumus; ortusque nostri partem patria vendicat, partem amici. Which is to say, in substance, that we are not born into this world *for ourselves alone, but to serve & give pleasure to our friends and country. For this reason, desiring to employ myself in some degree for the public good, I*

CENTAUR** WITH ARRIGHI**   MERGENTHALER TYPE LIBRARY

ABCDEFGHIJKLMNOPQRSTUVWXYZ&abcdefghijklmnopqrstuvwxyz1234567890$.,"":;!?

BITSTREAM CARMINA® MEDIUM   BITSTREAM TYPEFACE LIBRARY

ABCDEFGHIJKLMNOPQRSTUVWXYZ&abcdefghijklmnopqrstuvwxyz1234567890$.,"":;!?

BITSTREAM CARMINA MEDIUM ITALIC   BITSTREAM TYPEFACE LIBRARY

ABCDEFGHIJKLMNOPQRSTUVWXYZ&abcdefghijklmnopqrstuvwxyz1234567890$.,"":;!?

BITSTREAM CARMINA BOLD   BITSTREAM TYPEFACE LIBRARY

ABCDEFGHIJKLMNOPQRSTUVWXYZ&abcdefghijklmnopqrstuvwxyz1234567890$.,"":;!?

BITSTREAM CARMINA BOLD ITALIC   BITSTREAM TYPEFACE LIBRARY

ABCDEFGHIJKLMNOPQRSTUVWXYZ&abcdefghijklmnopqrstuvwxyz1234567890$.,"":;!?

BITSTREAM CARMINA BLACK   BITSTREAM TYPEFACE LIBRARY

ABCDEFGHIJKLMNOPQRSTUVWXYZ&abcdefghijklmnopqrstuvwxyz1234567890$.,"":;!?

BITSTREAM CARMINA BLACK ITALIC   BITSTREAM TYPEFACE LIBRARY

12/13 In considering fine and praiseworthy inventions, we must freely confess that printing has been and is to-day the best and most estimable–the invention by means of which two persons turning the press can get a greater number of books in a day than formerly could have been transcribed by several persons in a year. It is claimed that this art was invented at Mainz, a city of Germany, in the year 1442 by Jean Guttemberg, or, according to others, Guttenberg, an honorable German chevalier. It was at Mainz that after experimenting with an ink *which is used by printers to-day, he first began the practice of the art. Some persons prefer to*

10/11 In considering fine and praiseworthy inventions, *we must freely confess that printing has been and is to-day the best and most estimable–the invention by means of which two persons turning the press can get a greater number of books in a day than formerly could have been transcribed by several persons in a year.* It is claimed that this art was invented in Mainz, a city of Germany, in the year 1442 by Jean Guttemberg, or, according to others, Guttenberg, an honorable German chevalier. It was at Mainz that after experimenting with an ink which is used by printers to-day, he first began the practice of the art. Some persons prefer to attribute the invention to Jean Fauste & Yues Scheffey two years earlier, holding that our Guttemberg, Jean Mentel, Jean Prus, *Adolphe Rusche, Pierre Scheffec, Martin Flache, Huldric Han, Jean Froben, Adam Petri, Thomas Vuolffe, and*

BITSTREAM CARMINA® MEDIUM WITH MEDIUM ITALIC   BITSTREAM TYPEFACE LIBRARY

12/13 **In considering fine and praiseworthy inventions, we must freely confess that printing has been and is to-day the best and most estimable–the invention by means of which two persons turning the press can get a greater number of books in a day than formerly have been transcribed by several persons in a year. It is claimed that this art was invented at Mainz, a city of Germany, in the year 1442 by Jean Guttemberg, or, according to other sources, Guttenberg, an honorable German chevalier. *It was at Mainz that after experimenting with an ink which is used***

10/11 **In considering fine and praiseworthy inventions, we must freely confess that printing has been and is to-day the best and most estimable–the invention by means of which two persons turning the press can get a greater number of books in a day than formerly could have been transcribed by several persons in a year. It is claimed that this art was invented at Mainz, a city of Germany, in the year 1442 by Jean Guttemberg, or, according to others, Guttenberg, an honorable German chevalier. It was at Mainz that after experimenting with an ink which is used by printers to-day, he first began the practice of the art. *Some persons prefer to attribute the invention to Jean Fauste & Yues Scheffey two years earlier, holding that our Guttemberg, Jean Mentel, Jean Prus, Adol-***

BITSTREAM CARMINA BOLD WITH BOLD ITALIC   BITSTREAM TYPEFACE LIBRARY

12/13 **In considering fine and praiseworthy inventions, we must freely confess that printing has been and is to-day the best and most estimable–the invention by means of which two persons turning the press can get a greater number of books in a day than formerly could have been transcribed by several persons in a year. It is claimed that this art was invented at Mainz, a city of Germany, in the year 1442 by Jean Guttemberg, or, according to other sources, *Guttenberg, an honorable German chevalier. It was at Mainz that after***

10/11 **In considering fine and praiseworthy inventions, we must freely confess that printing has been and is to-day the best and most estimable–the invention by means of which two persons turning the press can get a greater number of books in a day than formerly could have been transcribed by several persons in a year. It is claimed that this art was invented at Mainz, a city of Germany, in the year 1442 by Jean Guttemberg, or, according to others, Guttenberg, an honorable German chevalier. It was at Mainz that after experimenting with an ink which is used by printers to-day, he first began the practice of the art. Some persons *prefer to attribute the invention to Jean Fauste & Yues Scheffey two years earlier,***

BITSTREAM CARMINA BLACK WITH BLACK ITALIC   BITSTREAM TYPEFACE LIBRARY

ABCDEFGHIJKLMNOPQRSTUVWXYZ&abcdefghijklmnopqrstuvwxyz1234567890$.,""'':;!?

TSI CAXTON** LIGHT   MERGENTHALER TYPE LIBRARY

ABCDEFGHIJKLMNOPQRSTUVWXYZ&abcdefghijklmnopqrstuvwxyz1234567890$.,""'':;!?

TSI CAXTON** LIGHT ITALIC   MERGENTHALER TYPE LIBRARY

ABCDEFGHIJKLMNOPQRSTUVWXYZ&abcdefghijklmnopqrstuvwxyz1234567890$.,""'':;!?

TSI CAXTON** BOOK   MERGENTHALER TYPE LIBRARY

ABCDEFGHIJKLMNOPQRSTUVWXYZ&abcdefghijklmnopqrstuvwxyz1234567890$.,""'':;!?

TSI CAXTON** BOOK ITALIC   MERGENTHALER TYPE LIBRARY

ABCDEFGHIJKLMNOPQRSTUVWXYZ&abcdefghijklmnopqrstuvwxyz1234567890$.,""'':;!?

TSI CAXTON** BOLD   MERGENTHALER TYPE LIBRARY

ABCDEFGHIJKLMNOPQRSTUVWXYZ&abcdefghijklmnopqrstuvwxyz1234567890$.,""'':;!?

TSI CAXTON** BOLD ITALIC   MERGENTHALER TYPE LIBRARY

SUPPLEMENTARY FACES 339

12/13 The invention of printing, one of the most momentous events in the history of civilization, has been the subject of most controversy. The rival claims of Gutenberg and Coster have been argued with considerable acrimony by a number of authorities. While the weight of opinion has credited the invention to Gutenberg, the case of the German has not been absolutely conclusive. In the first place, there exists no piece of printing in which the name of Gutenberg appears as the printer. In the second place, there was known no trustworthy printed or written *evidence dated during the contemporary period. And, in the third place, the cause of*

10/11 The invention of printing, one of the most momentous events in the history of civilization, has been the subject of most controversy. The rival claims of Gutenberg and Coster have been argued with considerable acrimony by a number of authorities. While the weight of opinion has credited the invention to Gutenberg, the case of the German has not been absolutely conclusive. In the first place, there exists no piece of printing in which the name of Gutenberg appears as the printer. In the second place, there was known no trustworthy printed or written evidence dated during the contemporary period. And, in the third place, the cause of Gutenberg suffered severe prejudice through the discovery by Hessels that a large proportion of the documents, on which his case *had been based, were rank forgeries, inspired by the over-enthusiastic nationalism of Bodmann, the ar-*

TSI CAXTON** LIGHT WITH LIGHT ITALIC   MERGENTHALER TYPE LIBRARY

12/13 The invention of printing, one of the most momentous events in the history of civilization, has been the subject of most controversy. The rival claims of Gutenberg and Coster have been argued with considerable acrimony by a number of authorities. While the weight of opinion has credited the invention to Gutenberg, the case of the German has not been absolutely conclusive. In the first place, there exists no piece of printing in which the name of Gutenberg appears as the printer. In the second place, there was known no trust*worthy printed or written evidence dated during the contemporary period. And, in*

10/11 The invention of printing, one of the most momentous events in the history of civilization, has been the subject of most controversy. The rival claims of Gutenberg and Coster have been argued with considerable acrimony by a number of authorities. While the weight of opinion has credited the invention to Gutenberg, the case of the German has not been absolutely conclusive. In the first place, there exists no piece of printing in which the name of Gutenberg appears as the printer. In the second place, there was known no trustworthy printed or written evidence dated during the contemporary period. And, in the third place, the cause of Gutenberg suffered severe prejudice through the discovery by Hessels that a large proportion of the docu*ments, on which his case had been based, were rank forgeries, inspired by the over-enthusiastic*

TSI CAXTON** BOOK WITH BOOK ITALIC   MERGENTHALER TYPE LIBRARY

12/13 **The invention of printing, one of the most momentous events in the history of civilization, has been the subject of most controversy. The rival claims of Gutenberg and Coster have been argued with considerable acrimony by a number of authorities. While the weight of opinion has credited the invention to Gutenberg, the case of the German has not been absolutely conclusive. In the first place, there exists no piece of printing in which the name of Gutenberg appears as the printer. In the second place, *there was known no trustworthy printed or written evidence dated dur-***

10/11 **The invention of printing, one of the most momentous events in the history of civilization, has been the subject of most controversy. The rival claims of Gutenberg and Coster have been argued with considerable acrimony by a number of authorities. While the weight of opinion has credited the invention to Gutenberg, the case of the German has not been absolutely conclusive. In the first place, there exists no piece of printing in which the name of Gutenberg appears as the printer. In the second place, there was known no trustworthy printed or written evidence dated during the contemporary period. And, in the third place, the cause of Gutenberg suffered severe prejudice through *the discovery by Hessels that a large proportion of the documents, on which his case had***

TSI CAXTON** BOLD WITH BOLD ITALIC   MERGENTHALER TYPE LIBRARY

ABCDEFGHIJKLMNOPQRSTUVWXYZ&abcdefghijklmnopqrstuvwxyz1234567890$.,""":;!?

BITSTREAM CHARTER®   BITSTREAM TYPEFACE LIBRARY

ABCDEFGHIJKLMNOPQRSTUVWXYZ&abcdefghijklmnopqrstuvwxyz1234567890$.,""":;!?

BITSTREAM CHARTER ITALIC   BITSTREAM TYPEFACE LIBRARY

ABCDEFGHIJKLMNOPQRSTUVWXYZ&abcdefghijklmnopqrstuvwxyz1234567890$.,""":;!?

BITSTREAM CHARTER BOLD   BITSTREAM TYPEFACE LIBRARY

ABCDEFGHIJKLMNOPQRSTUVWXYZ&abcdefghijklmnopqrstuvwxyz1234567890$.,""":;!?

BITSTREAM CHARTER BOLD ITALIC   BITSTREAM TYPEFACE LIBRARY

ABCDEFGHIJKLMNOPQRSTUVWXYZ&abcdefghijklmnopqrstuvwxyz1234567890$.,""":;!?

BITSTREAM CHARTER BLACK   BITSTREAM TYPEFACE LIBRARY

ABCDEFGHIJKLMNOPQRSTUVWXYZ&abcdefghijklmnopqrstuvwxyz1234567890$.,""":;!?

BITSTREAM CHARTER BLACK ITALIC   BITSTREAM TYPEFACE LIBRARY

SUPPLEMENTARY TYPEFACES   341

12/13 The invention of printing, one of the most momentous events in the history of civilization, has been the subject of most controversy. The rival claims of Gutenberg and Coster have been argued with considerable acrimony by a number of authorities. While the weight of opinion has credited the invention to Gutenberg, the case of the German has not been absolutely conclusive. In the first place, there exists no piece of printing in which the name of Gutenberg appears as the printer. In the second place, there was known no trustworthy printed or written evidence *dated during the contemporary period. And, in the third place, the cause of Gutenberg suffered*

10/11 The invention of printing, one of the most momentous events in the history of civilization, has been the subject of most controversy. The rival claims of Gutenberg and Coster have been argued with considerable acrimony by a number of authorities. While the weight of opinion has credited the invention to Gutenberg, the case of the German has not been absolutely conclusive. In the first place, there exists no piece of printing in which the name of Gutenberg appears as the printer. In the second place, there was known no trustworthy printed or written evidence dated during the contemporary period. And, in the third place, the cause of Gutenberg suffered severe prejudice through the discovery by Hessels that a large proportion of the documents, on which his case has been based, were *rank forgeries, inspired by the over-enthusiastic nationalism of Bodmann, the archivist at Mentz. The circum-*

BITSTREAM CHARTER® WITH ITALIC   BITSTREAM TYPEFACE LIBRARY

12/13 **The invention of printing, one of the most momentous events in the history of civilization, has been the subject of most controversy. The rival claims of Gutenberg and Coster have been argued with considerable acrimony by a number of authorities. While the weight of opinion has credited the invention to Gutenberg, the case of the German has not been absolutely conclusive. In the first place, there exists no piece of printing in which the name of Gutenberg appears as the printer. In the second place, there was known no *trustworthy printed or written evidence dated during the contemporary period. And,***

10/11 **The invention of printing, one of the most momentous events in the history of civilization, has been the subject of most controversy. The rival claims of Gutenberg and Coster have been argued with considerable acrimony by a number of authorities. While the weight of opinion has credited the invention to Gutenberg, the case of the German has not been absolutely conclusive. In the first place, there exists no piece of printing in which the name of Gutenberg appears as the printer. In the second place, there was known no trustworthy printed or written evidence dated during the contemporary period. And, in the third place, the cause of Gutenberg suffered severe prejudice through the discovery by Hessels that a large proportion of the documents, on which his case has been based, were rank *forgeries, inspired by the over-enthusiastic nation-***

BITSTREAM CHARTER BOLD WITH BOLD ITALIC   BITSTREAM TYPEFACE LIBRARY

12/13 **The invention of printing, one of the most momentous events in the history of civilization, has been the subject of most controversy. The rival claims of Gutenberg and Coster have been argued with considerable acrimony by a number of authorities. While the weight of opinion has credited the invention to Gutenberg, the case of the German has not been absolutely conclusive. In the first place, there exists no piece of printing in which the name of Gutenberg *appears as the printer. In the second place, there was not trustworthy***

10/11 **The invention of printing, one of the most momentous events in the history of civilization, has been the subject of most controversy. The rival claims of Gutenberg and Coster have been argued with considerable acrimony by a number of authorities. While the weight of opinion has credited the invention to Gutenberg, the case of the German has not been absolutely conclusive. In the first place, there exists no piece of printing in which the name of Gutenberg appears as the printer. In the second place, there was known no trustworthy printed or written evidence dated during the contemporary period. And, in the third place, the cause of Gutenberg *suffered severe prejudice through the discovery by Hessels that a large proportion of the***

BITSTREAM CHARTER BLACK WITH BLACK ITALIC   BITSTREAM TYPEFACE LIBRARY

ABCDEFGHIJKLMNOPQRSTUV
WXYZ&abcdefghijklmnopqrstuvwxyz
1234567890$.,"":;!?

COCHIN*   MERGENTHALER TYPE LIBRARY

*ABCDEFGHIJKLMNOPQRSTUVWXY
Ze3abcdefghijklmnopqrstuvwxyz123456789
0$.,"":;!?*

COCHIN* ITALIC   MERGENTHALER TYPE LIBRARY

**ABCDEFGHIJKLMNOPQRSTUV
WXYZ&abcdefghijklmnopqrstuvwx
yz1234567890$.,"":;!?**

COCHIN* BOLD   MERGENTHALER TYPE LIBRARY

***ABCDEFGHIJKLMNOPQRSTUVWX
YZe3abcdefghijklmnopqrstuvwxyz12345
67890$.,"":;!?***

COCHIN* BOLD ITALIC   MERGENTHALER TYPE LIBRARY

**ABCDEFGHIJKLMNOPQRSTUV
WXYZ&abcdefghijklmnopqrstuvwx
yz1234567890$.,"":;!?**

COCHIN* BLACK   MERGENTHALER TYPE LIBRARY

***ABCDEFGHIJKLMNOPQRSTUVWX
YZe3abcdefghijklmnopqrstuvwxyz1234
567890$.,"":;!?***

COCHIN* BLACK ITALIC   MERGENTHALER TYPE LIBRARY

12/13 The history of the Dutch book is famous. In the Middle Ages the art of the scribes and miniaturists flourished in the Netherlands to such a degree that their manuscripts are not considered inferior to the finest specimens of Italian and French origin; the Dutch incunabula are, especially by their woodcut illustrations, hardly surpassed, only equalled by Italian work. In the 17th century Holland regained a leading position in this sphere and the prints of Elzevir enjoy at present a world-wide fame. And although our books lack the grandeur of Italian manuscripts, the delicate grace *of a French impression (nor does the Dutch incunabulum display the pompous style of a Gutenberg*

10/11 The history of the Dutch book is famous. In the Middle Ages the art of the scribes and miniaturists flourished in the Netherlands to such a degree that their manuscripts are not considered inferior to the finest specimens of Italian and French origin; the Dutch incunabula are, especially by their woodcut illustrations, hardly surpassed, only equalled by Italian work. In the 17th century Holland regained a leading position in this sphere and the prints of Elzevir enjoy at present a world-wide fame. And although our books lack the grandeur of Italian manuscripts, the delicate grace of a French impression (nor does the Dutch incunabulum display the pompous style of a Gutenberg or Schoeffer work), they have undoubtedly a distinct character of their own, which bears the stamp of true art. They exhibit their *inmost artistic value only to the devout contemplator. We might parallel with the art of painting, especially of the Middle Ages:*

COCHIN* WITH ITALIC   MERGENTHALER TYPE LIBRARY

12/13 **The history of the Dutch book is famous. In the Middle Ages the art of the scribes and miniaturists flourished in the Netherlands to such a degree that their manuscripts are not considered inferior to the finest specimens of Italian and French origin; the Dutch incunabula are, especially by their woodcut illustrations, hardly surpassed, only equalled by Italian work. In the 17th century Holland regained a leading position in this sphere and the prints of Elzevir enjoy at present a world-wide fame. And although our books lack the grandeur of Italian manuscripts, *the delicate grace of a French impression (nor does the Dutch incunabulum display***

10/11 **The history of the Dutch book is famous. In the Middle Ages the art of the scribes and miniaturists flourished in the Netherlands to such a degree that their manuscripts are not considered inferior to the finest specimens of Italian and French origin; the Dutch incunabula are, especially by their woodcut illustrations, hardly surpassed, only equalled by Italian work. In the 17th century Holland regained a leading position in this sphere and the prints of Elzevir enjoy at present a world-wide fame. And although our books lack the grandeur of Italian manuscripts, the delicate grace of a French impression (nor does the Dutch incunabulum display the pompous style of a Gutenberg or Schoeffer work), they have undoubtedly a distinct character of their own, *which bears the stamp of true art. They exhibit their inmost artistic value only to the devout contemplator. We***

COCHIN* BOLD WITH BOLD ITALIC   MERGENTHALER TYPE LIBRARY

12/13 **The history of the Dutch book is famous. In the Middle Ages the art of the scribes and miniaturists flourished in the Netherlands to such a degree that their manuscripts are not considered inferior to the finest specimens of Italian and French origin; the Dutch incunabula are, especially by their woodcut illustrations, hardly surpassed, only equalled by Italian work. In the 17th century Holland regained a leading position in this sphere and the prints of Elzevir enjoy at present a world-wide fame. And although our *books lack the grandeur of Italian manuscripts, the delicate grace of a French im-***

10/11 **The history of the Dutch book is famous. In the Middle Ages the art of the scribes and miniaturists flourished in the Netherlands to such a degree that their manuscripts are not considered inferior to the finest specimens of Italian and French origin; the Dutch incunabula are, especially by their woodcut illustrations, hardly surpassed, only equalled by Italian work. In the 17th century Holland regained a leading position in this sphere and the prints of Elzevir enjoy at present a world-wide fame. And although our books lack the grandeur of Italian manuscripts, the delicate grace of a French impression (nor does the Dutch incunabulum display the pompous style of a Gutenberg or Schoeffer work), they *have undoubtedly a distinct character of their own, which bears the stamp of true art. They exhibit their***

COCHIN* BLACK WITH BLACK ITALIC   MERGENTHALER TYPE LIBRARY

ABCDEFGHIJKLMNOPQRSTUVWXYZ&abcdefghijklmnopqrstuvwxyz1234567890$.,""'':;!?

NICHOLAS COCHIN**   MERGENTHALER TYPE LIBRARY

ABCDEFGHIJKLMNOPQRSTUVWXYZ&abcdefghijklmnopqrstuvwxyz1234567890$.,""'':;!?

NICHOLAS COCHIN** BLACK   MERGENTHALER TYPE LIBRARY

ABCDEFGHIJKLMNOPQRSTUVWXYZ&abcdefghijklmnopqrstuvwxyz1234567890$.,""'' :;!?

DEVINNE   MERGENTHALER TYPE LIBRARY

ABCDEFGHIJKLMNOPQRSTUVWXYZ&abcdefghijklmnopqrstuvwxyz1234567890$.,""'':;!?

DEVINNE ITALIC   MERGENTHALER TYPE LIBRARY

ABCDEFGHIJKLMNOPQRSTUVWXYZ&abcdefghijklmnopqrstuvwxyz1234567890$.,""'':;!?

DIOTIMA*   MERGENTHALER TYPE LIBRARY

ABCDEFGHIJKLMNOPQRSTUVWXYZ&abcdefghijklmnopqrstuvwxyz1234567890$.,""'':;!?

DIOTIMA* ITALIC   MERGENTHALER TYPE LIBRARY

SUPPLEMENTARY FACES 345

12/13 The invention of printing, one of the most momentous events in the history of civilization, has been the subject of most controversy. The rival claims of Gutenberg and Coster have been argued with considerable acrimony by a number of authorities. While the weight of opinion has credited the invention to Gutenberg, the case of the German has not been absolutely conclusive. In the first place, there exists no piece of printing in which the name of Gutenberg appears as the printer. In the second place, there was known no trustworthy printed or written evidence dated during the contemporary period. And, in the third place, the cause of Gutenberg suffered severe prejudice through the discovery by Hessels that a large proportion of the documents, on which his case had been based, were rank forgeries, inspired by the over-enthusi-

10/11 The invention of printing, one of the most momentous events in the history of civilization, has been the subject of most controversy. The rival claims of Gutenberg and Coster have been argued with considerable acrimony by a number of authorities. While the weight of opinion has credited the invention to Gutenberg, the case of the German has not been absolutely conclusive. In the first place, there exists no piece of printing in which the name of Gutenberg appears as the printer. In the second place, there was known no trustworthy printed or written evidence dated during the contemporary period. And, in the third place, the cause of Gutenberg suffered severe prejudice through the discovery by Hessels that a large proportion of the documents, on which his case had been based, were rank forgeries, inspired by the over-enthusiastic nationalism of Bodmann, the archivist at Mentz.

The circumstantial evidence, however, has all pointed to Gutenberg as the father of the printing art, and the invention was very generally credited to him, particularly as there was never produced any direct and conclusive evidence to justify ascription of the

NICHOLAS COCHIN** WITH BLACK   MERGENTHALER TYPE LIBRARY

12/13 It is still a matter of conjecture whether Johann Gutenberg was the first to conceive the principle of casting movable [i.e., separate] metal types which he could arrange in words and sentences so that he could impress their faces on paper. There is, however, hardly a doubt, judging at least from the evidence available, that he was the first to make practical use of the idea, and that it is due to his ingenious application of it that the profound art of typography was born.

Whether he cast his letters in molds of sand or in metal matrices, is a question not *really material at this time; it is the far-reaching results of his inspiration that most*

10/11 It is still a matter of conjecture whether Johann Gutenberg was the first to conceive the principle of casting movable [i.e., separate] metal types which he could arrange in words and sentences so that he could impress their faces on paper. There is, however, hardly a doubt, judging at least from the evidence available, that he was the first to make practical use of the idea, and that it is due to his ingenious application of it that the profound art of typography was born.

Whether he cast his letters in molds of sand or in metal matrices, is a question not really material at this time; it is the far-reaching results of his inspiration that most concern us in this discussion. It seems quite probable that Gutenberg at first had little more *in mind than a desire to find some expedient by which to supplement with explanatory text the illustrations*

DEVINNE WITH ITALIC   MERGENTHALER TYPE LIBRARY

12/13 It is still a matter of conjecture whether Johann Gutenberg was the first to conceive the principle of casting movable [i.e., separate] metal types which he could arrange in words and sentences so that he could impress their faces on paper. There is, however, hardly a doubt, judging at least from the evidence available, that he was the first to make practical use of the idea, and that it is due to his ingenious application of it that the profound art of typography was born.

Whether he cast his letters in molds of *sand or in metal matrices, is a question not really material at this time; it is the far-reaching results of*

10/11 It is still a matter of conjecture whether Johann Gutenberg was the first to conceive the principle of casting movable [i.e., separate] metal types which he could arrange in words and sentences so that he could impress their faces on paper. There is, however, hardly a doubt, judging at least from the evidence available, that he was the first to make practical use of the idea, and that it is due to his ingenious application of it that the profound art of typography was born.

Whether he cast his letters in molds of sand or in metal matrices, is a question not really material at this time; it is the far-reaching results of his inspiration that most concern us in this discussion. It seems quite probable that Gutenberg at *first had little more in mind than a desire to find some expedient by which to supplement with explanatory text the*

DIOTIMA* WITH ITALIC   MERGENTHALER TYPE LIBRARY

ABCDEFGHIJKLMNOPQRSTUVWXYZ&abcdefghijklmnopqrstuvwxyz1234567890$.,''"":;!?

EGYPTIAN 505 LIGHT**   MERGENTHALER TYPE LIBRARY

ABCDEFGHIJKLMNOPQRSTUVWXYZ&abcdefghijklmnopqrstuvwxyz1234567890$.,''"":;!?

EGYPTIAN 505**   MERGENTHALER TYPE LIBRARY

ABCDEFGHIJKLMNOPQRSTUVWXYZ&abcdefghijklmnopqrstuvwxyz1234567890$.,''"":;!?

EGYPTIAN 505 MEDIUM**   MERGENTHALER TYPE LIBRARY

ABCDEFGHIJKLMNOPQRSTUVWXYZ&abcdefghijklmnopqrstuvwxyz1234567890$.,''"":;!?

EGYPTIAN 505 BOLD**   MERGENTHALER TYPE LIBRARY

ABCDEFGHIJKLMNOPQRSTUVWXYZ&abcdefghijklmnopqrstuvwxyz1234567890$.,''"":;!?

EGYPTIENNE F 75 BLACK**   MERGENTHALER TYPE LIBRARY

ABCDEFGHIJKLMNOPQRSTUVWXYZ&abcdefghijklmnopqrstuvwxyz1234567890$.,''"":;!?

EGYPTIENNE F 67 BOLD CONDENSED**

12/13 The history of the Dutch book is famous. In the Middle Ages the art of the scribes and miniaturists flourished in the Netherlands to such a degree that their manuscripts are not considered inferior to the finest specimens of Italian and French origin; the Dutch incunabula are, especially by their woodcut illustrations, hardly surpassed, only equalled by Italian work. In the 17th century Holland regained a leading position in this sphere and the prints of Elzevir enjoy at present a world-wide fame. And although our books lack the grandeur of Italian manuscripts, the delicate grace of a French impression (nor does the Dutch incunabulum

10/11 The history of the Dutch book is famous. In the Middle Ages the art of the scribes and miniaturists flourished in the Netherlands to such a degree that their manuscripts are not considered inferior to the finest specimens of Italian and French origin; the Dutch incunabula are, especially by their woodcut illustrations, hardly surpassed, only equalled by Italian work. In the 17th century Holland regained a leading position in this sphere and the prints of Elzevir enjoy at present a world-wide fame. And although our books lack the grandeur of Italian manuscripts, the delicate grace of a French impression (nor does the Dutch incunabulum display the pompous style of a Gutenberg or Schoeffer work), they have undoubtedly a distinct character of their own, which bears the stamp of true art. They exhibit their inmost artistic value only to the devout contemplator. We might par-

EGYPTIAN 505** LIGHT WITH REGULAR   MERGENTHALER TYPE LIBRARY

12/13 The history of the Dutch book is famous. In the Middle Ages the art of the scribes and miniaturists flourished in the Netherlands to such a degree that their manuscripts are not considered inferior to the finest specimens of Italian and French origin; the Dutch incunabula are, especially by their woodcut illustrations, hardly surpassed, only equalled by Italian work. In the 17th century Holland regained a leading position in this sphere and the prints of Elzevir enjoy at present a world-wide fame. And although our books lack the grandeur of Italian manuscripts, the delicate grace of a French impression (nor does the Dutch incunabulum

10/11 The history of the Dutch book is famous. In the Middle Ages the art of the scribes and miniaturists flourished in the Netherlands to such a degree that their manuscripts are not considered inferior to the finest specimens of Italian and French origin; the Dutch incunabula are, especially by their woodcut illustrations, hardly surpassed, only equalled by Italian work. In the 17th century Holland regained a leading position in this sphere and the prints of Elzevir enjoy at present a world-wide fame. And although our books lack the grandeur of Italian manuscripts, the delicate grace of a French impression (nor does the Dutch incunabulum display the pompous style of a Gutenberg or Schoeffer work), they have undoubtedly a distinct character of their own, which bears the stamp of true art. They exhibit their inmost artistic value only to the devout contemplator.

EGYPTIAN 505** MEDIUM WITH BOLD   MERGENTHALER TYPE LIBRARY

12/13 **The history of the Dutch book is famous. In the Middle Ages the art of the scribes and miniaturists flourished in the Netherlands to such a degree that their manuscripts are not considered inferior to the finest specimens of Italian and French origin; the Dutch incunabula are, especially by their woodcut illustrations, hardly surpassed, only equalled by Italian work. In the 17th century Holland regained a leading position in this sphere and the prints of Elzevir enjoy at present a world-wide fame. And although our books lack the grandeur of Italian manuscripts, the delicate grace**

10/11 The history of the Dutch book is famous. In the Middle Ages the art of the scribes and miniaturists flourished in the Netherlands to such a degree that their manuscripts are not considered inferior to the finest specimens of Italian and French origin; the Dutch incunabula are, especially by their woodcut illustrations, hardly surpassed, only equalled by Italian work. In the 17th century Holland regained a leading position in this sphere and the prints of Elzevir enjoy at present a world-wide fame. And although our books lack the grandeur of Italian manuscripts, the delicate grace of a French impression (nor does the Dutch incunabulum display the pompous style of a Gutenberg or Schoeffer work), they have undoubtedly a distinct character of their own, which bears the stamp of true

EGYPTIENNE F** 75 BLACK WITH 67 BOLD CONDENSED   MERGENTHALER TYPE LIBRARY

ABCDEFGHIJKLMNOPQRSTUVWX
YZ&abcdefghijklmnopqrstuvwxyz
1234567890$.,"":;!?

ITC ELAN** BOOK   MERGENTHALER TYPE LIBRARY

*ABCDEFGHIJKLMNOPQRSTUVWX
YZ&abcdefghijklmnopqrstuvwxyz
1234567890$.,"":;!?*

ITC ELAN** BOOK ITALIC   MERGENTHALER TYPE LIBRARY

ABCDEFGHIJKLMNOPQRSTUVWXYZ
&abcdefghijklmnopqrstuvwxyz123
4567890$.,"":;!?

ITC ELAN** MEDIUM   MERGENTHALER TYPE LIBRARY

*ABCDEFGHIJKLMNOPQRSTUVWXY
Z&abcdefghijklmnopqrstuvwxyz12
34567890$.,"":;!?*

ITC ELAN** MEDIUM ITALIC   MERGENTHALER TYPE LIBRARY

**ABCDEFGHIJKLMNOPQRSTUVWXY
Z&abcdefghijklmnopqrstuvwxyz1
234567890$.,"":;!?**

ITC ELAN** BOLD   MERGENTHALER TYPE LIBRARY

***ABCDEFGHIJKLMNOPQRSTUVWX
YZ&abcdefghijklmnopqrstuvwxyz
1234567890$.,"":;!?***

ITC ELAN** BOLD ITALIC   MERGENTHALER TYPE LIBRARY

SUPPLEMENTARY FACES 349

12/13 The invention of printing, one of the most momentous events in the history of civilization, has been the subject of most controversy. The rival claims of Gutenberg and Coster have been argued with considerable acrimony by a number of authorities. While the weight of opinion has credited the invention to Gutenberg, the case of the German has not been absolutely conclusive. In the first place, there exists no piece of printing in which the name of Gutenberg appears as the printer. In the second place, there was *known no trustworthy printed or written evidence dated during the contempo-*

10/11 The invention of printing, one of the most momentous events in the history of civilization, has been the subject of most controversy. The rival claims of Gutenberg and Coster have been argued with considerable acrimony by a number of authorities. While the weight of opinion has credited the invention to Gutenberg, the case of the German has not been absolutely conclusive. In the first place, there exists no piece of printing in which the name of Gutenberg appears as the printer. In the second place, there was known no trustworthy printed or written evidence dated during the contemporary period. And, in the third place, the cause of Gutenberg suffered severe prejudice through the discovery by Hessels *that a large proportion of the documents, on which his case had been based, were rank for-*

ITC ELAN** BOOK WITH BOOK ITALIC   MERGENTHALER TYPE LIBRARY

12/13 **The invention of printing, one of the most momentous events in the history of civilization, has been the subject of most controversy. The rival claims of Gutenberg and Coster have been argued with considerable acrimony by a number of authorities. While the weight of opinion has credited the invention to Gutenberg, the case of the German has not been absolutely conclusive. In the first place, there exists no piece of printing in which the name of Gutenberg appears as the printer. In the second place, there *was known no trustworthy printed or written evidence dated during the con-***

10/11 **The invention of printing, one of the most momentous events in the history of civilization, has been the subject of most controversy. The rival claims of Gutenberg and Coster have been argued with considerable acrimony by a number of authorities. While the weight of opinion has credited the invention to Gutenberg, the case of the German has not been absolutely conclusive. In the first place, there exists no piece of printing in which the name of Gutenberg appears as the printer. In the second place, there was known no trustworthy printed or written evidence dated during the contemporary period. And, in the third place, the cause of Gutenberg suffered severe prejudice through the discovery by Hessels *that a large proportion of the documents, on which his case had been based, were rank for-***

ITC ELAN** MEDIUM WITH MEDIUM ITALIC   MERGENTHALER TYPE LIBRARY

12/13 **The invention of printing, one of the most momentous events in the history of civilization, has been the subject of most controversy. The rival claims of Gutenberg and Coster have been argued with considerable acrimony by a number of authorities. While the weight of opinion has credited the invention to Gutenberg, the case of the German has not been absolutely conclusive. In the first place, there exists no piece of printing in which the name of Gutenberg appears as the printer. In *the second place, there was known no trustworthy printed or written evi-***

10/11 **The invention of printing, one of the most momentous events in the history of civilization, has been the subject of most controversy. The rival claims of Gutenberg and Coster have been argued with considerable acrimony by a number of authorities. While the weight of opinion has credited the invention to Gutenberg, the case of the German has not been absolutely conclusive. In the first place, there exists no piece of printing in which the name of Gutenberg appears as the printer. In the second place, there was known no trustworthy printed or written evidence dated during the contemporary period. And, in the third place, the cause of Gutenberg suffered severe preju-*dice through the discovery by Hessels that a large proportion of the documents, on which***

ITC ELAN** BOLD WITH BOLD ITALIC   MERGENTHALER TYPE LIBRARY

350 SUPPLEMENTARY FACES

ABCDEFGHIJKLMNOPQRSTUVWX YZ&abcdefghijklmnopqrstuvwxy z1234567890$.,""":;!?

ITC ELAN** BLACK   MERGENTHALER TYPE LIBRARY

ABCDEFGHIJKLMNOPQRSTUVWX YZ&abcdefghijklmnopqrstuvwxy z1234567890$.,""":;!?

ITC ELAN** BLACK ITALIC   MERGENTHALER TYPE LIBRARY

ABCDEFGHIJKLMNOPQRSTUVW XYZ&abcdefghijklmnopqrstuvwxyz123 4567890$.,"":;!?

ELECTRA*   MERGENTHALER TYPE LIBRARY

ABCDEFGHIJKLMNOPQRSTUVWX YZ&abcdefghijklmnopqrstuvwxyz12345 67890$.,"":;!?

ELECTRA* CURSIVE   MERGENTHALER TYPE LIBRARY

ABCDEFGHIJKLMNOPQRSTUVWX YZ&abcdefghijklmnopqrstuvwxyz123 4567890$.,'"":;!?

EUROSTILE**   MERGENTHALER TYPE LIBRARY

ABCDEFGHIJKLMNOPQRSTUVWX YZ&abcdefghijklmnopqrstuvwxyz12 34567890$.,'"":;!?

EUROSTILE** BOLD   MERGENTHALER TYPE LIBRARY

12/13 **The invention of printing, one of the most momentous events in the history of civilization, has been the subject of most controversy. The rival claims of Gutenberg and Coster have been argued with considerable acrimony by a number of authorities. While the weight of opinion has credited the invention to Gutenberg, the case of the German has not been absolutely conclusive. In the first place, there exists no piece of printing in which the name of Gutenberg appears as the printer. *In the second place, there was known no trustwor-***

10/11 **The invention of printing, one of the most momentous events in the history of civilization, has been the subject of most controversy. The rival claims of Gutenberg and Coster have been argued with considerable acrimony by a number of authorities. While the weight of opinion has credited the invention to Gutenberg, the case of the German has not been absolutely conclusive. In the first place, there exists no piece of printing in which the name of Gutenberg appears as the printer. In the second place, there was known no trustworthy printed or written evidence dated during the contemporary period. And, in the third place, the cause *of Gutenberg suffered severe prejudice through the discovery by Hessels that a large***

ITC ELAN** BLACK WITH BLACK ITALIC   MERGENTHALER TYPE LIBRARY

12/13 The invention of printing, one of the most momentous events in the history of civilization, has been the subject of most controversy. The rival claims of Gutenberg and Coster have been argued with considerable acrimony by a number of authorities. While the weight of opinion has credited the invention to Gutenberg, the case of the German has not been absolutely conclusive. In the first place, there exists no piece of printing in which the name of Gutenberg appears as the printer. In the second place, there was known no trustworthy printed or written evidence dated during the contemporary period. And, in the *third place, the cause of Gutenberg suffered severe prejudice through the discovery by Hessels*

10/11 The invention of printing, one of the most momentous events in the history of civilization, has been the subject of most controversy. The rival claims of Gutenberg and Coster have been argued with considerable acrimony by a number of authorities. While the weight of opinion has credited the invention to Gutenberg, the case of the German has not been absolutely conclusive. In the first place, there exists no piece of printing in which the name of Gutenberg appears as the printer. In the second place, there was known no trustworthy printed or written evidence dated during the contemporary period. And, in the third place, the cause of Gutenberg suffered severe prejudice through the discovery by Hessels that a large proportion of the documents, on which his case had been based, were rank forgeries, inspired by the over-enthusiastic nationalism *of Bodmann, the archivist at Mentz.*

The circumstantial evidence, however, has all pointed to

ELECTRA* WITH CURSIVE   MERGENTHALER TYPE LIBRARY

12/13 It is still a matter of conjecture whether Johann Gutenberg was the first to conceive the principle of casting movable [i.e., separate] metal types which he could arrange in words and sentences so that he could impress their faces on paper. There is, however, hardly a doubt, judging at least from the evidence available, that he was the first to make practical use of the idea, and that it is due to his ingenious application of it that the profound art of typography was born.

Whether he cast his letters in molds of **sand or in metal matrices, is a question not really material at this time; it is the**

10/11 It is still a matter of conjecture whether Johann Gutenberg was the first to conceive the principle of casting movable [i.e., separate] metal types which he could arrange in words and sentences so that he could impress their faces on paper. There is, however, hardly a doubt, judging at least from the evidence available, that he was the first to make practical use of the idea, and that it is due to his ingenious application of it that the profound art of typography was born.

Whether he cast his letters in molds of sand or in metal matrices, is a question not really material at this time; it is the far-reaching results of his inspiration that most concern us in this discussion. It seems quite probable that Gutenberg at **first had little more in mind than a desire to find some expedient by which to supplement with ex-**

EUROSTILE** WITH BOLD   MERGENTHALER TYPE LIBRARY

ABCDEFGHIJKLMNOPQRSTUVWXYZ&abcdefghijklmnopqrstuvwxyz1234567890$.,"":;!?

EUROSTILE** CONDENSED   MERGENTHALER TYPE LIBRARY

ABCDEFGHIJKLMNOPQRSTUVWXYZ&abcdefghijklmnopqrstuvwxyz1234567890$.,"":;!?

EUROSTILE** BOLD CONDENSED   MERGENTHALER TYPE LIBRARY

ABCDEFGHIJKLMNOPQRSTUVWXYZ&abcdefghijklmnopqrstuvwxyz1234567890$.,"":;!?

EUROSTILE** EXTENDED NO. 2   MERGENTHALER TYPE LIBRARY

ABCDEFGHIJKLMNOPQRSTUVWXYZ&abcdefghijklmnopqrstuvwxyz1234567890$.,"":;!?

EUROSTILE** BOLD EXTENDED NO. 2   MERGENTHALER TYPE LIBRARY

ABCDEFGHIJKLMNOPQRSTUVWXYZ&abcdefghijklmnopqrstuvwxyz1234567890$.,"":;!?

FAIRFIELD* MEDIUM   MERGENTHALER TYPE LIBRARY

ABCDEFGHIJKLMNOPQRSTUVWXYZ&abcdefghijklmnopqrstuvwxyz1234567890$.,"":;!?

FAIRFIELD* MEDIUM ITALIC   MERGENTHALER TYPE LIBRARY

12/13 It is still a matter of conjecture whether Johann Gutenberg was the first to conceive the principle of casting movable [i.e., separate] metal types which he could arrange in words and sentences so that he could impress their faces on paper. There is, however, hardly a doubt, judging at least from the evidence available, that he was the first to make practical use of the idea, and that it is due to his ingenious application of it that the profound art of typography was born.

Whether he cast his letters in molds of sand or in metal matrices, is a question not really material at this time; it is the far-reaching results of his **inspiration that most concern us in this discussion. It seems quite probable that Gutenberg at**

10/11 It is still a matter of conjecture whether Johann Gutenberg was the first to conceive the principle of casting movable [i.e., separate] metal types which he could arrange in words and sentences so that he could impress their faces on paper. There is, however, hardly a doubt, judging at least from the evidence available, that he was the first to make practical use of the idea, and that it is due to his ingenious application of it that the profound art of typography was born.

Whether he cast his letters in molds of sand or in metal matrices, is a question not really material at this time; it is the far-reaching results of his inspiration that most concern us in this discussion. It seems quite probable that Gutenberg at first had little more in mind than a desire to find some expedient by which to supplement with explana**tory text the illustrations cut on wood blocks — some method that would avoid the labor of engraving the text**

EUROSTILE** CONDENSED WITH BOLD CONDENSED   MERGENTHALER TYPE LIBRARY

12/13 It is still a matter of conjecture whether Johann Gutenberg was the first to conceive the principle of casting movable [i.e., separate] metal types which he could arrange in words and sentences so that he could impress their faces on paper. There is, however, hardly a doubt, judging at least from the evidence available, that he was the first to make practical use of the **idea, and that it is due to his ingenious application of it**

10/11 It is still a matter of conjecture whether Johann Gutenberg was the first to conceive the principle of casting movable [i.e., separate] metal types which he could arrange in words and sentences so that he could impress their faces on paper. There is, however, hardly a doubt, judging at least from the evidence available, that he was the first to make practical use of the idea, and that it is due to his ingenious application of it that the profound art of typography was born.

Whether he cast his letters in **molds of sand or in metal matrices, is a question not really ma-**

EUROSTILE** EXTENDED NO. 2 WITH BOLD EXTENDED NO. 2   MERGENTHALER TYPE LIBRARY

12/13 Lying in my bed, on the morning of the Feast of Kings, when I had had my sleep and rest, & my stomach had readily digested its light and pleasant repast, in the year that was reckoned as MDXXIII, I fell to musing and set the wheel of my memory awhirl thinking on a thousand little conceits, some serious & some joyous, among which there came to my mind a certain Antique letter which I had lately made for my lord the Treasurer for War, Maistre Jehan Groslier, Counsellor and Secretary to our Lord the King, lover of well-made letters and of all learned persons, by whom also he is *much loved & esteemed on both this & the other side of the mountains. And whilst thinking of this Attic*

10/11 Lying in my bed, on the morning of the Feast of Kings, when I had had my sleep and rest, & my stomach had readily digested its light and pleasant repast, in the year that was reckoned as MDXXIII, I fell to musing and set the wheel of my memory awhirl thinking on a thousand little conceits, some serious & some joyous, among which there came to my mind a certain Antique letter which I had lately made for my lord the Treasurer for War, Maistre Jehan Groslier, Counsellor and Secretary to our Lord the King, lover of well-made letters and of all learned persons, by whom also he is much loved & esteemed on both this & the other side of the mountains. And whilst thinking of this Attic Letter, there came of a sudden into my memory a pithy passage in the first book & eighth chapter of the *DeOfficiis of Cicero, where it is written: Non nobis solum nati sumus; ortusque nostri partem patria vendicat, partem*

FAIRFIELD* MEDIUM WITH MEDIUM ITALIC   MERGENTHALER TYPE LIBRARY

SUPPLEMENTARY FACES

ABCDEFGHIJKLMNOPQRSTUVWXYZ&abcdefghijklmnopqrstuvwxyz1234567890$.,'""`:;!?

ITC FENICE** LIGHT   MERGENTHALER TYPE LIBRARY

ABCDEFGHIJKLMNOPQRSTUVWXYZ&abcdefghijklmnopqrstuvwxyz1234567890$.,'""`:;!?

ITC FENICE** LIGHT ITALIC   MERGENTHALER TYPE LIBRARY

ABCDEFGHIJKLMNOPQRSTUVWXYZ&abcdefghijklmnopqrstuvwxyz1234567890$.,'""`:;!?

ITC FENICE** REGULAR   MERGENTHALER TYPE LIBRARY

ABCDEFGHIJKLMNOPQRSTUVWXYZ&abcdefghijklmnopqrstuvwxyz1234567890$.,'""`:;!?

ITC FENICE** REGULAR ITALIC   MERGENTHALER TYPE LIBRARY

ABCDEFGHIJKLMNOPQRSTUVWXYZ&abcdefghijklmnopqrstuvwxyz1234567890$.,'""`:;!?

ITC FENICE** BOLD   MERGENTHALER TYPE LIBRARY

ABCDEFGHIJKLMNOPQRSTUVWXYZ&abcdefghijklmnopqrstuvwxyz1234567890$.,'""`:;!?

ITC FENICE** BOLD ITALIC   MERGENTHALER TYPE LIBRARY

12/13 In considering fine and praiseworthy inventions, we must freely confess that printing has been and is to-day the best and most estimable — the invention by means of which two persons turning the press can get a greater number of books in a day than formerly could have been transcribed by several persons in a year. It is claimed that this art was invented at Mainz, a city of Germany, in the year 1442 by Jean Guttemberg, or, according to others, Guttenberg, an honorable German chevalier. It was at Mainz that after experimenting with an ink which is used by printers to-day, he first began the practice of the art. *Some persons prefer to attribute the invention to Jean Fauste & Yues Scheffey two years earlier, hold-*

10/11 In considering fine and praiseworthy inventions, we must freely confess that printing has been and is to-day the best and most estimable — the invention by means of which two persons turning the press can get a greater number of books in a day than formerly could have been transcribed by several persons in a year. It is claimed that this art was invented at Mainz, a city of Germany, in the year 1442 by Jean Guttemberg, or, according to others, Guttenberg, an honorable German chevalier. It was at Mainz that after experimenting with an ink which is used by printers to-day, he first began the practice of the art. Some persons prefer to attribute the invention to Jean Fauste & Yues Scheffey two years earlier, holding that our Guttemberg, Jean Mentel, Jean Prus, Adolphe Rusche, Pierre Scheffec, Martin Flache, Huldric Han, Jean Froben, Adam Petri, *Thomas Vuolffe, and others added improvements and spread the art of printing through all Germany and other*

ITC FENICE** LIGHT WITH LIGHT ITALIC   MERGENTHALER TYPE LIBRARY

12/13 In considering fine and praiseworthy inventions, we must freely confess that printing has been and is to-day the best and most estimable — the invention by means of which two persons turning the press can get a greater number of books in a day than formerly could have been transcribed by several persons in a year. It is claimed that this art was invented at Mainz, a city of Germany, in the year 1442 by Jean Guttemberg, or, according to others, Guttenberg, an honorable German chevalier. It was at Mainz that after experimenting with an ink which is used by *printers to-day, he first began the practice of the art. Some persons prefer to attribute the*

10/11 In considering fine and praiseworthy inventions, we must freely confess that printing has been and is to-day the best and most estimable — the invention by means of which two persons turning the press can get a greater number of books in a day than formerly could have been transcribed by several persons in a year. It is claimed that this art was invented at Mainz, a city of Germany, in the year 1442 by Jean Guttemberg, or, according to others, Guttenberg, an honorable German chevalier. It was at Mainz that after experimenting with an ink which is used by printers to-day, he first began the practice of the art. Some persons prefer to attribute the invention to Jean Fauste & Yues Scheffey two years earlier, holding that our Guttemberg, Jean Mentel, Jean Prus, Adolphe Rusche, Pierre *Scheffec, Martin Flache, Huldric Han, Jean Froben, Adam Petri, Thomas Vuolffe, and others added im-*

ITC FENICE** REGULAR WITH REGULAR ITALIC   MERGENTHALER TYPE LIBRARY

12/13 **In considering fine and praiseworthy inventions, we must freely confess that printing has been and is to-day the best and most estimable — the invention by means of which two persons turning the press can get a greater number of books in a day than formerly could have been transcribed by several persons in a year. It is claimed that this art was invented at Mainz, a city of Germany, in the year 1442 by Jean Guttemberg, or, according to others, Guttenberg, an honorable German chevalier. It was at Mainz that after ex-*perimenting with an ink which is used by printers to-day, he first began the prac-***

10/11 **In considering fine and praiseworthy inventions, we must freely confess that printing has been and is to-day the best and most estimable — the invention by means of which two persons turning the press can get a greater number of books in a day than formerly could have been transcribed by several persons in a year. It is claimed that this art was invented at Mainz, a city of Germany, in the year 1442 by Jean Guttemberg, or, according to others, Guttenberg, an honorable German chevalier. It was at Mainz that after experimenting with an ink which is used by printers to-day, he first began the practice of the art. Some persons prefer to attribute the invention to Jean Fauste & Yues Scheffey two years earlier, holding that our *Guttemberg, Jean Mentel, Jean Prus, Adolphe Rusche, Pierre Scheffec, Martin Flache, Huldric***

ITC FENICE** BOLD WITH BOLD ITALIC   MERGENTHALER TYPE LIBRARY

ABCDEFGHIJKLMNOPQRSTUV WXYZ&abcdefghijklmnopqrstuvwxyz1234567890$.,""":;!?

ITC FENICE** ULTRA   MERGENTHALER TYPE LIBRARY

ABCDEFGHIJKLMNOPQRSTUV WXYZ&abcdefghijklmnopqrstuvwxyz1234567890$.,""":;!?

ITC FENICE** ULTRA ITALIC   MERGENTHALER TYPE LIBRARY

ABCDEFGHIJKLMNOPQRSTUVWXYZ&abcdefghijklmnopqrstuvwxyz1234567890$.,""":;!?

FLOREAL HASS** LIGHT   MERGENTHALER TYPE LIBRARY

ABCDEFGHIJKLMNOPQRSTUVWXYZ&abcdefghijklmnopqrstuvwxyz1234567890$.,""":;!?

FLOREAL HASS**   MERGENTHALER TYPE LIBRARY

ABCDEFGHIJKLMNOPQRSTUVWXYZ&abcdefghijklmnopqrstuvwxyz1234567890$.,""":;!?

FLOREAL HASS** BOLD   MERGENTHALER TYPE LIBRARY

ABCDEFGHIJKLMNOPQRSTUVWXYZ&abcdefghijklmnopqrstuvwxyz1234567890$.,""":;!?

FLOREAL HASS** BLACK   MERGENTHALER TYPE LIBRARY

SUPPLEMENTARY FACES 357

12/13 **In considering fine and praiseworthy inventions, we must freely confess that printing has been and is to-day the best and most estimable — the invention by means of which two persons turning the press can get a greater number of books in a day than formerly could have been transcribed by several persons in a year. It is claimed that this art was invented at Mainz, a city of Germany, in the year 1442 by Jean Guttemberg, or, according to others, Guttenberg, an honorable German chevalier. It was at Mainz that after experimenting with**

10/11 **In considering fine and praiseworthy inventions, we must freely confess that printing has been and is to-day the best and most estimable — the invention by means of which two persons turning the press can get a greater number of books in a day than formerly could have been transcribed by several persons in a year. It is claimed that this art was invented at Mainz, a city of Germany, in the year 1442 by Jean Guttemberg, or, according to others, Guttenberg, an honorable German chevalier. It was at Mainz that after experimenting with an ink which is used by printers to-day, he first began the practice of the art. Some persons prefer to attribute the *invention to Jean Fauste & Yues Scheffey two years earlier, holding that our Guttemberg,***

ITC FENICE** ULTRA WITH ULTRA ITALIC   MERGENTHALER TYPE LIBRARY

12/13 In considering fine and praiseworthy inventions, we must freely confess that printing has been and is to-day the best and most estimable — the invention by means of which two persons turning the press can get a greater number of books in a day than formerly could have been transcribed by several persons in a year. It is claimed that this art was invented at Mainz, a city of Germany, in the year 1442 by Jean Guttemberg, or, according to others, Guttenberg, an honorable German chevalier. It was at Mainz that after experimenting with an ink which is used by printers to-day, he first began the practice of the art. Some

10/11 In considering fine and praiseworthy inventions, we must freely confess that printing has been and is to-day the best and most estimable — the invention by means of which two persons turning the press can get a greater number of books in a day than formerly could have been transcribed by several persons in a year. It is claimed that this art was invented at Mainz, a city of Germany, in the year 1442 by Jean Guttemberg, or, according to others, Guttenberg, an honorable German chevalier. It was at Mainz that after experimenting with an ink which is used by printers to-day, he first began the practice of the art. Some persons prefer to attribute the invention to Jean Fauste & Yues Scheffey two years earlier, holding that our Guttemberg, Jean Mentel, Jean Prus, Adolphe Rusche, Pierre Scheffec, Martin Flache, Huldric Han, Jean Froben, Adam Petri,

FLOREAL HASS** LIGHT WITH FLOREAL HASS**   MERGENTHALER TYPE LIBRARY

12/13 **In considering fine and praiseworthy inventions, we must freely confess that printing has been and is to-day the best and most estimable — the invention by means of which two persons turning the press can get a greater number of books in a day than formerly could have been transcribed by several persons in a year. It is claimed that this art was invented at Mainz, a city of Germany, in the year 1442 by Jean Guttemberg, or, according to others, Guttenberg, an honorable German chevalier. It was at Mainz that after experimenting with an ink which is used by printers to-**

10/11 **In considering fine and praiseworthy inventions, we must freely confess that printing has been and is to-day the best and most estimable — the invention by means of which two persons turning the press can get a greater number of books in a day than formerly could have been transcribed by several persons in a year. It is claimed that this art was invented at Mainz, a city of Germany, in the year 1442 by Jean Guttemberg, or, according to others, Guttenberg, an honorable German chevalier. It was at Mainz that after experimenting with an ink which is used by printers to-day, he first began the practice of the art. Some persons prefer to attribute the invention to Jean Fauste & Yues Scheffey two years earlier, holding that our Guttemberg, Jean Mentel, Jean Prus, Adolphe Rusche,**

FLOREAL HASS** BOLD WITH BLACK   MERGENTHALER TYPE LIBRARY

ABCDEFGHIJKLMNOPQRSTUVWXYZ&abcdefghijklmnopqrstuvwxyz1234567890$.,'''":;!?

FOLIO** LIGHT   MERGENTHALER TYPE LIBRARY

ABCDEFGHIJKLMNOPQRSTUVWXYZ&abcdefghijklmnopqrstuvwxyz1234567890$.,'''":;!?

FOLIO** LIGHT ITALIC   MERGENTHALER TYPE LIBRARY

ABCDEFGHIJKLMNOPQRSTUVWXYZ&abcdefghijklmnopqrstuvwxyz1234567890$.,'''":;!?

FOLIO** MEDIUM   MERGENTHALER TYPE LIBRARY

ABCDEFGHIJKLMNOPQRSTUVWXYZ&abcdefghijklmnopqrstuvwxyz1234567890$.,'''":;!?

FOLIO** BOLD   MERGENTHALER TYPE LIBRARY

ABCDEFGHIJKLMNOPQRSTUVWXYZ&abcdefghijklmnopqrstuvwxyz1234567890$.,'''":;!?

FOURNIER**   MERGENTHALER TYPE LIBRARY

ABCDEFGHIJKLMNOPQRSTUVWXYZ&abcdefghijklmnopqrstuvwxyz1234567890$.,'''":;!?

FOURNIER** ITALIC   MERGENTHALER TYPE LIBRARY

SUPPLEMENTARY FACES 359

12/13 In type-founding, types are cast in moulds containing at one end a copper matrix of the character. The aperture through which the melted metal is injected is at the end of the mould opposite the matrix, and a piece as long as the type, called the jet, extends through the aperture from the bottom of the type. Thus imperfections in the metal and variations of temperature spend themselves in the jet, leaving the body of the type comparatively perfect. The types thus cast go through various processes, such as breaking off the jet and ploughing in its place a shallow *groove across the foot, thus leaving each type two "feet" to stand upon, "rubbing,"*

10/11 In type-founding, types are cast in moulds containing at one end a copper matrix of the character. The aperture through which the melted metal is injected is at the end of the mould opposite the matrix, and a piece as long as the type, called the jet, extends through the aperture from the bottom of the type. Thus imperfections in the metal and variations of temperature spend themselves in the jet, leaving the body of the type comparatively perfect. The types thus cast go through various processes, such as breaking off the jet and ploughing in its place a shallow groove across the foot, thus leaving each type two "feet" to stand upon, "rubbing," etc.; and at last, set up in long rows, they pass under the eye of an expert, who, as he examines them carefully with a glass, rejects all in *which he detects any imperfections. In these processes an average of 10 per cent, is eliminated; so*

FOLIO** LIGHT WITH LIGHT ITALIC   MERGENTHALER TYPE LIBRARY

12/13 **In type-founding, types are cast in moulds containing at one end a copper matrix of the character.** The aperture through which the melted metal is injected is at the end of the mould opposite the matrix, and a piece as long as the type, called the jet, extends through the aperture from the bottom of the type. Thus imperfections in the metal and variations of temperature spend themselves in the jet, leaving the body of the type comparatively perfect. The types thus cast go through various processes, such as breaking off the jet and ploughing in its place a shallow groove across the foot, thus leav**ing each type two "feet" to stand**

10/11 In type-founding, types are cast in moulds containing at one end a copper matrix of the character. The aperture through which the melted metal is injected is at the end of the mould opposite the matrix, and a piece as long as the type, called the jet, extends through the aperture from the bottom of the type. Thus imperfections in the metal and variations of temperature spend themselves in the jet, leaving the body of the type comparatively perfect. The types thus cast go through various processes, such as breaking off the jet and ploughing in its place a shallow groove across the foot, thus leaving each type two "feet" to stand upon, "rubbing," etc.; and at last, set up in long rows, they pass under the eye of an expert, who, as he examines them carefully with a **glass, rejects all in which he detects any imperfections. In these processes an average**

FOLIO** MEDIUM WITH BOLD   MERGENTHALER TYPE LIBRARY

12/13 Lying in my bed, on the morning of the Feast of Kings, when I had had my sleep and rest, & my stomach had readily digested its light and pleasant repast, in the year that was reckoned as MDXXIII, I fell to musing and set the wheel of my memory awhirl thinking on a thousand little conceits, some serious & some joyous, among which there came to my mind a certain Antique letter which I had lately made for my lord the Treasurer for War, Maistre Jehan Groslier, Counsellor and Secretary to our Lord the King, lover of well-made letters and of all learned persons, by whom also he is much loved & *esteemed on both this & the other side of the mountains. And whilst thinking of this Attic Letter, there came of a*

10/11 Lying in my bed, on the morning of the Feast of Kings, when I had had my sleep and rest, & my stomach had readily digested its light and pleasant repast, in the year that was reckoned as MDXXIII, I fell to musing and set the wheel of my memory awhirl thinking on a thousand little conceits, some serious & some joyous, among which there came to my mind a certain Antique letter which I had lately made for my lord the Treasurer for War, Maistre Jehan Groslier, Counsellor and Secretary to our Lord the King, lover of well-made letters and of all learned persons, by whom also he is much loved & esteemed on both this & the other side of the mountains. And whilst thinking of this Attic Letter, there came of a sudden into my memory a pithy passage in the first book & eighth chapter of the DeOfficiis of Cicero, where it is *written: Non nobis solum nati sumus; ortusque nostri partem patria vendicat, partem amici. Which is to say, in substance, that*

FOURNIER** WITH ITALIC   MERGENTHALER TYPE LIBRARY

SUPPLEMENTARY FACES

ABCDEFGHIJKLMNOPQRSTUVWX
YZ&abcdefghijklmnopqrstuvwxyz
1234567890$.,'"";:!?

FRANKLIN   AGFA COMPUGRAPHIC TYPE LIBRARY

*ABCDEFGHIJKLMNOPQRSTUVWX
YZ&abcdefghijklmnopqrstuvwxyz
1234567890$.,'"";:!?*

FRANKLIN ITALIC   AGFA COMPUGRAPHIC TYPE LIBRARY

ABCDEFGHIJKLMNOPQRSTUVWXYZ&
abcdefghijklmnopqrstuvwxyz
1234567890$.,'"";:!?

FRANKLIN CONDENSED   AGFA COMPUGRAPHIC TYPE LIBRARY

*ABCDEFGHIJKLMNOPQRSTUVWXYZ&
abcdefghijklmnopqrstuvwxyz
1234567890$.,'"";:!?*

FRANKLIN CONDENSED ITALIC   AGFA COMPUGRAPHIC TYPE LIBRARY

ABCDEFGHIJKLMNOPQRSTU
VWXYZ&abcdefghijklmnopqrs
tuvwxyz1234567890$.,'"";:!?

FRANKLIN WIDE   AGFA COMPUGRAPHIC TYPE LIBRARY

*ABCDEFGHIJKLMNOPQRSTU
VWXYZ&abcdefghijklmnopqrs
tuvwxyz1234567890$.,'"";:!?*

FRANKLIN WIDE ITALIC   AGFA COMPUGRAPHIC TYPE LIBRARY

SUPPLEMENTARY FACES 361

12/13 In type-founding, types are cast in moulds containing at one end a copper matrix of the character. The aperture through whch the melted metal is injected is at the end of the mould opposite the matrix, and a piece as long as the type, called the jet, leaving the body of the type comparatively perfect. The types thus cast go through various processes, such as breaking off the jet and ploughing in its place a shallow groove across the foot, thus leaving each type two "feet" to stand upon, "rubbing," *etc.; and at last, set up in long rows, they pass under the eye of an expert,*

10/11 In type-founding, types are cast in moulds containing at one end a copper matrix of the character. The aperture through whch the melted metal is injected is at the end of the mould opposite the matrix, and a piece as long as the type, called the jet, leaving the body of the type comparatively perfect. The types thus cast go through various processes, such as breaking off the jet and ploughing in its place a shallow groove across the foot, thus leaving each type two "feet" to stand upon, "rubbing," etc.; and at last, set up in long rows, they pass under the eye of an expert, who, as he examines them carefully with a glass, rejects all in which he detects any imperfections. In these pro*cesses an average of 10 percent, is eliminated; so that of 100 lbs. cast only 90 lbs. are actually*

FRANKLIN WITH ITALIC   AGFA COMPUGRAPHIC TYPE LIBRARY

12/13 In type-founding, types are cast in moulds containing at one end a copper matrix of the character. The aperture through whch the melted metal is injected is at the end of the mould opposite the matrix, and a piece as long as the type, called the jet, leaving the body of the type comparatively perfect. The types thus cast go through various processes, such as breaking off the jet and ploughing in its place a shallow groove across the foot, thus leaving each type two "feet" to stand upon, "rubbing," etc.; and at last, set up in long rows, they pass under the eye of an expert, who, as he ex*amines them carefully with a glass, rejects all in which he detects any imperfections. In these*

10/11 In type-founding, types are cast in moulds containing at one end a copper matrix of the character. The aperture through whch the melted metal is injected is at the end of the mould opposite the matrix, and a piece as long as the type, called the jet, leaving the body of the type comparatively perfect. The types thus cast go through various processes, such as breaking off the jet and ploughing in its place a shallow groove across the foot, thus leaving each type two "feet" to stand upon, "rubbing," etc.; and at last, set up in long rows, they pass under the eye of an expert, who, as he examines them carefully with a glass, rejects all in which he detects any imperfections. In these processes *an average of 10 percent, is eliminated; so that of 100 lbs. cast only 90 lbs. are actually fit for delivery. Gen*

FRANKLIN CONDENSED WITH CONDENSED ITALIC   AGFA COMPUGRAPHIC TYPE LIBRARY

12/13 **In type-founding, types are cast in moulds containing at one end a copper matrix of the character. The aperture through whch the melted metal is injected is at the end of the mould opposite the matrix, and a piece as long as the type, called the jet, leaving the body of the type comparatively perfect. The types thus cast go through various processes, such as breaking off the jet and ploughing in its place a shallow *groove across the foot, thus leaving each type two "feet" to stand upon,***

10/11 In type-founding, types are cast in moulds containing at one end a copper matrix of the character. The aperture through whch the melted metal is injected is at the end of the mould opposite the matrix, and a piece as long as the type, called the jet, leaving the body of the type comparatively perfect. The types thus cast go through various processes, such as breaking off the jet and ploughing in its place a shallow groove across the foot, thus leaving each type two "feet" to stand upon, "rubbing," etc.; and at last, set up in long rows, they pass under the eye of an expert, who, as *he examines them carefully with a glass, rejects all in which he detects any imper*

FRANKLIN WIDE WITH WIDE ITALIC   AGFA COMPUGRAPHIC TYPE LIBRARY

ABCDEFGHIJKLMNOPQRSTUVWXYZ&
abcdefghijklmnopqrstuvwxyz
1234567890$.,''"":;!?

FRIZ QUADRATA   AGFA COMPUGRAPHIC TYPE LIBRARY

**ABCDEFGHIJKLMNOPQRSTUVWXYZ&
abcdefghijklmnopqrstuvwxyz
1234567890$.,''"":;!?**

FRIZ QUADRATA BOLD   AGFA COMPUGRAPHIC TYPE LIBRARY

ABCDEFGHIJKLMNOPQRSTUVWXYZ&
abcdefghijklmnopqrstuvwxyz
1234567890$.,'''':;!?

FRONTIERA 55   AGFA COMPUGRAPHIC TYPE LIBRARY

*ABCDEFGHIJKLMNOPQRSTUVWXYZ&
abcdefghijklmnopqrstuvwxyz
1234567890$.,'''':;!?*

FRONTIERA 56   AGFA COMPUGRAPHIC TYPE LIBRARY

**ABCDEFGHIJKLMNOPQRSTUVWXY
Z&abcdefghijklmnopqrstuvwxyz
1234567890$.,'''':;!?**

FRONTIERA 75   AGFA COMPUGRAPHIC TYPE LIBRARY

***ABCDEFGHIJKLMNOPQRSTUVWXY
Z&abcdefghijklmnopqrstuvwxyz
1234567890$.,'''':;!?***

FRONTIERA 76   AGFA COMPUGRAPHIC TYPE LIBRARY

SUPPLEMENTARY FACES 363

12/13 The invention of printing, one of the most momentous events in the history of civilization, has been the subject of most controversy. The rival claims of Gutenberg and Coster have been argued with considerable acrimony by a number of authorities. While the weight of opinion has credited the invention to Gutenberg, the case of the German has not been absolutely conclusive. In the first place, there exists no piece of printing in which the name of Gutenberg appears as the printer. In the second place, **there was known no trustworthy printed or written evidence dated during the con-**

10/11 The invention of printing, one of the most momentous events in the history of civilization, has been the subject of most controversy. The rival claims of Gutenberg and Coster have been argued with considerable acrimony by a number of authorities. While the weight of opinion has credited the invention to Gutenberg, the case of the German has not been absolutely conclusive. In the first place, there exists no piece of printing in which the name of Gutenberg appears as the printer. In the second place, there was known no trustworthy printed or written evidence dated during the contemporary period. And, in the third place, the cause of Gutenberg suffered severe prejudice through the discovery by Hessels that **a large proportion of the documents, on which his case had been based, were rank forgeries,**

FRIZ QUADRATA WITH BOLD   AGFA COMPUGRAPHIC TYPE LIBRARY

12/13 The invention of printing, one of the most momentous events in the history of civilization, has been the subject of most controversy. The rival claims of Gutenberg and Coster have been argued with considerable acrimony by a number of authorities. While the weight of opinion has credited the invention to Gutenberg, the case of the German has not been absolutely conclusive. In the first place, there exists no piece of printing in which the name of Gutenberg appears as the printer. In the second place, there was *known no trustworthy printed or written evidence dated during the contemporary*

10/11 The invention of printing, one of the most momentous events in the history of civilization, has been the subject of most controversy. The rival claims of Gutenberg and Coster have been argued with considerable acrimony by a number of authorities. While the weight of opinion has credited the invention to Gutenberg, the case of the German has not been absolutely conclusive. In the first place, there exists no piece of printing in which the name of Gutenberg appears as the printer. In the second place, there was known no trustworthy printed or written evidence dated during the contemporary period. And, in the third place, the cause of Gutenberg suffered severe prejudice through the discovery by Hessels that a large *proportion of the documents, on which his case had been based, were rank forgeries, inspired*

FRONTIERA 55 WITH 56   AGFA COMPUGRAPHIC TYPE LIBRARY

12/13 **The invention of printing, one of the most momentous events in the history of civilization, has been the subject of most controversy. The rival claims of Gutenberg and Coster have been argued with considerable acrimony by a number of authorities. While the weight of opinion has credited the invention to Gutenberg, the case of the German has not been absolutely conclusive. In the first place, there exists no piece of printing in which the name of Gutenberg appears as the printer. *In the second place, there was known no trustwor-***

10/11 **The invention of printing, one of the most momentous events in the history of civilization, has been the subject of most controversy. The rival claims of Gutenberg and Coster have been argued with considerable acrimony by a number of authorities. While the weight of opinion has credited the invention to Gutenberg, the case of the German has not been absolutely conclusive. In the first place, there exists no piece of printing in which the name of Gutenberg appears as the printer. In the second place, there was known no trustworthy printed or written evidence dated during the contemporary period. And, in the third place, the cause of *Gutenberg suffered severe prejudice through the discovery by Hessels that a large propor-***

FRONTIERA 75 WITH 76   AGFA COMPUGRAPHIC TYPE LIBRARY

ABCDEFGHIJKLMNOPQRSTUVWXYZ&abcdefghijklmnopqrstuvwxyz1234567890$.,"''":;!?

FRUTIGER* 45 LIGHT   MERGENTHALER TYPE LIBRARY

ABCDEFGHIJKLMNOPQRSTUVWXYZ&abcdefghijklmnopqrstuvwxyz1234567890$.,"''":;!?

FRUTIGER* 46 LIGHT ITALIC   MERGENTHALER TYPE LIBRARY

ABCDEFGHIJKLMNOPQRSTUVWXYZ&abcdefghijklmnopqrstuvwxyz1234567890$.,"''":;!?

FRUTIGER* 55   MERGENTHALER TYPE LIBRARY

ABCDEFGHIJKLMNOPQRSTUVWXYZ&abcdefghijklmnopqrstuvwxyz1234567890$.,"''":;!?

FRUTIGER* 56 ITALIC   MERGENTHALER TYPE LIBRARY

ABCDEFGHIJKLMNOPQRSTUVWXYZ&abcdefghijklmnopqrstuvwxyz1234567890$.,"''":;!?

FRUTIGER* 65 BOLD   MERGENTHALER TYPE LIBRARY

ABCDEFGHIJKLMNOPQRSTUVWXYZ&abcdefghijklmnopqrstuvwxyz1234567890$.,"''":;!?

FRUTIGER* 66 BOLD ITALIC   MERGENTHALER TYPE LIBRARY

SUPPLEMENTARY FACES 365

12/13 Lying in my bed, on the morning of the Feast of Kings, when I had had my sleep and rest, & my stomach had readily digested its light and pleasant repast, in the year that was reckoned as MDXXIII, I fell to musing and set the wheel of my memory awhirl thinking on a thousand little conceits, some serious & some joyous, among which there came to my mind a certain Antique letter which I had lately made for my lord the Treasurer for War, Maistre Jehan Groslier, Counsellor and Secretary to our Lord the King, lover of well-made letters and of all learned persons, by whom also he is much *loved & esteemed on both this & the other side of the mountains. And whilst thinking of*

10/11 Lying in my bed, on the morning of the Feast of Kings, when I had had my sleep and rest, & my stomach had readily digested its light and pleasant repast, in the year that was reckoned as MDXXIII, I fell to musing and set the wheel of my memory awhirl thinking on a thousand little conceits, some serious & some joyous, among which there came to my mind a certain Antique letter which I had lately made for my lord the Treasurer for War, Maistre Jehan Groslier, Counsellor and Secretary to our Lord the King, lover of well-made letters and of all learned persons, by whom also he is much loved & esteemed on both this & the other side of the mountains. And whilst thinking of this Attic Letter, there came of a sudden into my memory a pithy passage in the first book & eighth chapter of the DeOfficiis of *Cicero, where it is written: Non nobis solum nati sumus; ortusque nostri partem patria vendicat, partem*

FRUTIGER® 45 LIGHT WITH 46 LIGHT ITALIC   MERGENTHALER TYPE LIBRARY

12/13 Lying in my bed, on the morning of the Feast of Kings, when I had had my sleep and rest, & my stomach had readily digested its light and pleasant repast, in the year that was reckoned as MDXXIII, I fell to musing and set the wheel of my memory awhirl thinking on a thousand little conceits, some serious & some joyous, among which there came to my mind a certain Antique letter which I had lately made for my lord the Treasurer for War, Maistre Jehan Groslier, Counsellor and Secretary to our Lord the King, lover of *well-made letters and of all learned persons, by whom also he is much loved &*

10/11 Lying in my bed, on the morning of the Feast of Kings, when I had had my sleep and rest, & my stomach had readily digested its light and pleasant repast, in the year that was reckoned as MDXIII, I fell to musing and set the wheel of my memory awhirl thinking on a thousand little conceits, some serious & some joyous, among which there came to my mind a certain Antique letter which I had lately made for my lord the Treasurer for War, Maistre Jehan Groslier, Counsellor and Secretary to our Lord the King, lover of well-made letters and of all learned persons, by whom also he is much loved & esteemed on both this & the other side of the mountains. And whilst thinking of this Attic Letter, there came of a sudden into my mem*ory a pithy passage in the first book & eighth chapter of the DeOfficiis of Cicero, where it is*

FRUTIGER® 55 WITH 56 ITALIC   MERGENTHALER TYPE LIBRARY

12/13 **Lying in my bed, on the morning of the Feast of Kings, when I had had my sleep and rest, & my stomach had readily digested its light and pleasant repast, in the year that was reckoned as MDXXIII, I fell to musing and set the wheel of my memory awhirl thinking on a thousand little conceits, some serious & some joyous, among which there came to my mind a certain Antique letter which I had lately made for my lord the Treasurer for War, Maistre Jehan Groslier, Counsellor and Secretary to our Lord the King, lover *of well-made letters and of all learned persons, by whom also he is much loved***

10/11 **Lying in my bed, on the morning of the Feast of Kings, when I had had my sleep and rest, & my stomach had readily digested its light and pleasant repast, in the year that was reckoned as MDXIII, I fell to musing and set the wheel of my memory awhirl thinking on a thousand little conceits, some serious & some joyous, among which there came to my mind a certain Antique letter which I had lately made for my lord the Treasurer for War, Maistre Jehan Groslier, Counsellor and Secretary to our Lord the King, lover of well-made letters and of all learned persons, by whom also he is much loved & esteemed on both this & the other side of the mountains. And whilst thinking of this Attic Letter, there came of a sudden into *my memory a pithy passage in the first book & eighth chapter of the DeOfficiis of Cicero, where***

FRUTIGER® 65 BOLD WITH 66 BOLD ITALIC   MERGENTHALER TYPE LIBRARY

SUPPLEMENTARY FACES

ABCDEFGHIJKLMNOPQRSTUVWXYZ&abcdefghijklmnopqrstuvwxyz1234567890$.,"'":;!?

FRUTIGER* 75 BLACK   MERGENTHALER TYPE LIBRARY

ABCDEFGHIJKLMNOPQRSTUVWXYZ&abcdefghijklmnopqrstuvwxyz1234567890$.,"'":;!?

FRUTIGER* 76 BLACK ITALIC   MERGENTHALER TYPE LIBRARY

ABCDEFGHIJKLMNOPQRSTUVWXYZ&abcdefghijklmnopqrstuvwxyz1234567890$.,"'":;!?

FRUTIGER* 57 CONDENSED   MERGENTHALER TYPE LIBRARY

ABCDEFGHIJKLMNOPQRSTUVWXYZ&abcdefghijklmnopqrstuvwxyz1234567890$.,"'":;!?

FRUTIGER* 67 BOLD CONDENSED   MERGENTHALER TYPE LIBRARY

ABCDEFGHIJKLMNOPQRSTUVWXYZ&abcdefghijklmnopqrstuvwxyz1234567890$.,"'":;!?

FRUTIGER* 77 BLACK CONDENSED   MERGENTHALER TYPE LIBRARY

ABCDEFGHIJKLMNOPQRSTUVWXYZ&abcdefghijklmnopqrstuvwxyz1234567890$.,"'":;!?

FRUTIGER* 87 EXTRA BLACK CONDENSED   MERGENTHALER TYPE LIBRARY

SUPPLEMENTARY FACES 367

12/13 Lying in my bed, on the morning of the Feast of Kings, when I had had my sleep and rest, & my stomach had readily digested its light and pleasant repast, in the year that was reckoned as MDXXIII, I fell to musing and set the wheel of my memory awhirl thinking on a thousand little conceits, some serious & some joyous, among which there came to my mind a certain Antique letter which I had lately made for my lord the Treasurer for War, Maistre Jehan Groslier, Counsellor and Secretary to our Lord the King, lover of well-made letters and

10/11 Lying in my bed, on the morning of the Feast of Kings, when I had had my sleep and rest, & my stomach had readily digested its light and pleasant repast, in the year that was reckoned as MDXXIII, I fell to musing and set the wheel of my memory awhirl thinking on a thousand little conceits, some serious & some joyous, among which there came to my mind a certain Antique letter which I had lately made for my lord the Treasurer for War, Maistre Jehan Groslier, Counsellor and Secretary to our Lord the King, lover of well-made letters and of all learned persons, by whom also he is much loved & esteemed on both this & the other side of the mountains. And *whilst thinking of this Attic Letter, there came of a sudden into my memory a pithy*

FRUTIGER* 75 BLACK WITH 76 BLACK ITALIC   MERGENTHALER TYPE LIBRARY

12/13 Lying in my bed, on the morning of the Feast of Kings, when I had had my sleep and rest, & my stomach had readily digested its light and pleasant repast, in the year that was reckoned as MDXXIII, I fell to musing and set the wheel of my memory awhirl thinking on a thousand little conceits, some serious & some joyous, among which there came to my mind a certain Antique letter which I had lately made for my lord the Treasurer for War, Maistre Jehan Groslier, Counsellor and Secretary to our Lord the King, lover of well-made letters and of all learned persons, by whom also he is much loved & esteemed on both this & the other side of the **mountains. And whilst thinking of this Attic Letter, there came of a sudden into my mem-**

10/11 Lying in my bed, on the morning of the Feast of Kings, when I had had my sleep and rest, & my stomach had readily digested its light and pleasant repast, in the year that was reckoned as MDXXIII, I fell to musing and set the wheel of my memory awhirl thinking on a thousand little conceits, some serious & some joyous, among which there came to my mind a certain Antique letter which I had lately made for my lord the Treasurer for War, Maistre Jehan Groslier, Counsellor and Secretary to our Lord the King, lover of well-made letters and of all learned persons, by whom also he is much loved & esteemed on both this & the other side of the mountains. And whilst thinking of this Attic Letter, there came of a sudden into my memory a pithy passage in the first book & eighth chapter of the DeOfficiis of Cicero, where it is written: Non nobis solum nati sumus; ortusque nostri partem patria vendicat, partem amici. Which is to say, in substance, that we are not born into this world for ourselves alone, but to

FRUTIGER* 57 CONDENSED WITH 67 BOLD CONDENSED   MERGENTHALER TYPE LIBRARY

12/13 Lying in my bed, on the morning of the Feast of Kings, when I had had my sleep and rest, & my stomach had readily digested its light and pleasant repast, in the year that was reckoned as MDXXIII, I fell to musing and set the wheel of my memory awhirl thinking on a thousand little conceits, some serious & some joyous, among which there came to my mind a certain Antique letter which I had lately made for my lord the Treasurer for War, Maistre Jehan Groslier, Counsellor and Secretary to our Lord the King, lover of well-made letters and of all learned persons, by whom also he is much loved & esteemed on both this & the

10/11 Lying in my bed, on the morning of the Feast of Kings, when I had had my sleep and rest, & my stomach had readily digested its light and pleasant repast, in the year that was reckoned as MDXXIII, I fell to musing and set the wheel of my memory awhirl thinking on a thousand little conceits, some serious & some joyous, among which there came to my mind a certain Antique letter which I had lately made for my lord the Treasurer for War, Maistre Jehan Groslier, Counsellor and Secretary to our Lord the King, lover of well-made letters and of all learned persons, by whom also he is much loved & esteemed on both this & the other side of the mountains. And whilst thinking of this Attic Letter, there came of a sudden into my memory a pithy passage in the first book & eighth chapter of the DeOfficiis of Cicero, where it is written: Non nobis solum

FRUTIGER* 77 BLACK CONDENSED WITH 87 EXTRA BLACK CONDENSED   MERGENTHALER TYPE LIBRARY

ABCDEFGHIJKLMNOPQRSTUVWXYZ&abcdefghijklmnopqrstuvwxyz1234567890$.,""'':;!?

FUTURA** LIGHT   MERGENTHALER TYPE LIBRARY

ABCDEFGHIJKLMNOPQRSTUVWXYZ&abcdefghijklmnopqrstuvwxyz1234567890$.,""'':;!?

FUTURA** LIGHT ITALIC   MERGENTHALER TYPE LIBRARY

ABCDEFGHIJKLMNOPQRSTUVWXYZ&abcdefghijklmnopqrstuvwxyz1234567890$.,""'':;!?

FUTURA** BOOK   MERGENTHALER TYPE LIBRARY

ABCDEFGHIJKLMNOPQRSTUVWXYZ&abcdefghijklmnopqrstuvwxyz1234567890$.,""'':;!?

FUTURA**BOOK ITALIC   MERGENTHALER TYPE LIBRARY

ABCDEFGHIJKLMNOPQRSTUVWXYZ&abcdefghijklmnopqrstuvwxyz1234567890$.,""'':;!?

FUTURA** MEDIUM   MERGENTHALER TYPE LIBRARY

ABCDEFGHIJKLMNOPQRSTUVWXYZ&abcdefghijklmnopqrstuvwxyz1234567890$.,""'':;!?

FUTURA** MEDIUM ITALIC   MERGENTHALER TYPE LIBRARY

SUPPLEMENTARY FACES 369

¹²⁄₁₃ The present popularity of the old style has encouraged French type-founders to revive other early printed forms, but they seem to regard the imitation of early manuscript forms as a reversion to barbarism and ugliness. But this imitation has been cleverly done by artists who have undertaken to make designs for book titles and book covers. Some have gone far beyond early typographic models, selecting the early Roman letter the plain capital without serif or hair line, with an almost absolute uniformity of thick line. Others have copied and exaggerated *the mannerisms of mediaeval copyists and engravers, with all their faults,*

¹⁰⁄₁₁ The present popularity of the old style has encouraged French type-founders to revive other early printed forms, but they seem to regard the imitation of early manuscript forms as a reversion to barbarism and ugliness. But this imitation has been cleverly done by artists who have undertaken to make designs for book titles and book covers. Some have gone far beyond early typographic models, selecting the early Roman letter the plain capital without serif or hair line, with an almost absolute uniformity of thick line. Others have copied and exaggerated the mannerisms of mediaeval copyists and engravers, with all their faults, bundling words together without proper relief between lines, dividing them by periods and not by spaces, until they are *almost unreadable. The closely huddled and carelessly formed letters of Botticelli and other early Italian*

FUTURA** LIGHT WITH LIGHT ITALIC   MERGENTHALER TYPE LIBRARY

¹²⁄₁₃ The present popularity of the old style has encouraged French type-founders to revive other early printed forms, but they seem to regard the imitation of early manuscript forms as a reversion to barbarism and ugliness. But this imitation has been cleverly done by artists who have undertaken to make designs for book titles and book covers. Some have gone far beyond early typographic models, selecting the early Roman letter the plain capital without serif or hair line, with an almost absolute uniformity of thick line. Others have *copied and exaggerated the mannerisms of mediaeval copyists and engravers, with*

¹⁰⁄₁₁ The present popularity of the old style has encouraged French type-founders to revive other early printed forms, but they seem to regard the imitation of early manuscript forms as a reversion to barbarism and ugliness. But this imitation has been cleverly done by artists who have undertaken to make designs for book titles and book covers. Some have gone far beyond early typographic models, selecting the early Roman letter the plain capital without serif or hair line, with an almost absolute uniformity of thick line. Others have copied and exaggerated the mannerisms of mediaeval copyists and engravers, with all their faults, bundling words together without proper relief between lines, dividing them by periods and not by spaces, *until they are almost unreadable. The closely huddled and carelessly formed letters of Botticelli and*

FUTURA** BOOK WITH BOOK ITALIC   MERGENTHALER TYPE LIBRARY

¹²⁄₁₃ The present popularity of the old style has encouraged French type-founders to revive other early printed forms, but they seem to regard the imitation of early manuscript forms as a reversion to barbarism and ugliness. But this imitation has been cleverly done by artists who have undertaken to make designs for book titles and book covers. Some have gone far beyond early typographic models, selecting the early Roman letter the plain capital without serif or hair line, with an almost absolute uniformity of thick line. Others have copied and exagge*rated the mannerisms of mediaeval copyists and engravers, with all their faults, bundling*

¹⁰⁄₁₁ The present popularity of the old style has encouraged French type-founders to revive other early printed forms, but they seem to regard the imitation of early manuscript forms as a reversion to barbarism and ugliness. But this imitation has been cleverly done by artists who have undertaken to make designs for book titles and book covers. Some have gone far beyond early typographic models, selecting the early Roman letter the plain capital without serif or hair line, with an almost absolute uniformity of thick line. Others have copied and exaggerated the mannerisms of mediaeval copyists and engravers, with all their faults, bundling words together without proper relief between lines, dividing them by periods and not by spaces, until they are almost unreadable. The closely huddled and *carelessly formed letters of Botticelli and other early Italian engravers are even preferred by many artists to*

FUTURA** MEDIUM WITH MEDIUM ITALIC   MERGENTHALER TYPE LIBRARY

ABCDEFGHIJKLMNOPQRSTUVWXYZ&abcdefghijklmnopqrstuvwxyz1234567890$.,"":;!?

FUTURA** HEAVY   MERGENTHALER TYPE LIBRARY

ABCDEFGHIJKLMNOPQRSTUVWXYZ&abcdefghijklmnopqrstuvwxyz1234567890$.,"":;!?

FUTURA** HEAVY ITALIC   MERGENTHALER TYPE LIBRARY

ABCDEFGHIJKLMNOPQRSTUVWXYZ&abcdefghijklmnopqrstuvwxyz1234567890$.,"":;!?

FUTURA** BOLD   MERGENTHALER TYPE LIBRARY

ABCDEFGHIJKLMNOPQRSTUVWXYZ&abcdefghijklmnopqrstuvwxyz1234567890$.,"":;!?

FUTURA**BOLD ITALIC   MERGENTHALER TYPE LIBRARY

ABCDEFGHIJKLMNOPQRSTUVWXYZ&abcdefghijklmnopqrstuvwxyz1234567890$.,"":;!?

FUTURA** EXTRA BLACK   MERGENTHALER TYPE LIBRARY

ABCDEFGHIJKLMNOPQRSTUVWXYZ&abcdefghijklmnopqrstuvwxyz1234567890$.,"":;!?

FUTURA** EXTRA BLACK ITALIC   MERGENTHALER TYPE LIBRARY

SUPPLEMENTARY FACES 371

12/13 The present popularity of the old style has encouraged French type-founders to revive other early printed forms, but they seem to regard the imitation of early manuscript forms as a reversion to barbarism and ugliness. But this imitation has been cleverly done by artists who have undertaken to make designs for book titles and book covers. Some have gone far beyond early typographic models, selecting the early Roman letter the plain capital without serif or hair line, with an almost absolute uniformity of thick line. Others have *copied and exaggerated the mannerisms of mediaeval copyists and engravers, with*

10/11 The present popularity of the old style has encouraged French type-founders to revive other early printed forms, but they seem to regard the imitation of early manuscript forms as a reversion to barbarism and ugliness. But this imitation has been cleverly done by artists who have undertaken to make designs for book titles and book covers. Some have gone far beyond early typographic models, selecting the early Roman letter the plain capital without serif or hair line, with an almost absolute uniformity of thick line. Others have copied and exaggerated the mannerisms of mediaeval copyists and engravers, with all their faults, bundling words together without proper relief between lines, dividing them by periods and not by spaces, *until they are almost unreadable. The closely huddled and carelessly formed letters of*

FUTURA** HEAVY WITH HEAVY ITALIC   MERGENTHALER TYPE LIBRARY

12/13 **The present popularity of the old style has encouraged French type-founders to revive other early printed forms, but they seem to regard the imitation of early manuscript forms as a reversion to barbarism and ugliness. But this imitation has been cleverly done by artists who have undertaken to make designs for book titles and book covers. Some have gone far beyond early typographic models, selecting the early Roman letter *the plain capital without serif or hair line, with an almost absolute***

10/11 **The present popularity of the old style has encouraged French type-founders to revive other early printed forms, but they seem to regard the imitation of early manuscript forms as a reversion to barbarism and ugliness. But this imitation has been cleverly done by artists who have undertaken to make designs for book titles and book covers. Some have gone far beyond early typographic models, selecting the early Roman letter the plain capital without serif or hair line, with an almost absolute uniformity of thick line. Others have copied and exaggerated the mannerisms of mediaeval copyists and engravers, with *all their faults, bundling words together without proper relief between lines, divid-***

FUTURA** BOLD WITH BOLD ITALIC   MERGENTHALER TYPE LIBRARY

12/13 **The present popularity of the old style has encouraged French type-founders to revive other early printed forms, but they seem to regard the imitation of early manuscript forms as a reversion to barbarism and ugliness. But this imitation has been cleverly done by artists who have undertaken to make designs for book titles and book covers. Some have gone far beyond early typographic models, selecting the early Roman letter the plain capital without serif *or hair line, with an almost absolute uniformity of thick line. Others have***

10/11 **The present popularity of the old style has encouraged French type-founders to revive other early printed forms, but they seem to regard the imitation of early manuscript forms as a reversion to barbarism and ugliness. But this imitation has been cleverly done by artists who have undertaken to make designs for book titles and book covers. Some have gone far beyond early typographic models, selecting the early Roman letter the plain capital without serif or hair line, with an almost absolute uniformity of thick line. Others have copied and exaggerated the mannerisms of mediaeval copyists and engravers, with all their faults, *bundling words together without proper relief between lines, dividing them by periods and***

FUTURA** EXTRA BLACK WITH EXTRA BLACK ITALIC   MERGENTHALER TYPE LIBRARY

ABCDEFGHIJKLMNOPQRSTUVWXYZ&abcdefghijklm
nopqrstuvwxyz1234567890$.,"":;!?

FUTURA LIGHT CONDENSED   MERGENTHALER TYPE LIBRARY

ABCDEFGHIJKLMNOPQRSTUVWXYZ&abcdef
ghijklmnopqrstuvwxyz1234567890$.,"":;!?

FUTURA MEDIUM CONDENSED   MERGENTHALER TYPE LIBRARY

ABCDEFGHIJKLMNOPQRSTUVWXYZ&abcdefg
hijklmnopqrstuvwxyz1234567890$.,"":;!?

FUTURA BOLD CONDENSED   MERGENTHALER TYPE LIBRARY

*ABCDEFGHIJKLMNOPQRSTUVWXYZ&abcdefgh
ijklmnopqrstuvwxyz1234567890$.,"":;!?*

FUTURA BOLD CONDENSED ITALIC   MERGENTHALER TYPE LIBRARY

ABCDEFGHIJKLMNOPQRSTUVWXYZ&abcdefg
hijklmnopqrstuvwxyz1234567890$.,"":;!?

FUTURA EXTRA BLACK CONDENSED   MERGENTHALER TYPE LIBRARY

*ABCDEFGHIJKLMNOPQRSTUVWXYZ&abcdefg
hijklmnopqrstuvwxyz1234567890$.,"":;
!?*

FUTURA EXTRA BLACK CONDENSED ITALIC   MERGENTHALER TYPE LIBRARY

12/13 The present popularity of the old style has encouraged French type-founders to revive other early printed forms, but they seem to regard the imitation of early manuscript forms as a reversion to barbarism and ugliness. But this imitation has been cleverly done by artists who have undertaken to make designs for book titles and book covers. Some have gone far beyond early typographic models, selecting the early Roman letter the plain capital without serif or hair line, with an almost absolute uniformity of thick line. Others have copied and exaggerated the mannerisms of mediaeval copyists and engravers, with all their faults, bundling words together without proper relief between lines, dividing them by periods and not by spaces, until they are almost unreadable. The closely huddled and carelessly formed letters of Botticelli and other early Italian engravers are even preferred by many artists to the simple, severe, and easily read letters of chiseled inscriptions on the stones of ancient Rome. There has been an

10/11 The present popularity of the old style has encouraged French type-founders to revive other early printed forms, but they seem to regard the imitation of early manuscript forms as a reversion to barbarism and ugliness. But this imitation has been cleverly done by artists who have undertaken to make designs for book titles and book covers. Some have gone far beyond early typographic models, selecting the early Roman letter the plain capital without serif or hair line, with an almost absolute uniformity of thick line. Others have copied and exaggerated the mannerisms of mediaeval copyists and engravers, with all their faults, bundling words together without proper relief between lines, dividing them by periods and not by spaces, until they are almost unreadable. The closely huddled and carelessly formed letters of Botticelli and other early Italian engravers are even preferred by many artists to the simple, severe, and easily read letters of chiseled inscriptions on the stones of ancient Rome. There has been an eccentric departure in another direction. Some designer has asked these questions: Why copy letter forms of any origin? Why should letters always of the same style?

As printing began to develop, punch cutters departed more and more from the manuscripts of their time. Fewer ligatures were empoyled; more

FUTURA** LIGHT CONDENSED WITH MEDIUM CONDENSED   MERGENTHALER TYPE LIBRARY

12/13 **The present popularity of the old style has encouraged French type-founders to revive other early printed forms, but they seem to regard the imitation of early manuscript forms as a reversion to barbarism and ugliness. But this imitation has been cleverly done by artists who have undertaken to make designs for book titles and book covers. Some have gone far beyond early typographic models, selecting the early Roman letter the plain capital without serif or hair line, with an almost absolute uniformity of thick line. Others have copied and exaggerated the mannerisms of mediaeval copyists and engravers, with all their faults, bundling words together without proper relief *between lines, dividing them by periods and not by spaces, until they are almost unreadable. The closely***

10/11 **The present popularity of the old style has encouraged French type-founders to revive other early printed forms, but they seem to regard the imitation of early manuscript forms as a reversion to barbarism and ugliness. But this imitation has been cleverly done by artists who have undertaken to make designs for book titles and book covers. Some have gone far beyond early typographic models, selecting the early Roman letter the plain capital without serif or hair line, with an almost absolute uniformity of thick line. Others have copied and exaggerated the mannerisms of mediaeval copyists and engravers, with all their faults, bundling words together without proper relief between lines, dividing them by periods and not by spaces, until they are almost unreadable. The closely huddled and carelessly formed letters of Botticelli and other early Italian engravers are even preferred by many artists to the simple, severe, and easily read *letters of chiseled inscriptions on the stones of ancient Rome. There has been an eccentric departure in another direction. Some designer***

FUTURA** BOLD CONDENSED WITH BOLD CONDENSED ITALIC   MERGENTHALER TYPE LIBRARY

12/13 **The present popularity of the old style has encouraged French type-founders to revive other early printed forms, but they seem to regard the imitation of early manuscript forms as a reversion to barbarism and ugliness. But this imitation has been cleverly done by artists who have undertaken to make designs for book titles and book covers. Some have gone far beyond early typographic models, selecting the early Roman letter the plain capital without serif or hair line, with an almost absolute uniformity of thick line. Others have copied and exaggerated the mannerisms of mediaeval *copyists and engravers, with all their faults, bundling words together without proper relief***

10/11 **The present popularity of the old style has encouraged French type-founders to revive other early printed forms, but they seem to regard the imitation of early manuscript forms as a reversion to barbarism and ugliness. But this imitation has been cleverly done by artists who have undertaken to make designs for book titles and book covers. Some have gone far beyond early typographic models, selecting the early Roman letter the plain capital without serif or hair line, with an almost absolute uniformity of thick line. Others have copied and exaggerated the mannerisms of mediaeval copyists and engravers, with all their faults, bundling words together without proper relief between lines, dividing them by periods and not by spaces, until they are almost unreadable. The closely huddled and carelessly formed letters of Botticelli and other early Italian engravers are even preferred by many artists to the simple, severe, and easily read letters**

FUTURA** EXTRA BLACK CONDENSED WITH EXTRA BLACK CONDENSED ITALIC   MERGENTHALER TYPE LIBRARY

ABCDEFGHIJKLMNOPQRSTUV
WXYZ&abcdefghijklmnopqrstuvwxy
z1234567890$.,""":;!?

ITC GALLIARD**   MERGENTHALER TYPE LIBRARY

*ABCDEFGHIJKLMNOPQRSTUVW
XYZ&abcdefghijklmnopqrstuvwxyz123
4567890$.,""":;!?*

ITC GALLIARD** ITALIC   MERGENTHALER TYPE LIBRARY

**ABCDEFGHIJKLMNOPQRSTUV
WXYZ&abcdefghijklmnopqrstuvwxy
z1234567890$.,""":;!?**

ITC GALLIARD** BOLD   MERGENTHALER TYPE LIBRARY

***ABCDEFGHIJKLMNOPQRSTUVW
XYZ&abcdefghijklmnopqrstuvwxyz1234
567890$.,""":;!?***

ITC GALLIARD** BOLD ITALIC   MERGENTHALER TYPE LIBRARY

**ABCDEFGHIJKLMNOPQRSTUV
WXYZ&abcdefghijklmnopqrstuvw
xyz1234567890$.,""":;!?**

ITC GALLIARD** BLACK   MERGENTHALER TYPE LIBRARY

***ABCDEFGHIJKLMNOPQRSTUV
WXYZ&abcdefghijklmnopqrstuvwxyz
1234567890$.,""":;!?***

ITC GALLIARD** BLACK ITALIC   MERGENTHALER TYPE LIBRARY

SUPPLEMENTARY FACES 375

12/13 Lying in my bed, on the morning of the Feast of Kings, when I had had my sleep and rest, & my stomach had readily digested its light and pleasant repast, in the year that was reckoned as MDXXIII, I fell to musing and set the wheel of my memory awhirl thinking on a thousand little conceits, some serious & some joyous, among which there came to my mind a certain Antique letter which I had lately made for my lord the Treasurer for War, Maistre Jehan Groslier, Counsellor and Secretary to our Lord the King, lover of well-made letters and of all learned persons, by whom also *he is much loved & esteemed on both this & the other side of the mountains. And whilst thinking*

10/11 Lying in my bed, on the morning of the Feast of Kings, when I had had my sleep and rest, & my stomach had readily digested its light and pleasant repast, in the year that was reckoned as MDXXIII, I fell to musing and set the wheel of my memory awhirl thinking on a thousand little conceits, some serious & some joyous, among which there came to my mind a certain Antique letter which I had lately made for my lord the Treasurer for War, Maistre Jehan Groslier, Counsellor and Secretary to our Lord the King, lover of well-made letters and of all learned persons, by whom also he is much loved & esteemed on both this & the other side of the mountains. And whilst thinking of this Attic Letter, there came of a sudden into my memory a pithy passage in the first book & eighth chapter of the DeOfficiis of Cicero, *where it is written: Non nobis solum nati sumus; ortusque nostri partem patria vendicat, partem amici.*

ITC GALLIARD** WITH ITALIC   MERGENTHALER TYPE LIBRARY

12/13 **Lying in my bed, on the morning of the Feast of Kings, when I had had my sleep and rest, & my stomach had readily digested its light and pleasant repast, in the year that was reckoned as MDXXIII, I fell to musing and set the wheel of my memory awhirl thinking on a thousand little conceits, some serious & some joyous, among which there came to my mind a certain Antique letter which I had lately made for my lord the Treasurer for War, Maistre Jehan Groslier, Counsellor and Secretary to our Lord the King, lover of well-made *letters and of all learned persons, by whom also he is much loved & esteemed on both this & the***

10/11 **Lying in my bed, on the morning of the Feast of Kings, when I had had my sleep and rest, & my stomach had readily digested its light and pleasant repast, in the year that was reckoned as MDXXIII, I fell to musing and set the wheel of my memory awhirl thinking on a thousand little conceits, some serious & some joyous, among which there came to my mind a certain Antique letter which I had lately made for my lord the Treasurer for War, Maistre Jehan Groslier, Counsellor and Secretary to our Lord the King, lover of well-made letters and of all learned persons, by whom also he is much loved & esteemed on both this & the other side of the mountains. And whilst thinking of this Attic Letter, there came of a sudden into my memory a pithy passage in *the first book & eighth chapter of the DeOfficiis of Cicero, where it is written: Non nobis solum nati***

ITC GALLIARD** BOLD WITH BOLD ITALIC   MERGENTHALER TYPE LIBRARY

12/13 **Lying in my bed, on the morning of the Feast of Kings, when I had had my sleep and rest, & my stomach had readily digested its light and pleasant repast, in the year that was reckoned as MDXXIII, I fell to musing and set the wheel of my memory awhirl thinking on a thousand little conceits, some serious & some joyous, among which there came to my mind a certain Antique letter which I had lately made for my lord the Treasurer for War, Maistre Jehan Groslier, Counsellor and Secretary to our Lord the King, lover *of well-made letters and of all learned persons, by whom also he is much loved & es-***

10/11 **Lying in my bed, on the morning of the Feast of Kings, when I had had my sleep and rest, & my stomach had readily digested its light and pleasant repast, in the year that was reckoned as MDXIII, I fell to musing and set the wheel of my memory awhirl thinking on a thousand little conceits, some serious & some joyous, among which there came to my mind a certain Antique letter which I had lately made for my lord the Treasurer for War, Maistre Jehan Groslier, Counsellor and Secretary to our Lord the King, lover of well-made letters and of all learned persons, by whom also he is much loved & esteemed on both this & the other side of the mountains. And whilst thinking of this Attic Letter, there came of a sud-*den into my memory a pithy passage in the first book & eighth chapter of the DeOfficiis of Cicero, where it***

ITC GALLIARD** BLACK WITH BLACK ITALIC   MERGENTHALER TYPE LIBRARY

SUPPLEMENTARY FACES

ABCDEFGHIJKLMNOPQRSTU
VWXYZ&abcdefghijklmnopqrstu
vwxyz1234567890$.,""'':;!?

ITC GALLIARD** ULTRA   MERGENTHALER TYPE LIBRARY

*ABCDEFGHIJKLMNOPQRSTU
VWXYZ&abcdefghijklmnopqrstuv
wxyz1234567890$.,""'':;!?*

ITC GALLIARD** ULTRA ITALIC   MERGENTHALER TYPE LIBRARY

ABCDEFGHIJKLMNOPQRSTUVW
XYZ&abcdefghijklmnopqrstuvwxyz12
34567890$.,""'':;!?

SIMONCINI GARAMOND**   MERGENTHALER TYPE LIBRARY

*ABCDEFGHIJKLMNOPQRSTUVWX
YZ&abcdefghijklmnopqrstuvwxyz12345
67890$.,""'':;!?*

SIMONCINI GARAMOND** ITALIC   MERGENTHALER TYPE LIBRARY

ABCDEFGHIJKLMNOPQRSTUVWXYZ&abc
defghijklmnopqrstuvwxyz1234567890$.
,""'':;!?

ITC GARAMOND** ULTRA CONDENSED   MERGENTHALER TYPE LIBRARY

*ABCDEFGHIJKLMNOPQRSTUVWXYZ&ab
cdefghijklmnopqrstuvwxyz123456789
0$.,""'':;!?*

ITC GARAMOND** ULTRA CONDENSED ITALIC   MERGENTHALER TYPE LIBRARY

12/13 **Lying in my bed, on the morning of the Feast of Kings, when I had had my sleep and rest, & my stomach had readily digested its light and pleasant repast, in the year that was reckoned as MDXXIII, I fell to musing and set the wheel of my memory awhirl thinking on a thousand little conceits, some serious & some joyous, among which there came to my mind a certain Antique letter which I had lately made for my lord the Treasurer for War, Maistre Jehan Groslier, Counsellor and Secretary to our Lord the King, lover of well-made letters and of all**

10/11 **Lying in my bed, on the morning of the Feast of Kings, when I had had my sleep and rest, & my stomach had readily digested its light and pleasant repast, in the year that was reckoned as MDXXIII, I fell to musing and set the wheel of my memory awhirl thinking on a thousand little conceits, some serious & some joyous, among which there came to my mind a certain Antique letter which I had lately made for my lord the Treasurer for War, Maistre Jehan Groslier, Counsellor and Secretary to our Lord the King, lover of well-made letters and of all learned persons, by whom also he is much loved & esteemed on both this & the other side of the mountains. And whilst thinking of this *Attic Letter, there came of a sudden into my memory a pithy passage in the first book & eighth***

ITC GALLIARD** ULTRA WITH ULTRA ITALIC   MERGENTHALER TYPE LIBRARY

12/13 The present popularity of the old style has encouraged French type-founders to revive other early printed forms, but they seem to regard the imitation of early manuscript forms as a reversion to barbarism and ugliness. But this imitation has been cleverly done by artists who have undertaken to make designs for book titles and book covers. Some have gone far beyond early typographic models, selecting the early Roman letter the plain capital without serif or hair line, with an almost absolute uniformity of thick line. Others have copied and exaggerated the mannerisms of mediaeval *copyists and engravers, with all their faults, bundling words together without proper relief be-*

10/11 The present popularity of the old style has encouraged French type-founders to revive other early printed forms, but they seem to regard the imitation of early manuscript forms as a reversion to barbarism and ugliness. But this imitation has been cleverly done by artists who have undertaken to make designs for book titles and book covers. Some have gone far beyond early typographic models, selecting the early Roman letter the plain capital without serif or hair line, with an almost absolute uniformity of thick line. Others have copied and exaggerated the mannerisms of mediaeval copyists and engravers, with all their faults, bundling words together without proper relief between lines, dividing them by periods and not by spaces, until they are almost unreadable. The closely huddled and carelessly formed letters of *Botticelli and other early Italian engravers are even preferred by many artists to the simple, severe, and easily read*

SIMONCINI GARAMOND** WITH ITALIC   MERGENTHALER TYPE LIBRARY

12/13 From a letter by Benjamin Franklin to Noah Webster dated Dec. 26, 1789:

In examining the English Books, that were printed between the Restoration and the Accession of George the 2d, we may observe, that all *Substantives* were begun with a capital, in which we imitated our Mother Tongue, the German. This was more particularly useful to those, who were not well acquainted with the English; there being such a prodigious Number of our Words, that are both *Verbs* and *Substantives,* and spelt in the same manner, tho' often accented differently in Pronunciation.

This Method has, by the Fancy of Printers, of late Years been laid aside, from an Idea,

10/11 From a letter by Benjamin Franklin to Noah Webster dated Dec. 26, 1789:

In examining the English Books, that were printed between the Restoration and the Accession of George the 2d, we may observe, that all *Substantives* were begun with a capital, in which we imitated our Mother Tongue, the German. This was more particularly useful to those, who were not well acquainted with the English; there being such a prodigious Number of our Words, that are both *Verbs* and *Substantives,* and spelt in the same manner, tho' often accented differently in Pronunciation.

This Method has, by the Fancy of Printers, of late Years been laid aside, from an Idea, that suppressing the Capitals shows the Character to greater Advantage; those Letters prominent above the line disturbing its *even regular Appearance. The Effect of this Change is so considerable, that a learned Man of France, who*

ITC GARAMOND** ULTRA CONDENSED WITH ITALIC   MERGENTHALER TYPE LIBRARY

ABCDEFGHIJKLMNOPQRSTUVWXYZ& abcdefghijklmnopqrstuvwxyz1234567890$.,""'':;!?

ADOBE GARAMOND™ REGULAR   ADOBE TYPE LIBRARY

ABCDEFGHIJKLMNOPQRSTUVWXYZ& abcdefghijklmnopqrstuvwxyz1234567890$.,""'':;!?

ADOBE GARAMOND ITALIC   ADOBE TYPE LIBRARY

ABCDEFGHIJKLMNOPQRSTUVWXYZ& abcdefghijklmnopqrstuvwxyz1234567890$.,""'':;!?

ADOBE GARAMOND SEMIBOLD   ADOBE TYPE LIBRARY

ABCDEFGHIJKLMNOPQRSTUVWXYZ& abcdefghijklmnopqrstuvwxyz1234567890$.,""'':;!?

ADOBE GARAMOND SEMIBOLD ITALIC   ADOBE TYPE LIBRARY

ABCDEFGHIJKLMNOPQRSTUVWXYZ& abcdefghijklmnopqrstuvwxyz1234567890$.,""'':;!?

ADOBE GARAMOND BOLD   ADOBE TYPE LIBRARY

ABCDEFGHIJKLMNOPQRSTUVWXYZ& abcdefghijklmnopqrstuvwxyz1234567890$.,""'':;!?

ADOBE GARAMOND BOLD ITALIC   ADOBE TYPE LIBRARY

SUPPLEMENTARY FACES 379

12/13 In considering fine and praiseworthy inventions, we must freely confess that printing has been and is to-day the best and most estimable—the invention by means of which two persons turning the press can get a greater number of books in a day than formerly could have been transcribed by several persons in a year. It is claimed that this art was invented at Mainz, a city of Germany, in the year 1442 by Jean Guttemberg, or, according to others, Guttenberg, an honorable German chevalier. It was at Mainz that after experimenting with an ink which is used by printers to-day, he first began the practice of the art. *Some persons prefer to attribute the invention to Jean Fauste and Yues Scheffey two years earlier, holding that Guttem-*

10/11 In considering fine and praiseworthy inventions, we must freely confess that printing has been and is to-day the best and most estimable—the invention by means of which two persons turning the press can get a greater number of books in a day than formerly could have been transcribed by several persons in a year. It is claimed that this art was invented at Mainz, a city of Germany, in the year 1442 by Jean Guttemberg, or, according to others, Guttenberg, an honorable German chevalier. It was at Mainz that after experimenting with an ink which is used by printers to-day, he first began the practice of the art. Some persons prefer to attribute the invention to Jean Fauste and Yues Scheffey two years earlier, holding that our Guttemberg, Jean Mentel, Jean Prus, Adolphe Rusche, Pierre Scheffec, Martin Flache, Huldric Han, Jean Froben, Adam Petri, Thomas Vuolffe, *and, others added improvements and spread the art of printing through all Germany and other countries. In fact Conrad*

ADOBE GARAMOND REGULAR WITH ITALIC   ADOBE TYPE LIBRARY

12/13 **In considering fine and praiseworthy inventions, we must freely confess that printing has been and is to-day the best and most estimable—the invention by means of which two persons turning the press can get a greater number of books in a day than formerly could have been transcribed by several persons in a year. It is claimed that this art was invented at Mainz, a city of Germany, in the year 1442 by Jean Guttemberg, or, according to others, Guttenberg, an honorable German chevalier. It was at Mainz that after experimenting with an ink which is used by printers to-day, he first began the practice of the art.** *Some persons prefer to attribute the invention to Jean Fauste and Yues Scheffey two years earlier,*

10/11 **In considering fine and praiseworthy inventions, we must freely confess that printing has been and is to-day the best and most estimable—the invention by means of which two persons turning the press can get a greater number of books in a day than formerly could have been transcribed by several persons in a year. It is claimed that this art was invented at Mainz, a city of Germany, in the year 1442 by Jean Guttemberg, or, according to others, Guttenberg, an honorable German chevalier. It was at Mainz that after experimenting with an ink which is used by printers to-day, he first began the practice of the art. Some persons prefer to attribute the invention to Jean Fauste and Yues Scheffey two years earlier, holding that our Guttemberg, Jean Mentel, Jean Prus, Adolphe Rusche, Pierre Scheffec, Martin Flache, Huldric Han, Jean Froben, Adam Petri,** *Thomas Vuolffe, and, and many others added improvements and spread the art of printing through all Germany*

ADOBE GARAMOND SEMIBOLD WITH ITALIC   ADOBE TYPE LIBRARY

12/13 **In considering fine and praiseworthy inventions, we must freely confess that printing has been and is to-day the best and most estimable—the invention by means of which two persons turning the press can get a greater number of books in a day than formerly could have been transcribed by several persons in a year. It is claimed that this art was invented at Mainz, a city of Germany, in the year 1442 by Jean Guttemberg, or, according to others, Guttenberg, an honorable German chevalier. It was at Mainz that after experimenting with an ink which is used by printers to-day, he first began the practice of the art.** *Some persons prefer to attribute the invention to Jean Fauste and Yues Scheffey two years earlier,*

10/11 **In considering fine and praiseworthy inventions, we must freely confess that printing has been and is to-day the best and most estimable—the invention be means of which two persons turning the press can get a transcribed by several persons in a year. It is claimed that this art was invented at Mainz, a city of Germany, in the year 1442 by Jean Guttemberg, or, according to others, Guttenberg, an honorable German chevalier. It was at Mainz that after experimenting with an ink which is used by printers to-day, he first began the practice of the art. Some persons prefer to attribute the invention to Jean Fauste & Yues Scheffey two years earlier, holding that our Guttemberg, Jean Mentel, Jean Prus, Adolphe Rusche, Pierre Scheffec, Martin Flache, Huldric Han, Jean Froben, Adam Petri, Thomas Vuolffe, and others** *added improvements and spread the practised the art at Rome about the year 1400. In the beginning the technique*

ADOBE GARAMOND BOLD WITH ITALIC   ADOBE TYPE LIBRARY

ABCDEFGHIJKLMNOPQRSTUVWXYZ&abcdefghijklmnopqrstuvwxyz1234567890$.,''"":;!?

GARTH GRAPHIC   AGFA COMPUGRAPHIC TYPE LIBRARY

ABCDEFGHIJKLMNOPQRSTUVWXYZ&abcdefghijklmnopqrstuvwxyz1234567890$.,''"":;!?

GARTH GRAPHIC ITALIC   AGFA COMPUGRAPHIC TYPE LIBRARY

ABCDEFGHIJKLMNOPQRSTUVWXYZ&abcdefghijklmnopqrstuvwxyz1234567890$.,''"":;!?

GARTH GRAPHIC BOLD   AGFA COMPUGRAPHIC TYPE LIBRARY

ABCDEFGHIJKLMNOPQRSTUVWXYZ&abcdefghijklmnopqrstuvwxyz1234567890$.,''"":;!?

GARTH GRAPHIC BOLD ITALIC   AGFA COMPUGRAPHIC TYPE LIBRARY

ABCDEFGHIJKLMNOPQRSTUVWXYZ&abcdefghijklmnopqrstuvwxyz1234567890$.,''"":;!?

GARTH GRAPHIC EXTRA BOLD   AGFA COMPUGRAPHIC TYPE LIBRARY

ABCDEFGHIJKLMNOPQRSTUVWXYZ&abcdefghijklmnopqrstuvwxyz1234567890$.,''"":;!?

GARTH GRAPHIC BLACK   AGFA COMPUGRAPHIC TYPE LIBRARY

SUPPLEMENTARY FACES 381

12/13 It is still a matter of conjecture whether Johann Gutenberg was the first to conceive the principle of casting moveable [i.e., separate] metal types which he could arrange in words and sentences so that he could impress their faces on paper. There is, however, hardly a doubt, judging at least from the evidence available, that he was the first to make practical use of the idea, and that it is do to his ingenious application of it that the profound art of typography was born. Whether he cast his letters in molds of sand or in metal matrices, is a question *not really material at this time; it is the far-reaching results of his inspiration that most*

10/11 It is still a matter of conjecture whether Johann Gutenberg was the first to conceive the principle of casting moveable [i.e., separate] metal types which he could arrange in words and sentences so that he could impress their faces on paper. There is, however, hardly a doubt, judging at least from the evidence available, that he was the first to make practical use of the idea, and that it is do to his ingenious application of it that the profound art of typography was born. Whether he cast his letters in molds of sand or in metal matrices, is a question not really material at this time; it is the far-reaching results of his inspiration that most concern us in this discussion. It seems quite probable that Gutenberg at first had little more in mind than a desire to find *some expedient by which to supplement with explanatory text the illustrations cut on wood blocks--some method*

GARTH GRAPHIC WITH ITALIC   AGFA COMPUGRAPHIC TYPE LIBRARY

12/13 **It is still a matter of conjecture whether Johann Gutenberg was the first to conceive the principle of casting moveable [i.e., separate] metal types which he could arrange in words and sentences so that he could impress their faces on paper. There is, however, hardly a doubt, judging at least from the evidence available, that he was the first to make practical use of the idea, and that it is do to his in genious application of it that the profound art of typography was born. Whether he cast his letters in molds of sand or in metal matrices, is a question not really material**

10/11 **It is still a matter of conjecture whether Johann Gutenberg was the first to conceive the principle of casting moveable [i.e., separate] metal types which he could arrange in words and sentences so that he could impress their faces on paper. There is, however, hardly a doubt, judging at least from the evidence available, that he was the first to make practical use of the idea, and that it is do to his ingenious application of it that the profound art of typography was born. Whether he cast his letters in molds of sand or in metal matrices, is a question not really material at this time; it is the far-reaching results of his inspiration that most concern us in this discussion. It seems *quite probable that Gutenberg at first had little more in mind than a desire to find some exped-***

GARTH GRAPHIC BOLD WITH BOLD ITALIC   AGFA COMPUGRAPHIC TYPE LIBRARY

12/13 **It is still a matter of conjecture whether Johann Gutenberg was the first to conceive the principle of casting moveable [i.e., separate] metal types which he could arrange in words and sentences so that he could impress their faces on paper. There is, however, hardly a doubt, judging at least from the evidence available, that he was the first to make practical use of the idea, and that it is do to his in genious application of it that the profound art of typography was born. Whether he cast his letters in molds of sand or in metal matrices, is a**

10/11 **It is still a matter of conjecture whether Johann Gutenberg was the first to conceive the principle of casting moveable [i.e., separate] metal types which he could arrange in words and sentences so that he could impress their faces on paper. There is, however, hardly a doubt, judging at least from the evidence available, that he was the first to make practical use of the idea, and that it is do to his ingenious application of it that the profound art of typography was born. Whether he cast his letters in molds of sand or in metal matrices, is a question not really material at this time; it is the far-reaching results of his inspiration that most concern us in this discussion. It seems quite probable that Gutenberg at first had little more**

GARTH GRAPHIC EXTRA BOLD WITH BLACK   AGFA COMPUGRAPHIC TYPE LIBRARY

SUPPLEMENTARY FACES

ABCDEFGHIJKLMNOPQRSTUVWXYZ&abcdefghijklmnopqrstuvwxyz1234567890$.,''"":;!?

GOUDY OLD STYLE   MERGENTHALER TYPE LIBRARY

ABCDEFGHIJKLMNOPQRSTUVWXYZ&abcdefghijklmnopqrstuvwxyz1234567890$.,''"":;!?

GOUDY OLD STYLE ITALIC   MERGENTHALER TYPE LIBRARY

ABCDEFGHIJKLMNOPQRSTUVWXYZ&abcdefghijklmnopqrstuvwxyz1234567890$.,''"":;!?

GOUDY BOLD   MERGENTHALER TYPE LIBRARY

ABCDEFGHIJKLMNOPQRSTUVWXYZ&abcdefghijklmnopqrstuvwxyz1234567890$.,''"":;!?

GOUDY BOLD ITALIC   MERGENTHALER TYPE LIBRARY

ABCDEFGHIJKLMNOPQRSTUVWXYZ&abcdefghijklmnopqrstuvwxyz1234567890$.,''"":;!?

GOUDY HEAVYFACE   MERGENTHALER TYPE LIBRARY

ABCDEFGHIJKLMNOPQRSTUVWXYZ&abcdefghijklmnopqrstuvwxyz1234567890$.,''"":;!?

GOUDY HEAVYFACE ITALIC   MERGENTHALER TYPE LIBRARY

SUPPLEMENTARY FACES 383

12/13 Now, since architects, painters & others at times are wont to set an inscription on lofty walls, it will make for the merit of the work that they form the letters correctly. Accordingly I am minded here to treat briefly of this. And first I will give rules for a Latin Alphabet, and then for one of our common Text: since it is of these two sorts of letters we customarily make use in such work; and first, for the Roman letters: Draw for each a square of uniform size, in which the letter is to be contained. But when you draw in it the heavier limb of the letter, make this of the width of a tenth part of the square, and the lighter a *third as wide as the heavier: to follow this rule for all letters of the Alphabet.*

10/11 Now, since architects, painters & others at times are wont to set an inscription on lofty walls, it will make for the merit of the work that they form the letters correctly. Accordingly I am minded here to treat briefly of this. And first I will give rules for a Latin Alphabet, and then for one of our common Text: since it is of these two sorts of letters we customarily make use in such work; and first, for the Roman letters: Draw for each a square of uniform size, in which the letter is to be contained. But when you draw in it the heavier limb of the letter, make this of the width of a tenth part of the square, and the lighter a third as wide as the heavier: to follow this rule for all letters of the Alphabet.

First, make an A after this fashion: Indicate the angles of the square by the letters a. b. c. d. (and so do for all the *rest of the letters): then divide the square by two lines bisecting one another at right angles — the vertical e. f. the horizontal*

GOUDY OLD STYLE WITH ITALIC   MERGENTHALER TYPE LIBRARY

12/13 Now, since architects, painters & others at times are wont to set an inscription on lofty walls, it will make for the merit of the work that they form the letters correctly. Accordingly I am minded here to treat briefly of this. And first I will give rules for a Latin Alphabet, and then for one of our common Text: since it is of these two sorts of letters we customarily make use in such work; and first, for the Roman letters: Draw for each a square of uniform size, in which the letter is to be contained. But when you draw in it the heavier limb of the letter, make this of the width of a tenth part of *the square, and the lighter a third as wide as the heavier: to follow this rule for all letters of*

10/11 Now, since architects, painters & others at times are wont to set an inscription on lofty walls, it will make for the merit of the work that they form the letters correctly. Accordingly I am minded here to treat briefly of this. And first I will give rules for a Latin Alphabet, and then for one of our common Text: since it is of these two sorts of letters we customarily make use in such work; and first, for the Roman letters: Draw for each a square of uniform size, in which the letter is to be contained. But when you draw in it the heavier limb of the letter, make this of the width of a tenth part of the square, and the lighter a third as wide as the heavier: to follow this rule for all letters of the Alphabet.

First, make an A after this fashion: Indicate the angles of the square by the letters a. b. c. d. (and so do for *all the rest of the letters): then divide the square by two lines bisecting one another at right angles — the vertical*

GOUDY BOLD WITH BOLD ITALIC   MERGENTHALER TYPE LIBRARY

12/13 **Now, since architects, painters & others at times are wont to set an inscription on lofty walls, it will make for the merit of the work that they form the letters correctly. Accordingly I am minded here to treat briefly of this. And first I will give rules for a Latin Alphabet, and then for one of our common Text: since it is of these two sorts of letters we customarily make use in such work; and first, for the Roman letters: Draw for each a square of uniform size, in which the letter is to be contained. But when you draw**

10/11 **Now, since architects, painters & others at times are wont to set an inscription on lofty walls, it will make for the merit of the work that they form the letters correctly. Accordingly I am minded here to treat briefly of this. And first I will give rules for a Latin Alphabet, and then for one of our common Text: since it is of these two sorts of letters we customarily make use in such work; and first, for the Roman letters: Draw for each a square of uniform size, in which the letter is to be contained. But when you draw in it the heavier limb of the letter, make this of the width of a tenth part of the square, and the lighter a *third as wide as the heavier: to follow this rule for all letters of the Alphabet.***

GOUDY HEAVYFACE WITH ITALIC   MERGENTHALER TYPE LIBRARY

ABCDEFGHIJKLMNOPQRSTUVWXYZ&
abcdefghijklmnopqrstuvwxyz
1234567890$.,''"":;!?

MONOTYPE GOUDY SANS LIGHT   AGFA COMPUGRAPHIC TYPE LIBRARY

ABCDEFGHIJKLMNOPQRSTUVWXYZ&
abcdefghijklmnopqrstuvwxyz
1234567890$.,''"":;!?

MONOTYPE GOUDY SANS LIGHT ITALIC   AGFA COMPUGRAPHIC TYPE LIBRARY

ABCDEFGHIJKLMNOPQRSTUVWXYZ&
abcdefghijklmnopqrstuvwxyz
1234567890$.,''"":;!?

MONOTYPE GOUDY SANS MEDIUM   AGFA COMPUGRAPHIC TYPE LIBRARY

ABCDEFGHIJKLMNOPQRSTUVWXYZ&
abcdefghijklmnopqrstuvwxyz
1234567890$.,''"":;!?

MONOTYPE GOUDY SANS MEDIUM ITALIC   AGFA COMPUGRAPHIC TYPE LIBRARY

ABCDEFGHIJKLMNOPQRSTUVWXYZ
&abcdefghijklmnopqrstuvwxyz
1234567890$.,''"":;!?

MONOTYPE GOUDY SANS BOLD   AGFA COMPUGRAPHIC TYPE LIBRARY

ABCDEFGHIJKLMNOPQRSTUVWXY
Z&abcdefghijklmnopqrstuvwxyz
1234567890$.,''"":;!?

MONOTYPE GOUDY SANS EXTRA BOLD   AGFA COMPUGRAPHIC TYPE LIBRARY

SUPPLEMENTARY FACES 385

12/13 The history of the Dutch book is famous. In the Middle Ages the art of the scribes and miniaturists flourished in the Netherlands to such a degree that their manuscripts are not considered inferior to the finest specimens of Italian and French origin; the Dutch incunabula are, especially by their woodcut illustrations, hardly surpassed, only equalled by Italian work. In the 17th century Holland regained a leading position in this sphere and the prints of Elzevir enjoy at present a world-wide fame. And although our books lack the grandeur of Italian manuscripts, the delicate grace of a French impression (nor does the Dutch incunabulum display the pompous style of a Gutenberg or Schoeffer work), they have undoubtedly a distinct

12/13 The history of the Dutch book is famous. In the Middle Ages the art of the scribes and miniaturists flourished in the Netherlands to such a degree that their manuscripts are not considered inferior to the finest specimens of Italian and French origin; the Dutch incunabula are, especially by their woodcut illustrations, hardly surpassed, only equalled by Italian work. In the 17th century Holland regained a leading position in this sphere and the prints of Elzevir enjoy at present a world-wide fame. And although our books lack the grandeur of Italian manuscripts, the delicate grace of a French impression (nor does the Dutch incunabulum display the pompous style of a Gutenberg or Schoeffer work), they have undoubtedly a distinct character of their own, which bears the stamp of true art. They exhibit their inmost artistic value only to the devout contemplator. We might parallel with the art of painting, especially of the Middle Ages: there, too, the Dutchman is more reserved; his work

MONOTYPE GOUDY SANS LIGHT WITH LIGHT ITALIC   AGFA COMPUGRAPHIC TYPE LIBRARY

12/13 The history of the Dutch book is famous. In the Middle Ages the art of the scribes and miniaturists flourished in the Netherlands to such a degree that their manuscripts are not considered inferior to the finest specimens of Italian and French origin; the Dutch incunabula are, especially by their woodcut illustrations, hardly surpassed, only equalled by Italian work. In the 17th century Holland regained a leading position in this sphere and the prints of Elzevir enjoy at present a world-wide fame. And although our books lack the grandeur of Italian manuscripts, the delicate grace of a French impression (nor does the Dutch incunabulum display the pompous style of a Gutenberg or Schoeffer

12/13 The history of the Dutch book is famous. In the Middle Ages the art of the scribes and miniaturists flourished in the Netherlands to such a degree that their manuscripts are not considered inferior to the finest specimens of Italian and French origin; the Dutch incunabula are, especially by their woodcut illustrations, hardly surpassed, only equalled by Italian work. In the 17th century Holland regained a leading position in this sphere and the prints of Elzevir enjoy at present a world-wide fame. And although our books lack the grandeur of Italian manuscripts, the delicate grace of a French impression (nor does the Dutch incunabulum display the pompous style of a Gutenberg or Schoeffer work), they have undoubtedly a distinct character of their own, which bears the stamp of true art. They exhibit their inmost artistic value only to the devout contemplator. We might parallel with the art of painting, especially of the Middle Ages:

MONOTYPE GOUDY SANS MEDIUM WITH MEDIUM ITALIC   AGFA COMPUGRAPHIC TYPE LIBRARY

12/13 **The history of the Dutch book is famous. In the Middle Ages the art of the scribes and miniaturists flourished in the Netherlands to such a degree that their manuscripts are not considered inferior to the finest specimens of Italian and French origin; the Dutch incunabula are, especially by their woodcut illustrations, hardly surpassed, only equalled by Italian work. In the 17th century Holland regained a leading position in this sphere and the prints of Elzevir enjoy at present a world-wide fame. And although our books lack the grandeur of Italian manuscripts, the delicate grace of a French impression (nor does the Dutch**

12/13 **The history of the Dutch book is famous. In the Middle Ages the art of the scribes and miniaturists flourished in the Netherlands to such a degree that their manuscripts are not considered inferior to the finest specimens of Italian and French origin; the Dutch incunabula are, especially by their woodcut illustrations, hardly surpassed, only equalled by Italian work. In the 17th century Holland regained a leading position in this sphere and the prints of Elzevir enjoy at present a world-wide fame. And although our books lack the grandeur of Italian manuscripts, the delicate grace of a French impression (nor does the Dutch incunabulum display the pompous style of a Gutenberg or Schoeffer work), they have undoubtedly a distinct character of their own, which bears the stamp of true art. They exhibit their inmost artistic value only to the**

MONOTYPE GOUDY SANS BOLD WITH EXTRA BOLD   AGFA COMPUGRAPHIC TYPE LIBRARY

ABCDEFGHIJKLMNOPQRSTUVWX
YZ&abcdefghijklmnopqrstuvwxyz123456
7890$.,""":;!?

GRANJON* MERGENTHALER TYPE LIBRARY

*ABCDEFGHIJKLMNOPQRSTUVWXYZ
&abcdefghijklmnopqrstuvwxyz1234567890$
.,""":;!?*

GRANJON* ITALIC MERGENTHALER TYPE LIBRARY

ABCDEFGHIJKLMNOPQRSTUVWXYZ&abcd
efghijklmnopqrstuvwxyz1234567890$.,""":;!?

HARRY** THIN MERGENTHALER TYPE LIBRARY

ABCDEFGHIJKLMNOPQRSTUVWXYZ&abcdef
ghijklmnopqrstuvwxyz1234567890$.,""":;!?

HARRY** PLAIN MERGENTHALER TYPE LIBRARY

ABCDEFGHIJKLMNOPQRSTUVWXYZ&abc
defghijklmnopqrstuvwxyz1234567890$.,
""":;!?

HARRY** HEAVY MERGENTHALER TYPE LIBRARY

ABCDEFGHIJKLMNOPQRSTUVWXYZ&ab
cdefghijklmnopqrstuvwxyz1234567890$
.,""":;!?

HARRY** FAT MERGENTHALER TYPE LIBRARY

SUPPLEMENTARY FACES 387

12/13 **The present popularity of the old style has encouraged French type-founders to revive other** early printed forms, but they seem to regard the imitation of early manuscript forms as a reversion to barbarism and ugliness. But this imitation has been cleverly done by artists who have undertaken to make designs for book titles and book covers. Some have gone far beyond early typographic models, selecting the early Roman letter the plain capital without serif or hair line, with an almost absolute uniformity of thick line. Others have copied and exaggerated the mannerisms of mediaeval copyists and engravers, with all their *faults, bundling words together without proper relief between lines, dividing them by periods and not by*

10/11 The present popularity of the old style has encouraged French type-founders to revive other early printed forms, but they seem to regard the imitation of early manuscript forms as a reversion to barbarism and ugliness. But this imitation has been cleverly done by artists who have undertaken to make designs for book titles and book covers. Some have gone far beyond early typographic models, selecting the early Roman letter the plain capital without serif or hair line, with an almost absolute uniformity of thick line. Others have copied and exaggerated the mannerisms of mediaeval copyists and engravers, with all their faults, bundling words together without proper relief between lines, dividing them by periods and not by spaces, until they are almost unreadable. The closely huddled and carelessly formed letters of Botticelli and other early Italian engravers *are even preferred by many artists to the simple, severe, and easily read letters of chiseled inscriptions on the stones of ancient*

GRANJON* WITH ITALIC AND BOLD   MERGENTHALER TYPE LIBRARY

12/13 The present popularity of the old style has encouraged French type-founders to revive other early printed forms, but they seem to regard the imitation of early manuscript forms as a reversion to barbarism and ugliness. But this imitation has been cleverly done by artists who have undertaken to make designs for book titles and book covers. Some have gone far beyond early typographic models, selecting the early Roman letter the plain capital without serif or hair line, with an almost absolute uniformity of thick line. Others have copied and exaggerated the mannerisms of mediaeval copyists and engravers, with all their faults, bundling words together without proper **relief between lines, dividing them by periods and not by spaces, until they are almost unreadable.**

10/11 The present popularity of the old style has encouraged French type-founders to revive other early printed forms, but they seem to regard the imitation of early manuscript forms as a reversion to barbarism and ugliness. But this imitation has been cleverly done by artists who have undertaken to make designs for book titles and book covers. Some have gone far beyond early typographic models, selecting the early Roman letter the plain capital without serif or hair line, with an almost absolute uniformity of thick line. Others have copied and exaggerated the mannerisms of mediaeval copyists and engravers, with all their faults, bundling words together without proper relief between lines, dividing them by periods and not by spaces, until they are almost unreadable. The closely huddled and carelessly formed letters of Botticelli and other early Italian engravers are even preferred by many artists to the simple, severe, and easily read letters of chiseled inscriptions on the stones of ancient Rome. There has been an eccentric departure in another direction.

HARRY** THIN WITH PLAIN   MERGENTHALER TYPE LIBRARY

12/13 **The present popularity of the old style has encouraged French type-founders to revive other early printed forms, but they seem to regard the imitation of early manuscript forms as a reversion to barbarism and ugliness. But this imitation has been cleverly done by artists who have undertaken to make designs for book titles and book covers. Some have gone far beyond early typographic models, selecting the early Roman letter the plain capital without serif or hair line, with an almost absolute uniformity of thick line. Others have copied and exaggerated the mannerisms of mediaeval copyists and engravers, with all their faults, bundling words together without proper relief between lines, dividing them by periods**

10/11 The present popularity of the old style has encouraged French type-founders to revive other early printed forms, but they seem to regard the imitation of early manuscript forms as a reversion to barbarism and ugliness. But this imitation has been cleverly done by artists who have undertaken to make designs for book titles and book covers. Some have gone far beyond early typographic models, selecting the early Roman letter the plain capital without serif or hair line, with an almost absolute uniformity of thick line. Others have copied and exaggerated the mannerisms of mediaeval copyists and engravers, with all their faults, bundling words together without proper relief between lines, dividing them by periods and not by spaces, until they are almost unreadable. The closely huddled and carelessly formed letters of Botticelli and other early Italian engravers are even preferred by many artists to the simple, severe, and easily read letters of chiseled inscrip-

HARRY** HEAVY WITH FAT   MERGENTHALER TYPE LIBRARY

ABCDEFGHIJKLMNOPQRSTUVWXYZ&
abcdefghijklmnopqrstuvwxyz
1234567890$.,'"":;!?

HIROSHIGE BOOK   AGFA COMPUGRAPHIC TYPE LIBRARY

*ABCDEFGHIJKLMNOPQRSTUVWXYZ&
abcdefghijklmnopqrstuvwxyz
1234567890$.,'"":;!?*

HIROSHIGE BOOK ITALIC   AGFA COMPUGRAPHIC TYPE LIBRARY

**ABCDEFGHIJKLMNOPQRSTUVWXYZ
&abcdefghijklmnopqrstuvwxyz
1234567890$.,'"":;!?**

HIROSHIGE MEDIUM   AGFA COMPUGRAPHIC TYPE LIBRARY

***ABCDEFGHIJKLMNOPQRSTUVWXYZ
&abcdefghijklmnopqrstuvwxyz
1234567890$.,'"":;!?***

HIROSHIGE MEDIUM ITALIC   AGFA COMPUGRAPHIC TYPE LIBRARY

**ABCDEFGHIJKLMNOPQRSTUVWX
YZ&abcdefghijklmnopqrstuvwxyz
1234567890$.,'"":;!?**

HIROSHIGE BLACK   AGFA COMPUGRAPHIC TYPE LIBRARY

***ABCDEFGHIJKLMNOPQRSTUVWX
YZ&abcdefghijklmnopqrstuvwxyz
1234567890$.,'"":;!?***

HIROSHIGE BLACK ITALIC   AGFA COMPUGRAPHIC TYPE LIBRARY

12/13 In type-founding, types are cast in moulds containing at one end a copper matrix of the character. The aperture through whch the melted metal is injected is at the end of the mould opposite the matrix, and a piece as long as the type, called the jet, leaving the body of the type comparatively perfect. The types thus cast go through various processes, such as breaking off the jet and ploughing in its place a shallow groove across the foot, thus leaving each type two "feet" to stand upon, "rubbing," etc.; and at last, set up in long rows, they pass under the eye of an expert, who, as he examines them carefully with a glass, rejects all in which he detects any imperfections. In these pro-

10/11 In type-founding, types are cast in moulds containing at one end a copper matrix of the character. The aperture through whch the melted metal is injected is at the end of the mould opposite the matrix, and a piece as long as the type, called the jet, leaving the body of the type comparatively perfect. The types thus cast go through various processes, such as breaking off the jet and ploughing in its place a shallow groove across the foot, thus leaving each type two "feet" to stand upon, "rubbing," etc.; and at last, set up in long rows, they pass under the eye of an expert, who, as he examines them carefully with a glass, rejects all in which he detects any imperfections. In these processes an average of 10 percent, is eliminated; so that of 100 lbs. cast only 90 lbs. are actually fit for delivery. General Construction *of Type-setting Machinery.--With this exception of the Westcott machinery, all the American setters are made to*

HIROSHIGE BOOK WITH BOOK ITALIC   AGFA COMPUGRAPHIC TYPE LIBRARY

12/13 In type-founding, types are cast in moulds containing at one end a copper matrix of the character. The aperture through whch the melted metal is injected is at the end of the mould opposite the matrix, and a piece as long as the type, called the jet, leaving the body of the type comparatively perfect. The types thus cast go through various processes, such as breaking off the jet and ploughing in its place a shallow groove across the foot, thus leaving each type two "feet" to stand upon, "rubbing," etc.; and at last, set up in long rows, they pass under the eye of an expert, who, as he examines them carefully with a glass, rejects all in which he detects any

10/11 In type-founding, types are cast in moulds containing at one end a copper matrix of the character. The aperture through whch the melted metal is injected is at the end of the mould opposite the matrix, and a piece as long as the type, called the jet, leaving the body of the type comparatively perfect. The types thus cast go through various processes, such as breaking off the jet and ploughing in its place a shallow groove across the foot, thus leaving each type two "feet" to stand upon, "rubbing," etc.; and at last, set up in long rows, they pass under the eye of an expert, who, as he examines them carefully with a glass, rejects all in which he detects any imperfections. In these processes an average of 10 percent, is eliminated; so that of 100 lbs. cast only 90 lbs. are actually fit for delivery. *General Construction of Type-setting Machinery.--With this exception of the Westcott machinery, all the*

HIROSHIGE MEDIUM WITH MEDIUM ITALIC   AGFA COMPUGRAPHIC TYPE LIBRARY

12/13 **In type-founding, types are cast in moulds containing at one end a copper matrix of the character. The aperture through whch the melted metal is injected is at the end of the mould opposite the matrix, and a piece as long as the type, called the jet, leaving the body of the type comparatively perfect. The types thus cast go through various processes, such as breaking off the jet and ploughing in its place a shallow groove across the foot, thus leaving each type two "feet" to stand upon, "rubbing," etc.; *and at last, set up in long rows, they pass under the eye of an expert, who, as***

10/11 **In type-founding, types are cast in moulds containing moulds containing at one end a copper matrix of the character. The aperture through whch the melted metal is injected is at the end of the mould opposite the matrix, and a piece as long as the type, called the jet, leaving the body of the type comparatively perfect. The types thus cast go through various processes, such as breaking off the jet and ploughing in its place a shallow groove across the foot, thus leaving each type two "feet" to stand upon, "rubbing," etc.; and at last, set up in long rows, they pass under the eye of an expert, who, as he examines them carefully with a glass, rejects all in which he detects any imperfections. In these processes *an average of 10 percent, is eliminated; so that of 100 lbs. cast only 90 lbs. are actually fit for***

HIROSHIGE BLACK WITH BLACK ITALIC   AGFA COMPUGRAPHIC TYPE LIBRARY

ABCDEFGHIJKLMNOPQRSTUVWXYZ
&abcdefghijklmnopqrstuvwxyz1234
567890$.,"":;!?

ITC ISBELL** BOOK   MERGENTHALER TYPE LIBRARY

*ABCDEFGHIJKLMNOPQRSTUVWXY
Z&abcdefghijklmnopqrstuvwxyz123
4567890$.,"":;!?*

ITC ISBELL** BOOK ITALIC   MERGENTHALER TYPE LIBRARY

**ABCDEFGHIJKLMNOPQRSTUVWX
YZ&abcdefghijklmnopqrstuvwxyz12
34567890$.,"":;!?**

ITC ISBELL** MEDIUM   MERGENTHALER TYPE LIBRARY

*ABCDEFGHIJKLMNOPQRSTUVWXY
Z&abcdefghijklmnopqrstuvwxyz123
4567890$.,"":;!?*

ITC ISBELL** MEDIUM ITALIC   MERGENTHALER TYPE LIBRARY

**ABCDEFGHIJKLMNOPQRSTUVW
XYZ&abcdefghijklmnopqrstuvwx
yz1234567890$.,"":;!?**

ITC ISBELL** BOLD   MERGENTHALER TYPE LIBRARY

***ABCDEFGHIJKLMNOPQRSTUVW
XYZ&abcdefghijklmnopqrstuvwxy
z1234567890$.,"":;!?***

ITC ISBELL** BOLD ITALIC   MERGENTHALER TYPE LIBRARY

12/13 In considering fine and praiseworthy inventions, we must freely confess that printing has been and is to-day the best and most estimable — the invention by means of which two persons turning the press can get a greater number of books in a day than formerly could have been transcribed by several persons in a year. It is claimed that this art was invented at Mainz, a city of Germany, in the year 1442 by Jean Guttemberg, or, according to others, Guttenberg, an honorable German chevalier. It was at Mainz that after experimenting with an ink *which is used by printers to-day, he first began the practice of the art. Some persons*

10/11 In considering fine and praiseworthy inventions, we must freely confess that printing has been and is to-day the best and most estimable — the invention by means of which two persons turning the press can get a greater number of books in a day than formerly could have been transcribed by several persons in a year. It is claimed that this art was invented at Mainz, a city of Germany, in the year 1442 by Jean Guttemberg, or, according to others, Guttenberg, an honorable German chevalier. It was at Mainz that after experimenting with an ink which is used by printers to-day, he first began the practice of the art. Some persons prefer to attribute the invention to Jean Fauste & Yues Scheffey two years earlier, holding that our Guttemberg, Jean Mentel, Jean Prus, *Adolphe Rusche, Pierre Scheffec, Martin Flache, Huldric Han, Jean Froben, Adam Petri, Thomas*

ITC ISBELL** BOOK WITH BOOK ITALIC   MERGENTHALER TYPE LIBRARY

12/13 In considering fine and praiseworthy inventions, we must freely confess that printing has been and is to-day the best and most estimable — the invention by means of which two persons turning the press can get a greater number of books in a day than formerly could have been transcribed by several persons in a year. It is claimed that this art was invented at Mainz, a city of Germany, in the year 1442 by Jean Guttemberg, or, according to others, Guttenberg, an honorable German chevalier. It was at Mainz that after experimenting with an ink *which is used by printers to-day, he first began the practice*

10/11 In considering fine and praiseworthy inventions, we must freely confess that printing has been and is to-day the best and most estimable — the invention by means of which two persons turning the press can get a greater number of books in a day than formerly could have been transcribed by several persons in a year. It is claimed that this art was invented at Mainz, a city of Germany, in the year 1442 by Jean Guttemberg, or, according to others, Guttenberg, an honorable German chevalier. It was at Mainz that after experimenting with an ink which is used by printers to-day, he first began the practice of the art. Some persons prefer to attribute the invention to Jean Fauste & Yues Scheffey two years earlier, holding that our Guttemberg, *Jean Mentel, Jean Prus, Adolphe Rusche, Pierre Scheffec, Martin Flache, Huldric Han, Jean Froben, Adam*

ITC ISBELL** MEDIUM WITH MEDIUM ITALIC   MERGENTHALER TYPE LIBRARY

12/13 **In considering fine and praiseworthy inventions, we must freely confess that printing has been and is to-day the best and most estimable — the invention by means of which two persons turning the press can get a greater number of books in a day than formerly could have been transcribed by several persons in a year. It is claimed that this art was invented at Mainz, a city of Germany, in the year 1442 by Jean Guttemberg, or, according to others, Guttenberg, an honorable German chevalier. It was at Mainz that *after experimenting with an ink which is used by printers to-day, he first began***

10/11 **In considering fine and praiseworthy inventions, we must freely confess that printing has been and is to-day the best and most estimable — the invention by means of which two persons turning the press can get a greater number of books in a day than formerly could have been transcribed by several persons in a year. It is claimed that this art was invented at Mainz, a city of Germany, in the year 1442 by Jean Guttemberg, or, according to others, Guttenberg, an honorable German chevalier. It was at Mainz that after experimenting with an ink which is used by printers to-day, he first began the practice of the art. Some persons prefer to attribute the invention to Jean Fauste & Yues Scheffey two years earlier, holding that our Guttemberg, *Jean Mentel, Jean Prus, Adolphe Rusche, Pierre Scheffec,***

ITC ISBELL** BOLD WITH BOLD ITALIC   MERGENTHALER TYPE LIBRARY

SUPPLEMENTARY FACES

ABCDEFGHIJKLMNOPQRSTUVWXYZ&abcdefghijklmnopqrstuvwxyz1234567890$.,"""":;!?

ITC ISBELL** HEAVY   MERGENTHALER TYPE LIBRARY

ABCDEFGHIJKLMNOPQRSTUVWXYZ&abcdefghijklmnopqrstuvwxyz1234567890$.,"""":;!?

ITC ISBELL** HEAVY ITALIC   MERGENTHALER TYPE LIBRARY

ABCDEFGHIJKLMNOPQRSTUVWXYZ&abcdefghijklmnopqrstuvwxyz1234567890$.,"""":;!?

ITALIA** BOOK (ITC)   MERGENTHALER TYPE LIBRARY

ABCDEFGHIJKLMNOPQRSTUVWXYZ&abcdefghijklmnopqrstuvwxyz1234567890$.,"""":;!?

ITALIA** MEDIUM (ITC)   MERGENTHALER TYPE LIBRARY

ABCDEFGHIJKLMNOPQRSTUVWXYZ&abcdefghijklmnopqrstuvwxyz1234567890$.,"""":;!?

ITALIA** BOLD (ITC)   MERGENTHALER TYPE LIBRARY

12/13 **In considering fine and praiseworthy inventions, we must freely confess that printing has been and is to-day the best and most estimable — the invention by means of which two persons turning the press can get a greater number of books in a day than formerly could have been transcribed by several persons in a year. It is claimed that this art was invented at Mainz, a city of Germany, in the year 1442 by Jean Guttemberg, or, according to others, Guttenberg, an honorable German chevalier. It was at Mainz that after experimenting with**

10/11 **In considering fine and praiseworthy inventions, we must freely confess that printing has been and is to-day the best and most estimable — the invention by means of which two persons turning the press can get a greater number of books in a day than formerly could have been transcribed by several persons in a year. It is claimed that this art was invented at Mainz, a city of Germany, in the year 1442 by Jean Guttemberg, or, according to others, Guttenberg, an honorable German chevalier. It was at Mainz that after experimenting with an ink which is used by printers to-day, he first began the practice of the art. Some persons prefer to attribute the *invention to Jean Fauste & Yues Scheffey two years earlier, holding that our Guttemberg,***

ITC ISBELL** HEAVY WITH HEAVY ITALIC   MERGENTHALER TYPE LIBRARY

12/13 In considering fine and praiseworthy inventions, we must freely confess that printing has been and is to-day the best and most estimable — the invention by means of which two persons turning the press can get a greater number of books in a day than formerly could have been transcribed by several persons in a year. It is claimed that this art was invented at Mainz, a city of Germany, in the year 1442 by Jean Guttemberg, or, according to others, Guttenberg, an honorable German chevalier. It was at Mainz that after experimenting with an ink which is used by printers to-day, he first began the practice of the art. Some persons prefer to attribute the in-

10/11 In considering fine and praiseworthy inventions, we must freely confess that printing has been and is to-day the best and most estimable — the invention by means of which two persons turning the press can get a greater number of books in a day than formerly could have been transcribed by several persons in a year. It is claimed that this art was invented at Mainz, a city of Germany, in the year 1442 by Jean Guttemberg, or, according to others, Guttenberg, an honorable German chevalier. It was at Mainz that after experimenting with an ink which is used by printers to-day, he first began the practice of the art. Some persons prefer to attribute the invention to Jean Fauste & Yues Scheffey two years earlier, holding that our Guttemberg, Jean Mentel, Jean Prus, Adolphe Rusche, Pierre Scheffec, Martin Flache, Huldric Han, Jean Froben, Adam Petri, Thomas Vuolffe, and others added improvements and spread

ITALIA** BOOK (ITC) WITH MEDIUM (ITC)   MERGENTHALER TYPE LIBRARY

12/13 **In considering fine and praiseworthy inventions, we must freely confess that printing has been and is to-day the best and most estimable — the invention by means of which two persons turning the press can get a greater number of books in a day than formerly could have been transcribed by several persons in a year. It is claimed that this art was invented at Mainz, a city of Germany, in the year 1442 by Jean Guttemberg, or, according to others, Guttenberg, an honorable German chevalier. It was at Mainz that after experimenting with an ink which is used by printers to-day, he first began the practice of the art. Some persons prefer to**

10/11 **In considering fine and praiseworthy inventions, we must freely confess that printing has been and is to-day the best and most estimable — the invention by means of which two persons turning the press can get a greater number of books in a day than formerly could have been transcribed by several persons in a year. It is claimed that this art was invented at Mainz, a city of Germany, in the year 1442 by Jean Guttemberg, or, according to others, Guttenberg, an honorable German chevalier. It was at Mainz that after experimenting with an ink which is used by printers to-day, he first began the practice of the art. Some persons prefer to attribute the invention to Jean Fauste & Yues Scheffey two years earlier, holding that our Guttemberg, Jean Mentel, Jean Prus, Adolphe Rusche, Pierre Scheffec, Martin Flache, Huldric Han, Jean Froben, Adam Petri, Thomas Vuolffe, and others**

ITALIA** BOLD (ITC)   MERGENTHALER TYPE LIBRARY

ABCDEFGHIJKLMNOPQRSTUVW
XYZ&abcdefghijklmnopqrstuvwxyz1234
567890$.,""'':;!?

JANSON* TEXT 55   MERGENTHALER TYPE LIBRARY

ABCDEFGHIJKLMNOPQRSTUVWXYZ&abcdefghijklmnopqrstuvwxyz1234567890$.,""'':;!?

JANSON* TEXT 56 ITALIC   MERGENTHALER TYPE LIBRARY

ABCDEFGHIJKLMNOPQRSTUVWXYZ&abcdefghijklmnopqrstuvwxyz1234567890$.,""'':;!?

JANSON* TEXT 75 BOLD   MERGENTHALER TYPE LIBRARY

ABCDEFGHIJKLMNOPQRSTUVWXYZ&abcdefghijklmnopqrstuvwxyz1234567890$.,""'':;!?

JANSON* TEXT 76 BOLD ITALIC   MERGENTHALER TYPE LIBRARY

ABCDEFGHIJKLMNOPQRSTUVWXYZ&abcdefghijklmnopqrstuvwxyz1234567890$.,""'':;!?

JANSON* TEXT 95 BLACK   MERGENTHALER TYPE LIBRARY

ABCDEFGHIJKLMNOPQRSTUVWXYZ&abcdefghijklmnopqrstuvwxyz1234567890$.,""'':;!?

JANSON* TEXT 96 BLACK ITALIC   MERGENTHALER TYPE LIBRARY

SUPPLEMENTARY FACES 395

12/13 OBSERVATIONS ON COMPOSING. Although this essential point has been passed over with little notice by most writers upon this subject, still (so great are the evils resulting from ill-contracted habits, which naturally keep pace with our growth), we cannot avoid pointing out a few instances of the sure consequences attendant on them. There are many persons now employed in the art, who frequently, with great justice, inveigh in strong terms against the conduct of those unto whose care they were first entrusted, for suffering them to contract those ill-becoming postures *which are productive of knock knees, round shoulders, and other deformities. It is deeply to be regret-*

10/11 OBSERVATIONS ON COMPOSING. Although this essential point has been passed over with little notice by most writers upon this subject, still (so great are the evils resulting from ill-contracted habits, which naturally keep pace with our growth), we cannot avoid pointing out a few instances of the sure consequences attendant on them. There are many persons now employed in the art, who frequently, with great justice, inveigh in strong terms against the conduct of those unto whose care they were first entrusted, for suffering them to contract those ill-becoming postures which are productive of knock knees, round shoulders, and other deformities. It is deeply to be regretted, that those who undertake so important a charge, are not better qualified to fulfill that duty: instead of suffering the *tender shoot to grow wild and uncultivated, when the pruning-knife, in a gentle hand, with a little admonition, would*

JANSON* TEXT 55 WITH 56 ITALIC   MERGENTHALER TYPE LIBRARY

12/13 **OBSERVATIONS ON COMPOSING. Although this essential point has been passed over with little notice by most writers upon this subject, still (so great are the evils resulting from ill-contracted habits, which naturally keep pace with our growth), we cannot avoid pointing out a few instances of the sure consequences attendant on them. There are many persons now employed in the art, who frequently, with great justice, inveigh in strong terms against the conduct of those unto whose care they were first entrusted, for suffering *them to contract those ill-becoming postures which are productive of knock knees, round***

10/11 **OBSERVATIONS ON COMPOSING. Although this essential point has been passed over with little notice by most writers upon this subject, still (so great are the evils resulting from ill-contracted habits, which naturally keep pace with our growth), we cannot avoid pointing out a few instances of the sure consequences attendant on them. There are many persons now employed in the art, who frequently, with great justice, inveigh in strong terms against the conduct of those unto whose care they were first entrusted, for suffering them to contract those ill-becoming postures which are productive of knock knees, round shoulders, and other deformities. It is deeply to be regretted, that those who undertake so important a charge, are not better *qualified to fulfill that duty: instead of suffering the tender shoot to grow wild and uncultivated, when the***

JANSON* TEXT 75 BOLD WITH 76 BOLD ITALIC   MERGENTHALER TYPE LIBRARY

12/13 **OBSERVATIONS ON COMPOSING. Although this essential point has been passed over with little notice by most writers upon this subject, still (so great are the evils resulting from ill-contracted habits, which naturally keep pace with our growth), we cannot avoid pointing out a few instances of the sure consequences attendant on them. There are many persons now employed in the art, who frequently, with great justice, inveigh in strong terms against the conduct of those unto whose care *they were first entrusted, for suffering them to contract those ill-becoming pos-***

10/11 **OBSERVATIONS ON COMPOSING. Although this essential point has been passed over with little notice by most writers upon this subject, still (so great are the evils resulting from ill-contracted habits, which naturally keep pace with our growth), we cannot avoid pointing out a few instances of the sure consequences attendant on them. There are many persons now employed in the art, who frequently, with great justice, inveigh in strong terms against the conduct of those unto whose care they were first entrusted, for suffering them to contract those ill-becoming postures which are productive of knock knees, round shoulders, and other deformities. It is deeply *to be regretted, that those who undertake so important a charge, are not better qualified to***

JANSON* TEXT 95 BLACK WITH 96 BLACK ITALIC   MERGENTHALER TYPE LIBRARY

ABCDEFGHIJKLMNOPQRSTUVWXYZ&abcdefghijklmnopqrstuvwxyz1234567890$.,""'':;!?

JENSON (NICHOLAS)   MERGENTHALER TYPE LIBRARY

ABCDEFGHIJKLMNOPQRSTUVWXYZ&abcdefghijklmnopqrstuvwxyz1234567890$.,""'':;!?

KENNERLY   MERGENTHALER TYPE LIBRARY

ABCDEFGHIJKLMNOPQRSTUVWXYZ&abcdefghijklmnopqrstuvwxyz1234567890$.,""'':;!?

KENNERLY ITALIC   MERGENTHALER TYPE LIBRARY

ABCDEFGHIJKLMNOPQRSTUV WXYZ&abcdefghijklmnopqrstuvwxyz1234567890$.,""'':;!?

KENNERLY BOLD   MERGENTHALER TYPE LIBRARY

ABCDEFGHIJKLMNOPQRSTUVWXYZ&abcdefghijklmnopqrstuvwxyz1234567890$.,""'':;!?

KENNERLY BOLD ITALIC   MERGENTHALER TYPE LIBRARY

SUPPLEMENTARY FACES 397

12/13 The history of the Dutch book is famous. In the Middle Ages the art of the scribes and miniaturists flourished in the Netherlands to such a degree that their manuscripts are not considered inferior to the finest specimens of Italian and French origin; the Dutch incunabula are, especially by their woodcut illustrations, hardly surpassed, only equalled by Italian work. In the 17th century Holland regained a leading position in this sphere and the prints of Elzevir enjoy at present a world-wide fame. And although our books lack the grandeur of Italian manuscripts, the delicate grace of a French impression (nor does the Dutch incunabulum display the pompous style of a Gutenberg or Schoeffer work),

10/11 The history of the Dutch book is famous. In the Middle Ages the art of the scribes and miniaturists flourished in the Netherlands to such a degree that their manuscripts are not considered inferior to the finest specimens of Italian and French origin; the Dutch incunabula are, especially by their woodcut illustrations, hardly surpassed, only equalled by Italian work. In the 17th century Holland regained a leading position in this sphere and the prints of Elzevir enjoy at present a world-wide fame. And although our books lack the grandeur of Italian manuscripts, the delicate grace of a French impression (nor does the Dutch incunabulum display the pompous style of a Gutenberg or Schoeffer work), they have undoubtedly a distinct character of their own, which bears the stamp of true art. They exhibit their inmost artistic value only to the devout contemplator. We might parallel with the art of painting, especially of the Middle Ages: there, too, the

JENSON (NICHOLAS)   MERGENTHALER TYPE LIBRARY

12/13 The history of the Dutch book is famous. In the Middle Ages the art of the scribes and miniaturists flourished in the Netherlands to such a degree that their manuscripts are not considered inferior to the finest specimens of Italian and French origin; the Dutch incunabula are, especially by their woodcut illustrations, hardly surpassed, only equalled by Italian work. In the 17th century Holland regained a leading position in this sphere and the prints of Elzevir enjoy at present a world-wide fame. And although our books lack the grandeur of Italian manuscripts, the delicate *grace of a French impression (nor does the Dutch incunabulum display the pompous style*

10/11 The history of the Dutch book is famous. In the Middle Ages the art of the scribes and miniaturists flourished in the Netherlands to such a degree that their manuscripts are not considered inferior to the finest specimens of Italian and French origin; the Dutch incunabula are, especially by their woodcut illustrations, hardly surpassed, only equalled by Italian work. In the 17th century Holland regained a leading position in this sphere and the prints of Elzevir enjoy at present a world-wide fame. And although our books lack the grandeur of Italian manuscripts, the delicate grace of a French impression (nor does the Dutch incunabulum display the pompous style of a Gutenberg or Schoeffer work), they have undoubtedly a distinct character of their own, which bears the stamp of true art. They exhibit *their inmost artistic value only to the devout contemplator. We might parallel with the art of painting,*

KENNERLY WITH ITALIC   MERGENTHALER TYPE LIBRARY

12/13 **The history of the Dutch book is famous. In the Middle Ages the art of the scribes and miniaturists flourished in the Netherlands to such a degree that their manuscripts are not considered inferior to the finest specimens of Italian and French origin; the Dutch incunabula are, especially by their woodcut illustrations, hardly surpassed, only equalled by Italian work. In the 17th century Holland regained a leading position in this sphere and the prints of Elzevir enjoy at present a world-wide fame. And although our books *lack the grandeur of Italian manuscripts, the delicate grace of a French impression***

10/11 The history of the Dutch book is famous. In the Middle Ages the art of the scribes and miniaturists flourished in the Netherlands to such a degree that their manuscripts are not considered inferior to the finest specimens of Italian and French origin; the Dutch incunabula are, especially by their woodcut illustrations, hardly surpassed, only equalled by Italian work. In the 17th century Holland regained a leading position in this sphere and the prints of Elzevir enjoy at present a world-wide fame. And although our books lack the grandeur of Italian manuscripts, the delicate grace of a French impression (nor does the Dutch incunabulum display the pompous style of a Gutenberg or Schoeffer work), they have undoubtedly a distinct character of their *own, which bears the stamp of true art. They exhibit their inmost artistic value only to the devout*

KENNERLY BOLD WITH BOLD ITALIC   MERGENTHALER TYPE LIBRARY

ABCDEFGHIJKLMNOPQRSTUVWXYZ&abcdefghijklmnopqrstuvwxyz1234567890$.,""":;!?

ITC KORINNA**   MERGENTHALER TYPE LIBRARY

ABCDEFGHIJKLMNOPQRSTUVWXYZ&abcdefghijklmnopqrstuvwxyz1234567890$.,""":;!?

ITC KORINNA** KURSIV   MERGENTHALER TYPE LIBRARY

ABCDEFGHIJKLMNOPQRSTUVWXYZ&abcdefghijklmnopqrstuvwxyz1234567890$.,""":;!?

ITC KORINNA** BOLD   MERGENTHALER TYPE LIBRARY

ABCDEFGHIJKLMNOPQRSTUVWXYZ&abcdefghijklmnopqrstuvwxyz1234567890$.,""":;!?

ITC KORINNA** BOLD KURSIV   MERGENTHALER TYPE LIBRARY

ABCDEFGHIJKLMNOPQRSTUVWXYZ&abcdefghijklmnopqrstuvwxyz1234567890$.,""":;!?

ITC KORINNA** EXTRA BOLD   MERGENTHALER TYPE LIBRARY

ABCDEFGHIJKLMNOPQRSTUVWXYZ&abcdefghijklmnopqrstuvwxyz1234567890$.,""":;!?

ITC KORINNA** EXTRA BOLD KURSIV   MERGENTHALER TYPE LIBRARY

12/13 It is still a matter of conjecture whether Johann Gutenberg was the first to conceive the principle of casting movable [i.e., separate] metal types which he could arrange in words and sentences so that he could impress their faces on paper. There is, however, hardly a doubt, judging at least from the evidence available, that he was the first to make practical use of the idea, and that it is due to his ingenious application of it that the profound art of typography was born.

Whether he cast his letters in molds of sand or in metal matrices, is a question not really *material at this time; it is the far-reaching results of his inspiration that most concern*

10/11 It is still a matter of conjecture whether Johann Gutenberg was the first to conceive the principle of casting movable [i.e., separate] metal types which he could arrange in words and sentences so that he could impress their faces on paper. There is, however, hardly a doubt, judging at least from the evidence available, that he was the first to make practical use of the idea, and that it is due to his ingenious application of it that the profound art of typography was born.

Whether he cast his letters in molds of sand or in metal matrices, is a question not really material at this time; it is the far-reaching results of his inspiration that most concern us in this discussion. It seems quite probable that Gutenberg at first had little more in mind than a desire to find some expedient by which to *supplement with explanatory text the illustrations cut on wood blocks — some method that would*

ITC KORINNA** WITH KURSIV   MERGENTHALER TYPE LIBRARY

12/13 **It is still a matter of conjecture whether Johann Gutenberg was the first to conceive the principle of casting movable [i.e., separate] metal types which he could arrange in words and sentences so that he could impress their faces on paper. There is, however, hardly a doubt, judging at least from the evidence available, that he was the first to make practical use of the idea, and that it is due to his ingenious application of it that the profound art of typography was born.**

Whether he cast his letters in molds of sand or in metal matrices, is a question not *really material at this time; it is the far-reaching results of his inspiration that*

10/11 **It is still a matter of conjecture whether Johann Gutenberg was the first to conceive the principle of casting movable [i.e., separate] metal types which he could arrange in words and sentences so that he could impress their faces on paper. There is, however, hardly a doubt, judging at least from the evidence available, that he was the first to make practical use of the idea, and that it is due to his ingenious application of it that the profound art of typography was born.**

Whether he cast his letters in molds of sand or in metal matrices, is a question not really material at this time; it is the far-reaching results of his inspiration that most concern us in this discussion. It seems quite probable that Gutenberg at first had little more in mind than a desire to find some expedient by which to *supplement with explanatory text the illustrations cut on wood blocks — some method that would*

ITC KORINNA** BOLD WITH BOLD KURSIV   MERGENTHALER TYPE LIBRARY

12/13 **It is still a matter of conjecture whether Johann Gutenberg was the first to conceive the principle of casting movable [i.e., separate] metal types which he could arrange in words and sentences so that he could impress their faces on paper. There is, however, hardly a doubt, judging at least from the evidence available, that he was the first to make practical use of the idea, and that it is due to his ingenious application of it that the profound art of typography was born.**

Whether he cast his letters in molds of *sand or in metal matrices, is a question not really material at this time; it is the*

10/11 **It is still a matter of conjecture whether Johann Gutenberg was the first to conceive the principle of casting movable [i.e., separate] metal types which he could arrange in words and sentences so that he could impress their faces on paper. There is, however, hardly a doubt, judging at least from the evidence available, that he was the first to make practical use of the idea, and that it is due to his ingenious application of it that the profound art of typography was born.**

Whether he cast his letters in molds of sand or in metal matrices, is a question not really material at this time; it is the far-reaching results of his inspiration that most concern us in this discussion. It seems quite probable that Gutenberg at *first had little more in mind than a desire to find some expedient by which to supplement with*

ITC KORINNA** EXTRA BOLD WITH EXTRA BOLD KURSIV   MERGENTHALER TYPE LIBRARY

ABCDEFGHIJKLMNOPQRSTUVWX
YZ&abcdefghijklmnopqrstuvwxy
z1234567890$.,""'':;!?

ITC LUBALIN GRAPH** EXTRA LIGHT   MERGENTHALER TYPE LIBRARY

*ABCDEFGHIJKLMNOPQRSTUVWX
YZ&abcdefghijklmnopqrstuvwxy
z1234567890$.,""'':;!?*

ITC LUBALIN GRAPH** EXTRA LIGHT OBLIQUE   MERGENTHALER TYPE LIBRARY

ABCDEFGHIJKLMNOPQRSTUVWX
YZ&abcdefghijklmnopqrstuvwxyz
1234567890$.,""'':;!?

ITC LUBALIN GRAPH** BOOK   MERGENTHALER TYPE LIBRARY

*ABCDEFGHIJKLMNOPQRSTUVWX
YZ&abcdefghijklmnopqrstuvwxyz
1234567890$.,""'':;!?*

ITC LUBALIN GRAPH** BOOK OBLIQUE   MERGENTHALER TYPE LIBRARY

ABCDEFGHIJKLMNOPQRSTUVWX
YZ&abcdefghijklmnopqrstuvwx
yz1234567890$.,""'':;!?

ITC LUBALIN GRAPH** MEDIUM   MERGENTHALER TYPE LIBRARY

*ABCDEFGHIJKLMNOPQRSTUVWX
YZ&abcdefghijklmnopqrstuvwxy
z1234567890$.,""'':;!?*

ITC LUBALIN GRAPH** MEDIUM OBLIQUE   MERGENTHALER TYPE LIBRARY

SUPPLEMENTARY FACES 401

12/13 OBSERVATIONS ON COMPOSING. Although this essential point has been passed over with little notice by most writers upon this subject, still (so great are the evils resulting from ill-contracted habits, which naturally keep pace with our growth), we cannot avoid pointing out a few instances of the sure consequences attendant on them. There are many persons now employed in the art, who frequently, with great justice, inveigh in strong terms against the conduct of those unto *whose care they were first entrusted, for suffering them to contract those ill-*

10/11 OBSERVATIONS ON COMPOSING. Although this essential point has been passed over with little notice by most writers upon this subject, still (so great are the evils resulting from ill-contracted habits, which naturally keep pace with our growth), we cannot avoid pointing out a few instances of the sure consequences attendant on them. There are many persons now employed in the art, who frequently, with great justice, inveigh in strong terms against the conduct of those unto whose care they were first entrusted, for suffering them to contract those ill-becoming postures which are productive of knock knees, round shoulders, and other deformities. It is deeply to be regretted, that those *who undertake so important a charge, are not better qualified to fulfill that duty: instead of*

ITC LUBALIN GRAPH** EXTRA LIGHT WITH EXTRA LIGHT OBLIQUE   MERGENTHALER TYPE LIBRARY

12/13 OBSERVATIONS ON COMPOSING. Although this essential point has been passed over with little notice by most writers upon this subject, still (so great are the evils resulting from ill-contracted habits, which naturally keep pace with our growth), we cannot avoid pointing out a few instances of the sure consequences attendant on them. There are many persons now employed in the art, who frequently, with great justice, inveigh in strong terms against the conduct of those unto whose care they were *first entrusted, for suffering them to contract those ill-becoming postures which*

10/11 OBSERVATIONS ON COMPOSING. Although this essential point has been passed over with little notice by most writers upon this subject, still (so great are the evils resulting from ill-contracted habits, which naturally keep pace with our growth), we cannot avoid pointing out a few instances of the sure consequences attendant on them. There are many persons now employed in the art, who frequently, with great justice, inveigh in strong terms against the conduct of those unto whose care they were first entrusted, for suffering them to contract those ill-becoming postures which are productive of knock knees, round shoulders, and other deformities. It is deeply to be regretted, that those who under*take so important a charge, are not better qualified to fulfill that duty: instead of suffering*

ITC LUBALIN GRAPH** BOOK WITH BOOK OBLIQUE   MERGENTHALER TYPE LIBRARY

12/13 **OBSERVATIONS ON COMPOSING. Although this essential point has been passed over with little notice by most writers upon this subject, still (so great are the evils resulting from ill-contracted habits, which naturally keep pace with our growth), we cannot avoid pointing out a few instances of the sure consequences attendant on them. There are many persons now employed in the art, who frequently, with great justice, inveigh in strong terms against the conduct of those *unto whose care they were first entrusted, for suffering them to contract***

10/11 **OBSERVATIONS ON COMPOSING. Although this essential point has been passed over with little notice by most writers upon this subject, still (so great are the evils resulting from ill-contracted habits, which naturally keep pace with our growth), we cannot avoid pointing out a few instances of the sure consequences attendant on them. There are many persons now employed in the art, who frequently, with great justice, inveigh in strong terms against the conduct of those unto whose care they were first entrusted, for suffering them to contract those ill-becoming postures which are productive of knock knees, round shoulders, and other deformities. *It is deeply to be regretted, that those who undertake so important a charge, are not bet-***

ITC LUBALIN GRAPH** MEDIUM WITH MEDIUM OBLIQUE   MERGENTHALER TYPE LIBRARY

ABCDEFGHIJKLMNOPQRSTUVWX
YZ&abcdefghijklmnopqrstuvwxy
z1234567890$.,""":;!?

ITC LUBALIN GRAPH** DEMI   MERGENTHALER TYPE LIBRARY

*ABCDEFGHIJKLMNOPQRSTUVW
XYZ&abcdefghijklmnopqrstuvwx
yz1234567890$.,""":;!?*

ITC LUBALIN GRAPH** DEMI OBLIQUE   MERGENTHALER TYPE LIBRARY

**ABCDEFGHIJKLMNOPQRSTUVWXY
Z&abcdefghijklmnopqrstuvwxyz12
34567890$.,""":;!?**

ITC LUBALIN GRAPH** BOLD   MERGENTHALER TYPE LIBRARY

***ABCDEFGHIJKLMNOPQRSTUVWX
YZ&abcdefghijklmnopqrstuvwxyz
1234567890$.,""":;!?***

ITC LUBALIN GRAPH** BOLD OBLIQUE   MERGENTHALER TYPE LIBRARY

ABCDEFGHIJKLMNOPQRSTUVW
XYZ&abcdefghijklmnopqrstuvwxyz1234
567890$.,""":;!?

LUCIAN**   MERGENTHALER TYPE LIBRARY

**ABCDEFGHIJKLMNOPQRSTUV
WXYZ&abcdefghijklmnopqrstuvwxyz
1234567890$.,""":;!?**

LUCIAN** BOLD   MERGENTHALER TYPE LIBRARY

SUPPLEMENTARY FACES 403

12/13 OBSERVATIONS ON COMPOSING. Although this essential point has been passed over with little notice by most writers upon this subject, still (so great are the evils resulting from ill-contracted habits, which naturally keep pace with our growth), we cannot avoid pointing out a few instances of the sure consequences attendant on them. There are many persons now employed in the art, who frequently, with great justice, inveigh in strong terms against the conduct of those unto whose care *they were first entrusted, for suffering them to contract those ill-becoming*

10/11 OBSERVATIONS ON COMPOSING. Although this essential point has been passed over with little notice by most writers upon this subject, still (so great are the evils resulting from ill-contracted habits, which naturally keep pace with our growth), we cannot avoid pointing out a few instances of the sure consequences attendant on them. There are many persons now employed in the art, who frequently, with great justice, inveigh in strong terms against the conduct of those unto whose care they were first entrusted, for suffering them to contract those ill-becoming postures which are productive of knock knees, round shoulders, and other deformities. It is deeply to be regretted, that those *who undertake so important a charge, are not better qualified to fulfill that duty: instead of*

ITC LUBALIN GRAPH** DEMI WITH DEMI OBLIQUE   MERGENTHALER TYPE LIBRARY

12/13 **OBSERVATIONS ON COMPOSING. Although this essential point has been passed over with little notice by most writers upon this subject, still (so great are the evils resulting from ill-contracted habits, which naturally keep pace with our growth), we cannot avoid pointing out a few instances of the sure consequences attendant on them. There are many persons now employed in the art, who frequently, with great justice, inveigh in strong terms against the conduct of those *unto whose care they were first entrusted, for suffering them to contract***

10/11 **OBSERVATIONS ON COMPOSING. Although this essential point has been passed over with little notice by most writers upon this subject, still (so great are the evils resulting from ill-contracted habits, which naturally keep pace with our growth), we cannot avoid pointing out a few instances of the sure consequences attendant on them. There are many persons now employed in the art, who frequently, with great justice, inveigh in strong terms against the conduct of those unto whose care they were first entrusted, for suffering them to contract those ill-becoming postures which are productive of knock knees, round shoulders, and other deformities. It is deeply to be regretted, that those who undertake *so important a charge, are not better qualified to fulfill that***

ITC LUBALIN GRAPH** BOLD WITH BOLD OBLIQUE   MERGENTHALER TYPE LIBRARY

12/13 OBSERVATIONS ON COMPOSING. Although this essential point has been passed over with little notice by most writers upon this subject, still (so great are the evils resulting from ill-contracted habits, which naturally keep pace with our growth), we cannot avoid pointing out a few instances of the sure consequences attendant on them. There are many persons now employed in the art, who frequently, with great justice, inveigh in strong terms against the conduct of those unto whose care they were first entrusted, for suffering them to contract those ill-becoming postures which are productive of knock knees, round **shoulders, and other deformities. It is deeply to be regretted, that those who undertake so**

10/11 OBSERVATIONS ON COMPOSING. Although this essential point has been passed over with little notice by most writers upon this subject, still (so great are the evils resulting from ill-contracted habits, which naturally keep pace with our growth), we cannot avoid pointing out a few instances of the sure consequences attendant on them. There are many persons now employed in the art, who frequently, with great justice, inveigh in strong terms against the conduct of those unto whose care they were first entrusted, for suffering them to contract those ill-becoming postures which are productive of knock knees, round shoulders, and other deformities. It is deeply to be regretted, that those who undertake so important a charge, are not better qualified to fulfill that duty: instead of suffering the tender shoot to grow wild and uncultivated, when the pruning-**knife, in a gentle hand, with a little admonition, would have checked its improper growth, and trained it in a**

LUCIAN** WITH BOLD   MERGENTHALER TYPE LIBRARY

ABCDEFGHIJKLMNOPQRSTUVW
XYZ&abcdefghijklmnopqrstuvwxyz
1234567890$.,''"":;!?

MELIOR*   MERGENTHALER TYPE LIBRARY

*ABCDEFGHIJKLMNOPQRSTUVWX
YZ&abcdefghijklmnopqrstuvwxyz1
234567890$.,''"":;!?*

MELIOR* ITALIC   MERGENTHALER TYPE LIBRARY

**ABCDEFGHIJKLMNOPQRSTUVW
XYZ&abcdefghijklmnopqrstuvwxy
z1234567890$.,''"":;!?**

MELIOR* MEDIUM   MERGENTHALER TYPE LIBRARY

*ABCDEFGHIJKLMNOPQRSTUVW
XYZ&abcdefghijklmnopqrstuvwxy
z1234567890$.,''"":;!?*

MELIOR* MEDIUM ITALIC   MERGENTHALER TYPE LIBRARY

**ABCDEFGHIJKLMNOPQRSTUVWXY
Z&abcdefghijklmnopqrstuvwxyz1234
567890$.,''"":;!?**

MELIOR* BOLD   MERGENTHALER TYPE LIBRARY

***ABCDEFGHIJKLMNOPQRSTUVWX
YZ&abcdefghijklmnopqrstuvwxyz12
34567890$.,''"":;!?***

MELIOR* BOLD ITALIC   MERGENTHALER TYPE LIBRARY

12/13 In type-founding, types are cast in moulds containing at one end a copper matrix of the character. The aperture through which the melted metal is injected is at the end of the mould opposite the matrix, and a piece as long as the type, called the jet, extends through the aperture from the bottom of the type. Thus imperfections in the metal and variations of temperature spend themselves in the jet, leaving the body of the type comparatively perfect. The types thus cast go through various processes, such as breaking off the jet and ploughing in its *place a shallow groove across the foot, thus leaving each type two "feet" to stand*

10/11 In type-founding, types are cast in moulds containing at one end a copper matrix of the character. The aperture through which the melted metal is injected is at the end of the mould opposite the matrix, and a piece as long as the type, called the jet, extends through the aperture from the bottom of the type. Thus imperfections in the metal and variations of temperature spend themselves in the jet, leaving the body of the type comparatively perfect. The types thus cast go through various processes, such as breaking off the jet and ploughing in its place a shallow groove across the foot, thus leaving each type two "feet" to stand upon, "rubbing," etc.; and at last, set up in long rows, they pass under the eye of an expert, who, as he examines them care*fully with a glass, rejects all in which he detects any imperfections. In these processes an average of*

MELIOR* WITH ITALIC   MERGENTHALER TYPE LIBRARY

12/13 In type-founding, types are cast in moulds containing at one end a copper matrix of the character. The aperture through which the melted metal is injected is at the end of the mould opposite the matrix, and a piece as long as the type, called the jet, extends through the aperture from the bottom of the type. Thus imperfections in the metal and variations of temperature spend themselves in the jet, leaving the body of the type comparatively perfect. The types thus cast go through various processes, such as breaking off the jet and ploughing in its *place a shallow groove across the foot, thus leaving each type two "feet" to stand*

10/11 In type-founding, types are cast in moulds containing at one end a copper matrix of the character. The aperture through which the melted metal is injected is at the end of the mould opposite the matrix, and a piece as long as the type, called the jet, extends through the aperture from the bottom of the type. Thus imperfections in the metal and variations of temperature spend themselves in the jet, leaving the body of the type comparatively perfect. The types thus cast go through various processes, such as breaking off the jet and ploughing in its place a shallow groove across the foot, thus leaving each type two "feet" to stand upon, "rubbing," etc.; and at last, set up in long rows, they pass under the eye of an expert, who, as he examines them care*fully with a glass, rejects all in which he detects any imperfections. In these processes an average*

MELIOR* MEDIUM WITH MEDIUM ITALIC   MERGENTHALER TYPE LIBRARY

12/13 **In type-founding, types are cast in moulds containing at one end a copper matrix of the character. The aperture through which the melted metal is injected is at the end of the mould opposite the matrix, and a piece as long as the type, called the jet, extends through the aperture from the bottom of the type. Thus imperfections in the metal and variations of temperature spend themselves in the jet, leaving the body of the type comparatively perfect. The types thus cast go through various processes, such as breaking off the jet and *ughing in its place a shallow groove across the foot, thus leaving each type***

10/11 **In type-founding, types are cast in moulds containing at one end a copper matrix of the character. The aperture through which the melted metal is injected is at the end of the mould opposite the matrix, and a piece as long as the type, called the jet, extends through the aperture from the bottom of the type. Thus imperfections in the metal and variations of temperature spend themselves in the jet, leaving the body of the type comparatively perfect. The types thus cast go through various processes, such as breaking off the jet and ploughing in its place a shallow groove across the foot, thus leaving each type two "feet" to stand upon, "rubbing," etc.; and at last, set up in long rows, they pass under the eye of an expert, who, as *he examines them carefully with a glass, rejects all in which he detects any imperfections. In***

MELIOR* BOLD WITH BOLD ITALIC   MERGENTHALER TYPE LIBRARY

ABCDEFGHIJKLMNOPQRSTUVWXYZ&abcdefghijklmnopqrstuvwxyz1234567890$.,""";:!?

MINION™ REGULAR   ADOBE TYPE LIBRARY

ABCDEFGHIJKLMNOPQRSTUVWXYZ&abcdefghijklmnopqrstuvwxyz1234567890$.,""";:!?

MINION ITALIC   ADOBE TYPE LIBRARY

ABCDEFGHIJKLMNOPQRSTUVWXYZ&abcdefghijklmnopqrstuvwxyz1234567890$.,""";:!?

MINION SEMIBOLD   ADOBE TYPE LIBRARY

ABCDEFGHIJKLMNOPQRSTUVWXYZ&abcdefghijklmnopqrstuvwxyz1234567890$.,""";:!?

MINION SEMIBOLD ITALIC   ADOBE TYPE LIBRARY

ABCDEFGHIJKLMNOPQRSTUVWXYZ&abcdefghijklmnopqrstuvwxyz1234567890$.,""";:!?

MINION BLACK   ADOBE TYPE LIBRARY

ABCDEFGHIJKLMNOPQRSTUVWXYZ&abcdefghijklmnopqrstuvwxyz1234567890$.,""";:!?

MINION BOLD ITALIC   ADOBE TYPE LIBRARY

SUPPLEMENTARY FACES 407

12/13 In considering fine and praiseworthy inventions, we must freely confess that printing has been and is to-day the best and most estimable—the invention by means of which two persons turning the press can get a greater number of books in a day than formerly could have been transcribed by several persons in a year. It is claimed that this art was invented at Mainz, a city of Germany, in the year 1442 by Jean Guttemberg, or, according to others, Guttenberg, an honorable German chevalier. It was at Mainz that after experimenting with an ink which is used by printers to-day, he first began the practice of the art. *Some persons prefer to attribute the invention to Jean Fauste and Yues Scheffey two years earlier, holding that our*

10/11 In considering fine and praiseworthy inventions, we must freely confess that printing has been and is to-day the best and most estimable—the invention by means of which two persons turning the press can get a greater number of books in a day than formerly could have been transcribed by several persons in a year. It is claimed that this art was invented at Mainz, a city of Germany, in the year 1442 by Jean Guttemberg, or, according to others, Guttenberg, an honorable German chevalier. It was at Mainz that after experimenting with an ink which is used by printers to-day, he first began the practice of the art. Some persons prefer to attribute the invention to Jean Fauste and Yues Scheffey two years earlier, holding that our Guttemberg, Jean Mentel, Jean Prus, Adolphe Rusche, Pierre Scheffec, Martin Flache, Huldric Han, Jean Froben, *Adam Petri, Thomas Vuolffe, and others added improvements and spread the art of printing through all Germany*

MINION REGULAR WITH ITALIC   ADOBE TYPE LIBRARY

12/13 **In considering fine and praiseworthy inventions, we must freely confess that printing has been and is to-day the best and most estimable—the invention by means of which two persons turning the press can get a greater number of books in a day than formerly could have been transcribed by several persons in a year. It is claimed that this art was invented at Mainz, a city of Germany, in the year 1442 by Jean Guttemberg, or, according to others, Guttenberg, an honorable German chevalier. It was at Mainz that after experimenting with an ink which is used by printers to-day, he first began the practice of the art. *Some persons prefer to attribute the invention to Jean Fauste and Yues Scheffey***

10/11 **In considering fine and praiseworthy inventions, we must freely confess that printing has been and is to-day the best and most estimable—the invention by means of which two persons turning the press can get a greater number of books in a day than formerly could have been transcribed by several persons in a year. It is claimed that this art was invented at Mainz, a city of Germany, in the year 1442 by Jean Guttemberg, or, according to others, Guttenberg, an honorable German chevalier. It was at Mainz that after experimenting with an ink which is used by printers to-day, he first began the practice of the art. Some persons prefer to attribute the invention to Jean Fauste and Yues Scheffey two years earlier, holding that our Guttemberg, Jean Mentel, Jean Prus, Adolphe Rusche, Pierre Scheffec, Martin Flache, *Huldric Han, Jean Froben, Adam Petri, Thomas Vuolffe,* and others added improvements and spread the art of**

MINION SEMIBOLD WITH ITALIC   ADOBE TYPE LIBRARY

12/13 **In considering fine and praiseworthy inventions, we must freely confess that printing has been and is to-day the best and most estimable—the invention by means of which two persons turning the press can get a greater number of books in a day than formerly could have been transcribed by several persons in a year. It is claimed that this art was invented at Mainz, a city of Germany, in the year 1442 by Jean Guttemberg, or, according to others, Guttenberg, an honorable German chevalier. It was at Mainz that after experimenting with an ink which is used by printers to-day, he first began the practice of the art. *Some persons prefer to attribute the invention to Jean Fauste and Yues***

10/11 **In considering fine and praiseworthy inventions, we must freely confess that printing has been and is to-day the best and most estimable—the invention be means of which two persons turning the press can get a transcribed by several persons in a year. It is claimed that this art was invented at Mainz, a city of Germany, in the year 1442 by Jean Guttemberg, or, according to others, Guttenberg, an honorable German chavalier. It was at Mainz that after experimenting with an ink which is used by printers to-day, he first began the practice of the art. Some persons prefer to attribute the invention to Jean Fauste & Yues Scheffey two years earlier, holding that our Guttemberg, Jean Mentel, Jean Prus, Adolphe Rusche, Pierre Scheffec, Martin Flache, Huldric Han, Jean Froben, Adam Petri, Thomas Vuolffe, and others added improvements and spread the art of printing through all Germany and other countrie**

MINION BLACK WITH BOLD ITALIC   ADOBE TYPE LIBRARY

ABCDEFGHIJKLMNOPQRSTUVWX
YZ&abcdefghijklmnopqrstuvwxyz1
234567890$.,""":;!?

ITC MODERN NO. 216** LIGHT   MERGENTHALER TYPE LIBRARY

*ABCDEFGHIJKLMNOPQRSTUVWX
YZ&abcdefghijklmnopqrstuvwxyz1
234567890$.,""":;!?*

ITC MODERN NO. 216** LIGHT ITALIC   MERGENTHALER TYPE LIBRARY

ABCDEFGHIJKLMNOPQRSTUVWXY
Z&abcdefghijklmnopqrstuvwxyz123
4567890$.,""":;!?

ITC MODERN NO. 216** MEDIUM   MERGENTHALER TYPE LIBRARY

*ABCDEFGHIJKLMNOPQRSTUVWXY
Z&abcdefghijklmnopqrstuvwxyz123
4567890$.,""":;!?*

ITC MODERN NO. 216** MEDIUM ITALIC   MERGENTHALER TYPE LIBRARY

**ABCDEFGHIJKLMNOPQRSTUVWX
YZ&abcdefghijklmnopqrstuvwxyz1
234567890$.,""":;!?**

ITC MODERN NO. 216** BOLD   MERGENTHALER TYPE LIBRARY

***ABCDEFGHIJKLMNOPQRSTUVWX
YZ&abcdefghijklmnopqrstuvwxyz1
234567890$.,""":;!?***

ITC MODERN NO. 216** BOLD ITALIC   MERGENTHALER TYPE LIBRARY

SUPPLEMENTARY FACES 409

12/13 The invention of printing, one of the most momentous events in the history of civilization, has been the subject of most controversy. The rival claims of Gutenberg and Coster have been argued with considerable acrimony by a number of authorities. While the weight of opinion has credited the invention to Gutenberg, the case of the German has not been absolutely conclusive. In the first place, there exists no piece of printing in which the name of Gutenberg appears as the printer. In the second place, there was known no trust-*worthy printed or written evidence dated during the contemporary period. And, in*

10/11 The invention of printing, one of the most momentous events in the history of civilization, has been the subject of most controversy. The rival claims of Gutenberg and Coster have been argued with considerable acrimony by a number of authorities. While the weight of opinion has credited the invention to Gutenberg, the case of the German has not been absolutely conclusive. In the first place, there exists no piece of printing in which the name of Gutenberg appears as the printer. In the second place, there was known no trustworthy printed or written evidence dated during the contemporary period. And, in the third place, the cause of Gutenberg suffered severe prejudice through the discovery by Hessels that a large proportion of the docu-*ments, on which his case had been based, were rank forgeries, inspired by the over-enthusiastic*

ITC MODERN NO. 216** LIGHT WITH LIGHT ITALIC   MERGENTHALER TYPE LIBRARY

12/13 The invention of printing, one of the most momentous events in the history of civilization, has been the subject of most controversy. The rival claims of Gutenberg and Coster have been argued with considerable acrimony by a number of authorities. While the weight of opinion has credited the invention to Gutenberg, the case of the German has not been absolutely conclusive. In the first place, there exists no piece of printing in which the name of Gutenberg appears as the printer. In the second place, there was *known no trustworthy printed or written evidence dated during the contem-*

10/11 The invention of printing, one of the most momentous events in the history of civilization, has been the subject of most controversy. The rival claims of Gutenberg and Coster have been argued with considerable acrimony by a number of authorities. While the weight of opinion has credited the invention to Gutenberg, the case of the German has not been absolutely conclusive. In the first place, there exists no piece of printing in which the name of Gutenberg appears as the printer. In the second place, there was known no trustworthy printed or written evidence dated during the contemporary period. And, in the third place, the cause of Gutenberg suffered severe prejudice through the discovery by Hessels *that a large proportion of the documents, on which his case had been based, were rank for-*

ITC MODERN NO. 216** MEDIUM WITH MEDIUM ITALIC   MERGENTHALER TYPE LIBRARY

12/13 **The invention of printing, one of the most momentous events in the history of civilization, has been the subject of most controversy. The rival claims of Gutenberg and Coster have been argued with considerable acrimony by a number of authorities. While the weight of opinion has credited the invention to Gutenberg, the case of the German has not been absolutely conclusive. In the first place, there exists no piece of printing in which the name of Gutenberg appears as the printer. In the second place, *there was known no trustworthy printed or written evidence***

10/11 **The invention of printing, one of the most momentous events in the history of civilization, has been the subject of most controversy. The rival claims of Gutenberg and Coster have been argued with considerable acrimony by a number of authorities. While the weight of opinion has credited the invention to Gutenberg, the case of the German has not been absolutely conclusive. In the first place, there exists no piece of printing in which the name of Gutenberg appears as the printer. In the second place, there was known no trustworthy printed or written evidence dated during the contemporary period. And, in the third place, the cause of Gutenberg suffered severe prejudice *through the discovery by Hessels that a large proportion of the documents, on which his***

ITC MODERN NO. 216** BOLD WITH BOLD ITALIC   MERGENTHALER TYPE LIBRARY

ABCDEFGHIJKLMNOPQRST
UVWXYZ&abcdefghijklmnop
qrstuvwxyz1234567890$.,""'":;!?

CRAW MODERN**   MERGENTHALER TYPE LIBRARY

ABCDEFGHIJKLMNOPQRSTUVWXYZ&
abcdefghijklmnopqrstuvwxyz
1234567890$.,''"":;!?

MUSKETEER LIGHT   AGFA COMPUGRAPHIC TYPE LIBRARY

ABCDEFGHIJKLMNOPQRSTUVWXY
Z&abcdefghijklmnopqrstuvwxyz
1234567890$.,''"":;!?

MUSKETEER DEMI BOLD   AGFA COMPUGRAPHIC TYPE LIBRARY

ABCDEFGHIJKLMNOPQRSTUVWXYZ&
abcdefghijklmnopqrstuvwxyz
1234567890$.,''"":;!?

MUSKETEER   AGFA COMPUGRAPHIC TYPE LIBRARY

ABCDEFGHIJKLMNOPQRSTUVW
XYZ&abcdefghijklmnopqrstuvwxyz
1234567890$.,''"":;!?

MUSKETEER EXTRA BOLD   AGFA COMPUGRAPHIC TYPE LIBRARY

SUPPLEMENTARY FACES 411

12/13 It is still a matter of conjecture whether Johann Gutenberg was the first to conceive the principle of casting movable [i.e., separate] metal types which he could arrange in words and sentences so that he could impress their faces on paper. There is, however, hardly a doubt, judging at least from the evidence available, that he was the first to make practical use of the idea, and

10/11 It is still a matter of conjecture whether Johann Gutenberg was the first to conceive the principle of casting movable [i.e., separate] metal types which he could arrange in words and sentences so that he could impress their faces on paper. There is, however, hardly a doubt, judging at least from the evidence available, that he was the first to make practical use of the idea, and that it is due to his ingenious application of it that the profound art of typography was born.

Whether he cast his letters in molds of sand or in metal ma-

CRAW MODERN**   MERGENTHALER TYPE LIBRARY

12/13 It is still a matter of conjecture whether Johann Gutenberg was the first to conceive the principle of casting moveable [i.e., separate] metal types which he could arrange in words and sentences so that he could impress their faces on paper. There is, however, hardly a doubt, judging at least from the evidence available, that he was the first to make practical use of the idea, and that it is do to his ingenious application of it that the profound art of typography was born. Whether he cast his letters in molds of sand or in metal matrices, is a question not really material at this time; it is the far-reaching results of his **inspiration that most concern us in this discussion. It seems quite probable that**

10/11 It is still a matter of conjecture whether Johann Gutenberg was the first to conceive the principle of casting moveable [i.e., separate] metal types which he could arrange in words and sentences so that he could impress their faces on paper. There is, however, hardly a doubt, judging at least from the evidence available, that he was the first to make practical use of the idea, and that it is do to his ingenious application of it that the profound art of typography was born. Whether he cast his letters in molds of sand or in metal matrices, is a question not really material at this time; it is the far-reaching results of his inspiration that most concern us in this discussion. It seems quite probable that Gutenberg at first had little more in mind than a desire to find some expedient by which to supplement with explanatory text the illustrations cut on wood blocks--some **method that wold avoid the labor of engraving the text itself, some device that would produce more**

MUSKETEER LIGHT WITH DEMI BOLD   AGFA COMPUGRAPHIC TYPE LIBRARY

12/13 It is still a matter of conjecture whether Johann Gutenberg was the first to conceive the principle of casting moveable [i.e., separate] metal types which he could arrange in words and sentences so that he could impress their faces on paper. There is, however, hardly a doubt, judging at least from the evidence available, that he was the first to make practical use of the idea, and that it is do to his in genious application of it that the profound art of typography was born. Whether he cast his letters in molds of sand or in metal matrices, is a question not really material at this time; it **is the far-reaching results of his inspiration that most concern us in this discus-**

10/11 It is still a matter of conjecture whether Johann Gutenberg was the first to conceive the principle of casting moveable [i.e., separate] metal types which he could arrange in words and sentences so that he could impress their faces on paper. There is, however, hardly a doubt, judging at least from the evidence available, that he was the first to make practical use of the idea, and that it is do to his ingenious application of it that the profound art of typography was born. Whether he cast his letters in molds of sand or in metal matrices, is a question not really material at this time; it is the far-reaching results of his inspiration that most concern us in this discussion. It seems quite probable that Gutenberg at first had little more in mind than a desire to find some expedient by which to supplement with explanatory **text the illustrations cut on wood blocks--some method that would avoid the labor**

MUSKETEER WITH EXTRA BOLD   AGFA COMPUGRAPHIC TYPE LIBRARY

ABCDEFGHIJKLMNOPQRSTUVWXYZ&
abcdefghijklmnopqrstuvwxyz
1234567890$.,""'':;!?

NEWS GOTHIC LIGHT   AGFA COMPUGRAPHIC TYPE LIBRARY

ABCDEFGHIJKLMNOPQRSTUVWXYZ&
abcdefghijklmnopqrstuvwxyz
1234567890$.,""'':;!?

NEWS GOTHIC LIGHT ITALIC   AGFA COMPUGRAPHIC TYPE LIBRARY

ABCDEFGHIJKLMNOPQRSTUVWXYZ
&abcdefghijklmnopqrstuvwxyz
1234567890$.,""'':;!?

NEWS GOTHIC   AGFA COMPUGRAPHIC TYPE LIBRARY

ABCDEFGHIJKLMNOPQRSTUVWXYZ
&abcdefghijklmnopqrstuvwxyz
1234567890$.,""'':;!?

NEWS GOTHIC BOLD   AGFA COMPUGRAPHIC TYPE LIBRARY

ABCDEFGHIJKLMNOPQRSTUVWXYZ&
abcdefghijklmnopqrstuvwxyz
1234567890$.,""'':;!?

NEWS GOTHIC CONDENSED   AGFA COMPUGRAPHIC TYPE LIBRARY

ABCDEFGHIJKLMNOPQRSTUVWXYZ&
abcdefghijklmnopqrstuvwxyz
1234567890$.,""'':;!?

NEWS GOTHIC BOLD CONDENSED   AGFA COMPUGRAPHIC TYPE LIBRARY

12/13 The invention of printing, one of the most momentous events in the history of civilization, has been the subject of most controversy. The rival claims of Gutenberg and Coster have been argued with considerable acrimony by a number of authorities. While the weight of opinion has credited the invention to Gutenberg, the case of the German has not been absolutely conclusive. In the first place, there exists no piece of printing in which the name of Gutenberg appears as the printer. In the second place, there was known no trustworthy printed or written evidence dated *during the contemporary period. And, in the third place, the cause of Gutenberg suffered*

10/11 The invention of printing, one of the most momentous events in the history of civilization, has been the subject of most controversy. The rival claims of Gutenberg and Coster have been argued with considerable acrimony by a number of authorities. While the weight of opinion has credited the invention to Gutenberg, the case of the German has not been absolutely conclusive. In the first place, there exists no piece of printing in which the name of Gutenberg appears as the printer. In the second place, there was known no trustworthy printed or written evidence dated during the contemporary period. And, in the third place, the cause of Gutenberg suffered severe prejudice through the discovery by Hessels that a large proportion of the documents, on which his case had been based, were *rank forgeries, inspired by the over-enthusiastic nationalism of Bodmann, the archivist at Mentz. The*

NEWS GOTHIC LIGHT WITH LIGHT ITALIC   AGFA COMPUGRAPHIC TYPE LIBRARY

12/13 The invention of printing, one of the most momentous events in the history of civilization, has been the subject of most controversy. The rival claims of Gutenberg and Coster have been argued with considerable acrimony by a number of authorities. While the weight of opinion has credited the invention to Gutenberg, the case of the German has not been absolutely conclusive. In the first place, there exists no piece of printing in which the name of Gutenberg appears as the printer. In the second place, there was known no trustworthy printed or **written evidence dated during the contemporary period. And, in the third place, the**

10/11 The invention of printing, one of the most momentous events in the history of civilization, has been the subject of most controversy. The rival claims of Gutenberg and Coster have been argued with considerable acrimony by a number of authorities. While the weight of opinion has credited the invention to Gutenberg, the case of the German has not been absolutely conclusive. In the first place, there exists no piece of printing in which the name of Gutenberg appears as the printer. In the second place, there was known no trustworthy printed or written evidence dated during the contemporary period. And, in the third place, the cause of Gutenberg suffered severe prejudice through the discovery by Hessels that a large **proportion of the documents, on which his case had been based, were rank forgeries, inspired by the**

NEWS GOTHIC WITH BOLD   AGFA COMPUGRAPHIC TYPE LIBRARY

12/13 The invention of printing, one of the most momentous events in the history of civilization, has been the subject of most controversy. The rival claims of Gutenberg and Coster have been argued with considerable acrimony by a number of authorities. While the weight of opinion has credited the invention to Gutenberg, the case of the German has not been absolutely conclusive. In the first place, there exists no piece of printing in which the name of Gutenberg appears as the printer. In the second place, there was known no trustworthy printed or written evidence dated during the contemporary period. And, in the third place, the cause of Gutenberg suffered severe prejudice trough the discovery by Hessels that **a large proportion of the documents, on which his case had been based, were rank forgeries, inspired by the**

10/11 The invention of printing, one of the most momentous events in the history of civilization, has been the subject of most controversy. The rival claims of Gutenberg and Coster have been argued with considerable acrimony by a number of authorities. While the weight of opinion has credited the invention to Gutenberg, the case of the German has not been absolutely conclusive. In the first place, there exists no piece of printing in which the name of Gutenberg appears as the printer. In the second place, there was known no trustworthy printed or written evidence dated during the contemporary period. And, in the third place, the cause of Gutenberg suffered severe prejudice through the discovery by Hessels that a large proportion of the documents, on which his case had been based, were rank forgeries, inspired by the over-enthusiastic nationalism of Bodmann, the archivist at Mentz. The circumstantial evidence, however, has all pointed to Gutenberg as the father of the printing art, **and the invention was very generally credited to him, particularly as there was never produced any direct and conclusive evidence**

NEWS GOTHIC CONDENSED WITH BOLD CONDENSED   AGFA COMPUGRAPHIC TYPE LIBRARY

ABCDEFGHIJKLMNOPQRSTUVWXYZ
&abcdefghijklmnopqrstuvwxyz1234567890$.,'"":;!?

ITC NOVARESE** BOOK   MERGENTHALER TYPE LIBRARY

ABCDEFGHIJKLMNOPQRSTUVWXYZ
&abcdefghijklmnopqrstuvwxyz1234567890$.,'"":;!?

ITC NOVARESE** BOOK ITALIC   MERGENTHALER TYPE LIBRARY

ABCDEFGHIJKLMNOPQRSTUVWXYZ
&abcdefghijklmnopqrstuvwxyz1234567890$.,'"":;!?

ITC NOVARESE** MEDIUM   MERGENTHALER TYPE LIBRARY

ABCDEFGHIJKLMNOPQRSTUVWXYZ
&abcdefghijklmnopqrstuvwxyz1234567890$.,'"":;!?

ITC NOVARESE** MEDIUM ITALIC   MERGENTHALER TYPE LIBRARY

ABCDEFGHIJKLMNOPQRSTUVWXYZ&abcdefghijklmnopqrstuvwxyz1234567890$.,'"":;!?

ITC NOVARESE** BOLD   MERGENTHALER TYPE LIBRARY

ABCDEFGHIJKLMNOPQRSTUVWXYZ&abcdefghijklmnopqrstuvwxyz1234567890$.,'"":;!?

ITC NOVARESE** BOLD ITALIC   MERGENTHALER TYPE LIBRARY

SUPPLEMENTARY FACES 415

12/13 It is still a matter of conjecture whether Johann Gutenberg was the first to conceive the principle of casting movable [i.e., separate] metal types which he could arrange in words and sentences so that he could impress their faces on paper. There is, however, hardly a doubt, judging at least from the evidence available, that he was the first to make practical use of the idea, and that it is due to his ingenious application of it that the profound art of typography was born.

Whether he cast his letters in molds of sand or in metal matrices, is a question not *really material at this time; it is the far-reaching results of his inspiration that most concern us in this*

10/11 It is still a matter of conjecture whether Johann Gutenberg was the first to conceive the principle of casting movable [i.e., separate] metal types which he could arrange in words and sentences so that he could impress their faces on paper. There is, however, hardly a doubt, judging at least from the evidence available, that he was the first to make practical use of the idea, and that it is due to his ingenious application of it that the profound art of typography was born.

Whether he cast his letters in molds of sand or in metal matrices, is a question not really material at this time; it is the far-reaching results of his inspiration that most concern us in this discussion. It seems quite probable that Gutenberg at first had little more in mind than a desire to find some expedient by which to *supplement with explanatory text the illustrations cut on wood blocks — some method that would avoid the labor of engraving*

ITC NOVARESE** BOOK WITH BOOK ITALIC   MERGENTHALER TYPE LIBRARY

12/13 It is still a matter of conjecture whether Johann Gutenberg was the first to conceive the principle of casting movable [i.e., separate] metal types which he could arrange in words and sentences so that he could impress their faces on paper. There is, however, hardly a doubt, judging at least from the evidence available, that he was the first to make practical use of the idea, and that it is due to his ingenious application of it that the profound art of typography was born.

Whether he cast his letters in molds of sand or in metal matrices, is a question not *really material at this time; it is the far-reaching results of his inspiration that most concern us in this*

10/11 It is still a matter of conjecture whether Johann Gutenberg was the first to conceive the principle of casting movable [i.e., separate] metal types which he could arrange in words and sentences so that he could impress their faces on paper. There is, however, hardly a doubt, judging at least from the evidence available, that he was the first to make practical use of the idea, and that it is due to his ingenious application of it that the profound art of typography was born.

Whether he cast his letters in molds of sand or in metal matrices, is a question not really material at this time; it is the far-reaching results of his inspiration that most concern us in this discussion. It seems quite probable that Gutenberg at first had little more *in mind than a desire to find some expedient by which to supplement with explanatory text the illustrations cut on wood*

ITC NOVARESE** MEDIUM WITH MEDIUM ITALIC   MERGENTHALER TYPE LIBRARY

12/13 **It is still a matter of conjecture whether Johann Gutenberg was the first to conceive the principle of casting movable [i.e., separate] metal types which he could arrange in words and sentences so that he could impress their faces on paper. There is, however, hardly a doubt, judging at least from the evidence available, that he was the first to make practical use of the idea, and that it is due to his ingenious application of it that the profound art of typography was born.**

Whether he cast his letters in molds of sand or in metal matrices, is a question not *really material at this time; it is the far-reaching results of his inspiration that most concern*

10/11 **It is still a matter of conjecture whether Johann Gutenberg was the first to conceive the principle of casting movable [i.e., separate] metal types which he could arrange in words and sentences so that he could impress their faces on paper. There is, however, hardly a doubt, judging at least from the evidence available, that he was the first to make practical use of the idea, and that it is due to his ingenious application of it that the profound art of typography was born.**

Whether he cast his letters in molds of sand or in metal matrices, is a question not really material at this time; it is the far-reaching results of his inspiration that most concern us in this discussion. It seems quite probable that Gutenberg at first had little *more in mind than a desire to find some expedient by which to supplement with explanatory text the illustra-*

ITC NOVARESE** BOLD WITH BOLD ITALIC   MERGENTHALER TYPE LIBRARY

ABCDEFGHIJKLMNOPQRSTUVWXYZ
&abcdefghijklmnopqrstuvwxyz
1234567890$.,"''":;!?

ANTIQUE OLIVE   AGFA COMPUGRAPHIC TYPE LIBRARY

*ABCDEFGHIJKLMNOPQRSTUVWXYZ&
abcdefghijklmnopqrstuvwxyz
1234567890$.,"''":;!?*

ANTIQUE OLIVE ITALIC   AGFA COMPUGRAPHIC TYPE LIBRARY

**ABCDEFGHIJKLMNOPQRSTUVWXYZ
&abcdefghijklmnopqrstuvwxyz
1234567890$.,"''":;!?**

ANTIQUE OLIVE MEDIUM   AGFA COMPUGRAPHIC TYPE LIBRARY

***ABCDEFGHIJKLMNOPQRSTUVWXYZ
&abcdefghijklmnopqrstuvwxyz
1234567890$.,"''":;!?***

ANTIQUE OLIVE MEDIUM ITALIC   AGFA COMPUGRAPHIC TYPE LIBRARY

ABCDEFGHIJKLMNOPQRSTUVWXYZ&
abcdefghijklmnopqrstuvwxyz
1234567890$.,"''":;!?

ANTIQUE OLIVE LIGHT   AGFA COMPUGRAPHIC TYPE LIBRARY

**ABCDEFGHIJKLMNOPQRSTUVWXY
Z&abcdefghijklmnopqrstuvwx
yz1234567890$.,"''":;!?**

ANTIQUE OLIVE BOLD   AGFA COMPUGRAPHIC TYPE LIBRARY

SUPPLEMENTARY FACES 417

12/13 In considering fine and praiseworthy inventions, we must freely confess that printing has been and is to-day the best and most estimable-the invention by means of which two persons turning the press can get a greater number of books in a day than formerly could have been transcribed by several persons in a year. It is claimed that this art was invented at Mainz, a city of Germany, in the year 1442 by Jean Guttemberg, or, according to others, Guttenberg, an *honorable German chevalier. It was at Mainz that after experimenting with*

10/11 In considering fine and praiseworthy inventions, we must freely confess that printing has been and is to-day the best and most estimable-the invention by means of which two persons turning the press can get a greater number of books in a day than formerly could have been transcribed by several persons in a year. It is claimed that this art was invented at Mainz, a city of Germany, in the year 1442 by Jean Guttemberg, or, according to others, Guttenberg, an honorable German chevalier. It was at Mainz that after experimenting with with an ink which is used by printers to-day, he first began the practice of the art. Some persons prefer to at*tribute the invention to Jean Fauste & Yues Scheffey two years earlier, holding that our*

ANTIQUE OLIVE WITH ITALIC — AGFA COMPUGRAPHIC TYPE LIBRARY

12/13 **In considering fine and praiseworthy inventions, we must freely confess that printing has been and is to-day the best and most estimable-the invention by means of which two persons turning the press can get a greater number of books in a day than formerly could have been transcribed by several persons in a year. It is claimed that this art was invented at Mainz, a city of Germany, in the year 1442 by Jean Guttemberg, or, according to others, Guttenberg, an *honorable German chevalier. It was at Mainz that after experimenting with***

10/11 **In considering fine and praiseworthy inventions, we must freely confess that printing has been and is to-day the best and most estimable-the invention by means of which two persons turning the press can get a greater number of books in a day than formerly could have been transcribed by several persons in a year. It is claimed that this art was invented at Mainz, a city of Germany, in the year 1442 by Jean Guttemberg, or, according to others, Guttenberg, an honorable German chevalier. It was at Mainz that after experimenting with with an ink which is used by printers to-day, he first began the practice of the art. Some persons *prefer to attribute the invention to Jean Fauste & Yues Scheffey two years earlier,***

ANTIQUE OLIVE MEDIUM WITH MEDIUM ITALIC — AGFA COMPUGRAPHIC TYPE LIBRARY

12/13 In considering fine and praiseworthy inventions, we must freely confess that printing has been and is to-day the best and most estimable-the invention by means of which two persons turning the press can get a greater number of books in a day than formerly could have been transcribed by several persons in a year. It is claimed that this art was invented at Mainz, a city of Germany, in the year 1442 by Jean Guttemberg, or, according to others, Guttenberg, an honorable German chevalier. It was at Mainz that after ex**perimenting with an ink which is used by printers to-day, he first be**

10/11 In considering fine and praiseworthy inventions we must freely confess that printing has been and is to-day the best and most estimable-the invention by means of which two persons turning the press can get a greater number of books in a day than formerly could have been transcribed by several persons in a year. It is claimed that this art was invented at Mainz, a city of Germany, in the year 1442 by Jean Guttemberg, or, according to others, Guttenberg, an honorable German chevalier. It was at Mainz that after experimenting with with an ink which is used by printers to-day, he first began the practice of the art. Some persons prefer to attribute the invention to Jean Fauste & Yues Scheffey two years earlier, holding **that our Guttemberg, Jean Mentel, Jean Prus, Adolphe Rusche, Pierre Scheffec,**

ANTIQUE OLIVE LIGHT WITH BOLD — AGFA COMPUGRAPHIC TYPE LIBRARY

ABCDEFGHIJKLMNOPQRSTUVWXYZ&abcdefghijklmnopqrstuvwxyz1234567890$.,'''':;!?

OPTIMA*   MERGENTHALER TYPE LIBRARY

ABCDEFGHIJKLMNOPQRSTUVWXYZ&abcdefghijklmnopqrstuvwxyz1234567890$.,'''':;!?

OPTIMA* ITALIC   MERGENTHALER TYPE LIBRARY

ABCDEFGHIJKLMNOPQRSTUVWXYZ&abcdefghijklmnopqrstuvwxyz1234567890$.,'''':;!?

OPTIMA* MEDIUM   MERGENTHALER TYPE LIBRARY

ABCDEFGHIJKLMNOPQRSTUVWXYZ&abcdefghijklmnopqrstuvwxyz1234567890$.,'''':;!?

OPTIMA* MEDIUM ITALIC   MERGENTHALER TYPE LIBRARY

ABCDEFGHIJKLMNOPQRSTUVWXYZ&abcdefghijklmnopqrstuvwxyz1234567890$.,'''':;!?

OPTIMA* DEMI BOLD   MERGENTHALER TYPE LIBRARY

ABCDEFGHIJKLMNOPQRSTUVWXYZ&abcdefghijklmnopqrstuvwxyz1234567890$.,'''':;!?

OPTIMA* DEMI BOLD ITALIC   MERGENTHALER TYPE LIBRARY

SUPPLEMENTARY FACES 419

12/13 In considering fine and praiseworthy inventions, we must freely confess that printing has been and is to-day the best and most estimable — the invention by means of which two persons turning the press can get a greater number of books in a day than formerly could have been transcribed by several persons in a year. It is claimed that this art was invented at Mainz, a city of Germany, in the year 1442 by Jean Guttemberg, or, according to others, Guttenberg, an honorable German chevalier. It was at Mainz that after experimenting with an ink which is used by printers *to-day, he first began the practice of the art. Some persons prefer to attribute the invention*

10/11 In considering fine and praiseworthy inventions, we must freely confess that printing has been and is to-day the best and most estimable — the invention by means of which two persons turning the press can get a greater number of books in a day than formerly could have been transcribed by several persons in a year. It is claimed that this art was invented at Mainz, a city of Germany, in the year 1442 by Jean Guttemberg, or, according to others, Guttenberg, an honorable German chevalier. It was at Mainz that after experimenting with an ink which is used by printers to-day, he first began the practice of the art. Some persons prefer to attribute the invention to Jean Fauste & Yues Scheffey two years earlier, holding that our Guttemberg, Jean Mentel, Jean Prus, Adolphe Rusche, Pierre Scheffec, *Martin Flache, Huldric Han, Jean Froben, Adam Petri, Thomas Vuolffe, and others added improvements and*

OPTIMA* WITH ITALIC   MERGENTHALER TYPE LIBRARY

12/13 In considering fine and praiseworthy inventions, we must freely confess that printing has been and is to-day the best and most estimable — the invention by means of which two persons turning the press can get a greater number of books in a day than formerly could have been transcribed by several persons in a year. It is claimed that this art was invented at Mainz, a city of Germany, in the year 1442 by Jean Guttemberg, or, according to others, Guttenberg, an honorable German chevalier. It was at Mainz that after experi*menting with an ink which is used by printers to-day, he first began the practice of the*

10/11 In considering fine and praiseworthy inventions, we must freely confess that printing has been and is to-day the best and most estimable — the invention by means of which two persons turning the press can get a greater number of books in a day than formerly could have been transcribed by several persons in a year. It is claimed that this art was invented at Mainz, a city of Germany, in the year 1442 by Jean Guttemberg, or, according to others, Guttenberg, an honorable German chevalier. It was at Mainz that after experimenting with an ink which is used by printers to-day, he first began the practice of the art. Some persons prefer to attribute the invention to Jean Fauste & Yues Scheffey two years earlier, holding that our Gut*temberg, Jean Mentel, Jean Prus, Adolphe Rusche, Pierre Scheffec, Martin Flache, Huldric Han, Jean*

OPTIMA* MEDIUM WITH MEDIUM ITALIC   MERGENTHALER TYPE LIBRARY

12/13 **In considering fine and praiseworthy inventions, we must freely confess that printing has been and is to-day the best and most estimable — the invention by means of which two persons turning the press can get a greater number of books in a day than formerly could have been transcribed by several persons in a year. It is claimed that this art was invented at Mainz, a city of Germany, in the year 1442 by Jean Guttemberg, or, according to others, Guttenberg, an honorable German chevalier. It was at Mainz after experimenting with an ink *which is used by printers to-day, he first began the practice of the art. Some persons***

10/11 **In considering fine and praiseworthy inventions, we must freely confess that printing has been and is to-day the best and most estimable — the invention by means of which two persons turning the press can get a greater number of books in a day than formerly could have been transcribed by several persons in a year. It is claimed that this art was invented at Mainz, a city of Germany, in the year 1442 by Jean Guttemberg, or, according to others, Guttenberg, an honorable German chevalier. It was at Mainz that after experimenting with an ink which is used by printers to-day, he first began the practice of the art. Some persons prefer to attribute the invention to Jean Fauste & Yues Scheffey two years earlier, holding that our Guttemberg, Jean Mentel, Jean Prus, *Adolphe Rusche, Pierre Scheffec, Martin Flache, Huldric Han, Jean Froben, Adam Petri, Thomas***

OPTIMA* DEMI BOLD WITH DEMI BOLD ITALIC   MERGENTHALER TYPE LIBRARY

ABCDEFGHIJKLMNOPQRSTUVWXYZ&abcdefghijklmnopqrstuvwxyz1234567890$.,''"":;!?

OPTIMA* BOLD   MERGENTHALER TYPE LIBRARY

ABCDEFGHIJKLMNOPQRSTUVWXYZ&abcdefghijklmnopqrstuvwxyz1234567890$.,''"":;!?

OPTIMA* BOLD ITALIC   MERGENTHALER TYPE LIBRARY

ABCDEFGHIJKLMNOPQRSTUVWXYZ&abcdefghijklmnopqrstuvwxyz1234567890$.,''"":;!?

OPTIMA* BLACK   MERGENTHALER TYPE LIBRARY

ABCDEFGHIJKLMNOPQRSTUVWXYZ&abcdefghijklmnopqrstuvwxyz1234567890$.,''"":;!?

OPTIMA* BLACK ITALIC   MERGENTHALER TYPE LIBRARY

ABCDEFGHIJKLMNOPQRSTUVWXYZ&abcdefghijklmnopqrstuvwxyz1234567890$.,''"":;!?

OPTIMA* EXTRA BLACK   MERGENTHALER TYPE LIBRARY

ABCDEFGHIJKLMNOPQRSTUVWXYZ&abcdefghijklmnopqrstuvwxyz1234567890$.,''"":;!?

OPTIMA* EXTRA BLACK ITALIC   MERGENTHALER TYPE LIBRARY

SUPPLEMENTARY FACES 421

12/13 **In considering fine and praiseworthy inventions, we must freely confess that printing has been and is to-day the best and most estimable — the invention by means of which two persons turning the press can get a greater number of books in a day than formerly could have been transcribed by several persons in a year. It is claimed that this art was invented at Mainz, a city of Germany, in the year 1442 by Jean Guttemberg, or, according to others, Guttenberg, an honorable German chevalier. It was at Mainz that after experimenting with an ink which is *used by printers to-day, he first began the practice of the art. Some persons prefer to***

10/11 **In considering fine and praiseworthy inventions, we must freely confess that printing has been and is to-day the best and most estimable — the invention by means of which two persons turning the press can get a greater number of books in a day than formerly could have been transcribed by several persons in a year. It is claimed that this art was invented at Mainz, a city of Germany, in the year 1442 by Jean Guttemberg, or, according to others, Guttenberg, an honorable German chevalier. It was at Mainz that after experimenting with an ink which is used by printers to-day, he first began the practice of the art. Some persons prefer to attribute the invention to Jean Fauste & Yues Scheffey two years earlier, holding that our Guttemberg, Jean Mentel, Jean Prus, Adolphe *Rusche, Pierre Scheffec, Martin Flache, Huldric Han, Jean Froben, Adam Petri, Thomas Vuolffe, and others***

OPTIMA* BOLD WITH BOLD ITALIC   MERGENTHALER TYPE LIBRARY

12/13 **In considering fine and praiseworthy inventions, we must freely confess that printing has been and is to-day the best and most estimable — the invention by means of which two persons turning the press can get a greater number of books in a day than formerly could have been transcribed by several persons in a year. It is claimed that this art was invented at Mainz, a city of Germany, in the year 1442 by Jean Guttemberg, or, according to others, Guttenberg, an honorable German chevalier. It was at Mainz that after experi*menting with an ink which is used by printers to-day, he first began the practice***

10/11 **In considering fine and praiseworthy inventions, we must freely confess that printing has been and is to-day the best and most estimable — the invention by means of which two persons turning the press can get a greater number of books in a day than formerly could have been transcribed by several persons in a year. It is claimed that this art was invented at Mainz, a city of Germany, in the year 1442 by Jean Guttemberg, or, according to others, Guttenberg, an honorable German chevalier. It was at Mainz that after experimenting with an ink which is used by printers to-day, he first began the practice of the art. Some persons prefer to attribute the invention to Jean Fauste & Yues Scheffey two years earlier, holding that our Gut*temberg, Jean Mentel, Jean Prus, Adolphe Rusche, Pierre Scheffec, Martin Flache, Huldric Han, Jean***

OPTIMA* BLACK WITH BLACK ITALIC   MERGENTHALER TYPE LIBRARY

12/13 **In considering fine and praiseworthy inventions, we must freely confess that printing has been and is to-day the best and most estimable — the invention by means of which two persons turning the press can get a greater number of books in a day than formerly could have been transcribed by several persons in a year. It is claimed that this art was invented at Mainz, a city of Germany, in the year 1442 by Jean Guttemberg, or, according to others, Guttenberg, an honorable German chevalier. *It was at Mainz that after experimenting with an ink which is used by print-***

10/11 **In considering fine and praiseworthy inventions, we must freely confess that printing has been and is to-day the best and most estimable — the invention by means of which two persons turning the press can get a greater number of books in a day than formerly could have been transcribed by several persons in a year. It is claimed that this art was invented at Mainz, a city of Germany, in the year 1442 by Jean Guttemberg, or, according to others, Guttenberg, an honorable German chevalier. It was at Mainz that after experimenting with an ink which is used by printers to-day, he first began the practice of the art. Some persons prefer to attribute the invention to Jean Fauste *& Yues Scheffey two years earlier, holding that our Guttemberg, Jean Mentel, Jean Prus,***

OPTIMA* EXTRA BLACK WITH EXTRA BLACK ITALIC   MERGENTHALER TYPE LIBRARY

ABCDEFGHIJKLMNOPQRSTUVW
XYZ&abcdefghijklmnopqrstuvwxyz
1234567890$.,''"":;!?

PALATINO*   MERGENTHALER TYPE LIBRARY

*ABCDEFGHIJKLMNOPQRSTUVWX
YZ&abcdefghijklmnopqrstuvwxyz12345
67890$.,''"":;!?*

PALATINO* ITALIC   MERGENTHALER TYPE LIBRARY

**ABCDEFGHIJKLMNOPQRSTUVWX
YZ&abcdefghijklmnopqrstuvwxyz123
4567890$.,''"":;!?**

PALATINO* BOLD   MERGENTHALER TYPE LIBRARY

***ABCDEFGHIJKLMNOPQRSTUVWXY
Z&abcdefghijklmnopqrstuvwxyz12345
67890$.,''"":;!?***

PALATINO* BOLD ITALIC   MERGENTHALER TYPE LIBRARY

ABCDEFGHIJKLMNOPQRSTUVW
XYZ&abcdefghijklmnopqrstuvwxyz12
34567890 $.,"":;!?

TS PARSONS**   MERGENTHALER TYPE LIBRARY

*ABCDEFGHIJKLMNOPQRSTUVW
XYZ&abcdefghijklmnopqrstuvwxyz1
234567890 $.,"":;!?*

TS PARSONS** ITALIC   MERGENTHALER TYPE LIBRARY

SUPPLEMENTARY FACES 423

12/13 Lying in my bed, on the morning of the Feast of Kings, when I had had my sleep and rest, & my stomach had readily digested its light and pleasant repast, in the year that was reckoned as MDXXIII, I fell to musing and set the wheel of my memory awhirl thinking on a thousand little conceits, some serious & some joyous, among which there came to my mind a certain Antique letter which I had lately made for my lord the Treasurer for War, Maistre Jehan Groslier, Counsellor and Secretary to our Lord the King, lover of well-made letters and of all learned persons, *by whom also he is much loved & esteemed on both this & the*

10/11 Lying in my bed, on the morning of the Feast of Kings, when I had had my sleep and rest, & my stomach had readily digested its light and pleasant repast, in the year that was reckoned as MDXXIII, I fell to musing and set the wheel of my memory awhirl thinking on a thousand little conceits, some serious & some joyous, among which there came to my mind a certain Antique letter which I had lately made for my lord the Treasurer for War, Maistre Jehan Groslier, Counsellor and Secretary to our Lord the King, lover of well-made letters and of all learned persons, by whom also he is much loved & esteemed on both this & the other side of the mountains. And whilst thinking of this Attic Letter, there came of a sudden into my memory a pithy passage *in the first book & eighth chapter of the DeOfficiis of Cicero, where it is written: Non nobis solum nati sumus;*

PALATINO* WITH ITALIC   MERGENTHALER TYPE LIBRARY

12/13 **Lying in my bed, on the morning of the Feast of Kings, when I had had my sleep and rest, & my stomach had readily digested its light and pleasant repast, in the year that was reckoned as MDXXIII, I fell to musing and set the wheel of my memory awhirl thinking on a thousand little conceits, some serious & some joyous, among which there came to my mind a certain Antique letter which I had lately made for my lord the Treasurer for War, Maistre Jehan Groslier, Counsellor and Secretary to our Lord the King, lover of *well-made letters and of all learned persons, by whom also he is much loved &***

10/11 **Lying in my bed, on the morning of the Feast of Kings, when I had had my sleep and rest, & my stomach had readily digested its light and pleasant repast, in the year that was reckoned as MDXXIII, I fell to musing and set the wheel of my memory awhirl thinking on a thousand little conceits, some serious & some joyous, among which there came to my mind a certain Antique letter which I had lately made for my lord the Treasurer for War, Maistre Jehan Groslier, Counsellor and Secretary to our Lord the King, lover of well-made letters and of all learned persons, by whom also he is much loved & esteemed on both this & the other side of the mountains. And whilst thinking of this Attic Letter, there came of a sudden into my memory a pithy *passage in the first book & eighth chapter of the DeOfficiis of Cicero, where it is written: Non nobis***

PALATINO* BOLD WITH BOLD ITALIC   MERGENTHALER TYPE LIBRARY

12/13 In type-founding, types are cast in moulds containing at one end a copper matrix of the character. The aperture through which the melted metal is injected is at the end of the mould opposite the matrix, and a piece as long as the type, called the jet, extends through the aperture from the bottom of the type. Thus imperfections in the metal and variations of temperature spend themselves in the jet, leaving the body of the type comparatively perfect. The types thus cast go through various processes, such as breaking off the jet and ploughing in its place a shallow *groove across the foot, thus leaving each type two "feet" to stand upon, "rubbing," etc.;*

10/11 In type-founding, types are cast in moulds containing at one end a copper matrix of the character. The aperture through which the melted metal is injected is at the end of the mould opposite the matrix, and a piece as long as the type, called the jet, extends through the aperture from the bottom of the type. Thus imperfections in the metal and variations of temperature spend themselves in the jet, leaving the body of the type comparatively perfect. The types thus cast go through various processes, such as breaking off the jet and ploughing in its place a shallow groove across the foot, thus leaving each type two "feet" to stand upon, "rubbing," etc.; and at last, set up in long rows, they pass under the eye of an expert, who, as he examines them carefully with a glass, rejects all in *which he detects any imperfections. In these processes an average of 10 per cent, is eliminated; so that of 100*

TS PARSONS** WITH ITALIC   MERGENTHALER TYPE LIBRARY

ABCDEFGHIJKLMNOPQRSTUVWXYZ&abcdefghijklmnopqrstuvwxyz1234567890$.,""":;!?

PERPETUA**   MERGENTHALER TYPE LIBRARY

ABCDEFGHIJKLMNOPQRSTUVWXYZ&abcdefghijklmnopqrstuvwxyz1234567890$.,""":;!?

PERPETUA** ITALIC   MERGENTHALER TYPE LIBRARY

ABCDEFGHIJKLMNOPQRSTUVWXYZ&abcdefghijklmnopqrstuvwxyz1234567890$.,""":;!?

PERPETUA** BOLD   MERGENTHALER TYPE LIBRARY

ABCDEFGHIJKLMNOPQRSTUVWXYZ&abcdefghijklmnopqrstuvwxyz1234567890$.,""":;!?

PERPETUA** BOLD ITALIC   MERGENTHALER TYPE LIBRARY

ABCDEFGHIJKLMNOPQRSTUVWXYZ&abcdefghijklmnopqrstuvwxyz1234567890$.,""":;!?

PERPETUA** BLACK   MERGENTHALER TYPE LIBRARY

SUPPLEMENTARY FACES 425

12/13 In considering fine and praiseworthy inventions, we must freely confess that printing has been and is to-day the best and most estimable — the invention by means of which two persons turning the press can get a greater number of books in a day than formerly could have been transcribed by several persons in a year. It is claimed that this art was invented at Mainz, a city of Germany, in the year 1442 by Jean Guttemberg, or, according to others, Guttenberg, an honorable German chevalier. It was at Mainz that after experimenting with an ink which is used by printers to-day, he first began the practice of the art. Some persons prefer to attribute the invention to Jean Fauste & Yues *Scheffey two years earlier, holding that our Guttemberg, Jean Mentel, Jean Prus, Adolphe Rusche, Pierre Scheffec, Martin*

10/11 In considering fine and praiseworthy inventions, we must freely confess that printing has been and is to-day the best and most estimable — the invention by means of which two persons turning the press can get a greater number of books in a day than formerly could have been transcribed by several persons in a year. It is claimed that this art was invented at Mainz, a city of Germany, in the year 1442 by Jean Guttemberg, or, according to others, Guttenberg, an honorable German chevalier. It was at Mainz that after experimenting with an ink which is used by printers to-day, he first began the practice of the art. Some persons prefer to attribute the invention to Jean Fauste & Yues Scheffey two years earlier, holding that our Guttemberg, Jean Mentel, Jean Prus, Adolphe Rusche, Pierre Scheffec, Martin Flache, Huldric Han, Jean Froben, Adam Petri, Thomas Vuolffe, and others added improvements and spread the art of printing *through all Germany and other countries. In fact Conrad practised the art at Rome about the year 1400.*

PERPETUA** WITH ITALIC   MERGENTHALER TYPE LIBRARY

12/13 **In considering fine and praiseworthy inventions, we must freely confess that printing has been and is to-day the best and most estimable — the invention by means of which two persons turning the press can get a greater number of books in a day than formerly could have been transcribed by several persons in a year. It is claimed that this art was invented at Mainz, a city of Germany, in the year 1442 by Jean Guttemberg, or, according to others, Guttenberg, an honorable German chevalier. It was at Mainz that after experimenting with an ink which is used by printers to-day, he first *began the practice of the art. Some persons prefer to attribute the invention to Jean Fauste & Yues Schef-***

10/11 **In considering fine and praiseworthy inventions, we must freely confess that printing has been and is to-day the best and most estimable — the invention by means of which two persons turning the press can get a greater number of books in a day than formerly could have been transcribed by several persons in a year. It is claimed that this art was invented at Mainz, a city of Germany, in the year 1442 by Jean Guttemberg, or, according to others, Guttenberg, an honorable German chevalier. It was at Mainz that after experimenting with an ink which is used by printers to-day, he first began the practice of the art. Some persons prefer to attribute the invention to Jean Fauste & Yues Scheffey two years earlier, holding that our Guttemberg, Jean Mentel, Jean Prus, Adolphe Rusche, Pierre Scheffec, Martin Flache, *Huldric Han, Jean Froben, Adam Petri, Thomas Vuolffe, and others added improvements and spread the art of printing***

PERPETUA** BOLD WITH BOLD ITALIC   MERGENTHALER TYPE LIBRARY

12/13 **In considering fine and praiseworthy inventions, we must freely confess that printing has been and is to-day the best and most estimable — the invention by means of which two persons turning the press can get a greater number of books in a day than formerly could have been transcribed by several persons in a year. It is claimed that this art was invented at Mainz, a city of Germany, in the year 1442 by Jean Guttemberg, or, according to others, Guttenberg, an honorable German chevalier. It was at Mainz that after experimenting with an ink which is used by print-**

10/11 **In considering fine and praiseworthy inventions, we must freely confess that printing has been and is to-day the best and most estimable — the invention by means of which two persons turning the press can get a greater number of books in a day than formerly could have been transcribed by several persons in a year. It is claimed that this art was invented at Mainz, a city of Germany, in the year 1442 by Jean Guttemberg, or, according to others, Guttenberg, an honorable German chevalier. It was at Mainz that after experimenting with an ink which is used by printers to-day, he first began the practice of the art. Some persons prefer to attribute the invention to Jean Fauste & Yues Scheffey two years earlier, holding that our Guttemberg, Jean Mentel, Jean Prus,**

PERPETUA** BLACK   MERGENTHALER TYPE LIBRARY

ABCDEFGHIJKLMNOPQRSTUVWXYZ&abcdefghijklmnopqrstuvwxyz1234567890$.,""":;!?

PLANTIN** LIGHT   MERGENTHALER TYPE LIBRARY

ABCDEFGHIJKLMNOPQRSTUVWXYZ&abcdefghijklmnopqrstuvwxyz1234567890$.,""":;!?

PLANTIN** LIGHT ITALIC   MERGENTHALER TYPE LIBRARY

ABCDEFGHIJKLMNOPQRSTUVWXYZ&abcdefghijklmnopqrstuvwxyz1234567890$.,""":;!?

PLANTIN**   MERGENTHALER TYPE LIBRARY

ABCDEFGHIJKLMNOPQRSTUVWXYZ&abcdefghijklmnopqrstuvwxyz1234567890$.,""":;!?

PLANTIN** ITALIC   MERGENTHALER TYPE LIBRARY

ABCDEFGHIJKLMNOPQRSTUVWXYZ&abcdefghijklmnopqrstuvwxyz1234567890$.,""":;!?

PLANTIN** BOLD   MERGENTHALER TYPE LIBRARY

ABCDEFGHIJKLMNOPQRSTUVWXYZ&abcdefghijklmnopqrstuvwxyz1234567890$.,""":;!?

PLANTIN** BOLD ITALIC   MERGENTHALER TYPE LIBRARY

SUPPLEMENTARY FACES 427

12/13 The invention of printing, one of the most momentous events in the history of civilization, has been the subject of most controversy. The rival claims of Gutenberg and Coster have been argued with considerable acrimony by a number of authorities. While the weight of opinion has credited the invention to Gutenberg, the case of the German has not been absolutely conclusive. In the first place, there exists no piece of printing in which the name of Gutenberg appears as the printer. In the second place, there was known no trustworthy printed or written evidence dated during the *contemporary period. And, in the third place, the cause of Gutenberg suffered severe prejudice*

10/11 The invention of printing, one of the most momentous events in the history of civilization, has been the subject of most controversy. The rival claims of Gutenberg and Coster have been argued with considerable acrimony by a number of authorities. While the weight of opinion has credited the invention to Gutenberg, the case of the German has not been absolutely conclusive. In the first place, there exists no piece of printing in which the name of Gutenberg appears as the printer. In the second place, there was known no trustworthy printed or written evidence dated during the contemporary period. And, in the third place, the cause of Gutenberg suffered severe prejudice through the discovery by Hessels that a large proportion of the documents, on which his case had been based, were rank forgeries, *inspired by the over-enthusiastic nationalism of Bodmann, the archivist at Mentz.*

PLANTIN** LIGHT WITH LIGHT ITALIC   MERGENTHALER TYPE LIBRARY

12/13 The invention of printing, one of the most momentous events in the history of civilization, has been the subject of most controversy. The rival claims of Gutenberg and Coster have been argued with considerable acrimony by a number of authorities. While the weight of opinion has credited the invention to Gutenberg, the case of the German has not been absolutely conclusive. In the first place, there exists no piece of printing in which the name of Gutenberg appears as the printer. In the second place, there was known no trustworthy printed or written evidence dated during the *contemporary period. And, in the third place, the cause of Gutenberg suffered severe prejudice*

10/11 The invention of printing, one of the most momentous events in the history of civilization, has been the subject of most controversy. The rival claims of Gutenberg and Coster have been argued with considerable acrimony by a number of authorities. While the weight of opinion has credited the invention to Gutenberg, the case of the German has not been absolutely conclusive. In the first place, there exists no piece of printing in which the name of Gutenberg appears as the printer. In the second place, there was known no trustworthy printed or written evidence dated during the contemporary period. And, in the third place, the cause of Gutenberg suffered severe prejudice through the discovery by Hessels that a large proportion of the documents, on which his case had been based, were rank forgeries, *inspired by the over-enthusiastic nationalism of Bodmann, the archivist at Mentz.*

PLANTIN** WITH ITALIC   MERGENTHALER TYPE LIBRARY

12/13 **The invention of printing, one of the most momentous events in the history of civilization, has been the subject of most controversy. The rival claims of Gutenberg and Coster have been argued with considerable acrimony by a number of authorities. While the weight of opinion has credited the invention to Gutenberg, the case of the German has not been absolutely conclusive. In the first place, there exists no piece of printing in which the name of Gutenberg appears as the printer. In the second place, there was known no trustworthy printed or written evi-*dence dated during the contemporary period. And, in the third place, the cause of***

10/11 **The invention of printing, one of the most momentous events in the history of civilization, has been the subject of most controversy. The rival claims of Gutenberg and Coster have been argued with considerable acrimony by a number of authorities. While the weight of opinion has credited the invention to Gutenberg, the case of the German has not been absolutely conclusive. In the first place, there exists no piece of printing in which the name of Gutenberg appears as the printer. In the second place, there was known no trustworthy printed or written evidence dated during the contemporary period. And, in the third place, the cause of Gutenberg suffered severe prejudice through the discovery by Hessels that a large proportion of the documents, on which his case *had been based, were rank forgeries, inspired by the over-enthusiastic nationalism of Bodmann, the ar-***

PLANTIN** BOLD WITH BOLD ITALIC   MERGENTHALER TYPE LIBRARY

ABCDEFGHIJKLMNOPQRSTUVW
XYZ&abcdefghijklmnopqrstuvwxyz
1234567890$.,""":;!?

PRIMER* 54   MERGENTHALER TYPE LIBRARY

*ABCDEFGHIJKLMNOPQRSTUVWX
YZ&abcdefghijklmnopqrstuvwxyz12
34567890$.,""":;!?*

PRIMER* 54 ITALIC   MERGENTHALER TYPE LIBRARY

**ABCDEFGHIJKLMNOPQRSTUVWX
YZ&abcdefghijklmnopqrstuvwxyz12
34567890$.,""":;!?**

PRIMER* 54 SEMI BOLD   MERGENTHALER TYPE LIBRARY

*ABCDEFGHIJKLMNOPQRSTUVWXY
Z&abcdefghijklmnopqrstuvwxyz1234
567890$.,""":;!?*

PRIMER* 54 SEMI BOLD ITALIC   MERGENTHALER TYPE LIBRARY

**ABCDEFGHIJKLMNOPQRSTUVW
XYZ&abcdefghijklmnopqrstuvwxy
z1234567890$.,""":;!?**

PRIMER* 54 BOLD   MERGENTHALER TYPE LIBRARY

***ABCDEFGHIJKLMNOPQRSTUVWX
YZ&abcdefghijklmnopqrstuvwxyz1
234567890$.,""":;!?***

PRIMER* 54 BOLD ITALIC   MERGENTHALER TYPE LIBRARY

12/13 Now, since architects, painters & others at times are wont to set an inscription on lofty walls, it will make for the merit of the work that they form the letters correctly. Accordingly I am minded here to treat briefly of this. And first I will give rules for a Latin Alphabet, and then for one of our common Text: since it is of these two sorts of letters we customarily make use in such work; and first, for the Roman letters: Draw for each a square of uniform size, in which the letter is to be contained. But when you draw in it the heavier limb of the letter, make this of the *width of a tenth part of the square, and the lighter a third as wide as the heavier: to*

10/11 Now, since architects, painters & others at times are wont to set an inscription on lofty walls, it will make for the merit of the work that they form the letters correctly. Accordingly I am minded here to treat briefly of this. And first I will give rules for a Latin Alphabet, and then for one of our common Text: since it is of these two sorts of letters we customarily make use in such work; and first, for the Roman letters: Draw for each a square of uniform size, in which the letter is to be contained. But when you draw in it the heavier limb of the letter, make this of the width of a tenth part of the square, and the lighter a third as wide as the heavier: to follow this rule for all letters of the Alphabet.
 First, make an A after this fashion: Indicate the *angles of the square by the letters a. b. c. d. (and so do for all the rest of the letters): then divide the square by*

PRIMER* 54 WITH ITALIC   MERGENTHALER TYPE LIBRARY

12/13 Now, since architects, painters & others at times are wont to set an inscription on lofty walls, it will make for the merit of the work that they form the letters correctly. Accordingly I am minded here to treat briefly of this. And first I will give rules for a Latin Alphabet, and then for one of our common Text: since it is of these two sorts of letters we customarily make use in such work; and first, for the Roman letters: Draw for each a square of uniform size, in which the letter is to be contained. But when you draw in it the heavier limb *of the letter, make this of the width of a tenth part of the square, and the lighter a*

10/11 Now, since architects, painters & others at times are wont to set an inscription on lofty walls, it will make for the merit of the work that they form the letters correctly. Accordingly I am minded here to treat briefly of this. And first I will give rules for a Latin Alphabet, and then for one of our common Text: since it is of these two sorts of letters we customarily make use in such work; and first, for the Roman letters: Draw for each a square of uniform size, in which the letter is to be contained. But when you draw in it the heavier limb of the letter, make this of the width of a tenth part of the square, and the lighter a third as wide as the heavier: to follow this rule for all letters of the Alphabet.
 First, make an A after this fashion: Indicate the angles of the square by the letters a. b. c. d. (and so

PRIMER* 54 SEMI BOLD WITH SEMI BOLD ITALIC   MERGENTHALER TYPE LIBRARY

12/13 **Now, since architects, painters & others at times are wont to set an inscription on lofty walls, it will make for the merit of the work that they form the letters correctly. Accordingly I am minded here to treat briefly of this. And first I will give rules for a Latin Alphabet, and then for one of our common Text: since it is of these two sorts of letters we customarily make use in such work; and first, for the Roman letters: Draw for each a square of uniform size, in which the letter is to be contained. *But when you draw in it the heavier limb of the letter, make this of***

10/11 **Now, since architects, painters & others at times are wont to set an inscription on lofty walls, it will make for the merit of the work that they form the letters correctly. Accordingly I am minded here to treat briefly of this. And first I will give rules for a Latin Alphabet, and then for one of our common Text: since it is of these two sorts of letters we customarily make use in such work; and first, for the Roman letters: Draw for each a square of uniform size, in which the letter is to be contained. But when you draw in it the heavier limb of the letter, make this of the width of a tenth part of the square, and the lighter a third as wide as the heavier: to follow this rule for all letters of the Alphabet.
 *First, make an A after this fashion: Indicate***

PRIMER* 54 BOLD WITH BOLD ITALIC   MERGENTHALER TYPE LIBRARY

ABCDEFGHIJKLMNOPQRSTUVWXYZ
&abcdefghijklmnopqrstuvwxyz
1234567890$.,''"":;!?

RALEIGH LIGHT   AGFA COMPUGRAPHIC TYPE LIBRARY

ABCDEFGHIJKLMNOPQRSTUVWXYZ
&abcdefghijklmnopqrstuvwxyz
1234567890$.,''"":;!?

RALEIGH MEDIUM   AGFA COMPUGRAPHIC TYPE LIBRARY

ABCDEFGHIJKLMNOPQRSTUVWXYZ
&abcdefghijklmnopqrstuvwxyz
1234567890$.,''"":;!?

RALEIGH REGULAR   AGFA COMPUGRAPHIC TYPE LIBRARY

ABCDEFGHIJKLMNOPQRSTUVWXYZ
&abcdefghijklmnopqrstuvwxyz
1234567890$.,''"":;!?

RALEIGH BOLD   AGFA COMPUGRAPHIC TYPE LIBRARY

ABCDEFGHIJKLMNOPQRSTUVWXYZ
&abcdefghijklmnopqrstuvwxyz
1234567890$.,''"":;!?

RALEIGH DEMI BOLD   AGFA COMPUGRAPHIC TYPE LIBRARY

ABCDEFGHIJKLMNOPQRSTUVWXYZ
&abcdefghijklmnopqrstuvwxyz
1234567890$.,''"":;!?

RALEIGH EXTRA BOLD CONDENSED   AGFA COMPUGRAPHIC TYPE LIBRARY

SUPPLEMENTARY FACES 431

12/13 Now, since architects, painters & others at times are wont to set an inscription on lofty walls, it will make for the merit of the work that they form the letters correctly. Accordingly I am minded here to treat briefly of this. And first I will give rules for a Latin Alphabet, and then for one of our common Text: since it is of these two sorts of letters we customarily make use in such work; and first, for the Roman letters: Draw for each a square of uniform size, in which the letter is to be contained. But when you draw in it the heavier limb of the letter, make this of the width of a tenth part of the square, and the lighter a third as wide as the heavier:

10/11 Now, since architects, painters & others at times are wont to set an inscription on lofty walls, it will make for the merit of the work that they form the letters correctly. Accordingly I am minded here to treat briefly of this. And first I will give rules for a Latin Alphabet, and then for one of our common Text: since it is of these two sorts of letters we customarily make use in such work; and first, for the Roman letters: Draw for each a square of uniform size, in which the letter is to be contained. But when you draw in it the heavier limb of the letter, make this of the width of a tenth part of the square, and the lighter a third as wide as the heavier: to follow this rule for all letters of the Alphabet. First, make an A after this fashion: Indicate the angles of the square by the letters a. b. c. d. (and so do for all the rest of the letters): then divide the square by two lines

RALEIGH LIGHT WITH MEDIUM   AGFA COMPUGRAPHIC TYPE LIBRARY

12/13 Now, since architects, painters & others at times are wont to set an inscription on lofty walls, it will make for the merit of the work that they form the letters correctly. Accordingly I am minded here to treat briefly of this. And first I will give rules for a Latin Alphabet, and then for one of our common Text: since it is of these two sorts of letters we customarily make use in such work; and first, for the Roman letters: Draw for each a square of uniform size, in which the letter is to be contained. But when you draw in it the heavier limb of the letter, make this **of the width of a tenth part of the square, and the lighter a third as wide as the**

10/11 Now, since architects, painters & others at times are wont to set an inscription on lofty walls, it will make for the merit of the work that they form the letters correctly. Accordingly I am minded here to treat briefly of this. And first I will give rules for a Latin Alphabet, and then for one of our common Text: since it is of these two sorts of letters we customarily make use in such work; and first, for the Roman letters: Draw for each a square of uniform size, in which the letter is to be contained. But when you draw in it the heavier limb of the letter, make this of the width of a tenth part of the square, and the lighter a third as wide as the heavier: to follow this rule for all letters of the Alphabet. First, make an A after this fashion: Indicate the angles of the **square by the letters a. b. c. d. (and so do for all the rest of the letters): then divide the square by**

RALEIGH REGULAR WITH BOLD   AGFA COMPUGRAPHIC TYPE LIBRARY

12/13 **Now, since architects, painters & others at times are wont to set an inscription on lofty walls, it will make for the merit of the work that they form the letters correctly.** accordingly I am minded here to treat briefly of this. And first I will give rules for a Latin Alphabet, and then for one of our common Text: since it is of these two sorts of letters we customarily make use in such work; and first, for the Roman letters: Draw for each a square of uniform size, in which the letter is to be contained. But when you draw in it the heavier limb of the letter, **make this of the width of a tenth part of the square, and the lighter a third as**

10/11 **Now, since architects, painters & others at times are wont to set an inscription on lofty walls, it will make for the merit of the work that they form the letters correctly.** Accordingly I am minded here to treat briefly of this. And first I will give rules for a Latin Alphabet, and then for one of our common Text: since it is of these two sorts of letters we customarily make use in such work; and first, for the Roman letters: Draw for each a square of uniform size, in which the letter is to be contained. But when you draw in it the heavier limb of the letter, make this of the width of a tenth part of the square, and the lighter a third as the heavier: to follow this rule for all letters of the Alphabet. First, make an A after this fashion: **Indicate the angles of the square by the letters a. b. c. d. (and so do for all the rest of the letters**

RALEIGH DEMI BOLD WITH EXTRA BOLD   AGFA COMPUGRAPHIC TYPE LIBRARY

ABCDEFGHIJKLMNOPQRSTUVWXYZ&
abcdefghijklmnopqrstuvwxyz
1234567890$.,"":;!?

ROTIS SEMI SANS 55   AGFA COMPUGRAPHIC TYPE LIBRARY

**ABCDEFGHIJKLMNOPQRSTUVWXYZ&
abcdefghijklmnopqrstuvwxyz
1234567890$.,"":;!?**

ROTIS SEMI SANS 75   AGFA COMPUGRAPHIC TYPE LIBRARY

ABCDEFGHIJKLMNOPQRSTUVWXYZ&
abcdefghijklmnopqrstuvwxyz
1234567890$.,"":;!?

ROTIS SEMI SERIF 55   AGFA COMPUGRAPHIC TYPE LIBRARY

**ABCDEFGHIJKLMNOPQRSTUVWXYZ&
abcdefghijklmnopqrstuvwxyz
1234567890$.,"":;!?**

ROTIS SEMI SERIF 65   AGFA COMPUGRAPHIC TYPE LIBRARY

ABCDEFGHIJKLMNOPQRSTUVWXYZ&
abcdefghijklmnopqrstuvwxyz
1234567890$.,"":;!?

ROTIS SERIF 55   AGFA COMPUGRAPHIC TYPE LIBRARY

*ABCDEFGHIJKLMNOPQRSTUVWXYZ&
abcdefghijklmnopqrstuvwxyz
1234567890$.,"":;!?*

ROTIS SERIF 56   AGFA COMPUGRAPHIC TYPE LIBRARY

12/13 Lying in my bed, on the morning of the Feast of Kings, when I had had my sleep and rest, & my stomach had readily digested its light and pleasant repast, in the year that was reckoned as MDXXIII, I fell to musing and set the wheel of my memory awhirl thinking on a thousand little conceits, some serious and some joyous, which there came to my mind a certain Antique letter which I had lately made for my lord the Treasurer for War, Maistre Jehan Groslier, Counsellor and Secretary to our Lord the King, lover of well-made letters and of all learned persons, by whom also he is much loved & esteem**ed on both this & the other side of the mountains. And whilst thinking of this Attic Letter**

10/11 Lying in my bed, on the morning of the Feast of Kings, when I had had my sleep and rest, & my stomach had readily digested its light and pleasant repast, in the year that was reckoned as MDXXIII, I fell to musing and set the wheel of my memory awhirl thinking on a thousand little conceits, some serious and some joyous, among which there came to my mind a certain Antique letter which I had lately made for my lord the Treasurer for War, Maistre Jehan Groslier, Counsellor and Secretary to our Lord the King, lover of well-made letters and of all learned persons, by whom also he is much loved & esteemed on both this & the other side of the mountains. And whilst thinking of this Attic Letter, there came of a sudden into my memory a pithy passage in the first book & eighth chapter of the DeOfficiis of Cicero, where it is written: Non nobis solum **nati sumus; ortusque nostri partem patria vendicat, partem amici. Which is to say, in substance, that we**

ROTIS SEMI SANS 55 WITH 75   AGFA COMPUGRAPHIC TYPE LIBRARY

12/13 Lying in my bed, on the morning of the Feast of Kings, when I had had my sleep and rest, & my stomach had readily digested its light and pleasant repast, in the year that was reckoned as MDXXIII, I fell to musing and set the wheel of my memory awhirl thinking on a thousand little conceits, some serious and some joyous, among which there came to my mind a certain Antique letter which I had lately made for my lord the Treasurer for War, Maistre Jehan Groslier, Counsellor and Secretary to our Lord the King, lover of well-made letters and of all learned persons, by whom also he is much **loved & esteemed on both this & the other side of the mountains. And whilst thinking of this**

10/11 Lying in my bed, on the morning of the Feast of Kings, when I had had my sleep and rest, & my stomach had readily digested its light and pleasant repast, in the year that was reckoned as MDXXIII, I fell to musing and set the wheel of my memory awhirl thinking on a thousand little conceits, some serious and some joyous, among which there came to my mind a certain Antique letter which I had lately made for my lord the Treasurer for War, Maistre Jehan Groslier, Counsellor and Secretary to our Lord the King, lover of well-made letters and of all learned persons, by whom also he is much loved & esteemed on both this & the other side of the mountains. And whilst thinking of this Attic Letter, there came of a sudden into my memory a pithy passage in the first book & eighth chapter of the DeOfficiis of Cicero, where it is written: Non **nobis solum nati sumus; ortusque nostri partem patria vendicat, partem amici. Which is to say, in substance**

ROTIS SEMI SERIF 55 WITH 65   AGFA COMPUGRAPHIC TYPE LIBRARY

12/13 Lying in my bed, on the morning of the Feast of Kings, when I had had my sleep and rest, & my stomach had readily digested its light and pleasant repast, in the year that was reckoned as MDXXIII, I fell to musing and set the wheel of my memory awhirl thinking on a thousand little conceits, some serious and some joyous, among which there came to my mind a certain Antique letter which I had lately made for my lord the Treasurer for War, Maistre Jehan Groslier, Counsellor and Secretary to our Lord the King, lover of well-made letters and of all learned persons, by whom also he is much lov*ed & esteemed on both this & the other side of the mountains. And whilst thinking of this*

10/11 Lying in my bed, on the morning of the Feast of Kings, when I had had my sleep and rest, & my stomach had readily digested its light and pleasant repast, in the year that was reckoned as MDXXIII, I fell to musing and set the wheel of my memory awhirl thinking on a thousand little conceits, some serious and some joyous, among which there came to my mind a certain Antique letter which I had lately made for my lord the Treasurer for War, Maistre Jehan Groslier, Counsellor and Secretary to our Lord the King, lover of well-made letters and of all learned persons, by whom also he is much loved & esteemed on both this & the other side of the mountains. And whilst thinking of this Attic Letter, there came of a sudden into my memory a pithy passage in the first book & eighth chapter of the DeOfficiis of Cicero, where *it is written: Non nobis solum nati sumus; ortusque nostri partem patria vendicat, partem amici. Which is to say*

ROTIS SERIF 55 WITH 56   AGFA COMPUGRAPHIC TYPE LIBRARY

ABCDEFGHIJKLMNOPQRSTUVWX
YZ&abcdefghijklmnopqrstuvwxyz1
234567890$.,"":;!?

TS SCENARIO** LIGHT   MERGENTHALER TYPE LIBRARY

*ABCDEFGHIJKLMNOPQRSTUVWX
YZ&abcdefghijklmnopqrstuvwxyz1
234567890$.,"":;!?*

TS SCENARIO** LIGHT ITALIC   MERGENTHALER TYPE LIBRARY

**ABCDEFGHIJKLMNOPQRSTUVW
XYZ&abcdefghijklmnopqrstuvwx
yz1234567890$.,"":;!?**

TS SCENARIO** DEMI   MERGENTHALER TYPE LIBRARY

**ABCDEFGHIJKLMNOPQRSTUV
WXYZ&abcdefghijklmnopqrstu
vwxyz1234567890$.,"":;!?**

TS SCENARIO** BOLD   MERGENTHALER TYPE LIBRARY

ABCDEFGHIJKLMNOPQRSTUV
WXYZ&abcdefghijklmnopqrstuvwxyz
1234567890$.,"":;!?

SCOTCH NO. 2   MERGENTHALER TYPE LIBRARY

*ABCDEFGHIJKLMNOPQRSTUVWX
YZ&abcdefghijklmnopqrstuvwxyz12345
67890$.,"":;!?*

SCOTCH NO. 2 ITALIC   MERGENTHALER TYPE LIBRARY

12/13 In type-founding, types are cast in moulds containing at one end a copper matrix of the character. The aperture through which the melted metal is injected is at the end of the mould opposite the matrix, and a piece as long as the type, called the jet, extends through the aperture from the bottom of the type. Thus imperfections in the metal and variations of temperature spend themselves in the jet, leaving the body of the type comparatively perfect. The types thus cast go through various processes, such as *breaking off the jet and ploughing in its place a shallow groove across the foot,*

10/11 In type-founding, types are cast in moulds containing at one end a copper matrix of the character. The aperture through which the melted metal is injected is at the end of the mould opposite the matrix, and a piece as long as the type, called the jet, extends through the aperture from the bottom of the type. Thus imperfections in the metal and variations of temperature spend themselves in the jet, leaving the body of the type comparatively perfect. The types thus cast go through various processes, such as breaking off the jet and ploughing in its place a shallow groove across the foot, thus leaving each type two "feet" to stand upon, "rubbing," etc.; and at last, set up in long rows, they pass under the eye of an expert, who, as *he examines them carefully with a glass, rejects all in which he detects any imperfections. In these*

TS SCENARIO** LIGHT WITH LIGHT ITALIC   MERGENTHALER TYPE LIBRARY

12/13 **In type-founding, types are cast in moulds containing at one end a copper matrix of the character. The aperture through which the melted metal is injected is at the end of the mould opposite the matrix, and a piece as long as the type, called the jet, extends through the aperture from the bottom of the type. Thus imperfections in the metal and variations of temperature spend themselves in the jet, leaving the body of the type comparatively perfect. The types thus cast go through various processes, such as breaking off the jet and ploughing in its place a shallow**

10/11 In type-founding, types are cast in moulds containing at one end a copper matrix of the character. The aperture through which the melted metal is injected is at the end of the mould opposite the matrix, and a piece as long as the type, called the jet, extends through the aperture from the bottom of the type. Thus imperfections in the metal and variations of temperature spend themselves in the jet, leaving the body of the type comparatively perfect. The types thus cast go through various processes, such as breaking off the jet and ploughing in its place a shallow groove across the foot, thus leaving each type two "feet" to stand upon, "rubbing," etc.; and at last, set up in long rows, they pass **under the eye of an expert, who, as he examines them carefully with a glass, rejects all in**

TS SCENARIO** DEMI WITH BOLD   MERGENTHALER TYPE LIBRARY

12/13 In type-founding, types are cast in moulds containing at one end a copper matrix of the character. The aperture through which the melted metal is injected is at the end of the mould opposite the matrix, and a piece as long as the type, called the jet, extends through the aperture from the bottom of the type. Thus imperfections in the metal and variations of temperature spend themselves in the jet, leaving the body of the type comparatively perfect. The types thus cast go through various processes, such as breaking off the jet and ploughing in its place a shallow *groove across the foot, thus leaving each type two "feet" to stand upon, "rubbing," etc.; and at last,*

10/11 In type-founding, types are cast in moulds containing at one end a copper matrix of the character. The aperture through which the melted metal is injected is at the end of the mould opposite the matrix, and a piece as long as the type, called the jet, extends through the aperture from the bottom of the type. Thus imperfections in the metal and variations of temperature spend themselves in the jet, leaving the body of the type comparatively perfect. The types thus cast go through various processes, such as breaking off the jet and ploughing in its place a shallow groove across the foot, thus leaving each type two "feet" to stand upon, "rubbing," etc.; and at last, set up in long rows, they pass under the eye of an expert, who, as he examines them carefully with a glass, *rejects all in which he detects any imperfections. In these processes an average of 10 per cent. is eliminated; so that*

SCOTCH NO. 2 WITH ITALIC   MERGENTHALER TYPE LIBRARY

ABCDEFGHIJKLMNOPQRSTUVWXYZ&abcdefghijklmnopqrstuvwxyz1234567890$.,'"``:;!?

ITC SERIF GOTHIC** LIGHT   MERGENTHALER TYPE LIBRARY

ABCDEFGHIJKLMNOPQRSTUVWXYZ&abcdefghijklmnopqrstuvwxyz1234567890$.,'"``:;!?

ITC SERIF GOTHIC**   MERGENTHALER TYPE LIBRARY

ABCDEFGHIJKLMNOPQRSTUVWXYZ&abcdefghijklmnopqrstuvwxyz1234567890$.,'"``:;!?

ITC SERIF GOTHIC** BOLD   MERGENTHALER TYPE LIBRARY

ABCDEFGHIJKLMNOPQRSTUVWXYZ&abcdefghijklmnopqrstuvwxyz1234567890$.,'"``:;!?

ITC SERIF GOTHIC** EXTRA BOLD   MERGENTHALER TYPE LIBRARY

ABCDEFGHIJKLMNOPQRSTUVWXYZ&abcdefghijklmnopqrstuvwxyz1234567890$.,'"``:;!?

ITC SERIF GOTHIC** HEAVY   MERGENTHALER TYPE LIBRARY

ABCDEFGHIJKLMNOPQRSTUVWXYZ&abcdefghijklmnopqrstuvwxyz1234567890$.,'"``:;!?

ITC SERIF GOTHIC** BLACK   MERGENTHALER TYPE LIBRARY

12/13 It is still a matter of conjecture whether Johann Gutenberg was the first to conceive the principle of casting movable [i.e., separate] metal types which he could arrange in words and sentences so that he could impress their faces on paper. There is, however, hardly a doubt, judging at least from the evidence available, that he was the first to make practical use of the idea, and that it is due to his ingenious application of it that the profound art of typography was born.

Whether he cast his letters in molds of sand or in metal matrices, is a question not really material at this time; it is the far-reaching results of his inspiration that most concern us

10/11 It is still a matter of conjecture whether Johann Gutenberg was the first to conceive the principle of casting movable [i.e., separate] metal types which he could arrange in words and sentences so that he could impress their faces on paper. There is, however, hardly a doubt, judging at least from the evidence available, that he was the first to make practical use of the idea, and that it is due to his ingenious application of it that the profound art of typography was born.

Whether he cast his letters in molds of sand or in metal matrices, is a question not really material at this time; it is the far-reaching results of his inspiration that most concern us in this discussion. It seems quite probable that Gutenberg at first had little more in mind than a desire to find some expedient by which to supplement with explanatory text the illustrations cut on wood blocks — some method that would avoid the

ITC SERIF GOTHIC** LIGHT WITH ITC SERIF GOTHIC**   MERGENTHALER TYPE LIBRARY

12/13 **It is still a matter of conjecture whether Johann Gutenberg was the first to conceive the principle of casting movable [i.e., separate] metal types which he could arrange in words and sentences so that he could impress their faces on paper. There is, however, hardly a doubt, judging at least from the evidence available, that he was the first to make practical use of the idea, and that it is due to his ingenious application of it that the profound art of typography was born.**

Whether he cast his letters in molds of sand or in metal matrices, is a question not really material at this time; it is the far-reaching results of his inspiration that most con-

10/11 **It is still a matter of conjecture whether Johann Gutenberg was the first to conceive the principle of casting movable [i.e., separate] metal types which he could arrange in words and sentences so that he could impress their faces on paper. There is, however, hardly a doubt, judging at least from the evidence available, that he was the first to make practical use of the idea, and that it is due to his ingenious application of it that the profound art of typography was born.**

Whether he cast his letters in molds of sand or in metal matrices, is a question not really material at this time; it is the far-reaching results of his inspiration that most concern us in this discussion. It seems quite probable that Gutenberg at first had little more in mind than a desire to find some expedient by which to supplement with explanatory text the illustrations

ITC SERIF GOTHIC** BOLD WITH EXTRA BOLD   MERGENTHALER TYPE LIBRARY

12/13 **It is still a matter of conjecture whether Johann Gutenberg was the first to conceive the principle of casting movable [i.e., separate] metal types which he could arrange in words and sentences so that he could impress their faces on paper. There is, however, hardly a doubt, judging at least from the evidence available, that he was the first to make practical use of the idea, and that it is due to his ingenious application of it that the profound art of typography was born.**

Whether he cast his letters in molds of sand or in metal matrices, is a question not really material at this time; it is the far-

10/11 **It is still a matter of conjecture whether Johann Gutenberg was the first to conceive the principle of casting movable [i.e., separate] metal types which he could arrange in words and sentences so that he could impress their faces on paper. There is, however, hardly a doubt, judging at least from the evidence available, that he was the first to make practical use of the idea, and that it is due to his ingenious application of it that the profound art of typography was born.**

Whether he cast his letters in molds of sand or in metal matrices, is a question not really material at this time; it is the far-reaching results of his inspiration that most concern us in this discussion. It seems quite probable that Gutenberg at first had little more in mind than a desire to find some expedient by which to supplement with explanatory text the

ITC SERIF GOTHIC** HEAVY WITH BLACK   MERGENTHALER TYPE LIBRARY

ABCDEFGHIJKLMNOPQRSTUVWXYZ&abcdefghijklmnopqrstuvwxyz1234567890$.,""":;!?

ITC SOUVENIR** LIGHT   MERGENTHALER TYPE LIBRARY

ABCDEFGHIJKLMNOPQRSTUVWXYZ&abcdefghijklmnopqrstuvwxyz1234567890$.,""":,!?

ITC SOUVENIR** LIGHT ITALIC   MERGENTHALER TYPE LIBRARY

ABCDEFGHIJKLMNOPQRSTUVWXYZ&abcdefghijklmnopqrstuvwxyz1234567890$.,""":;!?

ITC SOUVENIR** MEDIUM   MERGENTHALER TYPE LIBRARY

ABCDEFGHIJKLMNOPQRSTUVWXYZ&abcdefghijklmnopqrstuvwxyz1234567890$.,""":;!?

ITC SOUVENIR** MEDIUM ITALIC   MERGENTHALER TYPE LIBRARY

ABCDEFGHIJKLMNOPQRSTUVWXYZ&abcdefghijklmnopqrstuvwxyz1234567890$.,""":;!?

ITC SOUVENIR** DEMI   MERGENTHALER TYPE LIBRARY

ABCDEFGHIJKLMNOPQRSTUVWXYZ&abcdefghijklmnopqrstuvwxyz1234567890$.,""":;!?

ITC SOUVENIR** DEMI ITALIC   MERGENTHALER TYPE LIBRARY

SUPPLEMENTARY FACES 439

12/13 The history of the Dutch book is famous. In the Middle Ages the art of the scribes and miniaturists flourished in the Netherlands to such a degree that their manuscripts are not considered inferior to the finest specimens of Italian and French origin; the Dutch incunabula are, especially by their woodcut illustrations, hardly surpassed, only equalled by Italian work. In the 17th century Holland regained a leading position in this sphere and the prints of Elzevir enjoy at present a world-wide fame. And although our books lack the grandeur of Italian manuscripts, the delicate *grace of a French impression (nor does the Dutch incunabulum display the pompous*

10/11 The history of the Dutch book is famous. In the Middle Ages the art of the scribes and miniaturists flourished in the Netherlands to such a degree that their manuscripts are not considered inferior to the finest specimens of Italian and French origin; the Dutch incunabula are, especially by their woodcut illustrations, hardly surpassed, only equalled by Italian work. In the 17th century Holland regained a leading position in this sphere and the prints of Elzevir enjoy at present a world-wide fame. And although our books lack the grandeur of Italian manuscripts, the delicate grace of a French impression (nor does the Dutch incunabulum display the pompous style of a Gutenberg or Schoeffer work), they have undoubtedly a distinct character of their own, which bears the stamp of true art. They exhibit their *inmost artistic value only to the devout contemplator. We might parallel with the art of painting, especially of*

ITC SOUVENIR** LIGHT WITH LIGHT ITALIC   MERGENTHALER TYPE LIBRARY

12/13 **The history of the Dutch book is famous. In the Middle Ages the art of the scribes and miniaturists flourished in the Netherlands to such a degree that their manuscripts are not considered inferior to the finest specimens of Italian and French origin; the Dutch incunabula are, especially by their woodcut illustrations, hardly surpassed, only equalled by Italian work. In the 17th century Holland regained a leading position in this sphere and the prints of Elzevir enjoy at present a world-wide fame. And although our books lack the grandeur of Italian manuscripts, *the delicate grace of a French impression (nor does the Dutch incunabulum***

10/11 The history of the Dutch book is famous. In the Middle Ages the art of the scribes and miniaturists flourished in the Netherlands to such a degree that their manuscripts are not considered inferior to the finest specimens of Italian and French origin; the Dutch incunabula are, especially by their woodcut illustrations, hardly surpassed, only equalled by Italian work. In the 17th century Holland regained a leading position in this sphere and the prints of Elzevir enjoy at present a world-wide fame. And although our books lack the grandeur of Italian manuscripts, the delicate grace of a French impression (nor does the Dutch incunabulum display the pompous style of a Gutenberg or Schoeffer work), they have undoubtedly a distinct character of their *own, which bears the stamp of true art. They exhibit their inmost artistic value only to the devout con-*

ITC SOUVENIR** MEDIUM WITH MEDIUM ITALIC   MERGENTHALER TYPE LIBRARY

12/13 **The history of the Dutch book is famous. In the Middle Ages the art of the scribes and miniaturists flourished in the Netherlands to such a degree that their manuscripts are not considered inferior to the finest specimens of Italian and French origin; the Dutch incunabula are, especially by their woodcut illustrations, hardly surpassed, only equalled by Italian work. In the 17th century Holland regained a leading position in this sphere and the prints of Elzevir enjoy at present a world-wide fame. And al-*though our books lack the grandeur of Italian manuscripts, the delicate grace***

10/11 **The history of the Dutch book is famous. In the Middle Ages the art of the scribes and miniaturists flourished in the Netherlands to such a degree that their manuscripts are not considered inferior to the finest specimens of Italian and French origin; the Dutch incunabula are, especially by their woodcut illustrations, hardly surpassed, only equalled by Italian work. In the 17th century Holland regained a leading position in this sphere and the prints of Elzevir enjoy at present a world-wide fame. And although our books lack the grandeur of Italian manuscripts, the delicate grace of a French impression (nor does the Dutch incunabulum display the pompous style of a Gutenberg or Schoeffer work), *they have undoubtedly a distinct character of their own, which bears the stamp of true art.***

ITC SOUVENIR** DEMI WITH DEMI ITALIC   MERGENTHALER TYPE LIBRARY

ABCDEFGHIJKLMNOPQRSTUVWX
YZ&abcdefghijklmnopqrstuvwxyz
1234567890$.,""":;!?

ITC STONE® INFORMAL   ADOBE TYPE LIBRARY

*ABCDEFGHIJKLMNOPQRSTUVWXYZ
&abcdefghijklmnopqrstuvwxyz12345
67890$.,""":;!?*

ITC STONE INFORMAL ITALIC   ADOBE TYPE LIBRARY

**ABCDEFGHIJKLMNOPQRSTUVW
XYZ&abcdefghijklmnopqrstuvwx
yz1234567890$.,""":;!?**

ITC STONE INFORMAL SEMIBOLD   ADOBE TYPE LIBRARY

***ABCDEFGHIJKLMNOPQRSTUVWX
YZ&abcdefghijklmnopqrstuvwxyz
1234567890$.,""":;!?***

ITC STONE INFORMAL SEMIBOLD ITALIC   ADOBE TYPE LIBRARY

**ABCDEFGHIJKLMNOPQRSTUV
WXYZ&abcdefghijklmnopqrst
uvwxyz1234567890$.,""":;!?**

ITC STONE INFORMAL BOLD   ADOBE TYPE LIBRARY

***ABCDEFGHIJKLMNOPQRSTUVW
XYZ&abcdefghijklmnopqrstuvwxy
z1234567890$.,""":;!?***

ITC STONE INFORMAL BOLD ITALIC   ADOBE TYPE LIBRARY

SUPPLEMENTARY FACES 441

12/13 Now, since architects, painters and others at times are wont to set an inscription on lofty walls, it will make for the merit of the work that they form the letters correctly. Accordingly I am minded here to treat briefly of this. And first I will give rules for a Latin Alphabet, and then for one of our common Text: since it is of these two sorts of letters we customarily make use in such work; and first, for the Roman letters: Draw for each a square of uniform size, in which the letter is to be contained. But when you draw in it the heavier limb of the letter, *make this of the width of a tenth part of the square, and the lighter a third as wide as the*

10/11 Now, since architects, painters and others at times are wont to set an inscription on lofty walls, it will make for the merit of the work that they form the letters correctly. Accordingly I am minded here to treat briefly of this. And first I will give rules for a Latin Alphabet, and then for one of our common Text: since it is of these two sorts of letters we customarily make use in such work; and first, for the Roman letters: Draw for each a square of uniform size, in which the letter is to be contained. But when you draw in it the heavier limb of the letter, make this of the width of a tenth part of the square, and the lighter a third as wide as the heavier: to follow this rule for all letters of the Alphabet.
First, make an A after this fashion: Indicate the angles of the square by the letters a. b. c. d. (and so do

ITC STONE INFORMAL WITH ITALIC   ADOBE TYPE LIBRARY

12/13 **Now, since architects, painters and others at times are wont to set an inscription on lofty walls, it will make for the merit of the work that they form the letters correctly. Accordingly I am minded here to treat briefly of this. And first I will give rules for a Latin Alphabet, and then for one of our common Text: since it is of these two sorts of letters we cus-tomarily make use in such work; and first, for the Roman letters: Draw for each a square of uniform size, in which the letter is to be contained. But *when you draw in it the heavier limb of the letter, make this of the width of a***

10/11 **Now, since architects, painters and others at times are wont to set an inscription on lofty walls, it will make for the merit of the work that they form the letters correctly. Accordingly I am minded here to treat briefly of this. And first I will give rules for a Latin Alphabet, and then for one of our common Text: since it is of these two sorts of letters we customarily make use in such work; and first, for the Roman letters: Draw for each a square of uniform size, in which the letter is to be contained. But when you draw in it the heavier limb of the letter, make this of the width of a tenth part of the square, and the lighter a third as wide as the heavier: to follow this rule for all letters of the Alphabet. *First, make an A after this fashion: Indicate the angles of the square by the letters***

ITC STONE INFORMAL SEMIBOLD WITH ITALIC   ADOBE TYPE LIBRARY

12/13 **Now, since architects, painters and others at times are wont to set an inscription on lofty walls, it will make for the merit of the work that they form the letters correctly. Accordingly I am minded here to treat briefly of this. And first I will give rules for a Latin Alphabet, and then for one of our common Text: since it is of these two sorts of letters we customarily make use in such work; and first, for the Roman letters: Draw for each a square of uniform size, in *which the letter is to be contained. But when you draw in it the heavier limb of***

10/11 **Now, since architects, painters and others at times are wont to set an inscription on lofty walls, it will make for the merit of the work that they form the letters correctly. Accordingly I am minded here to treat briefly of this. And first I will give rules for a Latin Alphabet, and then for one of our common Text: since it is of these two sorts of letters we customarily make use in such work; and first, for the Roman letters: Draw for each a square of uniform size, in which the letter is to be contained. But when you draw in it the heavier limb of the letter, make this of the width of a tenth part of the square, and the light*er a third as wide as the heavier: to follow this rule for all letters of the Alphabet.***

ITC STONE INFORMAL BOLD WITH ITALIC   ADOBE TYPE LIBRARY

ABCDEFGHIJKLM NOPQRSTUVWXYZ
& abcdefghijklmnopqrstuvwxyz12345
67890$.,"":;!?

ITC STONE® SANS   ADOBE TYPE LIBRARY

*ABCDEFGHIJKLM NOPQRSTUVWXYZ&
abcdefghijklmnopqrstuvwxyz1234567
890$.,"":;!?*

ITC STONE SANS ITALIC   ADOBE TYPE LIBRARY

**ABCDEFGHIJKLMNOPQRSTUVWXY
Z&abcdefghijklmnopqrstuvwxyz123
4567890$.,"":;!?**

ITC STONE SANS SEMIBOLD   ADOBE TYPE LIBRARY

***ABCDEFGHIJKLM NOPQRSTUVWXYZ&
abcdefghijklmnopqrstuvwxyz123456
7890$.,"":;!?***

ITC STONE SANS SEMIBOLD ITALIC   ADOBE TYPE LIBRARY

**ABCDEFGHIJKLMNOPQRSTUVWX
YZ&abcdefghijklmnopqrstuvwxy
z1234567890$.,"":;!?**

ITC STONE SANS BOLD   ADOBE TYPE LIBRARY

***ABCDEFGHIJKLMNOPQRSTUVWXYZ
&abcdefghijklmnopqrstuvwxyz123
4567890$.,"":;!?***

ITC STONE SANS BOLD ITALIC   ADOBE TYPE LIBRARY

12/13 Now, since architects, painters and others at times are wont to set an inscription on lofty walls, it will make for the merit of the work that they form the letters correctly. Accordingly I am minded here to treat briefly of this. And first I will give rules for a Latin Alphabet, and then for one of our common Text: since it is of these two sorts of letters we customarily make use in such work; and first, for the Roman letters: Draw for each a square of uniform size, in which the letter is to be contained. But when you draw in it the heavier limb of the letter, make this of the width of a *tenth part of the square, and the lighter a third as wide as the heavier: to follow this rule for all*

10/11 Now, since architects, painters and others at times are wont to set an inscription on lofty walls, it will make for the merit of the work that they form the letters correctly. Accordingly I am minded here to treat briefly of this. And first I will give rules for a Latin Alphabet, and then for one of our common Text: since it is of these two sorts of letters we customarily make use in such work; and first, for the Roman letters: Draw for each a square of uniform size, in which the letter is to be contained. But when you draw in it the heavier limb of the letter, make this of the width of a tenth part of the square, and the lighter a third as wide as the heavier: to follow this rule for all letters of the Alphabet.
First, make an A after this fashion: Indicate the angles *of the square by the letters a. b. c. d. (and so do for all the rest of the letters): then divide the square by two*

ITC STONE SANS WITH ITALIC   ADOBE TYPE LIBRARY

12/13 **Now, since architects, painters and others at times are wont to set an inscription on lofty walls, it will make for the merit of the work that they form the letters correctly. Accordingly I am minded here to treat briefly of this. And first I will give rules for a Latin Alphabet, and then for one of our common Text: since it is of these two sorts of letters we customarily make use in such work; and first, for the Roman letters: Draw for each a square of uniform size, in which the letter is to be contained. But when you draw in it the heavier limb of *the letter, make this of the width of a tenth part of the square, and the lighter a third as***

10/11 **Now, since architects, painters and others at times are wont to set an inscription on lofty walls, it will make for the merit of the work that they form the letters correctly. Accordingly I am minded here to treat briefly of this. And first I will give rules for a Latin Alphabet, and then for one of our common Text: since it is of these two sorts of letters we customarily make use in such work; and first, for the Roman letters: Draw for each a square of uniform size, in which the letter is to be contained. But when you draw in it the heavier limb of the letter, make this of the width of a tenth part of the square, and the lighter a third as wide as the heavier: to follow this rule for all letters of the Alphabet.
First, make an A after this fashion: Indicate the an-*gles of the square by the letters a. b. c. d. (and so do for all the rest of the letters): then divide the square by***

ITC STONE SANS SEMIBOLD WITH ITALIC   ADOBE TYPE LIBRARY

12/13 **Now, since architects, painters and others at times are wont to set an inscription on lofty walls, it will make for the merit of the work that they form the letters correctly. Accordingly I am minded here to treat briefly of this. And first I will give rules for a Latin Alphabet, and then for one of our common Text: since it is of these two sorts of letters we customarily make use in such work; and first, for the Roman letters: Draw for each a square of uniform size, in which the letter is to be contained. But when you *draw in it the heavier limb of the letter,***

10/11 **Now, since architects, painters and others at times are wont to set an inscription on lofty walls, it will make for the merit of the work that they form the letters correctly. Accordingly I am minded here to treat briefly of this. And first I will give rules for a Latin Alphabet, and then for one of our common Text: since it is of these two sorts of letters we customarily make use in such work; and first, for the Roman letters: Draw for each a square of uniform size, in which the letter is to be contained. But when you draw in it the heavier limb of the letter, make this of the width of a tenth part of the square, and the lighter a third as wide as the heavier: to follow this rule for all *letters of the Alphabet.First, make an A after this fashion: Indicate the angles of the square by the***

ITC STONE SANS BOLD WITH ITALIC   ADOBE TYPE LIBRARY

SUPPLEMENTARY FACES

ABCDEFGHIJKLMNOPQRSTUVWX
YZ&abcdefghijklmnopqrstuvwxyz
1234567890$.,"":;!?

ITC STONE® SERIF   ADOBE TYPE LIBRARY

ABCDEFGHIJKLMNOPQRSTUVWXY
Z&abcdefghijklmnopqrstuvwxyz1234
567890$.,"":;!?

ITC STONE SERIF ITALIC   ADOBE TYPE LIBRARY

ABCDEFGHIJKLMNOPQRSTUVW
XYZ&abcdefghijklmnopqrstuvwx
yz1234567890$.,"":;!?

ITC STONE SERIF SEMIBOLD   ADOBE TYPE LIBRARY

ABCDEFGHIJKLMNOPQRSTUVW
XYZ&abcdefghijklmnopqrstuvwxy
z1234567890$.,"":;!?

ITC STONE SERIF SEMIBOLD ITALIC   ADOBE TYPE LIBRARY

ABCDEFGHIJKLMNOPQRSTUV
WXYZ&abcdefghijklmnopqrst
uvwxyz1234567890$.,"":;!?

ITC STONE SERIF BOLD   ADOBE TYPE LIBRARY

ABCDEFGHIJKLMNOPQRSTUV
WXYZ&abcdefghijklmnopqrstu
vwxyz1234567890$.,"":;!?

ITC STONE SERIF BOLD ITALIC   ADOBE TYPE LIBRARY

12/13 Now, since architects, painters and others at times are wont to set an inscription on lofty walls, it will make for the merit of the work that they form the letters correctly. Accordingly I am minded here to treat briefly of this. And first I will give rules for a Latin Alphabet, and then for one of our common Text: since it is of these two sorts of letters we customarily make use in such work; and first, for the Roman letters: Draw for each a square of uniform size, in which the letter is to be contained. But when you draw in it the heavier limb *of the letter, make this of the width of a tenth part of the square, and the lighter a third as*

10/11 Now, since architects, painters and others at times are wont to set an inscription on lofty walls, it will make for the merit of the work that they form the letters correctly. Accordingly I am minded here to treat briefly of this. And first I will give rules for a Latin Alphabet, and then for one of our common Text: since it is of these two sorts of letters we customarily make use in such work; and first, for the Roman letters: Draw for each a square of uniform size, in which the letter is to be contained. But when you draw in it the heavier limb of the letter, make this of the width of a tenth part of the square, and the lighter a third as wide as the heavier: to follow this rule for all letters of the Alphabet.
First, make an A after this fashion: Indicate the angles of the square by the letters a. b. c. d. (and so

ITC STONE SERIF WITH ITALIC   ADOBE TYPE LIBRARY

12/13 **Now, since architects, painters and others at times are wont to set an inscription on lofty walls, it will make for the merit of the work that they form the letters correctly. Accordingly I am minded here to treat briefly of this. And first I will give rules for a Latin Alphabet, and then for one of our common Text: since it is of these two sorts of letters we customarily make use in such work; and first, for the Roman letters: Draw for each a square of uniform size, in which the letter is to be contained. But when *you draw in it the heavier limb of the letter, make this of the width of a tenth***

10/11 **Now, since architects, painters and others at times are wont to set an inscription on lofty walls, it will make for the merit of the work that they form the letters correctly. Accordingly I am minded here to treat briefly of this. And first I will give rules for a Latin Alphabet, and then for one of our common Text: since it is of these two sorts of letters we customarily make use in such work; and first, for the Roman letters: Draw for each a square of uniform size, in which the letter is to be contained. But when you draw in it the heavier limb of the letter, make this of the width of a tenth part of the square, and the lighter a third as wide as the heavier: to follow this rule for all letters of the *Alphabet.First, make an A after this fashion: Indicate the angles of the square by the letters***

ITC STONE SERIF SEMIBOLD WITH ITALIC   ADOBE TYPE LIBRARY

12/13 **Now, since architects, painters and others at times are wont to set an inscription on lofty walls, it will make for the merit of the work that they form the letters correctly. Accordingly I am minded here to treat briefly of this. And first I will give rules for a Latin Alphabet, and then for one of our common Text: since it is of these two sorts of letters we customarily make use in such work; and first, for the Roman letters: Draw for each a square of uniform size, in which the *letter is to be contained. But when you draw in it the heavier limb of the letter,***

10/11 **Now, since architects, painters and others at times are wont to set an inscription on lofty walls, it will make for the merit of the work that they form the letters correctly. Accordingly I am minded here to treat briefly of this. And first I will give rules for a Latin Alphabet, and then for one of our common Text: since it is of these two sorts of letters we customarily make use in such work; and first, for the Roman letters: Draw for each a square of uniform size, in which the letter is to be contained. But when you draw in it the heavier limb of the letter, make this of the width of a tenth part of the square, and the lighter a third as wide as the heavier: to *follow this rule for all letters of the Alphabet.* First, make an A after this fashion: Indicate**

ITC STONE SERIF BOLD WITH ITALIC   ADOBE TYPE LIBRARY

ABCDEFGHIJKLMNOPQRSTUVWXYZ
&abcdefghijklmnopqrstuvwxyz123456
7890$.,""'':;!?

TEKTON™   ADOBE TYPE LIBRARY

ABCDEFGHIJKLMNOPQRSTUVWXYZ
&abcdefghijklmnopqrstuvwxyz123456
7890$.,""'':;!?

TEKTON OBLIQUE   ADOBE TYPE LIBRARY

ABCDEFGHIJKLMNOPQRSTUVWX
YZ&abcdefghijklmnopqrstuvwxyz1
234567890$.,""'':;!?

WTC THADDEUS** REGULAR   MERGENTHALER TYPE LIBRARY

ABCDEFGHIJKLMNOPQRSTUVWX
YZ&abcdefghijklmnopqrstuvwxyz1
234567890$.,""'':;!?

WTC THADDEUS** REGULAR ITALIC   MERGENTHALER TYPE LIBRARY

ABCDEFGHIJKLMNOPQRSTUVWX
YZ&abcdefghijklmnopqrstuvwxyz1
234567890$.,""'':;!?

WTC THADDEUS** BOLD   MERGENTHALER TYPE LIBRARY

ABCDEFGHIJKLMNOPQRSTUVWX
YZ&abcdefghijklmnopqrstuvwxyz1
234567890$.,""'':;!?

WTC THADDEUS** BOLD ITALIC   MERGENTHALER TYPE LIBRARY

SUPPLEMENTARY FACES 447

12/13 In considering fine and praiseworthy inventions, we must freely confess that printing has been and is to-day the best and most estimable—the invention by means of which two persons turning the press can get a greater number of books in a day than formerly could have been transcribed by several persons in a year. It is claimed that this art was invented at Mainz, a city of Germany, in the year 1442 by Jean Guttemberg, or, according to others, Guttenberg, an honorable German chevalier. It was at Mainz that after experimenting with an ink which is used by printers to-day, he first began the practice of the art. Some persons prefer to attribute the invention to Jean Fauste and Yues Scheffey

10/11 In considering fine and praiseworthy inventions, we must freely confess that printing has been and is to-day the best and most estimable—the invention by means of which two persons turning the press can get a greater number of books in a day than formerly could have been transcribed by several persons in a year. It is claimed that this art was invented at Mainz, a city of Germany, in the year 1442 by Jean Guttemberg, or, according to others, Guttenberg, an honorable German chevalier. It was at Mainz that after experimenting with an ink which is used by printers to-day, he first began the practice of the art. Some persons prefer to attribute the invention to Jean Fauste and Yues Scheffey two years earlier, holding that our Guttemberg, Jean Mentel, Jean Prus, Adolphe Rusche, Pierre Scheffec, Martin Flache, Huldric Han, Jean Froben, Adam Petri, Thomas Vuolffe, and others added improvements and spread the art of print-

TEKTON WITH OBLIQUE   ADOBE TYPE LIBRARY

12/13 Lying in my bed, on the morning of the Feast of Kings, when I had had my sleep and rest, & my stomach had readily digested its light and pleasant repast, in the year that was reckoned as MDXXIII, I fell to musing and set the wheel of my memory awhirl thinking on a thousand little conceits, some serious & some joyous, among which there came to my mind a certain Antique letter which I had lately made for my lord the Treasurer for War, Maistre Jehan Groslier, Counsellor and Secretary to our Lord the King, lover of well-made letters and of all learned persons, by whom also he is much loved & esteemed

10/11 Lying in my bed, on the morning of the Feast of Kings, when I had had my sleep and rest, & my stomach had readily digested its light and pleasant repast, in the year that was reckoned as MDXXIII, I fell to musing and set the wheel of my memory awhirl thinking on a thousand little conceits, some serious & some joyous, among which there came to my mind a certain Antique letter which I had lately made for my lord the Treasurer for War, Maistre Jehan Groslier, Counsellor and Secretary to our Lord the King, lover of well-made letters and of all learned persons, by whom also he is much loved & esteemed on both this & the other side of the mountains. And whilst thinking of this Attic Letter, there came of a sudden into my memory a pithy passage in the first book & eighth chapter of the DeOfficiis of Cicero, where it is written: Non nobis solum nati

WTC THADDEUS** REGULAR WITH REGULAR ITALIC   MERGENTHALER TYPE LIBRARY

12/13 **Lying in my bed, on the morning of the Feast of Kings, when I had had my sleep and rest, & my stomach had readily digested its light and pleasant repast, in the year that was reckoned as MDXXIII, I fell to musing and set the wheel of my memory awhirl thinking on a thousand little conceits, some serious & some joyous, among which there came to my mind a certain Antique letter which I had lately made for my lord the Treasurer for War, Maistre Jehan Groslier, Counsellor and Secretary to our Lord the King, lover of well-made *letters and of all learned persons, by whom also he is much loved & esteemed***

10/11 **Lying in my bed, on the morning of the Feast of Kings, when I had had my sleep and rest, & my stomach had readily digested its light and pleasant repast, in the year that was reckoned as MDXXIII, I fell to musing and set the wheel of my memory awhirl thinking on a thousand little conceits, some serious & some joyous, among which there came to my mind a certain Antique letter which I had lately made for my lord the Treasurer for War, Maistre Jehan Groslier, Counsellor and Secretary to our Lord the King, lover of well-made letters and of all learned persons, by whom also he is much loved & esteemed on both this & the other side of the mountains. And whilst thinking of this Attic Letter, there came of a sudden into my memory a pithy passage *in the first book & eighth chapter of the DeOfficiis of Cicero, where it is written: Non nobis solum nati***

WTC THADDEUS** BOLD WITH BOLD ITALIC   MERGENTHALER TYPE LIBRARY

ABCDEFGHIJKLMNOPQRSTUVW
XYZ&abcdefghijklmnopqrstuvwxyz1
234567890$.,""'':;!?

ITC TIFFANY LIGHT   MERGENTHALER TYPE LIBRARY

*ABCDEFGHIJKLMNOPQRSTUVWX
YZ&abcdefghijklmnopqrstuvwxyz1234
567890$.,""'':;!?*

ITC TIFFANY LIGHT ITALIC   MERGENTHALER TYPE LIBRARY

ABCDEFGHIJKLMNOPQRSTUVW
XYZ&abcdefghijklmnopqrstuvwxyz
1234567890$.,""'':;!?

ITC TIFFANY MEDIUM   MERGENTHALER TYPE LIBRARY

*ABCDEFGHIJKLMNOPQRSTUVW
XYZ&abcdefghijklmnopqrstuvwxyz1
234567890$.,""'':;!?*

ITC TIFFANY MEDIUM ITALIC   MERGENTHALER TYPE LIBRARY

**ABCDEFGHIJKLMNOPQRSTUV
WXYZ&abcdefghijklmnopqrstuv
wxyz1234567890$.,""'':;!?**

ITC TIFFANY HEAVY   MERGENTHALER TYPE LIBRARY

***ABCDEFGHIJKLMNOPQRSTUV
WXYZ&abcdefghijklmnopqrstuv
wxyz1234567890$.,""'':;!?***

ITC TIFFANY HEAVY ITALIC   MERGENTHALER TYPE LIBRARY

ITC TIFFANY** LIGHT WITH LIGHT ITALIC — MERGENTHALER TYPE LIBRARY

12/13 In type-founding, types are cast in moulds containing at one end a copper matrix of the character. The aperture through which the melted metal is injected is at the end of the mould opposite the matrix, and a piece as long as the type, called the jet, extends through the aperture from the bottom of the type. Thus imperfections in the metal and variations of temperature spend themselves in the jet, leaving the body of the type comparatively perfect. The types thus cast go through various processes, such as breaking off the jet and ploughing in *its place a shallow groove across the foot, thus leaving each type two "feet" to stand*

10/11 In type-founding, types are cast in moulds containing at one end a copper matrix of the character. The aperture through which the melted metal is injected is at the end of the mould opposite the matrix, and a piece as long as the type, called the jet, extends through the aperture from the bottom of the type. Thus imperfections in the metal and variations of temperature spend themselves in the jet, leaving the body of the type comparatively perfect. The types thus cast go through various processes, such as breaking off the jet and ploughing in its place a shallow groove across the foot, thus leaving each type two "feet" to stand upon, "rubbing," etc.; and at last, set up in long rows, they pass under the eye of an expert, who, as he examines them carefully *with a glass, rejects all in which he detects any imperfections. In these processes an average of 10*

ITC TIFFANY** MEDIUM WITH MEDIUM ITALIC — MERGENTHALER TYPE LIBRARY

12/13 In type-founding, types are cast in moulds containing at one end a copper matrix of the character. The aperture through which the melted metal is injected is at the end of the mould opposite the matrix, and a piece as long as the type, called the jet, extends through the aperture from the bottom of the type. Thus imperfections in the metal and variations of temperature spend themselves in the jet, leaving the body of the type comparatively perfect. The types thus cast go through various processes, *such as breaking off the jet and ploughing in its place a shallow groove across*

10/11 In type-founding, types are cast in moulds containing at one end a copper matrix of the character. The aperture through which the melted metal is injected is at the end of the mould opposite the matrix, and a piece as long as the type, called the jet, extends through the aperture from the bottom of the type. Thus imperfections in the metal and variations of temperature spend themselves in the jet, leaving the body of the type comparatively perfect. The types thus cast go through various processes, such as breaking off the jet and ploughing in its place a shallow groove across the foot, thus leaving each type two "feet" to stand upon, "rubbing," etc.; and at last, set up in long rows, they pass under the eye of an *expert, who, as he examines them carefully with a glass, rejects all in which he detects any imper-*

ITC TIFFANY** HEAVY WITH HEAVY ITALIC — MERGENTHALER TYPE LIBRARY

12/13 **In type-founding, types are cast in moulds containing at one end a copper matrix of the character. The aperture through which the melted metal is injected is at the end of the mould opposite the matrix, and a piece as long as the type, called the jet, extends through the aperture from the bottom of the type. Thus imperfections in the metal and variations of temperature spend themselves in the jet, leaving the body of the type comparatively perfect. The types thus cast go through vari-**

10/11 **In type-founding, types are cast in moulds containing at one end a copper matrix of the character. The aperture through which the melted metal is injected is at the end of the mould opposite the matrix, and a piece as long as the type, called the jet, extends through the aperture from the bottom of the type. Thus imperfections in the metal and variations of temperature spend themselves in the jet, leaving the body of the type comparatively perfect. The types thus cast go through various processes, such as breaking off the jet and ploughing in its place a shallow groove across the *foot, thus leaving each type two "feet" to stand upon, "rubbing," etc.; and at***

ABCDEFGHIJKLMNOPQRSTUVWXYZ&abcdefghijklmnopqrstuvwxyz1234567890$.,""":;!?

TRAJANUS*   MERGENTHALER TYPE LIBRARY

ABCDEFGHIJKLMNOPQRSTUVWXYZ&abcdefghijklmnopqrstuvwxyz1234567890$.,""":;!?

TRAJANUS* ITALIC   MERGENTHALER TYPE LIBRARY

ABCDEFGHIJKLMNOPQRSTUVWXYZ&abcdefghijklmnopqrstuvwxyz1234567890$.,""":;!?

TRAJANUS* BOLD   MERGENTHALER TYPE LIBRARY

ABCDEFGHIJKLMNOPQRSTUVWXYZ&abcdefghijklmnopqrstuvwxyz1234567890$.,""":;!?

TRAJANUS* BOLD ITALIC   MERGENTHALER TYPE LIBRARY

ABCDEFGHIJKLMNOPQRSTUVWXYZ&abcdefghijklmnopqrstuvwxyz1234567890$.,""":;!?

TRAJANUS* BLACK   MERGENTHALER TYPE LIBRARY

ABCDEFGHIJKLMNOPQRSTUVWXYZ&abcdefghijklmnopqrstuvwxyz1234567890$.,""":;!?

TRAJANUS* BLACK ITALIC   MERGENTHALER TYPE LIBRARY

12/13 **OBSERVATIONS ON COMPOSING.** **Although this essential point has been passed over with little notice by most writers upon this subject, still (so great are the evils resulting from ill-contracted habits, which naturally keep pace with our growth), we cannot avoid pointing out a few instances of the sure consequences attendant on them. There are many persons now employed in the art, who frequently, with great justice, inveigh in strong terms against the** *conduct of those unto whose care they were first entrusted, for suffer-*

10/11 **OBSERVATIONS ON COMPOSING. Although this essential point has been passed over with little notice by most writers upon this subject, still (so great are the evils resulting from ill-contracted habits, which naturally keep pace with our growth), we cannot avoid pointing out a few instances of the sure consequences attendant on them. There are many persons now employed in the art, who frequently, with great justice, inveigh in strong terms against the conduct of those unto whose care they were first entrusted, for suffering them to contract those ill-becoming postures which are productive of knock knees, round shoulders, and other deformities. It is deeply to be re-** *gretted, that those who undertake so impor-*

UNIVERS® 75 BLACK WITH 76 BLACK ITALIC   MERGENTHALER TYPE LIBRARY

12/13 OBSERVATIONS ON COMPOSING. Although this essential point has been passed over with little notice by most writers upon this subject, still (so great are the evils resulting from ill-contracted habits, which naturally keep pace with our growth), we cannot avoid pointing out a few instances of the sure consequences attendant on them. There are many persons now employed in the art, who frequently, with great justice, inveigh in strong terms against the conduct of those unto whose care they were first entrusted, for suffer-

10/11 OBSERVATIONS ON COMPOSING. Although this essential point has been passed over with little notice by most writers upon this subject, still (so great are the evils resulting from ill-contracted habits, which naturally keep pace with our growth), we cannot avoid pointing out a few instances of the sure consequences attendant on them. There are many persons now employed in the art, who frequently, with great justice, inveigh in strong terms against the conduct of those unto whose care they were first entrusted, for suffering them to contract those ill-becoming postures which are productive of knock knees, round shoulders, and other deformities. It is deeply to be regretted, that those who undertake so important a charge,

UNIVERS® 85 EXTRA BLACK   MERGENTHALER TYPE LIBRARY

12/13 OBSERVATIONS ON COMPOSING. Although this essential point has been passed over with little notice by most writers upon this subject, still (so great are the evils resulting from ill-contracted habits, which naturally keep pace with our growth), we cannot avoid pointing out a few instances of the sure consequences attendant on them. There are many persons now employed in the art, who frequently, with great justice, inveigh in strong terms against the conduct of those unto whose care they were first entrusted, for suffering them to contract those ill-becoming postures which are productive of knock knees, round shoulders, and other deformities. It is deeply to be *regretted, that those who undertake so important a charge, are not better qualified to fulfill that duty:*

10/11 OBSERVATIONS ON COMPOSING. Although this essential point has been passed over with little notice by most writers upon this subject, still (so great are the evils resulting from ill-contracted habits, which naturally keep pace with our growth), we cannot avoid pointing out a few instances of the sure consequences attendant on them. There are many persons now employed in the art, who frequently, with great justice, inveigh in strong terms against the conduct of those unto whose care they were first entrusted, for suffering them to contract those ill-becoming postures which are productive of knock knees, round shoulders, and other deformities. It is deeply to be regretted, that those who undertake so important a charge, are not better qualified to fulfill that duty: instead of suffering the tender shoot to grow wild and uncultivated, when the pruning-knife, in a gentle hand, with a little admonition, would have checked its improper *growth, and trained it in a right course.*
  What to a learner may appear fatiguing, time and habit will

UNIVERS® 47 LIGHT CONDENSED WITH 48 LIGHT CONDENSED ITALIC   MERGENTHALER TYPE LIBRARY

SUPPLEMENTARY FACES

ABCDEFGHIJKLMNOPQRSTUVWXYZ&abcdefghijklmnopqrstuvwxyz1234567890$.,""':;!?

UNIVERS* 57 CONDENSED   MERGENTHALER TYPE LIBRARY

ABCDEFGHIJKLMNOPQRSTUVWXYZ&abcdefghijklmnopqrstuvwxyz1234567890$.,"":;!?

UNIVERS* 58 CONDENSED ITALIC   MERGENTHALER TYPE LIBRARY

ABCDEFGHIJKLMNOPQRSTUVWXYZ&abcdefghijklmnopqrstuvwxyz1234567890$.,"":;!?

UNIVERS* 67 BOLD CONDENSED   MERGENTHALER TYPE LIBRARY

ABCDEFGHIJKLMNOPQRSTUVWXYZ&abcdefghijklmnopqrstuvwxyz1234567890$.,"":;!?

UNIVERS* 68 BOLD CONDENSED ITALIC   MERGENTHALER TYPE LIBRARY

ABCDEFGHIJKLMNOPQRSTUVWXYZ&abcdefghijklmnopqrstuvwxyz1234567890$.,"'':;!?

UNIVERS* 53 EXTENDED   MERGENTHALER TYPE LIBRARY

ABCDEFGHIJKLMNOPQRSTUVWXYZ&abcdefghijklmnopqrstuvwxyz1234567890$.,"'':;!?

UNIVERS* 63 BOLD EXTENDED   MERGENTHALER TYPE LIBRARY

SUPPLEMENTARY FACES 463

12/13 OBSERVATIONS ON COMPOSING. Although this essential point has been passed over with little notice by most writers upon this subject, still (so great are the evils resulting from ill-contracted habits, which naturally keep pace with our growth), we cannot avoid pointing out a few instances of the sure consequences attendant on them. There are many persons now employed in the art, who frequently, with great justice, inveigh in strong terms against the conduct of those unto whose care they were first entrusted, for suffering them to contract those ill-becoming postures which are productive of knock knees, *round shoulders, and other deformities. It is deeply to be regretted, that those who under-*

10/11 OBSERVATIONS ON COMPOSING. Although this essential point has been passed over with little notice by most writers upon this subject, still (so great are the evils resulting from ill-contracted habits, which naturally keep pace with our growth), we cannot avoid pointing out a few instances of the sure consequences attendant on them. There are many persons now employed in the art, who frequently, with great justice, inveigh in strong terms against the conduct of those unto whose care they were first entrusted, for suffering them to contract those ill-becoming postures which are productive of knock knees, round shoulders, and other deformities. It is deeply to be regretted, that those who undertake so important a charge, are not better qualified to fulfill that duty: instead of suffering the tender shoot to grow wild and uncultivated, *when the pruning-knife, in a gentle hand, with a little admonition, would have checked its improper*

UNIVERS® 57 CONDENSED WITH 58 CONDENSED ITALIC   MERGENTHALER TYPE LIBRARY

12/13 **OBSERVATIONS ON COMPOSING. Although this essential point has been passed over with little notice by most writers upon this subject, still (so great are the evils resulting from ill-contracted habits, which naturally keep pace with our growth), we cannot avoid pointing out a few instances of the sure consequences attendant on them. There are many persons now employed in the art, who frequently, with great justice, inveigh in strong terms against the conduct of those unto whose care they were first entrusted, for suffering them to contract those ill-becoming postures which are productive of *knock knees, round shoulders, and other deformities. It is deeply to be regretted, that those***

10/11 **OBSERVATIONS ON COMPOSING. Although this essential point has been passed over with little notice by most writers upon this subject, still (so great are the evils resulting from ill-contracted habits, which naturally keep pace with our growth), we cannot avoid pointing out a few instances of the sure consequences attendant on them. There are many persons now employed in the art, who frequently, with great justice, inveigh in strong terms against the conduct of those unto whose care they were first entrusted, for suffering them to contract those ill-becoming postures which are productive of knock knees, round shoulders, and other deformities. It is deeply to be regretted, that those who undertake so important a charge, are not better qualified to fulfill that duty: instead of suffering the tender shoot to grow wild *and uncultivated, when the pruning-knife, in a gentle hand, with a little admonition, would have checked its***

UNIVERS® 67 BOLD CONDENSED WITH 68 BOLD CONDENSED ITALIC   MERGENTHALER TYPE LIBRARY

12/13 OBSERVATIONS ON COMPOS-ING. Although this essential point has been passed over with little notice by most writers upon this subject, still (so great are the evils resulting from ill-contracted habits, which naturally keep pace with our growth), we cannot avoid pointing out a few instances of the sure consequences attendant on them. There are many persons now employed in the art, who frequently, **with great justice, inveigh in strong terms against the con-**

10/11 OBSERVATIONS ON COMPOSING. Although this essential point has been passed over with little notice by most writers upon this subject, still (so great are the evils resulting from ill-contracted habits, which naturally keep pace with our growth), we cannot avoid pointing out a few instances of the sure consequences attendant on them. There are many persons now employed in the art, who frequently, with great justice, inveigh in strong terms against the conduct of those unto whose care they were first entrusted, for suffering them to contract those ill-becoming **postures which are productive of knock knees, round shoulders, and**

UNIVERS® 53 EXTENDED WITH 63 BOLD EXTENDED   MERGENTHALER TYPE LIBRARY

ABCDEFGHIJKLMNOPQRSTUVWXYZ&abcdefghijklmnopqrstuvwxyz1234567890$.,"":;!?

ITC USHERWOOD** BOOK   MERGENTHALER TYPE LIBRARY

ABCDEFGHIJKLMNOPQRSTUVWXYZ&abcdefghijklmnopqrstuvwxyz1234567890$.,"":;!?

ITC USHERWOOD** BOOK ITALIC   MERGENTHALER TYPE LIBRARY

ABCDEFGHIJKLMNOPQRSTUVWXYZ&abcdefghijklmnopqrstuvwxyz1234567890$.,"":;!?

ITC USHERWOOD** MEDIUM   MERGENTHALER TYPE LIBRARY

ABCDEFGHIJKLMNOPQRSTUVWXYZ&abcdefghijklmnopqrstuvwxyz1234567890$.,"":;!?

ITC USHERWOOD** MEDIUM ITALIC   MERGENTHALER TYPE LIBRARY

ABCDEFGHIJKLMNOPQRSTUVWXYZ&abcdefghijklmnopqrstuvwxyz1234567890$.,"":;!?

ITC USHERWOOD** BOLD   MERGENTHALER TYPE LIBRARY

ABCDEFGHIJKLMNOPQRSTUVWXYZ&abcdefghijklmnopqrstuvwxyz1234567890$.,"":;!?

ITC USHERWOOD** BOLD ITALIC   MERGENTHALER TYPE LIBRARY

12/13 In considering fine and praiseworthy inventions, we must freely confess that printing has been and is to-day the best and most estimable — the invention by means of which two persons turning the press can get a greater number of books in a day than formerly could have been transcribed by several persons in a year. It is claimed that this art was invented at Mainz, a city of Germany, in the year 1442 by Jean Guttemberg, or, according to others, Guttenberg, an honorable German chevalier. It was at Mainz that after experimenting with an ink which is *used by printers to-day, he first began the practice of the art. Some persons prefer to*

10/11 In considering fine and praiseworthy inventions, we must freely confess that printing has been and is to-day the best and most estimable — the invention by means of which two persons turning the press can get a greater number of books in a day than formerly could have been transcribed by several persons in a year. It is claimed that this art was invented at Mainz, a city of Germany, in the year 1442 by Jean Guttemberg, or, according to others, Guttenberg, an honorable German chevalier. It was at Mainz that after experimenting with an ink which is used by printers to-day, he first began the practice of the art. Some persons prefer to attribute the invention to Jean Fauste & Yues Scheffey two years earlier, holding that our Guttemberg, Jean Mentel, Jean Prus, *Adolphe Rusche, Pierre Scheffec, Martin Flache, Huldric Han, Jean Froben, Adam Petri, Thomas Vuolffe, and others*

ITC USHERWOOD** BOOK WITH BOOK ITALIC   MERGENTHALER TYPE LIBRARY

12/13 In considering fine and praiseworthy inventions, we must freely confess that printing has been and is to-day the best and most estimable — the invention by means of which two persons turning the press can get a greater number of books in a day than formerly could have been transcribed by several persons in a year. It is claimed that this art was invented at Mainz, a city of Germany, in the year 1442 by Jean Guttemberg, or, according to others, Guttenberg, an honorable German chevalier. It was at Mainz that after experimenting with an ink *which is used by printers to-day, he first began the practice of the art. Some persons*

10/11 In considering fine and praiseworthy inventions, we must freely confess that printing has been and is to-day the best and most estimable — the invention by means of which two persons turning the press can get a greater number of books in a day than formerly could have been transcribed by several persons in a year. It is claimed that this art was invented at Mainz, a city of Germany, in the year 1442 by Jean Guttemberg, or, according to others, Guttenberg, an honorable German chevalier. It was at Mainz that after experimenting with an ink which is used by printers to-day, he first began the practice of the art. Some persons prefer to attribute the invention to Jean Fauste & Yues Scheffey two years earlier, holding that our Guttemberg, Jean Mentel, Jean Prus, *Adolphe Rusche, Pierre Scheffec, Martin Flache, Huldric Han, Jean Froben, Adam Petri, Thomas*

ITC USHERWOOD** MEDIUM WITH MEDIUM ITALIC   MERGENTHALER TYPE LIBRARY

12/13 **In considering fine and praiseworthy inventions, we must freely confess that printing has been and is to-day the best and most estimable — the invention by means of which two persons turning the press can get a greater number of books in a day than formerly could have been transcribed by several persons in a year. It is claimed that this art was invented at Mainz, a city of Germany, in the year 1442 by Jean Guttemberg, or, according to others, Guttenberg, an honorable German chevalier. It was at Mainz that after experimenting with an ink which is used by printers to-day, he first began the practice**

10/11 **In considering fine and praiseworthy inventions, we must freely confess that printing has been and is to-day the best and most estimable — the invention by means of which two persons turning the press can get a greater number of books in a day than formerly could have been transcribed by several persons in a year. It is claimed that this art was invented at Mainz, a city of Germany, in the year 1442 by Jean Guttemberg, or, according to others, Guttenberg, an honorable German chevalier. It was at Mainz that after experimenting with an ink which is used by printers to-day, he first began the practice of the art. Some persons prefer to attribute the invention to Jean Fauste & Yues Scheffey two years earlier, holding that our *Guttemberg, Jean Mentel, Jean Prus, Adolphe Rusche, Pierre Scheffec, Martin Flache, Huldric Han,***

ITC USHERWOOD** BOLD WITH BOLD ITALIC   MERGENTHALER TYPE LIBRARY

SUPPLEMENTARY FACES   465

ABCDEFGHIJKLMNOPQRSTUVWX YZ&abcdefghijklmnopqrstuvwxyz1 234567890$.,""":;!?

UTOPIA™ REGULAR   ADOBE TYPE LIBRARY

ABCDEFGHIJKLMNOPQRSTUVWX YZ&abcdefghijklmnopqrstuvwxyz1 234567890$.,""":;!?

UTOPIA ITALIC   ADOBE TYPE LIBRARY

ABCDEFGHIJKLMNOPQRSTUVWX YZ&abcdefghijklmnopqrstuvwxyz1 234567890$.,""":;!?

UTOPIA SEMIBOLD   ADOBE TYPE LIBRARY

ABCDEFGHIJKLMNOPQRSTUVWX YZ&abcdefghijklmnopqrstuvwxyz1 234567890$.,""":;!?

UTOPIA SEMIBOLD ITALIC   ADOBE TYPE LIBRARY

ABCDEFGHIJKLMNOPQRSTUVWX YZ&abcdefghijklmnopqrstuvwxyz1 234567890$.,""":;!?

UTOPIA BOLD   ADOBE TYPE LIBRARY

ABCDEFGHIJKLMNOPQRSTUVWX YZ&abcdefghijklmnopqrstuvwxyz1 234567890$.,""":;!?

UTOPIA BOLD ITALIC   ADOBE TYPE LIBRARY

SUPPLEMENTARY FACES 467

12/13 It is still a matter of conjecture whether Johann Gutenberg was the first to conceive the principle of casting movable (i.e., separate) metal types which could be arranged in words and sentences so that he could impress their faces on paper. There is, however, hardly a doubt, judging at least from the evidence available, that he was the first to make practical use of the idea, and that it is due to his ingenious application of it that the profound art of typography was born.
Whether he cast his letters in molds of sand *or in metal matrices, is a question not really material at this time; it is the far-reaching re-*

10/11 It is still a matter of conjecture whether Johann Gutenberg was the first to conceive the principle of casting movable (i.e., separate) metal types which could be arranged in words and sentences so that he could impress their faces on paper. There is, however, hardly a doubt, judging at least from the evidence available, that he was the first to make practical use of the idea, and that it is due to his ingenious application of it that the profound art of typography was born.
Whether he cast his letters in molds of sand or in metal matrices, is a question not really material at this time; it is the far-reaching results of his inspiration that most concern us in this discussion. It seems quite probable that Gutenberg at first had *little more in mind than a desire to find some expedient by which to supplement with explana-*

UTOPIA REGULAR WITH ITALIC   ADOBE TYPE LIBRARY

12/13 **It is still a matter of conjecture whether Johann Gutenberg was the first to conceive the principle of casting movable (i.e., separate) metal types which could be arranged in words and sentences so that he could impress their faces on paper. There is, however, hardly a doubt, judging at least from the evidence available, that he was the first to make practical use of the idea, and that it is due to his ingenious application of it that the profound art of typography was born.
Whether he cast his letters in molds of *sand or in metal matrices, is a question not really material at this time; it is the far-***

10/11 **It is still a matter of conjecture whether Johann Gutenberg was the first to conceive the principle of casting movable (i.e., separate) metal types which could be arranged in words and sentences so that he could impress their faces on paper. There is, however, hardly a doubt, judging at least from the evidence available, that he was the first to make practical use of the idea, and that it is due to his ingenious application of it that the profound art of typography was born.
Whether he cast his letters in molds of sand or in metal matrices, is a question not really material at this time; it is the far-reaching results of his inspiration that most concern us in this discussion. It seems quite probable that Gutenberg at first *had little more in mind than a desire to find some expedient by which to supplement with explana-***

UTOPIA SEMIBOLD WITH ITALIC   ADOBE TYPE LIBRARY

12/13 **It is still a matter of conjecture whether Johann Gutenberg was the first to conceive the principle of casting movable (i.e., separate) metal types which could be arranged in words and sentences so that he could impress their faces on paper. There is, however, hardly a doubt, judging at least from the evidence available, that he was the first to make practical use of the idea, and that it is due to his ingenious application of it that the profound art of typography was born.
Whether he cast his letters in molds of *sand or in metal matrices, is a question not really material at this time; it is the far-***

10/11 **It is still a matter of conjecture whether Johann Gutenberg was the first to conceive the principle of casting movable (i.e., separate) metal types which could be arranged in words and sentences so that he could impress their faces on paper. There is, however, hardly a doubt, judging at least from the evidence available, that he was the first to make practical use of the idea, and that it is due to his ingenious application of it that the profound art of typography was born.
Whether he cast his letters in molds of sand or in metal matrices, is a question not really material at this time; it is the far-reaching results of his inspiration that most concern us in this discussion. It seems quite probable that Gutenberg at *first had little more in mind than a desire to find some expedient by which to supplement with ex-***

UTOPIA BOLD WITH ITALIC   ADOBE TYPE LIBRARY

ABCDEFGHIJKLMNOPQRSTUVWXYZ&abcdefghijklmnopqrstuvwxyz1234567890$.,""'':;!?

VERSAILLES* 45 LIGHT   MERGENTHALER TYPE LIBRARY

ABCDEFGHIJKLMNOPQRSTUVWXYZ&abcdefghijklmnopqrstuvwxyz1234567890$.,""'':;!?

VERSAILLES* 46 LIGHT ITALIC   MERGENTHALER TYPE LIBRARY

ABCDEFGHIJKLMNOPQRSTUVWXYZ&abcdefghijklmnopqrstuvwxyz1234567890$.,""'':;!?

VERSAILLES* 55   MERGENTHALER TYPE LIBRARY

ABCDEFGHIJKLMNOPQRSTUVWXYZ&abcdefghijklmnopqrstuvwxyz1234567890$.,""'':;!?

VERSAILLES* 56 ITALIC   MERGENTHALER TYPE LIBRARY

ABCDEFGHIJKLMNOPQRSTUVWXYZ&abcdefghijklmnopqrstuvwxyz1234567890$.,""'':;!?

VERSAILLES* 95 BLACK   MERGENTHALER TYPE LIBRARY

ABCDEFGHIJKLMNOPQRSTUVWXYZ&abcdefghijklmnopqrstuvwxyz1234567890$.,""'':;!?

VERSAILLES* 96 BLACK ITALIC   MERGENTHALER TYPE LIBRARY

SUPPLEMENTARY FACES 469

12/13 Now, since architects, painters & others at times are wont to set an inscription on lofty walls, it will make for the merit of the work that they form the letters correctly. Accordingly I am minded here to treat briefly of this. And first I will give rules for a Latin Alphabet, and then for one of our common Text: since it is of these two sorts of letters we customarily make use in such work; and first, for the Roman letters: Draw for each a square of uniform size, in which the letter is to be contained. But when you draw in it the heavier limb of the *letter, make this of the width of a tenth part of the square, and the lighter a third as*

10/11 Now, since architects, painters & others at times are wont to set an inscription on lofty walls, it will make for the merit of the work that they form the letters correctly. Accordingly I am minded here to treat briefly of this. And first I will give rules for a Latin Alphabet, and then for one of our common Text: since it is of these two sorts of letters we customarily make use in such work; and first, for the Roman letters: Draw for each a square of uniform size, in which the letter is to be contained. But when you draw in it the heavier limb of the letter, make this of the width of a tenth part of the square, and the lighter a third as wide as the heavier: to follow this rule for all letters of the Alphabet.
   First, make an A after this fashion: Indicate the *angles of the square by the letters a. b. c. d. (and so do for all the rest of the letters): then divide the*

VERSAILLES* 45 LIGHT WITH 46 LIGHT ITALIC   MERGENTHALER TYPE LIBRARY

12/13 Now, since architects, painters & others at times are wont to set an inscription on lofty walls, it will make for the merit of the work that they form the letters correctly. Accordingly I am minded here to treat briefly of this. And first I will give rules for a Latin Alphabet, and then for one of our common Text: since it is of these two sorts of letters we customarily make use in such work; and first, for the Roman letters: Draw for each a square of uniform size, in which the letter is to be contained. But when you draw in it the *heavier limb of the letter, make this of the width of a tenth part of the square, and*

10/11 Now, since architects, painters & others at times are wont to set an inscription on lofty walls, it will make for the merit of the work that they form the letters correctly. Accordingly I am minded here to treat briefly of this. And first I will give rules for a Latin Alphabet, and then for one of our common Text: since it is of these two sorts of letters we customarily make use in such work; and first, for the Roman letters: Draw for each a square of uniform size, in which the letter is to be contained. But when you draw in it the heavier limb of the letter, make this of the width of a tenth part of the square, and the lighter a third as wide as the heavier: to follow this rule for all letters of the Alphabet.
   First, make an A after this fashion: Indicate the *angles of the square by the letters a. b. c. d. (and*

VERSAILLES* 55 WITH 56 ITALIC   MERGENTHALER TYPE LIBRARY

12/13 **Now, since architects, painters & others at times are wont to set an inscription on lofty walls, it will make for the merit of the work that they form the letters correctly. Accordingly I am minded here to treat briefly of this. And first I will give rules for a Latin Alphabet, and then for one of our common Text: since it is of these two sorts of letters we customarily make use in such work; and first, for the Roman letters: Draw for each a square of uniform size, in which the letter is to be contained. But when you draw in it the**

10/11 **Now, since architects, painters & others at times are wont to set an inscription on lofty walls, it will make for the merit of the work that they form the letters correctly. Accordingly I am minded here to treat briefly of this. And first I will give rules for a Latin Alphabet, and then for one of our common Text: since it is of these two sorts of letters we customarily make use in such work; and first, for the Roman letters: Draw for each a square of uniform size, in which the letter is to be contained. But when you draw in it the heavier limb of the letter, make this of the width of a tenth part of the square, and the lighter a third as wide as the heavier: to follow this rule for all letters of the Alphabet.**

VERSAILLES* 95 BLACK WITH 96 BLACK ITALIC   MERGENTHALER TYPE LIBRARY

ABCDEFGHIJKLMNOPQRSTUVW
XYZ&abcdefghijklmnopqrstuvwxy
z1234567890$.,""":;!?

WALDBAUM**   MERGENTHALER TYPE LIBRARY

*ABCDEFGHIJKLMNOPQRSTUVW
XYZ&abcdefghijklmnopqrstuvwxy
z1234567890$.,""":;!?*

WALDBAUM** ITALIC   MERGENTHALER TYPE LIBRARY

ABCDEFGHIJKLMNOPQRSTUVWXY
Z&abcdefghijklmnopqrstuvwxyz123456
7890$.,"":;!?

WEISS**   MERGENTHALER TYPE LIBRARY

*ABCDEFGHIJKLMNOPQRSTUVWXYZ&
abcdefghijklmnopqrstuvwxyz1234567890$.,"":;
!?*

WEISS** ITALIC   MERGENTHALER TYPE LIBRARY

**ABCDEFGHIJKLMNOPQRSTUVWX
YZ&abcdefghijklmnopqrstuvwxyz1234
567890$.,"":;!?**

WEISS** BOLD   MERGENTHALER TYPE LIBRARY

**ABCDEFGHIJKLMNOPQRSTUVW
XYZ&abcdefghijklmnopqrstuvwxyz1
234567890$.,"":;!?**

WEISS** EXTRA BOLD   MERGENTHALER TYPE LIBRARY

12/13 Now, since architects, painters & others at times are wont to set an inscription on lofty walls, it will make for the merit of the work that they form the letters correctly. Accordingly I am minded here to treat briefly of this. And first I will give rules for a Latin Alphabet, and then for one of our common Text: since it is of these two sorts of letters we customarily make use in such work; and first, for the Roman letters: Draw for each a square of uniform size, in which the letter is to be contained. But when you draw in it the *heavier limb of the letter, make this of the width of a tenth part of the square, and*

10/11 Now, since architects, painters & others at times are wont to set an inscription on lofty walls, it will make for the merit of the work that they form the letters correctly. Accordingly I am minded here to treat briefly of this. And first I will give rules for a Latin Alphabet, and then for one of our common Text: since it is of these two sorts of letters we customarily make use in such work; and first, for the Roman letters: Draw for each a square of uniform size, in which the letter is to be contained. But when you draw in it the heavier limb of the letter, make this of the width of a tenth part of the square, and the lighter a third as wide as the heavier: to follow this rule for all letters of the Alphabet.
First, make an A after this fashion: Indicate the angles of the square by the letters a. b. c. d. (and so

WALDBAUM** WITH ITALIC   MERGENTHALER TYPE LIBRARY

12/13 Now, since architects, painters & others at times are wont to set an inscription on lofty walls, it will make for the merit of the work that they form the letters correctly. Accordingly I am minded here to treat briefly of this. And first I will give rules for a Latin Alphabet, and then for one of our common Text: since it is of these two sorts of letters we customarily make use in such work; and first, for the Roman letters: Draw for each a square of uniform size, in which the letter is to be contained. But when you draw in it the heavier limb of the letter, make this of the width of a tenth part of the square, and the lighter a *third as wide as the heavier: to follow this rule for all letters of the Alphabet.*

10/11 Now, since architects, painters & others at times are wont to set an inscription on lofty walls, it will make for the merit of the work that they form the letters correctly. Accordingly I am minded here to treat briefly of this. And first I will give rules for a Latin Alphabet, and then for one of our common Text: since it is of these two sorts of letters we customarily make use in such work; and first, for the Roman letters: Draw for each a square of uniform size, in which the letter is to be contained. But when you draw in it the heavier limb of the letter, make this of the width of a tenth part of the square, and the lighter a third as wide as the heavier: to follow this rule for all letters of the Alphabet.
First, make an A after this fashion: Indicate the angles of the square by the letters a. b. c. d. (and so do for all the *rest of the letters): then divide the square by two lines bisecting one another at right angles — the vertical e. f. the horizontal g. h.: then, in*

WEISS** WITH ITALIC   MERGENTHALER TYPE LIBRARY

12/13 Now, since architects, painters & others at times are wont to set an inscription on lofty walls, it will make for the merit of the work that they form the letters correctly. Accordingly I am minded here to treat briefly of this. And first I will give rules for a Latin Alphabet, and then for one of our common Text: since it is of these two sorts of letters we customarily make use in such work; and first, for the Roman letters: Draw for each a square of uniform size, in which the letter is to be contained. But when you draw in it the heavier limb of the letter, make this of the width of a tenth part of the square, and the **lighter a third as wide as the heavier: to follow this rule for all letters of the Alphabet.**

10/11 Now, since architects, painters & others at times are wont to set an inscription on lofty walls, it will make for the merit of the work that they form the letters correctly. Accordingly I am minded here to treat briefly of this. And first I will give rules for a Latin Alphabet, and then for one of our common Text: since it is of these two sorts of letters we customarily make use in such work; and first, for the Roman letters: Draw for each a square of uniform size, in which the letter is to be contained. But when you draw in it the heavier limb of the letter, make this of the width of a tenth part of the square, and the lighter a third as wide as the heavier: to follow this rule for all letters of the Alphabet.
First, make an A after this fashion: Indicate the angles of the square by the letters a. b. c. d. (and so do for all the **rest of the letters): then divide the square by two lines bisecting one another at right angles — the vertical e.**

WEISS** BOLD WITH EXTRA BOLD   MERGENTHALER TYPE LIBRARY

ABCDEFGHIJKLMNOPQRSTUVWXYZ&abcdefghijklmnopqrstuvwxyz1234567890$.,'"":;!?

ITC WEIDEMANN** BOOK   MERGENTHALER TYPE LIBRARY

ABCDEFGHIJKLMNOPQRSTUVWXYZ&abcdefghijklmnopqrstuvwxyz1234567890$.,'"":;!?

ITC WEIDEMANN** BOOK ITALIC   MERGENTHALER TYPE LIBRARY

ABCDEFGHIJKLMNOPQRSTUVWXYZ&abcdefghijklmnopqrstuvwxyz1234567890$.,'"":;!?

ITC WEIDEMANN** MEDIUM   MERGENTHALER TYPE LIBRARY

ABCDEFGHIJKLMNOPQRSTUVWXYZ&abcdefghijklmnopqrstuvwxyz1234567890$.,'"":;!?

ITC WEIDEMANN** MEDIUM ITALIC   MERGENTHALER TYPE LIBRARY

ABCDEFGHIJKLMNOPQRSTUVWXYZ&abcdefghijklmnopqrstuvwxyz1234567890$.,'"":;!?

ITC WEIDEMANN** BLACK   MERGENTHALER TYPE LIBRARY

ABCDEFGHIJKLMNOPQRSTUVWXYZ&abcdefghijklmnopqrstuvwxyz1234567890$.,'"":;!?

ITC WEIDEMANN** BLACK ITALIC   MERGENTHALER TYPE LIBRARY

SUPPLEMENTARY FACES 473

12/13 Lying in my bed, on the morning of the Feast of Kings, when I had had my sleep and rest, & my stomach had readily digested its light and pleasant repast, in the year that was reckoned as MDXXIII, I fell to musing and set the wheel of my memory awhirl thinking on a thousand little conceits, some serious & some joyous, among which there came to my mind a certain Antique letter which I had lately made for my lord the Treasurer for War, Maistre Jehan Groslier, Counsellor and Secretary to our Lord the King, lover of well-made letters and of all learned persons, by whom also he is much loved & esteemed on both this & the other *side of the mountains. And whilst thinking of this Attic Letter, there came of a sudden into my*

10/11 Lying in my bed, on the morning of the Feast of Kings, when I had had my sleep and rest, & my stomach had readily digested its light and pleasant repast, in the year that was reckoned as MDXXIII, I fell to musing and set the wheel of my memory awhirl thinking on a thousand little conceits, some serious & some joyous, among which there came to my mind a certain Antique letter which I had lately made for my lord the Treasurer for War, Maistre Jehan Groslier, Counsellor and Secretary to our Lord the King, lover of well-made letters and of all learned persons, by whom also he is much loved & esteemed on both this & the other side of the mountains. And whilst thinking of this Attic Letter, there came of a sudden into my memory a pithy passage in the first book & eighth chapter of the DeOfficiis of Cicero, where it is written: Non nobis solum nati sumus; ortusque *nostri partem patria vendicat, partem amici. Which is to say, in substance, that we are not born into this world for*

ITC WEIDEMANN** BOOK WITH BOOK ITALIC   MERGENTHALER TYPE LIBRARY

12/13 Lying in my bed, on the morning of the Feast of Kings, when I had had my sleep and rest, & my stomach had readily digested its light and pleasant repast, in the year that was reckoned as MDXXIII, I fell to musing and set the wheel of my memory awhirl thinking on a thousand little conceits, some serious & some joyous, among which there came to my mind a certain Antique letter which I had lately made for my lord the Treasurer for War, Maistre Jehan Groslier, Counsellor and Secretary to our Lord the King, lover of well-made letters and of all learned persons, by whom also he is much *loved & esteemed on both this & the other side of the mountains. And whilst thinking of this*

10/11 Lying in my bed, on the morning of the Feast of Kings, when I had had my sleep and rest, & my stomach had readily digested its light and pleasant repast, in the year that was reckoned as MDXXIII, I fell to musing and set the wheel of my memory awhirl thinking on a thousand little conceits, some serious & some joyous, among which there came to my mind a certain Antique letter which I had lately made for my lord the Treasurer for War, Maistre Jehan Groslier, Counsellor and Secretary to our Lord the King, lover of well-made letters and of all learned persons, by whom also he is much loved & esteemed on both this & the other side of the mountains. And whilst thinking of this Attic Letter, there came of a sudden into my memory a pithy passage in the first book & eighth chapter of the DeOfficiis of Cicero, where it is *written: Non nobis solum nati sumus; ortusque nostri partem patria vendicat, partem amici. Which is to say, in*

ITC WEIDEMANN** MEDIUM WITH MEDIUM ITALIC   MERGENTHALER TYPE LIBRARY

12/13 **Lying in my bed, on the morning of the Feast of Kings, when I had had my sleep and rest, & my stomach had readily digested its light and pleasant repast, in the year that was reckoned as MDXXIII, I fell to musing and set the wheel of my memory awhirl thinking on a thousand little conceits, some serious & some joyous, among which there came to my mind a certain Antique letter which I had lately made for my lord the Treasurer for War, Maistre Jehan Groslier, Counsellor and Secretary to our Lord the King, lover of well-made *letters and of all learned persons, by whom also he is much loved & esteemed***

10/11 **Lying in my bed, on the morning of the Feast of Kings, when I had had my sleep and rest, & my stomach had readily digested its light and pleasant repast, in the year that was reckoned as MDXXIII, I fell to musing and set the wheel of my memory awhirl thinking on a thousand little conceits, some serious & some joyous, among which there came to my mind a certain Antique letter which I had lately made for my lord the Treasurer for War, Maistre Jehan Groslier, Counsellor and Secretary to our Lord the King, lover of well-made letters and of all learned persons, by whom also he is much loved & esteemed on both this & the other side of the mountains. And whilst thinking of this Attic Letter, there came of a sudden into my memory a pithy passage *in the first book & eighth chapter of the DeOfficiis of Cicero, where it is written: Non nobis solum***

ITC WEIDEMANN** BLACK WITH BLACK ITALIC   MERGENTHALER TYPE LIBRARY

ABCDEFGHIJKLMNOPQRSTUV
WXYZ&abcdefghijklmnopqrstuvw
xyz1234567890$.,""'';:!?

WINDSOR OLD STYLE LIGHT   MERGENTHALER TYPE LIBRARY

**ABCDEFGHIJKLMNOPQRSTU
VWXYZ&abcdefghijklmnopqrst
uvwxyz1234567890$.,""'';:!?**

WINDSOR**   MERGENTHALER TYPE LIBRARY

ABCDEFGHIJKLMNOPQRSTUVWXYZ&abc
defghijklmnopqrstuvwxyz1234567890$.,""'';:!?

WINDSOR** LIGHT CONDENSED   MERGENTHALER TYPE LIBRARY

**ABCDEFGHIJKLMNOPQRSTUVWXYZ&abcd
efghijklmnopqrstuvwxyz1234567890$.,""'';:!?**

WINDSOR** ELONGATED   MERGENTHALER TYPE LIBRARY

ABCDEFGHIJKLMNOPQRSTUVWX
YZ&abcdefghijklmnopqrstuvwxyz1234567
890$.,""'';:!?

WORCESTER ROUND**   MERGENTHALER TYPE LIBRARY

*ABCDEFGHIJKLMNOPQRSTUVWXYZ
&abcdefghijklmnopqrstuvwxyz1234567890
$.,""'';:!?*

WORCESTER ROUND** ITALIC   MERGENTHALER TYPE LIBRARY

SUPPLEMENTARY FACES 475

12/13 In type-founding, types are cast in moulds containing at one end a copper matrix of the character. The aperture through which the melted metal is injected is at the end of the mould opposite the matrix, and a piece as long as the type, called the jet, extends through the aperture from the bottom of the type. Thus imperfections in the metal and variations of temperature spend themselves in the jet, leaving the body of the type comparatively perfect. The types thus cast go through various processes, such as breaking off the jet **and ploughing in its place a shallow groove across the foot, thus leaving**

10/11 In type-founding, types are cast in moulds containing at one end a copper matrix of the character. The aperture through which the melted metal is injected is at the end of the mould opposite the matrix, and a piece as long as the type, called the jet, extends through the aperture from the bottom of the type. Thus imperfections in the metal and variations of temperature spend themselves in the jet, leaving the body of the type comparatively perfect. The types thus cast go through various processes, such as breaking off the jet and ploughing in its place a shallow groove across the foot, thus leaving each type two "feet" to stand upon, "rubbing," etc.; and at last, set up in long rows, they pass under the eye of an expert, who, **as he examines them carefully with a glass, rejects all in which he detects any imperfec-**

WINDSOR OLD STYLE** LIGHT WITH WINDSOR**   MERGENTHALER TYPE LIBRARY

12/13 In type-founding, types are cast in moulds containing at one end a copper matrix of the character. The aperture through which the melted metal is injected is at the end of the mould opposite the matrix, and a piece as long as the type, called the jet, extends through the aperture from the bottom of the type. Thus imperfections in the metal and variations of temperature spend themselves in the jet, leaving the body of the type comparatively perfect. The types thus cast go through various processes, such as breaking off the jet and ploughing in its place a shallow groove across the foot, thus leaving each type two "feet" to stand upon, "rubbing," etc.; and at last, set up in long rows, they pass under the eye of an expert, who, as he examines **them carefully with a glass, rejects all in which he detects any imperfections. In these processes an average of 10 per cent, is**

10/11 In type-founding, types are cast in moulds containing at one end a copper matrix of the character. The aperture through which the melted metal is injected is at the end of the mould opposite the matrix, and a piece as long as the type, called the jet, extends through the aperture from the bottom of the type. Thus imperfections in the metal and variations of temperature spend themselves in the jet, leaving the body of the type comparatively perfect. The types thus cast go through various processes, such as breaking off the jet and ploughing in its place a shallow groove across the foot, thus leaving each type two "feet" to stand upon, "rubbing," etc.; and at last, set up in long rows, they pass under the eye of an expert, who, as he examines them carefully with a glass, rejects all in which he detects any imperfections. In these processes an average of 10 per cent, is eliminated; so that of 100 lbs. cast only 90 lbs. are actually fit for delivery.
General Construction of Type-setting Machinery. — With this exception of the Westcott machinery, all the American setters are made to take types from reservoirs

WINDSOR** LIGHT CONDENSED WITH ELONGATED   MERGENTHALER TYPE LIBRARY

12/13 In type-founding, types are cast in moulds containing at one end a copper matrix of the character. The aperture through which the melted metal is injected is at the end of the mould opposite the matrix, and a piece as long as the type, called the jet, extends through the aperture from the bottom of the type. Thus imperfections in the metal and variations of temperature spend themselves in the jet, leaving the body of the type comparatively perfect. The types thus cast go through various processes, such as breaking off the jet and ploughing in its place a shallow groove across the foot, thus leaving each type two "feet" to stand upon, *"rubbing," etc.; and at last, set up in long rows, they pass under the eye of an expert, who, as he examines*

10/11 In type-founding, types are cast in moulds containing at one end a copper matrix of the character. The aperture through which the melted metal is injected is at the end of the mould opposite the matrix, and a piece as long as the type, called the jet, extends through the aperture from the bottom of the type. Thus imperfections in the metal and variations of temperature spend themselves in the jet, leaving the body of the type comparatively perfect. The types thus cast go through various processes, such as breaking off the jet and ploughing in its place a shallow groove across the foot, thus leaving each type two "feet" to stand upon, "rubbing," etc.; and at last, set up in long rows, they pass under the eye of an expert, who, as he examines them carefully with a glass, rejects all in which he detects any imperfections. In these processes an average of 10 per cent, is eliminated; so that of 100 lbs. cast only 90 lbs. are actually fit for delivery.
General Construction of Type-setting Machinery. — With

WORCESTER ROUND** WITH ITALIC   MERGENTHALER TYPE LIBRARY

ABCDEFGHIJKLMNOPQRSTUVWXYZ&abcdefghijklmnopqrstuvwxyz1234567890$.,'"";!?

ITC ZAPF BOOK** LIGHT   MERGENTHALER TYPE LIBRARY

ABCDEFGHIJKLMNOPQRSTUVWXYZ&abcdefghijklmnopqrstuvwxyz1234567890$.,'"";!?

ITC ZAPF BOOK** LIGHT ITALIC   MERGENTHALER TYPE LIBRARY

ABCDEFGHIJKLMNOPQRSTUVWXYZ&abcdefghijklmnopqrstuvwxyz1234567890$.,'"";!?

ITC ZAPF BOOK** MEDIUM   MERGENTHALER TYPE LIBRARY

ABCDEFGHIJKLMNOPQRSTUVWXYZ&abcdefghijklmnopqrstuvwxyz1234567890$.,'"";!?

ITC ZAPF BOOK** MEDIUM ITALIC   MERGENTHALER TYPE LIBRARY

ABCDEFGHIJKLMNOPQRSTUVWXYZ&abcdefghijklmnopqrstuvwxyz1234567890$.,'"";!?

ITC ZAPF BOOK** DEMI   MERGENTHALER TYPE LIBRARY

ABCDEFGHIJKLMNOPQRSTUVWXYZ&abcdefghijklmnopqrstuvwxyz1234567890$.,'"";!?

ITC ZAPF BOOK** DEMI ITALIC   MERGENTHALER TYPE LIBRARY

SUPPLEMENTARY FACES 477

12/13 In considering fine and praiseworthy inventions, we must freely confess that printing has been and is to-day the best and most estimable — the invention by means of which two persons turning the press can get a greater number of books in a day than formerly could have been transcribed by several persons in a year. It is claimed that this art was invented at Mainz, a city of Germany, in the year 1442 by Jean Guttemberg, or, according to others, Guttenberg, an honorable German chevalier. It was at Mainz that after experimenting with an ink *which is used by printers to-day, he first began the practice of the art. Some persons*

10/11 In considering fine and praiseworthy inventions, we must freely confess that printing has been and is to-day the best and most estimable — the invention by means of which two persons turning the press can get a greater number of books in a day than formerly could have been transcribed by several persons in a year. It is claimed that this art was invented at Mainz, a city of Germany, in the year 1442 by Jean Guttemberg, or, according to others, Guttenberg, an honorable German chevalier. It was at Mainz that after experimenting with an ink which is used by printers to-day, he first began the practice of the art. Some persons prefer to attribute the invention to Jean Fauste & Yues Scheffey two years earlier, holding that our Guttemberg, Jean Mentel, Jean Prus, *Adolphe Rusche, Pierre Scheffec, Martin Flache, Huldric Han, Jean Froben, Adam Petri, Thomas*

ITC ZAPF BOOK** LIGHT WITH LIGHT ITALIC   MERGENTHALER TYPE LIBRARY

12/13 In considering fine and praiseworthy inventions, we must freely confess that printing has been and is to-day the best and most estimable — the invention by means of which two persons turning the press can get a greater number of books in a day than formerly could have been transcribed by several persons in a year. It is claimed that this art was invented at Mainz, a city of Germany, in the year 1442 by Jean Guttemberg, or, according to others, Guttenberg, an honorable German chevalier. It was at Mainz that after experimenting with an ink *which is used by printers to-day, he first began the practice of the art. Some persons*

10/11 In considering fine and praiseworthy inventions, we must freely confess that printing has been and is to-day the best and most estimable — the invention by means of which two persons turning the press can get a greater number of books in a day than formerly could have been transcribed by several persons in a year. It is claimed that this art was invented at Mainz, a city of Germany, in the year 1442 by Jean Guttemberg, or, according to others, Guttenberg, an honorable German chevalier. It was at Mainz that after experimenting with an ink which is used by printers to-day, he first began the practice of the art. Some persons prefer to attribute the invention to Jean Fauste & Yues Scheffey two years earlier, holding that our Guttemberg, Jean *Mentel, Jean Prus, Adolphe Rusche, Pierre Scheffec, Martin Flache, Huldric Han, Jean Froben, Adam*

ITC ZAPF BOOK** MEDIUM WITH MEDIUM ITALIC   MERGENTHALER TYPE LIBRARY

12/13 **In considering fine and praiseworthy inventions, we must freely confess that printing has been and is to-day the best and most estimable — the invention by means of which two persons turning the press can get a greater number of books in a day than formerly could have been transcribed by several persons in a year. It is claimed that this art was invented at Mainz, a city of Germany, in the year 1442 by Jean Guttemberg, or, according to others, Guttenberg, an honorable German chevalier. It was at Mainz *that after experimenting with an ink which is used by printers to-day, he first began***

10/11 **In considering fine and praiseworthy inventions, we must freely confess that printing has been and is to-day the best and most estimable — the invention by means of which two persons turning the press can get a greater number of books in a day than formerly could have been transcribed by several persons in a year. It is claimed that this art was invented at Mainz, a city of Germany, in the year 1442 by Jean Guttemberg, or, according to others, Guttenberg, an honorable German chevalier. It was at Mainz that after experimenting with an ink which is used by printers to-day, he first began the practice of the art. Some persons prefer to attribute the invention to Jean Fauste & Yues Scheffey *two years earlier, holding that our Guttemberg, Jean Mentel, Jean Prus, Adolphe Rusche, Pierre Schef-***

ITC ZAPF BOOK** DEMI WITH DEMI ITALIC   MERGENTHALER TYPE LIBRARY

ABCDEFGHIJKLMNOPQRSTUVWXYZ&abcdefghijklmnopqrstuvwxyz1234567890$.,""":;!?

ITC ZAPF INTERNATIONAL** LIGHT   MERGENTHALER TYPE LIBRARY

ABCDEFGHIJKLMNOPQRSTUVWXYZ&abcdefghijklmnopqrstuvwxyz1234567890$.,""":;!?

ITC ZAPF INTERNATIONAL** LIGHT ITALIC   MERGENTHALER TYPE LIBRARY

ABCDEFGHIJKLMNOPQRSTUVWXYZ&abcdefghijklmnopqrstuvwxyz1234567890$.,""":;!?

ITC ZAPF INTERNATIONAL** MEDIUM   MERGENTHALER TYPE LIBRARY

ABCDEFGHIJKLMNOPQRSTUVWXYZ&abcdefghijklmnopqrstuvwxyz1234567890$.,""":;!?

ITC ZAPF INTERNATIONAL** MEDIUM ITALIC   MERGENTHALER TYPE LIBRARY

ABCDEFGHIJKLMNOPQRSTUVWXYZ&abcdefghijklmnopqrstuvwxyz1234567890$.,""":;!?

ITC ZAPF INTERNATIONAL** DEMI   MERGENTHALER TYPE LIBRARY

ABCDEFGHIJKLMNOPQRSTUVWXYZ&abcdefghijklmnopqrstuvwxyz1234567890$.,""":;!?

ITC ZAPF INTERNATIONAL** DEMI ITALIC   MERGENTHALER TYPE LIBRARY

12/13 In considering fine and praiseworthy inventions, we must freely confess that printing has been and is to-day the best and most estimable — the invention by means of which two persons turning the press can get a greater number of books in a day than formerly could have been transcribed by several persons in a year. It is claimed that this art was invented at Mainz, a city of Germany, in the year 1442 by Jean Guttemberg, or, according to others, Guttenberg, an honorable German chevalier. It was at Mainz that after experimenting with an ink which is used by printers *to-day, he first began the practice of the art. Some persons prefer to attribute the invention*

10/11 In considering fine and praiseworthy inventions, we must freely confess that printing has been and is to-day the best and most estimable — the invention by means of which two persons turning the press can get a greater number of books in a day than formerly could have been transcribed by several persons in a year. It is claimed that this art was invented at Mainz, a city of Germany, in the year 1442 by Jean Guttemberg, or, according to others, Guttenberg, an honorable German chevalier. It was at Mainz that after experimenting with an ink which is used by printers to-day, he first began the practice of the art. Some persons prefer to attribute the invention to Jean Fauste & Yues Scheffey two years earlier, holding that our Guttemberg, Jean Mentel, Jean Prus, Adolphe Rusche, Pierre Scheffec, Martin Flache, *Huldric Han, Jean Froben, Adam Petri, Thomas Vuolffe, and others added improvements and spread the art of*

ITC ZAPF INTERNATIONAL** LIGHT WITH LIGHT ITALIC   MERGENTHALER TYPE LIBRARY

12/13 In considering fine and praiseworthy inventions, we must freely confess that printing has been and is to-day the best and most estimable — the invention by means of which two persons turning the press can get a greater number of books in a day than formerly could have been transcribed by several persons in a year. It is claimed that this art was invented at Mainz, a city of Germany, in the year 1442 by Jean Guttemberg, or, according to others, Guttenberg, an honorable German chevalier. It was at Mainz that after experimenting with an ink which is used by printers to-day, he first *began the practice of the art. Some persons prefer to attribute the invention to Jean Fauste*

10/11 In considering fine and praiseworthy inventions, we must freely confess that printing has been and is to-day the best and most estimable — the invention by means of which two persons turning the press can get a greater number of books in a day than formerly could have been transcribed by several persons in a year. It is claimed that this art was invented at Mainz, a city of Germany, in the year 1442 by Jean Guttemberg, or, according to others, Guttenberg, an honorable German chevalier. It was at Mainz that after experimenting with an ink which is used by printers to-day, he first began the practice of the art. Some persons prefer to attribute the invention to Jean Fauste & Yues Scheffey two years earlier, holding that our Guttemberg, Jean Mentel, Jean Prus, Adolphe Rusche, Pierre Scheffec, Martin Flache, *Huldric Han, Jean Froben, Adam Petri, Thomas Vuolffe, and others added improvements and spread the art of*

ITC ZAPF INTERNATIONAL** MEDIUM WITH MEDIUM ITALIC   MERGENTHALER TYPE LIBRARY

12/13 **In considering fine and praiseworthy inventions, we must freely confess that printing has been and is to-day the best and most estimable — the invention by means of which two persons turning the press can get a greater number of books in a day than formerly could have been transcribed by several persons in a year. It is claimed that this art was invented at Mainz, a city of Germany, in the year 1442 by Jean Guttemberg, or, according to others, Guttenberg, an honorable German chevalier. It was at Mainz that after experimenting with an ink which is used by *printers to-day, he first began the prac-***

10/11 **In considering fine and praiseworthy inventions, we must freely confess that printing has been and is to-day the best and most estimable — the invention by means of which two persons turning the press can get a greater number of books in a day than formerly could have been transcribed by several persons in a year. It is claimed that this art was invented at Mainz, a city of Germany, in the year 1442 by Jean Guttemberg, or, according to others, Guttenberg, an honorable German chevalier. It was at Mainz that after experimenting with an ink which is used by printers to-day, he first began the practice of the art. Some persons prefer to attribute the invention to Jean Fauste & Yues Scheffey two years earlier, holding that our *Guttemberg, Jean Mentel, Jean Prus, Adolphe Rusche, Pierre Scheffec, Martin Flache, Huldric***

ITC ZAPF INTERNATIONAL** DEMI WITH DEMI ITALIC   MERGENTHALER TYPE LIBRARY

ABCDEFGHIJKL
MNOPQRSTUVW
XYZ&abcdefghijklmnop
qrstuvwxyz1234567890$
.,""":;!?

48 POINT ARISTON   MERGENTHALER TYPE LIBRARY

ABCDEFGHIJKLMNOPQRSTUVWXYZ
&abcdefghijklmnopqrstuvwxyz1234567890$.,"":;!?

22 POINT ARISTON   MERGENTHALER TYPE LIBRARY

ABCDEFGHIJKL
MNOPQRSTUVW
XYZ&abcdefghijklmno
pqrstuvwxyz123456789
0$.,"":;!?

48 POINT ARISTON BOLD   MERGENTHALER TYPE LIBRARY

ABCDEFGHIJKLMNOPQRSTUVW
XYZ&abcdefghijklmnopqrstuvwxyz123456789
0$.,"":;!?

24 POINT ARISTON BOLD   MERGENTHALER TYPE LIBRARY

DISPLAY FACES: SCRIPTS and CURSIVES 481

ABCDEFGHIJK
LMNOPQRSTUV
WXYZ&abcdefghij
klmnopqrstuvwxyz1
234567890$.,""":;!?

48 POINT ARISTON EXTRA BOLD   MERGENTHALER TYPE LIBRARY

ABCDEFGHIJKLMNOPQRSTUV
WXYZ&abcdefghijklmnopqrstuvwxyz12
34567890$.,""":;!?

24 POINT ARISTON EXTRA BOLD   MERGENTHALER TYPE LIBRARY

ABCDEFGHIJKLMNOPQRST
UVWXYZ&abcdefghijklmnopqr
stuvwxyz1234567890$.,""":;!?

48 POINT BISON   MERGENTHALER TYPE LIBRARY

ABCDEFGHIJKLMNOPQRSTUVWXYZ&abcdefghijklmnop
qrstuvwxyz1234567890$.,""":;!?

24 POINT BISON   MERGENTHALER TYPE LIBRARY

DISPLAY FACES: SCRIPTS and CURSIVES

ABCDEFGHIJKLMN
OPQRSTUVWXYZ&ab
cdefghijklmnopqrstuvwxyz1
234567890$.,""'':;!?

48 POINT BRUSH SCRIPT   MERGENTHALER TYPE LIBRARY

ABCDEFGHIJKLMNOPQRSTUVWXYZ&abc
defghijklmnopqrstuvwxyz1234567890$.,"":;!?

24 POINT BRUSH SCRIPT   MERGENTHALER TYPE LIBRARY

ABCDEFGHIJKLM
NOPQRSTUVWXY
Z&abcdefghijklmnopqrstuv
wxyz1234567890$.,'''"":;!?

48 POINT CALLIGRAPHIA   MERGENTHALER TYPE LIBRARY

ABCDEFGHIJKLMNOPQRSTUVWXY
Z&abcdefghijklmnopqrstuvwxyz1234567890$.,'''"":;!?

24 POINT CALLIGRAPHIA   MERGENTHALER TYPE LIBRARY

ABCDEFGHIJKLMNOPQRS
TUVWXYZ&abcdefghijklmn
opqrstuvwxyz1234567890
$.,""":;!?

48 POINT CASCADE* SCRIPT   MERGENTHALER TYPE LIBRARY

ABCDEFGHIJKLMNOPQRSTUVWXYZ&abcdefghijk
lmnopqrstuvwxyz1234567890$.,""":;!?

24 POINT CASCADE* SCRIPT   MERGENTHALER TYPE LIBRARY

ABCDEFGHIJKLMNOPQ
RSTUVWXYZ&abcdefghijk
lmnopqrstuvwxyz12345678
90$.,""":;!?

48 POINT CHOC**   MERGENTHALER TYPE LIBRARY

ABCDEFGHIJKLMNOPQRSTUVWXYZ&abcdefghijkl
mnopqrstuvwxyz1234567890$.,""":;!?

24 POINT CHOC**   MERGENTHALER TYPE LIBRARY

484 DISPLAY FACES: SCRIPTS and CURSIVES

ABCDEFGH
IJKLMNOPQR
STUVWXYZ
&abcdefghijklmnopqrstuvwxyz
1234567890$., ""'' .;:!?

48 POINT CITADEL SCRIPT   AGFA COMPUGRAPHIC TYPE LIBRARY

ABCDEFGHIJKLMNOP
QRSTUVWXYZ &abcdefghijklmnopqrstu
vwxyz1234567890$., ""'' .;:!?

24 POINT CITADEL SCRIPT   AGFA COMPUGRAPHIC TYPE LIBRARY

ABCDEFGHIJKLM
NOPQRSTUVWXY
Z &abcdefghijklmnopqrs
tuvwxyz1234567890$
., ''"" .;:!?

48 POINT COMMERCIAL SCRIPT   AGFA COMPUGRAPHIC TYPE LIBRARY

ABCDEFGHIJKLMNOPQRSTUVWXY
Z &abcdefghijklmnopqrstuvwxyz1234567890$
.,""'';;!?

24 POINT COMMERCIAL SCRIPT   AGFA COMPUGRAPHIC TYPE LIBRARY

ABCDEFGHIJKLMNOP
QRSTUVWXYZ&abcdefghijklm
nopqrstuvwxyz1234567890$.,""'';;!?

48 POINT CORONET   MERGENTHALER TYPE LIBRARY

ABCDEFGHIJKLMNOPQRSTUVWXYZ&abcdefghijklmn
opqrstuvwxyz1234567890$.,""'';;!?

24 POINT CORONET   MERGENTHALER TYPE LIBRARY

ABCDEFGHIJKLMNO
PQRSTUVWXYZ&abcdefghi
jklmnopqrstuvwxyz1234567890$.,""'';;!?

46 POINT CORONET BOLD   MERGENTHALER TYPE LIBRARY

ABCDEFGHIJKLMNOPQRSTUVWXYZ&abcdefg
hijklmnopqrstuvwxyz1234567890$.,""'';;!?

24 POINT CORONET BOLD   MERGENTHALER TYPE LIBRARY

ABCDEFGHIJKLM
NOPQRSTUVWXYZ
&abcdefghijklmnopqrstuvwxyz123456789
0$.,""'':;!?

48 POINT DISKUS*   MERGENTHALER TYPE LIBRARY

ABCDEFGHIJKLMNOPQRSTUVWXYZ&
abcdefghijklmnopqrstuvwxyz1234567890$.,""'':;!?

24 POINT DISKUS*   MERGENTHALER TYPE LIBRARY

ABCDEFGHIJKL
MNOPQRSTUVWXY
Z&abcdefghijklmnopqrstuvwxyz123
4567890$.,""'':;!?

48 POINT DISKUS* BOLD   MERGENTHALER TYPE LIBRARY

ABCDEFGHIJKLMNOPQRSTUVWXYZ
&abcdefghijklmnopqrstuvwxyz1234567890$.,""'':;!?

24 POINT DISKUS* BOLD   MERGENTHALER TYPE LIBRARY

ABCDEFGHIJKLMNOPQRSTUV
WXYZ&abcdefghijklmnopqrstuvwx
yz1234567890$.,"":;!?

48 POINT DOM CASUAL   MERGENTHALER TYPE LIBRARY

ABCDEFGHIJKLMNOPQRSTUVWXYZ&abcdefghijklmnopqrstuvwxy
z1234567890$.,"":;!?

24 POINT DOM CASUAL   MERGENTHALER TYPE LIBRARY

ABCDEFGHIJKLMNOPQRSTU
VWXYZ&abcdefghijklmnopqrst
uvwxyz1234567890$.,"":;!?

48 POINT DOM CASUAL BOLD   MERGENTHALER TYPE LIBRARY

ABCDEFGHIJKLMNOPQRSTUVWXYZ&abcdefghijklmnopqrst
uvwxyz1234567890$.,"":;!?

24 POINT DOM CASUAL BOLD   MERGENTHALER TYPE LIBRARY

DISPLAY FACES: SCRIPTS and CURSIVES

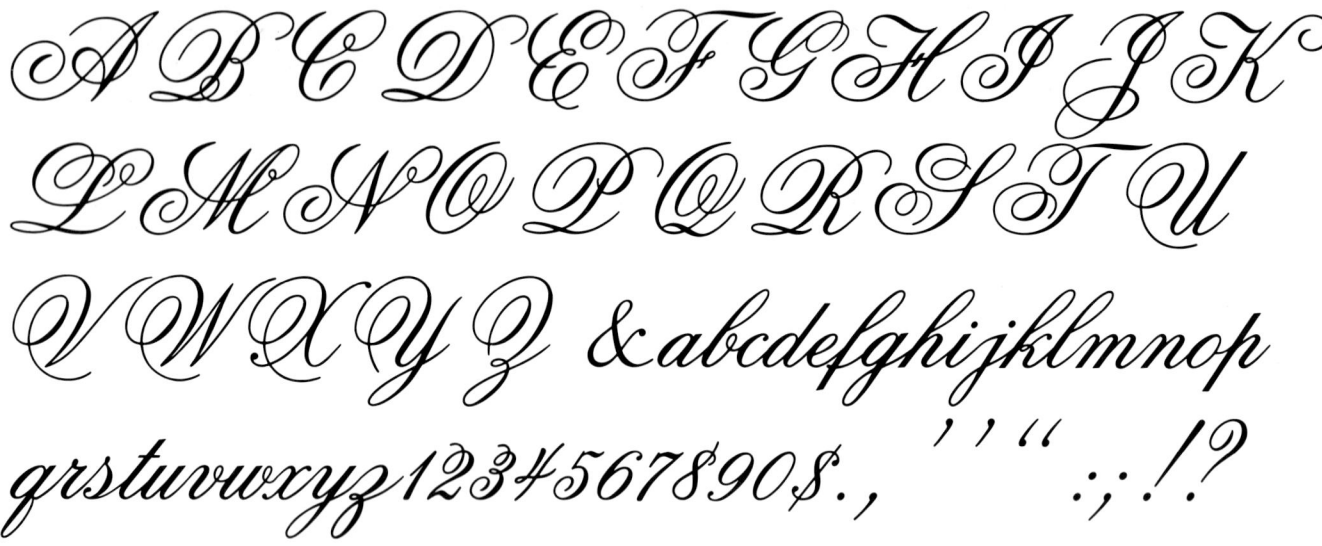

ABCDEFGHIJK LMNOPQRSTU VWXYZ &abcdefghijklmnop qrstuvwxyz1234567890$., ' ' " ".;.!?

48 POINT FLEMISH SCRIPT II   AGFA COMPUGRAPHIC TYPE LIBRARY

ABCDEFGHIJKLMNOPQRS TUVWXYZ &abcdefghijklmnopqrstuvwxyz1234567890$.,' ' " ".;.!?

24 POINT FLEMISH SCRIPT II   AGFA COMPUGRAPHIC TYPE LIBRARY

ABCDEFGHIJKL MNOPQRSTUVW XYZ &abcdefghijklmnopqrst uvwxyz1234567890$., ' ' " ".;.!?

48 POINT FLORENTINE SCRIPT II   AGFA COMPUGRAPHIC TYPE LIBRARY

ABCDEFGHIJKLMNOPQRST UVWXYZ &abcdefghijklmnopqrstuvwxyz1234567890$.,' ' " ".;.!?

24 POINT FLORENTINE SCRIPT II   AGFA COMPUGRAPHIC TYPE LIBRARY

ABCDEFGHIJKLM
NOPQRSTUVWXYZ
&abcdefghijklmnopqrstuvwxyz
1234567890$.,''":;!?

48 POINT FLORIDIAN SCRIPT   AGFA COMPUGRAPHIC TYPE LIBRARY

ABCDEFGHIJKLMNOPQRSTUVWXYZ&
abcdefghijklmnopqrstuvwxyz1234567890$.,''":;!?

24 POINT FLORIDIAN SCRIPT   AGFA COMPUGRAPHIC TYPE LIBRARY

ABCDEFGHIJKLMNOP
QRSTUVWXYZ&abcdefghij
klmnopqrstuvwxyz1234567890$
.,''":;!?

48 POINT FRENCH SCRIPT   AGFA COMPUGRAPHIC TYPE LIBRARY

ABCDEFGHIJKLMNOPQRSTUVWXYZ&abcdefghijklm
nopqrstuvwxyz1234567890$.,''":;!?

24 POINT FRENCH SCRIPT   AGFA COMPUGRAPHIC TYPE LIBRARY

490 DISPLAY FACES: SCRIPTS and CURSIVES

ABCDEFGHIJKLMNOP
QRSTUVWXYZ&abcdefghijk
lmnopqrstuvwxyz1234567890$.,'''':;!?
46 POINT GANDO RONDE* SCRIPT   MERGENTHALER TYPE LIBRARY

ABCDEFGHIJKLMNOPQRSTUVWXYZ&abcdefg
hijklmnopqrstuvwxyz1234567890$.,'''':;!?
24 POINT GANDO RONDE* SCRIPT   MERGENTHALER TYPE LIBRARY

ABCDEFGHIJKLMNOP
QRSTUVWXYZ&abcdefghijkl
mnopqrstuvwxyz1234567890$.,"":;!?
44 POINT GAVOTTE SCRIPT   MERGENTHALER TYPE LIBRARY

ABCDEFGHIJKLMNOPQRSTUVWXYZ&abcdefg
hijklmnopqrstuvwxyz1234567890$.,"":;!?
24 POINT GAVOTTE SCRIPT   MERGENTHALER TYPE LIBRARY

ABCDEFGHIJKLMN
OPQRSTUVWXYZ&abcde
fghijklmnopqrstuvwxyz12345678
90$.,""'';;!?

48 POINT IMPULS   MERGENTHALER TYPE LIBRARY

ABCDEFGHIJKLMNOPQRSTUVWXYZ&abc
defghijklmnopqrstuvwxyz1234567890$.,""'';;!?

24 POINT IMPULS   MERGENTHALER TYPE LIBRARY

ABCDEFGHIJKLM
NOPQRSTUVWXY
Z&abcdefghijklmnopqrstuvwxyz1
234567890$.,"":;!?

48 POINT JIFFY   MERGENTHALER TYPE LIBRARY

ABCDEFGHIJKLMNOPQRSTUVWXY
Z&abcdefghijklmnopqrstuvwxyz1234567890$.,"":;!?

24 POINT JIFFY   MERGENTHALER TYPE LIBRARY

DISPLAY FACES: SCRIPTS and CURSIVES

ABCDEFGHIJKLMNOPQRST
UVWXYZ&abcdefghijklmnopqr
stuvwxyz1234567890$.,"":;!?

46 POINT KAUFMANN   MERGENTHALER TYPE LIBRARY

ABCDEFGHIJKLMNOPQRSTUVWXYZ&abcdefghijklmnop
qrstuvwxyz1234567890$.,"":;!?

24 POINT KAUFMANN   MERGENTHALER TYPE LIBRARY

ABCDEFGHIJKLMNOP
QRSTUVWXYZ&abcdefgh
ijklmnopqrstuvwxyz12345
67890$.,"":;!?

48 POINT KAUFMANN BOLD   MERGENTHALER TYPE LIBRARY

ABCDEFGHIJKLMNOPQRSTUVWXYZ&abcdefghij
klmnopqrstuvwxyz1234567890$.,"":;!?

24 POINT KAUFMANN BOLD   MERGENTHALER TYPE LIBRARY

DISPLAY FACES: SCRIPTS and CURSIVES 493

abcdefghijklmnopq
rstuvwxyz&abcdefg
hijklmnopqrstuvwx
yz1234567890$.,""'":;!?

48 POINT LIBRA**   MERGENTHALER TYPE LIBRARY

abcdefghijklmnopqrstuvwxyz&abcdefg
hijklmnopqrstuvwxyz1234567890$.,""'":;!?

24 POINT LIBRA**   MERGENTHALER TYPE LIBRARY

ABCDEFGHIJKLMNOPQ
RSTUVWXYZ&abcdefghijklm
nopqrstuvwxyz1234567890$.,''"":;!?

48 POINT LINOSCRIPT*   MERGENTHALER TYPE LIBRARY

ABCDEFGHIJKLMNOPQRSTUVWXYZ&abcdefghijklm
nopqrstuvwxyz1234567890$.,''"":;!?

24 POINT LINOSCRIPT*   MERGENTHALER TYPE LIBRARY

DISPLAY FACES: SCRIPTS and CURSIVES

ABCDEFGHIJKLMNOPQR
STUVWXYZ&abcdefghijkl
mnopqrstuvwxyz1 23456
7890$.,"''":;!?

48 POINT LISBON   AGFA COMPUGRAPHIC TYPE LIBRARY

ABCDEFGHIJKLMNOPQRSTUVWXYZ&abcdefghijklm
nopqrstuvwxyz1234567890$.,"''":;!?

24 POINT LISBON   AGFA COMPUGRAPHIC TYPE LIBRARY

ABCDEFGHIJKLMNOPQR
STUVWXYZ&abcdefghijkl
mnopqrstuvwxyz1 23456
7890$.,"''":;!?

48 POINT LISBON ITALIC   AGFA COMPUGRAPHIC TYPE LIBRARY

ABCDEFGHIJKLMNOPQRSTUVWXYZ&abcdefghijklm
nopqrstuvwxyz1234567890$.,"''":;!?

24 POINT LISBON ITALIC   AGFA COMPUGRAPHIC TYPE LIBRARY

ABCDEFGHIJKLMNOP
QRSTUVWXYZ&abcdefg
hijklmnopqrstuvwxyz1234
567890$.,""'':;,!?

48 POINT LISBON CURSIVE   AGFA COMPUGRAPHIC TYPE LIBRARY

ABCDEFGHIJKLMNOPQRSTUVWXYZ&abcdefghij
klmnopqrstuvwxyz1234567890$.,""'':;,!?

24 POINT LISBON CURSIVE   AGFA COMPUGRAPHIC TYPE LIBRARY

ABCDEFGHIJKLMNOPQRSTUVWX
YZ&abcdefghijklmnopqrstuvwxyz
1234567890$.,"":;!?

48 POINT MARIGOLD   AGFA COMPUGRAPHIC TYPE LIBRARY

ABCDEFGHIJKLMNOPQRSTUVWXYZ&abcdefghijklmnopqrstuvwxyz
1234567890$.,"":;!?

24 POINT MARIGOLD   AGFA COMPUGRAPHIC TYPE LIBRARY

496 DISPLAY FACES: SCRIPTS and CURSIVES

ABCDEFGHIJKLMNOPQRSTUVWXYZ&abcdefghijklmnopqrstuvwxyz1234567890$.,""'':;!?

48 POINT MEDICI* SCRIPT   MERGENTHALER TYPE LIBRARY

ABCDEFGHIJKLMNOPQRSTUVWXYZ&abcdefghijklmnopqrstuvwxyz1234567890$.,""'':;!?

24 POINT MEDICI* SCRIPT   MERGENTHALER TYPE LIBRARY

ABCDEFGHIJKLMNOPQRSTUVWXYZ&abcdefghijklmnopqrstuvwxyz1234567890$.,""'':;!?

48 POINT MISTRAL**   MERGENTHALER TYPE LIBRARY

ABCDEFGHIJKLMNOPQRSTUVWXYZ&abcdefghijklmnopqrstuvwxyz1234567890$.,""'':;!?

24 POINT MISTRAL**   MERGENTHALER TYPE LIBRARY

DISPLAY FACES: SCRIPTS and CURSIVES 497

ABCDEFGHIJKLMNOPQRSTUVWXYZ&abcdefghijklmnopqrstuvwxyz1234567890$.,''"":;!?

48 POINT MURRAY   AGFA COMPUGRAPHIC TYPE LIBRARY

ABCDEFGHIJKLMNOPQRSTUVWXYZ&abcdefghijklmnopqrstuvwxyz1234567890$.,''"":;!?

24 POINT MURRAY   AGFA COMPUGRAPHIC TYPE LIBRARY

ABCDEFGHIJKLMNOPQRSTUVWXYZ&abcdefghijklmnopqrstuvwxyz1234567890$.,""":;!?

48 POINT MURRAY BOLD   AGFA COMPUGRAPHIC TYPE LIBRARY

ABCDEFGHIJKLMNOPQRSTUVWXYZ&abcdefghijklmnopqrstuvwxyz1234567890$.,""":;!?

24 POINT MURRAY BOLD   AGFA COMPUGRAPHIC TYPE LIBRARY

DISPLAY FACES: SCRIPTS and CURSIVES

ABCDEFGHIJKLMNOPQRSTUVWXYZ&abcdefghijklmnopqrstuvwxyz1234567890$.,""'':;!?

48 POINT NUPTIAL SCRIPT   MERGENTHALER TYPE LIBRARY

ABCDEFGHIJKLMNOPQRSTUVWXYZ&abcdefghijklmnopqrstuvwxyz1234567890$.,""'':;!?

24 POINT NUPTIAL SCRIPT   MERGENTHALER TYPE LIBRARY

ABCDEFGHIJKLMNOPQRSTUVWXYZ&abcdefghijklmnopqrstuvwxyz1234567890$.,""'':;!?

48 POINT OLD FASHION SCRIPT   AGFA COMPUGRAPHIC TYPE LIBRARY

ABCDEFGHIJKLMNOPQRSTUVWXYZ&abcdefghijklmnopqrstuvwxyz1234567890$.,""'':;!?

24 POINT OLD FASHION SCRIPT   AGFA COMPUGRAPHIC TYPE LIBRARY

DISPLAY FACES: SCRIPTS and CURSIVES 499

ABCDEFGHIJKLMNOPQRSTUVWXYZ&abcdefghijklmnopqrstuvwxyz1234567890$.,""":;!?

48 POINT ONDINE**   MERGENTHALER TYPE LIBRARY

ABCDEFGHIJKLMNOPQRSTUVWXYZ&abcdefghijklmnopqrstuvwxyz1234567890$.,""":;!?

24 POINT ONDINE**   MERGENTHALER TYPE LIBRARY

ABCDEFGHIJKLMNOPQRSTUVWXYZ&abcdefghijklmnopqrstuvwxyz1234567890$.,""":;!?

48 POINT OXFORD   AGFA COMPUGRAPHIC TYPE LIBRARY

ABCDEFGHIJKLMNOPQRSTUVWXYZ& abcdefghijklmnopqrstuvwxyz1234567890$.,""":;!?

24 POINT OXFORD   AGFA COMPUGRAPHIC TYPE LIBRARY

DISPLAY FACES: SCRIPTS and CURSIVES

ABCDEFGHIJKLM
NOPQRSTUVWXY
Z&abcdefghijklmnopqrstuvwxy
z1234567890$.,""'':;!?

48 POINT PARK AVENUE** SCRIPT   MERGENTHALER TYPE LIBRARY

ABCDEFGHIJKLMOPQRSTUVWXY
Z&abcdefghijklmnopqrstuvwxyz1234567890$.,""'':;!?

24 POINT PARK AVENUE** SCRIPT   MERGENTHALER TYPE LIBRARY

ABCDEFGHIJKLMNOPQRSTUVWX
YZ&abcdefghijklmnopqrstuvwxyz123456
7890$.,""'':;!?

48 POINT PARLIAMENT   MERGENTHALER TYPE LIBRARY

ABCDEFGHIJKLMNOPQRSTUVWXYZ&abcdefghijklmnopqrstuvwxyz1
234567890$.,""'':;!?

24 POINT PARLIAMENT   MERGENTHALER TYPE LIBRARY

DISPLAY FACES: SCRIPTS and CURSIVES 501

ABCDEFGHIJKLM
NOPQRSTUVWXY
Z&abcdefghijklmnopqrstuvwxy
z1234567890$.,'"'":;!?

48 POINT PIRANESI ITALIC   AGFA COMPUGRAPHIC TYPE LIBRARY

ABCDEFGHIJKLMNOPQRSTUVWXY
Z&abcdefghijklmnopqrstuvwxyz1234567890$.,'"'":;!?

24 POINT PIRANESI ITALIC   AGFA COMPUGRAPHIC TYPE LIBRARY

ABCDEFGHIJKLM
NOPQRSTUVWXYZ
&abcdefghijklmnopqrstuv
wxyz1234567890$.,'"'":;!?

48 POINT PRESENT* SCRIPT   MERGENTHALER TYPE LIBRARY

ABCDEFGHIJKLMNOPQRSTUVWXYZ&ab
cdefghijklmnopqrstuvwxyz1234567890$.,'"'":;!?

22 POINT PRESENT* SCRIPT   MERGENTHALER TYPE LIBRARY

DISPLAY FACES: SCRIPTS and CURSIVES

ABCDEFGHIJKLMNOP
QRSTUVWXYZ&abcdefghij
klmnopqrstuvwxyz1234567890$
.,'"":;!?

48 POINT QUILL   AGFA COMPUGRAPHIC TYPE LIBRARY

ABCDEFGHIJKLMNOPQRSTUVWXYZ&abcdefghijk
lmnopqrstuvwxyz1234567890$.,'"":;!?

24 POINT QUILL   AGFA COMPUGRAPHIC TYPE LIBRARY

ABCDEFGHJJKLMNOPQRST
UVWXYZ&abcdefghijklmnopqrst
uvwxyz1234567890$.,""::!?

44 POINT REPORTER NO. 2**   MERGENTHALER TYPE LIBRARY

ABCDEFGHJJKLMNOPQRSTUVWXYZ&abcdefghijklmn
opqrstuvwxyz1234567890$.,"":;!?

24 POINT REPORTER NO. 2**   MERGENTHALER TYPE LIBRARY

DISPLAY FACES: SCRIPTS and CURSIVES 503

ABCDEFGHIJKLMNO
PQRSTUVWXYZ&abcd
efghijklmnopqrstuvwxyz123456789
0$.,'"‚;:!?

48 POINT RIVIERA SCRIPT   AGFA COMPUGRAPHIC TYPE LIBRARY

ABCDEFGHIJKLMNOPQRSTUVWXYZ&abcde
fghijklmnopqrstuvwxyz1234567890$.,'"‚;:!?

24 POINT RIVIERA SCRIPT   AGFA COMPUGRAPHIC TYPE LIBRARY

ABCDEFGHIJKLMNOP
QRSTUVWXYZ&abcdefg
hijklmnopqrstuvwxyz1234
567890$.,'"‚;:!?

48 POINT SALLWEY SCRIPT   MERGENTHALER TYPE LIBRARY

ABCDEFGHIJKLMNOPQRSTUVWXYZ&abcd
efghijklmnopqrstuvwxyz1234567890$.,'"‚;:!?

24 POINT SALLWEY SCRIPT   MERGENTHALER TYPE LIBRARY

DISPLAY FACES: SCRIPTS and CURSIVES

ABCDEFGHIJK
LMNOPQRSTUV
WXYZ &abcdefghijklmnopq
rstuvwxyz1234567890$.,'"":;!?

46 POINT SHELLEY* VOLANTE SCRIPT   MERGENTHALER TYPE LIBRARY

ABCDEFGHIJKLMNOPQRSTUVW
XYZ &abcdefghijklmnopqrstuvwxyz1234567890$.,'"":;!?

22 POINT SHELLEY* VOLANTE SCRIPT   MERGENTHALER TYPE LIBRARY

ABCDEFGHIJKL
MNOPQRSTUVW
XYZ &abcdefghijklmnopq
rstuvwxyz1234567890$
.,'"":;!?

48 POINT SIGNET ROUNDHAND   AGFA COMPUGRAPHIC TYPE LIBRARY

ABCDEFGHIJKLMNOPQRS
TUVWXYZ &abcdefghijklmnopqrstuvwxyz
1234567890$.,'"":;!?

24 POINT SIGNET ROUNDHAND   AGFA COMPUGRAPHIC TYPE LIBRARY

DISPLAY FACES: SCRIPTS and CURSIVES 505

ABCDEFGHIJK
LMNOPQRSTUV
WXYZ&abcdefghijkl
mnopqrstuvwxyz1234
567890$.,"":;!?

48 POINT SNELL ROUNDHAND* BLACK SCRIPT   MERGENTHALER TYPE LIBRARY

ABCDEFGHIJKLMNOPQRSTUV
WXYZ&abcdefghijklmnopqrstuvwxyz123456
7890$.,"":;!?

24 POINT SNELL ROUNDHAND* BLACK SCRIPT   MERGENTHALER TYPE LIBRARY

ABCDEFGHIJKLMNO
PQRSTUVWXYZ&abdefg
hijklmnopqrstuvwxyz1234567890$
.,''""::;!?

48 POINT STUYVESANT   AGFA COMPUGRAPHIC TYPE LIBRARY

ABCDEFGHIJKLMNOPQRSTUVWXYZ&abcdefg
hijklmnopqrstuvwxyz1234567890$.,''"":;!?

24 POINT STUYVESANT   AGFA COMPUGRAPHIC TYPE LIBRARY

DISPLAY FACES: SCRIPTS and CURSIVES

ABCDEFGHIJKLMNO
PQRSTUVWXYZ&abcdef
ghijklmnopqrstuvwxyz1234567890$
.,""'":;!?

48 POINT TYPO UPRIGHT   AGFA COMPUGRAPHIC TYPE LIBRARY

ABCDEFGHIJK LM NOPQR STUVWX YZ&abcde
fghijklmnopqrstuvwxyz1234567890$.,""'":;!?

24 POINT TYPO UPRIGHT   AGFA COMPUGRAPHIC TYPE LIBRARY

ABCDEFGHIJKLMNOP
QRSTUVWXYZ&abcdefg
hijklmnopqrstuvwxyz12345
67890$.,""'":;!?

48 POINT VENTURE* SCRIPT   MERGENTHALER TYPE LIBRARY

ABCDEFGHIJKLMNOPQRSTUVWXYZ&abcde
fghijklmnopqrstuvwxyz1234567890$.,""'":;!?

24 POINT VENTURE* SCRIPT   MERGENTHALER TYPE LIBRARY

DISPLAY FACES: SCRIPTS and CURSIVES

ABCDEFGHIJKLMNOPQRSTUVWXYZ&abcdefghijklmnopqrstuvwxyz1234567890$.,"";:!?

48 POINT VISIGOTH   AGFA COMPUGRAPHIC TYPE LIBRARY

ABCDEFGHIJKLMNOPQRSTUVWXYZ&abcdefghijklmnopqrstuvwxyz1234567890$.,"";:!?

24 POINT VISIGOTH   AGFA COMPUGRAPHIC TYPE LIBRARY

Sample setting of Visigoth, a typeface designed by calligrapher Arthur Baker.

ARACHNE

Ah mad Arachne! so I saw you there—
already half turned spider—on the shreds
of what you wove to be your own despair

Excerpt from THE DIVINE COMEDY of Dante Alighieri

DISPLAY FACES: ECCENTRICS, ROMANTICS and PERIOD FACES

ABCDEFGHIJKLMNOPQRSTUVWXYZ&
1234567890$.,''"";:;!?
30 POINT ANTIQUE   AGFA COMPUGRAPHIC TYPE LIBRARY

ABCDEFGHIJKLMNOPQRSTUVWXYZ&
1234567890$.,''"";:;!?
30 POINT AMERICAN ANTIQUE   AGFA COMPUGRAPHIC TYPE LIBRARY

ABCDEFGHIJKLMNOPQRSTUVWXYZ&
1234567890$.,''"";:;!?
30 POINT CALLIOPE ANTIQUE   AGFA COMPUGRAPHIC TYPE LIBRARY

ABCDEFGHIJKLMNOPQRSTUVWXYZ&
1234567890$.,''"";:;!?
30 POINT FEDERAL ANTIQUE   AGFA COMPUGRAPHIC TYPE LIBRARY

ABCDEFGHIJKLMNOPQ
RSTUVWXYZ&123456789
0$.,'"":;!?
38 POINT CHARLEMAGNE™ REGULAR   ADOBE TYPE LIBRARY

ABCDEFGHIJKLMNOP
QRSTUVWXYZ&123456
7890$.,'"":;!?
38 POINT CHARLEMAGNE BOLD   ADOBE TYPE LIBRARY

DISPLAY FACES: ECCENTRICS, ROMANTICS and PERIOD FACES 509

ABCDEFGHIJKLMNOP
QRSTUVWXYZ&123456
7890$.,''"":;!?

30 POINT CHEVALIER   AGFA COMPUGRAPHIC TYPE LIBRARY

ABCDEFGHIJKLMNOPQRSTUVWXYZ
&abcdefghijklmnopqrstuvwxyz12345
67890$.,'"":;!?

30 POINT CHISEL   AGFA COMPUGRAPHIC TYPE LIBRARY

ABCDEFGHIJKLMNOPQRSTUVWXY
Z&abcdefghijklmnopqrstuvwxyz12
34567890$.,""":;!?

30 POINT CHWAST BUFFALO** BLACK CONDENSED   MERGENTHALER TYPE LIBRARY

ABCDEFGHIJKLMNOPQRSTUVWXYZ&
1234567890$.,"";:!?

30 POINT COMPUTER   AGFA COMPUGRAPHIC TYPE LIBRARY

ABCDEFGHIJKLMNOPQRSTUVWXYZ&
1234567890$.,'"":;!?

30 POINT COMPUTER OUTLINE   AGFA COMPUGRAPHIC TYPE LIBRARY

ABCDEFGHIJKLMNOPQRST
UVWXYZ&1234567890$
.,'"":;!?

30 POINT COPPERPLATE LIGHT   AGFA COMPUGRAPHIC TYPE LIBRARY

DISPLAY FACES: ECCENTRICS, ROMANTICS and PERIOD FACES

ABCDEFGHIJKLMNOPQRST
UVWXYZ&1234567890$":;!?
30 POINT COPPERPLATE HEAVY   AGFA COMPUGRAPHIC TYPE LIBRARY

ABCDEFGHIJKLMNOPQRSTUVWXYZ
&1234567890$..""":;!?
30 POINT DAVIDA**   MERGENTHALER TYPE LIBRARY

ABCDEFGHIJKLMNOPQRSTUVWXY
Z&abcdefghijklmnopqrstuvwxyz1234
567890$..""":;!?
30 POINT DEVENDRA*   MERGENTHALER TYPE LIBRARY

ABCDEFGHIJKLMNOPQRSTUVWXYZ&1234567890$":;!?
30 POINT ECCENTRIC   AGFA COMPUGRAPHIC TYPE LIBRARY

ABCDEFGHIJKLMNOPQRS
TUVWXYZ&ABCDEFGHIJKL
MNOPQRSTUVWXYZ1234567890$
.,"":;!?
30 POINT ENGRAVURE   AGFA COMPUGRAPHIC TYPE LIBRARY

ABCDEFGHIJKLMNOPQRSTU
VWXYZ&abcdefghijklmnopqrs
tuvwxyz1234567890$.,""":;!?
30 POINT EUCLID   AGFA COMPUGRAPHIC TYPE LIBRARY

DISPLAY FACES: ECCENTRICS, ROMANTICS and PERIOD FACES

ABCDEFGHIJKLMNOPQRSTU
VWXYZ&abcdefghijklmnopqrs
tuvwxyz1234567890$.,""";;!?

30 POINT EUCLID BOLD   AGFA COMPUGRAPHIC TYPE LIBRARY

ABCDEFGHIJKLMNOPQRSTUVWXYZ&abcd
efghijklmnopqrstuvwxyz1234567890$.,""":,;!?

30 POINT FANTAIL   MERGENTHALER TYPE LIBRARY

ABCDEFGHIJKLMNOPQRSTUVWXY
Z&abcdefghijklmnopqrstuvwxyz123
4567890$.,""";;!?

30 POINT FEHRLE* DISPLAY   MERGENTHALER TYPE LIBRARY

ABCDEFGHIJKLMNOPQR
STUVWXYZ&abcdefghijklmnopq
rstuvwxyz1234567890$.,""":,;!?

31 POINT FETTE FRAKTUR BOLD   ADOBE TYPE LIBRARY

ABCDEFGHIJKLMNOPQRSTUVWXY
Z&abcdefghijklmnopqrstuvwxyz
1234567890$.,""":,;!?

30 POINT ITC FRANKLIN GOTHIC CONTOUR   AGFA COMPUGRAPHIC TYPE LIBRARY

512   DISPLAY FACES: ECCENTRICS, ROMANTICS and PERIOD FACES

ABCDEFGHIJKLMNOPQRSTUVW
XYZ&abcdefghijklmnopqrstuvw
xyz1234567890$.,"";;!?
30 POINT ITC FRANKLIN GOTHIC OUTLINE SHADOW   AGFA COMPUGRAPHIC TYPE LIBRARY

ABCDEFGHIJKLMNOP
QRSTUVWXYZ
30 POINT BEN FRANKLIN INITIALS   AGFA COMPUGRAPHIC TYPE LIBRARY

ABCDEFGHIJKLMNOPQRST
UVWXYZ&1234567890$
.,""::;!?
30 POINT GLENN SHADED   AGFA COMPUGRAPHIC TYPE LIBRARY

ABCDEFGHIJKLMNOPQRS
TUVWXYZ&1234567890$
.,""::;!?
30 POINT GOLD NUGGET   AGFA COMPUGRAPHIC TYPE LIBRARY

ABCDEFGHIJKLMNOPQRSTUVW
XYZ&abcdefghijklmnopqrstuvwxyz12
34567890$.,"";:;!?
30 POINT GOUDY HANDTOOLED   MERGENTHALER TYPE LIBRARY

ABCDEFGHIJKLMNOPQRSTUVWXYZ
&abcdefghijklmnopqrstuvwxyz12345
67890$.,"":;!?
30 POINT HOBO   MERGENTHALER TYPE LIBRARY

DISPLAY FACES: ECCENTRICS, ROMANTICS and PERIOD FACES

ABCDEFGHIJKLMNOPQRSTUVWXYZ&abcdefghijklmnopqrstuvwxyz 1234567890$.,""'':;!?

30 POINT ITC KABEL CONTOUR   AGFA COMPUGRAPHIC TYPE LIBRARY

ABCDEFGHIJKLMNOPQRSTUVWXYZ&abcdefghijklmnopqrstuvwxyz1234567890$.,""'':;!?

30 POINT KABEL* SHADED   MERGENTHALER TYPE LIBRARY

ABCDEFGHIJKLMNOPQRSTUVWXYZ&abcdefghijklmnopqrstuvwxyz1234567890$.,""'':;!?

30 POINT KISMET   MERGENTHALER TYPE LIBRARY

ABCDEFGHIJKLMNOPQRSTUVWXYZ&1234567890$.,""'':;!?

38 POINT LITHOS™ EXTRA LIGHT   ADOBE TYPE LIBRARY

ABCDEFGHIJKLMNOPQRSTUVWXYZ&1234567890$.,""'':;!?

38 POINT LITHOS LIGHT   ADOBE TYPE LIBRARY

514 DISPLAY FACES: ECCENTRICS, ROMANTICS and PERIOD FACES

ABCDEFGHIJKLMNOPQRSTUVWXYZ&123456789 0$.,"":;!?
38 POINT LITHOS REGULAR   ADOBE TYPE LIBRARY

ABCDEFGHIJKLMNOPQRSTUVWXYZ&1234567890$.,"":;!?
38 POINT LITHOS BOLD   ADOBE TYPE LIBRARY

ABCDEFGHIJKLMNOPQRSTUVWXYZ&1234567890$.,"":;!?
38 POINT LITHOS BLACK   ADOBE TYPE LIBRARY

ABCDEFGHIJKLMNOPQRSTUVWXYZ&abcdefghijklmnopqrstuvwxyz1234567890$.,"":;!?
30 POINT LONDON TEXT   MERGENTHALER TYPE LIBRARY

ABCDEFGHIJKLMNOPQRSTUVWXYZ&abcdefghijklmnopqrstuvwxyz1234567890$.,"":;!?
30 POINT LUTHER FRACTUR*   MERGENTHALER TYPE LIBRARY

DISPLAY FACES: ECCENTRICS, ROMANTICS and PERIOD FACES 515

ABCDEFGHIJKLMNOPQRSTUVWXYZ&abcdefghij
klmnopqrstuvwxyz1234567890$.,""'":;!?

30 POINT MACBETH   MERGENTHALER TYPE LIBRARY

ABCDEFGHIJKLMNOPQRSTUVWXYZ&abcdefghij
klmnopqrstuvwxyz1234567890$.,""'":;!?

30 POINT ITC MACHINE**   MERGENTHALER TYPE LIBRARY

ABCDEFGHIJKLMNOPQRSTUVWXYZ&abcdefghij
klmnopqrstuvwxyz1234567890$.,""'":;!?

30 POINT ITC MACHINE** BOLD   MERGENTHALER TYPE LIBRARY

ABCDEFGHIJKLMNOPQRSTUVWXYZ&abcdefghij
klmnopqrstuvwxyz1234567890$.,""'":;!?

30 POINT McCOLLOUGH   AGFA COMPUGRAPHIC TYPE LIBRARY

ABCDEFGHIJKLMNOPQRSTUVWXYZ&abcdefghijkl
mnopqrstuvwxyz1234567890$.,""'":;!?

30 POINT MIKADO BLACK   MERGENTHALER TYPE LIBRARY

ABCDEFGHIJKLMNOPQRSTUVWXYZ&
1234567890$.,""'":;!?

30 POINT MIQUE   AGFA COMPUGRAPHIC TYPE LIBRARY

ABCDEFGHIJKLMNOPQRSTUV
WXYZ&abcdefghijklmnopqrstuvwxyz
1234567890$.,""'":;!?

30 POINT MODERN BLACKLETTER   AGFA COMPUGRAPHIC TYPE LIBRARY

DISPLAY FACES: ECCENTRICS, ROMANTICS and PERIOD FACES

ABCDEFGHIJKLMNOPQRSTUVWXYZ&ABCDEFG
HIJKLMNOPQRSTUVWXYZ1234567890$.,""'':;!?
30 POINT NEW BOSTONIAN   AGFA COMPUGRAPHIC TYPE LIBRARY

ABCDEFGHIJKLMNOPQR
STUVWXYZ&abcdefghijklm
nopqrstuvwxyz1234567890$
.,"":;!?
30 POINT NUBIAN   MERGENTHALER TYPE LIBRARY

ABCDEFGHIJKLMNOPQRSTUV
WXYZ&abcdefghijklmnopqrstuvwxyz
1234567890$.,"":;!?
30 POINT OLD ENGLISH   AGFA COMPUGRAPHIC TYPE LIBRARY

ABCDEFGHIJKLMNOPQRSTUVW
XYZ&abcdefghijklmnopqrstuvwxyz12
34567890 $.,"":;!?
30 POINT TS PARSONS**   MERGENTHALER TYPE LIBRARY

ABCDEFGHIJKLMNOPQRSTUV
WXYZ&abcdefghijklmnopqrstu
vwxyz1234567890$.,"":;!?
30 POINT PIERROT**   MERGENTHALER TYPE LIBRARY

ABCDEFGHIJKLMNOPQRSTUVWXYZ&abcdefghijklmnopqrstu
vwxyz1234567890$.,"":;!?
30 POINT PLAYBILL**   MERGENTHALER TYPE LIBRARY

ABCDEFGHIJKLMNOPQ
RSTUVWXYZ&1234567
890$.,"";;!?
30 POINT PROFIL   AGFA COMPUGRAPHIC TYPE LIBRARY

ABCDEFGHIJKLMNOPQRSTUVWXYZ&123
4567890$.,"";;!?
30 POINT QUARTZ 45 LIGHT   MERGENTHALER TYPE LIBRARY

ABCDEFGHIJKLMNOPQRSTUVWXYZ&123
4567890$.,"";;!?
30 POINT QUARTZ 75 BOLD   MERGENTHALER TYPE LIBRARY

ABCDEFGHIJKLMNOPQRSTU
VWXYZ&abcdefghijklmnopqrst
uvwxyz1234567890$.,"";;!?
30 POINT RAINBOW BASS*   MERGENTHALER TYPE LIBRARY

ABCDEFGHIJKLMNOPQRSTUVWXYZ&
abcdefghijklmnopqrstuvwxyz12345678
90$.,"";;!?
30 POINT RAPHAEL   AGFA COMPUGRAPHIC TYPE LIBRARY

ABCDEFGHIJKLMNOPQRSTUVW
XYZ&1234567890$.,"";;!?
30 POINT STENCIL   MERGENTHALER TYPE LIBRARY

DISPLAY FACES: ECCENTRICS, ROMANTICS and PERIOD FACES

ABCDEFGHIJKLMNOPQRSTUVWXYZ
&1234567890$.,"":;!?
30 POINT STOP   MERGENTHALER TYPE LIBRARY

ABCDEFGHIJKLMNOPQRSTUVWXYZ&abcdefghijklmnopqrstuvwxyz1234567890$.,"":;!?
30 POINT TSI TANGO**   MERGENTHALER TYPE LIBRARY

ABCDEFGHIJKLMNOPQRSTUVWXYZ&1234567890$.,"":;!?
30 POINT TEA CHEST   MERGENTHALER TYPE LIBRARY

ABCDEFGHIJKLMNOPQRSTUVWXYZ&1234567890$.,"":;!?
28 POINT THUNDERBIRD EXTRA CONDENSED   AGFA COMPUGRAPHIC TYPE LIBRARY

ABCDEFGHIJKLMNOPQRSTUVWXYZ&1234567890$.,"":;!?
38 POINT TRAJAN™ REGULAR   ADOBE TYPE LIBRARY

ABCDEFGHIJKLMNOPQRSTUVWXYZ&1234567890$.,"":;!?
38 POINT TRAJAN BOLD   ADOBE TYPE LIBRARY

ABCDEFGHIJKLMNOPQRSTUVWXYZ
&1234567890$.,'"";:!?

30 POINT UMBRA   MERGENTHALER TYPE LIBRARY

ABCDEFGHIJKLMNOPQRSTUV WXYZ&abcdefghijklmnopqrst uvwxyz1234567890$.,'"";:!?

30 POINT ZARANA   AGFA COMPUGRAPHIC TYPE LIBRARY

Composed solely of typographic ornaments, this ornate portico of a classic temple appears on a folded sheet in a French type specimen book issued in Paris in 1745 by Nicolas Gando.

DISPLAY FACES: OUTLINES

ABCDEFGHIJKLMNOPQRSTU
VWXYZ&abcdefghijklmnopqr
stuvwxyz1234567890$.,''"":;!?

30 POINT AMERICANA** OUTLINE   MERGENTHALER TYPE LIBRARY

ABCDEFGHIJKLMNOPQRSTUVWXYZ
&abcdefghijklmnopqrstuvwxyz123
4567890$.,''"":;!?

30 POINT ITC BAUHAUS** HEAVY OUTLINE   MERGENTHALER TYPE LIBRARY

ABCDEFGHIJKLMNOPQRSTU
VWXYZ&abcdefghijklmnopqr
stuvwxyz1234567890$.,''"":;!?

30 POINT BLOC   MERGENTHALER TYPE LIBRARY

ABCDEFGHIJKLMNOPQRSTUVWXY
Z&abcdefghijklmnopqrstuvwxyz12
34567890$.,''""::!?

30 POINT CHWAST BUFFALO** BLACK CONDENSED OUTLINE   MERGENTHALER TYPE LIBRARY

ABCDEFGHIJKLMNOPQRSTUVWX
YZ&abcdefghijklmnopqrstuvwxyz12345
67890$.,''"":;!?

30 POINT CLOISTER OPEN FACE   MERGENTHALER TYPE LIBRARY

ABCDEFGHIJKLMNOPQRSTUV
WXYZ&abcdefghijklmnopqrst
uvwxyz1234567890$.,''"":;!?
30 POINT COOPER BLACK OUTLINE   MERGENTHALER TYPE LIBRARY

ABCDEFGHIJKLMNOPQRSTUVWXYZ
&abcdefghijklmnopqrstuvwxyz
1234567890$.,''"":;!?
30 POINT ITC FRANKLIN GOTHIC OUTLINE   AGFA COMPUGRAPHIC TYPE LIBRARY

ABCDEFGHIJKLMNOPQRST
UVWXYZ&abcdefghijklmno
pqrstuvwxyz1234567890$.
,''"":;!?
30 POINT GILL SANS** ULTRA BOLD OUTLINE (KAYO)   MERGENTHALER TYPE LIBRARY

ABCDEFGHIJKLMNOPQRSTUVWXYZ
&abcdefghijklmnopqrstuvwxyz
1234567890$.,''"":;!?
30 POINT GLOBE GOTHIC OUTLINE   AGFA COMPUGRAPHIC TYPE LIBRARY

ABCDEFGHIJKLMNOPQRSTUVWXYZ&
abcdefghijklmnopqrstuvwxyz
1234567890$.,''"":;!?
30 POINT GOTHIC OUTLINE CONDENSED   AGFA COMPUGRAPHIC TYPE LIBRARY

DISPLAY FACES: OUTLINES

ABCDEFGHIJKLMNOPQRSTUVWXY
Z&abcdefghijklmnopqrstuvwxyz
1234567890$.,''"":;!?
30 POINT HOBO OUTLINE   AGFA COMPUGRAPHIC TYPE LIBRARY

ABCDEFGHIJKLMNOPQRSTUVWXY
Z&abcdefghijklmnopqrstuvwxyz
1234567890$.,''"":;!?
30 POINT ITC KABEL OUTLINE   AGFA COMPUGRAPHIC TYPE LIBRARY

ABCDEFGHIJKLMNOPQRSTUV
WXYZ&abcdefghijklmnopqrstuv
wxyz1234567890$.,''"":;!?
30 POINT ITC KORINNA BOLD OUTLINE   AGFA COMPUGRAPHIC TYPE LIBRARY

ABCDEFGHIJKLMNOPQRSTUVW
XYZ&abcdefghijklmnopqrstuvw
xyz1234567890$.,''"":;!?
30 POINT REVUE OUTLINE CONDENSED   AGFA COMPUGRAPHIC TYPE LIBRARY

ABCDEFGHIJKLMNOPQRSTUV
WXYZ&abcdefghijklmnopqrst
uvwxyz1234567890$
.,''"":;!?
30 POINT REVUE SHADOW   AGFA COMPUGRAPHIC TYPE LIBRARY

ABCDEFGHIJKLMNOPQRSTUVWXYZ&abcdefghijklm
nopqrstuvwxyz1234567890$.,'"":;!?
30 POINT ROMAN STYLUS   AGFA COMPUGRAPHIC TYPE LIBRARY

ABCDEFGHIJKLMNOPQRST
UVWXYZ&abcdefghijklmnop
qrstuvwxyz1234567890$
.,'"":;!?
30 POINT ITC SOUVENIR OUTLINE   AGFA COMPUGRAPHIC TYPE LIBRARY

ABCDEFGHIJKLMNOPQRSTUVWX
YZ&1234567890$.,'"":;!?
30 POINT STENCIL OUTLINE   AGFA COMPUGRAPHIC TYPE LIBRARY

ABCDEFGHIJKLMNOPQRSTUVWXYZ&
abcdefghijklmnopqrstuvwxyz
1234567890$.,'"":;!?
30 POINT ITC SERIF GOTHIC BOLD OUTLINE   AGFA COMPUGRAPHIC TYPE LIBRARY

ABCDEFGHIJKLMNOPQRSTU
VWXYZ&abcdefghijklmnopqrst
uvwxyz1234567890$.,'"":;!?
30 POINT WINDSOR** OUTLINE   MERGENTHALER TYPE LIBRARY

ABCDEFGHIJKLMNOPQRSTUVW
XYZ&abcdefghijklmnopqrstuvwxyz12
34567890$.,'"":;!?
30 POINT WORCESTER ROUND** OUTLINE   MERGENTHALER TYPE LIBRARY

524 DISPLAY FACES: DIGITIZED WOOD TYPE

ABCDEFG
HIJKLMN
OPQRSTUV
WXYZ&?01
23456789

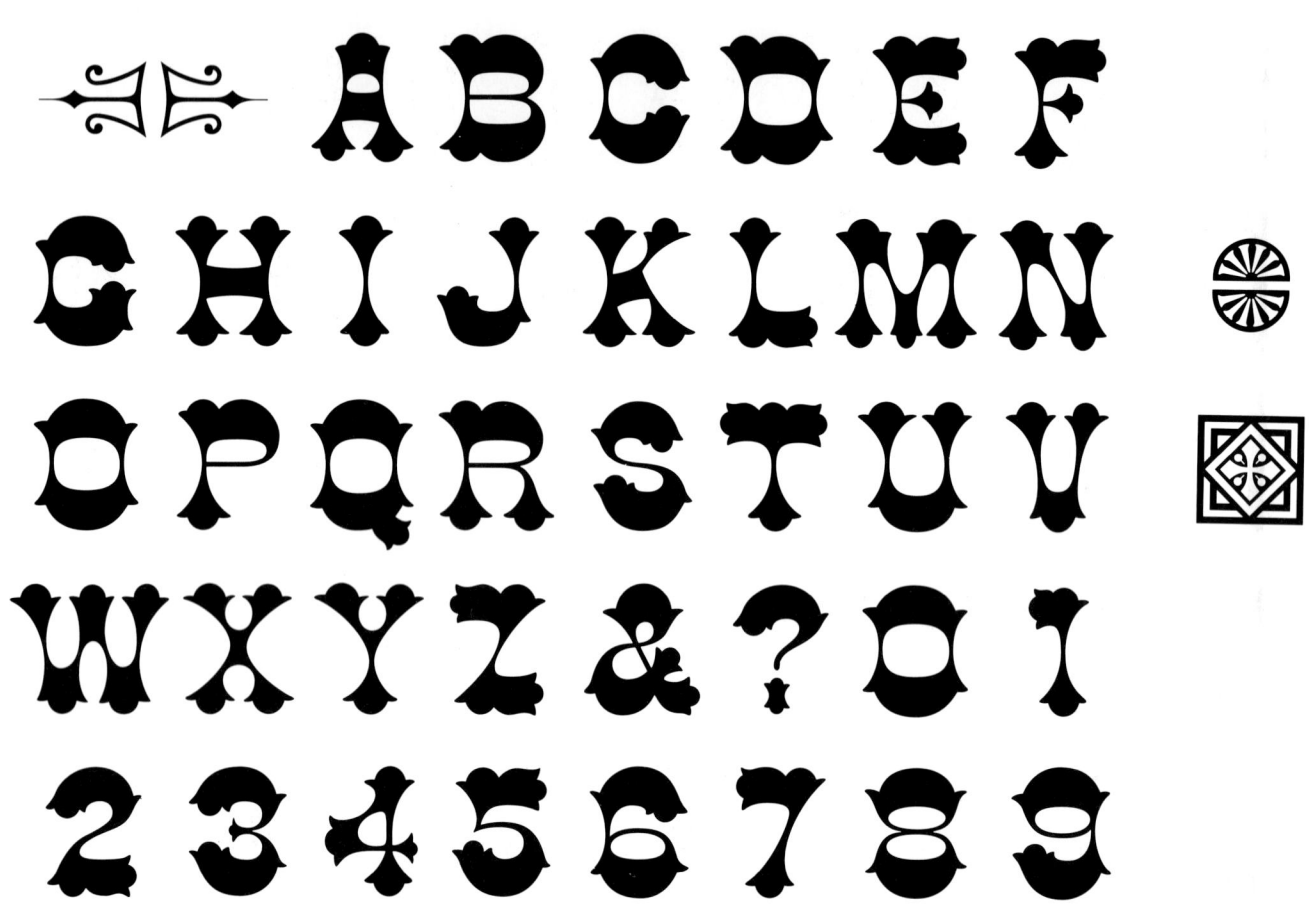

COTTONWOOD   ADOBE TYPE LIBRARY

IRONWOOD   ADOBE TYPE LIBRARY

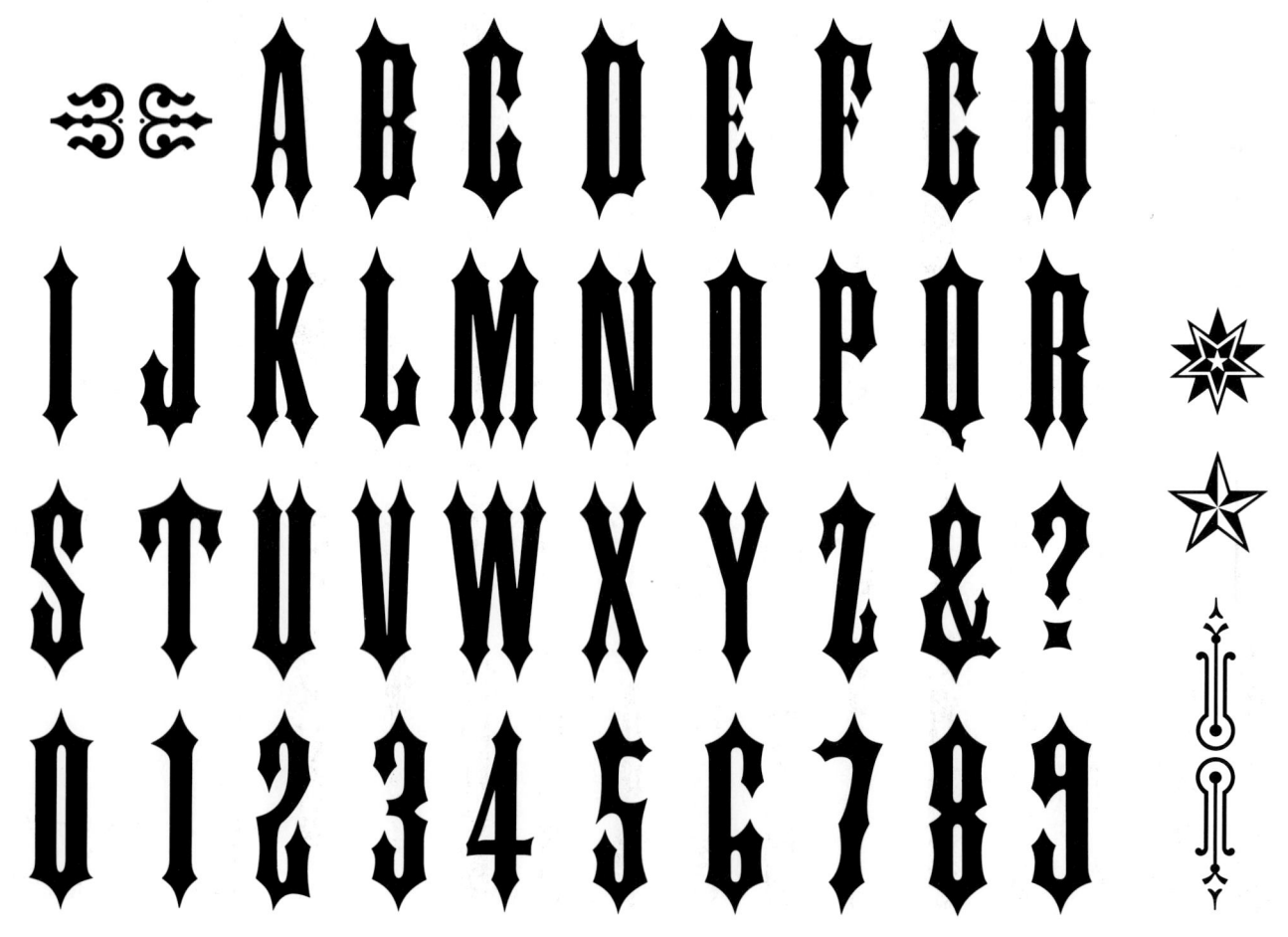

ABCDEFGH
IJKLMNOPQR
STUVWXYZ&?
0123456789

DISPLAY FACES: DIGITIZED WOOD TYPE 525

ABCDEFG
HIJKLMNO
PQRSTUVW
XYZ&?!0I
23456789

JUNIPER   ADOBE TYPE LIBRARY

PONDEROSA   ADOBE TYPE LIBRARY

ABCDEFGHIJK
LMNOPQRSTUVWXY
Z&?!0123456789

Ornaments shown are from the Adobe Type Library

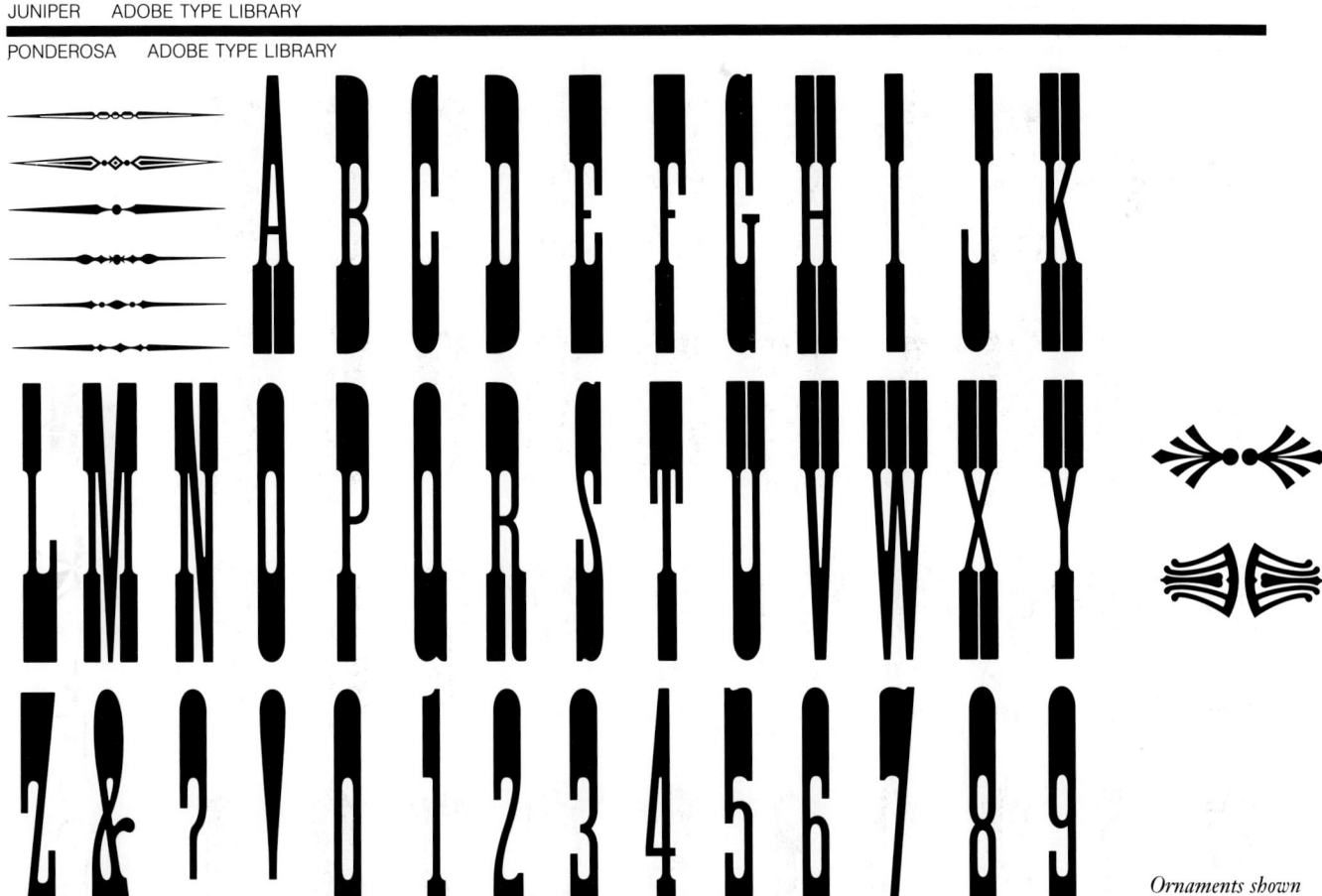

Types were selected from the following three vendors for showing as one-line specimens. Many are duplicates or close approximations to types shown among the families of type and the supplemental and display faces. Some are virtually identical to others except for different names. Others vary only in the relative size of the type face to the type body. These listings identify types available from vendors that may not receive showings elsewhere in this book. Most types are now, or in future will be, available to all major typeface suppliers. These showings will help identify sources of selected faces proprietary to Adobe, Bitstream and ITC as of 1990.

Selections from the
ADOBE TYPE LIBRARY

Bauer Bodoni®
Roman
Italic
Bold
Bold Italic
Black
Black Italic
Bold Condensed
Black Condensed

Linotype Centennial* 55
45 Light
46 Light Italic
56 Italic
75 Bold
76 Bold Italic
95 Black
96 Black Italic

Concorde®
Concorde
Italic
Bold
Bold Italic

Corona*
Corona
Italic
Bold

Excelsior*
Excelsior
Italic
Bold

Fette Fraktur

Lucida®
Roman
Italic
Bold
Bold Italic

Lucida Sans
Roman
Italic
Bold
Bold Italic

Meridien*
Roman
Italic
Medium
Medium Italic
Bold
Bold Italic

MESQUITE™

Parisian™

PONDEROSA™

Post Antiqua®
Post Antiqua
Bold

Reporter® No. 2

Sabon*
Roman
Italic
Bold
Bold Italic

Tempo™
Heavy Condensed
Heavy Condensed Italic

Times* Ten
Roman
Italic
Bold
Bold Italic

University Roman

* TRADEMARKS OF LINOTYPE AG AND/OR ITS SUBSIDIARIES

ONE LINE SPECIMENS: BITSTREAM TYPEFACE LIBRARY 527

Selections from the
BITSTREAM TYPE LIBRARY

Aldine 401
Roman
Italic
Bold
Bold Italic

Amazone™

Americana™
Roman
Italic
Bold
Extra Bold
Extra Bold Condensed

Aurora
Condensed
Bold Condensed

BALLOON™
LIGHT
BOLD
EXTRA BOLD

Bernhard Modern™
Roman
Italic
Bold
Bold Italic

Bernhard Tango™

Candida®
Roman
Italic
Bold

Cloister Black™

Compacta
Light
Roman
Italic
Bold
Bold Italic
Black

DECORATED
035
Bitstream version of Profil®

Dutch 801
Roman
Italic
Semi-Bold
Semi-Bold Italic
Bold
Bold Italic
Extra Bold
Extra Bold Italic
Roman/Head
Italic/Head
Bitstream version of Times Roman®

Engravers' Old English™
Regular
Bold

Exotic 350
Light
Demi-Bold
Bold
Bitstream version of Peignot®

Flareserif 821
Light
Roman
Bold

Folio®
Light
Light Italic
Book
Medium
Bold
Extra Bold
Bold Condensed

Formal Script 421
Bitstream version of Ondine™

Freeform 710
Bitstream version of Eckmann™

Geometric
Slabserif 703
Light
Light Italic
Medium
Medium Italic
Bold
Bold Italic
Extra Bold
Extra Bold Italic
Medium Condensed
Bold Condensed
Extra Bold Condensed
Bitstream version of Memphis®

Handel Gothic™

Humanist 521
Light
Light Italic
Roman
Italic
Bold
Bold Italic
Extra Bold
Ultra Bold
Condensed
Bold Condensed
Extra Bold Condensed

Incised 901
Light
Roman
Italic
Bold
Black
Bold Condensed
Compact
Nord
Nord Italic
Bitstream version of Antique Olive™

Industrial 736
Roman
Italic
Bitstream version of Torino™

Kuenstler 480
Roman
Italic
Bold
Bold Italic
Black
Bitstream version of Trump Mediaeval™

Lapidary 333
Roman
Italic
Bold
Bold Italic
Black

Latin 725
Roman
Italic
Medium
Medium Italic
Bold
Bold Italic
Bitstream version of Meridien®

Matt Antique
Roman
Italic
Bold

MAXIMUS

News 701
Roman
Italic
Bold
Bitstream version of Ionic No.5®

News 702
Roman
Italic
Bold
Bold Italic
Bitstream version of Excelsior®

News Gothic™
Light
Light Italic
Roman
Italic
Demi
Demi Italic
Bold
Bold Italic
Condensed
Condensed Italic
Bold Condensed
Bold Condensed Italic
Extra Condensed
Bold Extra Condensed

Normande
Roman
Italic

Revival 565
Roman
Italic
Bold
Bold Italic
Bitstream version of Berling

Schneidler™
Light
Light Italic
Roman
Italic
Medium
Medium Italic
Bold
Bold Italic
Black
Black Italic

Seagull™
Light
Medium
Bold
Heavy

SHOTGUN
REGULAR
BLANKS

Square 721
Roman
Bold
Condensed
Bold Condensed
Extended
Bold Extended
Bitstream version of Eurostile™

Staccato 222
Bitstream version of Mistral™

Swiss 721
Thin
Thin Italic
Light
Light Italic
Roman
Italic
Medium
Medium Italic
Bold
Bold Italic
Heavy
Heavy Italic
Black
Black Italic
Black No. 2
Light Condensed
Light Condensed Italic
Condensed
Condensed Italic
Bold Condensed
Bold Condensed Italic
Black Condensed
Black Condensed Italic
Light Extended
Extended
Bold Extended
Black Extended
Bold Outline
Black Outline
Bold Condensed Outline
Bold Rounded
Black Rounded
Bitstream version of Helvetica®

Transitional 511
Roman
Italic
Bold
Bold Italic
Bitstream version of Caledonia®

Transitional 521
Roman
Cursive
Bold
Bitstream version of Electra®

Transitional 551
Medium
Medium Italic
Bitstream version of Fairfield™

Vineta

Zapf Calligraphic 801
Roman
Italic
Bold
Bold Italic
Bitstream version of Palatino®

Zapf Elliptical 711
Roman
Italic
Bold
Bold Italic
Bitstream version of Melior®

Zapf Humanist 601
Roman
Italic
Demi
Demi Italic
Bold
Bold Italic
Ultra
Ultra Italic
Bitstream version of Optima®

Selections from the
ITC TYPE LIBRARY

ITC American Typewriter®
Light
Light Italic
Medium
Medium Italic
Bold
Bold Italic
Light Condensed
Medium Condensed
Bold Condensed

ITC Avant Garde Gothic®
Extra Light
Extra Light Oblique
Book
Book Oblique
Medium
Medium Oblique
Demibold
Demibold Oblique
Bold
Bold Oblique
Book Condensed
Medium Condensed
Demibold Condensed
Bold Condensed

ITC Barcelona®
Book
Book Italic
Medium
Medium Italic
Bold
Bold Italic
Heavy
Heavy Italic

ITC Bauhaus®
Light
Medium
Demibold
Bold
Heavy

ITC Benguiat®
Book
Book Italic
Medium
Medium Italic
Bold
Bold Italic
Book Condensed
Book Condensed Italic
Medium Condensed
Medium Condensed Italic
Bold Condensed
Bold Condensed Italic

ITC Benguiat Gothic®
Book
Book Italic
Medium
Medium Italic
Bold
Bold Italic
Heavy
Heavy Italic

ITC Berkeley Oldstyle®
Book
Book Italic
Medium
Medium Italic
Bold
Bold Italic
Black
Black Italic

ITC Bookman®
Light
Light Italic
Medium
Medium Italic
Demibold
Demibold Italic
Bold
Bold Italic

ITC Caslon No. 224®
Book
Book Italic
Medium
Medium Italic
Bold
Bold Italic
Black
Black Italic

ITC Century®
Light
Light Italic
Book
Book Italic
Bold
Bold Italic
Ultra
Ultra Italic
Light Condensed
Light Condensed Italic
Book Condensed
Book Condensed Italic
Bold Condensed
Bold Condensed Italic
Ultra Condensed
Ultra Condensed Italic

ITC Cheltenham®
Light
Light Italic
Book
Book Italic
Bold
Bold Italic
Ultra
Ultra Italic
Light Condensed
Light Condensed Italic
Book Condensed
Book Condensed Italic
Bold Condensed
Bold Condensed Italic
Ultra Condensed
Ultra Condensed Italic

ITC Clearface®
Regular
Regular Italic
Bold
Bold Italic
Heavy
Heavy Italic
Black
Black Italic

ITC Cushing®
Book
Book Italic
Medium
Medium Italic
Bold
Bold Italic
Heavy
Heavy Italic

ITC Élan®
Book
Book Italic
Medium
Medium Italic
Bold
Bold Italic
Black
Black Italic

ITC Eras®
Light
Book
Medium
Demi
Bold
Ultra

ITC Esprit®
Book
Book Italic
Medium
Medium Italic
Bold
Bold Italic
Black
Black Italic

ITC Fenice®
Light
Light Italic
Regular
Regular Italic
Bold
Bold Italic
Ultra
Ultra Italic

ITC Flora™
Medium
Bold

ITC Franklin Gothic®
Book
Book Italic
Medium
Medium Italic
Demi
Demi Italic
Heavy
Heavy Italic

Friz Quadrata
Friz Quadrata
Friz Quadrata Bold

ITC Galliard®
Roman
Italic
Bold
Bold Italic
Black
Black Italic
Ultra
Ultra Italic

ITC Gamma®
Book
Book Italic
Medium
Medium Italic
Bold
Bold Italic
Black
Black Italic

ITC Garamond®
Light
Light Italic
Book
Book Italic
Bold
Bold Italic
Ultra
Ultra Italic
Light Condensed
Light Condensed Italic
Book Condensed
Book Condensed Italic
Bold Condensed
Bold Condensed Italic
Ultra Condensed
Ultra Condensed Italic

ITC Giovanni™
Book
Book Italic
Bold
Bold Italic
Black
Black Italic

ITC Golden Type™
Original
Bold
Black

ITC Goudy Sans
Book
Book Italic
Medium
Medium Italic
Bold
Bold Italic
Black
Black Italic

ITC Isadora
Regular
Bold

ITC Isbell
Book
Book Italic
Medium
Medium Italic
Bold
Bold Italic
Heavy
Heavy Italic

Italia
Book
Medium
Bold

ITC Jamille
Book
Book Italic
Bold
Bold Italic
Black
Black Italic

ITC Kabel
Book
Medium
Demi
Bold
Ultra

ITC Korinna
Regular
Kursiv Regular
Bold
Kursiv Bold
Extra Bold
Kursiv Extra Bold
Heavy
Kursiv Heavy

ITC Leawood
Book
Book Italic
Medium
Medium Italic
Bold
Bold Italic
Black
Black Italic

ITC Lubalin Graph
Extra Light
Extra Light Oblique
Book
Book Oblique
Medium
Medium Oblique
Demi
Demi Oblique
Bold
Bold Oblique

ITC Mixage
Book
Book Italic
Medium
Medium Italic
Bold
Bold Italic
Black
Black Italic

ITC Modern No. 216
Light
Light Italic
Medium
Medium Italic
Bold
Bold Italic
Heavy
Heavy Italic

ITC New Baskerville
Roman
Italic
Semi Bold
Semi Bold Italic
Bold
Bold Italic
Black
Black Italic

ITC Newtext
Light
Light Italic
Book
Book Italic
Regular
Regular Italic
Demi
Demi Italic

ITC Novarese
Book
Book Italic
Medium
Medium Italic
Bold
Bold Italic
Ultra

ITC Pacella
Book
Book Italic
Medium
Medium Italic
Bold
Bold Italic
Black
Black Italic

ITC Panache
Book
Book Italic
Bold
Bold Italic
Black
Black Italic

ITC Quorum
Light
Book
Medium
Bold
Black

ITC Serif Gothic
Light
Regular
Bold
Extra Bold
Heavy
Black

ITC Slimbach
Book
Book Italic
Medium
Medium Italic
Bold
Bold Italic
Black
Black Italic

ITC Souvenir
Light
Light Italic
Medium
Medium Italic
Demi
Demi Italic
Bold
Bold Italic

ITC Stone Informal
Medium
Medium Italic
Semi Bold
Semi Bold Italic
Bold
Bold Italic

ITC Stone Sans
Medium
Medium Italic
Semi Bold
Semi Bold Italic
Bold
Bold Italic

ITC Stone Serif
Medium
Medium Italic
Semi Bold
Semi Bold Italic
Bold
Bold Italic

ITC Symbol
Book
Book Italic
Medium
Medium Italic
Bold
Bold Italic
Black
Black Italic

ITC Tiepolo
Book
Book Italic
Bold
Bold Italic
Black
Black Italic

ITC Tiffany
Light
Light Italic
Medium
Medium Italic
Demi
Demi Italic
Heavy
Heavy Italic

ITC Usherwood
Book
Book Italic
Medium
Medium Italic
Bold
Bold Italic
Black
Black Italic

ITC Veljovic
Book
Book Italic
Medium
Medium Italic
Bold
Bold Italic
Black
Black Italic

ITC Weidemann
Book
Book Italic
Medium
Medium Italic
Bold
Bold Italic
Black
Black Italic

ITC Zapf Book
Light
Light Italic
Medium
Medium Italic
Demi
Demi Italic
Heavy
Heavy Italic

ITC Zapf Chancery
Light
Light Italic
Medium
Medium Italic
Demi
Bold

ITC Zapf International
Light
Light Italic
Medium
Medium Italic
Demi
Demi Italic
Heavy
Heavy Italic

This listing shows the range of the excellent ITC Typeface Collection. ITC develops and licenses typefaces to vendors and type suppliers. Many of these faces appear elsewhere in this book among family, supplementary and display faces.

ONE LINE SPECIMENS: ITC DISPLAY FACES

ITC AKI LINES®
ITC American Typewriter Bold Outline®
ITC Bauhaus Heavy®
ITC Bauhaus Heavy Outline®
ITC Bernase Roman®
ITC Bolt Bold®
ITC/LSC Book Regular Roman®
ITC/LSC Book Regular Italic®
ITC/LSC Book Bold Roman®
ITC/LSC Book Bold Italic®
ITC/LSC Book X-Bold Roman®
ITC/LSC Book X-Bold Italic®
ITC Bookman Outline with Swash®
ITC Bookman Contour with Swash®
ITC BUSORAMA LIGHT®
ITC BUSORAMA MEDIUM®
ITC BUSORAMA BOLD®
ITC Caslon Headline®
ITC/LSC Caslon Light No.223®
ITC/LSC Caslon Light No.223 Italic®
ITC/LSC Caslon Regular No.223®
ITC/LSC Caslon Regular No.223 Italic®
ITC/LSC Caslon Bold No.223®
ITC/LSC Caslon Bold No.223 Italic®
ITC/LSC Caslon X-Bold No.223®
ITC/LSC Caslon X-Bold No.223 Italic®
ITC Cheltenham Outline®
ITC Cheltenham Outline Shadow®
ITC Cheltenham Contour®
ITC Clearface Outline®
ITC Clearface Contour®
ITC Clearface Outline Shadow®

ITC/LSC Condensed®
ITC/LSC Condensed Italic®
ITC Didi®
ITC Eras Outline®
ITC Eras Contour®
ITC Fat Face®
ITC Firenze®
ITC Franklin Gothic Outline®
ITC Franklin Gothic Outline Shadow®
ITC Franklin Gothic Contour®
ITC Gorilla®
ITC Grizzly®
ITC Grouch®
ITC Honda®
ITC Kabel Outline®
ITC Kabel Contour®
ITC Korinna Bold Outline®
ITC MACHINE®
ITC MACHINE BOLD®
ITC/LSC Manhattan™
ITC Milano Roman®
ITC NEON®
ITC PIONEER®
ITC Ronda Light®
ITC Ronda®
ITC Ronda Bold®
ITC Serif Gothic Bold Outline®
ITC/L&C Stymie Hairline®
ITC Tom's Roman®
ITC Upright Regular®
ITC Upright Neon®

APPENDIX

Sources of Illustrations

Illustrations, courtesy of the Pierpont Morgan Library, on pages two through five, are listed below with their accession numbers:

Page two:
PML 27002 (ChL ff 386) GRADUALE ROMANUM
PML 23506.7 BIBLIA GERMANICA

Page three:
PML 14 PSALTER, LATIN, MAINZ

Pages four and five:
B PML 18395 Pliny: HISTORIA NATURALIS, de Spira
C PML 674 (ChL f 1762) Chaucer, CANTERBURY TALES
D PML 373 (ChL f 1017) Colonna: HYPNEOTOMACHIA POLIPHILI
E PML 16203 Geoffrey Tory: CHAMPFLEURY
G PML 62954 Trissino: CANZIONE
H PML 2170

Illustrations **A** *and* **F** *identified as* Westvaco *on pages 4 and 5 are from* WESTVACO INSPIRATIONS 212, 1959, HISTORY of PAPER and TYPOGRAPHIC DESIGN, *designed by Bradbury Thompson.*

Illustrations from the Pierpont Morgan Library for pages 72 and 287, together with accession numbers:
M 860, f.96 FOUR GOSPELS, St. Luke
M 860, f.15 FOUR GOSPELS, St. Matthew

Trademark and Copyright Notices

Asterisks appearing on identification lines under types from the Mergenthaler Type Library, are referenced as follows:

*Trademark of Allied Corporation
**Licensed Trademark.

Bitstream Amerigo, Bitstream Carmina, and Bitstream Charter are registered trademarks of Bitstream Inc. Caledonia, Corona, Electra, Excelsior, Helvetica, Melior, Memphis, Meridien, Optima, Palatino, Peignot, Profil, and Times Roman are registered trademarks and Eckmann, Eurostile, Fairfield, Ionic No.5, Ondine, and Trump Mediaeval are trademarks of Linotype AG and/or its subsidiaries. Times Roman is also a registered trademark of the Monotype Corporation plc. Americana, Balloon, Bernhard Modern, Bernhard Tango, Cloister Black, Engraver's Old English, and News Gothic are trademarks of the Kinsley-ATF Type Corporation. Antique Olive and Mistral are trademarks of Fonderie Olive. Handel Gothic is a trademark of Fotostar International. Candida and Folio are registered trademarks and Schneidler is a trademark of Fundicion Tipografica Neufville S.A. Seagull is a trademark of Ingrama S.A. Torino is a trademark of Societá Nebiolo. Amazone is a trademark of Tetterode Nederland (Lettergieterij Amsterdam).

Design: Ben Rosen
Text set in Janson Text 55 & 56
Headings set in Helvetica Heavy